Abortion in the Early Middle Ages
c. 500–900

YORK MEDIEVAL PRESS

York Medieval Press is published by the University of York's Centre for Medieval Studies in association with Boydell & Brewer Limited. Our objective is the promotion of innovative scholarship and fresh criticism on medieval culture. We have a special commitment to interdisciplinary study, in line with the Centre's belief that the future of Medieval Studies lies in those areas in which its major constituent disciplines at once inform and challenge each other.

Editorial Board (2017)

Professor Peter Biller (Dept of History): General Editor
Professor T. Ayers (Dept of History of Art)
Dr Henry Bainton (Dept of English and Related Literature): Secretary
Dr J. W. Binns (Dept of English and Related Literature)
Dr K. P. Clarke (Dept of English and Related Literature)
Dr K. F. Giles (Dept of Archaeology)
Professor W. Mark Ormrod (Dept of History)
Dr L. J. Sackville (Dept of History)
Dr Hanna Vorholt (Dept of History of Art)
Professor J. G. Wogan-Browne (English Faculty, Fordham University)

Consultant on Manuscript Publications

Professor Linne Mooney (Dept of English and Related Literature)

All enquiries of an editorial kind, including suggestions for monographs and essay collections, should be addressed to: The Academic Editor, York Medieval Press, Department of History, University of York, Heslington, York, YO10 5DD (E-mail: pete.biller@york.ac.uk).

Details of other York Medieval Press volumes are available from Boydell & Brewer Ltd.

Abortion in the Early Middle Ages
c. 500–900

Zubin Mistry

THE UNIVERSITY of York

YORK MEDIEVAL PRESS

© Zubin Mistry 2015

All rights reserved. Except as permitted under current legislation
no part of this work may be photocopied, stored in a retrieval system,
published, performed in public, adapted, broadcast,
transmitted, recorded or reproduced in any form or by any means,
without the prior permission of the copyright owner

The right of Zubin Mistry to be identified as
the author of this work has been asserted in accordance with
sections 77 and 78 of the Copyright, Designs and Patents Act 1988

First published 2015
Paperback edition 2017

A York Medieval Press publication
in association with The Boydell Press
an imprint of Boydell & Brewer Ltd
PO Box 9, Woodbridge, Suffolk IP12 3DF, UK
and of Boydell & Brewer Inc.
668 Mt Hope Avenue, Rochester, NY 14620–2731, USA
website: www.boydellandbrewer.com
and with the
Centre for Medieval Studies, University of York

ISBN 978 1 903153 57 4 hardback
ISBN 978 1 903153 75 8 paperback

A CIP catalogue record for this book is available
from the British Library

The publisher has no responsibility for the continued existence or accuracy of
URLs for external or third-party internet websites referred to in this book, and
does not guarantee that any content on such websites is, or will remain, accurate
or appropriate

CONTENTS

Acknowledgments		vi
Abbreviations		x
Note on Translation		xiii
Introduction: Thinking about Abortion in the Early Middle Ages		1
1.	From Hope of Children to Object of God's Care: Abortion in Classical and Late Antique Society	23
2.	The Word of God: Abortion and Christian Communities in Sixth-Century Gaul	56
3.	Church and State: Politicizing Abortion in Visigothic Spain	93
4.	Medicine for Sin: Reading Abortion in Early Medieval Penitentials	126
5.	Tradition in Practice: Abortion under the Carolingians	165
6.	Legislative Energies: Disputing Abortion in Law-Codes	207
7.	Interior Wound: The Rumour of Abortion in the Divorce of Lothar II and Theutberga	238
8.	Unnatural Symbol: Imagining *Abortivi* in the Early Middle Ages	262
Afterword		296
Bibliography		300
Index		334

ACKNOWLEDGMENTS

This book was written in two immensely stimulating intellectual environments. The School of History at Queen Mary University of London was the setting for the final stages. The bulk of it was researched and written at University College London. I arrived at Gordon Square as a classicist with little intention of moving beyond the fall of Rome. By the time I left a decade or so later, something had happened. I owe a special collective thanks to teachers and, later, colleagues at the History department at UCL, including (but not exclusively) its critical mass of medievalists.

Ideas developed in chapters four, six and eight were presented in conference and seminar papers delivered at the *Gender & History* symposium at York in September 2012, the Earlier Middle Ages seminar at the Institute of Historical Research, London, in February 2013, and the Matrix of the World workshop at Rome in November 2013; I am grateful for helpful comments and suggestions by participants. I (finally) had the pleasure of meeting Marianne Elsakkers at a Generation to Reproduction conference at Cambridge in December 2012 and soon found a copy of 'Reading Between the Lines' in my hands. Normally a liberal lender of books, I jealously guard my copy.

My debts have steadily accumulated over the years. Simon Corcoran, Jack Lennon, James Palmer and John Sabapathy provided serendipitous references. Julian Barr, Roy Flechner, Karl Heidecker, Yitzhak Hen, Rachel Stone and Charles West generously shared unpublished work. Conrad Barwa (best man in multiple senses), Bill MacLehose and Sophie Page read and commented in detail on previous incarnations of chapters. (I fondly remember Bill's knack for making me laugh at my mixed metaphors and other crimes against the English language). Yitzhak Hen read chapter two, Karl Heidecker and Rachel Stone chapter seven. David d'Avray provided comments on chapters three and seven, and much else besides. Miri Rubin saved me from a clanger late in the day. All remaining errors and infelicities (and mixed metaphors) are mine.

Pete Biller has been an inspiration on the page, a careful and charitable reader when the roles have been reversed, and a consistent source of wisdom, wit and encouragement off the page. I owe an even bigger debt to Antonio Sennis as supervisor, colleague and friend. It is no exaggeration to say that I would never have migrated to the Early Middle Ages without Antonio.

I am grateful to the Isobel Thornley Fund for a grant towards the cost of publication and Clive Burgess for his kindness during the application process.

Acknowledgments

I owe huge thanks to Caroline Palmer, not least for her endless reserves of both patience and encouragement, together with her colleagues at Boydell and Brewer. Camila Gatica Mizala generously helped me with Spanish. I finally tracked down the cover image thanks to the kind help of Thomas Sureau, Mary Shepard and Painton Cowen.

I owe the biggest debt of all to my family. My sister, Zeenia, was my dearest friend and confidante throughout my postgraduate years. Her gifts for languages and laughter were matched by her gift for cooking crêpes at unearthly hours.

Harpreet Palray has been the *sine qua non* as I struggled to finish this book. It has intruded upon our first year of marriage (a scouting mission for the cover image took place during an anniversary trip to Paris). Her support has been unfailing. It's now my turn to play the Caryatid.

Finally, this book would never have been possible without the love and support of my parents. It is dedicated to them.

This book is produced with the generous assistance of a grant from Isobel Thornley's Bequest to the University of London

ABBREVIATIONS

AS	Acta Sanctorum
Asbach, *Poenitentiale*	F. B. Asbach, *Das Poenitentiale Remense und der sogen. Excarpsus Cummeani: Überlieferung, Quellen und Entwicklung zweier kontinentaler Bußbücher aus der 1. Hälfte des 8. Jahrhunderts* (Regensburg, 1975)
Bezler, *Paenitentialia*	F. Bezler, *Paenitentialia Hispaniae*, CCSL 156A (Turnhout, 1998)
Bieler, *Irish Penitentials*	L. Bieler, *The Irish Penitentials, with an appendix by D. A. Binchy* (Dublin, 1963)
CCCM	Corpus Christianorum Continuatio Medievalis
CCH 2	G. Martínez Díez, *La Colección canónica hispana 2: Colecciones derivadas* (Madrid, 1976)
CCH 3	G. Martínez Díez and F. Rodríguez, *La Colección canónica hispana 3: Concilios griegos y africanos* (Madrid, 1982)
CCH 4	G. Martínez Díez and F. Rodríguez, *La Colección canónica hispana 4: Concilios galos, concilios hispanos: primera parte* (Madrid, 1984)
CCH 5	G. Martínez Díez and F. Rodríguez, *La Colección canónica hispana 5: Concilios hispanos: segunda parte* (Madrid, 1992)
CCSA	Corpus Christianorum Series Apocryphorum
CCSL	Corpus Christianorum Series Latina
CSEL	Corpus Scriptorum Ecclesiasticorum Latinorum
Elsakkers, RBL	M. Elsakkers, 'Reading Between the Lines: Old Germanic and Early Christian Views on Abortion' (unpublished Ph.D. dissertation, University of Amsterdam, 2010)
EME	*Early Medieval Europe*
Finsterwalder, *Canones*	P. W. Finsterwalder, *Die Canones Theodori Cantauriensis und ihre Überlieferungsreformen* (Weimar, 1929)

Heist, *Vitae*	W. W. Heist, *Vitae sanctorum Hiberniae, ex codice olim Salmanticensi, nunc Bruxellensi* (Brussels, 1965)
v. Hörmann, 'Bußbücherstudien IV'	W.v. Hörmann, 'Bußbücherstudien IV', *Zeitschrift der Savigny-Stiftung für Rechtsgeschichte, Kanonische Abteilung* 4 (1914), 358–483
JECS	*Journal of Early Christian Studies*
JEH	*Journal of Ecclesiastical History*
JHMAS	*Journal of the History of Medicine and Allied Sciences*
JHS	*Journal of the History of Sexuality*
Kerff, 'Paenitentiale Pseudo-Gregorii'	F. Kerff, 'Das Paenitentiale Pseudo-Gregorii: Eine kritische Edition', in *Aus Archiven und Bibliotheken: Festschrift für Raymund Kottje zum 65. Geburtstag* (Frankfurt, 1992), pp. 161–88
Kottje, *Paenitentialia*	R. Kottje, *Paenitentialia minora Franciae et Italiae saeculi VIII–IX*, CCSL 156 (Turnhout, 1994)
LA	*Lex Alamannorum*
LB	*Lex Baiwariorum*
LF	*Lex Frisionum*
LH	Gregory of Tours, *Libri historiarum decem*
LM	*Laterculus Malalianus*
LR	*Lex Ribuaria*
LV	*Lex Visigothorum*
Meens, *Boeteboek*	R. Meens, *Het tripartite boeteboek: Overlevering en betekenis van vroegmiddeleeuwse biechtvoorschriften* (Hilversum, 1994)
MGH	Monumenta Germaniae Historica
--- AA	Auctores antiquissimi
--- Capit.	Capitularia regum Francorum
--- Capit. N.S.	Capitularia regum Francorum, Nova series
--- Capit. episc.	Capitularia episcoporum
--- Conc.	Concilia
--- Epp.	Epistolae
--- Epp. sel.	Epistolae selectae in usum scholarum ex Monumenta Germaniae Historicis separatim editae
--- Fontes iuris	Fontes iuris Germanici antiqui in usum scholarum separatim editi
--- Formulae	Formulae Merowingici et Karolini aevi
--- LL	Leges
--- LNG	Leges nationum Germanicarum
--- Poetae	Poetae Latini medii aevi

--- QQ	Quellen zur Geistesgeschichte des Mittelalters
--- SS	Scriptores
--- SRG	Scriptores rerum Germanicarum in usum scholarum separatim editi
--- SRG, N.S.	Scriptores rerum Germanicarum, Nova series
--- SRM	Scriptores rerum Merovingicarum
Munier, *Concilia Africae*	C. Munier, *Conciliae Africae a.345–a.525*, CCSL 149 (Turnhout, 1974)
Munier, *Concilia Galliae*	C. Munier, *Concilia Galliae a.314–a.506*, CCSL 148 (Turnhout, 1963)
P&P	*Past & Present*
PG	Patrologia Graeca
PL	Patrologia Latina
Plummer, *Vitae*	C. Plummer, *Vitae sanctorum Hiberniae*, 2 vols. (Oxford, 1910)
Schmitz, *Bußbücher*	H. J. Schmitz, *Die Bußbücher und die Bußdisziplin der Kirche*, 2 vols. (Mainz, 1883–98)
SC	Sources Chrétiennes
SCH	Studies in Church History
SHM	*Social History of Medicine*
TTH	Translated Texts for Historians
van Rhijn, *Paenitentiale*	C. van Rhijn, *Paenitentiale Pseudo-Theodori*, CCSL 156B (Turnhout, 2009)
Wasserschleben, *Bußordnungen*	F. W. H. Wasserschleben, *Die Bußordnungen der abendländischen Kirche* (Halle, 1851)

NOTE ON TRANSLATION

First, the easier part. All translations are my own except where otherwise noted. Latin sources: in almost all instances the Latin text is provided in the footnotes. Greek sources: many are quoted from translation; in some cases words of particular interest are provided in the main body of the text. I have relied wholly on translations of sources in Coptic or Syriac.

Now, the harder part. I am deeply aware of the hazards of 'dangerous modern vocabulary', modern words which 'insidiously imply ... past capacity to think similarly'.[1] The problem is compounded most obviously by the electric resonance of words in modern discourse on abortion; and less obviously by linguistic evolutions of words for abortion in English (and, for that matter, Latin).[2] There is no simple solution but a few tendencies ought to be highlighted.

First, in most cases I lean towards more literal translations from (occasionally knotty) Latin.

Second, Latin nouns like *aborsus* or *abortio* and verbs like *abortare* could mean either (in everyday speech) abortion or miscarriage; or (in medical language) therapeutic or spontaneous abortion. In other words, Latin did not have separate words for abortion and miscarriage. In almost all cases, I translate and refer to abortion (and not to miscarriage or spontaneous abortion). The rationale is not to elide perspectives on abortion and miscarriage (indeed, I will caution against doing this in chapters six and eight), but to reflect the Latin.

Third, most allusions to abortion used other words; for instance, to kill the infant or fetus or child or offspring etc. in the womb. Here, the dangers of modern vocabulary are especially acute. Fetus, for example, can be used as a politically deliberate alternative to, say, child (and vice versa). I have decided to be consistent when translating relevant nouns: *conceptus*, what has been conceived; *fetus*, fetus; *infans*, infant; *partus*, offspring; *filius*, child (or son where *filia*, daughter, is mentioned too). The approach risks, on occasion, diluting nuances which can be reasonably guessed at; but it reduces the risk, I hope, of unwittingly imposing modern resonances.

---

[1] P. Biller, *The Measure of Multitude: Population in Medieval Thought* (Oxford, 2000), p. 137.
[2] On which, see M. Lemmens, *Lexical Perspectives on Transitivity and Ergativity: Causative Constructions in English* (Amsterdam, 1998), pp. 191–218.

INTRODUCTION
Thinking about Abortion in the Early Middle Ages

According to the apostle Paul, Eve's sin led to the fall; but she would be saved by childbearing. The author of a sixth-century biblical commentary thought carefully about the implications of Paul's words: *'But she will be saved by generation of children*. Not Eve, but woman: because Eve was used as an example, it was not being said specifically about her, through generation of children, by rearing, not by killing or aborting.'[1] The good works of the righteous widow, Paul went on to write, included bringing up children. Again, concern over abortion entered the author's mind as he interpreted Paul's words: '*If she brought up children*, if she brought up those born, and not by receiving abortion, nor has she killed [children] already born.'[2]

Our commentator was not alone in considering abortion as an obstacle to salvation. A Carolingian poem probably from the late ninth century commemorated a Merovingian bishop who had once saved a soul by thwarting an abortion. Many early medieval bishops acted on abortion from the pulpit or council chamber, but Germanus of Paris (d. 576) had acted from his mother's womb:

> [W]hen, before he was born to the world,
> He shone in mother's womb through a miracle of virtue:
> Mother had conceived him more quickly than usual,
> By drinking poisons she wanted an abortion flung out,
> Unaware a woman duly brings forth in the seventh month
> Any offspring that moves on the seventieth day.
> But whom divine providence had prepared for the world,
> No detriments could harm, no potions either;
> A warrant preserved the chosen one and rendered untouched;
> The mother, lest she became a parricide, was thwarted.

---

[1] '*Salvabitur autem per filiorum generationem*. Non Eva, sed mulier: quia Eva ad exemplum adducta est, non de ipsa proprie dicebatur, per filiorum generationem, nutriendo, et non necando, nec abortiendo', Pseudo-Primasius, *Commentaria in epistolas B. Pauli*, PL 68, col. 664A–B (1 Tim. 2. 15 italicized); see p. 277 n.60 below for details on this commentary.

[2] '*Si filios educavit*. Si natos educavit, et aborsum non accipiendo, aut iam natum non occidit', *Commentaria in epistolas B. Pauli*, col. 668A (1 Tim. 5. 10 italicized).

He who wanted John to rejoice in the womb,
Brought forth Germanus here through a miracle before birth.³

Childbearing was one path to salvation in early medieval Christianity. Monasticism offered a different path defined by the renunciation of sexuality and its consequences, including childbearing. In a story about another saint written in Ireland perhaps around the turn of the ninth century, renunciation was taken so seriously that a nun's pregnancy could miraculously vanish without a trace:

> On another day, making a journey, Áed came to a place of other holy virgins ... But gazing upon the virgin who was serving him, holy Áed saw that her womb was swelling and carrying a child. At once, he stood up without food to take flight from that place. Then she confessed before all that she had secretly sinned and did penance. And holy Áed blessed her womb, and immediately the infant in her womb disappeared as if it did not exist.⁴

From the episcopal fetus to the evanescent fetus, the sinning noblewoman to the sinning nun, the miracles of Germanus and Áed encapsulate the variety of responses to abortion in early medieval societies. I begin with these miraculous examples because they represent a historical layer yet to be excavated within histories of abortion. Scratch beneath the surface and there are further layers.

Both miracle stories were retellings of older tales. The poem which commemorated the uterine miracle of Germanus was a literary reincarnation (and not the first) of a miracle story originally narrated in the later sixth century by an author who had known the bishop personally. It had become deeply lodged in Parisian lore by the time the west Frankish king Odo (d. 898) capitalized on Germanus's aura in the face of Viking threats and political instability.⁵ Áed's striking miracle was also a literary reincarnation, but with a gender twist.

---

³ '... cum ante natus quam fuisset saeculo, / In matris floruit alvo virtutis miraculo: / Mater illum quod plus cito concepisset solito, / Voluit venenis haustis abortivum proici, / Nescia septimo mense mulierem fundere / Rite partum, qui movetur die septagesimo. / Quem tamen divina mundo maiestas providerat, / Nulla laedunt nocimenta, nulla maleficia; / Vas electum conservatur integrumque redditur; / Genetrix, ne parricida fieret, eripitur. / Qui Iohannem exultare voluit in utero, / Hic Germanum ante partum extulit miraculo.', *De vita et miraculis beatissimi Germani antistitis* 1.3–8, MGH Poetae 4.1, p. 124.

⁴ 'Quadam autem die, Aidus, iter agens, venit ad aliarum sanctarum virginum locum ... Intuens autem sanctus Aidus virginem que sibi ministrabat, vidit quod uterus illius, partum gestans, intumescebat. Et cito surrexit ille sine cibo, ut ab isto loco fugeret. Tunc illa coram omnibus confessa est quod occulte peccasset et penitentiam egit. Sanctus autem Aidus benedixit uterum eius, et statim infans in utero eius evanuit quasi non esset.', *Vita Aidi* 15, ed. Heist, *Vitae*, p. 172.

⁵ Reading between the lines of Paul de Winterfeld's comments in MGH Poetae 4.1, p. 123, the poem was probably composed in this political context, on which see S. MacLean, *Kingship and Politics in the Late Ninth Century: Charles the Fat and the End of the Carolingian Empire* (Cambridge, 2003), pp. 57–62.

2

The author had adapted a disappearing pregnancy motif originally from the seventh-century hagiography of a female saint, Brigit of Kildare.

But these historical memories have dissipated in the afterlives of Áed and Germanus. In one later medieval redaction of Áed's life the infant disappeared from the text before it could disappear from the narrative. A diluted story of reconciliation after sexual sin was left behind.[6] Even more strikingly, in Migne's edition of the Brigidine original, an ellipsis is all that remains of a motif which did not pass the nineteenth-century censor.[7] The opening sentence of Germanus's entry in a modern version of *Butler's Lives of the Saints* looks more promising: 'Germanus was lucky to survive beyond childhood.' But the entry quickly tells another story in which Germanus survived an attempted poisoning in childhood.[8] If you walk around the aisles of Saint-Germain-des-Prés today, you may spot the depiction of a woman lifting a cup to her mouth with one hand while the other rests on her swelling navel. The thirteenth-century stained glass is a rare hint of a memory which has faded over time.[9]

This book is an attempt to recover these memories. It tells the history of how individuals and communities, ecclesiastical and secular authorities, construed abortion as a social, religious and political problem between c. 500 and c. 900, and the neglected variety of their responses. Church tradition is an important and inevitable part of the story. The church cast a large shadow over almost every facet of life in the Early Middle Ages – abortion was no different. Shadows do not stand still, however, and this book will capture the slow movements of church tradition. But the church was not the only social and cultural force in early medieval societies, even if it is the force now most visible to us. Women and fetuses are a vital part of the story, and we must try to detect the forces through which some fetuses could become 'unwanted children' in the eyes of some women as well as their families and communities.

This book is also about the cultural significance of abortion in early medieval societies. Our story will meet with other stories about men and women, church and state, orthodoxy and heresy, marriage and monasticism, writers and readers, authors and audiences, the letter and spirit of the law, the weight of the past and the energies of the present. We must re-examine the conventional sources for such histories – principally, canon law, penitential literature

---

[6] *Vita Aidi*, ed. Plummer, *Vitae*, I, p. 38.
[7] *Vita Brigitae*, PL 72, col. 780C. On the original significance and later fates of these miracles from Irish hagiography, see Z. Mistry, 'The Sexual Shame of the Chaste: "Abortion Miracles" in Early Medieval Saints' Lives', *Gender & History* 25.3 (2013), 607–20.
[8] *Butler's Lives of the Saints*, new concise ed., ed. P. Burns (London, 2003), p. 243.
[9] See M.B. Shepard, 'The St. Germain Windows from the Thirteenth-Century Lady Chapel at Saint-Germain-des-Prés', in *The Cloisters: Studies in Honor of the Fiftieth Anniversary*, ed. E.C. Parker (New York, 1992), pp. 283–302.

and law-codes. But we must also move beyond the boundaries of such histories to embrace the miracles of saints, interpretations of scriptural abortion in biblical commentaries, the forgotten afterlives of apocryphal texts, uncomfortable imaginings of resurrected fetuses in theological treatises, a baffling abortion accusation within a ninth-century political controversy and polemical letters whose authors likened rivals to fetuses flung from the womb.

But first of all we need to see that the stories which early medieval communities once told themselves, and the historically specific intricacies of what abortion signified to them, have scarcely been audible within the handful of stories we now tell about abortion in the Early Middle Ages.

Dark ages: The historiography of abortion in the Early Middle Ages

Old habits die hard. In the broader history of attitudes to abortion, the centuries from roughly 500 to 1000 remain the dark ages. Widening the net to include studies of related subjects – contraception, and infanticide and infant abandonment – does not make much difference.[10] A contrast with antiquity is illuminating. The centuries from Aristotle to Augustine are well served by a body of scholarship sufficiently voluminous to make the task of summarizing it a difficult exercise in selection and omission.[11] Since 1971 the field has even had its own repository of source material assembled by a historian of law. Enzo Nardi's compendious if flawed volume, which starts as far back as the fifth century BCE, reaches the sixth century CE.[12] Unlike the Early Middle Ages, antiquity has been subject to real historiographical debates on abortion. The biggest debate of all has had repercussions beyond the end of the classical world. It is easily distilled into a simple question: evolution or revolution? Did Christian opposition to abortion evolve (if spectacularly) out of Greco-Roman values? Or was Christian opposition to abortion a moral revolution which

---

[10] Contraception (though see below on John Noonan): coverage of the Early Middle Ages in large scale diachronic histories is cursory, understandably so given that their authors tend to be modern historians; see A. McLaren, *A History of Contraception: From Antiquity to the Present Day* (Oxford, 1990); R. Jütte, *Contraception: A History*, trans. V. Russell (Cambridge, 2008). Infant abandonment is better served. The picture of widespread social structures for reception of abandoned infants in medieval societies, including child oblation in monasteries, in J. E. Boswell, *The Kindness of Strangers: The Abandonment of Children from Late Antiquity to the Renaissance* (London, 1988), has been debated. M. de Jong, *In Samuel's Image: Child Oblation in the Early Medieval West* (Leiden, 1996), emphasizes the religious over the social function of oblation. The extent to which social structures for the reception of abandoned infants were either intended or functioned as alternatives to abortion has been little considered; the evidence, as we shall see, is intermittent.

[11] See p. 24 below.

[12] E. Nardi, *Procurato aborto nel mondo greco-romano* (Milan, 1971).

broke with Greco-Roman values?[13] The debate takes for granted that rejection of abortion was deeply woven into the moral systems developed by early and late antique Christians.

The story of abortion in the centuries to come naturally slipped into this groove. It is typically framed as the conservation of a heritage (however one defines its origins).[14] There is another reason for the hermeneutic of continuity. Coverage of the Early Middle Ages has been dominated by Catholic theologians and church lawyers. While other periods in church history with bigger names (like Augustine and Aquinas) have become battlegrounds for debates between pro-life and pro-choice Catholics, the Early Middle Ages have largely been interpreted by scholars consolidating, rather than contesting, official Catholic teaching.[15] In the 1940s Roger John Huser and Giuseppe Palazzini provided concise historical commentaries on canon law on abortion with some limited consideration of other ecclesiastical regulations like penitentials as well as secular law.[16] In the following decades the rise of fractious abortion politics, particularly in the USA, together with internal Catholic debates, initially over the permissibility of artificial contraception but later extending to the morality of early-term abortion, catalyzed more analytical interest in the history of church teaching. The scales at which authors wrote coincided with a noticeable linguistic divide. In the USA broad-ranging surveys of western, predominantly Christian, attitudes to the morality of abortion by theologians

---

[13] See, for example, R. Crahay, 'Les moralistes anciens et l'avortement', *L'antiquité classique* 10 (1941), 9–23, effectively arguing for revolution against F. J. Dölger, 'Das Lebensrecht des ungeborenen Kindes und die Fruchtabtreibung in der Bewertung der heidnischen und christlichen Antike', *Antike und Christentum: Kultur und religionsgeschichte Studien* 4 (1934), 1–61. S. K. Dickison, 'Abortion in Antiquity', *Arethusa* 6.1 (1973), 159–66, criticizes Nardi's *Aborto* for similar reasons.

[14] Cf. Nardi, *Aborto*, pp. 638–82.

[15] For examples of these debates (and their general avoidance of the Early Middle Ages), see D. C. Maguire and J. Burtchaell, 'The Catholic Legacy on Abortion: A Debate', in *On Moral Medicine: Theological Perspectives on Medical Ethics*, ed. S. E. Lammers and A. Verhey (Grand Rapids, 1998), pp. 586–99; D. A. Dombrowski and R. Deltete, *A Brief, Liberal, Catholic Defense of Abortion* (Urbana, 2000). The likes of Augustine and Aquinas have, to my mind, been distorted by attempts to appropriate them for pro-life or pro-choice positions; see pp. 49, 29ln.128 below. For a recent work which thinks more carefully than most about the content and contexts of medieval intellectual thought and its modern implications, see F. Amerini, *Aquinas on the Beginning and End of Human Life*, trans. M. Henninger (Cambridge MA, 2013); for a comparable study of Jewish thought, see E. Lepicard, 'The Embryo in Ancient Rabbinic Literature: Between Religious Law and Didactic Narratives: An Interpretative Essay', *History and Philosophy of the Life Sciences* 32 (2010), 21–42.

[16] R. J. Huser, *The Crime of Abortion in Canon Law: An Historical Synopsis and Commentary* (Washington DC, 1942); G. Palazzini, *Ius fetus ad vitam eiusque tutela in fontibus ac doctrina canonica usque ad saeculum xvi* (Urbania, 1943).

contained chapters or sections on the Early Middle Ages.¹⁷ On the continent a spate of articles published in canon law or theology journals focussed more closely on patristic thought up to the hazy area between the late antique and early medieval worlds, and on early medieval canon law and penitential literature.¹⁸

The best known work produced in this context was written by an American Catholic layman and lawyer who had previously examined the church's evolving stance on usury. John Noonan is best known for his *magnum opus* on contraception published in 1965, though he also wrote a historical essay on the church's historical position on abortion.¹⁹ Noonan encapsulates the complex subtexts of twentieth-century Catholic historical scholarship on abortion. On the one hand, Noonan, like Connery and others, wrote as an interlocutor in modern abortion debates.²⁰ His picture of an (almost) unwavering Christian tradition on abortion from antiquity through the Middle Ages to modernity has been criticized as a 'pro-life heritage tale'.²¹ On the other hand, Noonan's more scholarly *Contraception* was the work of an American Catholic who advocated a cautious relaxation of the church's strictures against artificial contraception. After the publication of *Contraception* Noonan was invited to serve on a Vatican commission to re-examine birth control. By the end of the decade he had publicly voiced his disappointment at the reiteration of Catholic doctrine in the 1968 papal encyclical, *Humanae Vitae*.²²

---

[17] J. R. Connery, *Abortion: The Development of the Roman Catholic Perspective* (Chicago, 1977); G. Grisez, *Abortion: The Myths, the Realities, and the Arguments* (New York, 1970).

[18] Patristic thought: A. M. Dubarle, 'La Bible et les pères ont-il parlé de la contraception?', *La vie spirituelle*, suppl. 63 (1962), 573–610; A. M. Dubarle, 'La contraception chez Césaire d'Arles', *La vie spirituelle*, suppl. 67 (1963), 515–19. Canonical and penitential literature: R. S. Callewaert, 'Les pénitentiels au moyen âge et les pratiques anticonceptionelles' *La vie spirituelle*, suppl. 74 (1965), 339–66; B. Honings, 'L'aborto nei libri penitenziali Irlandesi: convergenza morale e divergenze pastorali', reprinted in *Una componente della mentalità occidentale: penitenziali nell'alto medio evo*, ed. M. G. Muzzarelli (Bologna, 1980), pp. 155–84; B. Honings, 'L'aborto in alcuni decretali episcopali: una reazione decretale all'arbitrarietà penitenziale', *Apollinaris* 49 (1976), 201–17.

[19] J. T. Noonan, *Contraception: A History of its Treatment by the Catholic Theologians and Canonists* (Cambridge MA, 1965); J. T. Noonan, 'An Almost Absolute Value in History', in *The Morality of Abortion: Legal and Historical Perspectives*, ed. J. T. Noonan (Cambridge MA, 1970), pp. 1–59.

[20] Noonan edited the volume in which 'Almost Absolute Value' appeared. It included contributions from big-name Christian moral philosophers as debate over abortion intensified in the years leading up to the US Supreme Court's momentous *Roe v. Wade* ruling in 1973; cf. J. R. Connery, 'The Ancients and the Medievals on Abortion: The Consensus the Court Ignored', in *Abortion and the Constitution: Reversing Roe v. Wade through the Courts*, ed. D. J. Horan et al. (Washington DC, 1987), pp. 123–35.

[21] C. M. Condit, *Decoding Abortion Rhetoric: Communicating Social Change* (Urbana, 1990), pp. 43–58.

[22] K. Starr, 'Judge John T. Noonan, Jr. A Brief Biography', *Journal of Law and Religion* 11.1 (1994–5), 151–76. For the broader American Catholic context, see L. W. Tentler,

Introduction

Noonan's *Contraception* is the outlier, not because of his politics but because of the historical depth and evidential breadth with which he examined church tradition on contraception. Along the way, Noonan provided important insights, if not an overarching argument, on abortion too, including recognition that the conceptual boundaries between abortion and contraception in ancient and medieval thought do not overlap neatly with modern distinctions.[23] One of *Contraception*'s innovations was its attempt to contextualize ecclesiastical and, to a lesser extent, secular responses to contraception. First, as we just saw, this appears in the sense of wariness over distorting ancient and medieval texts with modern mental associations. For example, Noonan warned against the 'retrospective rationalization' of imputing protodemographic thought as if early medieval authors, just like modern historians, discerned and discussed the effects of post-Roman population decline.[24] Second, Noonan situates the development of doctrine in its social and intellectual context. One persistent thread in Noonan's narrative is reaction. Thus, eye-catching debates over sexual practices and marital theologies of heretical or rival religious groups – Gnostics in early Christianity, Manichaeans in Augustine's North Africa, Priscillianists in sixth-century Iberia, Cathars in twelfth- and thirteenth-century France – were crucial incubators for thought. Admittedly, Noonan's picture of the Early Middle Ages also very strongly emphasized continuity. Dark age monks were a prelude to the 'theologians of a more speculative age'. At the same time, he attempted to contextualize this continuity through brisk but focussed accounts of Spanish church councils, insular and continental penitentials and Frankish canon law.[25]

In the other works on abortion, including Noonan's essay on abortion, the central thread was church tradition as it appeared to twentieth-century Catholics: the transmission of patristic and conciliar thought on abortion. Some early medieval material (penitentials and law-codes) occupied an ancillary or otherwise peripheral place in these historical narratives depending on how their authors could connect them to the central thread.[26] Other material integral to early medieval, if not modern, Christianity (like saints' lives) was altogether neglected. The resulting picture was a narrower narrative of continuity. For suitable visual metaphors, think Caravaggio's 'St Jerome Writing'

Catholics and Contraception: An American History (Ithaca, NY 2004). It is a mark of Noonan's scholarship that traditionalist Catholics have used *Contraception* as a resource to argue against his position on contraception; cf. J. E. Smith, *Humanae Vitae: A Generation Later* (Washington DC, 1991), pp. 2–7.

[23] *Contraception*, pp. 88–91.
[24] Ibid., p. 144.
[25] Ibid., pp. 143–70 (quotation at p. 170).
[26] The summary of church tradition by a French Jesuit (imprisoned at Dachau in 1944-5 after his involvement in the Résistance), M. Riquet, 'Christianisme et population', *Population* 4 (1949), 615–30, was unusual for its uncomplicated integration of penitentials.

or Goya's 'St Gregory the Great', monkish figures stooped over books as they faithfully transcribe the enduring doctrine of the church. The early medieval world was obscured by a patristic shadow and later medieval thought was the light in the distance:

> In the period from 450 to 1100, when monks and bishops were the chief transmitters of Christian moral ideas, the teaching on abortion was reiterated ... The early Christian and patristic attitudes were faithfully preserved in the various channels communicating the teaching of past authority and instilling its observance.[27]

So far, the historiographical story has unfolded outside history departments. This is not a criticism. As in the history of marriage, theologians and church lawyers laid important groundwork.[28] Any study of the handling of abortion in the Early Middle Ages would have to engage, among other things, with the deep-lying tectonics of tradition.

As medieval historians ventured more deeply into new territories like the history of sexuality, Noonan's work became an important resource. Évelyne Patlagean and Jean-Louis Flandrin drew contrasting pictures of deliberate avoidance of offspring in marriage – respectively, a minimalist picture for early Byzantium and a less restrictive picture for the Christian West in the *longue durée* – but their work focussed on contraception (and Noonan's *Contraception*) more than abortion.[29] Engagement with early medieval abortion from within history departments has taken longer to get going. Of course, historians have had encounters with abortion in the course of research into a range of other subjects in the Early Middle Ages, including sexuality and marriage, women's history, magic, popular religion, penance, hagiography, law and, of course, history of medicine.[30] Occasional summaries appear from time to time.[31] So too have a few works which address abortion in specific

---

[27] Noonan, 'Almost Absolute Value', pp. 18–19; cf. Grisez, *Abortion*, p. 150.
[28] D. L. d'Avray, *Medieval Marriage: Symbolism and Society* (Oxford, 2005), pp. 9–15.
[29] É. Patlagean, 'Birth Control in the Early Byzantine Empire', J.-L. Flandrin, 'Contraception, Marriage, and Sexual Relations in the Christian West', both in *Biology of Man in History: Selections from the 'Annales'*, ed. R. Forster and O. Ranum, trans. E. Forster and P. M. Ranum (Baltimore, 1975), pp. 1–22, 23–47; both were originally published in French in *Annales E.S.C.* in 1969.
[30] I highlight relevant works at appropriate moments in subsequent chapters rather than list them here in what would inevitably be a bloated footnote.
[31] B. D. H. Miller, 'She who hath drunk any potion...', *Medium Aevum* 31 (1962), 188–93; S. Crawford, 'Infanticide, Abandonment and Abortion in the Graeco-Roman and Early Medieval World: Archaeological Perspectives', in *Childhood and Violence in the Western Tradition*, ed. L. Brockliss and H. Montgomery (Oxford, 2010), pp. 59–67; cf. F. S. Paxton, 'Birth and Death', in *The Cambridge History of Christianity Volume 3: Early Medieval Christianities, c. 600–c.1100*, ed. T. F. X. Noble and J. M. H. Smith (Cambridge, 2008), pp. 383–98.

texts and contexts.[32] But the overall picture is clear. Until fairly recently, there was little sustained work on early medieval abortion written by or for early medievalists.

The turn of the millennium witnessed the historiographical turning point. Over the last decade or so a Dutch scholar, Marianne Elsakkers, has conducted detailed research on three main bodies of early medieval sources on abortion: secular law-codes; ecclesiastical regulations (in an opposite tendency to Catholic scholarship, Elsakkers focusses more on penitentials than canon law); and medical texts (though here Elsakkers's work is more selective than panoramic).[33] Elsakkers's work has become the indispensable starting point and a testament to the neglected quantity of source material. The form in which her work appears – several published articles and book chapters alongside an unpublished doctoral thesis which also includes unpublished articles – precludes a grand narrative.[34] We will return to specific arguments and interpretations of sources in subsequent chapters.[35] Here, I want to highlight certain key approaches and themes.

Elsakkers's thesis concludes with the remark, 'condemnations and prohibitions of abortion in ... early medieval secular and ecclesiastical texts indicate that abortion happened'.[36] She is ultimately interested in practice as much as thought, though she is rightly cautious about its scale. Crucially, however, across Elsakkers's oeuvre male-authored texts provide brief glimpses of 'women's business'.[37] Or, to quote the final sentence of one article, '[u]ltimately, everything boils down to the *secreta mulierum*'.[38] Given that this picture is drawn from ecclesiastical and legal prescriptive texts, an implicit corollary is that early medieval regulations largely gendered abortion as a female offence.

Second, by 'reading between the lines', Elsakkers traces distinct opinions on abortion within and across genres of texts, and considers their rationales.

[32] Recently, for example, M. B. Callan, 'Of Vanishing Fetuses and Maidens Made-Again: Abortion, Restored Virginity, and Similar Scenarios in Medieval Irish Hagiography', *JHS* 21.2 (2012), 282–96.

[33] The collection of ecclesiastical and legal material in a chapter on the unborn child in H. Schwarz, *Der Schutz des Kindes im Recht des frühen Mittelalters* (Siegburg, 1993), was an important precursor to Elsakkers's work.

[34] I refer to Elsakkers's published articles and book chapters in their original context (which is how I first encountered them), though they are included in her thesis; I refer to unpublished work (both the main body of her thesis and unpublished articles included within it) as Elsakkers, RBL, which is available online; I am immensely grateful to Marianne Elsakkers for kindly giving me a hard copy in December 2012.

[35] Although parts of this book are written *pace* Elsakkers, awareness of disagreement ought not to be interpreted as unawareness of debt.

[36] RBL, p. 507.

[37] Ibid., p. 494.

[38] 'Genre Hopping: Aristotelian Criteria for Abortion in Germania', in *Germanic Texts and Latin Models: Medieval Reconstructions*, ed. K. E. Olsen *et al.* (Leuven, 2001), p. 92 (italics in original).

Thus, distinctions in fetal development with which some legal texts addressed abortion by assault (abortion unintended by a woman and caused through violence by another party) were attempts to assess harm to women. The more developed the fetus, the later the pregnancy and the greater the risk.[39] Elsakkers also distinguishes between 'hard-line' and 'tolerant' ecclesiastical approaches to abortion, the latter embodied in patristic and penitential texts which invoked distinctions in fetal developments.[40] Alongside her interest in these contrasts, Elsakkers's work also explores connections, the possibilities of 'genre-hopping' by which ideas migrated across genres and social practices. Thus, she hears echoes of embryological texts in some law-codes alongside louder reverberations of sermons in others.[41]

Elsakkers's close reading of texts has put early medieval *thought* on abortion back onto the map. Throughout this book, I will draw on comparative material, both historical and anthropological, to sharpen how we understand this thought. The Later Middle Ages and its scholarship are no different – comparative material rather than the same old thing writ large – but two important works on the Later Middle Ages raise questions for this book.

Peter Biller's *Measure of Multitude* runs to just over 500 pages. Fewer than ten pages are on ninth-century pastoral responses to avoidance of offspring but, as we shall see in a later chapter, these pages are as thought-provoking as anything else that has been written on ecclesiastical responses to abortion in the Early Middle Ages. *Measure of Multitude* excavates what medieval intellectuals thought about population – medieval demographic thought as opposed to medieval demography – principally from the twelfth century onward. A major theme is avoidance of offspring in medicine, canon law and theological commentaries, and pastoral and confessional literature.[42] As his own ideas took shape, Biller recalls the experience of reading John Baldwin's study of the social and economic views of Peter the Chanter and other intellectuals at Paris around the turn of the thirteenth century:

> [Baldwin's] works gave a sharp twist to the character of the theme 'medieval thought'. Usually conceived as abstract and speculative, 'medieval thought' in Baldwin's hands became something very different: medieval academics looking at and discussing hard contemporary realities[.][43]

---

[39] See pp. 115–16, 216, 223–4 below. I borrow the expression 'abortion by assault' from S. M. Butler, 'Abortion by Assault: Violence against Pregnant Women in Thirteenth and Fourteenth-Century England', *Journal of Women's History* 17.4 (2005), 9–31.
[40] 'Genre Hopping'.
[41] See p. 218 n.48, below.
[42] *Measure of Multitude*, pp. 135–212.
[43] Ibid., pp. 1–2; Biller is referring to J. W. Baldwin, *Masters, Princes, and Merchants: The Social Views of Peter the Chanter and his Circle*, 2 vols. (Princeton, 1970).

Introduction

Some years back, as I struggled with the dispiriting possibility that the repetitive texts I was reading really were just 'abstract compendi[a] of suppositious crimes and unnatural sins, thought up in the cloister by the tortuous intellect of the clerical scribe', *Measure of Multitude* had much the same effect on me.[44] The texts began to come to life. It is a mark of its influence that I will *not* be claiming to have unearthed early medieval Peter the Chanters. For, *Measure of Multitude* is above all about contextualizing thought. Contemporary realities, intellectual contexts and textual practices in the twelfth century and beyond speak of a different world: the renaissance in learned medicine, given fresh impetus by the influx of texts from the Arabic world; the gravitational orbit of canonical and theological discussion around Gratian and Peter Lombard; the pastoral revolution following the rise of mendicant orders and the mandatory obligation of lay confession after 1215. But we can still ask similar questions to those posed in *Measure of Multitude* – and in a similar spirit. How did our authors actually think about abortion? What about contraception? (Or should that be 'contraception'?) Why did they bother mentioning abortion? What were the intellectual and practical contexts? Can we detect responses to concrete contemporary realities? The answers may well look different. After reading *Measure of Multitude*, however, we must at least take seriously the possibility that early medieval authors did occasionally put down their reed pens and look at the societies in which they lived, even if their works often incline us to imagine little more than faceless scribes focussed squarely upon the books from which they copied.

Wolfgang Müller's *Criminalization of Abortion* tackles the question of when, why and how abortion became a criminal offence in the Middle Ages.[45] Focussing on the twelfth to sixteenth centuries, Müller's book is a history of crime as legal concept and criminalization as legal practice which focuses on the example of abortion (both voluntary abortion by women with or without accomplices or unintentional abortion caused by other parties). Müller distinguishes between three conceptualizations of abortion as an offence with corresponding forms of redress: (a) as sin, the violation of sacred or canon law, subject to forms of ecclesiastical discipline such as penance, excommunication or (in the case of clerics) loss of office; (b) as tort, an offence against an individual and, by extension, his or her kin-group, subject to monetary (or equivalent) compensation agreed by norms of dispute settlement possibly overseen by judiciaries but instigated by private initiatives; (c) and as crime, an offence not solely against an individual but also against public order or the common good, subject to 'top-down' investigative procedure and punitive justice.

The complex processes by which crime became conceptually possible and legally practicable were sparked off by the shift to 'downward justice' from

---

[44] See p. 163 below on the quotation.
[45] These are treacherous waters; cf. the polemical yet scholarly J. W. Dellapenna, *Dispelling the Myths of Abortion History* (Durham NC, 2006).

the twelfth century and culminated in criminalization of abortion in some jurisdictions by the end of the Middle Ages. In the Early Middle Ages, Müller argues, abortion was handled as a sin and as a tort – but not as a crime. Indeed, to think of criminalization of abortion (or, for that matter, criminalization at all) during the Early Middle Ages would be 'anachronistic and in disregard of contemporary conceptual capabilities'.[46] These ideal types in legal history – crime, tort, sin – and Müller's narrative on criminalization will form an important background to discussion of early medieval law-codes. I want to keep spoiler alerts to a minimum in this introduction, so for the time being it is worth signalling that Müller's important book also draws attention to the complex relation between legal theory and legal practice.[47] Looks, we shall see, can be deceiving.

Thinking about abortion: The aims of *Abortion in the Early Middle Ages*

This book is indebted to the scholarship summarized above but it is also premised on a deeper feeling that the sources have far more to tell than the scholarship has recognized. The complex and historically specific cultural significance of abortion in the Early Middle Ages has been underestimated. The book is about the practice(s) of responding to abortion in the Early Middle Ages. It is an attempt to historicize early medieval thought without enveloping it between ancient and later medieval thought. At its heart lie four key propositions:

1. Authors (and readers) actively deliberated on abortion
This book emphasizes thought. To discern it, however, we need to adjust our expectations. The scholarship to which this book is indebted has helpfully collected many (but not all) excerpts on abortion from important bodies of source material, principally canon law collections, penitentials and law-codes. Like objects assembled for display in a museum exhibit, this scholarly act of collection tells a story. Of course, it cannot be the full story. Many things have not been put on display. Equally importantly, what has been put on display has been relocated and something is always lost in the process of relocation. It

---

[46] W. P. Müller, *The Criminalization of Abortion in the West: Its Origins in Medieval Law* (Ithaca NY, 2012), pp. 34–44, on the Early Middle Ages (quotations at pp. 2, 22); his monograph is a thematically focussed development of ideas explored in W. P. Müller, *Die Abtreibung: Anfänge der Kriminalisierung* (Cologne, 2000).

[47] See *Criminalization*, pp. 66–74, 134–48, on the rise and demise of *percussio* (abortion by assault) as a felony subject to royal justice in English law between the late twelfth and mid fourteenth century. One strand of the story is plaintiffs using the threat of recourse to royal justice as a way of upping the stakes in pursuit of private compensation; what looks like abortion-as-crime in theory looks more like abortion-as-tort on the ground.

is a mistake, I think, to read the excerpts collected by scholars collectively as if they amounted to a sustained discourse on abortion. In reality, they are fragments of thought. They were originally embedded within broader initiatives on pastoral care, clerical education, ecclesiastical reform, political practice and social regulation. Like any fragments, we need to piece together where they came from before they were snapped off to see what they originally looked like.

2. Church tradition on abortion was an evolving practice

Most of these fragments originated in reams of repetitive and derivative texts. On first reading, many of these texts can act like sedatives on the modern reader (ninth-century retellings of the miracles of Germanus and Áed are exceptional stimulants). Where is the thought? Over-privileging originality or mistaking resourcefulness for mere repetition will be fatal to the dual task of bringing thought back to life and seeing tradition in practice.

By painstakingly close textual and contextual analysis; by thinking carefully about authors *and* readers, texts *and* variants; by recognizing uses of the past in addressing needs in the present; and by taking a worm's eye view rather than a bird's eye view, we begin to see a picture of tradition which looks rather different from the abstract and unflinching tradition outlined by the likes of Huser and Palazzini. In the ninth century, for example, we will see a compiler using a ruling, issued five centuries earlier and originally focussed on women who resorted to abortion to hide sexual sin, to address concerns over the sexual misconduct of clerics, an urgent question for Carolingian kings and the episcopate alike. Indeed, the Carolingian 'long ninth century' lies at the core of this book because of, not in spite of, the recirculation of a large body of material from preceding centuries. Moreover, when the Carolingian episcopate debated what to do with this material, they were debating the balance between authority and innovation within church tradition. The dialectic between authority and innovation and precious glimpses of what some of the biggest Carolingian names, including Rabanus Maurus and Hincmar of Rheims, did with the material allow us to see what tradition looked like in practice.

3. Different practices generated different perspectives on abortion

I follow a modern philosopher in conceiving of tradition as a 'historically extended, socially embodied argument' sustained by 'continuities of conflict'.[48] An obvious conflict was: *Is abortion murder?* But there were other conflicts too: *Does it depend on intention or effect? Who should be held responsible for abortion? Men too? Apothecaries? How should we deal with them?* There was one especially deep conflict. Did top-down regulations and bottom-up customs on

---

[48] A. MacIntyre, *After Virtue: A Study in Moral Theory*, 2nd edn (London, 1985), pp. 204–25 (quotations at p. 222).

sexual transgression risk making abortion a tempting recourse? At least some of our ecclesiastical authors recognized this conflict.

We will also trace differences of which our authors might not have been quite so aware. In particular, the variable gendering of abortion as an offence, including intersections between gender and religious or social status, which has also been neglected by scholars. But we must tread carefully when dealing with these differences. One group of texts concentrated upon abortion voluntarily perpetrated by women (and sometimes men); a further sub-set added in the complicating question of fetal development. Another group of texts concentrated upon abortion unintentionally induced by male (rarely female, according to their presumptions) violence; again, a further sub-set added in questions of fetal development. This is a rough-around-the-edges contrast between a significant proportion of ecclesiastical and secular legislation on abortion. Why the differences? Were they different answers to the same questions, or were they answering different questions? And were there affinities between uses of distinctions in fetal development? Answers to such questions need to recognize the different priorities of different practices in early medieval society. Ideas did not simply float around. Sharply differing perspectives – contrast a seventh-century Spanish king, who issued a law which threatened men and women who aborted their own children with a sadistic twist on the 'eye for an eye' of Old Testament justice, with a contemporary Spanish bishop, who edited this law for the king's son but elsewhere likened the inanimate fetus to little more than blood or semen – must be rooted in distinct social, intellectual and political practices.

4. Beware the embryology of the gaps
Embryological theories from late antique texts circulated in early medieval manuscripts. They often imagined the processes of formation and animation in the womb with startling numerical (and numerological) precision.[49] One scholarly reflex is to extract ideas from embryologies to fill the gaps in texts on abortion. The next step is to assume that early medieval jurists and compilers did much the same.[50] But, counter-intuitively, the assumption that the authors of our texts extracted ideas from embryological texts which they then applied to abortion is problematic. To my eyes, surface affinities between embryological and normative texts dissolve upon closer inspection.[51] The exception will prove the rule. In one chapter we will see a demonstrable connection

---

[49] See M. Elsakkers, 'The Early Medieval Latin Vocabulary of Abortion and Embryology', in *Science Translated: Latin and Vernacular Translations of Scientific Treatises in Medieval Europe*, ed. P. de Leemans *et al.* (Leuven, 2008), pp. 377–413, on Augustine, Macrobius and Vindicianus. For another example see Ausonius's poem, *De ratione puerperii maturi*, MGH AA 5.2, pp. 155–6; see p. 293, below, on Isidore of Seville's *Etymologiae*.

[50] Elsakkers, 'Vocabulary'.

[51] See, for example, pp. 218 n.48, 224 below.

Introduction

between the handling of abortion in penitential teaching and embryological ideas in a text. But rather like their author, a learned Greek monk who had once received a Byzantine medical education and subsequently happened to become the most important bishop in later seventh-century England, such a connection is an anomaly. His teaching would circulate widely but there are also hints that contemporaries lacked the intellectual grounding to make immediate sense of his ideas about fetal life and that his later readers drew different conclusions too.[52]

We must beware the embryology of the gaps. There is a risk, I concede, of setting the bar too high.[53] Further research might well clarify the reach of texts and their embryological ideas. But my point is that we should be wary of consulting embryological texts when reading ecclesiastical or legal texts as if they were the equivalents of modern embryology textbooks (not least because we know so well from modern debates that people draw different conclusions from the same textbooks) instead of asking what intellectual work distinctions in fetal development were actually doing in different texts and practical contexts.

There is another reason for caution. Most embryological texts in circulation were not, strictly speaking, medical embryologies.[54] They elaborated numerological or allegorical readings of fetal development; the fetus was the means to other intellectual ends. These embryologies number among a little-studied wealth of early medieval texts which imagined the fetus. The pervasion of evocations and symbolic representations of the fetus in early medieval culture is no surprise. The central moment in Christian theology, Christ's incarnation, began in Mary's womb. But integrating these cultural and religious expressions into historical study of abortion requires care because, as a growing body of inter-disciplinary scholarship is showing, the mental association between speaking about the fetus and speaking about abortion is a modern cultural reflex which premodern cultures did not share. The final chapter will investigate this interdisciplinary development and its implications for the study of abortion.

Abortion in the Early Middle Ages will cumulatively flesh out these arguments (and others) through detailed textual and contextual analysis of a broad range of texts. Not only texts which directly address abortion, but also other texts which less directly illuminate the handling of abortion: canon law collections, penitentials, sermons, letters, law-codes, formularies, charters (really, a single charter and, alas, probably a forgery), saints' lives,

---

[52] See pp. 145–56 below.
[53] As Peter Biller has wisely warned me.
[54] Perhaps the most significant exception was Vindicianus's *Gynaecia*, on which see L. Cilliers, 'Vindicianus' *Gynaecia* and Theories on Generation and Embryology from the Babylonians up to Graeco-Roman Times', in *Magic and Rationality in Ancient Near Eastern and Graeco-Roman Medicine*, ed. H. J. Horstmanshoff (Leiden, 2004), pp. 343–67.

chronicles, historical narratives, scripture, apocrypha, biblical commentaries, eschatology and so on. Different sources and contexts will require different approaches. For now, we should foreground two things about this body of material as a whole.

First, the most glaringly obvious thing: abortion, a deliberate or accidental physiological process experienced by women, was discussed in male-authored texts.[55] Women often exist as little more than a category of thought within these texts. Indeed, we will encounter the names of nine women directly in relation to abortion. It gets worse. Four of these were from the classical world (two of them fictional), two from late antiquity and one from the Byzantine east. This leaves just two women from the early medieval west; Germanus's mother was one of them (our poet did not divulge her name, but earlier texts did). It does not help that the Early Middle Ages is the age before case histories of abortion can be written. I cast envious glances at early modern historians who can hear the voices of women, albeit mediated or manipulated, in records of real cases directly or indirectly involving abortion.[56]

But my envy does not end there. Early modern historians hear other voices, also mediated or manipulated, the voices of men involved as witnesses or defendants in such cases: husbands, fathers, brothers, lovers, abusers.[57] These voices too are largely inaudible in the Early Middle Ages, which points to an important qualification. The majority of our male-authored texts were written by a specific cohort of men: clerics or monks. These men might not have authored every single kind of text (I assume, for example, that not all legal scribes were clerics) but they still predominate as copyists, readers and inter-

---

[55] Possibly one text might have been written in a nunnery, on which see p. 142 n.74. Another, *Vita Balthildis*, on which see pp. 91–2, was almost certainly composed by a nun, but it spoke about infanticide rather than abortion.

[56] See, for example, F. Egmond, 'Incestuous Relations and their Punishment in the Dutch Republic', *Eighteenth-Century Life* 25.3 (2001), 20–42; J. Ferraro, *Nefarious Crimes, Contested Justice: Illicit Sex and Infanticide in the Republic of Venice, 1557–1789* (Baltimore, 2008); B. R. Baernstein and J. Christopoulos, 'Interpreting the Body in Early Modern Italy: Pregnancy, Abortion and Adulthood', *P&P* 223 (2014), 41–75. Female voices in later medieval cases or letters seeking pardon can be heard too, for which see Müller, *Criminalization*. For absorbing use of oral history to explore experiences of birth control before the advent of the pill, see S. Szreter and K. Fisher, *Sex before the Sexual Revolution: Intimate Life in England 1918–1963* (Cambridge, 2010), pp. 229–67.

[57] In addition to the works just cited, see J. Christopoulos, 'Nonelite Male Perspectives on Procured Abortion, Rome circa 1600', *I Tatti Italian Studies in the Renaissance* 17.1 (2014), 155–74. These works, incidentally, suggest some other important things: (1) early modern authorities did not always gender abortion as a female offence; (2) details about abortion frequently appear in evidence for prosecution of other offences (like incest or *stuprum*, the deflowering of women, an offence in some Italian city-states); (3) legal precepts – which is effectively all that we have from the Early Middle Ages – look very different in legal practice; the implementation and interpretation of laws followed changeable and uneven rhythms.

preters. They were, to borrow a phrase Kyle Harper has used to describe their intellectual ancestors, a 'small, strident band of vociferous dissenters'.[58] It may be premature to think of the clerical caste as a 'third gender' in the ninth century or earlier.[59] Nonetheless, the men who make up the majority of authors and audiences of our texts were a masculine minority in early medieval societies, and sometimes they will tell us this in no uncertain terms.

Second, my approach to this body of material will lean very much towards the micro over the macro. It is not exactly microhistory but this book is punctuated with microhistorical moments and animated by a simple but crucial idea in microhistory: 'microscopic observation will reveal factors previously unobserved'.[60] After an opening survey of classical and late antiquity, the scale at which the roughly chronological organization of the book operates will vary from church communities and textual communities up to a series of 'micro-Christendoms' from the early sixth to late ninth centuries.[61]

The linguistic and cultural zones of these centuries justify certain limits. Except for a very brief detour here and there, I do not discuss the Greek East after the fourth century; there is certainly an interesting history yet to be fully explored.[62] I will not return to Anglo-Saxon England or early medieval Ireland after the seventh century and I do not seek to cover Scandinavia. To spell it out: I do not discuss texts on abortion written in vernaculars. Here, too, there are important histories waiting to be written.[63]

I must mention one further point here. A large corpus of medical texts circulated in the Early Middle Ages, some copies of classical and late antique medical texts, some adaptations, and some altogether newer works. A significant number of medical manuscripts survive too, predominantly from the Carolingian period onwards.[64] Many texts, from herbals and pharmacopaeia

[58] *From Shame to Sin: The Christian Transformation of Sexual Morality in Late Antiquity* (Cambridge MA, 2013), p. 135.
[59] R. Stone, 'Gender and Hierarchy: Archbishop Hincmar of Rheims (845–882) as a Religious Man', in *Religious Men and Masculine Identity in the Middle Ages*, ed. P. H. Cullum and K. J. Lewis (Woodbridge, 2013), pp. 31–4.
[60] G. Levi, 'On Microhistory', in *New Perspectives on Historical Writing*, ed. P. Burke (Cambridge, 1991), p. 97. A confession: I had not seen my research in this light until Antonio Sennis suggested the connection to me some years ago.
[61] The term is taken from a chapter in P. Brown, *The Rise of Western Christendom*, 2nd edn (Oxford, 2003), pp. 355–79.
[62] E. Poulakou-Rebelakou, E. Lasceratos and S. G. Marketos, 'Abortions in Byzantine Times (325–1453 AD)', *Vesalius* 2.1 (1996), 19-25; M.-H. Congourdeau, 'Les variations du désir d'enfant à Byzance', in *Becoming Byzantine: Children and Childhood in Byzantium*, ed. A. Papaconstantinou and A.-M. Talbot (Washington DC, 2009), pp. 35–63. See Huser, *Crime*, pp. 31–2, on eastern canon law.
[63] See, for example, L. Lövkrona, 'Gender, Power and Honour: Child Murder in Premodern Sweden', *Ethnologia Europaea* 32.1 (2004), 5–14
[64] For the manuscripts, see A. Beccaria, *I codici di medicina del periodo presalernitano (secoli IX, X e XI)* (Rome, 1956); E. Wickersheimer, *Les manuscrits latins de médecine du haut Moyen Âge dans les bibliothèques de France* (Paris, 1966). For an overview of Latin

to gynaecological works, included details of drugs, recipes, drinks, amulets and other things besides for provoking menstruation, expelling dead fetuses, purging the womb after childbirth or miscarriage, preventing conception and causing abortion. In readers' minds, these texts and their prescriptions may be strongly associated with the historical study of practice rather than thought.[65] But they also raise questions about thought. How, if at all, did early medieval medicine construe and respond to abortion as a problem? How should we interpret recipes for causing abortion alongside others for expelling dead fetuses or provoking menstruation? How were older texts read and used as their readerships evolved over time? Did medical texts or practice influence non-medical perspectives? Did medicine absorb the values of Christianizing societies? How was reproductive knowledge gendered?

These are huge questions in a field which, despite important new work, remains underdeveloped (as the title of the best introduction to it captures) and relatively quarantined from other areas of early medieval historiography.[66] Cursory answers would be hypocritical and this book is already long enough.[67] Let us at least recognize a deep cultural tension. Take the Carolingian context. Copies of older medical texts, it appears, were more likely to contain direct information on causing abortion than younger texts composed from the eighth century onward. In an important unpublished study of recipe books from eighth- to tenth-century manuscripts, Elsakkers has managed to identify just three clear references to abortifacients.[68] Here is one of them, from a ninth-century *receptarium* or recipe-book: 'A condemned

gynaecological works circulating in the early medieval west, see M. Green, 'The Transmission of Ancient Theories of Female Physiology and Disease through the Early Middle Ages' (unpublished Ph.D. dissertation, Princeton University, 1985), pp. 130–94.

[65] See J. M. Riddle, *Contraception and Abortion from the Ancient World to the Renaissance* (Cambridge MA, 1992) and J. M. Riddle, *Eve's Herbs: A History of Contraception and Abortion in the West* (Cambridge MA, 1997), for arguments that ancient and medieval reproductive technologies contained effective contraceptives and oral abortifacients; and that the information in (overwhelmingly male-authored) medical texts was only a subset of a body of knowledge which was widely diffused through oral transmission (principally between women). For powerful critiques of Riddle's positivist reading of texts, neglect of the gendered contexts of medical knowledge and practice, and problematic assumptions about the relationship between medical texts and the societies in which they were read, see H. King, *Hippocrates' Women: Reading the Female Body in Classical Greece* (London, 1998), pp. 132–56; M. Green, 'Gendering the History of Women's Healthcare', *Gender & History* 20.3 (2008), 487–518.

[66] P. Horden, 'What's Wrong with Early Medieval Medicine?', *SHM* 24.1 (2011), 5–25.

[67] As I finish writing this book, I have just begun a new research project exploring constructions of and responses to infertility and childlessness in the Carolingian period. One strand of this research will closely examine the texts and social contexts of reproductive medicine in the eighth to tenth centuries.

[68] '*Proicit, purgat et sanat*: Emmenagogues and Purgatives for Women's Diseases in Early Medieval Recipe Books', in Elsakkers, RBL, pp. 283–324.

Introduction

potion. Throw magic herbs and gargle[?] three times if they will not have bones and it expels human marrow of however many days.'[69]

Was this written (or indeed read) with a frown or a wink? Was it suppression of knowledge or a subterfuge to communicate it? It is hard to know. This *receptarium* was one of several recipe-books and plenty of other medical material in a composite manuscript; the earlier part contained text from the Old Testament. It was written at St Gall, one of the great Carolingian centres of learning, where it nestled on the shelves alongside a wealth of other volumes including ecclesiastical regulations and legal texts. The St Gall manuscript is not representative of early medieval or specifically Carolingian medicine (the challenge of early medieval medicine is that no manuscript is).[70] I do not quote it to suggest systematic suppression of reproductive knowledge in early medieval medical texts. But there were frowns or winks at St Gall, and they point to a big question. How did such different forms of knowledge about abortion, practical and moral, co-exist on the same shelves? An answer is beyond the task of this book but my hope is that it will make the question feel all the more urgent.

* * *

The handling of abortion in the Early Middle Ages is not reducible to the preservation of a heritage. We must start with a scrutiny of that heritage. Chapter one is a highly selective survey of Greco-Roman, Jewish and Christian responses to abortion in classical and late antiquity. It examines distinct perspectives on abortion generated by specific social and literary practices (from Roman law to medical ethics, from apologetics to satire) as well as more widely dispersed moral tropes and mental associations. I will try to highlight the intricacy and tensions masked by long-standing ideas about Greco-Roman and Christian *Zeitgeister*. The survey and its underlying selectivity also has ulterior motives. One is to introduce texts which had long early medieval careers (and readers are already advised to bookmark p. 44 below). Another is to emphasize that many other texts did not. The inheritance of Rome, to borrow Chris Wickham's useful expression, was partial.[71]

Roman moralists tended to view abortion through a civic lens. The sermons of the famous preacher, Caesarius of Arles, show that even in the still Romanized towns of southern Gaul in the sixth century, bishops viewed abortion as a church community problem. Caesarius is no stranger to histories of

---

[69] 'Potio denoncupata. Herba maleficia proice et ter guga si ossa non habuerint et medulla hominina quamlibet diuturnas expellit', *St Galler Receptarium (A)* 141 (St Gall, Stiftsbibliothek, Ms. 44, fols. 337–54), ed. J. Jörimann, *Frühmittelalterliche Rezeptarien* (Zurich, 1925), p. 30; see too Elsakkers, '*Proicit*', p. 314, and Beccaria, *Codici*, pp. 364–8, on the manuscript.

[70] Horden, 'What's Wrong', 17–18.

[71] C. Wickham, *The Inheritance of Rome: A History of Europe from 400 to 1000* (London, 2009).

birth control but his rhetoric on abortion has not been studied in the context of his attempts to form a Christian community in southern Gaul through the transformative power of the spoken word. Abortion was one node in a network of pastoral concerns and we will pay particular attention to how Caesarius tied sin to gender. By the later sixth century Caesarius's model for forming Christian communities through the power of the word had been eclipsed by an alternative style of community religion centred on the cult of saints and memories of their miracles. Two important witnesses to this religious evolution, Venantius Fortunatus and Gregory of Tours, also happened to write two strikingly different miracle stories involving abortion and dead infants. Enter Germanus (we will finally learn his mother's name). Their oeuvres are important too for imagining how unwanted pregnancies and responses to them were the product of different social, cultural and familial forces in early Merovingian society.

But not political forces. In chapter three, however, we shall encounter a rather different picture in Visigothic Iberia. By the seventh century, abortion had become politicized in a specific Visigothic sense: condemnation was loudly expressed in the ideological idiom of unity which characterized royal discourse following the Visigothic conversion from Arianism to Catholicism in 589. Religion and politics, it seems, had converged. The interplay between church and state is discernible too in the historical layers of Visigothic law, where the slowly dissolving residue of Roman law met with newer infusions of politicized rhetoric. But this is only one strand of the story. Another is how churchmen addressed abortion in moments of localized ecclesiastical reform. We will see surface anxieties over heresy – not just any old heresy, but the 'national' heresy, Priscillianism – and deeper concerns over pastoral care and clerical education.

Pastoral care and clerical education were integral to the sources which allow us to see most clearly how clerics and bishops actively thought about abortion: penitentials. Chapter four demonstrates how penitentials can be used to recapture, in Alexander Murray's words, 'nuances of thought easily ignored'.[72] By the eighth century, three penitential rulings on abortion had emerged in three distinct traditions of penitential composition. On visits to different micro-Christendoms – early Ireland, Merovingian Francia and Anglo-Saxon England – we will recover the highly specific preoccupations which generated these very different approaches to abortion. The rest of the chapter will turn from the thought of authors to the thought of readers. What makes the penitentials such tricky texts – their highly derivative nature – also makes it possible to see the thoughts of one very specific kind of reader: penitential compilers who ordered and tweaked their sources.

Penitentials have been marginalized from church tradition in twentieth-century histories of abortion. But chapter five demonstrates that the tex-

---

[72] *Suicide in the Middle Ages, volume II: The Curse on Self-Murder* (Oxford, 2000), p. 266.

Introduction

ture of tradition in the ninth century was more uneven than the smooth picture in older narratives suggests. There was no clear dichotomy between penitential rulings and conciliar canons, though there was a creative tension between authority and innovation in the development of church tradition on abortion. We will contextualize what counted as authoritative on abortion in Carolingian contexts together with authors' improvisations when confronted with problems not directly addressed by tradition. Building on an ingenious suggestion made in Peter Biller's ninth-century detour,[73] the final part of the chapter will examine the reflexivity of some Carolingian authors who wrote about abortion – and perhaps even their responsiveness to real life.

There were other traditional frameworks for dealing with abortion. Chapter six examines the frameworks found in sources which, at the surface, provide a sustained non-ecclesiastical voice on abortion in the Early Middle Ages: law-codes. Different practices generating different perspectives will be key to understanding the distinctive legal framework for handling abortion in older law-codes preserved in Carolingian manuscripts. Answers to important questions surrounding the relation between ecclesiastical and legal norms, and the applicability of legal ideal types (tort, sin and crime) will become more complicated when we turn to younger law-codes from the eighth and ninth centuries, and what they might tell us about how even older law-codes were interpreted and contested in practice.

The big problem is that we do not have any surviving cases. Or do we? One accusation of abortion against a named woman survives from the Early Middle Ages, but it has scarcely entered histories of abortion. By a quirk of history the accused was a Carolingian queen and the accusation was part of the opening act to a *cause célèbre* which dominated Carolingian political life in the 850s and 860s: the divorce of Lothar II and Theutberga. Chapter seven is a microhistorical examination of this episode. There are challenges. To understand the accusation, detective work is required to establish a subtle revision to the conventional narrative of the case. But there are also opportunities, not least the chance to see what a Carolingian legal expert, Hincmar of Rheims, thought about the accusation – and also the resources he drew upon when discussing it. The plural of anecdote is not data. What can the exceptional accusation against Theutberga really tell us about the handling of abortion? Certainly, that mud sometimes sticks to those who throw it, but also the huge gulf between regulations in theory and regulations in practice.

Theutberga also teaches us, as if we were in need of reminding, that women and their experiences are elusive. The final chapter turns to another elusive historical subject: the aborted fetus. It focuses on a neglected theme in speculative thought and symbolic language: *abortivi*, aborted fetuses, stillborn infants, or miscarried children. Chapter eight will examine discussion of *abortivi* in eschatology to explore the conceptual tensions raised by the doctrines

---

[73] *Measure of Multitude*, pp. 178–85.

of bodily resurrection and original sin. It was in this intellectual context, more than anywhere else, that thinkers struggled to visualize the bodies of fetuses, dead or alive. The rest of the chapter will turn to *abortivi* as a metaphor in scriptural interpretation. In particular, *abortivi* were a polemical ecclesiological image. But they were no innocent victims. *Abortivi* stood for problem groups – heretics, sinners, Jews – flung from the womb of the mother church. By inverting our expectations of what a culture antipathetic to abortion looks like, such images epitomize the complex cultural significance of abortion in the Early Middle Ages.

1

From Hope of Children to Object of God's Care: Abortion in Classical and Late Antique Society

The following lines come from the *Sibylline Oracles*:

> Those who defiled their flesh with vicious acts,
> And who undid the belt of maidenhood
> In secret union; who their unborn load
> Aborted, or cast out the child, once born,
> Unlawfully; witches and poisoners
> Them too the wrath of heavenly, deathless God
> Shall fasten to the pillar, where a stream
> Of quenchless fire flows round[.][1]

The second book of the *Sibylline Oracles* was composed by Hellenistic Jews at some point between 30 BCE and 250 CE, and was later heavily redacted by Christian hands. Whether written by Jewish authors or Christian redactors, this graphic visualization of the punishment awaiting those who practised abortion represented a response to abortion which was genuinely distinctive in Greco-Roman society. Yet the authors wrote in Ancient Greek, a *lingua franca* of the Roman Empire; in hexameters, the metre of classical epic; and in the guise of the Sibyls, the famed prophetesses of Greco-Roman religion.[2] In some manuscripts the second book of the *Sibylline Oracles* was interpolated with a passage from the *Sentences* of Pseudo-Phocylides, another Hellenistic Jewish composition, though some scholars once believed it was the work of Christians. Written in the name of Phocylides, an archaic Greek poet, the *Sentences* bluntly rejected abortion and infant exposure: 'Do not let a woman destroy the unborn babe in her belly, nor after its birth throw it before the dogs and the vultures as a prey'.[3]

The Early Middle Ages inherited only fractions and fragments of networks of ideas on abortion from classical and late antiquity. The categories by which

---

[1] *Sibylline Oracles* 2.279–86, trans. J. L. Lightfoot, *The Sibylline Oracles: With Introduction, Translation, and Commentary on the First and Second Books* (Oxford, 2007), p. 320 (Greek text at p. 301). All dates in this chapter are CE rather than BCE, unless otherwise noted.

[2] J. J. Collins, 'Sibylline Oracles', in *The Old Testament Pseudepigrapha*, 2 vols., ed. J. H. Charlesworth (London, 1983), I, pp. 317–24, 330–4; E. Koskenniemi, *The Exposure of Infants among Jews and Christians in Antiquity* (Sheffield, 2009), p. 26.

[3] *Sentences* 184–5, translation quoted from Koskenniemi, *Exposure*, p. 37; for the Greek text, see W. T. Wilson, *The Sentences of Pseudo-Phocylides* (Berlin, 2005), p. 221.

scholars have attempted to impose order on this huge body of material – Roman, Jewish, Christian, with further subcategories like Stoic, Hellenistic, Gnostic, and so on – approximately correspond to real intellectual and social boundaries. But the *Sibylline Oracles* and *Sentences* are reminders that these boundaries were both mobile and porous – and that the early medieval inheritance was partial.

This chapter surveys attitudes to abortion in classical and late Roman as well as early and late antique Christian texts. It is highly selective, anticipating the needs of subsequent chapters.[4] I have side-lined numerous sources with great reluctance (not least because my interest in the history of abortion was first sparked while still a student of the ancient world) together with several important topics including: ancient Greek perspectives;[5] abortion in classical medicine (except for medical ethics);[6] Greco-Roman as well as Jewish influences on Christian attitudes (Stoic, Pythagorean, Orphic – possibilities which are not mutually exclusive);[7] philosophical and theological discussion of conception, embryogenesis and animation;[8] and extensive comparison with attitudes to infanticide and infant exposure.[9]

[4] In addition to works mentioned at p. 4–5 in the introduction, on attitudes in classical and late antiquity, see K. Hopkins, 'Contraception in the Roman Empire', *Comparative Studies in Society and History* 8 (1965), 124–51; R. Etienne, 'La conscience médicale antique et la vie des enfants', *Annales de démographie historique* (1973), 15–46; L. P. Wilkinson, 'Classical Approaches to Population and Family Planning', *Population and Development Review* 4.3 (1978), 439–55; E. Eyben, 'Family Planning in Graeco-Roman Antiquity', *Ancient Society* 11/12 (1980–1), 5–82; P. Carrick, *Medical Ethics in Antiquity: Philosophical Perspectives on Abortion and Euthanasia* (Dordrecht, 1985); P. Salmon, *Les limitations des naissances dans la société romaine* (Brussels, 1999); K. Kapparis, *Abortion in the Ancient World* (London, 2002). Studies focussing especially on Christian attitudes include M. J. Gorman, *Abortion and the Early Church: Christian, Jewish and Pagan Attitudes in the Graeco-Roman World* (Downers Grove, 1982); G. Bonner, 'Abortion and Early Christian Thought', in *Abortion and the Sanctity of Human Life*, ed. J. H. Channer (Exeter, 1985), pp. 93–122; Koskenniemi, *Exposure*.

[5] Kapparis, *Abortion*, contains more Greek material than most. My bibliographical soundings in the next few footnotes are – the reader will already have guessed – selective.

[6] In addition to works by John Riddle, see too M.-T. Fontanille, *Avortement et contraception dans la médécine gréco-romaine* (Montrouge, 1977); A. Keller, *Die Abortiva in der römischen Kaiserzeit* (Stuttgart, 1988); P. Prioreschi, 'Contraception and Abortion in the Graeco-Roman World', *Vesalius* 1.2 (1995), 77–87.

[7] Stoicism: Noonan, *Contraception*, pp. 46–9, 76–81. Pythagoreanism: K. L. Gaca, 'The Reproductive Technology of the Pythagoreans', *Classical Philology* 95.2 (2000), 113–32. Orphism: D. Shanzer, 'Voices and Bodies: The Afterlife of the Unborn', *Numen* 56 (2009), 326–65. On Judaism, see p. 37 below.

[8] M.-H. Congourdeau, 'Genèse d'un regard Chrétien sur l'embryon', in *Naissance et petite enfance dans l'antiquité*, ed. V. Dasen (Fribourg, 2004), pp. 349–62; J.-B. Gourinat, 'L'embryon végétatif et la formation de l'âme selon les stoïcens', and V. Boudon-Millot, 'La naissance de la vie dans la théorie médicale et philosophique de Galien', both in *L'embryon formation et animation: Antiquité grecque et latine, traditions hébraïque, chrétienne et islamique*, ed. L. Brisson *et al.* (Paris, 2008), pp. 59–77, 79–84.

[9] See p. 27 n.22 below, together with Koskenniemi, *Exposure*.

One big question ought to be foregrounded, however. It concerns the relationship between Roman and Christian *Zeitgeister*. Did Christian rejection of abortion inject wholly new values into Greco-Roman society?[10] Or did Christianity develop pre-existing values? A definitive answer is beyond the scope of this chapter, but it does carry implications for what an answer (and, by implication, what the historical study of attitudes to abortion) should look like. It must root attitudes to abortion in questions of sex and gender, of the city of God and the cities of men, of writers and audiences, of origins and receptions. These questions are often overshadowed by what tends to become the inevitable crux: was the fetus regarded as human, abortion as murder?[11] The survey below deliberately avoids conjuring up a misleadingly coherent Roman *Zeitgeist* on abortion or, for that matter, an overly coherent Christian *Zeitgeist*. It resists using the lens of later Christian opposition to interpret Roman attitudes, whether in terms of 'indifference' or a kind of *praeparatio evangelica*; and it suggests that, if Christian rhetoric and regulations were genuinely distinctive in Greco-Roman society, they were not altogether uniform. It also emphasizes how different kinds of social and literary practices generated different perspectives on abortion, an emphasis which will be key in subsequent chapters.

The hope of children: Attitudes to abortion in the Roman Empire

An agonizing decision faced the eponymous heroine of a classical Greek romance, Chariton's *Callirhoe*. By a twist and turn of events, Callirhoe found herself unjustly enslaved to one man, Dionysius, but pregnant with the child of her husband, Chaereas. She eventually decided to keep the child after seeing a vision of her husband in a dream. But, speaking to the infant in her womb as she agonized, Callirhoe could also discern reasons for having an abortion: 'What sort of life will you face? To what future shall I bear you, without father or country, and a slave? You had better die before your birth.'[12] Like Callirhoe, when classical jurists, medical authors and moralists saw abortion, they also saw questions concerning social reproduction, personal status and gendered power. We begin with an examination of two distinct kinds

---

[10] A monograph by a sociologist, R. Stark, *The Rise of Christianity: A Sociologist Reconsiders History* (Princeton, 1996), especially pp. 95–128, argues ambitiously but problematically that the demographic consequences of a gulf in values, including rejection of abortion, explains the rise of Christianity; but see the robust critique by E. A. Castelli, 'Gender, Theory, and the Rise of Christianity: A Response to Rodney Stark', *JECS* 6.2 (1998), 227–57.

[11] Neglected problems with using premodern texts about fetuses in histories of abortion will be addressed in the final chapter.

[12] *Callirhoe* 2.8, ed. and trans. G. P. Goold, *Callirhoe: Chariton* (Cambridge MA, 1995), p. 121; cf. Kapparis, *Abortion*, pp. 121–4.

of practice – legal and medical – which generated distinct perspectives on abortion in Roman society before turning to moral tropes about abortion in Roman literature.

Seeing like a state: Abortion in Roman law
Roman law viewed abortion through two specific lenses: husbands' interests in safeguarding the inheritance of legitimate children and regulation of drugs or poisons.[13] A rescript issued under the father-and-son emperors Septimius Severus and Caracalla in the early third century typified one approach. It subjected a woman (by implication, married) who had an abortion to temporary exile because 'it can seem shameful that she cheated her husband of children with impunity'.[14] Jurists lent this legal approach an aura of antiquity. Tryphoninus, another jurist active under Septimius Severus, connected the rescript to a case originally recounted by Cicero (d. 43 BCE). A woman from Miletus, a Greek city in Asia Minor, received a capital sentence for deliberately having an abortion after receiving a bribe from rival heirs. In fact, Tryphoninus did not fully explain the background. In Cicero's account the woman had been recently widowed. Her deceased husband's interests were at stake. Cicero agreed with the sentence because she had injured the 'parent's hope, the memory of his name, the provisions of a race, the heir of a family and a future citizen of the republic'.[15] Nonetheless, for Tryphoninus, the point was clear. Any woman who 'has brought violence upon her insides after a divorce, because she is pregnant, so that she does not procreate a son for a hated husband, ought to be forced into temporary exile, which has been written by our most noble emperors'.[16] Abortion could harm male interests. Safeguarding these interests was not just a legal thought experiment.[17]

---

[13] For overviews of Roman law on abortion, see M. Hirt, 'La législation romaine et les droits des enfants', in *Naissance*, pp. 282–3; Eyben, 'Family Planning', 28–32; Elsakkers, RBL, pp. 329–31, 369–71; and key texts and commentary in Nardi, *Aborto*, pp. 413–58.

[14] 'indignum enim videri potest impune eam maritum liberis fraudasse', *Digest* 47.11.4, ed. T. Mommsen with P. Krueger, trans. A. Watson, *The Digest of Justinian*, 4 vols. (Philadelphia, 1985), IV, p. 784 (all translations are my own, though I have consulted Watson's translation).

[15] 'spem parentis, memoriam nominis, subsidium generis, heredem familiae, designatum rei publicae civem', *Pro Cluentio* 11.32; Latin text quoted from Nardi, *Aborto*, pp. 216–17; cf. Kapparis, *Abortion*, pp. 193–4.

[16] 'visceribus suis post divortium, quod praegnas fuit, vim intulerit, ne iam inimico marito filium procrearet, ut temporali exilio coerceatur, ab optimis imperatoribus nostris rescriptum est', *Digest* 48.19.39 (= Tryphoninus, *Disputationes* 10), IV, p. 854. The same measure (exile for abortion) appears without the accompanying rationale in a quotation from Ulpian in *Digest* 48.8.8, IV, p. 820.

[17] See the complex procedures attempting to balance male interest in heirs with female interest in social reputation in response to what was presumably a real post-divorce case in *Digest* 25.4.1–15, II, pp. 740–2: a man accused his ex-wife of being pregnant, which she denied.

The second legal approach focussed on the use and abuse of drugs, *venenae*, a term which could also mean poisons. Roman jurists discussed and debated the parameters of legal regulations on drugs, including interpretation of a law dating back to Republican Rome, the *Lex Cornelia de sicariis et veneficiis*.[18] Jurists thought carefully, for instance, about potential problems with the use of drugs in medical practice, including midwifery.[19] One provision clarified that drugs for healing (*ad sanandum*) did not fall under the remit of the law, but added that a senatorial decree penalized any woman 'who not with bad intention, but with bad example, has given a drug for conception, from which a woman who received it has died'.[20] The third-century jurist Paulus brought supply of specifically abortifacient drugs within the remit of the law. Anyone who dispensed an abortifacient or aphrodisiac drink (*abortionis aut amatorium poculum*) was liable to be sent to the mines or, if from the upper class, exiled to an island because, 'although [perpetrators] may do no harm, nonetheless ... the matter sets a bad example'. Bad example was ill-defined but it was related to the possibility that such drugs imperilled a woman's life rather than the life of the fetus she carried.[21]

The principal laws quoted above were collected in the *Digest*, part of the great legal project undertaken during the reign of Justinian (d. 565). From the perspective of late Roman Christian emperors and their jurists, Roman legal approaches to abortion formed part of an inheritance that was centuries old. The impact of Christianization on Roman law after the conversion of Constantine can be felt in several areas, including in law on infant exposure and abandonment. A rescript from 374 issued under Valentinian I, Valens and Gratian made infanticide a capital offence under the *Lex Cornelia*. This law channelled Christianizing dynamics through established legal tradition, though subsequent fifth- and sixth-century law on infant exposure and abandonment increased the distance between classical and late Roman law.[22] But

---

[18] J. B. Rives, 'Magic, Religion, and Law: The Case of the *Lex Cornelia de sicariis et veneficiis*', in *Religion and Law in Classical Rome*, ed. C. Ando and J. Rüpke (Stuttgart, 2006), pp. 49–54. See, for example, *Digest* 48.8.3.1, IV, p. 819.

[19] Addressing midwives (*obstetrices*), *Digest* 9.2.9, I, pp. 279–80, distinguished between giving a medicine (*medicamentum*) to a woman, which she used and subsequently died from, and actually administering it.

[20] 'quae non quidem malo animo, sed malo exemplo medicamentum ad conceptionem dedit ex quo ea quae acceperat decesserit', *Digest* 48.8.3.2, IV, p. 819. The measure probably envisaged fertility drugs, though Noonan, *Contraception*, pp. 26–7, suggests that it envisaged drugs for thwarting as well as promoting fertility.

[21] 'etsi dolo non faciant, tamen ... mali exempli res est', *Digest* 48.19.38.3, IV, p. 853. Rives, 'Magic', pp. 53–4, sees in Paulus's comment an increasing legal hostility towards sexualized use of *venenae* in the early empire.

[22] *Codex Theodosianus* 9.14.1, ed. T. Mommsen and P. M. Meyer, *Theodosiani Libri xvi cum Constitutionibus Simmondianis*, vol. I.2, 2nd edn (Berlin, 1954), p. 457. For late Roman law on infant exposure, see Boswell, *Kindness*, pp. 162–3, 170–2, 189–94; T. S. Miller, *The Orphans of Byzantium: Child Welfare in the Christian Empire* (Washington DC, 2003), pp. 148–52; K. Harper, *Slavery in the Late Roman World, AD 275–425* (Cambridge, 2011), pp. 391–423.

no clear equivalents on abortion were issued. The closest thing to new legislation on abortion appeared in late Roman imperial legislation on divorce and remarriage, which possibly had abortion in mind. The sixth-century legal compilation, the *Novellae*, reiterated a law of Theodosius II (d. 450) which granted a husband the right to divorce his wife if she was guilty of specific offences, including being a druggist or poisoner (*venefica*). A similar law – a man could divorce his wife if it were proven, among other things, that she was a *medicamentaria* (druggist) or *malefica* (sorceress) – had been issued a century or so earlier by Constantine (d. 337).[23] Both laws might have envisaged (or have been interpreted as envisaging) recourse to abortion.[24] Nonetheless, in Roman law abortion constituted a public offence insofar as it harmed husbands' interests or risked women's lives. But it was never punishable as the killing of a fetus.

The science of healing: Abortion and medical ethics
Different practices generated different perspectives on what made abortion problematic. For medical writers abortion raised questions about professional conduct and the nature of medicine. The modern temptation is to start with the Hippocratic Oath. Precisely what the Oath's provision on abortion might have originally meant and the extent to which it represented the mainstream of ancient Greek (let alone Roman) medical ethics remains debated.[25] Thinking in terms of reception is more illuminating. In the first century

---

[23] Respectively, *Novellae* 22.15.2 (22.15.1 provided a list of offences for which a wife could divorce her husband), ed. R. Schoell and G. Kroll, *Corpus Iuris Civilis*, vol. 3 (Berlin, 1912), pp. 155–6; *Codex Theodosianus* 3.16.1, I.2, pp. 155–6. Constantine might be connected to abortion in a different sense. His wife Fausta died in 326 after suffocating in a hot bath. D. Woods, 'On the Death of the Empress Fausta', *Greece & Rome* 45.1 (1998), 70–86, has proposed the theory that Fausta was pregnant with the child of Constantine's eldest son (Fausta's step-son) Crispus, who was executed the same year; and, perhaps coerced by Constantine, she had died in a failed abortion attempt (some medical texts, including Soranus's *Gynecology*, included immersion in hot water in abortifacient prescriptions).

[24] Cf. Elsakkers, RBL, p. 334.

[25] The Oath prohibited giving a destructive or abortifacient pessary (*pesson phthorion*) to a woman. Some modern interpreters have argued that the Oath ought to be interpreted literally as a prohibition on administering this kind of pessary rather than a prohibition on abortion per se: see, for example, Riddle, *Contraception*, pp. 7–10; S.H. Miles, *The Hippocratic Oath and the Ethics of Medicine* (Oxford, 2004), pp. 81–94. Like V. Nutton, *Ancient Medicine* (London, 2004), p. 337 n.90, this strikes me as an improbable and overly literalistic interpretation. Questions of social and intellectual context (and the distorting effect of the Oath's modern resonance) are more intriguing, on which see L. Edelstein, 'The Hippocratic Oath: Text, Translation and Interpretation', reprinted in *Ancient Medicine: Selected Papers of Ludwig Edelstein*, ed. O. Temkin and C. L. Temkin (Baltimore, 1967), pp. 3–63; Carrick, *Medical Ethics*, pp. 81–7; V. Nutton, 'Beyond the Hippocratic Oath', *Clio Medica* 24 (1993), 10–37; H. von Staden, '"In a Pure and Holy Way": Personal and Professional Conduct in the Hippocratic Oath', *JHMAS* 51.4 (1996), 404–37.

Scribonius Largus, physician to the emperor Claudius, used Hippocrates to frame the ethics of medicine. According to Scribonius, Hippocrates had prohibited teaching about abortifacients or prescribing them to pregnant women. His position was not exactly premised on the idea that destroying the fetus was murder. If people thought that to injure (*laedere*) the 'uncertain hope of a person' was wrong, then how much worse was it to kill (*nocere*) a perfected being? Abortion compromised the integrity of 'medicine, the science of healing, not of killing'.[26]

Scribonius's construal of medical ethics might well be an outlier, for his work was not widely read.[27] Another author, whose Greek work (and its Latin reincarnations) was, makes clear that abortion was subject to ethical and even physiological disagreement among doctors. Soranus of Ephesus famously distinguished between *atokion* (contraceptive), which 'does not let conception take place', *phthorion* (abortifacient), which 'destroys what has been conceived' and *ekbolion* (expulsive), which some regarded as 'synonymous with abortion' but others considered distinct because it entailed 'shaking and leaping'.[28] Soranus also reported a 'controversy'. Some doctors refused to prescribe abortifacients because of the Hippocratic injunction against abortion. According to this camp, the core obligation of medicine was to 'guard and preserve what has been engendered by nature'. Other doctors prescribed abortifacients 'with discrimination' on medical grounds such as when uterine abnormalities made childbirth dangerous, and 'they say the same about contraceptives as well'. Soranus sympathized with this second position, reasoning that it was 'safer to prevent conception from taking place than to destroy the fetus'.[29]

There were multiple conceptions of medical ethics and professional norms. Galen chided medical authors for divulging information on abortifacients because many were risibly ineffective and those which did work

---

[26] 'spem dubiam hominis'; 'scientia enim sanandi, non nocendi est medicina', *Compositiones*, ed. S. Sconnochia, *Scribonii Largi Compositiones* (Leipzig, 1983), pp. 2–3. Scribonius included instructions for an emmenagogue and for therapeutic after-care following childbirth or abortion (presumably in the sense of miscarriage), *Compositiones* 106, 126, pp. 57–8, 63–4.

[27] Nutton, *Ancient Medicine*, pp. 172–4.

[28] Soranus explicitly referred to the Hippocratic text, *On the Nature of the Child*, in which a slave-girl was advised to jump up and down vigorously to induce abortion; cf. A. E. Hanson, 'Continuity and Change: Three Case Studies in Hippocratic Gynecological Therapy and Theory', in *Ancient History and Women's History*, ed. S.B. Pomeroy (Chapel Hill, 1991), pp. 98–9 n.10.

[29] *Gynecology* 1.60, trans. O. Temkin, *Soranus' Gynecology* (Baltimore, 1956), pp. 62–3. On Soranus and late antique Latin adaptations of his work, see A. E. Hanson and M. H. Green, 'Soranus of Ephesus: *Methodicorum princeps*', in *Aufstieg und Niedergang der römischen Welt* II.37, ed. W. Hasse and H. Temporini (Berlin, 1994), pp. 968–1075. This passage did not enter the most famous Latin adaptation of Soranus's work, Muscio's *Genecia*, ed. V. Rose, *Sorani Gynaeciorum vetus translatio latina* (Leipzig, 1882).

were dangerous.³⁰ Pliny the Elder (d. 79), whose *Naturalis historia* provides an intriguing non-professional perspective on medical (and non-medical) reproductive technologies, refused in principle to provide information on abortifacients except by way of providing warnings.³¹ He did not quite live up to his professed reticence, though much of his relevant information concerned expelling fetuses already dead in the womb and his references to abortion tended to carry warnings. He justified mentioning information on an *atocium* – an amulet containing worms cut out from a particular kind of spider – because 'some women's fecundity, teeming with children, needs such indulgence'.³²

The plurality of perspectives represented, in part, different responses to the tension between safeguarding maternal health and medicine as healing. The tension was palpable in the *Euporiston*, a fourth-century work by Theodorus Priscianus. The third book, adapted from Soranus, was devoted to gynaecology and contained a section on abortion. 'It is never right to give an abortive to anyone,' it began before quickly referring to Hippocrates.³³ But Priscianus also recognized that complications such as uterine abnormalities or a woman's age could precipitate dangerous obstetric emergencies. He likened the difficult choice to pruning the branches of a tree or emptying overloaded ships of their cargo during a storm. Nine abortifacient remedies followed.³⁴

The obstetric emergencies which these recipes were designed to avoid were real dangers.³⁵ The most extreme recourse was embryotomy, the surgical excision of living or dead fetuses from the womb. A powerful evocation of the medical dilemma appeared in a tangent on embryotomy in *De anima*, a theological treatise by the early Christian author Tertullian (d. *c.* 225). Tertullian used embryotomy, taught (so he claimed) by the medical heavyweights Hippocrates, Asclepiades, Herophilus, Erasistratus and even the milder (*mitior*) Soranus, to refute the argument that the soul was not conceived in the womb but only later after birth. If embryotomy killed a fetus, Tertullian

---

[30] See Kapparis, *Abortion*, pp. 15, 29.
[31] *Naturalis historia* 25.7.25, ed. C. Mayhoff, *C. Plinii Secundi Naturalis historiae libri XXXVII*, 6 vols. (Stuttgart, 1967–70), IV, p. 124.
[32] 'aliquarum fecunditas plena liberis tali venia indiget', *Naturalis historia* 29.27.85, IV, p. 398; on Pliny's pro-natalist approach to recording reproductive information, see R. Flemming, *Medicine and the Making of Roman Women: Gender, Nature, and Authority from Celsus to Galen* (Oxford, 2000), pp. 164, 168–70.
[33] 'Abortivum dare nulli umquam fas est', *Euporiston* 3.6, ed. V. Rose, *Theodori Prisciani Euporiston libri III* (Leipzig, 1894), p. 240.
[34] *Euporiston* 3.6, pp. 240–4.
[35] For relevant palaeopathological and archaeological evidence, see D. Gourevitch 'Chirurgie obstétricale dans le monde romaine: césarienne et embryotomie', in *Naissance*, pp. 245–60; A. L. McClanan, '"Weapons to Probe the Womb": The Material Culture of Abortion and Contraception in the Early Byzantine Period', in *The Material Culture of Sex, Procreation and Marriage in Premodern Europe*, ed. A. L. McClanan and K. R. Encarnación (New York, 2002), pp. 33–58.

reasoned, then the fetus had been alive and animate. He also conveyed some practical details. A special surgical device prised open the womb while an attached blade dissected the fetus. Another instrument with a copper spike took the fetus's life. Tertullian's position on the morality of embryotomy is more difficult to interpret.[36] He described the practice as a crime (*scelus*), a throat-slitting (*iugulatio*) and a furtive robbery (*caecum latrocinium*) performed with a gruesome spiked instrument he called the embryo-slayer (a Greek word, *embruosphaktê*).[37] But Tertullian's charged language was also flecked with acknowledgment that the predicament raised difficult choices. The infant in the womb was 'butchered with necessary cruelty' because it threatened to become a 'matricide unless it dies'.[38]

Embryotomy was a final resort. In other words, most medical and moral discussion of abortion focussed on much earlier (and more ambiguous) stages of pregnancy. Nonetheless, Tertullian's tangent dramatized the core medical tension between the life of the fetus and the life of the mother, between healing-not-killing and killing-to-heal. It also demonstrates that a medicalized construal of the problem of abortion could migrate beyond the works of medical writers. Rabbinic jurists and late medieval casuists alike addressed the delicate balancing act between maternal and fetal life.[39] Despite the survival of Latin versions of medical oaths in early medieval manuscripts, however, comparable migrations of medical dilemmas into discussions by early medieval religious specialists will be much harder to find.[40]

[36] Contrast O. Temkin, 'The Idea of Respect for Life in the History of Medicine', in *Respect for Life: In Medicine, Philosophy, and the Law*, ed. O. Temkin (Baltimore, 1977), p. 9, with arguments that Tertullian was opposed to the practice in Noonan, 'Almost Absolute Value', p. 13 and F. Kudlien, 'Medical Ethics and Popular Ethics in Greece and Rome', *Clio Medica* 5 (1970), 104. See now the nuanced reading in J. A. Barr, 'Tertullian's Attitude to Uterine Offpsring', (unpublished Ph.D. dissertation, University of Queensland, 2013), pp. 79–80. I am grateful to Julian Barr for kindly giving me an electronic copy of his thesis.

[37] *De anima* 25.4–6, ed. J. H. Waszink, *Tertullianus: Opera II*, CCSL 2 (Turnhout, 1954), pp. 819–20.

[38] 'trucidatur necessaria crudelitate … matricida, ni moriturus', *De anima* 25.4, p. 820.

[39] Rabbinic approaches in the Talmud: D. Schiff, *Abortion in Judaism* (Cambridge, 2002), pp. 27–57; Y. M. Barilan, 'Abortion in Jewish Religious Law: Neighbourly Love, Imago Dei, and a Hypothesis on the Medieval Blood Libel', *Review of Rabbinic Judaism* 8.1 (2005), 1–34. Late medieval casuistry: Müller, *Criminalization*, pp. 100–22. See pp. 267–71 below on Augustine's discussion of embryotomical excision of dead fetuses in *Enchiridion*.

[40] On versions of the Hippocratic Oath (including prohibitions on abortion) in early medieval medical manuscripts, see L. MacKinney, 'Medical Ethics and Etiquette in the Early Middle Ages: The Legacy of Hippocrates', *Bulletin of the History of Medicine* 26.1 (1952), 1–31; C. R. Galvão-Sobrinho, 'Hippocratic Ideals, Medical Ethics, and the Practice of Medicine in the Early Middle Ages: The Legacy of the Hippocratic Oath', *JHMAS* 51.4 (1996), 438–55; M. Elsakkers, 'Late Antique and Early Medieval Remnants of the Hippocratic Oath: Early General Prohibitions of Abortion', in *RBL*, pp. 273–80.

Worthy of public contempt: Themes in Roman moralizing

It is hard to find non-medical sources which neutrally reported or, more strongly, supported abortion as opposed to infant exposure.[41] Plenty of Roman historians, philosophers and *litterateurs* construed abortion as problematic. Tacitus (d. *post* 117) constructed a picture of Germanic societies as pro-natalist communities in which 'capping the number of children' was a *flagitium*, a disgrace.[42] His *Germania* will be of little use to us when examining later Germanic societies, not least because Tacitus wrote on Germany with contrasting mores at Rome in mind.[43] A deeply rooted cultural reflex conditioned authors to adopt a civic perspective and see abortion in terms of social reproduction.[44] The reflex is even visible in an author often seen as inaugurating a new moral perspective later adopted by Christian thinkers, the first-century Stoic philosopher, Musonius Rufus.[45] Musonius's emphasis on procreation as a *sine qua non* in marital sex and his noticeable refusal to uphold sexual double standards certainly anticipated some Christian construals of marital morality. Fundamentally, however, Musonius regarded abortion as a civic vice and large families as a healthy union of individual and civic virtue. Thus, the 'lawgivers, whose special function it was by careful search to discern what is good for the state and what is bad' had forbidden abortion and incentivized large families.[46]

Men might have devised every imaginable form of sexual deviation, Pliny once wrote, but women had invented abortion.[47] Roman moral tropes about abortion sharply gendered abortion as a female offence. The gendering reflected the social structuring of marriage and reproduction. In the Greco-Roman marriage system legitimate heirs could only be produced in marriage and marriage could only be contracted with a free woman of good standing

---

[41] The reason may lie partly in the fact that infant exposure was often a husband's decision. In addition to works mentioned at p. 27 n. 22, see J. Evans Grubb, 'Infanticide and Infant Exposure', in *The Oxford Handbook of Childhood and Education in the Classical World*, ed. J. Evans Grubb *et al.* (Oxford, 2013), pp. 83–107. Abortion from a (literally) political perspective in Ancient Greece was a different matter; on Plato and Aristotle, see Eyben, 'Family Planning', 32–8, the special issue of *Arethusa* 8.2 (1975), and, more broadly, Kapparis, *Abortion*.

[42] 'Numerum liberorum finire ... flagitium habetur', *Germania* 19.2, ed. M. Winterbottom and R. M. Ogilvie, *Cornelii Taciti Opera Minora* (Oxford, 1975), p. 47.

[43] R. Langlands, *Sexual Morality in Ancient Rome* (Cambridge, 2006), pp. 321–32.

[44] See, for example, Polybius (d. *c.* 118 BCE) on the underpopulation of Hellenistic cities, quoted in Eyben, 'Family Planning', 24.

[45] Eyben, 'Family Planning', 40–2; more broadly on Musonius's thought, see M. Nussbaum, 'The Incomplete Feminism of Musonius Rufus, Platonist, Stoic, and Roman', in *The Sleep of Reason: Erotic Experience and Sexual Ethics in Ancient Greece and Rome*, ed. M. Nussbaum and J. Sihvola (Chicago, 2002), especially pp. 308–13.

[46] *Fragment* 15, ed. and trans. C. E. Lutz, 'Musonius Rufus "The Roman Socrates"', *Yale Classical Studies* 10 (1947), 97. Musonius probably had Augustan marriage legislation in mind and overstretched its meaning: Eyben, 'Family Planning', 26.

[47] *Naturalis historia* 10.83.172, II, p. 270.

(as opposed to, say, a prostitute). Anything which compromised legitimacy or female reputation went against the social grain.[48] In recycled tropes, women – implicitly freeborn and reputable in terms of status – allegedly resorted to abortion to conceal sexual transgression, which contradicted their reproductive role in the sexual economy, or for trivial motives, which compromised the ideals of good reputation which allowed them to exercise that role. Medical writers were not inoculated against these presumptions. Although Soranus discerned the toll that reproduction took on female bodies more critically than most, his ethical 'discrimination' precluded aiding those who wanted to cover up adultery or preserve 'youthful beauty'.[49]

Moralists were obsessed with the idea that women were obsessed with their physical appearance. Writing from exile to his mother Helvia, Seneca the Younger (d. 65) juxtaposed her moral decency (*pudicitia*) with the indecency (*impudicitia*) of her female contemporaries, who sauntered in public with too much make-up but not enough clothes. Unlike so many women obsessed by their appearance, 'you never concealed your swelling womb as if it were an unsightly burden or cut out the hopes of children conceived within your insides'.[50] In a second-century story about the rhetor Favorinus in Aulus Gellius's *Noctes Atticae*, the obsession dovetailed with another: breast-feeding. While visiting the home of a pupil who had recently become a father, Favorinus learned that the family would be employing wet-nurses. He was appalled at this semi-motherhood (*dimidiatum matris genus*) in which women refused to breast-feed in case, Favorinus casually assumed, nursing marred their beauty. They were no different from women who 'struggle through cunning ruses so that the very fetuses conceived in their bodies are aborted in case the surface of the belly should get wrinkled'.[51] If 'killing a person in its very beginnings, while it is being shaped and given life at the hands of nature the maker, deserve[d] public contempt and communal scorn', how different was depriving an infant of nourishment?[52]

These moral tropes – and others associating abortion with female adultery, to which we shortly turn – are easily misdiagnosed as symptoms of a Roman

---

[48] See the excellent analytical summary in Harper, *Slavery*, pp. 285–91.
[49] *Gynecology* 1.60, p. 63.
[50] 'numquam ... tumescentem uterum abscondisti quasi indecens onus, nec intra viscera tua conceptas spes liberorum elisisti', *De consolatione ad Helviam* 16.3, ed. L. D. Reynolds, *L. Annaei Senecae Dialogorum libri duodecim* (Oxford, 1977), p. 311; translation adapted from Langlands, *Sexual Morality*, p. 76.
[51] 'commenticiis fraudibus nituntur, ut fetus quoque ipsi in corpore suo concepti aboriantur, ne aequor illud ventris inrugetur', *Noctes Atticae* 12.1.8, ed. C. Hosius, *A. Gellii Noctium Atticarum libri XX*, 2 vols. (Leipzig, 1967), II, p. 27.
[52] 'Quod cum sit publica detestatione communique odio dignum in ipsis hominem primordiis, dum fingitur, dum animatur, inter ipsas artificis naturae manus interfectum ire', *Noctes Atticae* 12.1.9, II, p. 27. On rhetorical use of nursing to convey broader ideas about education of children, see W. Keulen, *Gellius the Satirist: Roman Cultural Authority in Attic Nights* (Leiden, 2009), pp. 32–5.

'abortion epidemic' to which Christianity responded;⁵³ or, conversely, as evidence of women's assertion of bodily autonomy in defiance of onerous public and private pressures.⁵⁴ Suzanne Dixon is scathing; though 'taken for centuries as evidence of [the] moral decline of Roman society', they were little more than 'scuttlebut', tendentious caricatures which articulated masculine anxieties at the same times as they offered authors diverting material for pompous prose or playful narratives.⁵⁵

The risks lie not only in imagining the practice of abortion, but also in excavating public morality from literary texts. Abortion was (and is) a solemn subject, but not all authors played by the rules. Ovid (d. 17/18) wrote two infamous poems about an abortion by his probably fictitious lover Corinna (*Amores* 2.13–14). Ovid rehearsed the arguments: abortion was dangerous (women who killed in the womb often perished themselves); unnatural (even tigresses and lionesses would not slay their own children); frivolous (Corinna wanted to avoid stretch-marks, *rugae*); and anti-social (what if the mothers of great figures had aborted them?). Ovid even imagined the callous cry of bystanders in the funeral procession for a woman who died in abortion: *merito*, she got what she deserved.⁵⁶ Unsurprisingly, there has been a tendency to decipher these arguments as imprints of public morality in Augustan Rome as if Ovid was a spokesman for popular sentiment.⁵⁷ But there are

---

⁵³ Gorman, *Abortion*, p. 26; cf. comparable assumptions in Nardi, *Aborto*, pp. 200–3; Stark, *Rise of Christianity*, pp. 119–21; Huser, *Crime*, p. 12.

⁵⁴ Kapparis, *Abortion*, p. 130: 'abortion could represent a rebellion against male authority and an expressed desire for self-determination'; cf. A. Rousselle, *Porneia: On Desire and the Body in Antiquity*, trans. F. Pheasant (Oxford, 1988), pp. 44–6. Kapparis structures his monograph with distinct chapters on male and female perspectives, a problematic distinction given male authorship of all relevant texts. Freeborn women exercised agency within a tightly circumscribed social space, on which see Harper, *Slavery*, pp. 281–91. Within this social space, abortions were as likely to have been acts of desperation as defiance. Plutarch (d. 120) sympathetically recorded a story about a Spartan girl who lost her virginity before marriage and had an abortion. She 'bore up so bravely, not uttering a single sound, that her delivery took place without the knowledge of her father and others who were near. For the confronting of indecorum with decorum gained the victory over the poignant distress of her pains.', *Moralia* 242C, ed. and trans. F. C. Babbitt, *Plutarch's Moralia, vol. 3, 172a–263c* (s.l., 1931), p. 469.

⁵⁵ *Reading Roman Women: Sources, Genres, and Real Life* (London, 2001), pp. 59–65 (quotations at pp. 61, 59).

⁵⁶ *Amores* 2.14, especially ll.7–8 (stretch–marks), ll.13–22 (Roman version of the 'Beethoven argument'), ll.35–6 (tigresses and lionesses), ll.37–40 (funeral), ed. E. J. Kenney, *P. Ovidii Nasonis Amores; Medicamina faciei femineae; Ars amatoria; Remedia amoris* (Oxford, 1961), pp. 60–1.

⁵⁷ W. J. Watts, 'Ovid, the Law, and Roman Society on Abortion', *Acta Classica* 16 (1973), 89–101; M.-K. Gamel, '*Non sine caede*: Abortion Politics and Poetics in Ovid's *Amores*', *Helios* 16 (1989), 183–206; cf. Eyben, 'Family Planning', 51; Nardi, *Aborto*, p. 240.

hints of parody, of a 'comic pro-life elegy', too.[58] The list of extraordinary individuals who would never have existed if they had been aborted took a mischievous political turn – if Venus had aborted Aeneas, there would be no Caesars, including no Augustus[59] – before the wickedly bathetic climax: if Ovid's mother had aborted him, he would never have become a poetic lover. Finally, there was one distinctively Roman perspective on abortion which Ovid did not adopt: the marital gaze, and with good reason. The image of Ovid as straight-talking spokesman for public morality is hard to square with a rather different image of Ovid in the poem immediately preceding the pair on abortion. There, he triumphantly sneaks past the doorman and Corinna's husband to reach his prize: her bosom.[60]

Words can be dangerous. Written around the turn of second century, Juvenal's vicious sixth satire on women – not so much flesh-and-blood Roman women as imagined inversions of the idealized Roman wife[61] – is a case in point. Unlike poor women, rich women shirked the toils of childbirth and nursing. For 'hardly any woman lies in labour on a gilded bed, so powerful are the skills and drugs of the woman who manufactures sterility and takes contracts to kill humans inside the belly'.[62] Juvenal's term to describe the aborted fetus might look momentous: *homo*, a human being.[63] But was it? Martial (d. 102/4), too, used the same term, *homo*, in an epigram about another 'huge crime' (*scelus ingens*) perpetrated by a certain Ponticus. The crime in question? Masturbation. The epigram, a case of (there is no delicate way to put this) one man calling another a wanker, culminated in a tongue-in-cheek rebuke from Nature herself: 'That stuff you waste with your fingers, Ponticus, is human'.[64] Like Martial, Juvenal used *homo* pointedly. But neither had penned a proto pro-life poem. Those who quote Juvenal on fetal *homines* rarely quote what came next, his jarring counsel to husbands: better to give her the potion yourself or 'you'd perhaps turn out to be father of an Ethiopian.

---

[58] V. Rimell, *Martial's Rome: Empire and the Ideology of Epigram* (Cambridge, 2008), p. 110.

[59] On the mischief, see A. Richlin, *The Garden of Priapus: Sexuality and Aggression in Roman Humour*, rev. edn (New Haven, 1992), p. 159; P. J. Davis, *Ovid and Augustus: A Political Reading of Ovid's Erotic Poems* (London, 2006), p. 78.

[60] See too Ovid's morally complex imagining of a failed abortion attempt by a figure from myth, Canace, pregnant with her brother's child in *Heroides* 11.33–44, ed. and trans. G. Showerman, *Ovid: Heroides and Amores* (London, 1914), pp. 134–5.

[61] P. Watson, 'Juvenal's *scripta matrona*: Elegiac Resonances in Satire 6', *Mnemosyne*, 4th s., 60.4 (2007), 628–40.

[62] 'sed iacet aurato vix ulla puerpera lecto. / tantum artes huius, tantum medicamina possunt, / quae steriles facit atque homines in ventre necandos / conducit', *Satura* 6.594-7, ed. and trans. S. M. Braund, *Juvenal and Persius* (Cambridge MA, 2004), pp. 288–9.

[63] Cf. Eyben, 'Family Planning', 54; Kapparis, *Abortion*, p. 36.

[64] 'istud quod digitis, Pontice, perdis, homo est', *Epigrammata* 9.41, ed. D. R. Shackleton-Bailey, *M. Valerii Martialis Epigrammata* (Stuttgart, 1990), p. 291; cf. Rimell, *Martial's Rome*, pp. 109–11.

Soon your will would be monopolized by your discoloured heir – whom you'd never want to see in the morning light'.⁶⁵ Ovid and Juvenal suggest that abortion slotted into a recognizable nexus of moral themes in Roman society – but, significantly, that there was also a cultural space for parodic twists and satirical inflation of these themes.⁶⁶

Two final thoughts accompany a few final texts. Perhaps these are exceptional, but even exceptions hint at cultural possibilities. First, on gendering. It was at least intelligible for Roman writers to absorb the squalid connotations of abortion when casting aspersions on the reputation of powerful men. The empress Octavia was publicly accused of infertility, exiled on dubious charges of adultery and abortion, and finally executed in AD 62. But in his account Tacitus attacked her husband and accuser, Nero (d. 68), for his merciless slander of Octavia.⁶⁷ More pertinently, widely reported stories about the emperor Domitian (d. 96) alleged that he had seduced his niece, Julia Flavia (d. 91), and forced her into an abortion from which she died. He became a perfect *exemplum* in Juvenal's satire on moral hypocrisy. Domitian had resurrected draconian laws at the precise moment 'when Julia was unsealing her fertile womb with numerous abortion-inducers and pouring out lumps which resembled her uncle'.⁶⁸ In both cases, authors refused to interpret rumours of abortion through conventional moral tropes about women.

Second, there was evidently significant philosophical debate over when life began in the womb, when bodies were formed and souls were created.⁶⁹ The extent to which such discussions were really about abortion (or were applied to the question of abortion) is often taken for granted. But a curious second-century tract, *Whether what is carried in the womb is a living being*, explicitly made the connection. After outlining various positions on the question, the tract elaborated a richly metaphysical embryology to argue emphatically that the fetus was a living being. The climax was a rallying cry for embryonic vengeance for abortion:

> Come out of the recesses without the fear that you [embryos] might be deprived of your generation, or lose your family and your fortune. The slander of many, and the wickedness of those who commit crimes against nature

---

⁶⁵ 'esses / Aethiopis fortasse pater, mox decolor heres / impleret tabulas numquam tibi mane videndus', *Satura* 6.599–601, pp. 288–91.

⁶⁶ See pp. 285–6 on what may be the closest things to early medieval jokes about abortion.

⁶⁷ P. Murgatroyd, 'Tacitus on the Death of Octavia', *Greece & Rome* 55.2 (2008), 263–73.

⁶⁸ 'cum tot abortivis fecundam Iulia vulvam / solveret et patruo similes effunderet offas', *Satura* 2.32–3, pp. 150–1. I am grateful to Jack Lennon for this reference. For (less grotesque) allusions to the rumour, see Pliny the Younger, *Ep.* 4.11.6, ed. R. A. B. Mynors, *C. Plinii Caecili Secundi epistolarum libri decem* (Oxford, 1963), p. 110; Suetonius, *De vita Caesarum* 8.22, ed. and trans. J. C. Rolfe, *Suetonius*, 2 vols. (s.l., 1914), I, pp. 382–3.

⁶⁹ Kapparis, *Abortion*, pp. 33–52.

will not erase you. You yourselves will become the avengers like Pericles, Peisistratus, Paris, like Alexander the Macedonian and Hercules.[70]

The tract is idiosyncratic – it recognizes that its arguments run against more culturally dominant views. Moreover, it resembles a rhetorical exercise more than a philosophical treatise. Nonetheless, sharp rejection of abortion was at least an intelligible rhetorical pose, a recognizable moral niche, in Greco-Roman society.

The object of God's concern: Abortion and Christianity

The *Didache*, literally meaning teaching or training, was a brief manual written in the later first or early second century for a very early Christian community. The second rule of training commenced with ten offences, including murder and sexual transgression. After a pair of prohibitions on magical practice and making potions came a prohibition on forms of child-murder: 'You will not murder offspring by means of abortion [*ou phoneuseis teknon en phthorą*] / (and) you will not kill [him/her] having been born'.[71] Opposition to abortion and infanticide was integrated into the value systems of Christian communities from a very early stage.

These value systems did not emerge *ex nihilo*. The *Epistle of Barnabas*, roughly contemporaneous with the *Didache*, contained a similar prohibition of abortion and infanticide. The two works are otherwise rather different. Both texts had probably used a common source and the likelihood is that this common source was a Jewish text. As Erkki Koskenniemi has recently stressed, the Jewish milieus out of which early Christian values evolved have been underappreciated in histories of abortion. Ethical norms given condensed expression in the *Didache* and *Epistle of Barnabas* stand in a line of texts, including the *Sibylline Oracles* and Pseudo-Phocylides, which problematized abortion and infanticide.[72] Origins, however, did not fully predetermine subsequent trajectories.

Identity politics: Apologists on abortion

Christian rhetoric on abortion was genuinely distinctive in Greco-Roman society. But distinctiveness was also an image deliberately cultivated by

---

[70] *Whether what is carried in the womb is a living being* 3; translation from the appendix (with introduction and comments) in Kapparis, *Abortion*, pp. 201–13 (quotation at p. 210).

[71] *Didache* 2.2 [A8–9], ed. and trans. A. Milavec, *The Didache: Faith, Hope, and Life of the Earliest Christian Communities, 50–70 C.E.* (New York, 2003), p. 15.

[72] Koskenniemi, *Exposure*, pp. 29–30, 89–91, on the *Didache*, *Epistle to Barnabas* and their lost source, and, more broadly, pp. 15–87 on Jewish tradition from the Pentateuch to the Talmud. Bonner, 'Abortion', p. 106, who bluntly describes the second *Sibylline Oracle* as Christian, provides a small example of Koskenniemi's contention.

apologists in the second and third centuries. There was a subtle paradox. Apologists claimed Christian communities as networks of counter-cultural moral excellence, and their rhetoric gives the impression of a chasm in values between Christian communities and Greco-Roman society. Yet their works were also intended to resonate with non-Christian audiences, and their arguments drew substantively and stylistically on Greco-Roman literature. As a recent study of the oeuvre of one of these apologists suggests, the chasm looks wider from a distance than it does up close.[73]

When writing a defence of Christians addressed to the provincial governors of the Roman empire, Tertullian deflected rumours that Christians practised cannibalism by emphasizing religious aversion to bloodshed, a line of argument also adopted by Athenagoras when he wrote to the emperors Marcus Aurelius and Commodus in 176/7. Rejection of abortion encapsulated Christian rejection of all murder and violence:

> Since murder is altogether forbidden for us, it is not permissible even to destroy what has been conceived in the womb, while blood is still being gathered into a human. To prevent birth is the hastening of murder, and it does not matter whether someone takes away a soul that is born or destroys one that is nascent. What will be a human is human; the whole fruit is already in the seed.[74]

Tertullian also outlined a potted history of child sacrifice with religious roots in the pantheon of Greco-Roman religion. Minucius Felix, probably writing after Tertullian in the early third century, made similar arguments in a dialogue between a pagan, Caecilius, and a Christian, the eponymous Octavius. Using Octavius as his mouthpiece, Minucius rooted the social practice of infant exposure and abortion in aberrant religion too. Child-murder was the *disciplina* of the gods. After all, Saturn devoured his own offspring.[75] It was not Christians who strangled their own children or left them for the beasts and birds to consume. Nor, like some women, did they 'extinguish the beginning

---

[73] Barr, 'Tertullian's Attitude', thoroughly examines the substance and context of Tertullian's thought on abortion and fetal life, with an important emphasis on Tertullian's rhetorical strategies.

[74] 'Nobis vero homicidio semel interdicto etiam conceptum utero, dum adhuc sanguis in hominem delibatur, dissolvere non licet. Homicidii festinatio est prohibere nasci, nec refert, natam quis eripiat animam an nascentem disturbet. Homo est qui est futurus; etiam fructus omnis iam in semine est.', *Apologeticum* 9.8, ed. E. Dekkers, *Tertullianus: Opera I*, CCSL 1 (Turnhout, 1954), p. 103; see similar rhetoric in another apologetic work by Tertullian, *Ad nationes* 1.15.1–6, ed. J. G. Ph. Borleffs, CCSL 1, pp. 33–4, and Athenagoras, *Legatio* 36.6, ed. and trans. W. R. Schoedel, *Athenagoras: Legatio et De Resurrectione* (Oxford, 1972), p. 85.

[75] *Octavius* 30.3, ed. C. Halm, *M. Minucii Felicis Octavius*, CSEL 2 (Vienna, 1867), p. 43; cf. Tertullian, *Apologeticum* 9.2, p. 102, for similar claims about child-sacrifice to Saturn in Africa within living memory.

of a future human in their own organs and commit *parricidium* before they give birth by drinking up medicaments'.[76]

Both Tertullian and Minucius pointedly described child-murder as *parricidium*.[77] Like paedophilia today, *parricidium* was a technical term with an electric resonance. In Roman legal tradition *parricidium* entailed the murder of close relatives (including affines), though it progressively absorbed other socially transgressive bloodshed too, like the murder of patrons. *Parricidium* was among the most shocking crimes. The third-century jurist Modestinus described the punishment for murder of parents or grandparents (offenders would be sewn into a sack with a dog, cock, monkey and snake before being flung into the sea) as ancestral tradition.[78] In Minucius's day, however, *parricidium* did not typically denote the murder of children, a legal shift which occurred later in the fourth century.[79] By describing abortion and infanticide as *parricidium*, Minucius and Tertullian were refracting the Roman idiom of public morality to articulate the superiority of Christian moral norms.

Divine love and divine punishment: The revelation of abortion
Just after addressing embryotomy in *De anima*, Tertullian rhetorically called upon the testimony of scripture, the 'live wombs of the most holy women and the infants not only breathing there but even prophesying'.[80] Rebecca's womb was disturbed by the conflict between the unborn twins Jacob and Esau (Gen. 25. 22–3). Elizabeth rejoiced after John the Baptist leapt in her womb (Luke 1. 41). Mary glorified the Lord growing within her (Luke 1. 46). Tertullian ended with Jeremiah 1. 5, 'Before I formed you in the womb, I knew you', to underline his point: God crafts us in the womb.[81] Although the proximity to the embryotomy tangent is suggestive, Tertullian fell short of directly approaching abortion through scripture. Other early Christians did not.

Scriptural silence on abortion, often taken for granted today, is a product of the interpretative communities and cultural contexts in which scripture is read. It also depends on what counts as scripture. For Methodius of Olympus (d. *c.* 311) scripture spoke loudly and clearly on abortion. God was the supreme craftsman who 'mould[ed] us like wax within the womb from moist and infinitesimal seed' and solicitously ensured that the 'fetus is not strangled

---

[76] 'sunt quae in ipsis visceribus medicaminibus epotis originem futuri hominis extinguant et parricidium faciant, antequam pariant', *Octavius* 30.2, p. 43.
[77] Noonan, 'Almost Absolute Value', pp. 11–12; cf. Tertullian, *Apologeticum* 9.4, p. 102.
[78] *Digest* 48.9.9, IV, p. 822.
[79] On *parricidium*, see E. M. Lassen, 'The Ultimate Crime: Parricidium and the Concept of Family in the Late Roman Republic and Early Empire', *Classica et Mediaevalia* 43 (1993), 147–62.
[80] 'viventes uteros sanctissimarum feminarum nec modo spirantes iam illic infantes, verum etiam prophetantes', *De anima* 26.1, p. 821.
[81] *De anima* 26.2–5, pp. 821–2.

by the pressure of the fluids that course over it in its narrow confines'. This was why, Methodius continued, 'all babies, even those from unlawful unions, are entrusted at birth to the keeping of guardian angels':

> Whereas if they came into existence contrary to the will and ordinance of that blessed nature of God, how could they be committed to angels to be brought up with great gentleness and indulgence? And if they are to accuse their own parents, how could they summon them before the judgment seat of Christ with bold confidence[?][82]

Methodius drew this image of divine care for nascent life and divine punishment for parents who failed to nourish it from the 'divinely inspired scriptures'. The specific text he had in mind was the oldest surviving Christian depiction of hell, the *Apocalypse of Peter*, a Greek apocalyptic text composed in the first half of the second century.[83] Methodius was referring to a particular passage from the *Apocalypse of Peter* which graphically visualized the punishments awaiting those who practised abortion and infant exposure.[84] Women who 'abort their children and wipe out the work of God which he had formed' were enclosed in a feculent pit. Bolts of lightning shot out from their aborted infants, a 'drill in the eye of those who by this adultery have brought about their destruction'.[85] Similarly, naked men and women were confronted by the infants they had killed, who complained to God that their parents had 'despised and cursed [us] and violated your commandment and put [us] to death. And they cursed the angel who formed [us].' Beasts formed out of congealed milk leaking from the women's breasts tormented them and their husbands because 'they forsook the commandment of God and killed their children. But their children will be given to the angel Temlakos, but those who killed them will be punished forever.'[86] Women aborted, men and women exposed. Although the gendering of the offences may be a hint of gendered expectations among contemporaries, the text did not simply use abortion as a sign to expose specifically female sin. It was abortion, not sexual sin, which was being punished. On Patrick Gray's reading, the 'exhortative result' was

---

[82] *Symposium* 2.6, trans. H. Musurillo, *The Symposium: A Treatise on Charity* (New York, 1958), pp. 55–6.

[83] D. D. Buchholz, *Your Eyes Will Be Opened: A Study of the Greek (Ethiopic) Apocalypse of Peter* (Atlanta, 1988). Only a few Greek fragments have survived. For the full text we must rely on an Ethiopic version.

[84] For close readings of this passage (*Apocalypse of Peter* 8), see Buchholz, *Your Eyes Will Be Opened*, pp. 316–2; P. Gray, 'Abortion, Infanticide, and the Social Rhetoric of the Apocalypse of Peter', *JECS* 9.3 (2001), 313–37; Shanzer, 'Voices', 331–43.

[85] *Apocalypse of Peter* 8.1–4, ed. and trans. Buchholz, *Your Eyes Will Be Opened*, pp. 203–5. Buchholz provides the Ethiopic text with two parallel translations, a literal translation and a freer translation. Here and below I quote from the literal translation. The Ethiopic text may not correspond exactly to the Greek text which Methodius and others read.

[86] *Apocalypse of Peter* 8.5–10, pp. 205–7.

a plea against resorting to abortion even if to conceal sexual sin.[87] This was how Methodius interpreted the *Apocalypse of Peter* when he invited readers to imitate the divine gaze on 'all babies, even those from unlawful unions'.

Neither the *Apocalypse of Peter's* popularity nor its ultimate authority should be exaggerated. By the sixth century it had definitively 'lost its battle for recognition' in the scriptural canon.[88] Nonetheless, it did both shape and express responses to abortion in Christian communities until at least the fourth century. In the very late second century Clement of Alexandria (d. *c.* 215) added his own detail. After they were 'delivered to a care-taking (*temelouchos*) angel', aborted infants would be given a chance to grow up and reach the 'better abode', salvation. They were covered by a kind of eschatological insurance, which safeguarded them from eternal punishment even if they failed in the task because they had suffered such a great wrong.[89]

The *Apocalypse of Peter* and its use by Methodius and Clement encapsulated what abortion meant to generations of early Christians. Abortion was murder. This was not premised on an abstract conception of the status of the fetus, however; fetal existence was understood relationally. First, in relation to divine love; more than a human being, the fetus was a child of God. To kill the fetus was to kill the 'object of God's concern' and to counteract the 'creative power [through which God] transforms his archetypes and remodels them according to the image of Christ'.[90] This was a pre-Augustinian theological imaginary, a moral universe before infant baptism and its underlying doctrine of grace. Victims of abortion and infanticide would be entrusted to angels, not demons, in the afterlife.[91] Second, in relation to parents; abortion perverted what it meant to be a parent. The *Apocalypse of Peter's* 'tactics of intimidation', the accusing cries and electric glares of infants killed by their parents, were part of an emerging discourse on parenthood within early Christianity.[92]

---

[87] Gray, 'Abortion', 321–3 (quotation at 322); see Koskenniemi, *Exposure*, pp. 107–8, on a comparable point about 'infants who are proofs of illicit connections' made by Gregory of Nyssa (d. *c.* 394) in a treatise on theodicy, *De infantibus qui praemature abripiuntur*.

[88] Buchholz, *Your Eyes Will Be Opened*, pp. 20–79 (quotation at p. 41); A. Jakab, 'The Reception of the Apocalypse of Peter in Ancient Christianity', in *The Apocalypse of Peter*, ed. J. N. Bremmer and I. Czachesz (Leuven, 2003), pp. 174–86.

[89] *Eclogae Propheticae* 48–9 (with *Eclogae Propheticae* 41 on infanticide); text and translation (with further comments) quoted from Buchholz, *Your Eyes Will Be Opened*, pp. 22–9. Incidentally, the punishments appear the other way around: abortion was punished by mammary beasts, infanticide by lightning bolts.

[90] Respectively, Athenagoras, *Legatio* 36.6, p. 85, Methodius, *Symposium* 2.6, p. 55; cf. P. Brown, *The Body and Society: Men, Women and Sexual Renunciation in Early Christianity* (London, 1988), p. 439.

[91] See pp. 266–77 below on the rather different fate of aborted infants in early medieval eschatology.

[92] Shanzer, 'Voices', at 341. On parenthood and abortion in early Christianity, see C. Osiek and D. L. Balch, *Families in the New Testament World: Households and House Churches* (Louisville, 1997), pp. 165–6; C. B. Horn and J. W. Martens, 'Let the Little

Within the fold: Abortion in Christian communities

Apologists situated abortion well outside the boundaries of Christian communities. But, as the *Apocalypse of Peter* envisaged, Christians could be implicated in abortion too. The abrasion between ideal and practice produced loud grating in Christian communities. Here, I set aside ideas and practices attributed to heretical groups like the Phibionites who, the heresiologue Epiphanius of Salamis (d. 403) alleged, ground down the bodies of fetuses extracted from the wombs of pregnant women before mixing them with honey and spices to consume in disgusting feasts. Noonan and others have emphasized the role of anti-procreative ideas and practices attributed to 'heretical' groups in prompting 'orthodox' responses, and we will return to this theme in chapter three.[93] Instead, I focus on allegations of abortion as individual misconduct within intra-Christian disputes.

Tertullian rhetorically used abortion in an acerbic commentary on a new custom at Carthage. People were encouraging young women who had renounced marriage to stand unveiled in church. The custom fatally neglected, in Peter Brown's words, the 'social conventions that human frailty demanded'.[94] It was only a matter of time, Tertullian warned, before fallen virgins would do things to their own wombs to avoid being exposed as mothers, for 'God knows how many infants he has guided to be formed and carried to birth intact after their mothers had long fought against them'.[95] 'Such virgins,' Tertullian sneered, 'readily conceive and happily give birth and, besides, to [children] just like their fathers'.[96] But abortion was a rhetorical weapon wielded against men too. In a treatise against remarriage addressed to his wife, Tertullian framed procreation as one of the burdens facing married couples, burdens 'compelled by the laws, overcome by *parricidia*'.[97] Similarly, in another treatise addressed to an anonymous brother in faith, Tertullian

---

Children Come to Me': Childhood and Children in Early Christianity (Washington DC, 2009), pp. 223–5.

[93] Noonan, *Contraception*, pp. 56–106 (especially on Gnostics), 107–39 (on Augustine, though overemphasizing Manichaeanism and underplaying debates with Jovinian and Pelagius), and see too pp. 171–99 (on Cathars); cf. Patlagean, 'Birth Control'. On Epiphanius and the Phibionites, see M. A. Wiliiams, *Rethinking 'Gnosticism': An Argument for Dismantling a Dubious Category* (Princeton, 1996), pp. 179–80; J. Jacobsen Buckley, 'Libertines or Not: Fruit, Bread, Semen, and Other Body Fluids in Gnosticism', *JECS* 2.1 (1994), 18–20.

[94] *Body and Society*, pp. 80–2 (quotation at p. 81).

[95] 'Scit Deus quot iam infantes et perfici et perduci ad partum integros duxerit, debellatos aliquamdiu a matribus', *De virginibus velandis* 14.4, ed. E. Dekkers, CCSL 2, p. 1224.

[96] 'Facillime semper concipiunt et felicissime pariunt ... virgines, et quidem simillimos patribus', ibid.

[97] 'quae legibus coguntur, quae parricidiis expugnatur', *Ad Uxorem* 1.5.2, ed. A. Kroymann, CCSL 1, p. 379.

argued (slightly oddly) that second marriages after the loss of a wife made abortion tempting from a male perspective.[98]

Across the Mediterranean world churchmen resorted to insinuations of abortion to attack ecclesiastical rivals. In the midst of heated North African controversy over the readmission of Christians scared into performing pagan sacrifices during religious persecution, Cyprian of Carthage (d. 258) called into question the character of a rival presbyter. Novatus had 'struck his wife's womb with his heel and through a hasty abortion squeezed out his offspring in *parricidium*. And now he dares to condemn the hands of those who sacrificed when he is more deadly with his feet, with which his son was killed while he was being born.'[99] Across the sea in Rome, a splenetic attack by Hippolytus (d. 235) criticized Pope Callistus I for allowing young women from the aristocracy to take up low-class or unfree partners as *de facto* husbands. The attack is a snapshot of social values in transition. Callistus had permitted unions which were not recognized by Roman law. Hippolytus's attack represented a 'very patrician viewpoint' on marriages which cut too far across social boundaries. But Callistus was also attacked for enabling abortion. These wealthy ladies 'began to try even to bind themselves round with medicines against conception in order to abort what they had conceived because they were unwilling either to have a child from a slave or from one of lower class'. Hippolytus held Callistus ultimately responsible for 'teaching at the same time adultery and murder'.[100]

These polemics presupposed that rejection of abortion was deeply woven into the ideological fabric of Christian communities. But they also hint at the challenges of finding appropriate ways to regulate these communities. A startling story from the fifth-century *Apophthegmata Patrum*, a collection of anecdotes and aphorisms from ascetics in the Egyptian desert, dramatically depicted the possibility of redemption. A certain monk, Apollo, had a dark past as an 'uncouth' shepherd who had never said a single prayer in his life. Walking in the fields one day Apollo had chanced upon a pregnant woman and, 'urged by the devil, he had said, "I should like to see how the child lies in her womb." So he ripped her up and saw the foetus'. Deeply distressed by his crime, Apollo signed up to the ascetic ranks in the desert, where 'prayer

---

[98] *De exhortatione castitatis* 12.5, ed. A. Kroymann, CCSL 2, pp. 1032–3. On both texts, see Barr, 'Tertullian's Attitude', pp. 69–72.

[99] 'uterus uxoris calce percussus et abortione properante in parricidium partus expressus. Et damnare nunc audet sacrificantium manus, cum sit ipse nocentior pedibus, quibus filius qui nascebatur occisus est.', *Ep.* 52.2.5, ed. G.F. Diercks, *Cyprianus, Epistularium: Epistulae 1–57*, CCSL 3B (Turnhout, 1994), p. 248. Novatus is not to be confused with Novatian, the more famous rigorist in this debate.

[100] *Elenchus* 9.12.24; translation (with further comments) quoted from A. Brent, *Hippolytus and the Roman Church in the Third Century: Communities in Tension before the Emergence of the Monarch-Bishop* (Leiden, 1995), pp. 520–3 (quotation at p. 521); I set aside the thorny question of whether Hippolytus was the author of this text, discussed at length in Brent's monograph.

became his activity by night and day'. Daily he begged God for forgiveness and, in time, 'he was sure that God had forgiven him all his sins, including the murder of the woman; but for the child's murder, he was in doubt'. Finally, an old man approached Apollo and told him, 'God has forgiven you even the death of the child, but he leaves you in grief because that is good for your soul.'[101]

Conciliar prohibition: Elvira and Ancyra
Back in the cities, the challenge for bishops lay in balancing the needs of individual souls and the collective conscience of communities. The earliest explicit evidence for how bishops negotiated this takes the form of two early church councils from the western and eastern ends of the empire. One council met in Hispania Baetica (roughly, modern-day Andalusia) in the opening decade or two of the fourth century, though a precise dating is elusive.[102] Bishops gathered at the ancient town of Elvira discussed a range of issues: how best to handle local officials who upheld the imperial cult during persecution, disputes over landowning, matters concerning clerics, and so on. A conspicuous number of canons from Elvira – well over a third – concerned sex, marriage and gender roles.[103] One such canon addressed married women who killed their own children:

> If any woman has conceived through adultery in her husband's absence and has killed after the crime, it has been decided that she should not be given communion in the end [i.e. at her death], because she doubled her crime.[104]

Was this about abortion or infanticide?[105] Another canon issued at Elvira was clearly about infanticide. It stipulated that 'if a female catechumen conceived through adultery and strangled [the infant], it has been decided that she is baptized in the end'.[106] The earlier canon on married women, by contrast,

---

[101] *Apophthegmata Patrum* (Apollo 2), trans. B. Ward, *The Sayings of the Desert Fathers: The Alphabetical Tradition* (London, 1975), p. 31; on this and other stories of child sacrifice in the *Apophthegmata Patrum*, see C. T. Schroeder, 'Child Sacrifice in Egyptian Monastic Culture: From Familial Renunciation to Jephthah's Lost Daughter', *JECS* 20.2 (2012), 269–302.

[102] The dating of the council of Elvira remains debated. One key question is how to relate the council's measures to the Diocletianic persecution inaugurated in 303. See J. Streeter, 'Appendix to Chapter 2: The Date of the Council of Elvira', in G. E. M. de Ste. Croix, *Christian Persecution, Martyrdom, and Orthodoxy* (Oxford, 2006), pp. 99–104.

[103] For a detailed study, see S. Laeuchli, *Power and Sexuality: The Emergence of Canon Law at the Synod of Elvira* (Philadelphia, 1972).

[104] 'Si qua per adulterium absente marito suo conceperit idque post facinus occiderit, placuit nec in finem dandam esse communionem, eo quod geminaverit scelus', Council of Elvira, c.63, *CCH 4*, p. 262.

[105] Nardi, *Aborto*, pp. 489–91, suggests the latter.

[106] 'Catecumina si per adulterium conceperit et praefocaverit, placuit eam in finem baptizari', Council of Elvira, c.68, p. 264.

was ambiguous. But, in fact, the ambiguity was useful. As we shall see, in ecclesiastical legislation what was said about abortion was often easily turned to infanticide, and vice versa. Infanticide, just like abortion, was readily perceived as a response to sexual transgression.

The bishops at Elvira prioritized the social surveillance of women within their communities. Their presumptions are telling. Adultery and child-murder happened when husbands were absent. Elsewhere women could not receive or send mail unless signed off by their husbands. Admittedly, abortion was not completely reduced to a sign of female sexual transgression. In that slightly macabre pun, the crimes (adultery and abortion/infanticide) were doubled – literally twinned. But the irony is that in one of the earliest surviving prohibitions of abortion issued by Christian authorities, some of the most distinctive features of Christian ideas about abortion were diluted. In fact, the moral priorities at Elvira formed part of a wider cultural momentum in late antiquity, the 'creation of moral forces that had never been limited to Christianity, [for] Pagans and Jews also liked to see their womenfolk reduced to order in the same manner'.[107]

Far to the east in the Greek-speaking part of the empire another council, which met at Ancyra (modern-day Ankara) in 314 addressed the same core questions:

> About women who fornicate (*ekporneuousôn*) and either kill their offspring (*anairousôn ta gennômena*) or endeavour to cause abortion (*spoudazousôn phthoria poiein*), an earlier ruling excluded them until death, and some have agreed to this. But, finding it more humane, we have determined a period of ten years according to the appointed degrees.[108]

There was no ambiguity here. Infanticide and abortion – both framed in terms of sexual sin. As at Elvira, abortion signified sexual transgression. But here the framing was subtly different. Fornication was a more open category than adultery. Moreover if abortion was a sign of sexual transgression, it was a sign that was problematic in itself too.

It is commonly assumed that the 'earlier ruling' was a reference to Elvira but, to my mind, the dating problem, the vast geographical distance and the wording (Elvira had stipulated that the wife who committed child-murder should not receive communion at death) make the identification problematic. In fact, this question is a distraction from the really significant point. Although Ancyra and Elvira might be the oldest surviving ecclesiastical regulations on abortion, they were not the earliest regulations. Over half a century earlier, for instance, Cyprian had claimed that Novatus had been on the cusp of being

---

[107] Brown, *Body and Society*, pp. 206–7 (quotation at p. 207); cf. A. Rousselle, 'Body Politics in Ancient Rome', in *A History of Women, vol. 1: From Ancient Goddesses to Christian Saints*, ed. P. S. Pantel (Cambridge MA, 1992), pp. 333–5.

[108] Council of Ancyra, c. 21, ed. R. B. Rackham, 'The Text of the Canons of Ancyra', *Studia biblica et ecclesiastica* 3 (1891), 153.

expelled from the priesthood and excluded from communion for his *parricidium*. The case was due to be adjudicated by bishops but proceedings had been put on hold after the outbreak of religious persecution under Decius in 250.[109] Condensed within Ancyra's reference to the 'more humane' period of separation from communion 'according to the appointed degrees' lay pre-existing, if negotiable, patterns for handling abortion in Christian communities.

The reader is advised to bookmark the beginning of this section. References to Ancyra and Elvira will recur in the following chapters, for they formed the core of western canonical tradition on abortion. Their influence was not equal. Ironically, the Greek canon from Ancyra, translated into Latin and augmented more than once, enjoyed an earlier and more consistent circulation across the Latin west whereas Elvira's dissemination beyond the Iberian peninsula is harder to see before the seventh century.

Church fathers: Western examples

From the fourth century onward Christian writers continued to discuss abortion and related questions like infant exposure in different contexts. A few examples will convey the varieties of style and substance with which western church fathers addressed abortion.[110] Ambrose of Milan (d. 397) inserted a comment on the reproductive strategies of the rich and poor in a rich theological exploration of the six days of creation. Reaching the fifth day, Ambrose elaborated a kind of moral ornithology, lessons to be learned from the behaviour of birds. If only people cared for their children as much as crows cared for their offspring. Instead, whereas crows did everything they could to feed their young, women quickly stopped nursing. Even worse, rich women shunned nursing altogether. Ambrose sketched out a socially stratified picture of family limitation. 'The poor,' he noted matter-of-factly, 'cast off and expose their little children and deny them when found'.[111] He reserved a more stinging rebuke for the rich, who 'deny their own fetuses in the womb and extinguish the children of their own belly with parricidal liquids in the generative womb, a life taken away before it is given', all to avoid splitting up fortunes between multiple heirs.[112]

Aside from the language of *parricidium*, Ambrose's tangent reads like a

---

[109] Cyprian, *Ep.* 52.3, p. 619.

[110] One unfortunate side-effect of my selection is to replicate the historiographical tendency to concentrate on the most famous names and neglect relevant works by the likes of Lucifer of Cagliari, Optatus of Milevis, and Zeno of Verona; see Nardi, *Aborto*, pp. 481–582.

[111] 'pauperiores abiciunt parvulos et exponunt et deprehensos abnegant', *Hexameron* 5.18.58, ed. C. Schenkl, *Sancti Ambrosii opera, pars prima*, CSEL 32.1 (Vienna, 1896), p. 184.

[112] 'in utero proprios negant fetus et parricidalibus sucis in ipso genitali alvo pignera sui ventris extinguunt, priusque aufertur vita quam traditur', *Hexameron* 5.18.58, p. 184.

rhetorical set-piece learned by rote from older Roman moralizing.[113] Other authors spoke about abortion more urgently and with specifically Christian problems in mind. In the early 380s Jerome (d. 420) had become acquainted with a circle of aristocratic Roman women, including Paula, who had got religion in a big way. He mentioned abortion in a famous letter of spiritual guidance addressed to Eustochium, the adolescent daughter of Paula and an aspiring female ascetic. His gleeful attack on moral corruptions in the church turned to the sexual lapses of vowed virgins. Such women hid their lapses unless betrayed by a swelling womb or wailing infant. Some resorted to drastic remedies:

> Others drink up sterility and perpetrate the murder of an unborn human. Some, after they have realized that they have conceived, turn to poisons of abortion and frequently dying together themselves are led down to hell guilty of three crimes as self-murderers, adulterers against Christ and *parricidae* of their unborn children.[114]

Jerome's letter was widely quoted in subsequent centuries, so we do well to remember how divisive it was in the late fourth century.[115] His moral concerns were expressed with characteristic bluntness as part of a fractious 'ascetic campaign' on the place of sexual renunciation in Christianity. The fall-out would eventually force him out of Rome.[116] Crucially, however, lapses and desperate cover-ups by vowed virgins would not have struck Jerome's contemporaries as moral delusions. In 383, while Jerome was still at Rome, Ambrose found himself embroiled in an ecclesiastical dispute further north when Indicia, a family friend and professed virgin, was accused of giving birth within the confines of a monastery before killing the child.[117] The importance

---

[113] Two tropes – moral lessons from birds, the reproductive strategies of the rich and poor – appear in Musonius's discussion of family limitation in *Fragment* 15, p. 99. On another – nursing and idealized maternity – see above on Seneca and Favorinus.

[114] 'Aliae vero sterilitatem praebibunt et necdum nati hominis homicidium faciunt. Nonnullae, cum se senserint concepisse de scelere, aborti venena meditantur et frequenter etiam ipsae commortuae trium criminum reae ad inferos perducuntur, homicidae sui, Christi adulterae, necdum nati filii parricidae', *Ep.*22.13, ed. I. Hilberg, *Sancti Eusebii Hieronymi epistulae pars I: Epistulae I–LXX*, CSEL 54 (Vienna, 1910), p. 160, with comments on Jerome's likely sources in N. Adkin, *Jerome on Virginity: A Commentary on the Libellus de virginitate servanda (Letter 22)* (Cambridge, 2003), pp. 108–11.

[115] A. Cain, *The Letters of Jerome: Asceticism, Biblical Exegesis, and the Construction of Christian Authority in Late Antiquity* (Oxford, 2009), p. 102.

[116] J. N. D. Kelly, *Jerome: His Life, Writings, and Controversies* (London, 1975), pp. 91–103 (quotation at p. 101); see too Brown, *Body and Society*, pp. 366–86.

[117] See D. Elliott, *The Bride of Christ Goes to Hell: Metaphor and Embodiment in the Lives of Pious Women, 200–1500* (Philadelphia, 2010), pp. 51–5; K. C. Kelly, *Performing Virginity and Testing Chastity in the Middle Ages* (London, 2005), pp. 33–5.

of sexual renunciation in late antique Christianity spawned a new category of unwanted pregnancies.

But another cultural shift, the 'silent withdrawal of the city', affected how Christian authors addressed abortion by the married.[118] When Augustine of Hippo (d. 430), who wrote most extensively on abortion among patristic authors, scrutinized avoidance of offspring, he naturally adopted a domestic perspective, not the civic perspective of a Musonius Rufus or Tacitus. The intellectual contexts were decidedly public. As John Noonan emphasized, discussion of avoidance of offspring was generated by theological dispute (and personal slander) over the practice and place of marriage in the Christian social order, though seeing these polemics as battles between orthodoxy and heresy implies battle-lines which were clearer than they appeared to many contemporaries. The subtext, by contrast, was intensely personal. Augustine wrote about sexual misbehaviour and, perhaps, avoidance of offspring with more intimate knowledge than most. As a younger man, a relationship with a faithful concubine lasting well over a decade had produced just one son. Rueful memories of sexual relationships and his own moral failure occasionally surface in his treatises on marriage.[119]

In the early 390s Jovinian, a Roman monk, had argued that both the married and sexually continent could reach spiritual perfection. The overkill of Jerome's misogamous counter-attack had already complicated the debate by the time Augustine attempted a more moderate response in *De bono coniugali*.[120] At one point, Augustine considered whether an unmarried man and woman in a faithful sexual relationship, albeit one premised on lust rather than procreation, could be regarded as married. It was conceivable, he replied, so long as they stayed faithful and did not actively avoid having children, even if children were not the reason they were together. More specifically, so long as 'they do not ensure that none are born either through reluctance to have children born to them or through taking some evil means to frustrate such births'.[121]

Augustine expanded on this theme some years later in *De nuptiis et concupiscentia*, written in 418/420 after the Pelagian theologian Julian of Eclanum had accused him of condemning marriage. Augustine noted how some couples 'unfurl the good reputation [of marriage] to cover shamefulness'.[122] But

---

[118] Brown, *Body and Society*, p. 439.
[119] See P. Brown, *Augustine of Hippo: A Biography*, new edn (London, 2000), pp. 79–81, and Brown, *Body and Society*, pp. 392–3, on a self-critical quiver-of-the-lip moment in *De bono coniugali* 5, just after a passage quoted below at n.121; cf. B. D. Shaw, 'The Family in Late Antiquity: The Experience of Augustine', *P&P* 115 (1987), 45.
[120] Brown, *Body and Society*, p. 377.
[121] 'non ... vitaverint ut vel nolint sibi nasci filios vel etiam opere aliquo malo agant ne nascantur', *De bono coniugali* 5, ed. and trans. M. Walsh, *Augustine: De bono coniugali, De sancta virginitate* (Oxford, 2001), pp. 10–11.
[122] 'honestum nomen velandae turpitudini obtendunt', *De nuptiis et concupiscentia*

their cover was blown when they tried to rid themselves of children because, by exposing their children, their 'hidden shamefulness is dragged into the light and revealed as manifest cruelty'.[123] Abortion was another cruelty which undid marriage:

> [T]his lustful cruelty or cruel lust [reaches the point] that it procures poisons of sterility and, if nothing else has worked, destroys and pours out by some means fetuses conceived in the womb, by wanting its offspring to die before it lives or, if it was already alive in the womb, to be killed before being born. Again, if both are like this, they are not spouses ... But if both are not like this, then I dare say that either she is in a sense her husband's whore or he his wife's adulterer.[124]

The cruelty of lust (*libido crudelis*) conveyed the destructive culmination of uncontrolled sexual desire, the lustfulness of cruelty (*libidinosa crudelitas*) captured the sexual aetiology of child-murder. Abortion was perpetrated by spouses, not isolated women. Augustine had domesticated abortion.

In *De nuptiis* Augustine spoke of wanting offspring to die before it lives and killing before birth if the offspring was alive, a hint of perplexing questions about the ambiguous beginnings of life in the womb which he addressed at greater length in other intellectual contexts. Examination of the relevant works will be deferred until the final chapter. One reason is to avoid a tangent on how best to reconstruct Augustine's position on abortion from his marital treatises, theological works and (sometimes neglected) sermons and letters. To do justice to the intricacy of Augustine's thought, the tangent would risk becoming lengthy, not least because interpretation has been complicated by a 'whose Augustine is it anyway?' debate between pro-choice and pro-life contemporary Christians.[125]

There is another more fundamental reason. Noonan referred to Augustine's works, including *De nuptiis*, as the '*loci classici* on abortion in the West'.[126] One

---

1.15.17, ed. C. F. Urba and J. Zycha, *Sancti Aureli Augustini (sect. VIII, pars II)*, CSEL 42 (Vienna, 1902), p. 229.

[123] 'in lucem premitur et occulta turpitudo manifesta crudelitate convincitur', *De nuptiis* 1.15.17, p. 230.

[124] 'haec libidinosa crudelitas vel libido crudelis, ut etiam sterilitatis venena procuret et si nihil valuerit, conceptos fetus aliquo modo intra viscera extinguat ac fundat, volendo suum prolem prius interire quam vivere, aut si in utero iam vivebat, occidi quam nasci. Prorsus si ambo tales sunt, coniuges non sunt ... si autem non ambo sunt tales, audeo dicere: aut illa est quodam modo mariti meretrix aut ille adulter uxoris', *De nuptiis* 1.15.17, p. 230.

[125] Contrast, for example, D. A. Dombrowski, 'St. Augustine, Abortion and Libido Crudelis', *Journal of the History of Ideas* 49.1 (1988), 151–6, subsequently reiterated in Dombroski and Deltete, *Defense of Abortion*, with K. Cassidy, 'A Convenient Untruth: The Pro-Choice Invention of an Era of Abortion Freedom', in *Catholicism and Historical Narrative: A Catholic Engagement with Historical Scholarship*, ed. K. Schmiesing (Lanham MD, 2014), pp. 77–80.

[126] 'Almost Absolute Value', p. 17.

can understand why. Thanks to its inclusion in Ivo of Chartres' *Decretum* and, later, Gratian's *Decretum*, the 'cruel lust' passage was disseminated widely from the twelfth century.[127] But while there are traces of how early medieval readers grappled with ideas from Augustine's eschatology and exegesis, comparable traces from *De nuptiis* or *De bono coniugali* are conspicuous by their general absence. My point is about how, not whether, these works were being read. It is not that *De nuptiis* and *De bono coniugali* had no early medieval readers; but that there is surprisingly little evidence that their ideas on abortion were being extracted by these readers.[128]

There is one more complication. Obviously, Augustine's name carried immense authority in the Early Middle Ages. But – or, in fact, because of this – plenty of works or excerpts by authors who wrote long after his death also carried Augustine's name.[129] In sum, the Augustine on abortion reconstructed by selectively extracting and excluding ideas from multiple works was not – if he ever really existed[130] – Augustine as he appeared to his contemporaries nor, crucially, as he appeared to early medieval readers.

Church fathers: Eastern examples

We end with two final examples from eastern fathers. Neither appears to have had a direct influence on the Latin west in the Early Middle Ages, but both distil important questions about attitudes to abortion.

The first example concerns the status of the fetus. A preamble is necessary. Certainly by the fourth century churchmen were discussing whether and how the status of the fetus should affect the handling of abortion. Abortion was always a sin, but was abortion always murder? One of Jerome's letters contained a passing remark (which also found its way into Gratian's *Decretum*) on how 'seeds are gradually formed in wombs and it is not reputed homicide until the mixed elements receive the likeness of limbs', though in context it is unclear whether Jerome was endorsing or merely reporting this idea.[131] Nonetheless, the basis for it could also be found in an Old Testament

---

[127] Biller, *Measure of Multitude*, pp. 158–63, referring to the passage as *Aliquando*; cf. Noonan, 'Almost Absolute Value', p. 20. Gratian also included a passing comment from Jerome on fetal formation, on which see n.131 below.

[128] A case in point from the ninth century: a Carolingian mirror for a layman by Jonas of Orléans (d. 843), *De institutione laicali*, PL 106, cols. 121–278, quoted *De bono coniugali* and other works by Augustine, but did not obviously reproduce any passages on abortion.

[129] We will encounter examples; see pp. 58 n.9, 174–5, below.

[130] In the final chapter, we will see that reconstructed Augustines have been stripped of his epistemological uncertainty and theological presumptions on the fate of unbaptized infants.

[131] 'semina paulatim formantur in uteris et tam diu non reputatur homicidium, donec elementa confusa suas imagines membraque susicipiant', *Ep.* 122.4, ed. Hilberg, CSEL 56, p. 16; in context, Jerome was elaborating a metaphor of spiritual pregnancy, the conception of faith by pregnant souls. As we shall see in the final

passage; more specifically, in certain versions of an Old Testament passage. The famous expression an 'eye for an eye' comes from Exodus 21. 22–5, which established Mosaic law covering a scenario where two men fight and one of them hits a pregnant woman. The Hebrew text made a distinction depending on the consequences: a fine for harm or a life for a life. (It is commonly assumed that the Hebrew text was originally concerned solely with harm, fatal or otherwise, to the mother, though Erkki Koskenniemi has recently argued that the story of its original meaning is just as complicated as the story of its subsequent interpretations). In the Septuagint, the Greek translation of the Hebrew Bible made roughly in the third century BCE, the passage became a distinction between a fine for destroying the 'unformed' fetus, and a life for destroying the 'formed' fetus. The formed/unformed distinction was available to Latin-speakers in Vetus Latina (Old Latin) translations of the bible, which used the Septuagint, but not in the Vulgate of Jerome, who had used Hebrew texts.[132] The scenario addressed in Exodus 21. 22–5 did not actually address voluntary abortion by a woman, but an abortion inadvertently induced through violence. Nonetheless, some Jewish authors like Philo and Josephus did draw on the passage when criticizing abortion, infanticide and infant exposure (though neither used it to make a moral distinction between destruction of formed and unformed fetuses).[133] Some late antique Christian authors at least found the distinction intelligible when confronted with the Septuagint or Vetus Latina texts.[134]

There was disagreement on the applicability of such distinctions when considering abortion. Basil of Caesarea (d. 379) hinted at it in a letter responding to questions from a certain Amphilochius. One of these questions must have concerned abortion. Here is Basil's reply:

> The woman who deliberately has an abortion is held guilty of murder. And any fine distinction (*akribologia*) as to its being completely formed or unformed (*ekmemorphōmenou kai anexeikonistou*) is not admissible amongst us. For in this case not only is the child about to be born vindicated, but also she who plotted against herself, since women usually die from such attempts. And there is added to this crime the destruction of the embryo, a

> chapter, drawing ideas about the morality of abortion from this kind of symbolic language requires care. See Huser, *Crime*, pp. 41–3, on Gratian.

[132] On the different texts and interpretations of Exodus in Hebrew, Greek and Latin, see especially E. Koskenniemi, 'Right to Life and Jewish-Christian Ethics in the Roman World: A Case Study of the Fighting Men and the Unhappy Birth', in *Encounters of the Children of Abraham from Ancient to Modern Times*, ed. A. Laato and P. Lindqvist (Leiden, 2010), pp. 47–73; see too B. S. Jackson, 'The Problem of Exod. XXI 22–5 (*Ius talionis*)', *Vetus Testamentum* 23.3 (1973), 273–304; Schiff, *Abortion*, pp. 1–17; E. van Staalduine-Sullivan, 'Between Legislative and Linguistic Parallels: Exodus 21:22–25 in its Context', in *The Interpretation of Exodus: Studies in honour of Cornelis Houtman*, ed. R. Roukema (Leuven, 2006), pp. 207–24.

[133] Koskenniemi, *Exposure*, pp. 30–6.

[134] See pp. 289–91 below on Augustine's thoughts on Exodus 21. 22–5

second murder (*phthora tou embruon, heteros phonos*) – at least according to the intent (*kata ... tēn epinoian*) of those who dare these deeds.[135]

Basil regarded obsessive precision (*akribologia*) about fetal development as a blind alley. Abortion was murder not because of the ontological status of the fetus but because of intentionality, the motive (*epinoia*) of the woman who aborted. Basil's approach to abortion entered canon law – but in the Byzantine church, not in the Latin west.[136] In fact, in a later chapter we will encounter the irony that the western churchman most likely to have been familiar with what Basil wrote on abortion was responsible for introducing the very kind of distinction which Basil rejected into ecclesiastical regulations. At the same time, indirect echoes of Basil's stress on intentionality will be audible too.

The second example concerns the gendering of abortion. Abortion provided Christian (and non-Christian) moralists with ample opportunities to go to town on female sexual misbehaviour and social misconduct. But we have also seen that abortion could be a rhetorical tool in character assassinations of men. John Chrysostom (d. 407), a famous preacher in Antioch and later, though more unhappily, in Constantinople, refused to let the buck stop with women in a sermon attacking drunkenness and fornication – no coincidence, because heavy drinking often led to visits to brothels. Chrysostom made the social observation that when children were conceived on such visits, their births were a source of shame and embarrassment to free men. But prostitutes often resorted to abortion, and here Chrysostom posed some tough questions:

> Why sow where the ground makes it its care to destroy the fruit? Where there are many efforts at abortion? Where there is murder before the birth? For you do not even let the harlot continue a mere harlot, but make her a murderess also. You see how drunkenness leads to whoredom, whoredom to adultery, adultery to murder; or rather to a something even worse than murder. For I have no name to give it, since it does not take off the thing born, but prevents its being born.

In a casual squint, we might see older tropes.[137] Focus more carefully, however, and something unusual was happening. Chrysostom claimed that recourse to abortion was cosmetic, designed to maintain female beauty. But

---

[135] *Ep.* 188.2, ed. and trans. R. Deferrari, *Saint Basil: The Letters*, 4 vols. (London, 1926–34), III, pp. 20–3 (my translation slightly modifies Deferrari's). It seems that Basil was familiar with the Ancyran canon. He concluded that such women should be excluded from communion for ten years, not for their whole lives, and that the manner of their repentance was more important than the length of time. In another canon within the letter (*Ep.* 188.8), Basil also emphasized that women who gave drugs for abortion were equally culpable as murderers.

[136] On the canon's influence and later interpretations in eastern canon law, see Huser, *Crime*, pp. 22–4, 30–1.

[137] For example, Riddle, *Contraception*, p. 19, summarizes Chrysostom's argument as women (not specified as prostitutes) have abortions '[i]n order to look pretty'.

Classical and Late Antique Society

he was not channelling the spirit of Roman moralists. It was a professional necessity, he reluctantly acknowledged, for prostitutes to preserve their figures for the male eye. No wonder they resorted to abortion, 'thereby heaping on your head a great pile of fire'. Historians have focussed on Chrysostom's rhetoric on abortion as 'a something worse than murder'.[138] But too few have noticed that his direct addressees here were men. Tough on crime but tougher on the causes of crime, Chrysostom elaborated an aetiology of abortion which held men ultimately responsible, for 'though the daring deed is hers, yet the causing (*aitia*) of it is yours'. Male lust perverted the female body by making a 'chamber of procreation a chamber for murder'. Even worse, some men turned their marriage beds into sites of sin where the 'mingle of mischief is the greater [because] poisonings are applied not to the womb that is prostituted, but to the injured wife'. When we remember that prostitution (and images of the prostitute as antithesis to respectable wives) had long been central to the sexual economies of late Roman cities, we can begin to grasp how provocative Chrysostom's rhetoric really was. In effect: at least stop treating your wives like whores.[139]

The tenacity with which Chrysostom emphasized male culpability for abortion was, to my mind, unique. His words highlight one of the neglected themes in the history of attitudes to abortion: the gendering of abortion. In the chapters that follow, we will encounter a pervasive tendency to gender abortion as a female sin. But we will also have to learn to be sensitive to variations in the social and religious status of imagined female perpetrators; and also to different construals of male responsibility for abortion. Not just licentious husbands, sexually abusive relatives and profligate priests, but also those men professionally obliged to preach against abortion.

* * *

In classical and late antiquity writers construed abortion as a moral problem in a variety of ways. Different practices generated different perspectives. Contrasting intellectual and practical contexts generated contrasting rhetorical style and moral substance. The relation between Jewish origins, Greco-Roman milieus and Christian evolutions was complex. Beneath these categories – Jewish, 'pagan', Christian – lie further complexities: the brusque simplicity of the Judaicized Sibyl alongside the intricate casuistry of the Talmud; the cultivated traditionalism of Seneca alongside the cultural idiosyncrasy of

---

[138] Cf. Gorman, *Abortion*, pp. 72–3.
[139] *Homily 24 on the Epistles to the Romans*, trans. J. B. Morris and W. H. Simcox, *The Homilies of S. John Chrysostom, Archbishop of Constantinople on the Epistle of S. Paul the Apostle to the Romans*, 3rd edn (Oxford, 1877), pp. 413–14 (translation slightly amended and modernized); for the Greek text (and a Latin translation), see PG 60, cols. 621–8 (*aitia* at col. 627). See Harper, *From Shame to Sin*, pp. 161–7, on Chrysostom's handling of prostitution and married sexuality.

Musonius Rufus; the assertiveness of Tertullian alongside the agonizing of Augustine.

There were distinctive breaks with classical priorities. The civic perspective gave way to ecclesial and domestic perspectives. The gaze of God supplanted the gaze of husbands as nascent life in the womb evolved from the hope of children to the object of divine love. Yet the distance between Athens and Jerusalem was not always as large as Tertullian would have preferred. Like the *limes* of the Roman Empire, borders were not permanently fixed and boundaries were porous. If some Christians refused to characterize abortion as a female sin, others casually retained the sexual double standards of Roman social values. The approach to abortion adopted by apologists around the turn of the third century contrasted significantly with approaches adopted by contemporary Roman jurists. Yet the laws zealously upheld by later Christian emperors retained the values of a Modestinus every bit as much as they absorbed the values of a Minucius Felix.

Rejection of abortion formed part of the inheritance of Rome, to appropriate Chris Wickham's useful phrase I cited earlier. But, as this opening chapter demonstrates, it was a complicated inheritance. Early and late antique Christian opposition has been characterized as a novel and unanimous cultural dynamic: the 'form[ation] of a new standard higher than any which then existed in the world';[140] the 'new morality' of 'these new moralists';[141] a 'novel moral-viewpoint';[142] a 'notion that human life, even in its embryonic and wailing forms, demands a sacred respect';[143] the ascent of an 'absolute position';[144] or at least an 'almost absolute value'.[145] The sense of unanimous rejection of abortion, a new *Zeitgeist*, is a distorting truth. It is not altogether wrong, but it obscures the intricacies and tensions within Christian responses to abortion. Rejection of abortion marked the moral excellence of Christian life, but also the moral frailties of Christian communities. Child-murder was a 'pagan' structure of sin, but Christians committed it too. Abortion uncovered faultlines in the sexual lives of the married, but also in the sexual renunciation of those who rejected marriage. Abortion was illuminated by divine love and by divine punishment.

What the Early Middle Ages actually inherited was selective and sometimes surprising. Thus, Augustine will be part of the story in the chapters that follow, but his role will be more marginal than some may anticipate. Apocryphal acts and apocalypses, as much as canonical scripture, will enter the

---

[140] W. E. H. Lecky, *History of European Morals from Augustus to Charlemagne*, 3rd edn, 2 vols. (London, 1877), II, p. 20.
[141] 'la morale nouveau … ces nouveaux moralistes', Crahay, 'Les moralistes', 22.
[142] Huser, *Crime*, p. 12.
[143] 'le sentiment que la vie humaine, même dans ses formes embryonnaires et vagissantes, exige un respect sacré', Riquet, 'Christianisme', 622.
[144] Kapparis, *Abortion*, p. 51.
[145] Noonan, 'Almost Absolute Value'.

story in sixth-century Gaul. While the dissolving residue of Roman anxieties over poisons will still be detectable in sixth- and seventh-century Spain, the Roman legal obsession with marital rights will be largely invisible in the very different legal systems of post-Roman kingdoms. Political fragmentation also widened a linguistic divide, which filtered out not just Hellenistic Jewish but also many eastern Christian writings. Conversely, works by 'pagan' authors trickled through alongside a sprawling corpus of western Christian texts. From the later eighth century Carolingian churchmen were increasingly collating and consulting late antique councils on abortion. Some of them were also reading Juvenal and Ovid. None of them, it seems, were reading Basil or Chrysostom on abortion.

The real story of this book, however, is not the story of how an inheritance was carefully handed down from generation to generation like a precious family heirloom. The Early Middle Ages was not a historical courier which delivered a sealed moral doctrine from Augustine to Gratian. When early medieval churchmen and rulers spoke about abortion, they sometimes drew on the past. But they were speaking in the present tense – and few more eloquently than a famed preacher from southern Gaul in the opening decades of the sixth century.

2

The Word of God: Abortion and Christian Communities in Sixth-Century Gaul

Readers of a canon law collection originally compiled in early eighth-century Ireland would have encountered a striking idea. Any woman who took potions to avoid conceiving would be 'guilty of as many murders as [children] she ought to have conceived or born'.[1] Did this mean that contraception was child-murder? That every sperm was sacred? There was no specialized intellectual discourse on abortion in the Early Middle Ages against which to make immediate sense of the idea. Condemnation of abortion was integrated into broader attempts to educate the clergy and define the boundaries of Christian communities.

'It cannot be successfully argued,' wrote John Noonan, 'that the monastic code on marital morality was worked out by persons with no pastoral responsibilities or sympathies'.[2] Even this pioneering historian of birth control understated the significance of 'pastoral responsibilities'. A tradition of condemnation was the effect of a wider pastoral momentum – tradition or even traditions. In comparison with classical Greek philosophers, Talmudic thinkers or later medieval casuists, mitigating voices will be harder to hear and dissenting voices altogether silent. A corpus of early medieval ecclesiastical texts consistently condemned abortion. But abortion did not consistently throw up a single moral problem. Abortion threw up a range of practical and intellectual problems – moral, social, sexual, ecclesiological, eschatological – which early medieval churchmen construed and responded to differently. The task of the rest of this book will be to identify, connect and, sometimes, keep separate distinct threads across this corpus. There was no single perspective on abortion within the church, but a spectrum of focal points and blindspots. One reason for this is plain. Insofar as there was a western ecclesiastical tradition on abortion, it was developed and adapted to needs in the present. On closer inspection this tradition was the aggregate of localized attempts to educate and discipline the clergy, and to shape the beliefs and practices of communities.

---

[1] 'quantoscumque concipere vel parere debuerit, tantorum homicidiorum rea esse', *Collectio canonum Hibernensis* 44.4, ed. R. Flechner, *A Study, Edition and Translation of the Hibernensis with Commentary* (Dublin, forthcoming), p. 393 (translation mine). I am grateful to Roy Flechner for sharing his new edition of the *Hibernensis* with me prior to publication.

[2] Noonan, *Contraception*, p. 143.

Textual tools produced to these ends, including canonical collections, penitentials and sermons, form our principal evidence for how churchmen thought about abortion. These texts resist historical investigation, and not only because some are difficult to date and contextualize precisely. Most are derivative, generic and lacking in individuality. Excerpts from one text were recycled in countless others. Recycling constitutes a visible and very real continuity; but continuity can also obscure particularity. The idea quoted above is a case in point. The Irish canonical collection was recycling a phrase originally coined centuries earlier. The phrase was included in a section of canons devoted primarily to women who had taken religious vows. By contrast, when the phrase was originally coined it was addressed to married women. Surface continuities obscure deeper particularities. To miss these particularities is to miss the evolving priorities and practices through which churchmen construed and responded to abortion as a problem, and the different strategies by which they integrated condemnation of abortion into attempts to define and regulate Christian communities.

This chapter will concentrate on the historical moment when the 'so many conceptions, so many murders' phrase surfaced in a body of sermons associated with Caesarius of Arles, an expert preacher in sixth-century Gaul. His homiletic denunciations of abortion were just one way of using the power of the word to define the Christian community. But sixth-century Gaul also saw the rise of an alternative approach to forming Christian communities centred on cults of saints. The final portion of this chapter will examine how questions of abortion – and also the dynamics by which certain conceptions became unwanted by individuals, families and communities – were handled by Venantius Fortunatus and Gregory of Tours, two important witnesses to this alternative style of Christianity as community religion.

Tearful threats: Abortion in the preaching of Caesarius of Arles

Between 502 and 542 Caesarius served as bishop of Arles. These were decades of political instability during which the town ultimately passed from Visigothic to Merovingian hands.[3] An influential if controversial church leader, Caesarius is best known for his sermons, of which over 200 survive. By the turn of the sixth century there was already a strong culture of preaching in Gaul, though Caesarius became its most famous proponent and practitioner.[4] He was deeply influenced by the ideas of the rhetorician Julianus Pomerius

---

[3] The fundamental study is W. E. Klingshirn, *Caesarius of Arles: The Making of a Christian Community in Late Antique Gaul* (Cambridge, 1994). See W. E. Klingshirn, 'Church Politics and Chronology: Dating the Episcopacy of Caesarius of Arles', *Revue des études Augustiniennes* 38 (1992), 80–88, on his dates.

[4] L. K. Bailey, *Christianity's Quiet Success: The Eusebius Gallicanus Sermon Collection and the Power of the Church in Late Antique Gaul* (Notre Dame, 2010), pp. 16–28; H.

about pastoral rhetoric. God's word had to be communicated in language which even the poorly educated could grasp.[5]

Caesarius's hagiographers remembered their mentor gently encouraging some with 'sweet speech' but resorting to 'sharper language' when the sins of his flock warranted it.[6] Abortion was one sin which needed 'sharper language'. Caesarius is no stranger to histories of birth control. One theologian writing in the midst of the Catholic debate on artificial contraception in the 1960s concluded that his novelty lay in sharp clarity rather than doctrinal or moral originality.[7] Elsewhere, historians have been magnetically attracted to his most striking phrase on the subject.[8] But by lifting a few of Caesarius's distinctive phrases out of the sermons, instead of examining how abortion featured within and across them, scholars have paid insufficient attention to how and why Caesarius integrated denunciation of abortion into his attempts to form Christian communities in southern Gaul.

The first step in understanding what abortion meant to this indefatigable preacher, and the message which his lay and clerical contemporaries encountered, is to examine how abortion featured within individual sermons. In the decades since Germanus Morin's seminal edition a few new sermons have been added to the Caesarian corpus while the attribution of others has been questioned. There is a growing murmur among scholars that a reappraisal of the corpus is needed. The problem lies in precisely what made Morin's labours such an important scholarly development in the first place: the huge number of manuscripts across which Caesarius's sermons are anonymously or pseudonymously scattered.[9] Six edited sermons addressed abortion, though the scholarly murmur has raised some questions about two of these.

The best starting point is *sermo* 1. Far longer than other sermons, *sermo* 1

G. J. Beck, *The Pastoral Care of Souls in South-East France during the Sixth Century* (Rome, 1950), pp. 258–83.

[5] A. Ferreiro, '"*Frequenter legere*": The Propagation of Literacy, Education and Divine Wisdom in Caesarius of Arles', *JEH* 43.1 (1992), 5–15; C. Leyser, *Authority and Asceticism from Augustine to Gregory the Great* (Oxford, 2000), pp. 77–83. On the encounter with Pomerius, see too Klingshirn, *Caesarius*, pp. 75–82.

[6] *Life of Caesarius* 1.17, trans. W. E. Klingshirn, *Caesarius of Arles: Life, Testament, Letters*, TTH 19 (Liverpool, 1994), p. 17.

[7] A. M. Dubarle, 'La contraception chez saint Césaire d'Arles', *La vie spirituelle*, suppl. 67 (1963), 115–19.

[8] Alongside Noonan, *Contraception*, pp. 145–7, and Nardi, *Aborto*, pp. 599–605, see C. W. Atkinson, *The Oldest Vocation: Christian Motherhood in the Middle Ages* (Ithaca NY, 1991), pp. 86–7; G. Clark, *Women in Late Antiquity: Pagan and Christian Lifestyles* (Oxford, 1994), pp. 83–4.

[9] Cf. Leyser, *Authority*, pp. 81–82 n.3. Many of Caesarius's sermons circulated under Augustine's name. The authors of the *Hibernensis*, quoted at the beginning of this chapter, attributed the 'so many conceptions, so many homicides' phrase to Augustine. For a brief summary of editorial developments on Caesarius's corpus, see M.-J. Delage, 'Un évêque au temps du invasion', in *Césaire d'Arles et la Christianisation de la Provence*, ed. D. Bertrand *et al.* (Paris, 1994), pp. 22–4.

was in fact a letter to fellow Gallic bishops probably written in the 520s when Caesarius's influence was at its height. The letter set out a vision of ideal episcopal practice, in which the obligation to preach quickly became a recurring refrain. Preaching had to be incessant and ubiquitous. Not just at church, but also at banquets, conversations, gatherings, even when out and about on the road. The divine word should drown out the cacophony of 'quickfire gossip and biting jokes'.[10] Ineloquence was no excuse because 'there is no need for a bishop to preach with such eloquence that can scarcely reach the understanding of a few people'.[11] In a string of rhetorical questions Caesarius listed the sins against which priests had to speak out – who cannot denounce perjury, adultery and so on – until he came to abortion:

> Who is there who cannot say ... no woman should take any potions for abortion, because she should not doubt that she will have to bring herself before Christ's tribunal for as many cases as those she has killed, whether already born or just conceived? Who cannot warn that no woman should take potions so that she is unable to conceive nor should she harm the nature within her which God has wished to be fruitful; because she will be held guilty of as many murders as [children] she had been able to conceive or give birth to and, unless she has undergone a worthy penance, will be condemned to eternal death in hell. A woman who does not want to have children should enter into a religious pact with her husband: for chastity is the only sterility for the Christian woman.[12]

Condensed into these lines were key Caesarian themes: the prospect of final judgment; fertility as God-willed; the distinctive demands of Christian sexual morality. They drew attention to abortion in its overlap with infanticide and preventing conception, and also to the grave obligation to preach about it. The stakes were high. Priests too would be answerable at final judgment for

---

[10] 'otiosis fabulis et mordacibus iocis', *Sermo* 1.10, ed. and trans. M. J. Delage, *Césaire d'Arles: Sermons au people I*, SC 175 (Paris, 1971), p. 240. I have used Delage's edition for *sermo* 1; all other sermons are quoted from Morin's edition.

[11] 'non oporteat pontificem eloquio praedicare, quod vix ad paucorum potest intellegentiam pervenire', *Sermo* 1.12, p. 242. This rhetoric is classic Caesarius; see E. Auerbach, *Literary Language and its Public in Late Latin Antiquity and in the Middle Ages*, trans. R. Manheim (Princeton, 1965), pp. 88–95.

[12] 'Quis est qui non possit dicere ... nulla mulier aliquas potiones ad aborsum accipiat, quia, quantoscumque aut iam natos aut adhuc conceptos occiderit, cum tantis causis ante tribunal Christi se ducendam esse non dubitet? Quis est qui admonere non possit, ut nulla mulier potiones accipiat, ut iam concipere non queat, nec damnet in se naturam, quam Deus voluit esse fecundam; quia, quantoscumque concipere vel parere potuerat, tantorum homicidiorum rea tenebitur, et, nisi digna paenitentia subvenerit, in gehenna aeterna morte damnabitur; mulier, quae iam non vult habere filios, religiosum cum viro suo ineat pactum: christianae enim feminae sterilitas sola sit castitas', *Sermo* 1.12, p. 248.

any souls who 'perished through their negligence after suffering a famine of God's word'.[13]

Caesarius's call to homiletic arms provided the weapons too, the very lines with which to preach, for the evidence of the remaining sermons strongly suggests that these were well rehearsed lines from his own preaching. Condemnation of abortion was woven into two sermons which gave broad overviews of Christian values. Caesarius began *sermo* 19 by giving thanks to God for the opportunity to visit after various duties had kept him away, possibly a trace of original delivery to a rural or suburban congregation. The broad thematic range of the sermon complements this; Christians who only received intermittent preaching needed a primer in what it meant to be a Christian. After distinguishing *cotidiana peccata*, everyday sins atoned for through almsgiving and good works, from *crimina capitalia*, graver sins which cast perpetrators down to hell, he catalogued unacceptable practices. One cluster of practices – consulting magical practitioners about illnesses – provided a thread leading into a final meditation on physical and spiritual health.

The healthy, Caesarius explained, could be spiritually sick and the sick spiritually healthy. Life's vicissitudes called for gratitude to God both for convalescence from illness and for spiritual advantages imparted by sickness (the healthy more readily turned to sin because they were unencumbered by illness). Ultimately, spiritual gratitude was essential 'because [God] knows what we need, when it is better for us to grow ill or be healthy'.[14] Immediately, he moved on to abortion:

> And relying on your charity I warn all your daughters out of paternal concern that no woman should take potions for abortion and kill her children whether conceived or born; but she must rear however many she has conceived herself or hand them to others for rearing; because on judgment day she will appear as a murderer accused of however many she has killed.[15]

A non-sequitur? Ostensibly, yes, but I shall suggest otherwise below. The sermon then ended with encouragement to remember the message.

Sermo 200 also used abortion to mark the boundaries of the Christian community. An adaptation of a sermon by Augustine, it focussed on the induction of *conpetentes*, catechumens.[16] Caesarius marked out the new standards

---

[13] 'per neglegentiam passi famem verbi Dei perierint', *Sermo* 1.15, p. 258.

[14] 'quia ipse novit quid nobis oporteat, quando aegrotare aut sanos esse conveniat', *Sermo* 19.5, ed. G. Morin, *Sancti Caesarii Arelatensis Sermones*, CCSL 103–4 (Turnhout, 1953), p. 7.

[15] 'Nam et hoc praesumens de caritate vestra omnes filias vestras pro solicitudine paterna admoneo, ut nulla mulier potiones ad avorsum accipiat, nec filios suos aut conceptos aut natos occidat; sed quantoscumque conceperit, aut ipsa nutriat, aut nutriendos aliis tradat: quia quantoscumque occiderit, pro tantis homicida in die iudicii rea apparebit', *Sermo* 19.5, p. 91.

[16] The extent of Caesarius's efforts in converting non-Catholic Christians and Jews is sketchy: Klingshirn, *Caesarius*, pp. 178–9. His controversial ransoming of

expected of catechumens upon entry into the Christian community. In particular, any *conpetentes* guilty of certain serious sins committed 'at the devil's instigation' needed to cleanse themselves through prayer and penitence before baptism.[17] Caesarius identified these sins as 'theft or murder or adultery … or if a woman catechumen has at any time taken diabolical potions for abortion and has killed her children either still poised in the womb or already born, which is a very grave sin'.[18] A little later in the sermon he reinforced the message with a cautionary image:

> Since the womb of the mother church has conceived every catechumen through Christ's inspiration, they should practise nothing unjust or dishonest, in case by chance they convulse the maternal organs through their wrongdoing and the holy mother throws them forth like an abortion before a proper birth.[19]

This ecclesiological metaphor played on the idea of the church as a mother and baptismal initiation as birth. Similarly, a sermon on the biblical twins Jacob and Esau explained that the biblical twins were born from Isaac's seed 'just as the Christian people is procreated from the single baptism of our lord saviour and from the single womb of the church'.[20] Elsewhere, offspring destroying their mother's womb stood for sin. Envy consumed the soul in which it is conceived 'just as they say vipers are born after tearing and bursting apart the very maternal womb in which they were conceived'.[21] The metaphor in *sermo* 200 warned catechumens awaiting the birth of baptism not to end up stillborn by bringing on their own mother's abortion through sin.

A more focussed sermon for a martyr's feast, *sermo* 44 encapsulated Caesarius's sexual morality. The connection between feast and flesh was no accident because receiving the sacrament on martyrs' feasts required sexual abstinence beforehand. The sermon showcased one of Caesarius's characteristic rhetorical techniques: confrontations with hypothetical objectors, a

---

Burgundian and Frankish prisoners after the Ostrogothic relief of a besieged Arles in 508 was partly motivated by a desire to convert imprisoned Arian and pagan soldiers: W. E. Klingshirn, 'Charity and Power: Caesarius of Arles and the Ransoming of Captives in sub-Roman Gaul', *Journal of Roman Studies* 75 (1985), 183–203.

[17] 'persuadente diabolo', *Sermo* 200.4, p. 810.
[18] 'aut furtum aut homicidium aut adulterium…aut si mulier conpetens potiones diabolicas aliquando ad avorsum accepit, et filios suos aut adhuc in utero positos aut etiam natos occidit – quod satis grave peccatum est', *Sermo* 200.4, p. 810.
[19] 'Et quia omnes conpetentes uterus matris ecclesiae Christo inspirante concepit, nihil iniustum aut inhonestum exerceant; ne forte male agendo viscera materna concutiant, et ante legitimum partum velud avorsum eos mater sancta proiciat', *Sermo* 200.5, pp. 810–11.
[20] 'sicut de uno baptismo domini salvatoris et de uno ecclesiae utero procreatur populus christianus', *Sermo* 86.4, pp. 355–6.
[21] 'Et sicut aiunt viperas dilacerato et disrupto illo ipso materno utero, in quo conceptae sunt, nasci', *Sermo* 90.5, p. 373.

technique which also reminded clerical readers that congregations did not always (or even often) listen politely. Caesarius anticipated someone protesting that sexual sin was *parvum*, paltry, no big deal. He conceded that it was not the worst kind of sin but, if habitual, sexual sin polluted the soul just as tiny raindrops filled up rivers drop by drop. Would anyone tolerate so many 'paltry blows' to the body or so many stains and rips on one's clothes?[22]

Earlier in the sermon Caesarius staged a similar rhetorical confrontation in a tangent on abortion which followed a brief caution against premarital sex. Young men and women corrupted by premarital sex (which Caesarius called 'adultery') subsequently entered marriage with living bodies but dead souls. Possibly following a train of thought between premarital sex and avoidance of offspring, he moved on to abortion in a string of familiar phrases.[23] Then, in the most withering of his denunciations of abortion, he rhetorically confronted the *mulier ingenua*, freewoman, who hypocritically shrank from procreation:

> But the freeborn woman, who takes death-dealing potions so that she does not conceive, I would like to know if she would like her servant-girls or tenants to do this. Because just as every woman wants slaves to be born for her, who can be in service to her, so she should also rear however many [children] she has conceived herself or hand them to others for rearing; otherwise she either refuses to conceive or, which is worse, wants to kill those who might have been good Christians. And with what conscience does she want slaves to be born from her servant-girls while she refuses to engender those who could become Christians?[24]

The two remaining sermons, 51 and 52, were the most thematically coherent sermons to address abortion. But there is a slight question mark, if not quite an outright challenge, over their attribution to Caesarius. Both sermons survive in a single manuscript, an eighth-century homiliary, which is roughly

---

[22] *Sermo* 44.6, p. 198. On this rhetorical technique, see Delage, SC 175, pp. 197–201; Klingshirn, *Caesarius*, pp. 14, 209. On boisterous congregations, see Bailey, *Christianity's Quiet Success*, pp. 17–18.

[23] 'Nulla mulier potiones ad avorsum accipiat, nec filios nec conceptos aut iam natos occidat; quia, quaecumque hoc fecerit, ante tribunal Christi sciat se causam cum illis quos occiderit esse dicturam. Sed nec illas diabolicas potiones mulieres accipere, per quas iam non possint concipere. Mulier quaecumque hoc fecerit, quantoscumque parere potuerat, tantorum homicidiorum se ream esse cognoscat', *Sermo* 44.2, p. 196.

[24] 'Mulier autem ingenua, quae mortiferas potiones accipit ut non concipiat, velim scire si hoc ancillas vel colonas suas facere vellet. Et ideo quomodo unaquaeque vult ut sibi nascantur mancipia, que illi serviant, ita et illa, quantoscumque conceperit, aut ipsa nutriat, aut nutriendos aliis tradat; ne forte illos aut concipere nolit, aut, quod est gravius, occidere velit, qui boni christiani esse potuerant. Et qua conscientia sibi ab ancillis suis vult mancipia nasci, cum ipsa nolit eos qui christiani possint fieri generare?', *Sermo* 44.2, p. 196.

contemporaneous with Boniface's missionary efforts on the continent. Some scholars have associated it with the Anglo-Saxon missionary Burchard of Würzburg (d. 753).[25] Yitzhak Hen's recent study concludes that the homiliary was produced for a missionary priest in Boniface's circle and offers further reasons for connecting it to Burchard or his associates.[26] In his earlier work on Merovingian religion Hen drew attention to the conspicuously small number of sermons in Caesarius's corpus which addressed paganism and superstition. For Hen, this paucity 'reinforce[s] the notion that paganism and superstitions were marginal phenomena within the Merovingian cultural milieu'. One supplement to Hen's broader argument is the possibility that the sermons which only survive in the homiliary, including 51 and 52, were composed (or adapted) in eighth-century Francia rather than sixth-century Gaul; or, if still Caesarian, that their limited diffusion points to limited use until the turn of the eighth century when clerical fixation on pagan and superstitious practices became stronger.[27]

An examination of parenthood and childlessness, *sermo* 51 conveyed a core message: fertility and sterility were both part of God's plan. Good deeds were like surrogate children who raised their parents to heaven whereas flesh and blood children were often a source of trouble. Parents resorted to fraud or outright theft to amass wealth for their children and, ironically, older children impatient for their inheritances subsequently hankered after their own parents' deaths. The sermon took pains not to overstep the mark. Of course not all children were quite so malicious and it was perfectly reasonable to want to have children.

Childlessness presented its own temptations. People 'to whom God did not want to give children' could resort to 'certain herbs, devilish characters or sacrilegious amulets' and thereby 'fight against Christ's plan with cruel and impious audacity'.[28] The gender focus sharpened: 'For just as women whom God wants to have more children should take no potions [through] which they cannot have a conception, so too those women whom God wanted to

---

[25] Würzburg, Universitätsbibliothek, M. p. th. f. 28; cf. CCSL 103–4, pp. xliii–xlv, and G. Morin, 'L'homéliaire de Burchard de Würzburg: contribution à la critique des sermons de saint Césaire d'Arles', *Revue bénédictine* 13 (1896), 97–111.

[26] Y. Hen, 'The Contents and Aims of the so-called Homiliary of Burchard of Würzburg', in *Sermo Doctorum: Compilers, Preachers, and their Audiences in the Early Medieval West*, ed. M. Diesenberger *et al.* (Turnhout, 2013), pp. 127–52. I am grateful to Yitzhak Hen for sharing his book chapter with me prior to publication.

[27] Y. Hen, *Culture and Religion in Merovingian Gaul, A.D. 481–751* (Leiden, 1995), pp. 162–7 (quotation at p. 165); cf. Y. Hen, 'Paganism and Superstition in the time of Gregory of Tours: une question mal posée!', in *The World of Gregory of Tours*, ed. K. Mitchell and I. Wood (Leiden, 2002), pp. 229–40.

[28] 'cui deus filios dare noluerit, non eos de aliquis erbis vel diabolicis characteribus aut sacrilegis ligaturis habere conentur…contra dispensationem Christi crudeli et impio ausu pugnare', *Sermo* 51.4, p. 229.

remain sterile ought to desire and seek after this from God alone'.[29] Again, the familiar phrases kicked in. 'Those women whom God wanted to be fertile' should rear the children they conceived or hand them over to be reared by others; and the judgment day tribunal awaited them for murders of those conceived or born.[30] More unusually there was a clear patristic borrowing. When women 'through sacrilegious potions try to kill their own children within themselves', they became guilty of three crimes: suicide, adultery against Christ and parricide of their unborn children.[31] This was lifted from Jerome's letter to Eustochium. The subtext was slightly lost in translation insofar as *Christi adulterae* had originally referred to professed virgins rather than married women. Nonetheless, tying the threads back together, women who tried to have children 'by any kind of sacrilegious medicines' acted badly; and those who killed children conceived or born sinned more gravely, for 'by taking sacrilegious potions so they do not conceive they harm the nature within them, which God wanted to be fertile'.[32]

Aside from the quotation from Jerome and the marked emphasis on 'sacrilegious' and 'diabolical' means, the handling of abortion in *sermo* 51 was otherwise through phrases found in other sermons. *Sermo* 52, however, elaborated on abortion in a more extensive way than any other sermon. The core theme was the devil's malign influence. A martyr was 'anyone who gave witness to Christ in the name of justice'.[33] Caesarius called upon his congregation to become martyrs by speaking out against diabolical temptations such as consulting augurs, sorcerers and soothsayers. Under the devil's influence foolish men worshipped days and months, and foolish women set down their looms on Thursdays in honour of Jupiter. Some lunatics even believed that they could move the moon with their incantations.

Escape from childbearing was another manifestation of diabolical deception: 'Does not the devil clearly work his deceits, dearest, when he persuades some women, after they have borne two or three children, to kill the remaining ones or those already born, or to take a potion for abortion'?[34] Their reason was a fear that by having more children they could not be rich. The result was a perversion of maternity:

---

[29] 'Sicut enim mulieres, quas deus vult plures habere filios, nullas potationes debent accipere, <per> quas conceptum habere non possint, ita et illae, quas deus stereles voluit permanere, de solo deo hoc debent desiderare vel petere', *Sermo* 51.4, p. 229.
[30] 'Illae enim mulieres, quas deus vult esse fecundas', *Sermo* 51.4, p. 229.
[31] 'dum per sacrilegas potiones filios suos in seipsis occidere conantur', *Sermo* 51.4, p. 229.
[32] 'vel certe unde non concipiant potiones sacrilegas accipiendo damnant in se naturam, quam deus voluit esse fecundam', *Sermo* 51.4, p. 229.
[33] 'quicumque testimonium pro iustitia dederit Christo', *Sermo* 52.1, p. 230.
[34] 'Nonne, carissimi, aperte diabolus exercet deceptiones suas, quando aliquibus mulieribus persuadet, ut postquam duos aut tres filios genuerint, reliquos aut iam natos occident, aut poculum avorsionis accipiant', *Sermo* 52.4, p. 231.

> What do they believe when they do this other than that God cannot feed and guide those whom he ordered to be born? And quite possibly they kill some who might have served God better or obeyed their very parents with a perfect love. For which they take poisonous potions in a sacrilegious and parricidal rite to render the life of their children imperfect in an early death within the maternal organs, and through this sort of remedy they drink a cup of bereavement with this cruel potion.[35]

By taking potions for abortion women did not realize that they inflicted harm upon their infants and upon themselves:

> What pitiable conviction. They think that the poison, which passes through their drink, is separate from them; and they are unaware that when they draw out in a death what has been conceived in their organs, they are conceiving in sterility. For even if at this point no little infant can be found which could be killed within the fold of the maternal body, it is nonetheless true that the very nature within the person is harmed. Why, unhappy mother or really the step-mother of an unborn child, why do you seek medicines from without which will be eternally harmful? If you want it, you have healthier remedies within you. Do you not want to have a child? Draw up a religious pact with your husband; let him accept an end to childbearing for the virtue of purity. Chastity is the only sterility for a truly faithful woman.[36]

Were these Caesarius's words, the words of an eighth-century compiler – or something in between? The passage is long and unique, and an argument against attributing it to Caesarius could certainly be made, though it is impossible to answer definitively.[37] There are nonetheless hints of Caesarius. The clearest hint comes at the end of the passage, which leads up to his unmistakeable phrase on chastity as birth control. But, more broadly, the passage is flecked through with Caesarian themes: abortion deprived earthly and

---

[35] 'Et haec facientes quid aliud credunt, nisi quod illos, quos deus iusserit nasci, pascere et gubernare non possit? Et forsitan illos occidunt, qui aut deum melius servire aut ipsis parentibus perfecto amore potuerant oboedire. Pro qua re sacrilegio aut parricidali ritu venenatas potiones accipiunt, ut inperfectam filiorum vitam inmatura morte per viscera materna transmittant, et per quoddam remedium cum quodam potu crudele bibant poculum orbitatis.', *Sermo* 52.4, p. 231.

[36] 'Lugenda persuasio! alienum a se putant illud quod per earum haustum transit venenum; et nesciunt quia hoc genere, dum conceptum in visceribus excipiunt morte, in sterelitate concipiunt. Quod si adhuc infantolus qui possit occidi intra sinum materni corporis non invenitur, non minus est quod ipsa intra hominem natura damnatur. Quid, infelix mater, immo non geniti filii iam noverca, quid medicamenta in perpetuum nocitura de foris requiris? Tecum, si velis, intra habes salubriora remedia. Vis iam non habere filium? Relegiosum cum viro conscribe pactum: de virtute pudicitiae finem partus accipiat. Fidelissimae feminae sterelitas sola sit castitas', *Sermo* 52.4, pp. 231–2.

[37] Yitzhak Hen has suggested to me in a personal communication that *sermo* 51 looks Caesarian while *sermo* 52 might be a reworking of Caesarian topics and preoccupations, while cautioning that the Latin would be unusual for an eighth-century text.

heavenly society of its rightful denizens, contravened God's will and entailed a form of self-harm. No other early medieval authority combined these ideas on abortion. If these were not Caesarius's words, then they were the words of someone grappling with Caesarius's ideas on abortion at some point between the sixth and eighth centuries. The remainder of *sermo* 52 outlined other problematic practices, such as mothers consulting soothsayers or sorcerers to heal their ailing children, before concluding with an exhortation to avoid 'every one of the devil's traps'.[38]

Creating an idiom of condemnation
None of these sermons focussed primarily, let alone exclusively, on abortion. Passages on abortion formed portions of sermons dealing with a broader array of subjects. But as the survey emphasizes, denunciation of abortion was a way of defining the Christian community and its values in late antique Gaul. Moreover, Caesarius spoke about abortion in a way which was designed to resonate. Scholars have not fully recognized the originality of his rhetoric. Caesarius was well versed in and respectful of patristic predecessors. Plagiarism was a preacher's virtue, not a vice.[39] But while *sermo* 200 adapted a sermon by Augustine and *sermo* 51 incorporated a single quotation from Jerome, his actual words on abortion did not lean conspicuously on identifiable patristic sources.[40]

We can safely assume that Caesarius did encounter ideas on abortion in his own reading, for there was one relevant late antique text with which he was certainly familiar. It graphically imagined the eternal torments from which Caesarius wanted to save his flock. There is a small twist, however. The text in question has scarcely entered histories of church tradition on abortion because it lies beyond the periphery of modern constructions of that tradition. The *Visio Pauli* was a Latin translation of a third-century Greek apocalyptic text probably composed in Egypt. It was circulating by the end of the fifth century.[41] The *Visio Pauli* recounted the apostle Paul's vision of heaven and hell with lurid details of sins and corresponding punishments provided by an angelic guide. It is a striking text. Men and women chew on their own tongues in punishment for mocking the word of God in church. Others are hung from their eyebrows for committing adultery. Paul even prays that the damned

---

[38] 'omnes insidias diaboli', *Sermo* 52.5–6, pp. 232–3.
[39] For an overview of Caesarius's sources, see Delage's comments in SC 175, pp. 94–110.
[40] Nardi, *Aborto*, p. 604, quotes a passage from a pseudo-Ambrosian sermon with affinities to Caesarius's rhetoric on abortion, though the direction of influence is unclear.
[41] A. Hilhorst, 'The Apocalypse of Paul: Previous History and Afterlife', in *The Visio Pauli and the Gnostic Apocalypse of Paul*, ed. J. M. Bremmer and I. Czachesz (Leuven, 2007), pp. 1–23.

receive an infernal sabbatical, a rest from their torments every Sunday.[42] Caesarius was definitely aware of Paul's encounter with the damned. In a dozen or so sermons he quoted a line from the *Visio Pauli*, the 'burdens of the world have made them wretched', about those who reneged on ascetic vocations.[43] This phrase explained why men and women were punished by being dressed in rags full of pitch. Just a few lines earlier (within the same chapter in modern editions) the immediately preceding punishment saw men and women strangled in flames. These were 'women who defile the image of God [and] bring forth infants from the womb, and these are the men who lie with them'. Crying out for vengeance to God and his angels, their murdered infants protested that their parents 'dished us up for the dogs and to be trampled over by pigs, [and] they threw others into the river'.[44]

The *Visio Pauli* provides one picture of the torments which Caesarius imagined when he 'tearfully threatened with eternal punishment'.[45] But in his preaching Caesarius concentrated on the moment of final judgment more than subsequent punishment. He developed his own idiom of condemnation, a series of phrases and ideas which recurred across his sermons:

- Prohibition on killing children whether born or conceived/still in the womb (1.12, 19.5, 44.2, 51.4, 52.4, 200.4)
- On judgment day Christ's tribunal will charge women of as many murders as children killed (1.12, 19.5, 44.2, 51.4)
- Taking potions to avoid conception harms one's nature and contravenes God's will (1.12, 51.4, 52.4)
- Thwarting conception is murder (1.12, 44.2, 51.4)
- Chastity is the only acceptable 'sterility' (1.12, 52.4)

---

[42] *Visio Pauli* 37 (tongue-chewing), 39 (eyebrow suspension), 43–44 (no more Sunday roast), ed. T. Silverstein and A. Hilhorst, *Apocalypse of Paul: A New Critical Edition of the Three Long Latin Versions* (Geneva, 1997), pp. 144–6, 156–62. This edition prints several Latin texts synoptically. I have quoted from the edition based on the oldest manuscript containing the complete so-called 'long Latin' version (Paris, Bibliothèque nationale de France, MS nouv. acq. lat. 1631) written in what looks like ninth-century Carolingian minuscule but with elements of Merovingian Latin; see ibid., pp. 11–13, 23–8.

[43] *Visio Pauli* 40, p. 151. B. Fischer, 'Impedimenta mundi fecerunt eos miseros', *Vigiliae Christianae* 5 (1951), 84–7, first identified the *Visio Pauli* as Caesarius's source.

[44] 'Haec sunt mulieres commaculantes plasmam dei, proferentes ex utero infantes, et ii sunt viri concubentes cum eis ... dederunt nos in escam canibus et in conculcationem porcis, alios proiecerunt in flumine', *Visio Pauli* 40, p. 150. J.K. Elliott, *The Apocryphal New Testament: A Collection of Apocryphal Christian Literature in an English Translation* (Oxford, 1993), p. 616, interprets this as a reference to abortion, though I. Czachesz, 'Torture in Hell and Reality: The Visio Pauli', in *Visio Pauli*, pp. 130–1, implies otherwise. Coincidentally, the Coptic version of this text adds, '... and did not permit us to grow up into righteous men and to serve God'; Caesarius expressed a similar idea in *sermo* 44.2.

[45] *Life of Caesarius* 1.17, p. 17.

– Women should rear their children or give them to others for rearing (19.5, 44.2, 51.4)

Sermons lie in between oral performance and literary consumption. They occupy an 'especially indistinct position' between the spoken and written word.[46] Some were produced before the event, others were produced after it – and others still were produced but never delivered. In the case of Caesarius's sermons, this 'indistinct position' was the product of design as much as accident. Preaching was strongly associated with the episcopate in late antique Gaul. But Caesarius was no episcopal protectionist. He dispatched ready-made homiletic materials not only to bishops but also to clerics 'located far away in the Frankish lands, Gaul, Italy, Spain, and other provinces [so that] they could preach in their own churches'. In so doing, his hagiographers added, he 'diffused the fragrance of Christ far and wide'.[47]

Caesarius's sermons were both performative texts for a lay audience and pedagogical texts for a clerical readership. Their dual function and double audience is an important interpretative key. Ironically, the scholarly fixation on just one or two phrases reflects the care with which Caesarius chose his words. The rhetorical resonance of Latin phrases like *nec filios suos aut conceptos aut natos occidat* or *quantoscumque concipere vel parere potuerat, tantorum homicidiorum rea tenebitur* is difficult to convey in English. These awkward-to-translate contrasts (*aut ... aut*) and connections (*quantos ... tantorum*) were carefully composed mnemonics for preachers and their congregations. Their recurrence across different sermons reflects the importance of memory. Caesarius 'taught from memory' and might well have preached extempore.[48] He idealized his sermons as seeds from which the word of God could take root and grow fruitful through the spiritual cross-pollination of speech within the community: 'Let one say to another: I heard my bishop speak about chastity. Let another say: I also remember that he preached about almsgiving'. If each person remembered just a few *sententiae*, between them all they could remember the whole message and, with Christ's help, bring them to fruition in their lives.[49] The style and substance of his characteristic *sententiae* on abortion were designed to stick in the minds not only of lay audiences but also of clerical readers. As Lisa Bailey has emphasized, set phrases and images were a tool for 'enabling preaching, but also controlling its content'.[50] Through these recurring expressions Caesarius was attempting to generate a discourse on

---

[46] Bailey, *Christianity's Quiet Success*, p. 22; cf. T. N. Hall, 'The Early Medieval Sermon', in *The Sermon*, Typologie des sources du Moyen Age Occidental 81–3, ed. B. M. Kienzle (Turnhout, 2000), pp. 228–9.
[47] *Life of Caesarius* 1.55, p. 37; see, for example, *sermo* 2, pp. 18–19, the preface to a book of sermons which Caesarius circulated.
[48] *Life of Caesarius* 1.54, p. 36; cf. Klingshirn, *Caesarius*, pp. 12–14.
[49] *Sermo* 6.8, p. 36.
[50] Bailey, *Christianity's Quiet Success*, p. 22.

abortion within the Christian community while regulating the shape it took. But the message on abortion was more than the sum total of the mnemonics which Caesarius recycled. To understand it, we must understand the broader cluster of moral concerns with which Caesarius was preoccupied and the pastoral strategies he adopted to address them.

Gendering abortion: focal points and blind spots
Caesarius almost entirely isolated women as the culprits of abortion. His picture of what motivated women was far from comprehensive. The connection between abortion and sexual transgression was possibly tacit in just one sermon.[51] His characteristic phrase about chastity as the only legitimate *sterilitas* typified Caesarius's real focus: married women. Here, there was some reflection on material concerns. Some women resorted to abortion 'fearing that they cannot be rich if they were to have more children'.[52] The rhetorical encounter with the freeborn woman (*ingenua*), who expected a human production line from her slave-girls while withholding her own reproductive labour, played on a comparable idea. But this was about the pressure to maintain wealth rather than the difficulty of enduring poverty. Conrad Leyser has rightly called into question the image of Caesarius preaching non-stop to country bumpkins in rural Provence.[53] Recognizing the class focus of Caesarius's discourse on abortion complements Leyser's corrective. When he did speak about abortion in a more specific way, Caesarius was speaking about reasonably well-to-do women. His rhetoric on abortion was probably not unrelated to his most important constituency: the urban elite in Arles.[54]

Caesarius's almost exclusive gender focus was the consequence of a broader pastoral strategy. As Lisa Bailey has recently argued in a study of how the sermons tackled drunkenness and sexual promiscuity, Caesarius found it rhetorically useful to tie sin to gender. His sermons painted a picture of late antique lad culture. Men bragged over who had slept with the most slave-girls.[55] At boozy banquets drunkards ridiculed those who drank less than them for not being real men.[56] For Caesarius, drinking and debauchery were not just a question of individual sins but of a culture of sin premised

---

[51] See p. 62 above on *sermo* 44.1–2.
[52] 'timentes ne forte, si plures filios habuerint, divites esse non possent', *Sermo* 52.4, p. 231.
[53] Leyser, *Authority*, pp. 84–90.
[54] Both I. Réal, *Vies de saints, vie de famille: Représentation et système de la parenté dans le Royaume mérovingien (481–751) après les sources hagiographiques* (Turnhout, 2001), p. 399, and B. Filotas, *Pagan Survivals, Superstitions and Popular Cultures in Early Medieval Pastoral Literature* (Toronto, 2005), pp. 277–8, recognize the class focus of Caesarius's message on abortion. On the place of *ingenui* in sixth-century Gallic society, see A. E. Jones, *Social Mobility in Late Antique Gaul: Strategies and Opportunities for the Non-Elite* (Cambridge, 2009), pp. 130–57.
[55] *Sermo* 42.3, p. 187.
[56] *Sermo* 46.1, 47.1, pp. 205, 211.

on a misconception of what it meant to be a man. Caesarius countered by reconstructing sixth-century lad culture as a form of masculinity gone wrong. Virility, he argued, should be premised upon self-discipline rather than excess. Binge-drinking and sexual promiscuity represented deficiencies, not distinctions, in masculinity.[57]

As a social practice abortion was presumably as hushed as male promiscuity and drunkenness were brash. But like his handling of promiscuity and drunkenness, Caesarius's handling of abortion tied sin to gender. He critiqued abortion in the light of a particular kind of idealized femininity: motherhood. Abortion inverted the ideal. Across the sermons Caesarius complained that women killed their own children in the womb. *Sermo* 52 accentuated the desecration of maternity wrought by the 'parricidal rite' of abortion. By drinking up potions for sterility women sipped from the 'cup of bereavement' and rendered the 'life of their children imperfect in an early death within the maternal womb'.

This sermon even played rhetorically with the inversion when it described the woman who aborted as the stepmother (*noverca*) of a child not yet born. Whether or not we attribute these lines within *sermo* 52 to Caesarius, they were not the first to exploit a rhetorical association between abortion and *novercae*. In the later fifth century, the Christian poet Dracontius surveyed humanity's sins. After reaching infanticide, by which the souls of blameless infants were snatched away, Dracontius moved onto abortion: 'If only the cruel hand simply struck those who were born! But they also hasten to strike those not yet born in the belly'.[58] The aborting adulteress was even more abhorrent than the infanticidal *noverca*: 'Here the stepmother has less audacity with those born to others than the mother who does this. The stepmother's right hand sends those already born to the shades, the mother forces children to die before they are born'.[59] Like Caesarius, Dracontius drew attention to the peril of drinking up potions, though, unlike Caesarius, he insinuated that the motive was to hide adultery.[60] The negative social image of the *noverca* is also discernible in sixth-century texts. Gregory of Tours described how the second wife of the Burgundian king Sigismund machinated against his son 'as is the wont of stepmothers'.[61] Venantius Fortunatus echoed the idea that a

---

[57] L. Bailey, '"These are not men": Sex and Drink in the Sermons of Caesarius of Arles', *JECS* 15.1 (2007), 23–43, especially 31–5.

[58] 'Iam genitos utinam tantum fera dextra feriret! / Et necdum natos properant in ventre ferire', *De laudibus Dei* 2.321–2, ed. and trans. C. Moussy, *Dracontius Œuvres tome I: Louanges de Dieu, Livres I et II* (Paris, 1985), p. 209.

[59] 'Minus ecce noverca / audet in externos genitos quam mater agit rem. / Dextra novercalis iam natos mittit ad umbras, / ante mori genetrix quam nasci pignora cogit', *De laudibus Dei* 2.327–30, p. 211.

[60] Cf. 'Externos pariterque suos furit impia mater / conceptus damnare, sui nec cura pericli est', *De laudibus Dei* 2.323–4, p. 211.

[61] 'sicut novercarum mos est', *LH* 3.5, MGH SRM 1.1, pp. 100–1. On *novercae* in Merovingian and Carolingian society, see B. Kasten, 'Stepmothers in Frankish Legal

woman could undo maternity through her misdeeds when he described Eve as our collective 'mother through birth, but stepmother through sin'.[62] To call a woman who aborted a *noverca* was to make a provocative point: abortion mutilated a woman's identity as mother.

Abortion also risked a more physical sort of mutilation. Through abortion women visited physical harm upon themselves and, even worse, risked their own lives. Often, unbeknown to themselves, they conceived in sterility. This sterility was not a passive state but a more actively disruptive force. Whether or not it killed an infant in the womb, it damaged a woman's natural capacity to bear children and rejected God's will. This was a kind of harm (*damnare*) which flirted with damnation.

Finally, reproduction was social. The *ingenua* who shrank from procreation nonetheless insisted that her slave-girls bore children. She did this precisely to perpetuate a certain social order. Here, Caesarius shared more than one assumption with this imagined hypocrite. First, in late antique Gaul and other early medieval societies, status profoundly affected individual agency in sex, marriage and reproduction. Neither Caesarius nor *ingenuae* questioned the social expectation that masters and mistresses would influence reproduction among their slaves.[63] Second, both Caesarius and these imagined hypocrites presumed that women bore a special responsibility for perpetuating the social order. Where they diverged was on which kind of social reproduction should take precedence. Caesarius aimed to form a community that welcomed children who could become good Christians.

It should be stressed that Caesarius, the author of the first western *regula* for nuns, was no crude pronatalist. He discouraged people from trying to have children by any means whatsoever. Moreover, in contemporary conceptions of sanctity the spiritual connotations of maternity could be transposed onto men. Caesarius's hagiographers drew upon maternal and other images of nurturing women to convey his holiness. He loved his enemies 'not only with a paternal but also a maternal affection'.[64] By lopping off silver embellishments from columns and handing over chalices and censers to ransom Burgundian captives, he acted as a kind of spiritual midwife who 'made the womb of the mother [church] open up for children; he did not cause it to be

---

Life', in *Law, Laity and Solidarities: Essays in honour of Susan Reynolds*, ed. P. Stafford et al. (Manchester, 2001), pp. 47–67.

[62] 'mater de genere sed noverca de crimine', *Carm.* 10.2, MGH AA 4.1, p. 230.

[63] Gregory of Tours tells the story of a duke's cruel response upon learning that two of his servants had married. He had the pair buried alive in a sadistic twist on a promise that the two would never be separated: *LH* 5.3, pp. 196–8. The story, like Caesarius's point in *sermo* 44, was meant to illustrate bad moral decisions; but it did not call into question masters' control over their slaves' relationships. On the neglected *longue durée* of attitudes to slave marriage, see D. L. d'Avray, 'Slavery, Marriage and the Holy See: From the Ancient World to the New World', *Rechtgeschichte/Legal History* 20 (2012), 347–51.

[64] *Life of Caesarius* 1.53, p. 36.

harmed'.⁶⁵ The contrast with the fluidity of gender in sixth-century sanctity strengthens the impression that Caesarius's construction of abortion as a female sin was the product of a deliberate pastoral strategy.

But it was a pastoral strategy in tension with what Caesarius had to say about sexual and marital morality. Although sexual renunciation was a higher calling than marriage, Caesarius did consider marriage properly practised to be spiritually virtuous. On the sliding scale of sanctity the married had their own niche and corresponding biblical model for emulation: while virgins looked upon Mary and widows upon Anna, wives were to model themselves upon Susanna. Married couples who preserved mutual fidelity and had intercourse with a desire for children would number with Job, Sara, Susanna and others in heaven.⁶⁶

Antoni Zurek has rightly contrasted Augustine's conception of three goods of marriage (faithfulness, procreation and sacramentality) with Caesarius's narrower emphasis on procreation as the defining norm in marital sexuality.⁶⁷ But chastity, the proper exercise of sexuality in marriage, was inextricable from what made procreation normative in conceptions of marriage. Caesarius's emphasis on procreation was not premised upon the teleology of the sexual act or genital organs along the lines of some modern natural law arguments (the natural function of the sexual act and sexual organs is ordered to procreation, therefore the sexual act has to be open to procreation). Rather, for Caesarius the absence of procreative intention revealed that one had been conquered by lust. After his rebuke of the *ingenua* in *sermo* 44 Caesarius turned to chastity by addressing men. A good Christian man would not know his wife except from a desire for children. Imagine, he asked, if a man sowed his land in a single year as often as he slept with his wife when overcome by lust. The point was that 'no land which is sown frequently within a single year can yield proper fruit, as you well know'.⁶⁸ But, crucially, the field did not represent the female body, it represented men's own bodies and repeated sowing stood for the debilitating effect of lust upon it.⁶⁹ Similarly, Caesarius enjoined men to abstain from their wives on Sundays, feast-days and during menstruation. Worse for drink, he noted with disdain, some men did not spare pregnant wives from their sexual advances. Children born of liturgically or

---

⁶⁵ 'aperire fecit filiis matris viscera, non dampnari', *Vita Caesarii* 1.33, MGH SRM 3, p. 469; translation adapted from *Life of Caesarius* 1.33, p. 25.

⁶⁶ *Sermo* 6.7, p. 35.

⁶⁷ On Caesarius's sexual morality, see A. Zurek, 'L'etica coniugale in Cesario di Arles: Rapporti con Agostino e nuovi orientamenti', *Augustinianum* 25 (1985), 565–78; Klingshirn, *Caesarius*, pp. 190–3.

⁶⁸ 'sicut optime nostis, nulla terra poterit dare legitimum fructum, in qua frequenter in uno anno fuerit seminatum', *Sermo* 44.3, p. 197.

⁶⁹ Cf. 'Quod ergo non vult aliquis in agro suo, quare faciat in corpore suo?', ibid.; on this image, see A. Salvatore, *Sermo humilis, Sensus mysticus: Esegesi e linguaggio da Paolino di Nola a Cesario di Arles* (Naples, 1995), pp. 84–5.

physiologically transgressive intercourse, he warned, would turn out to be lepers or epileptics.[70]

The pastoral challenge was that double standards in sexual mores were the norm in sixth-century society. Sexually dissolute men insisted that their wives came to marriage as virgins.[71] People acted as if God had given separate rules to men and to women, forgetting that there was a single redemption for both sexes.[72] Caesarius used an etymological commonplace – man (*vir*) came from strength (*virtus*) and woman (*mulier*) from weakness (*mollities*) – to highlight the hypocrisy by which men expected their wives to battle against lust while they succumbed to lust's first blow.[73]

Caesarius did not mince his words on sexual double standards any more than he did on abortion. Precisely because of this there was a tension at the heart of his message. In critiquing sexual double standards perhaps Caesarius truly did 'sp[eak] up in defense of women'.[74] Caesarius visualized the breakdown of social order during the siege of Arles in 507/8 most powerfully when he painfully relived sexualized violence, the 'mothers of families abducted, pregnant women cut apart'.[75] However, as Suzanne Wemple has put it, '[e]ven this sympathetic observer of women's plight failed to perceive that men might have been more responsible for abortions and infanticides than women in a society where double sexual standards prevailed'.[76] The isolation of women as the culprits of abortion complemented, rather than countered, the sexual double standards which Caesarius attacked elsewhere. The contrast with Augustine is illuminating. Augustine had addressed abortion and preventing conception in moral advice addressed to husbands as well as wives. Although Caesarius situated abortion within marriage, by tying sin to gender he did not clearly address his message on abortion to those who, on his own terms, needed to hear it most: husbands.

---

[70] *Sermo* 44.7, p. 199. Gregory of Tours' story of a severely deformed boy cured by Martin of Tours played on the same association, for the boy had been conceived on a Sunday: *De virtutibus Martini* 2.24, MGH SRM 1.2, p. 167.

[71] *Sermo* 43.2, pp. 190–1.

[72] *Sermo* 42.3, pp. 186–7; cf. the account of the council of Mâcon (585), at which the arguments of a bishop who believed that woman (*mulier*) could not be included within the term person (*homo*) had to be refuted by reference to the Old Testament, in Gregory of Tours, *LH* 8.20, pp. 386–7.

[73] *Sermo* 43.1, p. 190. A detail in a story about a chaste marriage related by Gregory of Tours echoes this social expectation. The new bride was saddened on her wedding bay because she wished to pursue an ascetic life. Her new husband agreed to abstain from intercourse and, in thanking him, she conceded that sexual renunciation was a harder commitment for men than for women ('Difficile est sexum virilem mulieribus ista praestare'): *LH* 1.47, p. 31.

[74] S. F. Wemple, *Women in Frankish Society: Marriage and the Cloister 500 to 900* (Philadelphia, 1981), p. 24.

[75] 'matres familias abductas, praegnantes abscisas', *Sermo* 70.2, p. 297.

[76] Wemple, *Women*, p. 24.

Relying on charity: Envisaged community responses

Caesarius instructed women to let others adopt any children whom they could not rear themselves. Precisely who these others might have been is not immediately clear. It may be tempting to think of monasteries as possible sources of support. But Caesarius's *regula* for the nuns of St Jean at Arles tentatively set the age of entry at six or seven years and explicitly criticized parents who tried to use the monastery as a boarding school for their daughters.[77] Slightly earlier and later evidence of regulation on abandoned infants, however, provides glimpses of social practices which Caesarius had in mind.

First, there were the fifth-century councils in southern Gaul. The council of Vaison (442) outlined the preferred procedure when anyone found an abandoned infant, a ruling that was repeated at another council at Arles which met at some point between 442 and 506. After the rescuer had informed the local church, the priest would announce the discovery of the child to the people. Parents had ten days to reclaim their infant and the rescuer was eligible for compensation. But if parents tried to reclaim their infant after this period or pursued a case against the rescuer, they would be liable (curiously enough) to the penalties for murder. The real point of this ruling was to protect those who had found abandoned infants from litigation which would discourage others from doing the same.[78] Caesarius knew these rulings well. The council of Agde (506), an important moment early on in Caesarius's episcopate, declared that previous conciliar enactments on abandoned infants were to be observed, a reference to Vaison or Arles.[79]

Second, a late sixth-century model document from the earliest surviving formulary, the *Formulae Andecavenses*, outlined what should happen if the poor attached to a church found an abandoned *sanguinolentus* (literally, 'covered in blood'). After gaining approval from the priest and making genuine attempts to identify the parents, the rescuers were entitled to sell the infant to a third party.[80] Again the point was to provide legal protection for those who found abandoned infants.

---

[77] de Jong, *In Samuel's Image*, pp. 18–23, 32–6.

[78] Council of Vaison, cc. 9–10, Council of Arles, c.51, both ed. Munier, *Concilia Galliae*, pp. 100–1, 124; cf. Boswell, *Kindness*, pp. 172–3. On the Arles council, including an argument that it probably occurred *c.* 490/502 under Caesarius's predecessor and relative, Aeonius, see R. Mathisen, 'The "Second Council of Arles" and the Spirit of Compilation and Codification in Late Roman Gaul', *JECS* 5.4 (1997), 511–54.

[79] Council of Agde, c.24, ed. Munier, *Concilia Galliae*, p. 200; see Klingshirn, *Caesarius*, pp. 97–104, on this council.

[80] 'Incipit carta de sanguinolento, quem de matricola suscipi', *Formulae Andecavenses* 49, MGH Formulae, p. 21; trans. A. Rio, *The Formularies of Angers and Marculf: Two Merovingian Legal Handbooks*, TTH 46 (Liverpool, 2008), pp. 90–1, with pp. 248–54, on the thorny question of dating. An eighth-century *formula* on abandoned infants can be found in *Formulae Turonenses*, MGH Formulae, p. 141, though it afforded less secure legal protection to rescuers of foundlings; on both documents see Boswell, *Kindness*, pp. 202–3, 217.

The rescue of abandoned infants was sufficiently conceivable – but also contestable – to require both conciliar action and legal documentation. At least one sermon suggests that not everyone in the Christian community supported such social practices on the abandoned infants. Here, we must return to the apparent non-sequitur near the end of *sermo* 19. To reiterate: after a theologically focussed account of attitudes to sickness and health Caesarius moved on to abortion with the phrase, 'And relying on your charity, I advise all your daughters, out of paternal concern, that no woman should take potions for abortion [etc.]'. The allusion to charity is a clue to what was really going on. Caesarius hoped that his admonitions would ripple through the community as Christians reminded one another of their sins. But Caesarius also recognized that he needed his listeners' charity in receiving these admonitions and elsewhere he often cushioned moral criticisms with appeals for this receptive charity.[81] In *sermo* 19 the appeal to charity functioned in both ways. It was the source of the admonition, a paternal concern over his spiritual daughters' sins, but also a cushion for what was an address to fathers in particular. This was *not* a non-sequitur, for the preceding theology of health and sickness emphasized divine providence: God always knows what is best for us. Might this have included having a pregnant daughter? In societies where the hierarchical nature of parent-children relations is pronounced and unwed mothers become a source of shame or dishonour to family groups, recourse to abortion is often a response to direct or anticipated parental pressure.[82] Like Roman society before him and Carolingian society centuries later, Caesarius's society fits the bill and, as we shall see below, Gregory of Tours gives us no reason to see the later sixth century any differently. And yet there is scarcely any discussion by ancient or medieval authors of abortion in terms of direct or anticipated parental pressure. Caesarius's model for paternal imitation in *sermo* 19 was an exception to the rule. Insofar as it implied that not all fathers would offer such admonitions to their daughters, it was also a critique – but a subtle, even cautious, critique, which suggests that this familial context was tricky ground for a bishop.

Abortion as sacrilege and 'homicidal contraception'
Scholars interested in popular religion have increasingly questioned the idea that Caesarius's condemnations of ritual practices straightforwardly reflect pagan survivals. Beneath his 'indiscriminate polemic' against practices like bathing in rivers to mark the feast of John the Baptist lay a 'complicated

[81] G. de Nie, 'Caesarius of Arles and Gregory of Tours: Two Sixth-Century Bishops and "Christian Magic"', reprinted in G. de Nie, *Word, Image and Experience: Dynamics of Miracle and Self-Perception in Sixth-Century Gaul* (Aldershot, 2003), V, pp. 176–9.
[82] See pp. 235–6 below on the *Vita Haimhrammi*. On parental pressure *towards* abortion exerted on married women by in-laws (in the sense of parents of husbands) in modern Taiwan, see M. L. Moskowitz, *The Haunting Fetus: Abortion, Sexuality, and the Spirit World in Taiwan* (Honolulu, 2001), pp. 24–5.

diversity of religious intentions'.[83] Early Christian polemicists had constructed an aetiology of abortion which rooted the practice in the bloody tales of the Greco-Roman pantheon. Early medieval pastors like Caesarius did not have the luxury of encountering abortion (or pretending to) outside the Christian community. Where Caesarius associated abortion in some measure with superstitious practices, he did not construct abortion as a 'pagan' sin. Stylistically and substantially he used such associations to give clarity to the values which he wanted to define the community.[84]

Take the devil. Potions for abortion were 'diabolical' in *sermo* 44 and the devil instigated serious sins in *sermo* 200. *Sermo* 52 was all about the devil and made clear what was latent in other sermons: the devil's persuasion was a form of obfuscation. Women did not realize the self-harm and murder they wrought when they drank up potions for abortion. By uncovering the devil's malign persuasion Caesarius was rhetorically uncovering the true nature of abortion.

Both *sermo* 51 and 52 placed an accent on abortion as a form of sacrilege. When Caesarius called potions (and other practices) sacrilegious, he was drawing attention to means and ends which violated or bypassed divine power.[85] In *sermo* 51, 'devilish spells and sacrilegious amulets' were the means by which the childless desperately sought fertility and by which the fertile tried to bring about sterility. Such responses to sterility or fertility entailed fighting against the will of Christ. The ideas of sacrilege as recourse to non-divine power and diabolical obfuscation are also crucial to understand one of the most striking features of *sermo* 52, which reserved an especially fierce invective against mothers who sought out remedies for their sick children. Instead of seeking the church's medicine (anointing with oil) or even help from doctors, mothers sought out soothsayers and sorcerers, wrote spells and wore charms on their necks.[86] What connected this to abortion was the devil. Through his cunning women cruelly (*crudeliter*) killed their children through abortion and – this is striking – even more cruelly (*crudelius*) healed them through spells.[87] Here, the rhetorical strategy was to transfer the moral resonance of abortion, the cruel murder of children at the devil's instigation, onto the desperation with which some mothers tried to heal their children.

---

[83] Klingshirn, *Caesarius*, p. 210, with *Sermo* 33.4; cf. R. Markus, 'From Caesarius to Boniface: Christianity and Paganism in Gaul', in *The Seventh Century: Change and Continuity*, ed. J. Fontaine and J. N. Hillgarth (London, 1992), pp. 154–72; Klingshirn, *Caesarius*, pp. 209–26; Hen, *Culture*, pp. 154–67.

[84] R. Markus, *The End of Ancient Christianity* (Cambridge, 1990), pp. 206–7.

[85] Hen, *Culture*, p. 161.

[86] Cf. D. C. Skemer, *Binding Words: Textual Amulets in the Middle Ages* (University Park PA., 2006), pp. 40–1. On Caesarius's cautiously favourable attitude to medical practitioners, see Jones, *Social Mobility*, pp. 273–8.

[87] *Sermo* 52.5, p. 232.

These connotations are relevant to making sense of his most striking idea: so many possible conceptions, so many murders. Caesarius persistently described abortion as the taking of life. Abortion was to kill (*occidere* is used across all of the relevant sermons, with *homicidium* in *sermo* 1 and 19). The relational dimension was significant. Abortion was maternal murder. The killing field was within the womb, within the folds of the maternal body. Furthermore, the sermons eroded any distinctions between killing before or after birth. As a pastoral strategy this rested on the presumption that killing infants was recognizably wrong for the audience. Apart from recalling the sad fate of young infants who had been snatched away from their mothers and flung half-dead onto the road during the siege of Arles, Caesarius did not otherwise address infanticide separately.[88]

How did the so many possible conceptions, so many murders idea fit in? The extensive discussion of abortion in *sermo* 52 provides a clue. The aim of this passage had been to uncover how women harmed themselves in abortion – physically and spiritually. Even if there was no little infant within the womb, women harmed their own natures; strikingly, the passage rhetorically filled the womb with the diminutive *infantolus* at the very point when it imagined uterine emptiness. But the preceding lines also hinged on the deep ambiguity of what drinking potions for abortion actually entailed. Women were unaware that they conceived in sterility, that they received what had been conceived with death. This was one way of addressing the ambiguity of ending life scarcely before it had begun. Whether or not these were Caesarius's words, they suggest that the so many conceptions, so many murders idea was a response to the ambiguity of abortion. Caesarius's most striking phrase on abortion was not premised on the idea that every sperm is sacred. Rather, it played on the unsettling possibility that women were murdering their own children when they drank up potions.

Caesarius's ideas on abortion were communicated within his province and beyond during his lifetime. In the long term, they spread far beyond southern Gaul. In the eighth and ninth centuries Frankish reformers and missionaries evidently found his medium and message useful. But, as the fate of his most striking phrase on abortion suggests, later users put his words to new uses. Even if the two sermons which have only survived in the eighth-century Würzburg homiliary (51 and 52) should still be seen as Caesarius's, they evidently struck a chord within an eighth-century clerical culture in which ideas about 'paganism' were intensifying.[89] Neither the specificity of what abortion signified for Caesarius nor the multiple subsequent uses of Caesarius are

---

[88] *Sermo* 70.2, p. 297.
[89] On this intensified discourse on 'paganism' from the eighth century onward, in addition to Hen, *Culture*, see J. Palmer, 'Defining Paganism in the Carolingian World', *EME* 15.4 (2007), 402–25; J. Couser, 'Inventing Paganism in Eighth-Century Bavaria', *EME* 18.1 (2010), 26–42.

wholly reducible to the transmission of older ideas on abortion. Caesarius was addressing abortion in the present tense and so too were those who borrowed his words centuries later.

But we cannot take it for granted that Caesarius's ideas on abortion caught on in Merovingian Gaul in the short to medium term. The passing of southern Gaul from Visigothic to Merovingian hands weakened Caesarius's position later in his career. This is one reason for his relatively muted direct influence, certainly outside monastic contexts, in later sixth- and seventh-century Francia.[90] Another reason was that Caesarius's text-based approach to forming Christian communities was eclipsed by the coalescence of Christian communities around the material relics and textual commemorations of saints. Yet, if the story of abortion and the forming of Christian communities in sixth-century Gaul starts with Caesarius, it does not end with him. Towards the end of the sixth century another bishop came to be associated with saving women from the sin of abortion in a startlingly different sense.

Saving souls from the womb: The *Vita Germani*

The bishop in question was Germanus of Paris. His intervention in an attempted abortion was commemorated in a saint's life by Venantius Fortunatus, the Italian-born writer who made a career of composing literary works for ecclesiastical and aristocratic audiences in Gaul during the second half of the sixth century. The two had become acquaintances soon after Fortunatus's arrival in Gaul in the mid 560s. Germanus was the dedicatee of Fortunatus's life of one of his predecessors, Marcellus. Naturally enough, Fortunatus wrote a life of Germanus after his patron's death in 576.[91]

Much of the *Vita Germani* is typical of Fortunatus's hagiographical output. The first sentence raises no eyebrows. Germanus was born into a respectable family.[92] But the opening then narrated a startling miracle. Before his birth, the fetal Germanus miraculously survived his mother's attempt to abort him:

> Blessed Germanus, bishop of Paris, a native of the territory of Autun, was born of well bred and respected parents, his father Eleutherius and also his

---

[90] Cf. Klingshirn, *Caesarius*, pp. 271–86.
[91] *Vita Marcelli* 1, MGH AA 4.2, p. 49. For Fortunatus's biography see B. Brennan, 'The Career of Venantius Fortunatus', *Traditio* 41 (1985), 49–78; J. W. George, *Venantius Fortunatus: A Latin Poet in Merovingian Gaul* (Oxford, 1992), pp. 4–34. See M. Roberts, *The Humblest Sparrow: The Poetry of Venantius Fortunatus* (Ann Arbor, 2009), pp. 123–39, for a detailed reading of one poem (*Carm.* 2.9) celebrating Germanus's episcopal leadership.
[92] See S. Coates, 'Venantius Fortunatus and the Image of Episcopal Authority in Late Antique and Early Merovingian Gaul', *English Historical Review* 115, no. 464 (2000), 1115–18, on aristocratic background as an indicator of episcopal status in Fortunatus's hagiography.

mother Eusebia. Since she had conceived him in her womb within a short space of time after another [child], his mother, moved by womanly shame, wanted to kill the infant before birth; and since she did not harm him after taking a potion to throw out an abortion, she would lie on her belly to suffocate by her weight he whom she could not harm by poison. Mother was in battle with her child, but the infant was resisting from the womb; there was a fight between woman and her insides. The matron was being struck but the infant was not being harmed; the bundle was struggling so that the mother would not become a parricide. So it happened that protected he emerged safe and sound and rendered his mother innocent. Here was a prophecy of the future, to have performed a miracle before he even reached birth.[93]

Much of the rest of the *vita* showcased Germanus's sanctity as bishop in a parade of episcopal miracles, but only after a young Germanus had also survived an attempted poisoning by a relative eager to obtain his inheritance.[94]

If Germanus's miraculous survival in the womb might well be unique in hagiography, it nonetheless fits with broader hagiographical impulses. The passage from conception to birth often signalled the sanctity of holy men and women. Stories of saints conceived by ageing couples after prolonged barrenness, for example, echoed the stories of biblical couples such as Abraham and Sara.[95] Prophecies before birth, sometimes in the form of a pregnant mother's vision or dream, were another way of signalling the inception of sanctity.[96] Gregory of Tours' life of Nicetius of Lyon began with God's annunciation to the prophet Jeremiah, 'Before I formed you in the womb, I knew you, and before you were born I consecrated you' (Jeremiah 1. 5), before explaining that God had wanted to reveal Nicetius's future sanctity to his mother, Artemia,

---

[93] 'Beatus igitur Germanus Parisiorum pontifex, territorii Augustidunensis indigena, patre Eleutherio, matre quoque Eusebia, honestis honoratisque parentibus procreatus. Cuius genetrix, pro eo quod hunc post alterum intra breve spatium concepisset in utero, pudore mota muliebra [muliebri, in manuscript variants and Krusch's older edition], cupiebat ante partum infantem extinguere, et accepta potione, ut abortivum proiceret, nec noceret, incubabat in ventre, ut pondere praefocaret, quem veneno non laederet. Certabatur mater cum parvulo, renitebat infans ab utero: erat ergo pugna inter mulierem et viscera. Laedebatur matrona nec nocebatur infantia; obluctabatur sarcina, ne genetrix fieret parricida. Id actum est, ut servatus incolomis ipse inlaesus procederet et matrem redderet innocentam. Erat hinc futura praenoscere ante fecisse virtutem, quam nasci contingerit', *Vita Germani* 1, MGH SRM 7, p. 372; this is Bruno Krusch's revision of his older edition in MGH AA 4.2 (*Vita Germani* 1.1–4, at pp. 11–12).

[94] *Vita Germani* 2, p. 373; his antagonist is described as *mater parentis* after a reference to Stratidius, one of Germanus's *propinqui*.

[95] J. T. Schulenburg, *Forgetful of their Sex: Female Sanctity and Society, ca. 500–1100* (Chicago, 1998), pp. 221–4.

[96] I. Moreira, 'Dreams and Divination in Early Medieval Canonical and Narrative Sources: The Question of Clerical Control', *Catholic Historical Review* 89.4 (2003), 635–41.

before anyone else. Accordingly, when her husband told a pregnant Artemia that he was being earmarked for the bishopric at Geneva, the saint's mother begged him not to pursue it because she was carrying the future bishop in her womb.[97]

Germanus's birth story, a 'prophecy of the future', typifies what Isabel Moreira has called the 'Merovingian penchant for predestined saints'.[98] But predestined holiness met with another hagiographical impulse. Family members frequently represented familial obligations, social conventions or secular priorities inimical to sanctity – and often little else. Aside from a reference to their high social status, the only other detail about Caesarius's parents given by his hagiographers was their incomprehension at their young son's insistence on donating his clothes to the poor.[99] Germanus's mother Eusebia epitomized, in John Kitchen's words, the 'hagiographic tendency to accord the saint's kin a significant function in the narrative only when a member of the family initiates the conflict'.[100]

The extended uterine conflict with which the *vita Germani* opens served a dual hagiographical function: it prophesied Germanus's sanctity and dramatized the overcoming of familial opposition. But what was the message on abortion encoded in this miracle? The answer concerns both Merovingian women and Merovingian bishops.

Moved by womanly pudor: *The depiction of Eusebia*
Eusebia is an early medieval rarity: a named woman implicated in abortion. The thick description of the opening to the *Vita Germani*, the prolonged martial imagery, conveyed her increasing desperation to get rid of her child. It is tempting to read the opening as a whisper of the burden of childrearing and desire for family planning among Merovingian women.[101] More specifically, it might well be a whisper of the desire to space births within marriage. But it is easy to miss how Fortunatus framed Eusebia's action. She did not attempt abortion just because she had conceived another child so quickly; but because she was 'moved by womanly *pudor*' after conceiving another child so quickly. John Kitchen has argued that Fortunatus carefully avoided casting Germanus's mother in a sympathetic light. But Fortunatus's depiction of Eusebia's motivation is more ambivalent than Kitchen allows. If not wholly sympathetic, neither was it the kind of moral caricature with which Caesarius had denounced *ingenuae* some decades earlier.[102]

---

[97] *Liber vitae patrum* 8.1, MGH SRM 1.2, pp. 240–1.
[98] I. Moreira, *Dreams, Visions, and Spiritual Authority in Merovingian Gaul* (Ithaca NY, 2000), p. 176.
[99] *Life of Caesarius* 1.3, p. 10.
[100] J. Kitchen, *Saints' Lives and the Rhetoric of Gender* (Oxford, 1998), p. 27.
[101] Cf. ibid., p. 27.
[102] Cf. 'The position of the phrase *pudore mota muliebri* [viz. in a subordinate clause] is significant because the reference to shame ... cannot assume primary impor-

It is worth pausing here to recognize the complex sensibility towards pregnancy, childbirth and motherhood found across Fortunatus's oeuvre. At a symbolic level his models of sanctity, most obviously the abbess Radegund of Poitiers, were spiritual mothers as much as virile female ascetics.[103] In his occasional poetry Fortunatus was sensitive to motherhood in a more fleshly sense. His *consolatio* for the widower Dagaulf on the passing of his young wife Vilithuta, who died in childbirth at the age of seventeen, shows pained awareness of the dangers of pregnancy. The expectant Vilithuta was 'pregnant with her own destruction'. 'Bearing a soul, her own soul was robbed' in childbirth. Their child was 'buried in birth' and 'born in the mouth of death'.[104] On Emma Southon's reading, Fortunatus's *consolatio* stressed the death of the infant over Vilithuta's death.[105] But Fortunatus was noticeably reticent about one thing. While the poem culminated in reassurance of Vilithuta's heavenly fate, the fate of the infant went unmentioned. A fifth-century funerary inscription from southern Gaul for an infant captured the emotional struggle for parents who lost their unbaptized infants. The 'little Theudosius, whose parents in purity of mind intended to bury him in the holy baptismal font, was snatched away by shameless death'. His parents clung onto the hope that the 'child will be heir to Christ'.[106] Fortunatus's reticence was a small mercy. Elsewhere, an epitaph composed for the mother of two young sons conveyed the message that childbearing was sanctifying. These twins 'born of a single womb and buried in similar fate' had died young. One, Patrick, had died at the age of five, while the other, John, had died in his white baptismal garments. But they were not to be mourned because their 'blessed life' had made 'sinless men' of them. The

tance. To give greater prominence to the emotional factor by elaborating on it would risk casting the mother in a sympathetic light. If the mother is regarded sympathetically, then her role as an opponent would become ambiguous. Once ambiguity is introduced, the hagiographer loses the possibility of characterizing the circumstance as an occasion of highly polarized conflict between the hero and his mother', Kitchen, *Saints' Lives*, pp. 27–8. To my mind, this raises the question of why Fortunatus included reference to Eusebia's motivation at all.

[103] See G. de Nie, '"Consciousness Fecund through God": From Male Fighter to Spiritual Bride-Mother in Late Antique Female Sanctity', in *Sanctity and Motherhood: Essays on Holy Mothers in the Middle Ages* (New York, 1995), pp. 140–51; G. de Nie, 'Fatherly and Motherly Curing in Sixth-Century Gaul: Saint Radegund's *mysterium*', reprinted in de Nie, *Word, Image and Experience*, XIII, pp. 53–86; S. Coates, 'Regendering Radegund? Fortunatus, Baudonivia and the Problem of Female Sanctity in Merovingian Gaul', in *Gender and Christian Religion*, SCH 34, ed. R. N. Swanson (Woodbridge, 1998), pp. 37–50.

[104] 'damno feta suo, quae pariendo perit'; 'sic animam generans anima spoliatur et ipsa'; 'nascendo sepultus ... natus in ore necis', *Carm.* 4.26, ll.45, 49, 55–6, MGH AA 4.1, p. 96; cf. George, *Venantius Fortunatus*, pp. 93–4.

[105] E. Southon, 'Fatherhood in Late Antique Gaul', in *Families in the Roman and Late Antique World*, ed. M. Harlow and L. Larsson Lovén (London, 2012), p. 247

[106] Translation of this epitaph, now in a church at Brignoles, from P. Cramer, *Baptism and Change in the Early Middle Ages, c. 200–c. 1150* (Cambridge, 1993), p. 131.

twins were happy souls, *felices animae,* in heaven, and their *felix* mother, 'who deserved to experience the light [of heaven] through her childbearing', now rested in peace.¹⁰⁷

Like other early medieval ecclesiastical authors Fortunatus also used the uglier side of carnality to illumine the beauty of virginity. In the later 560s Fortunatus wrote a long poem for Radegund's community of nuns at Poitiers. One section of this poem graphically imagined the trials and traumas when birth went wrong. The pregnant woman 'does not conceal a stiffening womb with a fetus closed within, she lies down, saddened and wearied by the proof'. In childbirth, the 'heaving of body and soul between gasps', her life hangs in the balance until finally a 'monster comes into being':

> Unruly skin alone swelled out, beyond all human appearance
> so that it shames (*pudeat*) the mother that she bore it with love.
> Fleeing from her own relatives, ashamed, she carries it away
> until she destroys the burden, deposited in a sack.¹⁰⁸

This graphic depiction of perilous childbirth culminating in the clandestine abandonment of a misshapen, premature infant was ultimately meant to valorize virginity. But Fortunatus's imagining of the experience of miscarriage noticeably evoked mental trauma as well as physical strain. It invited psychological pity as well as physical disgust. He valorized virginity precisely because he was sensitive to these traumas and strains. In the allusion to concealing stillbirth from relatives lay a flicker of the social and familial pressures to which Merovingian women were subject. The reference to Eusebia's *pudor* in the *Vita Germani* was written, then, by an author for whom an ability to imagine the physical perils and psychological anguish of women's reproductive labour was part of his professional expertise.¹⁰⁹

Of course, Eusebia's *pudor* was not tinged with moral approbation like the 'sacred *pudor*' which raised virgins to heaven.¹¹⁰ *Pudor* did evoke a sense of public shame. Fortunatus's prose *vita* of Hilary of Poitiers tells the story of two merchants who decided to give a slab of wax as an offering to the saint. One

---

[107] 'uno utero geniti simili sunt sorte sepulti'; 'quos tulit innocuos vita beata viros'; 'quae meruit partu lumina ferre suo', *Carm.* 4.22, ll.2–3, 12, MGH AA 4.1, p. 93.

[108] 'non premit incluso torpentia viscera fetu / aut gravefacta iacet pignore maesta suo'; 'inter anehelantes animae seu corporis aestus'; 'crescit hydrus'; 'ultra hominis habitum tantum cutis effera turget, / ut pudeat matrem hoc quod amore gerit. / se fugiens propriis verecunda parentibus aufert, / donec depositum sarcina solvat onus', *Carm.* 8.3, ll.325–7, 330–4, pp. 189–90; translation adapted from Elliott, *Bride of Christ*, p. 91. On this poem and the circumstances of its composition see B. Brennan, 'Deathless Marriage and Spiritual Fecundity in Venantius Fortunatus' De virginitate', *Traditio* 51 (1996), 73–97, and see too B. H. Rosenwein, *Emotional Communities in the Early Middle Ages* (Ithaca NY, 2006), pp. 117–19, for a nuanced reading of this and other passages from *De virginitate*.

[109] Cf. Wemple, *Women*, p. 150–1.

[110] Cf. 'et quascumque sacer vexit ad astra pudor', *Carm.* 8.3, p. 182.

of the merchants begrudged the donation in his heart. Miraculously the wax placed before the altar divided into equal halves, but one half rolled away. This was a public sign of the saint's rejection of half-hearted offerings. The merchant admitted to the offence after he was overcome by *pudor*.[111]

Like the tight-fisted merchant's *pudor*, Eusebia's *pudor* hinted at shame related to public exposure; specifically, to the shame of conceiving another child in quick succession. Postpartum abstinence together with other forms of sexual abstinence connected with female physiology was commonly enjoined by churchmen in the Early Middle Ages.[112] Historians have understandably read postpartum abstinence norms in terms of a specifically Christian connection between sex and spiritual impurity. But they have scarcely attempted to imagine the social experience of such norms in light of comparable postpartum norms and taboos surrounding infant wellbeing, maternal health and parental responsibility in other societies. Eusebia's *pudor* entailed worrying about what the neighbours might think and, as anthropologists know well, what the neighbours might think is no trivial matter.[113] Here, we might recall the class distinctions with which Caesarius had urged sexual restraint upon the urban elite in Arles a few decades earlier. Lepers, he snorted, were born to *rustici*, country bumpkins, who did not know how to control themselves.[114] Eusebia's *pudor* anticipated that something between a moral fault and social *faux pas* would be publicized through the birth of a second child in quick succession. Fortunatus framed the circumstances in which Eusebia's pregnancy became unwanted in terms of a social pressure which would have been recognizable to his audience – or recognizable as something which bishops, following Caesarius, wanted to become a social pressure – just as the designs upon inheritance behind the attempt to poison Germanus were later in the narrative.

---

[111] 'inmensi pudoris reatu perculsus', *Liber de virtutibus sancti Hilarii* 11.33, MGH AA 4.2, p. 10.

[112] J.-L. Flandrin, *Un temps pour embrasser: Aux origines de la morale sexuelle occidentale (VIe–IXe siècle)* (Paris, 1983), pp. 12–18; J. A. Brundage, *Law, Sex, and Christian Society in Medieval Europe* (Chicago, 1987), pp. 155–7.

[113] In modern Gambia, where postpartum abstinence is integral to birth-spacing, 'goat seed' is an insult for a woman who bears children in quick succession: C. Bledsoe, *Contingent Lives: Fertility, Time, and Aging in West Africa* (Chicago, 2002), pp. 91–161 ('goat seed' insult at p. 103). In parts of Indian society marital abstinence for physiological as well as liturgical reasons cuts across religious boundaries and bears a resemblance to the sexual regimen envisaged in penitentials; see P. Chattopadhayay-Dutt, *Loops and Roots: The Conflict between Official and Traditional Family Planning in India* (New Delhi, 1995), pp. 209–14. For a cross-cultural survey of postpartum abstinence norms, see E. Abbott, *A History of Celibacy* (Cambridge MA, 2001), pp. 295–9.

[114] *Sermo* 44.7, p. 199; Gregory of Tours, *LH* 7.7, p. 330, notes Guntram's amazement upon hearing that Fredegund claimed to be pregnant having given birth four months earlier.

The fetal Germanus as episcopal saint

If Fortunatus's allusion to Eusebia's motivation was nuanced, the core message about Germanus was less subtle. Throughout his hagiographic output, miracles demonstrated episcopal charism and authority. Miracles had, in Simon Coates's words, a 'liturgical value: they incorporated the values represented by the episcopal saint into a system of values promulgated by preaching and the performance of the sacraments'. A large number of miracles performed by Germanus pertained one way or another to sacramental life. For example, Germanus cured a woman of blindness and on the next day she joined the people in procession at mass.[115] Such healing miracles dramatized the creation of 'unified, Christian, communities by reintegrating those who had been cut off from the services of the Church' and the 'reception of the sinner into the Christian community'.[116] Germanus's first miracle foretold his future role as bishop. The miracle lay in his mother's salvation as much as his own survival. While still a mere bundle he fought back to prevent his mother from becoming a *parricida*. By successfully fighting for his life, he 'rendered his mother innocent'.

The opening to the *vita Germani* uniquely condensed a distinctive way of imagining the fetus as saint, describing abortion as a conflict between mother and child, and marking the inauguration of Germanus's episcopacy long before his ordination. Unlike Caesarius's sermons, Fortunatus's miracle story has not entered histories of the church tradition on abortion. The privileging of canon law and conciliar rulings within such histories ignores other kinds of textual activity central to the values of Christian communities in the Early Middle Ages. Like Caesarius's sermons, Fortunatus's *vitae* can be imagined as performative texts, as textual centrepieces within ceremonial liturgies in which bishops attempted to cement their ties to prominent predecessors in front of their communities. Miracle stories within them were explicitly designed to stick in the memory.[117] These stories were propaganda pieces which publicized the bishop's capacity to reintegrate sinners. But, in dealing with sin, they also served a catechetical purpose. Germanus's first miracle was a compressed morality tale about the sin of abortion, a morality tale of which Caesarius would have approved. At the end of the battle (*certamen*) between mother and child, and fight (*pugna*) between a woman and her own body, Eusebia had been saved by childbearing and a bishop had fought for her salvation from her womb.[118]

---

[115] *Vita Germani* 33, p. 392.
[116] Coates, 'Venantius Fortunatus', 1129.
[117] R. Collins, 'Observations on the Form, Language and Public of the Prose Biographies of Venantius Fortunatus in the Hagiography of Merovingian Gaul', in *Columbanus and Merovingian Monasticism*, ed. H. B. Clarke and M. Brennan (Oxford, 1981), pp. 108–13; cf. *Vita Germani* 19, 23, pp. 384, 386.
[118] Here I depart from Shanzer, 'Voices', 351, who reads the *Vita Germani* as a text

Sixth-Century Gaul

Throw out your infant:
Unwanted pregnancy and the writings of Gregory of Tours

The miraculous story of Germanus's birth quickly caught on in Merovingian Gaul. Gregory of Tours, one of Fortunatus's episcopal patrons, certainly knew about it.[119] Gregory's absence from histories of abortion is more justifiable than Fortunatus's, for none of his writings directly addressed abortion. But they do offer two intriguing stories of unwanted pregnancies culminating in dead infants.

Dead infants and sexual sin
One story appeared in the *Liber in gloria martyrum*, a collection of miracle tales. Told to Gregory by a spiritual backpacker from Gaul who had been healed of leprosy in the holy land, it concerned an adulterous woman in Jericho. This unnamed woman was a serial infanticide, for 'whenever she gave birth to a child conceived from prostitution, immediately she suffocated the child and buried it in the ground, so that what was not concealed from God and his angels would be hidden to men'.[120] On the feast of the Epiphany – no coincidence, one imagines – the woman accompanied crowds gathered on the banks of the river Jordan. But as she approached to bathe, the waters ebbed away from her feet. Onlookers asked what crime she had committed. The woman confessed to the murders and asked for their prayers. The bathers collectively prayed for God to forgive her, whereupon she dropped dead. This happened, Gregory speculated in an aside, 'so that the crime that had been pardoned could never be repeated'.[121] Here, the motive for child-murder was concealing sexual sin, as the woman had explained in her public confession: 'Already I have murdered seven children born to me whom I conceived in immorality and feared to acknowledge. Yesterday I struck [and killed] my eighth child'.[122]

The story of the woman at Jericho balanced redress and redemption. An altogether more startling story appeared in another work which is often

---

which 'refer[s] neutrally to abortions'. This overlooks the stark moral colouring of abortion in the miracle, though it does capture the ambivalent depiction of Eusebia.
[119] Gregory pointed readers to Fortunatus's *Vita Germani* and its miracles (*virtutes*) in *LH* 5.8, p. 204.
[120] 'quotiens ab scorto concipiens partum edidisset, statim suffocatum terrae reconderet, ut scilicet fieret occultum hominibus, quae Deo et eius angelis non latebant', *Liber in gloria martyrum* 87, MGH SRM 1.2, p. 96; trans. R. Van Dam, *Gregory of Tours: Glory of the Martyrs*, TTH 3 (Liverpool, 1988), pp. 111–12 (here and below translations are Van Dam's). See *Liber in gloria martyrum* 18, pp. 49–50, on the deacon John from whom Gregory had obtained this story.
[121] 'ne crimen indultum iteraretur ulterius', *Liber in gloria martyrum* 87, p. 97.
[122] 'Septem iam a me parvulos editos interfeci, quos de incesto concipiens metui publicare, octavum adhuc die praeterita sugillavi', *Liber in gloria martyrum* 87, p. 97.

overlooked.¹²³ The *De miraculis beati Andreae apostoli* was a sixth-century epitome of a Latin version of the apocryphal *Acts of Andrew*, an epitome which Max Bonnet argued should be attributed to Gregory.¹²⁴ Scholarly interest in the epitome has concentrated on its use in reconstructing the now-lost *Acts of Andrew*, which was probably composed in the second or early third century and to which various Greek and Coptic fragments are related.¹²⁵ This scholarly interest has nonetheless thrown up two interesting features of Gregory's epitome. First, the original *Acts of Andrew* almost certainly represented a Gnostic strain of Christianity. Strong encratic traces which rejected marriage and sexuality would have been present in the Latin version which Gregory encountered. Second, and relatedly, where comparison with other fragments is possible, it is clear that Gregory made alterations to dilute these traces from a text which, he wrote euphemistically in the preface, was 'deemed apocryphal by some because of its excessive verbosity'.¹²⁶ Gregory evidently found some of his source material unsettling. In one story, for example, the apostle intervened to prevent two marriages between first cousins. In the original Andrew condemned marriage *tout court*. In Gregory's doctored account, however, Andrew carefully explained that he was condemning incest, not marriage, 'since God had ordered man and woman to be joined from the beginning'.¹²⁷

Our story concerned a woman called Caliopa, who had illicitly conceived a child in a union with a murderer (illicit because one could not marry a murderer under Roman law).¹²⁸ She suffered agonizing labour pains and could not bring forth the child. She asked her sister to invoke the aid of Diana, the

---

¹²³ Cf. I. Wood, 'The Individuality of Gregory of Tours', in *World of Gregory of Tours*, p. 28 (including n.2).

¹²⁴ See Max Bonnet's introductory comments in MGH SRM 1.2, pp. 371–6; cf. J. Flamion, *Les Actes Apocryphes de l'Apôtre André: Les Actes d'André et de Mathias, de Pierre et d'André et les textes apparentés* (Paris, 1911), pp. 50–5; J. M. Prieur's comments in *Acta Andreae*, CCSA 5–6 (Turnhout, 1989), pp. 8–12.

¹²⁵ See, for example, L. van Kampen, 'Acta Andreae and Gregory's "*De miraculis Andreae*"', *Vigiliae Christianae* 45.1 (1991), 18–26.

¹²⁶ 'propter nimium verbositatem a nonnullis apocrifus dicebatur', *De miraculis beati Andreae apostoli*, MGH SRM 1.2, p. 377; translations are my own though I have consulted Prieur's French translation in CCSA 5–6, pp. 555–651 and D. R. MacDonald's English translation in *The Acts of Andrew and the Acts of Andrew and Matthias in the City of the Cannibals* (Atlanta, 1990), pp. 188–317, both of which reproduce Bonnet's edition.

¹²⁷ 'cum ab initio Deus masculum iungi praecipisset et feminam', *De miraculis beati Andreae apostoli* 11, p. 382; cf. T. Adamik, 'Eroticism in the *Liber de miraculis beati Andreae apostoli* of Gregory of Tours', in *The Apocryphal Acts of Andrew*, ed. J. N. Bremmer (Leuven, 2000), pp. 39–40. See G. Quispel, 'An Unknown Fragment of the Acts of Andrew (Pap. Copt. Utrecht N. 1)', *Vigiliae Christianae* 10.1 (1956), 137–9, for another example: Gregory retained a story in which a proconsul's wife leaves him but toned down encratic emphases on divorce and rebellion against authority.

¹²⁸ Adamik, 'Eroticism', p. 44–5.

goddess with the requisite know-how in midwifery (*studium obstetricandi*), only to be reproached by a demon who insisted that she sought out the apostle instead. When Andrew finally arrived, he rebuked Caliopa before saving her life:

> 'Rightly you are suffering this, you are undergoing intolerable pains, who married badly [and] conceived with a conman. On top of this you consulted demons, who can help no-one, not even themselves. Now, believe in Jesus Christ and throw out the infant [*proice puerperium*]. But what you conceived unworthily will come out dead.' The woman believed and, after everyone left the chamber, she threw out [*proiecit*] a dead child; and thus she was freed from pains.[129]

No Greek or Coptic fragment survives to which we can compare Gregory's version of this unpleasant story. Elements within it – Caliopa's name, the invocation of Diana, the very setting in the apostolic era – would have struck Gregory and his readers as exoticisms from a different time and place. Given Gregory's tendency to make alterations, it is intriguing that this was the version which passed the censor. In the preface Gregory had explicitly said that his small volume included the *miracula admiranda*, miracles worthy of wonder.[130] Tamás Adamik has suggested that Gregory's rationale for including this story was to give moral instruction.[131] But what exactly was worthy of wonder here? What was the moral message?

Andrew's rebuke certainly conveyed a forceful message on recourse to healing outside the church, a message which Gregory would have found congenial.[132] The rebuke also drew attention to sexual sin, even if the legal reason why Caliopa's union was illicit might have been lost in translation. But readers of Gregory's epitome – and it did not languish in a single manuscript copy[133] – might well have found Andrew's imperative, *proice puerperium*, more jarring. This verb (*proicere*) in this context (pregnancy) carried potentially uncomfortable connotations of abortion and infant abandonment. In Caesarius's cautionary image for catechumens, sinners were literally projected from the womb. Eusebia had similarly tried to project Germanus in abortion. *Proicere* could also refer to infant abandonment and names like Proiectus were sometimes

---

[129] 'Recte haec pateris, quae male nupsisti, quae doloso concipiens, dolores intolerabiles sustines. Insuper consuluisti daemonia, quae neque ulli neque sibi prodesse possunt. Crede nunc Iesum Christum, filium Dei, et proice puerperium. Verumtamen mortuum egredietur quod indigne concepisti'. Credidit mulier, et egredientibus cunctis de cubiculo, proiecit partum mortuum; et sic a doloribus liberata est', *De miraculis beati Andreae apostoli* 25, p. 391.

[130] *De miraculis beati Andreae apostoli*, p. 377.

[131] Adamik, 'Eroticism', p. 45.

[132] On Gregory's hagiographical activism, see R. Van Dam, *Saints and their Miracles in Late Antique Gaul* (Princeton, 1993).

[133] J. Contreni, 'Reading Gregory of Tours in the Middle Ages', in *World of Gregory of Tours*, pp. 428–9, counts at least eleven surviving copies.

given to foundlings in late antiquity.[134] Gregory's readers might well have been struck more by Andrew's sadistic words than by his oxytocic miracle. The apostle seemed to sanction the idea that the offspring of certain unions were better off dead.[135] Admittedly, the temptation for readers of the *De miraculis Andreae* to draw conclusions was complicated by Gregory's spiritual health warning in the preface. Indeed, apocrypha on Andrew were regarded with increasing suspicion in the late antique and early medieval west because they were strongly associated with heretical groups like Manichaeans and Priscillianists.[136] Many readers encountered the *De miraculis Andreae* and its strange miracles as x-rated literature.

Unwanted sexual unions in Merovingian society
But the story does not quite end there. Gregory's other writings suggest that the idea which a reader of the *De miraculis Andreae* encountered on the page – offspring of certain unions were so problematic that they were better off dead – was not wholly alien to Merovingian society. Gregory's oeuvre contains several stories in which problematic sexual unions generated social conflict and sometimes culminated in horrific violence. Reading between the lines, the stories allow us to imagine why the conceptions of certain children were problematic for individuals and communities in Merovingian society.

Adultery and other transgressive sexual unions were socially explosive. An abbot by the name of Dagulf, a serial adulterer, was killed along with his lover when her husband caught them in bed. Gregory, in moralizing mode here, added that the story was a warning for clerics to shun the company of unrelated women.[137] Elsewhere, a priest from Le Mans and a bit of a ladies' man (*amator mulierum*) was only saved from his lover's angry relatives by the intervention of Aetherius, bishop of Lisieux. After moving to another city the woman (Gregory calls her a *scortum*, a whore) even cut her hair and dressed like a man to evade detection. But she was an *ingenua* born of well-to-do parents and her relatives soon tracked the couple down. They took the priest prisoner; he was only saved after Aetherius managed to ransom him for 20 *solidi*. The woman had no such luck; her kin burned her alive.[138]

In another story sexual scandal pitted one family against another. One man's wife was another man's daughter. Rumours spread in Paris that a

---

[134] Eyben, 'Family Planning', 25 n.72.
[135] Perhaps this was one rationale for some severely truncated early modern and modern editions of the *De miraculis beati Andreae apostoli*. The edition in PL 71, cols. 1261–4, prints the prologue, passion of Andrew and epilogue, with single sentence summaries of other chapters. This, in turn, was a reproduction of Theodorus Ruinart's severely truncated seventeenth-century edition; cf. Bonnet's comments, MGH SRM 1.2, p. 375.
[136] See Prieur's comments, CCSA 5–6, pp. 100–16.
[137] LH 8.19, pp. 385–6.
[138] LH 6.36, pp. 306–7.

woman had left her husband and started a sexual relationship with another man. The husband's relatives confronted her father and threatened to kill her in case the disgrace (*stuprum*) dishonoured their family. The father determined to swear an oath to prove his daughter's innocence, but the oath-swearing at the tomb of St Denis descended into a bloodbath when the husband's allies accused the father of perjury. After the bodies were cleared and the blood was rinsed away, the woman hung herself rather than face a trial.[139]

We must tread carefully. Gregory's stories about sex and its consequences were more like crafted anecdotes, 'ben trovati', rather than records of real episodes.[140] They were shaped in part by a moral schema which privileged the ascetic over the sexually active.[141] They were also manifestations of what Walter Goffart has called Gregory's 'prescriptive satire'. As a satirist Gregory 'painted a distorted verbal picture of the Gaul he lived in so as to show its true moral nature'.[142] The satirist inflates social mores to the point that they appear grotesque. But there is something there to be inflated. Gregory's stories about sex were extremes, perhaps, but extremes that amplified contemporary social impulses. Sixth-century legal regulations, covering everything from inappropriate tactility to sexually degrading insults against women, reflected comparable impulses towards the stifling protection of kinswomen in order to preserve family honour.[143] If the stories had the capacity to surprise, amuse or shock Gregory's contemporaries, the dynamics of family honour on which they hinged were altogether more familiar.

Some relevant stories, however, were not satirical. Two appeared in the same work as the story of the woman from Jericho, the *Liber de gloria martyrum*, a work whose purpose was in part catechetical. Both told of women wrongly accused of adultery by their husbands. In each case, the accused woman was ordered to undergo the ordeal of water by judges deaf to her protestations of innocence. In one version the wife was hurled into the Saône with a rock tied to her neck (as she was flung her husband shouted cruelly, 'With these abundant waters cleanse your fornications ... with which you have stained my bed'). When her relatives searched for her body the next day, they found her alive after she had been miraculously suspended above the

---

[139] *LH* 5.32, p. 237.
[140] D. Shanzer, 'History, Romance, Love, and Sex in Gregory of Tours' *Decem libri historiarum*', in *World of Gregory of Tours*, pp. 412–13.
[141] J. A. McNamara, 'Chastity as a Third Gender in the History and Hagiography of Gregory of Tours', in *World of Gregory of Tours*, pp. 199–209.
[142] *The Narrators of Barbarian History (A.D. 550–800): Jordanes, Gregory of Tours, Bede, and Paul the Deacon* (Princeton, 1988), pp. 197–203 (quotations at pp. 200–1).
[143] On these regulations see G. Halsall, 'Material Culture, Sex, Gender, Sexuality and Transgression in Sixth-Century Gaul', in G. Halsall, *Cemeteries and Society in Merovingian Gaul: Selected Studies in History and Archaeology, 1992–2009* (Leiden, 2010), pp. 349–54.

river.¹⁴⁴ In the other version of what looks like a motif, an Arlesian woman was flung into the Rhône. She floated, miraculously, through the intercession of St Genesius.¹⁴⁵ The same scenario with different local details suggests that the motif struck a chord. In both cases, the narrative took for granted that husbands' desire for retributive justice was given community sanction and that women received divine protection because of their innocence. The work in which these stories were written was probably used in liturgical readings or sermons. Two questions arise when we imagine them read aloud to an audience. What if the women had been guilty? And would this question have occurred to Gregory's listeners?

Gregory's writings are a useful resource for thinking about unwanted pregnancies. First, even if they were moralistic tales or grotesque satires of contemporary attitudes, by testifying to the repercussions of adulterous and other sexual unions Gregory's stories also suggest how the conception of certain children could become unwanted by individuals and communities in Merovingian society. Pregnancy and birth could disclose illicit relations and carry serious consequences for women and even men. Avoiding such disclosure was a question of social, even physical, survival.

Second, relevant social pressures emanated from more than one direction. Stories of disputes between and within kin-groups were written with a certain detachment (or mock detachment) and set against the backdrop of familial honour codes. Others involving clerics of different grades prompted closer authorial involvement and moral signposting. Gregory might well have exaggerated when he wrote that the entire population of Tours was incensed when rumours spread that their bishop Brictius had fathered the child of his laundress, also a nun.¹⁴⁶ For, as Gregory noted elsewhere, not all of his contemporaries took the problem of clerical and especially episcopal sexuality as seriously as he did. When two quarrelling bishops, Palladius of Saintes and Bertchramnus of Bordeaux, flung false allegations of adultery and fornication at one another, many onlookers laughed while others, Gregory noted in a moralizing signpost, were saddened that the 'devil's tares were sprouting forth among priests of the Lord'.¹⁴⁷ The fallout of clerical and even episcopal sex scandals was another dynamic through which pregnancies could become

---

¹⁴⁴ 'Ablute nunc aquis abundantibus fornicationes ... tuas, quibus saepe maculasti stratum meum', *Liber in gloria martyrum* 69, pp. 84–5.
¹⁴⁵ *Liber in gloria martyrum* 68, pp. 83–4.
¹⁴⁶ 'surrexit omnis populus Toronorum in ira', *LH* 2.1, p. 37; cf. Shanzer, 'History, Romance', pp. 400–1.
¹⁴⁷ 'inter sacerdotes Domini taliter zezania diabuli pollularet', *LH* 8.7, pp. 375–6. In a striking seventh-century correspondence between one of Gregory's successors, Chrodobert of Tours, and Importunus of Paris, the two Merovingian bishops traded in coarse sexual insults and allegations of promiscuity. Remarkably, the letters, preserved with the *Formulae Senonenses*, look like they were intentionally copied as model letters: 'insulting missives clearly had their place among the range of writings necessary for a bishop to conduct his affairs in Merovingian Francia', A.

unwanted. When we return to seventh- and eighth-century Merovingian Francia in chapter four, we will encounter penitential canons which addressed abortion specifically in the context of clerical sexuality.

* * *

The different social pressures that we can reconstruct by reading Gregory's works reemphasize the class focus with which Caesarius and Fortunatus had viewed abortion. Specificity is significant. Medium and message on abortion were shaped by specific, if evolving, dynamics of Christianization in sixth-century Gaul to an extent historians of abortion have inadequately recognized in their reading of Caesarius and neglect of Fortunatus, both of whom integrated the rejection of abortion into their definitions of the Christian community. Neither Caesarius nor Fortunatus was simply a vehicle for older condemnations of abortion, and allusions to apocryphal literature in this chapter show that the nature of church tradition on abortion as it appeared to sixth-century ecclesiastical authors was more variegated than later constructions of this tradition have recognized.

Although Caesarius's sermons and Fortunatus's *vita* were read in subsequent centuries – and we will encounter such readings in later chapters – the intricacy of what abortion signified to them was not simply cloned. Their individuality is important. This is not to deny that underlying their texts were contexts of collaboration between networks of bishops and clerics. Their works were community texts. But they also reflect individual initiatives and sensibilities. Corporate action on abortion was less visible in sixth-century Gaul than it would be even a century later in Gaul and elsewhere.

One final absence is worth noting. The texts examined in this chapter were not the only texts to address abortion in sixth-century Gaul. Some early canonical collections possibly produced in Gaul contained the Ancyran canon on abortion.[148] Moreover, the sixth century witnessed the codification and early revision of Salic law, which contained some articles on different permutations of abortion induced by violence. Discussion of these articles will be deferred until a broader analysis of legal approaches to abortion in Germanic law in chapter seven. As we shall see, it is difficult to join up the dots between the handling of abortion in Salic law and the handling of abortion within Christian communities by Caesarius and Fortunatus. The rationalities and underlying practices were distinct. Moreover, 'top-down', secular Merovingian measures against abortion as an entanglement of parental murder and sexual transgression are impossible to find. The closest thing to an exception is a brief reference in Merovingian hagiography; in other words, it does not really amount to much of an exception. The *vita* of Balthild (d. 680), the wife of Clovis II,

---

Rio, *Legal Practice and the Written Word in the Early Middle Ages* (Cambridge, 2009), pp. 51–2 (quotation at p. 52).
[148] See p. 99 below on the *Quesnelliana*.

possibly written by a nun at Chelles shortly after Balthild's death, related how this controversial Frankish queen had stamped out an 'impious tendency, by which many people were endeavouring to kill rather than rear their offspring'. The reason was the excessive tax burden, which Balthild managed to abolish.[149] Aside from this reference to infanticide rather than abortion, moralizing about child-murder in late antique and Merovingian Gaul was monopolized by ecclesiastical authors thinking in terms of Christian communities. In contemporary Visigothic Spain, by contrast, abortion became politicized. By the end of the seventh century a distinctive official discourse on abortion had emerged in Spain which was shaped by the interplay between religious and royal impulses, and by the tension between thinking about abortion in terms of Christian communities and Christian kingdoms.

---

[149] 'impia ... consuetudo, pro qua plures homines sobolem suam interire potius quam nutrire studebant', *Vita Balthildis* 6, MGH SRM 2, p. 488 (from the older A-text); on authorship, see C. T. Schroeder, 'Francia as "Christendom": The Merovingian *Vita domnae Balthildis*', *Medieval Encounters* 4.3 (1998), 265 n.1.

3

Church and State:
Politicizing Abortion in Visigothic Spain

In a letter apparently written in the late sixth century a certain Tarra asked for the Visigothic king's help in a difficult matter. All that we know about Tarra comes from this letter. He had been a monk at the monastery of Cauliana, near Mérida, but he now found himself expelled after rumours spread that he had visited a prostitute. Tarra protested his innocence. He did not know a single prostitute in Mérida or the surrounding province. A widower turned monk, no woman had touched his lips since the death of his wife. Tarra maintained that he had been banished without a fair hearing. Tarra's Germanic name and, more importantly, his conspicuous emphasis on orthodox credentials – at one point, he swore an oath in the name of the three members of the Trinity – suggest that he might have been an Arian Goth who had recently entered the Catholic fold just as Reccared, the king he was writing to, had done. If so, Tarra's letter conveys not only the disruption that rumours of sexual misconduct could wreak upon religious communities but also tensions lurking beneath the 'ideological screen' of 'social unanimity' in Visigothic society after the formalization of Reccared's conversion at the third council of Toledo in 589.[1]

Tarra's Latin has its quirks. He described his expulsion in a striking way. Wrongly accused, he claimed, 'they have flung me out like an uncondemned abortion from the womb and all the earth above me mourned; no one could be found who would know me well'.[2] The last two clauses are found in Mozarabic liturgy for the Monday after Palm Sunday.[3] The initial image, however, was Tarra's own. Effectively, he likened his fellow monks to abortionists who had expelled him from the womb of the monastery. This was more than just an idiosyncratic image within an idiosyncratic letter. Tarra's image provides a glimpse of the complex cultural significance of abortion in the Early Middle

---

[1] S. Castellanos, 'The Significance of Social Unanimity in a Visigothic Hagiography: Keys to an Ideological Screen', *JECS* 11.3 (2003), 413–14. For an overview of textual problems surrounding the letter, including the possibility that it was a deliberate reworking of an original petition produced at the royal chancery in the seventh century, see I. Velázquez, 'El *Suggerendum* de Tarra a Recaredo', *Antiquité Tardive* 4 (1996), 291–8.

[2] 'ut vulbe aborsum proiecerunt indemnatum et luxit super me omnis terra; non est inventus, qui me cognoscerat bene', ed. J. Gil, *Miscellanea Wisigothica* (Sevilla, 1972), p. 29.

[3] *Breviarium Gothicum*, PL 86, col. 574D.

Ages. Metaphors of abortion, often wielded in polemical contexts, have their own history, to which we turn in the final chapter. More immediately, there was a cultural background in Visigothic Spain against which it made sense to use abortion imagery in a petition to the king. By the late sixth century abortion was being discussed at various official levels. Churchmen, rulers and their legislators negotiated a range of concerns, from sexual transgression to the state of the fetus, from the health of the body politic to the healing of the body of the church.

The hiatus in records of church councils dealing with abortion after the councils of Ancyra and Elvira in the early fourth century came to an end in the mid sixth century when a local council and a canonical collection associated with another issued pronouncements on abortion. This was not the only kind of legislation on abortion in Visigothic Spain. By the time of its revision and promulgation in the mid seventh century, Visigothic law addressed abortion as comprehensively as any other post-Roman law-code. Beneath its seventh-century form lay accumulated layers of laws on abortion. Older laws from at least two earlier legislative moments can be excavated beneath the distinctive topsoil of a seventh-century addition ascribed to a Visigothic king. This law of Chindaswinth (d. 653) is the most striking exception to a broader rule in the history of abortion in the Early Middle Ages: it is difficult to associate rulers directly with legislation on abortion. Another significant exception was Reccared (d. 601). An intriguing canon which certainly covered infanticide and probably abortion too was issued during the formalization of his conversion at Toledo in 589.

At one level Visigothic royal pronouncements on abortion represented a convergence between church and state. Discourse on abortion was articulated in the ideological idiom of unity. Certainly after Reccared's conversion the idea of a Christian society was inextricable from the delineation of royal power. But at another level this politicization existed in tension with emerging pastoral approaches to abortion. Across the evidence different kinds of active deliberation on abortion are detectable, but it was shaped by the distinctive priorities and rationalities of localized conciliar action and centralizing royal legislation.

Killing those conceived in sin: The council of Lérida (546)

Reccared's conversion marks a watershed in the Iberian conciliar record. Before Toledo III councils were localized gatherings which concentrated on matters such as episcopal rights, liturgical questions and clerical behaviour. They are largely thin on context, with scant indication of specific reasons why bishops had convened. Unlike some national councils after 589, pre-conversion councils did not stand for the entire Iberian church.[4]

---

[4] R. L. Stocking, *Bishops, Councils, and Consensus in the Visigothic Kingdom, 589–633*

Visigothic Spain

Held in 546, the council of Lérida is typical of the pre-Toledo III record in all but one regard. A number of its canons on matters including incest, sexual violation of widows or nuns, and parents who presented their children for heretical (presumably Arian) baptism addressed the laity as well as the clergy. It also contained a ruling on abortion which articulated concerns over both lay and clerical sexual transgression:

> Those who have strived to kill or have assaulted in mothers' wombs by any potions what was wrongly conceived [and] made in adultery, communion is to be granted to adulterers of either sex after a period of seven years, provided that they persist in lamentation and humility for all their life; it is not allowed for them to recover the office of ministry, but from the moment of receiving communion they must number among the chorus of penitents. For the poisoners themselves communion may only be granted at death, if they have lamented their crimes for their entire life.[5]

We need to disentangle the canon from its survival and reception in later canonical collections. The bishops at Lérida did make passing references to canonical precedent. The final canon on what to do when a bishop died referred to the 'ancient authority of the canons' while another on rebaptism referred to the 'statutes of the Nicaean synod'.[6] But the practical reality of canonical sources available to Spanish bishops in the mid sixth century was more limited than these references might suggest.[7] At any rate, the abortion canon neither referred to nor resembles either of the two possible precedents from Ancyra and Elvira. There is nothing to indicate, then, that the bishops at Lérida were consciously responding to these earlier enactments. When thinking about its initial promulgation it is misleading to read the Léridan canon in a chain with the late antique canons on abortion as if, for instance, the bishops of Lérida consciously wanted to mitigate the longer penances stipulated in these earlier councils, respectively up to death (Elvira) and ten years (Ancyra).

This is where disentanglement becomes necessary. The rulings of all three councils – Elvira, Ancyra, Lérida – were included in the most important

---

(Ann Arbor, 2000), pp. 35–44; cf. R. Collins, *Early Medieval Spain: Unity in Diversity 400–1000* (New York, 1995), pp. 116–18.

[5] 'Ii vero qui male conceptos ex adulterio factos vel editos necare studuerint, vel in uteris matrum potionibus aliquibus colliscrint, in utroque sexu adulteris post septem annorum curricula communio tribuatur, ita tamen ut omni tempore vitae suae fletibus et humilitati insistant; officium eis ministrandi recuperare non liceat, attamen in choro psallentium a tempore receptae communionis intersint. Ipsis veneficis in exitu tantum, si facinora sua omni tempore vitae suae defleverint, communio tribuatur', Council of Lérida, c.2, *CCH* 4, p. 300; canons addressing lay behaviour include c.4 (incest), c.6 (sexual violation of widows/nuns) and c.13 (heretical baptism).

[6] 'prisca auctoritas canonum', 'Nicaeni synodi statuta', Council of Lérida, cc. 16, 9, pp. 307, 304.

[7] Stocking, *Bishops,* pp. 38–40.

Hispanic canonical collection, the *Collectio Hispana*, compiled in different recensions during the seventh century. The *Hispana* was a large collection which brought together Greek, African, Gallic and Spanish conciliar canons, including from Elvira, Ancyra and Lérida. The *Hispana* was organized chronologically; the abortion canons from these three councils were nowhere near one another. However, the seventh-century *Excerpta Hispana*, which accompanied the *Hispana* in some manuscripts, provided short references to conciliar canons arranged by topic. The *Excerpta* functioned as an index to the *Hispana*, which readers could use to pinpoint the canons they were after. Canons on abortion, including from Elvira, Ancyra and Lérida, appeared under the title, 'On parents who kill their children', within a book on marriage and sexual sin.[8] Thus, readers of the *Hispana* who had access to the *Excerpta* would have been able to encounter a conciliar tradition on abortion. They might have noticed what appeared to be a reduction in penance. Back in the sixth-century context, however, the bishops at Lérida were not consciously reducing the penance.

Admittedly, we can only speculate on this context, the circumstances surrounding the council. A precise answer is elusive, though some conciliar rulings may represent traces of actual disciplinary cases.[9] Before analysing the distinct elements of the canon it is worth pausing to note how they were put together. The overall meaning is clear, though the wording is slightly clumsy. While the final sentence passes muster, the grammatical subject jumps around in the inelegantly connected opening clauses (up to *insistant* in the Latin) and the reference to clerical culprits was noticeably tacked on.[10] The effort is of greater interest than the execution. Clumsiness points to ideas being brought together. Whether we attribute it to assembled bishops or a scribe (here we cannot escape the form in which the canon survived) the thought process was along the lines of, 'don't forget what happens if a priest is involved'.

The textual clumsiness is far more revealing than any *faux* numerology of penances. The canon was an attempt to scrutinize abortion with different culprits, accomplices and behavioural contexts in mind. First, the behavioural context: adultery. The connection between sexual transgression and abortion or infanticide was nothing new, but the Léridan canon very carefully specified that transgressors could be men as well as women. Abortion was a sign of transgression against a sexual order which, theoretically at least, made demands of male as well as female minds and bodies. Clerical minds and bodies were not exempt. The canon added a further permutation of male cul-

---

[8] 'De parentibus qui filios suos necant', *Excerpta Hispana* 5.10.1–6, *CCH* 2, p. 175.
[9] Cf. Collins, *Early Medieval Spain*, p. 117.
[10] A ninth- or tenth-century manuscript (Vatican, Biblioteca Apostolica Vaticana, MS latin 1341) added: 'si vero clerici fuerint, eis officium [etc.]', *CCH* 4, p. 300. This manuscript is the only complete witness to the *Hispana Gallica Augustodensis*, a mid ninth century adaptation of the *Hispana*, on which see L. Kéry, *Canonical Collections of the Early Middle Ages (ca. 400–1140)* (Washington DC, 1999), pp. 69–70.

pability in the form of the slightly garbled reference to loss of clerical office. Ironically, the disciplinary repercussions of an offence with strong associations of hiding sexual sin were distinctly public.

Within this behavioural context the bishops addressed both abortion and infanticide. They described infanticide as attempting to kill (*necare studuere*) those conceived in sin. The description of abortion, using potions to attack (*potionibus aliquibus collidere*) those conceived in sin, was more unusual insofar as *collidere* carried connotations of physical violence, of battering or beating.[11] At any rate those who administered the means for abortion were most severely punished and, in light of the earlier emphasis on both sexes, it is likely that 'poisoners' (*veneficis* is a masculine or feminine ending) envisaged men and women. The bishops envisaged a specific division of labour; both men and women endeavoured to kill an infant or launch an attack in the womb. The wording is open-ended, incidentally, about whether or not such attempts were successful. The bishops might well have been thinking about intent.[12] Nonetheless, whether *venefici* actually supplied or administered the various potions or simply offered relevant knowledge, they were deemed to have done something even worse.

The adultery-abortion frame did not, presumably, imply that abortion was licit in other contexts nor by punishing those who provided potions for abortion most severely were the bishops arguing that abortion was morally worse than infanticide. Likewise, the precise nature of male culpability for abortion was not spelled out. A man could coax or cajole a woman into taking an abortifacient potion, but he could not of course take it himself. Nonetheless, in thinking through abortion from multiple angles the Léridan canon presented disciplinary guidelines on the permutations of abortion for bishops who encountered future disciplinary cases.

Doctrinal theory and pastoral practice: Martin of Braga's canon on abortion

The context surrounding the next canon is less elusive. It takes us beyond the periphery of Visigothic political control to the kingdom of the Sueves in the north-west of the Iberian peninsula, a few decades before its conquest by Reccared's father, Leovigild, in 585. The canon is associated with Martin of Braga, who had journeyed west from his native Pannonia by the middle of the sixth century and subsequently became an important monastic and episcopal

---

[11] Elsakkers, RBL, p. 383 n.53. The terminological difference distinguished between abortion and infanticide, but presumably this leads Müller, *Criminalization*, p. 36 (with n.23) to characterize the Léridan canon as an 'anticipat[ion of] the scholastic distinction between prehuman and human life in the maternal womb'; cf. Nardi, *Aborto*, p. 619 n.91.

[12] Huser, *Crime*, p. 25.

figure in the Galician church.[13] Strictly speaking, the canon in question was not a conciliar enactment but a version of an older canon found in a canonical collection which was inserted after the records for the second council of Braga (572), at which Martin had presided as bishop of Braga. Martin explained in the preface that he had compiled this collection, the *Capitula ex orientalium patrum synodis*, for Nitigisius, the bishop of Lugo.[14] He put it together at some point between 569, when Lugo and Braga were separated as episcopal provinces, and the aftermath of Braga II, which had brought together Martin and Nitigisius as senior bishops. As the title suggests, the *Capitula* looked to eastern councils for much of its material. Though it was not labelled as such, the abortion canon clearly expanded on the Ancyran canon:

> If any woman has fornicated and killed the infant who was subsequently born, or has strived to have an abortion *and kill what has been conceived, or indeed has taken pains so that she does not conceive, whether in adultery or legitimate marriage,* earlier canons decreed that such women are to receive communion at death. Out of clemency, however, we judge that *such women, or those women complicit in these same crimes,* are to undertake ten years penance.[15]

Martin's canon brought attempts at preventing conception under the same heading as abortion and infanticide by clearly distinguishing between killing born infants, killing what has been conceived (*conceptum*) and doing something in order not to conceive (*ut non concipiat*). By including marriage as a behavioural context the canon did not solely associate abortion with sexual transgression. Yet, at the same time it gendered abortion as female sin in a particularly stark way by retaining the original focus on women and adding a reference to female accomplices (*consciae*). The bishops at Lérida had made every effort to think about male as well as female involvement with abortion. A few decades later here was another bishop who went to the opposite extreme.

---

[13] A. Ferreiro, 'The Missionary Labors of St. Martin of Braga in 6th Century Galicia', *Studia Monastica* 23 (1981), 11–26. On Martin's influence outside Galicia, see Y. Hen, 'Martin of Braga's *De correctione rusticorum* and its Uses in Frankish Gaul', in *Medieval Transformations: Texts, Power, and Gift in Context,* ed. E. Cohen and M. B. de Jong (Leiden, 2001), pp. 35–49.

[14] The preface is translated in R. Somerville and B. Brasington, *Prefaces to Canon Law Books in Latin Christianity: Selected Translations, 500–1245* (New Haven, 1998), pp. 53–4.

[15] 'Si qua mulier fornicaverit et infantem qui exinde fuerit natus occiderit, et quae studuerit abortum facere *et quod conceptum est necare aut certe ut non concipiat elaborat, sive ex adulterio sive ex legitimo coniugio,* has tales mulieres in mortem recipere communionem priores canones decreverunt. Nos tamen pro misericordia *sive tales mulieres sive conscias scelerum ipsarum* decem annis agere poenitentiam iudicamus', *Capitula* 77, ed. C. W. Barlow, *Martini episcopi Bracarensi opera omnia* (New Haven, 1950), p. 142 (my italics).

Visigothic Spain

In his search for the earliest conciliar ruling on contraception John Noonan found it in Martin's canon. For Noonan, however, the 'first apparent church legislation against contraception is ... an interpolation'. While some subsequent canonical collections reproduced the 'accurate' version of the Ancyran canon, others adopted 'Martin's concoction'.[16] 'Concoction' is too strong. There was no sleight of hand exactly, certainly not from the perspective of subsequent readers. The canon was preserved in several later collections as a conciliar ruling in its own right, distinct from the Ancyran canon.[17] The association with a council and, indeed, with Martin himself gave it a distinct authority, though moderately attentive readers would have spotted the affinities between the two canons. Significantly, Martin was not the only – or even the first – Latin compiler to tweak the Ancyran canon. The *Quesnelliana*, a later fifth-/early sixth-century collection of Gallic or Roman origin contained an addition to the opening clause on women who fornicated and killed their children: 'and also those women who act with them to strike out what has been conceived from the womb'.[18] Again, the emphasis was on abortion as female sin, though Martin's reworking, which is worded differently and attached to the final clause, was independent. Nor were other versions quite as 'accurate' as Noonan imagined. Dionysius Exiguus also included this addition to the opening clause of the Ancyran canon in his influential collection, through which it reached countless others.[19] Likewise the *Hispana* reproduced this version.[20] Canons were not uncommonly rearranged and changed by compilers, and in the preface Martin had declared his intention to remedy scribal errors and ambiguous translations. Why did Martin include and amend the Ancyran abortion canon?[21]

---

[16] Noonan, *Contraception*, p. 149.

[17] *Excerpta Hispana* 5.10.1, 4, p. 175, refers separately to the Ancyran canon and Martin's canon (as 'third council of Braga').

[18] 'sed et eas quae agunt secum ut utero conceptos excutiant', *Collectio Quesnelliana*, PL 56, col. 441A–B; on this collection, see Kéry, *Canonical Collections*, p. 27. Several divergences entered through multiple Latin translations made from the fifth century, though these are still understudied since the observations made over a century ago by Rackham, 'Canons of Ancyra', 159–61.

[19] *Codex canonum ecclesiasticum*, PL 67, col. 155A; one example of early influence from the sixth century is Cresconius, *Concordia canonum* 103, PL 88, col. 881C. Noonan, *Contraception*, p. 149, erroneously refers to Dionysius Exiguus's 'unchanged text'.

[20] Council of Ancyra, c.21, *CCH* 3, p. 101.

[21] Here, I make the assumption that he did. Claude Barlow, the editor of Martin's works, suggested that discrepancies between Greek canonical texts and Martin's versions should be explained by his use of different Greek originals which have not survived. Barlow points to the example of a ninth-century Syriac canonical collection full of eastern conciliar material which does not precisely correspond to any surviving Greek texts. Although the Syriac discrepancies might themselves have originated in translation rather than in a now lost Greek original, Barlow's suggestion is perfectly possible. But there are good and bad reasons for entertaining the possibility. To my mind, Barlow was excessively reluctant to regard the

Heresy hunting: A Priscillianist detour

Noonan's answer was, in a word, heresy. He argued that the canon was an 'attempt to protect conception from attack' against a 'background of Manichaean danger'. This 'Manichaean danger' took the guise of Priscillianism, the movement associated with the Galician bishop Priscillian, beheaded at Trier on charges of sorcery in 385 on the order of the western emperor, Magnus Maximus.[22] Priscillianism was strongly associated with Manichaeism – or, more precisely, some opponents of Priscillian and his followers made this connection – and Manichaeism in turn had long been tainted with allegations of deviant practices and ideas on sexuality and marriage. Orthodoxy needs heresy, and a marked feature of Noonan's broader narrative is heretical anti-procreative ideas and practices prompting the articulation and solidification of orthodox ideas on avoidance of offspring. His analysis of several late antique thinkers, especially Augustine, remains important even if we regard heresy less as a straightforward concrete reality and more as a mutable rhetorical tool, sometimes deployed by and sometimes deployed against figures later regarded as solidly orthodox. But did Priscillianism carry strong anti-procreative connotations in sixth-century Galicia? And, if so, did these Manichaean dangers prompt Martin's reworking?

Noonan deduced the 'background of Manichaean danger' from the activity of the first council of Braga. Presided over by Lucretius, the bishop of Braga, the council met in 561 with Martin, at this point the bishop of Dumium, also in attendance. Braga I represented a vital moment in the Galician church. Though the exact *annus mirabilis* is not known, the council was convening after the conversion of the Suevic kings from Arian to Catholic Christianity. Indeed, the council had been ordered to convene by King Ariamir.[23] In the opening address Lucretius set out three items on the episcopal agenda: to re-endorse what he called the 'statutes of faith'; to regain familiarity with earlier canons; and to issue new canons on improper clerical practice. The rationale was clear. After years in the wilderness, the Galician church needed to re-educate the clergy and reenergize ecclesiastical networks. Braga I might not have been as extravagantly stage-managed as the formalization of Reccared's conversion at Toledo in 589, but it was nonetheless a key moment in the Galician church.

amendments as Martin's: 'I cannot agree that Martin would arbitrarily have altered the provisions of the canon law as he found them ... [I]t must be conjectured that he had a different Greek original', *Opera omnia*, pp. 6–7. But there is no reason to regard alterations as arbitrary.

[22] For studies of Priscillian's ideas, followers and opponents, see H. Chadwick, *Priscillian of Avila: The Occult and the Charismatic in the Early Church* (Oxford, 1976); V. Burrus, *The Making of a Heretic: Gender, Authority, and the Priscillianist Controversy* (Berkeley, 1995).

[23] On the murky Suevic conversion, including the vexed question of whether Ariamir was in fact the first Suevic king to convert, see E. A. Thompson, 'The Conversion of the Spanish Suevi to Catholicism', in *Visigothic Spain: New Approaches*, ed. E. James (Oxford, 1980), pp. 77–92.

Priscillianism enters the scene through the statutes of faith. 'Although,' Lucretius acknowledged, 'the contagion of the Priscillian heresy was once detected and condemned in the provinces of Spain', he encouraged the bishops to be vigilant spiritual doctors in case anyone living in the farthest reaches of their provinces remained 'infected'.[24] The statutes of faith rehearsed two fifth-century anti-Priscillianist measures, with which the assembled bishops were expected to be familiar: a rule of faith proscribing Priscillianist heresies, commissioned by the first council of Toledo (400) and quickly sent to Balconius, the bishop of Braga, in the first decades of the fifth century; and a letter written by Pope Leo I 'at that time when the abominable poisons of the Priscillian sect were slithering in these regions'.[25] Written in 447, Leo's letter was a response to Turibius of Astorga, who had described Priscillian's followers and asked for the pope's intervention in a letter which has not survived. The rule of faith was read out for the bishops, copies of which they apparently held in their hands, though its measures were not transcribed for the conciliar record. Next, Lucretius turned to Leo's letter as a reminder that the 'fabrications of the Priscillianist heresy had once been abominated and condemned from the seat of the blessed apostle Peter'.[26]

The bishops then endorsed seventeen *relecta*, or reiterations, almost all of which were adapted from Leo's letter. One of these addressed marriage and procreation: 'If anyone condemns human marriage and shudders at the procreation of children, as Mani and Priscillian said, let him be anathema'.[27] Noonan based his reading of Martin's canon as an 'attempt to protect conception from attack' on this anathema against heretical misogamy and anti-procreationism. The next *relectum*, which Noonan did not quote, anathematized anyone who 'says that the forming of the human body is the work of the devil, and conceptions in mothers' wombs are fashioned by the work of demons'. At the surface this *relectum*, like the preceding one, could be read as evidence for Priscillianist anti-procreative ideas. But the real focus was on the theological repercussions of anti-materialism. Anyone who thought that the coming-into-being of flesh in the womb was the handiwork of demons 'does not believe in the resurrection of the flesh for this reason, as Mani and

---

[24] 'Nam licet iam olim Priscillianae haeresis contagio Hispaniarum provinciis detecta sit et damnata', Council of Braga (I) 2, ed. Barlow, *Opera omnia*, p. 196.

[25] 'eo tempore quo in his regionibus nefandissima Priscillianae sectae venena serpebant', Council of Braga (I) 2, p. 196.

[26] 'abominata iam olim a sede beatissimi Petri apostoli et damnata Priscillianae haeresis figmenta', Council of Braga (I) 2, p. 196.

[27] 'Si quis coniugia humana damnat et procreationem nascentium perhorrescit, sicut Manichaeus et Priscillianus dixerunt, anathema sit', Council of Braga (I) 3.11, p. 108. A comparable ruling from the first council of Toledo, held in 400, concentrated on marriage rather than procreation: 'Si quis dixerit vel crediderit coniugia hominum, quae secundum legem divinam licita habentur, execrabilia esse, anathema sit', Council of Toledo (I), c.16 (*regula fidei*), CCH 4, p. 344.

Priscillian have said'. And the next two canons outlined other repercussions of anti-materialist ideas ascribed to Mani and Priscillian.[28]

If we take a step back and survey the *relecta*, a tendency becomes clear. Take the first four *relecta*, which anathematized various ideas about the incarnation and Trinity. Arianism was the elephant in the room. These opening *relecta* effectively addressed aspects of Arian theology without explicitly mentioning Arianism. Instead the ideas were ascribed to a range of heretical figures, with one name consistently cropping up:

> ... like Sabellius and Priscillian said.
> ... like the Gnostics and Priscillian said.
> ... like Paul of Samosata and Photinus and Priscillian said
> ... like Cerdon, Marcion, Mani and Priscillian said.[29]

The bishops at Braga were doing what Gallic and Spanish bishops had been doing for well over a century: making Priscillian say what they wanted him to say. Over the course of the fifth and sixth centuries Priscillianism became, in Raymond Van Dam's words, a 'stereotyped image of evils and immoralities'. Priscillianism even eclipsed Manichaeism 'as a homebred idiom of heresy with which people articulated unacceptable aspects of their communities'.[30] Leo's response to Turibius in 447 is a good example. This was the main source for the two *relecta* concerned with procreation (neither of which reproduced all of Leo's rhetoric: for example, against the idea that demons formed children in their mother's wombs, Leo countered, 'such grotesque opinions are the works of demons, who do not form people in the bellies of women, but fashion such errors in heretics' hearts'). Leo evidently gained much of his information on Priscillianism from Turibius's letter to him and he simply transposed the *conflatus* of deviant thought and practice which he associated with Manichaeism onto Priscillianism.[31]

The *relectum* on heretical antipathy towards marriage and procreation, to which Noonan drew attention, must be placed into context. It possibly had anti-materialist theology in mind more than immoral practices. Moreover,

---

[28] 'Si quis plasmationem humani corporis diaboli dicit esse figmentum, et conceptiones in uteris matrum operibus dicit daemonum figurari, propter quod et resurrectionem carnis non credit, sicut Manichaeus et Priscillianus dixerunt, anathema sit', Council of Braga (I), 3.12, p. 108, with 3.13 (on the belief that the creation of all flesh was the work of malign angels) and 3.14 (on the belief that meat was impure).

[29] Council of Braga (I), 3.1–4, p. 107.

[30] R. Van Dam, *Leadership and Community in Late Antique Gaul* (Berkeley, 1985), pp. 88–114 (quotation at p. 108). Burrus, *Making of a Heretic*, pp. 21–4, provides an interesting critique of Van Dam's reading of the Priscillianist controversy in the fourth century. To my mind, however, Van Dam's account of the manipulated memory of Priscillianism in the fifth century and beyond remains extremely insightful.

[31] 'figmenta sunt daemonum, qui non in feminarum ventribus formant homines, sed in haereticorum cordibus tales fabricantur errores', *Ep.* 15, PL 54, cols. 683C–4B; cf. Van Dam, *Leadership*, pp. 112–14.

when talking about the infectious Priscillianist sect the bishops at Braga quite naturally – and tellingly – slipped into the past tense. Priscillian himself was a convenient mouthpiece for an astonishing array of heresies. Unsurprisingly, in a Galician context it was only natural that a home-grown heretic featured prominently in any who's-who of heresy. In sum, Noonan's sense of 'Manichaean danger' which imperilled conception itself is overstated.

One final and ironic absence at Braga is worth noting. Priscillian, like so many ecclesiastical figures caught up in heated disputes, was subject to rumour and gossip in his own day, though contemporary accounts were actually rather thin on concrete allegations of sexual misconduct.[32] A story recorded by Sulpicius Severus (d. c. 425), however, not only gave concrete details but even implicated Priscillian in an abortion. Travelling to Rome with two supporters in 380 in order to plead his case, Priscillian journeyed across southern Gaul. Expelled from Bordeaux, Priscillian nonetheless attracted a swelling band of followers, a 'disgusting and shameful retinue, with wives and even other unrelated women'.[33] Numbering among this group was a woman who would be beheaded with Priscillian at Trier, Euchrotia, the widow of an Aquitanian rhetor, Delphidius, together with her daughter, Procula. A rumour spread about this girl, 'who, according to people's conversation, pregnant through Priscillian's debauchery had driven her child away from her through plants'.[34] Contemporaries at least in southern Gaul knew this tale. Ausonius of Bordeaux (d. c. 395) knew both women. When writing about their late husband and father, Ausonius presented Delphidius's death as a blessing which 'spared him from his aberrant daughter's mistake and wife's punishment'.[35] But even by the fifth century this mud was being rinsed. Leo had referred to widespread rumours of immoral practices but without really offering any substantive details. It is possible that he was aware of rumours like the scandal referred to by Sulpicius Severus and Ausonius, but

---

[32] See A. Ferreiro, 'Priscillianism and Nicolaitism', *Vigiliae Christianae* 52.4 (1998), 180–8.

[33] 'turpi sane pudibundoque comitatu, cum uxoribus atque alienis etiam feminis', *Chronica* 2.48, ed. G. de Senneville-Grave, *Chroniques, Sulpice Sévère*, SC 441 (Paris, 1999), p. 97.

[34] 'de qua fuit in sermone hominum Priscilliani stupro gravidam partum sibi graminibus abegisse', *Chronica* 2.48, p. 97. Cf. Burrus, *Making of a Heretic*, p. 95: 'Priscillian "the magician" might well be thought to command a knowledge of abortifacient herbs, whose use was part of both the magician's and the physician's lore. And many Gallic Christians would readily believe that Priscillian the "Manichaean" secretly indulged in promiscuous sexual relations and condoned the use of contraception or abortion, while publicly exhorting Christians to live lives of continence.'

[35] 'errore quod non deviantis filiae / poenaque laesus coniugis', *Professores* 6.37–8, MGH AA 5.2, p. 59; cf. D.E. Trout, *Paulinus of Nola: Life, Letters, and Poems* (Berkeley, 1999), p. 74.

it is more likely that he was simply referring to 'ubiquitous word of mouth misinformation'.[36]

By the time the bishops convened at Braga in the middle of the sixth century, the mud of concrete sexual allegations seems to have been washed away from the historical memory of Priscillianism. What was remembered was the experience of Priscillianism in ecclesiastical power struggles, disputes over ordinations, rites and liturgy, and even suspicions of political rapports with Suevic overlords.[37] The Suevic conversion inaugurated a new beginning and Priscillianism was a rhetorically useful way of reaffirming the identity of the Galician church. Far from being a danger, Priscillianism offered the bishops at Braga an opportunity.

Back to Braga: Educating the clergy
When we shift forward over a decade to 572, around the time when Martin's canon was presented to Nitigisius, there are only the slightest flickers of concern over Priscillianism at Braga II, the records of which Martin might well have authored.[38] Braga II concentrated on defining and clarifying the duties of being a bishop. Admittedly, before this the records of Braga I, presumably including the *relecta*, were read out at Martin's prompting to remind bishops of the previous council's decrees. But thereafter the council issued only one ruling which possibly implied a reference to Priscillianism.[39] Finally, when we turn to Martin's *Capitula* itself, Priscillianism is also more distant than at Braga I, which is not to say that it was entirely absent. Henry Chadwick suggested that some of the eastern canons were chosen 'for their evident bearing on the Priscillianist problem'. Setting aside the question of just how much of a problem Priscillianism really was by the 570s, it is telling that all of the canons which Chadwick identified in this category were about ecclesiastical organization and liturgical practice. Aware of the sexual practices alleged of Manichaeans and Priscillianists alike, Chadwick did not count Martin's adaptation of the Ancyran abortion canon among this number.[40]

Noonan read the dynamics of heresy disputes, which he rightly identified as one important catalyst for thought in late antiquity, into sixth-century Galicia just as his account of twelfth- and thirteenth-century developments

---

[36] Ferreiro, 'Priscillianism', p. 390.
[37] M. J. Violante Branco, 'St. Martin of Braga, the Sueves and Gallaecia', in *The Visigoths: Studies in Culture and Society*, ed. A. Ferreiro (Leiden, 1999), pp. 70–2.
[38] Barlow, *Opera omnia*, p. 83.
[39] See Chadwick, *Priscillian*, p. 230, on this enactment which addressed liturgy; cf. Violante Branco, 'St. Martin of Braga', p. 88.
[40] Chadwick, *Priscillian*, pp. 228–9; cf. his comment on rumours of Procula's abortion at p. 37: 'Manichees were known to hold that procreation should be avoided, and horrified orthodox Catholics by openly advising married couples to confine sexual intercourse to the 'safe period' of the menstrual cycle. They were naturally accused of justifying abortion.'

in church doctrine overemphasized the reaction to the Cathars. Both here and in the twelfth and thirteenth centuries, pastoral practice and education of the clergy were of crucial, if less immediately conspicuous, importance.[41] The best understanding of why Martin included the canon lies in recognizing the needs of the Galician bishops at this critical juncture. Both Bragan councils attempted to remould a cohesive ecclesiastical structure through a canonically educated episcopate and clergy. The organizational principle governing Martin's *Capitula* reflected these concerns. His choice and arrangement of canons was intended for the benefit of his episcopal colleagues and clerics under their charge. The novelty of his approach to ecclesiastical regulations should not be underestimated. The *Capitula* is only the second surviving systematic canonical collection.[42] Martin arranged canons into distinct sections depending on whether they addressed bishops and clerics or the laity (including the abortion canon). As he explained in his preface, he did this so that 'anyone can locate more quickly whatever chapter he wishes to know about'.[43] Another aim, not expressed in the preface but embodied in the canons themselves and epitomized by his other works, was to adapt what he wrote according to the pastoral needs of the laity.[44] The augmentations to and very inclusion of the abortion canon were the fruits of thinking about abortion with these needs in mind: different intentions and effects of potions (preventing conception or killing what has been conceived); different contexts (adultery or marriage); and different forms of complicity. Rather than a memory of Priscillianism – and it would be a strange remembrance if a canon which very deliberately mentioned legitimate marriage as the context of child murder and avoidance of offspring was addressing the same concerns as Braga I's anathema against those who shuddered at the very thought of marriage – Martin's canon was a condensed set of guidelines produced within a broader programme of episcopal and clerical instruction.

---

[41] See the critique of Noonan's overemphasis on the Cathars in P. Biller,' Birth-Control in the West in the Thirteenth and Fourteenth Centuries', *P&P* 94 (1982), 8–12.

[42] The earliest systematic collection was Fulgentius Ferrandus's, *Breviatio canonum* composed in the 530s or 540s, which contained an abbreviated version of the Ancyran canon: 'Vt mulieres fornicantes quae parvulos suos necant aut aborsu <excutiant> decem annis paenitentiam agant', *Breviatio canonum* 150, ed. Munier, *Conciliae Africae*, p. 300.

[43] Somerville and Brasington, *Prefaces to Canon Law Books*, p. 54.

[44] See Violante Branco, 'St. Martin of Braga', pp. 90–6, on Martin's sensitivity to what he perceived as the differing pastoral needs of the Galician elite and poorly educated inhabitants of the countryside.

Discipline of bishops and judges: The third council of Toledo (589)

The final Hispanic council under scrutiny was very different from the localized gatherings at Lérida and Braga. Toledo III marked the formal alignment between Visigothic rule and the Catholic church through the conversion of Reccared. In subsequent narratives the council became the historical turning point when the political and sacred intersected,[45] but even in 589 the council was deliberately designed to be a momentous occasion.

The records of Toledo III are complex. They contain a narrative account of deliberations and ceremonies as well as actual conciliar rulings. After three days of fasting, Reccared's public profession of the Catholic faith, which emphasized his own role in driving out Arian heresy, was read out aloud. Next, an assembly of bishops, clergy and nobles was invited to issue a public repudiation of Arianism. Finally, the assembled bishops issued canons on various subjects with a subscription confirming their rulings from Reccared himself.[46]

The relevant canon appeared within the rulings issued by the bishops. Their enactments, however, bore the imprint of an envisaged interplay between religious and secular authority, between ecclesiastical and royal officials. It is signalled in the canon's title in later recensions of the *Hispana*, 'That bishops together with judges clamp down on murderers of children with sharper discipline':[47]

> While many complaints are brought before the ears of the sacred council, among them is a reported practice of such great cruelty that the ears of the presiding bishops cannot bear it, namely that in certain parts of Spain parents eager to fornicate, ignorant of piety, slay their own children. If it is burdensome for them to have a greater number of children, they should first scold themselves from fornication, for since they contract marriage for the sake of producing offspring, those *who demonstrate that they are joined not for children but for lust by killing their own fetuses* are held guilty of both parricide and fornication. Accordingly this great evil has been brought to the attention of King Reccared, our most glorious lord, whose glory has deemed it worthy to order the judges in those parts to investigate carefully this dreadful outrage with bishop[s] and forbid it with determined severity. Therefore this sacred synod regretfully decides that bishops of the localities

---

[45] S. Castellanos, 'Creating New Constantines at the End of the Sixth Century', *Historical Research* 85 (2012), 556–75.

[46] This section is particularly indebted to the rich reading of Toledo III in Stocking, *Bishops*, pp. 59–88.

[47] 'Ut episcopi cum iudicibus necatores filiorum acriori disciplina corripiant', *CCH* 5, p. 105. This is the title found in the Iuliana recension of the *Hispana*, named after Julian of Toledo and dated to c. 681. A marginally different version of this title can be found in the slightly later Vulgata recension, ibid., p. 107.

should painstakingly search out said wickedness with the judge and forbid it with fiercer discipline short of capital punishment.[48]

Before turning to the interplay between religion and politics, it is worth emphasizing why this canon ought to be understood as a reference to abortion as well as infanticide, for it has not entered all histories of abortion. The canon unequivocally addressed child-murder in the sense of infanticide. The basis for thinking that it also addressed abortion is the reference to parents killing their own fetuses (italicized above).[49] A secondary argument is that the abortion reading would have readily occurred to anyone who encountered the text of this canon. Treating infanticide and abortion together as entanglements of murder and sexual sin was perfectly in keeping with other ecclesiastical action in the sixth century. More novel was the moral topography: the location of these practices within a Christian kingdom rather than a church community. The bishops could scarcely bear to listen to what they were told was rife throughout Spain and the proposed response entailed a punishment rather than a penance. What lay behind this distinctive idiom of condemnation, an idiom which would later echo in seventh-century Visigothic law?

Reccared's shadow looms over this and other canons at Toledo III. It spoke of the king's active involvement in overseeing a response to a problem within his kingdom. This was in keeping with Reccared's modus operandi in 589. The momentum behind it originated in an ideology of royal power aimed at

---

[48] 'Dum multae querellae ad aures sancti concilii deferentur, inter cetera tantae crudelitatis est opus nuntiatum quantum ferre consedentium aures sacerdotum non possent, ut in quasdam Spaniae partes filios suos parentes interimant, fornicationi avidi, nescii pietatis. Quibus si taedium est filios numerosius agere, prius se ipsos debent castigare a fornicatione, nam dum causa propagandae prolis sortiantur coniugia, ii et parricidio et fornicatione tenentur obnoxii *qui fetus necando proprios docent se non pro filiis sed pro libidine sociari*. Proinde tantum nefas ad cognitionem gloriosissimi domni nostri Reccaredi regis perlatum est, cuius gloria dignata est iudicibus earundem partium imperare ut hoc horrendum facinus diligenter cum sacerdote perquirant et adhibita severitate prohibeant. Ergo et sacerdotes locorum haec sancta synodus dolentius convenit ut idem scelus cum iudice curiosius quaerant et sine capitali vindicta acriori disciplina prohibeant.', Council of Toledo (III), c.17, *CCH* 5, pp. 123–4 (my italics).

[49] Elsakkers, RBL, pp. 384–5, also reads c.17 in terms of infanticide and abortion, though she translates the italicized quotation as, 'those who demonstrate [how] to kill their own fetuses, because they do not unite to have children, but for lust'. It is not entirely implausible that *fetus* could be taken to mean a very young infant. This is presumably how one later adaptor of the *Hispana* understood it when he decided to change *fetus* to *filios*; this variant is noted in the critical apparatus for l.857, *CCH* 5, p. 124, and appears in the key manuscript witness to the *Hispana Gallica Augustodensis*, on which see above p. 96 n.10. The handful of early medieval examples of *fetus* in this sense which I have come across refer to the offspring of animals, not humans. Some examples: Cassiodorus, *Variae* 1.24.3, MGH AA 12, p. 27 (*fetus* of hawks); *Vita Eparchii* 3, MGH SRM 3, p. 554 (*fetus* of a goat); Jordanes, *Getica* 52.220, MGH AA 5.1, p. 114 (*foetus* – note the orthography – of storks).

consolidating a centralized monarchy, a 'prestige policy' initially dynamized by Reccared's father, Leovigild.[50] The trumpeting of Reccared's conversion at Toledo III developed this policy by using the language of religious unification to represent the stability of the kingdom and by stressing the king's role in maintaining that stability. Reccared styled himself as the prime mover in a process of canonical renewal inaugurated by the council and channelled the council's energy towards defining his own authority. As Rachel Stocking has emphasized, he defined his God-given role as renovator of the *mos canonicus*, the canonical way of life, in his kingdom. This *mos canonicus* had to be observed by his subjects and functioned as both a symbol and an instrument of his authority. Safeguarding the faith and morals of his people was inextricably tied to the delineation of Reccared's royal power.[51]

But the bishops were not passive in response to Reccared's ideological claims. Rachel Stocking has brought to light how the episcopal canons at Toledo III captured moments of negotiation between bishops and king. Their variances never spilled over into overt disagreement but there are discernible whispers of friction as each side attempted to capitalize on the new opportunities opened up by the other.[52] The canon on abortion and infanticide is one of several which carry the marks of a complex negotiation of power. The preceding canon, on idolatry, had also spoken of a widely cast jurisdiction. The sacrilege of idolatry was rife 'through all of Spain and Gaul' and local bishops were urged to join local judges in response. The canon on *necatores filiorum* was even more strongly marked with this jurisdictional overlap – but, reading between the lines, the bishops' response was not entirely supportive. Both canons were examples of the idealized arrangement by which separate hierarchies of centralized power – metropolitan bishops directing counterparts and inferiors in localities, the king directing his judges – were brought together. But the *necatores filiorum* canon tellingly omitted certain details. The manner of the cooperation between bishops and judges was not specified, a lacuna underlined by the fact that the preceding canon threatened uncooperative bishops with excommunication. The specifics of investigative procedures and judicial practicalities were all left out. Moreover, the bishops added their own detail: capital punishment was to be avoided. As Stocking has argued, from the bishops' perspective the canon represented a compromise between drawing upon Reccared's boost to their authority as fellow agents of the *mos canonicus* and leaving intact the configurations of ecclesiastical power in localities.[53]

---

[50] P. C. Díaz and M. R. Valverde, 'The Theoretical Strengths and Practical Weakness of the Visigothic Monarchy of Toledo', in *Rituals of Power from Late Antiquity to the Early Middle Ages*, ed. F. Theuws and J. L. Nelson (Leiden, 2000), pp. 60–77 (quotation at p. 75).

[51] Stocking, *Bishops*, pp. 68–71.

[52] Ibid., pp. 71–7.

[53] Ibid., pp. 80–2.

Visigothic Spain

Recognizing the royal-episcopal interplay is not to reduce discourse on infanticide and abortion to a political manipulation of moral sentiments, but these moral sentiments were expressed in terms which are inseparable from this interplay. The *horrendum facinus* which made the bishops shudder was defined more as a crime against the body politic than as a sin within a community addressed at Lérida or Braga. If the Toledan canon was a statement of negotiation between royal and episcopal power, then the Bragan and Léridan canons were precisely the kinds of localized action that the bishops at Toledo III wanted to safeguard.

No depravity is worse: Visigothic law on abortion

The previous chapter on the integration of abortion within attempts to define Christian communities in sixth-century Gaul did not discuss Salic law, which was also first codified in the early sixth century. The handling of abortion in Salic and other Germanic law-codes was distinct from the handling of abortion by churchmen. Most obviously, these law-codes did not directly address women who voluntarily underwent abortion. Examination of law-codes – and also of the reasons for this difference – will be deferred until a later chapter. Visigothic law is the exception for three inter-connected reasons. First, Visigothic law is typically regarded as the most Romanized of the post-Roman codes. An affinity to Roman legal ideas is discernible in some Visigothic material on abortion, though this affinity should not be overstated and was increasingly diluted in later Visigothic legislation. Second, certainly by the time of this later legislation, the interplay between religious and political ideals conspicuously shaped the handling of abortion in Visigothic law. Third – and, in part, consequently – Visigothic law addressed abortion more comprehensively than any other post-Roman law-code. Visigothic law addressed women who voluntarily underwent abortion, those who supplied the means for abortion and other parties who brought about abortion in pregnant women by physical violence. No other early medieval law-code was as comprehensive as Visigothic law.

This did not happen in a single step, however. In its surviving forms Visigothic law contained seven articles, which taken together addressed multiple permutations of abortion. The *Lex Visigothorum* was issued in 654 by Chindaswinth's son, Recceswinth (d. 672).[54] Subsequent modifications to the *Lex Visigothorum* were made under Erwig in 681 and new laws were added under Egica (d. 702) and Wittiza (d. 710). For our purposes the question of differences between later recensions can be largely ignored because these

---

[54] P. D. King, 'King Chindasvind and the First Territorial Law-Code of the Visigothic Kingdom', in *Visigothic Spain*, pp. 131–57, argues that the *Lex Visigothorum* was a revision of a code issued by Chindaswinth around a decade earlier.

did not significantly affect articles on abortion. The question of earlier phases of Visigothic law-making, however, is relevant. In all of its surviving forms the *Lex Visigothorum* brought together laws attributed to named seventh- or eighth-century kings (mainly Chindaswinth or Recceswinth) together with laws labelled as *antiquae*, 'ancient laws'. *Antiquae* likely originated from one of two earlier codes, both of which represented important moments in Visigothic law-making: a fifth-century code issued by Euric (d. 484), which survives in a few fragments, and Leovigild's sixth-century revision of this code, which has not survived.[55]

Patrick Wormald characterized earlier legislation by Euric and Leovigild as attempts by rulers to 'accommodat[e] what they believed to be the customs of their followers who formed their military power-base, within kingdoms whose legal culture was at least residually Roman'.[56] This Roman residue is clearly detectable in a law on second marriages, which safeguarded the interests of deceased men whose widows remarried or 'committed adultery' within a year of their deaths. The deceased's children or, in their absence, other heirs would be entitled to half of the widow's property. In spelling out the rationale the article referred to abortion: 'We have especially subjected such a woman to this penalty in case left pregnant by her husband she should extinguish the hope of offspring before it is born when she rushes into a second marriage through immoderate desire or perpetrates adultery.'[57] This article clearly owed something to Roman law on second marriages and elsewhere Roman law had addressed women who cheated their husbands of heirs.[58] The obsession over safeguarding the hope of offspring (*spes partus*) of a husband and father-to-be was a Roman residue and this article is the most straightforward example of Visigothic legislators drawing on Roman legal principles in addressing abortion.

But when we turn to the seven articles which directly addressed abortion Roman echoes become progressively quieter. All but one of these articles pre-dated the promulgation of the *Lex Visigothorum* in the mid seventh century: six were *antiquae*, only one was a law issued under Chindaswinth's name.

---

[55] P. D. King, *Law and Society in the Visigothic Kingdom* (Cambridge, 1972), pp. 1–21; Collins, *Early Medieval Spain*, pp. 24–30, 121–8. I set aside the question of whether some laws were issued under kings between Leovigild and Chindaswinth.

[56] P. Wormald, 'The *Leges Barbarorum*: Law and Ethnicity in the Post-Roman West', in *Regna and Gentes: The Relationship between Late Antique and Early Medieval Peoples and Kingdoms in the Transformation of the Roman World*, ed. H.-W. Goetz et al. (Leiden, 2003), p. 36.

[57] 'Quam idcirco mulierem precipue huic volumus subiacere dispendio, ne hec, que a marito gravida relinquitur, dum inmoderato desiderio ad secundi coniugii vota festinat vel adulterium perpetrat, spem partus, priusquam nascatur, extinguat.', *LV* 3.2.1, MGH LNG 1, p. 133.

[58] *Codex Justinianus* 5.9.2, *CIC* 2, p. 201, addresses the scenario of a woman remarrying within a year and stipulated a minimum of ten months. The wording is not identical, though this law also refers to rushing into (*festinare*) marriage.

They appeared in the sixth book on crimes involving physical harm, which covered subjects ranging from criminal accusations to homicide. Under the heading, 'On those who strike out people's offspring' (*De excutientibus hominum partum*), the articles on abortion appeared after a cluster of articles on magical practices and poisoning, and before another cluster on wounds and injuries.

Supply and demand: Potions for abortion (LV 6.3.1)
The articles on abortion can be divided into three groups. In its surviving form the first article (6.3.1) stands alone:

> If anyone has given a potion for abortion or killing an infant to a pregnant woman, he should be killed; *and the woman who seeks to make a potion for abortion*, if she is a slave-girl, she should receive 200 lashes; if she is a freeborn woman, she should lose her personal status and be handed over as a slave to whomever we order.[59]

The supplier of an abortifacient drink (*potio* does not have the same 'eye of newt' connotations as potion in modern English) faced execution. But there are two ambiguities in the Latin. Literally, a distinction was being made in the opening between potions for abortion or (*aut*) potions for infanticide. But given that the recipient of the potion was a pregnant woman it makes sense to read *pro necando infante* as an explanation of the effect of the potion for abortion.[60] Also, the opening of the second segment (italicized above) could refer to those who prepared such drinks or to those who tried to obtain them. The latter reading makes best sense of the fact that women were specified here whereas the suppliers were simply described as anyone (*quis*).[61]

This opening *antiqua* is not reducible to a prohibition of poisons rather

---

[59] 'Si quis mulieri pregnanti potionem ad avorsum aut pro necando infante dederit, occidatur; *et mulier, que potionem ad aborsum facere quesibit*, si ancilla est, CC flagella suscipiat; si ingenua est, careat dignitate persone et cui iusserimus servitura tradatur', *LV* 6.3.1, p. 260 (my italics). Karl Zeumer's edition in MGH LNG 1 prints versions of the code made under Reccesswinth and Erwig. In addition to manuscript variants, the latter includes some additions. Where there are divergences, I have quoted from the former.

[60] Cf. M. Elsakkers, 'Gothic Bible, Vetus Latina and Visigothic Law: Evidence for a Septuagint-based Gothic version of Exodus', *Sacris Erudiri* 44 (2005), 62. The generally taught rule in Latin is that *aut* is an exclusive disjunction, a stronger 'or', whereas *vel* is a weaker 'or', more likely to be an inclusive disjunction, though the historical use of *vel* and *aut* is more complicated (to say nothing of the vexed nature of disjunction in logic).

[61] D. W. Amundsen, 'Visigothic Medical Legislation', *Bulletin of the History of Medicine* 45.6 (1971), 567, translates the italicized segment as 'the woman who seeks to prepare a potion for abortion'; Amundsen clearly understands this to mean a 'third-party' manufacturer rather than a woman who voluntarily chooses to undergo abortion. By contrast, Elsakkers, RBL, p. 331 n.17, translates, 'the woman who asked [this person] for a potion to commit abortion' (Elsakkers's parenthesis).

than of abortion per se.⁶² Nor was it a wholesale derivation from Roman law, which had punished supply but not demand of abortifacient or aphrodisiac poisons.⁶³ Use of poisons certainly concerned Visigothic legislators just as it concerned secular and ecclesiastical legislators across the early medieval west. The preceding cluster of articles in the *Lex Visigothorum* included one on poisoners (*venefici*), which stipulated that freemen and slaves would be punished alike for preparing poisons; if the recipient died, *venefici* would be punished with a 'most shameful death'; if the recipient survived, *venefici* would be handed over for him to do with as he pleased.⁶⁴ But there was no mention of the morally loaded terms *veneficium* or *maleficium* in the *antiqua* on abortifacient potions. Even more importantly, the Visigothic articles on poisoning were later laws issued by Chindaswinth.

It is usually impossible to ascertain the origins of specific *antiquae* but the usual uncertainty does not fully apply here. This *antiqua* was possibly a sixth-century revision, even a mutation, of fifth-century Visigothic law. Karl Zeumer reconstructed fragments of Euric's code from the chance fact that compilers of Bavarian law in the eighth century happened to use it as a source. He noticed something about the putative form of this article in Euric's code. It began, 'If any woman has given to someone a potion to cause abortion, if she is a slave-girl, she should receive 200 lashes [etc.]'.⁶⁵ Some details – the woman who sought an abortion and capital punishment for those who abetted her – were not there; what later became the woman's punishment was here the punishment for supplying the potion. Zeumer believed that this original form, which flowed into a law addressing abortion by assault (to which we turn below), had been dramatically altered in the Leovigildian revision: 'According to [Euric's code] abortion was a crime against a pregnant woman and without her volition, according to Leovigild's version it was also with a woman's consent and desire'.⁶⁶ We can add that Leovigild's revision did not assume, as the earlier version had, that it was only women who supplied the

---

⁶² Cf. M. Elsakkers, 'Inflicting Serious Bodily Harm: The Visigothic *Antiquae* on Violence and Abortion', *Tijdschrift voor Rechtgeschiedenis* 71.1–2 (2003), 56 n.8: 'This law is in fact rather a condemnation of the use of poison than a prohibition of abortion'. This reading is revised in Elsakkers, RBL, p. 332: 'the Visigothic lawgiver added a provision that punishes the woman who is contemplating deliberate abortion'.

⁶³ Paulus's *sententia* on the *Lex Cornelia de sicariis et veneficis* was preserved in Visigothic Spain through Alaric's early sixth-century *Breviarium*: *Breviarium Alarici (PS)* 5.25.8, ed. G. Haenel, *Lex Romana Visigothorum* (Leipzig, 1849), p. 436.

⁶⁴ 'morte ... turpissima', *LV* 6.2.1–4 (6.2.3 on *venefici*), pp. 257–60.

⁶⁵ 'Si quae mulier alii potionem dederit, ut avorsum faceret, si ancilla est, CC flagella suspiciat [etc.]', *Codicis Euriciani leges restitutae* 3, MGH LNG 1, p. 29.

⁶⁶ 'Abortus crimen secundum textum antiquiorem contra mulierem gravidam et sine eius voluntate, secundum Leovigildi formam etiam consentiente vel petente ipsa muliere fit', MGH LNG 1, p. 29 n.1.

potions. But it did assume, unlike the earlier version, that women ought to be punished for seeking such potions.

In effect, a sixth-century development in Visigothic law now punished demand alongside supply. This further diluted any affinity to the Roman legal approach to abortion as a species of poisoning. It is also another strong hint that abortion was being spoken about by those at the top of society in the later sixth century. The timing is significant. It occurred before Reccared's conversion. Catholic authorities did not have a monopoly on problematizing abortion. The legislative efforts under an Arian king effectively treated abortion as a public offence. The next groups of articles on abortion provide evidence of pre-conversion legislators extracting and applying concepts from scripture when addressing abortion by assault.

Injury and murder: Abortion by assault (LV 6.3.2–6)
The *Lex Visigothorum* comfortably shifted between handling offences through punishments and through compensations exchanged between offenders and victims or their families while lacking the jurisprudential vocabulary with which to articulate a formal distinction between them.[67] But this terminological absence is more of a problem for historians seeking to distinguish between crime and tort than it was for seventh-century legislators, who even oscillated between punishments and compensations within single articles. The next sequence of *antiquae* addressing other parties who caused pregnant women to abort through physical violence offers some examples. Under the title, 'If a freeman causes a freewoman to abort', the first of these established a scenario assessed through two primary factors: whether or not the pregnant woman died; and, if she was not injured, how developed the fetus was:

> If anyone has beaten a pregnant woman by any sort of blow or through any other means causes a freewoman to abort, and after that she has died, he should be punished for homicide. But if only her offspring is struck out, and the woman was in no way injured, and a freeman is known to have done this to a freewoman, if he killed a formed infant he should pay 150 *solidi*; but if unformed, he should pay back 100 *solidi* for what he did.[68]

Marianne Elsakkers has associated the language in this article with the language used to distinguish between the formed (*formatus* or *deformatus*) and unformed (*informatus*) fetus in late antique texts which cited Vetus Latina

---

[67] Cf. King, *Law*, p. 87.
[68] 'Si quis mulierem gravidam percusserit, quocumque hictu aut per aliquam occasionem mulierem ingenuam abortare fecerit, et exinde mortua fuerit, pro homicidio puniatur. Si autem tantummodo partus excutiatur, et mulier in nullo debilitata fuerit, et ingenuus ingenue hoc intulisse cognoscitur, si formatum infantem extincxit, CL solidos reddat; si vero informem, C solidos pro facto restituat', *LV* 6.3.2, p. 261. Zeumer's reconstruction has some differences and only runs up to the mention of the offspring being killed; see ibid., p. 29.

versions of Exodus 21. 22–3. Versions of this passage quoted by Augustine and Origen (through Rufinus's Latin translation) not only used the same terminology but even described the fetus as *infans*. Elsakkers has plausibly speculated that the Visigothic terminology was extracted from the Latin descendants of Septuagintal versions of Exodus 21. 22–3, though we will return to the question of what conceptual work the distinction was doing below.[69]

Under the title, 'If a freewoman compels a freewoman to abort', the next *antiqua* considered the same scenario but where the assailant was a woman.

> If a freewoman has struck out the offspring of a freewoman through any violence or other means or it is known that she [viz. the victim] has been injured through this, she will be punished with the same penalty as the freeman condemned above.[70]

The article stipulated that the previous permutations also applied. But the legislator was slightly sloppy, for the reference to punishment for causing harm here points to an oversight in *LV* 6.3.2, which had explicitly treated death of the woman and destruction of the infant, but did not articulate what happened if a woman was not fatally injured. Although the scenario of violent abortion was addressed in other Germanic law-codes, this pair of articles was unusual in specifying that assailants could be women.

Introducing servile status into the scenario, the next three articles covered other configurations of assailant and victim:

> If a freeman has made a slave-girl suffer an abortion, he should be forced to pay 20 *solidi* to the slave-girl's master.[71]
> If a slave has struck out the offspring of a freewoman, he should be publicly beaten with 200 lashes and handed over to become the freewoman's slave.[72]
> If a slave made a slave-girl abort, the slave's master should be forced to give 10 *solidi*, and the slave himself should receive 200 lashes on top.[73]

Here, the line between punishments and compensations became especially blurred. Slaves could not pay compensations, though their masters could, and corporal punishment was the principal recompense that could be exacted

---

[69] Elsakkers, 'Gothic Bible', also argues that *LV* 6.3.2 is evidence for the existence of a Gothic version of Exodus.
[70] 'Si mulier ingenua per aliquam violentiam aut occasionem ingenue partum excusserit aut eam ex hoc debilitasse cognoscitur, sicut et ingenui superioris damni pena multetur', *LV* 6.3.3, p. 261.
[71] 'Si ingenuus ancille aborsum fecerit pati, XX solidos domino ancille cogatur inferre', *LV* 6.3.4, p. 261.
[72] 'Si servus ingenue partum excusserit, ducentenis flagellis publice verberetur et tradatur ingenue serviturus', *LV* 6.3.5, p. 261.
[73] 'Si ancillam servus abortare fecerit, X solidos dominus servi ancille domino dare cogatur, et ipse servus CC insuper flagella suscipiat', *LV* 6.3.6, p. 262.

directly from them. Taken as a group these *antiquae* form a sequence. But it is a sequence which shows signs of having been assembled in separate parts. The descriptive terms are not consistent (strike a pregnant woman; strike out the child of a woman through violence; make a woman suffer abortion; etc.) nor are the titles.[74]

Violently induced abortion clearly raised two main questions further complicated by the status of victim and assailant: injury, potentially fatal, to the woman and destruction of the fetus. Balancing these questions when interpreting the sequence is trickier than first meets the eye. This becomes especially clear if we momentarily turn to another area of Visigothic law, the law of property and damages. The eighth book of the *Lex Visigothorum* addressed those who caused mares and cows to abort. The comparison is not altogether far-fetched. A freewoman might have been a person before the law but an *ancilla*, like a mare, was legally someone else's property. Striking out the offspring of a pregnant mare required compensation in the form of a yearling: a foal for a foal.[75] More complicatedly, 'If anyone has caused someone else's pregnant cow to abort, he should be compelled to restore another [cow] along with her calf to the owner and he should himself receive the one whose offspring he struck out'.[76] In this second article the compensation was by implication both for injury to the parturient animal and for destruction of its offspring.

The *antiquae* on (human) abortion, by contrast, lack the clarity of the articles on mares and cows. They also had the added complication of the formed/unformed distinction. On the basis of some correspondence between the compensations owed by freemen/freewomen or punishments exacted from slaves for abortion by assault and those for injuries in the subsequent section on wounding and injury, Elsakkers has argued that the penalties throughout the sequence were for injuries to pregnant women and that the function of the formed/unformed distinction was to differentiate the severity of these injuries. On this reading the formed/unformed distinction has to be understood gynocentrically. It was not distinguishing between stages of fetal development so much as between stages of pregnancy, approximating to modern notions of 'early-term' and 'late-term' abortion. Destruction of the formed fetus warranted a larger compensation because 'late-term' abortion entailed a graver health hazard to the woman.[77]

---

[74] Additionally, only some parts of *LV* 6.3.2 are found in Zeumer's reconstructed Eurician fragment; see p. 113 n.68 above.

[75] 'Si quis quocumque pacto partum eque pregnantis excusserit, pulletrum anniculum illi, cuius fuerat, mox reformet', *LV* 8.4.5, p. 332.

[76] 'Si quis vaccam pregnantem abortare fecerit alienam, talem aliam cum vitulo domino reformare cogatur et illa, cui partum excussit, ipse accipiat. Hec et de aliis quadrupedibus forma servetur.', *LV* 8.4.6, p. 332.

[77] Elsakkers, 'Inflicting' and 'Gothic Bible'; L. Oliver, *The Body Legal in Barbarian Law* (Toronto, 2011), pp. 196–7, follows Elsakkers's reading.

It is true that there is some numerical correspondence between the fines or number of lashes in articles on abortion and those on bodily injuries. For instance, the 100 *solidi* stipulated for destruction of the unformed infant matched the compensations for causing certain serious bodily injuries such as a broken bone or a hacked off nose. But reading rationales into these correspondences is more problematic. There are other correspondences too; 100 *solidi* was, for example, the compensation stipulated for certain kinds of manslaughter. Indeed, an argument could be made that 100 *solidi* was a way of signalling that abortion by assault was like a manslaughter scenario rather than a way of signalling that the unformed infant was like a bodily appendage, worth more than a thumb (50 *solidi*) but certainly no more than a hand (100 *solidi*). Fundamentally, however, all of these correspondences are undermined by the fact that every single one of these 100 *solidi* compensations for bodily injuries appeared in later laws issued by Chindaswinth or Recceswinth. They could not have influenced the older *antiquae* on abortion.[78]

Pace Elsakkers the simplest reading of the first two articles in this sequence (6.3.2–3) is that they were addressing this class of violence against pregnant women *and* destruction of the fetus. The 150/100 *solidi* compensations were specified expressly 'if the woman was in no way harmed' and constituted recompense for having destroyed (*extinguere*) the formed/unformed infant, which after all had been the point of the distinction in Old Latin versions of Exodus.[79] Subsequent copyists of the *Lex Visigothorum* clearly grappled with these amounts; several stipulated 200 or even 250 *solidi* for the formed infant.[80] What they were grappling with was the social value to be placed on the infant before birth. Admittedly, there remains some ambiguity over how to interpret the three subsequent *antiquae* on servile assailants and/or victims (6.3.4–6), which did not explicitly refer back to the formed/unformed distinction. Their abbreviated form and inconsistent descriptive terms make it difficult to say for certain whether they were stipulating compensations and corporal punishment for injuries against the pregnant woman or for the loss of an *infans*, and different users of the *Lex Visigothorum* might have reached different conclusions.[81]

---

[78] LV 6.4.1 (broken bone, 100 *solidi*), 6.4.3 (lost nose, 100 *solidi*, amputated hand, amputated thumb; Chindaswinth), 6.5.4 (manslaughter during a quarrel, 100 *solidi*; Recceswinth), pp. 263–6, 271; in theory it could be argued that although the abortion articles were older, the fines might have been (re)calibrated when the *Lex Visigothorum* was promulgated, though this would be difficult to substantiate.

[79] Elsakkers's reading also implies a distinction between the injury suffered in a physical attack and the injury suffered in a miscarriage caused by the attack which is difficult to square with the text of *LV* 6.3.2.

[80] These variants for *LV* 6.3.2, p. 261, are found in a sizeable number of significantly later medieval manuscripts, though a few date from the tenth century.

[81] A thirteenth-century manuscript (Codex Toletanus, armarii 43. nr. 7, 4°) adds, 'but on account of the harm he will be subject to the laws [*pro lesione autem legibus adicetur*]', to *LV* 6.3.4, p. 261; this does not settle the question but does imply that one

Visigothic Spain

What is clearer is that social status affected social value. Some women and their infants were worth more compensation than others. There is a danger of overstressing the concern about violence against pregnant women just as there is of reading in a putative 'right to life'.[82] If anything, the opening *antiqua* in the sequence (6.3.2) slightly fudged the issue of injuries suffered by pregnant women. The scenario became a homicide if the woman died and compensation was stipulated for the destruction of the *infans* specifically if she had not been harmed – but what about non-fatal injuries? The next *antiqua* (6.3.3) suggests that such injuries were on the legislator's mind. But the carelessness is telling and narrowly defined the priorities of a husband, father or other male relative in this scenario. As is not uncommon when reading early medieval legal texts on violence, what appears on the surface to be a measure designed to protect women looks less solicitous of women's welfare upon closer inspection.

An eye for an eye: Chindaswinth on abortion (LV 6.3.7)
The final article, which was ascribed to Chindaswinth, dramatically altered the tenor of Visigothic law on abortion:

> Nothing is worse than the depravity of those who disregarding piety become killers of their own children. Because it is reported that their vice has grown in the provinces of our kingdom to such a degree that men as well as women are found to be the executors of this crime, prohibiting this dissoluteness we decree that if a freewoman or slave-girl has killed her born son or daughter, or if while still having it in her womb has either received a potion for abortion or has presumed to destroy her own offspring by whichever means, whenever a judge of the province or territory has discovered such a deed, he should not only condemn she who does this deed to a public death, or if he should wish to spare her life, he should not hesitate to destroy all the vision of her eyes, but also, if it has been clear that her husband had ordered or permitted such things, he should not hesitate to subject him to the same punishment.[83]

---

later medieval reader interpreted the article in terms of destruction of the infant and added in the question of injury to the woman.

[82] Cf. King, *Law*, p. 240: 'It is not the least mark of the level of Visigothic civilization that it upheld the right to live even of the unborn child'.

[83] 'Nihil est eorum pravitate deterius, qui, pietatis inmemores, filiorum suorum necatores existunt. Quorum quia vitium per provincias regni nostri sic inolevisse narratur, ut tam viri quam femine sceleris huius auctores esse repperiantur, ideo hanc licentiam proibentes decernimus, ut, seu libera seu ancilla natum filium filiamve necaverit, sive adhuc in utero habens, aut potionem ad avorsum acceperit, aut alio quocumque modo extinguere partum suum presumserit, mox provincie iudex aut territorii talem factum reppererit, non solum operatricem criminis huius publica morte condemnet, aut si vite reservare voluerit, omnem visionem oculorum eius non moretur extinguere, sed etiam si maritum eius talia iussisse vel permisisse patuerit, eundem etiam vindicte simili subdere non recuset', LV 6.3.7, p. 262.

Elsakkers has characterized Chindaswinth's law as a 'Caesarian sermon in legal guise'.[84] There is an echo of Caesarius in the title to this law, 'On those who kill their children whether born or in the womb'.[85] But the article is even more reminiscent of the Toledan canon, which had also complained of killers of children (*necatores filiorum*) who forgot all notions of piety. In fact it is very possible that this law was written in reference to the Toledan canon, which is not to say that they completely overlap. Whereas child murder and sexual sin, *parricidium* and *fornicatio*, had been inextricable in the Toledan canon, the connection was absent here.[86] But as at Toledo III reports of abortion and infanticide were said to have been flooding in from all over the realm; and men were implicated alongside women. Moreover, the severe punishment may reflect awareness of the final part of the Toledan canon, which had suggested that bishops should resort to severe discipline short of capital punishment. Blinding mimicked the offence which it punished by destroying (*extinguere*) the culprit's vision just as s/he had destroyed (*extinguere*) the child. This was a sadistic twist on Exodus: if not a life for a life, then an eye for a life.

The punishment was brutal and the rhetoric was highly charged. It is one manifestation of a broader shift across seventh-century additions to Visigothic law. One law, which penalized masters who tricked freeborn women into marrying their slaves, began, 'audacities of the depraved must be resisted so that the reins of depravity are not further relaxed'.[87] Another law, which insisted that women had to be younger than their husbands, warned that children born of unions between older women and mere boys would be defective.[88] Across the laws issued by Chindaswinth, Recceswinth and other later Visigothic kings, *necatores filiorum* were not the only offenders subjected to fierce moralizing. *Masculorum concubitores*, men who voluntarily slept with other men, were to be castrated because that 'crime must not be left unpunished which is always reckoned worthy of detesting as an execrable depravity of morals'.[89] And a suspension of the prohibition on divorce in clear cases of female fornication was justified by asserting that if it was a *crimen* to violate someone else's wife, then a woman who voluntarily did this ought to be condemned even more strongly.[90] In keeping with this new phase of Visigothic law-making, Chindaswinth's article on *necatores filiorum* drew on religious

---

[84] Elsakkers, 'Gothic Bible', 68.
[85] 'De his, qui filios suos aut natos aut in utero necant', *LV* 6.3.7, p. 262; cf. 'filios suos aut adhuc in utero positos aut etiam natos occidit', Caesarius, *Sermo* 200.4.
[86] Possibly the reference to 'dissoluteness' (*licentia*) envisages sexual sin.
[87] 'Resistendum est pravorum ausibus, ne pravitatis amplius frena laxentur', *LV* 3.2.7 (Chindaswinth), p. 137.
[88] *LV* 3.1.4 (Recceswinth), pp. 124–6.
[89] 'Non relinquendum est scelus inultum, quod detestandum semper execrabile morum pravitate censetur', *LV* 3.5.4 (Chindaswinth), p. 163; cf. the rhetoric in a later addition on 'sodomites', *LV* 3.5.7 (Egica), p. 165.
[90] *LV* 3.6.2 (Chindaswinth), p. 167.

ideas about offences in diagnosing a problem which afflicted the kingdom and necessitated a severe response from the political centre.

On the surface Chindaswinth's article and those on other offences including homosexual acts suggests the growing power of the church to shape legislation.[91] Beneath the surface, however, matters were more complicated. The underlying principle – murder of children by parents is abhorrent – was clearly consonant with ideas articulated by churchmen. But the application and articulation of this principle was shaped by what law-making meant to Visigothic kings in the mid seventh century. By the time Chindaswinth and Recceswinth were legislating, the sacrality of Visigothic kingship had become crucial to the definition and exercise of royal power.[92] Issuing laws which absorbed religious ideas was a means by which Chindaswinth, Recceswinth and their successors delineated and consolidated their authority. This was an intensified version of the God-given role which Reccared had claimed for himself at Toledo III, a role which cast the king as 'head of the public body', who was 'possessed of the eyes with which to search out what was noxious and of the mind to reach decisions by which the dependent and subject part might be ruled'.[93] Abortion and infanticide were two such noxious elements. If these offences – or reports of them – within the king's realm constituted a menace to the health of the public body, they also provided an opportunity for kings to articulate a response which transposed moral associations derived from religious ideas onto reassertions of royal authority. The relationship between church and ruler during the reigns of Chindaswinth and Recceswinth was anything but straightforward. Like other articles, the law on *necatores filiorum* tells us as much about the configuration of religion and politics from a royal perspective as about the church per se. This was abortion politicized Visigothic style.[94]

Through the accumulation of successive layers Visigothic law had come to cover abortion comprehensively. Taken together, the punishments and compensations stipulated within these layers complicate Wolfgang Müller's broader contention that the criminalization of abortion was a later medieval legislative development. First, crime and tort are useful ideal types when thinking about early medieval law if they are seen as existing along a continuum. If

---

[91] Elsakkers, RBL, p. 333, sees 'clerical influence, because [LV 6.3.7] reads like a vehement sermon'.
[92] A. Barbero and M. I. Loring, 'The Catholic Visigothic Kingdom', in *The New Cambridge Medieval History Volume 1: c. 500–c. 700*, ed. P. Fouracre (Cambridge, 2005), pp. 355–60, identify the intensification of sacral monarchy with the reigns of Sisenand (d. 636) and Chintila (d. 639/40).
[93] King, *Law*, p. 32.
[94] For a *longue durée* picture of relations between ruler and church, see A. Fear, 'God and Caesar: The Dynamics of Visigothic Monarchy', in *Every Inch a King: Comparative Studies on Kings and Kingship in the Ancient and Medieval Worlds*, ed. L. Mitchell and C. Melville (Leiden, 2013), pp. 285–302.

not at their point of origin then certainly by the time of their incorporation into the *Lex Visigothorum*, the *antiquae* on abortion by assault complicate attempts to disentangle tort from crime. These *antiquae* were exceptions to a broader rule, for much of the system of compensation and tariffs for personal injury, murder, sexual transgression and other offences entered was established through seventh-century additions to Visigothic law.[95] In some instances related to murder and adultery, royal justice cast a shadow over compensation between kin-groups to the point that regulated pursuit of private justice was framed not only as a public good but even a civic duty. For instance, one of Chindaswinth's laws encouraged adultery charges against wives because some women could sway their husbands' minds through potions or magic to such an extent that they did not want to accuse them publicly. Chindaswinth extended the right to bring adultery charges to sons and other relatives. Crucially, he went even further in making provisions for instances when sons were negligent or relatives unenthusiastic (literally referring to *tepiditas*, lukewarmness), and declared that the king would then determine how the case would be handled if it came to his attention. Elsewhere both Recceswinth and Chindaswinth decreed that relatives and even strangers could make homicide accusations. The latter explicitly reasoned that the right of anyone to lodge a murder accusation would act as a deterrent.[96] Given the fraught nature of official Visigothic discourse on abortion by the mid seventh century, it is quite plausible that the notion of private justice as public good and civic duty infused interpretations of the older *antiquae* on abortion by assault.

Second, and more straightforwardly, Visigothic law did criminalize abortion on any reasonable understanding of crime. Even if it was expressed in terms of royal ideology rather than jurisprudential theory and even if its practical applicability is questionable, Chindaswinth's article was a 'top-down' measure which defined abortion and infanticide as offences against the public body and subjected these offences to royally sanctioned punishment.[97] Less spectacularly, but no less significantly, the opening *antiqua* on abortion also criminalized supply and demand of abortifacient potions. In sum, the handling of abortion in Visigothic law entailed criminalization of voluntary abortion as well as a framework for dispute settlement in cases of abortion by assault. In comparative legal terms, the handling of abortion was unique in the early medieval west, and it carried traces, stronger and weaker, of Roman legal priorities, scriptural concepts, ecclesiastical moral sentiments and royal ideology without being reducible to any of these.

[95] Cf. Wormald, 'Leges barbarorum', p. 36.
[96] Adultery accusations: *LV* 3.4.13 (Chindaswinth), pp. 152–5; homicide accusations: *LV* 6.5.14 (Recceswinth), 6.5.15 (Chindaswinth) pp. 280–1; cf. King, *Law*, p. 88.
[97] C. Martin, *La géographie du pouvoir dans l'Espagne visigothique* (Villeneuve-d'Asq, 2003), p. 167 n.125, suggests that Chindaswinth's law 'corresponde plus à une déclaration de principes moraux qu'à une mesure législative destinée à produire des effets immédiats'.

Visigothic Spain

Convergence: entangling sex and murder

Legal, royal and ecclesiastical discourse on abortion in the sixth and seventh centuries shared several commonalities. With the exception of Martin's canon, all of the Visigothic material on abortion was deliberately gender inclusive. Abortion and infanticide were not solely female sins, and Chindaswinth's law even specified male insistence or complaisance. Another striking thread was the idea of abortion (and infanticide) as a double offence. Abortion entangled sexual sin and murder. In Martin of Braga's canon this was implicit in the behavioural contexts carefully specified: both adultery and legitimate marriage. In the Léridan and Toledan canons abortion and infanticide were forms of murder which uncovered two forms of sexual transgression: adultery by women and men, even clerics, which resulted in children conceived in sin (Lérida) and fornication by women and men in legitimate marriage (Toledo).

The association between abortion and sexual unions which were sinful either inherently or in practice played on a kind of circular reasoning: abortion was a way of hiding sexual sin, so it was also a way of uncovering sexual sin. Resorting to abortion implied getting rid of *male concepti*, children conceived in sin; to put it differently, no one would have any reason to get rid of the *bene concepti*. Abortion was a sign, though it functioned differently from the Roman abortion–adultery association insofar as both the sign (abortion/infanticide) and what it signalled (transgressive sexual unions) were problematic. This was certainly a moralizing association, but there is reason not to dismiss it altogether as a moralistic phantasm. Here, the overwhelmingly prescriptive and aspirational nature of so much evidence for Visigothic Spain is useful, for the very texts which read abortion as a sign of sexual transgression also suggest different pressures through which children became unwanted.

A powerful example appeared in a council held during the reign of Recceswinth. The ninth council of Toledo (655), a provincial rather than national council, addressed the problem of clerics who fathered children in extramarital sexual unions. The bishops ruefully noted that existing disciplinary measures had not curbed these offences.[98] Their solution was to visit the sins of the father upon his children, who would lose their inherited status and become enslaved to whichever church their wayward fathers were meant to be serving.[99] Such children of clerics were unwanted children in bishops' eyes because of the circumstances in which they were conceived and, whether or not it had the desired effect, their ruling aimed to function as a deterrent:

---

[98] The kind of measures the bishops had in mind was a canon issued at the fourth council of Toledo, a national council held in 633. Clerics who slept with unrelated women or slave-girls would be referred to their bishops and relegated to penitence for a period of time: Council of Toledo (IV), c.43, *CCH* 5, p. 227. Presumably the canon at Toledo IX addressed the married lower clergy; Council of Toledo (III), c.5, pp. 112–14, went further in demanding that bishops, presbyters and deacons observe chastity with their wives.

[99] Council of Toledo (IX), c.10, *CCH* 5, pp. 503–4.

in effect, they wanted such children to become unwanted in the eyes of clerics too. The number of legal and conciliar rulings against sexual transgression by clerics suggests that clerical sexual scandal troubled rulers and bishops alike.[100] The Léridan canon's mention of clerics implicated in abortion was an earlier manifestation of a more enduring concern.

Insofar as Visigothic law codified or attempted to reflect custom, legal measures also suggest that the problematization of certain sexual unions was generated by 'bottom-up' social impulses as well as 'top-down' ecclesiastical or royal impulses.[101] Disclosure of these unions could entail severe consequences for women and men. The repercussions for married women were unsurprisingly stark. Husbands could kill adulterous wives and their lovers with impunity.[102] Unmarried women too were subject to strong sanctions. A betrothed girl found guilty of 'adultery' could be enslaved, along with her lover, to the man she was meant to marry.[103] A father could kill his own daughter if she committed adultery within his home, a right which extended to brothers or paternal uncles if the father was not alive.[104] Legal measures which viewed widows suspiciously represent one manifestation of a broader surveillance of female sexuality.[105] Women involved in sexual unions which cut across status distinctions were also vulnerable to severe consequences. Where sexual liaisons took place between a woman and her slave or freedman, both parties could be publicly scourged before a judge and even burned alive.[106] All of these measures were legal possibilities rather than social inevitabilities. The social or physical death stipulated by law might have been 'top-down' measures, but the values they represented were not 'top-down' impositions alien to Visigothic society.

In practice, of course, disclosure often rested on conflicting testimonies. Chindaswinth's law on adultery accusations recognized this and made provisions for slaves to testify against adulterous masters and mistresses 'because it is difficult to get the truth, as [proof of] adultery of women is lacking through [testimony of] free persons, since this vice is accustomed to be perpetrated secretly'.[107] As much as any other form of testimony, pregnancy or the birth of a child could tilt the evidential balance dramatically. The stakes were high for

---

[100] Cf. King, *Law*, pp. 152–3; Stocking, *Bishops*, pp. 161–5, 179–80.
[101] For a survey of relevant legal provisions see G. Ausenda, 'Kinship and Marriage among the Visigoths', in *The Visigoths from the Migration Period to the Seventh Century: An Ethnographic Perspective*, ed. P. Heather (Woodbridge, 1999), pp. 163–5.
[102] *LV* 3.4.4, p. 149; cf. *LV* 3.4.1, 3, pp. 147–8; a single woman who committed adultery with a married man would be handed over to his wife in *LV* 3.4.9, pp. 150–1 (all *antiquae*).
[103] *LV* 3.4.2 (*antiqua*), pp. 147–8.
[104] Fathers could kill a 'filiam in adulterium', which may mean a daughter caught in the act, according to *LV* 3.4.5 (*antiqua*), p. 149.
[105] Cf. *LV* 3.5.6 (Egica), pp. 164–5.
[106] *LV* 3.2.3 (*antiqua*), p. 134.
[107] 'Verum quia difficile fieri potest, ut per liberas personas mulieris adulterium

women, though men too could have reasons for preventing the disclosure of sexual transgression through pregnancy or the birth of a child.[108]

Illicit sexual unions were a junction at which familial, social and religious pressures converged in problematizing the conception and birth of certain children, and the raw fact of pregnancy rendered women particularly vulnerable to these pressures. Prescriptive texts, with their moralizing association between abortion and illicit unions, cannot straightforwardly be read as a historical record of actual practice. But there was a fit between the social map of sexual relations and the moral location of abortion within it. This fit also entailed an inherent tension. Ecclesiastical and legal sanctions against sexual transgression gave formal expression to the kinds of pressures which, other ecclesiastical and legal sanctions lamented, led to child-murder.

As Martin's canon, the Toledan canon and Chindaswinth's law recognized, however, unwanted children could also be conceived in unions which were legitimate per se. Toledo III provides the most intriguing perspective. Earlier in the sixth century Caesarius had addressed what we would call family planning, but in the context of well-to-do Arlesian women. The bishops at Toledo went further. Their recognition of the burden (*taedium*) of having too many children was novel – and unlike Caesarius they addressed men as well as women. But *taedium* was interpreted through the lens of sexual sin. Couples tired of parental *taedium* were enjoined to refrain from sex, for marital sex was perverted into *fornicatio* when there was a desire not to have more children. It is worth stressing that infanticide as well as abortion were switched from signs of transgressive sexual unions to signs of sexual transgression within legitimate unions. Toledo III stated explicitly that by killing their children men and women revealed (*docere*) that the marriage was premised on lust, not procreation.

The reference to *parricidium* at Toledo III rendered explicit what was implicit in other canonical and legal material. Abhorrence at child-murder and the value of the infant was not premised on an abstract value attached to life. *Parricidium* was not just a particularly intense way of referring to murder – it drew attention to murders in which victim and culprit(s) were in a relation. Child-murder was understood relationally and situating child-murder within marriage sharpened the relational dimension: men and women were killing their *own* children. Abortion was a form of child-murder which enacted a grotesque inversion of the norms of marriage, the union of husbands and wives in the hope of becoming parents.

* * *

indagetur, dum frequenter hoc vitium occulte perpetrari sit solitum', *LV* 3.4.13, p. 155; *LV* 3.4.3 (*antiqua*), p. 148, also implies that proving adultery could be tricky.
[108] See also *LV* 3.3.1 (*antiqua*), pp. 139–40: a man who violently abducted a girl and was proven to have sexually violated her would be publicly flogged and enslaved to the girl's parents.

Abortion in the Early Middle Ages

The moral sentiments embedded in legal and ecclesiastical sources on abortion overlapped considerably. But this convergence co-existed with a tension which lurked close to the surface in the Toledan canon. The application of these sentiments varied according to the different practices and rationalities of conciliar consensus and royal law-making. The canons from Lérida and Braga were independent, localized initiatives integrated into broader programmes of clerical education. In specifying different kinds of acts, actors, accomplices and circumstances, they functioned as condensed guidelines for negotiating the problem of abortion within Christian communities. Those subject to their penitential provisions might well have found the experience punitive. Insofar as it entailed a process of separation from communion, penitence was not a private affair. But as well as signalling moral values to the broader community and individual perpetrators alike, the procedures outlined at Lérida and Braga also implied an end-goal: the reintegration of sinners within the community. By contrast, royal legislation on abortion, certainly Chindaswinth's law, was concerned with cleansing the kingdom rather than healing those who polluted it through wrongdoing. The Toledan canon represented an uneasy balancing act between these distinct rationalities, between maintaining the health of the body politic and the health of the body of the church.

Logically, there was a tension. The extent to which it was experienced as such by Visigothic judges and bishops is less clear. The *Lex Visigothorum* suggests that the functioning of the law depended on collaborative interactions between ecclesiastical and royal officials.[109] So too do the circumstances surrounding its promulgation. Recceswinth had given Braulio of Saragossa, a bishop to whom we shall return in the final chapter, the task of effectively copy-editing the forthcoming code.[110] At the same time, the idiom of unity in which bishops and kings alike expressed their aspirational visions for the kingdom and communities within it masked friction between church and monarch as well as very real limitations on episcopal and royal power.[111]

The key point is that the most striking features of Visigothic discourse on abortion were also its most peculiar. Visigothic Spain ultimately witnessed the criminalization of abortion in theory, if not in practice, articulated in a fierce rhetoric produced by the interplay of church and sovereign. But neither Reccared's initiative nor Chindaswinth's law marked a Constantinian watershed in the broader history of abortion in the early medieval west. Visigothic Spain is an exception to Wolfgang Müller's thesis on the criminalization of abortion in early medieval law-codes.[112] Beyond the Iberian peninsula it was

---

[109] S. Koon and J. Wood, 'Unity from Disunity: Law, Rhetoric and Power in the Visigothic Kingdom', *European Review of History/Revue européene d'histoire* 16.6 (2009), 801.

[110] C. H. Lynch, *Saint Braulio (631–651): His Life and Writings* (Washington DC, 1938), pp. 136–40.

[111] Koon and Wood, 'Unity', 804.

[112] I set aside the afterlife of Visigothic ecclesiastical and legal material in the Christian

Visigothic Spain

the kind of projects embodied at Lérida and Braga, and their underlying concern with episcopal discipline, clerical education and pastoral practice, which provided the context for thought and action on abortion. A significant tool in such projects took the form of a specific kind of ecclesiastical text which first emerged roughly contemporaneously with the councils at Lérida and Braga. Tracing active deliberation on abortion within these texts is a crucial part of the history of abortion in the early medieval west. This chapter has ultimately argued that Spain holds a distinctive place within that history. It is in keeping with this that these new ecclesiastical texts only arrived belatedly in Spain from the ninth century, long after their initial emergence in the sixth century, in part because they represented an evolution in penance explicitly rejected as an abomination by some Spanish bishops: penitentials.[113]

kingdoms which developed north of al-Andalus after the Arab conquest of 711. There is, I strongly suspect, an interesting story to be told. See R. Collins, '"Sicut lex Gothorum continet": Law and Charters in Ninth- and Tenth-Century León and Castile', *English Historical Review* 100, no. 396 (1985), 511, for reference to a case involving a cleric from the kingdom of León who had compelled a mistress into having an abortion. Bishops and secular judges confiscated his property but spared him from capital punishment.

[113] Council of Toledo (III), c.11, p. 128.

4

Medicine for Sin:
Reading Abortion in Early Medieval Penitentials

Penitentials once had a bad name. In one widely quoted assessment penitentials were a 'deplorable feature of the medieval church [and it] is hard to see how anyone could busy himself with such literature and not be the worse for it'.[1] Over recent decades, however, painstaking textual and codicological research, new critical editions, revisionist histories of penance and increasingly sophisticated use of penitentials in historical research have transformed scholarship on the penitentials. Allusion to the penitentials' older reputation is well on its way to becoming a cliché.[2]

Penitentials listed specific sins and corresponding penances, usually in the form of periods of fasting. Some also included prologues or epilogues outlining theologies of sin and reconciliation. Penitentials have traditionally been associated with the development of confession and so-called private penance, though more recent scholarship has expanded our picture of the use of penitentials together with the social and religious functions of penance in dispute settlement, canon law and political culture. Their emergence in early Ireland roughly coincided with conciliar rulings on abortion issued in sixth-century Spain and they soon spread to Anglo-Saxon England and Merovingian Gaul. By the ninth century they had become a significant if controversial textual resource for Carolingian bishops and clerics.[3]

---

[1] Charles Plummer (writing in 1896) quoted in M. E. Meyer, 'Early Anglo-Saxon Penitentials and the Position of Women', *Haskins Society Journal* 2 (1990), 49.

[2] R. Meens, 'Penitential Questions: Sin, Satisfaction and Reconciliation in the Tenth and Eleventh Centuries', *EME* 14.1 (2006), 1–6; R. Meens, 'The Historiography of Early Medieval Penance', in *A New History of Penance*, ed. A. Firey (Leiden, 2008), pp. 73–95.

[3] While older works on penance and penitentials, including A. J. Frantzen, *The Literature of Penance in Anglo-Saxon England* (New Brunswick, 1983) and A. J. Frantzen, *Mise à jour du fascicule no. 27* (Turnhout, 1985), a revision of C. Vogel, *Les 'libri paenitentiales'*, Typologie des Sources du Moyen Age Occidental, vol. 27 (Turnhout, 1978), remain valuable, the standard introduction will surely now become R. Meens, *Penance in Medieval Europe 600–1200* (Cambridge, 2014). Unfortunately, this new overview of penance by an expert on penitentials was published just as I was finishing the manuscript for this book. I have had a limited opportunity to digest Meens's insights as well as benefit from his mastery of penitential manuscripts and a sizeable body of German scholarship.

Rewriting penitentials into the history of abortion

Penitentials constitute the most significant corpus of material on how early medieval clerics and bishops thought about abortion. One reason is related to why Protestant and Catholic historians found penitentials uncomfortable in the nineteenth and early twentieth centuries: their detailed scrutiny of sexual sin.[4] New penitentials were composed and older penitentials copied or adapted throughout the period under study. The majority addressed abortion. Several which did not were briefer addenda within manuscripts containing penitentials which did.[5] Penitentials offer snapshots of the different concerns that abortion evoked together with different responses which mingled the care of souls and a kind of social discipline. Scholars interested in abortion as well as sexuality and magic have sifted through penitential rulings on abortion.[6] Their works provide valuable insights into specific penitential rulings on abortion and add up to a very useful inventory.[7]

One problem with works written before the renaissance in penitential scholarship is no fault of their authors: basic details and raw materials, including dating and editions of penitentials, have since been revised. A deeper contention underlying this chapter and the next, however, is that penitentials have been inadequately written into the history of abortion. First, penitentials have been marginalized in narratives of church tradition on abortion owing to a combination of once respectable but now problematic interpretations of early ninth-century Carolingian responses to penitentials and anachronistic conceptions of what counted as authoritative in the early medieval church. I examine this marginalization in the next chapter. Second, and more immediately, analysis of abortion rulings has been characterized by the kinds of methodological shortcomings which, Pierre Payer has argued, also characterize use of penitentials in studies of sexuality. Penitentials have been 'exploited for their sexual content with little critical attention to the texts themselves as

---

[4] D. Janes, 'Sex and Text: The Afterlife of Medieval Penance in Britain and Ireland', in *Medieval Sexuality: A Casebook*, ed. A. Harper and C. Proctor (London, 2008), pp. 32–44.

[5] For example, although *Vindobense C* did not address abortion, it forms part of a ninth-century manuscript containing a combined version of two penitentials which did: see R. Meens, '"*Aliud benitenciale*": The Ninth-Century *Paenitentiale Vindobense C*', *Mediaeval Studies* 66 (2004), 1–26. The most significant penitentials which did not address abortion were *Cummeani* and older versions of *Egberti*.

[6] Scholars typically refer to penitential canons. I refer – slightly artificially – to penitential rulings as opposed to canons because of a tendency in historiography on abortion to make a strong distinction between penitentials and canonical collections, a distinction which will be critiqued in the next chapter. I retain separate terms for the sake of clarity and to avoid loading the argumentative die with terminology.

[7] The most thorough survey of abortion in penitentials is Elsakkers, RBL, pp. 393–459; see too Honings, 'L'aborto nei libri penitenziali Irlandesi', Honings, 'L'aborto in alcuni decretali episcopali', and Palazzini, *Ius fetus*, pp. 89–98. I refer to other works on specifics below.

documents ... written in time and place, with or without authorial attribution, with sources, spread, and influence'.[8] One common tendency is to lift rulings from individual penitentials and present them in a loosely chronological or thematic chain. Scholars have focussed on durations of penance, often using Ancyra's ten-year penance as the yardstick; and also to graduations of penance according to stages of fetal development. There has been far less sensitivity to other variances (for instance, in terminology across rulings or in arrangements of rulings across penitentials) and what such variances can tell us about how compilers and readers thought about abortion. The problem, at root, is decontextualization. Attaching great importance to, for example, the difference between rulings which distinguished between stages of fetal development and those which did not ignores the fact that both approaches were included in most penitentials by the end of the eighth century. Similarly, a chronological picture concentrating on wholly new rulings overshadows amendments of older ones and even implies a replacement narrative whereby some canons superseded others. The earliest penitentials discussed in this chapter originated in sixth- and seventh-century Ireland, but all of them were reproduced by and have survived because of copyists in Carolingian scriptoria.

Developments in scholarship on the penitentials simultaneously necessitate and provide the means for more careful use of the penitentials in the history of abortion. Some early medieval historians remain wary over the penitentials' value in cultural and social history, so it is worth establishing how and why they are useful.[9] With the possible exception of some earlier texts, penitential compilation was highly derivative. Compilation was not always the same thing as mere copying, however. The 'peculiarity' of the penitentials lay in what Alexander Murray describes as their 'capacity to fuse plagiarism with originality'.[10] Their peculiarity also presents an opportunity. By paying close attention to small details – rephrasing, excision, abbreviation, (re)arrangement and, occasionally, additions to or of canons – it is possible to find traces of active deliberation on a range of subjects.[11] When compared with more detailed discussion of abortion in later medieval confessional and canonical literature, such traces look slight.[12] The thought they represent is tightly compressed, but they are traces of deliberation all the same.

---

[8] P. J. Payer, 'Confession and the Study of Sex in the Middle Ages', in *Handbook of Medieval Sexuality*, ed. V. L. Bullough and J. A. Brundage (New York, 1996), p. 5. Here, I do not have Elsakkers's scholarship in mind.

[9] R. Stone, *Morality and Masculinity in the Carolingian Empire* (Cambridge, 2012), pp. 33–5, sounds a note of reasonable caution.

[10] Murray, *Curse on Self-Murder*, p. 251.

[11] R. Meens, 'Religious Instruction in the Frankish Kingdoms', in *Medieval Transformations*, pp. 55–64.

[12] Biller, *Measure of Multitude*, pp. 185–212; see too T. N. Tentler, *Sex and Confession on the Eve of the Reformation* (Princeton, 1977), pp. 162–232; J. Christopoulos, 'Abortion

Contextualizing this deliberation is crucial. Penitentials were undoubtedly textual tools of one sort or another, but questions remain over why they were produced and how they were used. Rob Meens's important survey of 106 eighth- to tenth-century manuscripts identifies three main manuscript contexts: manuscripts for episcopal use; canon law manuscripts; and manuscripts for pastoral use, at least some of which reached the level of local priests alongside liturgical, canonical and other ecclesiastical texts. These manuscript contexts point to at least three distinct but overlapping functions of penitentials: a catechetical function in instructing the clergy in Christian morality; a juridical function in providing guidelines for bishops confronted with disciplinary cases; and a pastoral function in providing practical guidelines for priests acting as confessors.[13] There are limitations. Manuscript contexts cannot elucidate the earliest penitentials (though textual criticism and historical context can be illuminating) and, incidentally, composition of new penitentials clearly designed to reach the hands of local priests actually seems to have decreased after c. 900.[14] Nonetheless, the three principal functions are important in contextualizing active deliberation on abortion. Rulings on abortion were produced through textual practices orientated towards clerical education, church discipline and pastoral care of the laity. These were the reasons why readers used penitentials, the uses which compilers anticipated when copying, rewriting and rearranging rulings. A corollary is that bishops and clerics, not the laity, were the immediate audience of penitentials, an audience which will be especially important in understanding certain rulings on abortion.

The ideas and practices outlined in penitentials only reached the laity to the extent that penitentials were incorporated into structures of pastoral care in specific localities. This raises questions over the relation between penitentials and real-life behaviour in more than one sense. First, to what extent did penitentials shape how people thought and behaved? To put it differently, to what extent did the laity regularly participate in the confessional and penitential practices envisaged by penitentials? Chronological and regional variations together with uncertainty over early medieval parish or proto-parish structures inevitably complicate any answers. Useful maximalist and minimalist positions have been outlined respectively by Rob Meens and Alexander

and the Confessional in Counter-Reformation Italy', *Renaissance Quarterly* 65.2 (2012), 443–84.

[13] R. Meens, 'The Frequency and Nature of Early Medieval Penance', in *Handling Sin: Confession in the Middle Ages*, ed. P. Biller and A. J. Minnis (York, 1998), pp. 39–47. For evidence of penitentials (and other texts besides) reaching local priests, see too C. I. Hammer, 'Country Churches, Clerical Inventories and the Carolingian Renaissance in Bavaria', *Church History* 49.1 (1980), 5–17; Y. Hen, 'Knowledge of Canon Law among Rural Priests: The Evidence of two Carolingian manuscripts from around 800', *Journal of Theological Studies*, n.s., 50.1 (1999), 117–34.

[14] S. Hamilton, *The Practice of Penance 900–1050* (Woodbridge, 2001), pp. 44–50; R. Meens, 'Penitentials and the Practice of Penance in the Tenth and Eleventh Centuries', *EME* 14.1 (2006), 7–21.

Murray.[15] It should be stressed, however, that a minimalist position on lay confession is not an argument that penitentials were not put to use at all, an argument which is practically impossible to square with the manuscript evidence. Indeed, penitentials tell us what the clergy (or at least some clerical authors) thought more clearly than they tell us how the laity thought and behaved. Using penitentials to discern active deliberation on abortion is perfectly compatible with a minimalist position on how much the laity actually confessed their sins in the centuries before annual confession was made mandatory by the Fourth Lateran Council in 1215. Murray has himself made magisterial use of penitential rulings to retrace the contours of clerical thought on suicide.[16]

Second, to what extent do penitentials capture responses to actual behaviour? Everyone knows the rule of thumb when dealing with prescriptive texts: at least some people were getting up to whatever was prohibited. Perceptions of real-life behaviour certainly must have affected how compilers deliberated on abortion and related practices. Peter Biller has convincingly argued that we can see responses to real-life behaviour in some later medieval confessors' manuals.[17] Such responsiveness is harder to see, however, in early medieval penitentials. The prohibition-implies-practice rule of thumb becomes decidedly shaky with such derivative texts.[18] The understandable tendency is to concentrate on novel rulings or additions, especially if they are noticeably specific, as possible responses to real-life behaviour or even individual cases, though this is difficult to demonstrate decisively. But, to complicate matters, in the next chapter we will also encounter a moment when a churchman used fourth-century conciliar canons to address real-life questions in the ninth century. We must resist the false dichotomy by which penitential rulings must be either alert responses to real-life practices or little more than literary reiterations mechanically copied by scribes. There is a grey area between these alternatives which envisages penitential rulings as anticipations of what was needed in clerical education, episcopal discipline and pastoral care. Their authors might not have seen abortion happen, but they did see societies and communities in which it was conceivable to them that abortion could happen. As with any set of prescriptive guidelines a feedback loop between top-down ideals and on-the-ground realities was desirable. But it was not a *sine qua non*

---

[15] Respectively, Meens, 'Frequency', including pp. 40–1 on Franz Kerff's arguments for seeing the penitentials as quasi-canon law for use by bishops in synodal inquisitions; A. Murray, 'Confession before 1215', *Transactions of the Royal Historical Society*, 6th s., 9 (1993), 51–81.

[16] *Curse on Self-Murder*, pp. 252–69.

[17] For a useful anticipation of ideas developed in *Measure of Multitude*, see P. Biller, 'Confessors' Manuals and the Avoiding of Offspring', in *Handling Sin*, pp. 165–87.

[18] For example, Hen, *Culture*, pp. 180–9, argues that rulings on so-called pagan practices in early Frankish penitentials represent 'literary conventions' (at p. 180) rather than real-life behaviour in Merovingian Gaul.

and where such feedback loops did exist in the Early Middle Ages, few have left traces in the written record.

Chronology remains a problem. Many penitentials must still be read in dated nineteenth-century editions. This is one reason why the boundary separating this chapter from the next is self-consciously porous. It is roughly structured around criticisms of penitentials by Carolingian bishops in the early decades of the ninth century. This chapter will concentrate on penitentials compiled before *c.* 800, though many of these survive in ninth-century or later manuscripts and some post-800 compositions will pass through the net. But the main end point will be 'mixed' penitentials produced on the continent in the eighth century, 'mixed' in the sense that they drew on three distinct traditions (and three distinct abortion rulings) of older penitential composition. This chapter will scrutinize these rulings and the contexts in which they originated in early Ireland, Merovingian Gaul and Anglo-Saxon England, before turning to how the process of compiling lengthier penitentials on the continent affected the meanings of abortion rulings, and how readers of penitentials encountered them. The task requires the kind of 'dense exercise in deduction' to which Alexander Murray has subjected penitential rulings on suicide. Minute alterations – a feminine ending becoming masculine, or elaborations of penances graduated according to clerical grades – are as significant as they are easy to miss. Since painstaking detail is crucial, I hope, like Murray, that the reader is not 'rendered breathless'. Or, at least, that breathlessness is a worthwhile occupational hazard in the hunt for 'nuances of thought easily ignored'.[19]

Uncovering Sexual Sin: The *P. Vinniani* and *P. Columbani*

The earliest penitential ruling on abortion takes us to early medieval Ireland. It originated in perhaps the oldest surviving penitential, *Vinniani*, composed in mid to late sixth century Ireland by a certain Vinniaus. A precise date is elusive, though clear use of *Vinniani* in a penitential attributed to Columbanus gives a reason to suppose that it was written before Columbanus's departure for Gaul in *c.* 591.[20] Although *Vinniani* was not as directly influential as two other penitentials with Irish connections, *Columbani* and *Cummeani*, versions of the relevant rulings entered numerous later penitentials because of their inclusion in *Columbani*. In one sense, Vinniaus was writing in a monastic context. In a short epilogue Vinniaus explained that he had written a 'few

---

[19] Murray, *Curse on Self-Murder*, pp. 257, 266.
[20] See T. M. Charles-Edwards, *Early Christian Ireland* (Cambridge, 2000), pp. 291–3, on the long-disputed question of whether the author should be identified with Finnian of Clonard (d. 549) or Finnian of Moville (d. 589), a question which overlaps with uncertainty over the identity of Columbanus's teacher, variously called Findbarr, Vinniau and Finnio in Adomnan's *Vita Columbae*.

things about the remedies of penance' for the 'sons of his bowels ... so that all evil deeds may be destroyed by all people'.²¹ The overwhelming majority of *Vinniani*'s canons, however, applied to clerics or laypeople, suggesting that Vinniaus was writing with a mixed community including *manaig* or lay monastic tenants coalesced around a monastery in mind.²²

After opening rulings on sinful thoughts and intentions, a sequence addressed violence and murder. Compared with subsequent penitentials, *Vinniani* had plenty of moralizing asides. In one aside Vinniaus very carefully emphasized the extra responsibilities of the clergy compared with the laity. A layman received a lighter penance, Vinniaus reasoned, 'because he is a man of the world, his guilt is lighter in this world and his reward less in the future'.²³ Thereafter, the bulk of *Vinniani* addressed mainly clerical sins (*Vinniani* 10–29) followed by lay sins (*Vinniani* 35–47). This is our first strong clue to understanding the thought processes behind the relevant ruling. Despite considerable interest in lay sin, including sexual sin, abortion was addressed in the clerical section.

After dealing with clerical fornication in quite some detail, Vinniaus turned to magical practices. First he addressed a scenario in which a cleric or woman, a male or female *malificus/a*, in some way harmed (we will return to a semantically awkward Latin verb, *decipere*, in the section on *Columbani* below) someone through their *maleficium*.²⁴ 'It is an immense sin,' he added, 'but can be redeemed through penance', six years in this case.²⁵ Next, if the offender (still by implication a cleric or woman) had harmed no-one but 'had given [something] to someone out of dissolute love', he or she received a whole year's penance.²⁶ The next ruling (*Vinniani* 20) was effectively the third in a triad on different forms of *maleficium*. The perpetrator, however, was now female:

---

[21] 'pauca de penitentiae remediis ... suis visceralibus filiis ... ut ab omnibus omnia deleantur hominibus facinora', *P. Vinniani*, ed. and trans. Bieler, *Irish Penitentials*, p. 92–4; translations of all penitentials from this edition are mine, though I have consulted Bieler's translation.

[22] Meens, *Penance*, pp. 48–52. The organization of the early Irish church, especially as early as the sixth century, remains a vexed question, on which see R. Sharpe, 'Churches and Communities in Early Medieval Ireland: Towards a Pastoral Model', in *Pastoral Care before the Parish*, ed. J. Blair and R. Sharpe (Leicester, 1992), pp. 81–109; Charles-Edwards, *Early Christian Ireland*, pp. 241–64.

[23] 'quia homo seculi huius est, culpa levior in hoc mundo et premium minus in futuro', *P. Vinniani* 6, p. 76.

[24] The relevant manuscript (the second manuscript in p. 133 n.29 below) has *malificacus* for *malifica vel malificus*. On the connotations of *maleficium*, a term which is difficult to translate because it could refer to wrongdoing by natural as well as magical means, see V.I.J. Flint, *The Rise of Magic in Early Medieval Europe* (Oxford, 1991), pp. 13–21, 51–4.

[25] 'inmane peccatum est sed per penitentiam redimi potest', *P. Vinniani* 18, p. 78.

[26] 'sed pro inlecebroso amore dederat alicui', *P. Vinniani* 19, p. 78.

> If a woman has destroyed someone's offspring by her *maleficium*, she should do penance for half a year with an allowance of bread and water, and abstain from wine and from meat for two years and [fast] for six Lents with bread and water.[27]

Breathlessness is an occupational hazard from the earliest penitential ruling on abortion. There are textual and semantic complications. My translation of *Vinniani* 20 is deliberately open: 'If a woman has destroyed someone's offspring'. 'Someone' could refer to a woman (as in another woman's child) or to a man (as in a woman's child by a man). It is likely that different readers read it in different ways. The Latin text in Wasserschleben's older edition requires the first interpretation: 'If any woman has taken away [that problematic verb, *decipere*, again] the child of another woman [etc.]'.[28] The difference stems from divergences between the two ninth-century manuscript witnesses to *Vinniani*. In Ludwig Bieler's estimation the manuscript on which Wasserschleben based his edition better preserved the order of the original but is less reliable on wording. Bieler justified his translation, 'child she has conceived of somebody', by pointing to the ruling which immediately follows:[29]

> But if, as we have said, she bears a child and her sin is manifest, six years, as is the judgment about a cleric, and in the seventh she should be joined to the altar, and then we say that she can restore her crown and ought to don a white robe and be pronounced a virgin.[30]

This ruling assumed a spiritual, rather than physical, conception of virginity. A woman could earn back her crown (*corona*), in other words restore her virginity.[31] The rest of the ruling elaborated on the comparison with fornicating clerics, who would likewise be restored to their office after seven years. The rationale for the duration of penance, incidentally, was scriptural: a just man

---

[27] 'Si mulier maleficio suo partum alicuius perdiderit, dimedium annum cum pane et aqua peniteat per mensura et duobus annis abstineat a vino et a carnibus et sex quadragesimas <ieiunet> cum pane et aqua', *P. Vinniani* 20, pp. 78–80. In subsequent quotations from penitentials I will not include the Latin text for penances unless of particular interest.

[28] 'Si aliqua mulier maleficio suo partum alicujus femine deciperit', *P. Vinniani* 20, ed. Wasserschleben, *Bußordnungen*, p. 112.

[29] The manuscripts in question are St. Gall, Stiftsbibliothek, Ms 150 and Vienna, Österreichische Nationalbibliothek, Ms. lat. 2233 (Theol. Lat. 725): see Bieler, *Irish Penitentials*, pp. 17, 79, 243 n.7. The order of these rulings is the same in Wasserschleben's edition.

[30] 'Si autem genuerit, ut diximus, filium et manifestum peccatum eius fuerit, vi. annis, sicut iudicatum est de clerico, et in septimo iungatur altario, et tunc dicimus posse renovare coronam et induere vestimentum album debere et virginem nuncupare', *P. Vinniani* 21, p. 80.

[31] On recovered virginity in Irish Christianity, see K. Ritari, *Saints and Sinners in Early Christian Ireland: Moral Theology in the Lives of Saints Brigit and Columba* (Turnhout, 2009), p. 95; Callan, 'Vanishing Fetuses', 282–96.

fell and rose seven times (Proverbs 24. 16). Read on its own *Vinniani* 20 could have been taken in either sense outlined above. Moreover, reading *partus* as a young infant rather than a fetus (which is how *partus* was used in Latin versions of the Ancyran canon), by itself the ruling could have been read as covering infanticide.[32] Taken together with *Vinniani* 21 on the lapsed virgin, however, *Vinniani* 20 implied getting rid of a child before the manifestation of sin through childbirth.

In relative terms, the penance in *Vinniani* 20 seems lenient: half a year on bread and water, and abstention from wine and meat for two years. The vowed virgin who did *not* kill her child, by contrast, received six years in total. Hugh Connolly has concluded that 'Finnian did not accord to the foetus the same status as a human being after the moment of birth'.[33] There is something to this. With some exceptions, penitentials tended not to treat abortion as severely as other offences, including homicide or adultery. But conceiving fetal status too narrowly is misleading. For Vinniaus fetal status was inextricable from the circumstances surrounding conception and from the repercussions of birth.

Greatest ruin: The turbulence of sexual sin
Before the *maleficium* rulings Vinniaus scrutinized four permutations of what he called the *ruina* of fornication: clerical sexual sin. The key questions were habituation and social visibility. Like the virgin who lapsed, a cleric who fornicated lost his crown (*corona*). If his sin was an isolated incident which was 'hidden from people but came before the attention of God' it received one year of fasting.[34] He would not lose his office because, Vinniaus added, 'sins can be absolved in secret by penance'.[35] In the next scenario if a cleric habitually fornicated without its becoming public knowledge, his penance was three years and he lost his clerical office 'because it is not a smaller thing to sin before God than before people'.[36] But there were degrees of *ruina*. Fathering a child was the *ruina maxima*: 'If any of the clerics has fallen to the greatest ruin and begotten a child, the crime of fornication and homicide is great, but it can be redeemed through penance and God's mercy'.[37] This was the ruling

[32] Cf. Elsakkers, RBL, p. 441.
[33] H. Connolly, *The Irish Penitentials and Their Significance for the Sacrament of Penance Today* (Portland, 1995) p. 67; cf. Nardi, *Aborto*, p. 621.
[34] 'celatum est hominibus sed notuit coram Deo', *P. Vinniani* 10, p. 76; with two years of abstention from wine and meat.
[35] 'Dicimus enim in absconso absolui esse peccata per penitentiam', *P. Vinniani* 10, p. 76.
[36] 'quia non minus est peccare coram Deo quam coram hominibus', *P. Vinniani* 11, p. 76; with three years of abstention from wine and meat. Incidentally, loss of clerical office risked publicizing what had not come to public attention.
[37] 'Si qui<s> autem clericorum ruina maxima ceciderit et genuerit filium et ipsum occiderit, magnum est crimen fornicatio et homicidium, sed redimi potest per penitentiam et misericordiam Dei', *P. Vinniani* 12, p. 76.

to which *Vinniani* 21 later referred back. Intriguingly, the duration of penance was the same as the penance for the cleric whose fornication was habitual but not public knowledge, though Vinniaus stressed the quality of the penance, undertaken with tears of contrition, and prayers day and night. As well as losing his office in this case, the offending cleric would be exiled until the seventh year, whereupon he could be restored at the discretion of a bishop or priest.[38] There was one final permutation, a slightly rushed addition, which reemphasizes that durations of penance did not always operate according to a strictly calibrated calculus of moral gravity: 'But if he has not killed the child, lesser sin but same penance'.[39]

Only one other ruling in *Vinniani* addressed children who were unwanted because sinfully conceived. Although it appeared within the section on lay sins, the ruling concerned *puellae Dei*, nuns. A layman who 'defiled a girl of God and she has lost her crown and he has begotten a child from her' would do penance for three years, including no intercourse with his wife for the first year. The penance was reduced if the *puella Dei* did not bear a child. There was no mention of attempts to abort or kill such an infant.[40]

The 'ethical elite' at the summit of early Irish Christian communities justified its position in part through its special sexual status. Disclosure of sexual sin through the birth of children to clerics or nuns undermined the hierarchical patterning of these communities.[41] It is not surprising, then, that Vinniaus almost exclusively thought about children born of sinful conceptions in terms of clerics and nuns.[42] When addressing responses to the conception or birth of such children in the form of abortion or infanticide he did not address laypeople at all. The focus is telling. His penitential rulings on abortion and infanticide were shaped by questions of social visibility and community repercussions when the sexual sins of clerics or nuns became public knowledge.

Coincidentally, a rather different seventh-century Irish source, a precursor to one of the miracle stories with which this book began, handled the disappearance of children conceived in sin in a comparable way. In *c.* 680 Cogitosus, a monk of Kildare, wrote a *vita* of one of the most eminent early Irish saints: Brigit of Kildare. One startling miracle motif concerned Brigit's encounter with a pregnant nun:

---

[38] *Vinniani* 12, pp. 76–8.
[39] 'Si autem non occiderit filium, minus peccatum sed eadem penitentia', *P. Vinniani* 13, p. 78
[40] 'puellam Dei maculaverit et coronam suam perdiderit et genuerit filium ex ea', *P. Vinniani* 36–7, p. 88.
[41] L. Bitel, 'Sex, Sin and Celibacy in Early Medieval Ireland', *Proceedings of the Harvard Celtic Colloquium* 7 (1987), 81–6 (quotation at 84).
[42] The only exception is *P. Vinniani* 39–40 on men who slept with their slave-girls; they had to perform penance and, if a slave-girl bore a child, emancipate her.

> With a strength of faith most powerful and ineffable, [Brigit] faithfully blessed a woman who, after a vow of integrity, had fallen into youthful concupiscence, whose womb was now swelling with pregnancy; and, after the conception disappeared in the womb without childbirth or pain she restored her healthy to penitence.[43]

The great temptation in the study of early Irish hagiography, especially Brigidine hagiography, is to excavate pagan fossils from Christian texts. On some readings this brief story offers a glimpse of 'traditional heathen customs' or even of Brigit the fertility goddess.[44] More recently, Maeve Callan has argued that Irish penitentials and hagiography capture a 'remarkably permissive attitude' to abortion, and that 'female abortionists in the penitentials ... might be said to some extent represent the morality of "ordinary" Irish Christians'.[45] But the story's *dramatis personae* and monastic context, and its appearance in texts which sought to promote Christian ideals every bit as much as *Vinniani* did, suggest we should resist drawing conclusions primarily about the pagan past or even lay contemporaries.[46] Miracle stories often took the form of healing. In this case the affliction which needed healing was the problem of pregnancy for an individual and, by implication, a community defined by sexual renunciation. Through her benediction Brigit managed to bring about the end of abortion without quite resorting to the means. Instead of the bloody effusion of abortion the conception simply disappeared 'without childbirth or pain', a reference to Eve's curse in Genesis 3. 16. The miracle lay in averting the painful birth of an unwanted child together with the painful symbolism of having that child as a member of a community defined by chastity.[47]

---

[43] 'Potentissima enim et ineffabili fidei fortitudine, quamdam feminam, post votum integritatis, fragilitate humana in juvenili voluptatis desiderio lapsam, et habentem jam praegnantem ac tumescentem uterum, fideliter benedixit: et evanescente in vulva conceptu, sine partu et sine dolore eam sanam ad penitentiam restituit', *Vita Brigitae* 9, AS Feb. I, col. 136F; translation (and numeration) adapted from S. Connolly and J.-M. Picard, 'Cogitosus's *Life of St. Brigit*: Content and Value', *Journal of the Royal Society of Antiquaries of Ireland* 117 (1987), 16. A very similar version of this motif appears in the anonymous *Vita prima Brigitae* 16, AS Feb. I, col. 133C; trans. S. Connolly, 'Vita Prima Sanctae Brigitae: Background and Historical Value', *Journal of the Royal Society of Antiquaries of Ireland* 119 (1989), 45. Both translations are based on unpublished editions. I set aside the much debated question of which *vita* is older.

[44] Respectively, D. Herlihy, 'Households in the Early Middle Ages: Symmetry and Sainthood', in *Households: Comparative and Historical Studies of the Domestic Group*, ed. R. McC. Netting *et al.* (Berkeley, 1984), pp. 389–90; M. Condren, *The Serpent and the Goddess: Women, Religion, and Power in Celtic Ireland* (San Francisco, 1989), pp. 75–6.

[45] Callan, 'Vanishing Fetuses', 282, 295.

[46] An argument made more broadly by K. Ritari, 'The Image of Brigit as a Saint: Reading the Latin Lives', *Peritia* 21 (2010), 191–207.

[47] For a more detailed version of this interpretation, including discussion of later variants of the motif in the *vitae* of two male saints, Áed and Cainnech, see Mistry, 'Sexual Shame'.

The apparent leniency of *Vinniani* 20 was the flipside of Vinniaus's severity towards clerics who fathered or nuns who gave birth to children. It stemmed from the need to protect the sexual status which defined the spiritual elite in Christian communities. In a sense leniency did represent a position on the status of the fetus, but fetal status was evaluated in terms of circumstances of conception as much as embryological knowledge. The thought processes underlying the first penitential ruling on abortion gravitated around the social visibility and repercussions of sexual sin by those meant to be distinguished by their special sexual status. Of course, a reader of *Vinniani* 20 would not necessarily have aligned with these moral priorities. When we turn to *Columbani* it becomes clear that subsequent readers brought their own thought processes to *Vinniani*'s ruling on abortion. Interestingly, however, some early readers went in the opposite direction and thought of men.

In case he is guilty of murder: The P. Columbani

Thanks to Columbanus, the Irish missionary who journeyed to Gaul in the last decade of the sixth century, these were readers on the continent. Columbanus has long been assigned a seminal role in the history of penance but the image of Columbanus as a penitential revolutionary on the continent is being increasingly challenged.[48] A diversity of penitential practices and ecclesiastical reform impulses pre-dated Columbanus's arrival in Gaul.[49]

What was genuinely novel were the textual tools he brought with him, though they were soon integrated into Merovingian ecclesiastical practice. This process is inscribed upon *Columbani*, the penitential which circulated under Columbanus's name. In his reconstruction of the process by which *Columbani* was assembled Thomas Charles-Edwards has identified five originally separate compositions:

A (i)   penitential for monks – serious sins
A (ii) penitential for monks – minor sins
B (i)   penitential for clerics
B (ii) penitential for the laity
B (iii) penitential for monks – minor sins

Each section, it seems, was written separately before ultimately being brought together in a single manuscript together with what would become an influential prologue, which likened confessors to spiritual doctors and

---

[48] M. de Jong, 'Transformations of Penance', in *Rituals of Power*, pp. 185–224; Meens, *Penance*, pp. 70–81.

[49] On pre-existing forms of penance on the continent, see Meens, *Penance*, pp. 25–34; R. Price, 'Informal Penance in Early Medieval Christendom', in *Retribution, Repentance, and Reconciliation*, SCH 40, ed. K. Cooper and J. Gregory (Woodbridge, 2004), pp. 29–32.

emphasized the diversity of spiritual cures for different ailments of the soul. Penance had to be tailored to individual penitents.[50]

For our purposes the place to look is B (i), the clerical penitential, which drew on A (i) and the clerical section from *Vinniani* as sources. Once again abortion appeared in the midst of clerical sins:

> If *anyone* has *destroyed* somebody by *maleficium*, he should do penance for three years on an allowance of bread and water, and abstain from wine and meat for three further years, and then finally be received in communion in the seventh year. But if anyone has been a *maleficus* out of love, and has destroyed no-one, if a cleric he should do penance for a whole year on bread and water, if a layman for half a year, if a deacon for two, if a priest for three; *especially if through this anyone has ensnared the child of a woman*, let each one add six Lents on top *in case he is guilty of murder*.[51]

This was clearly an adaptation of the triad on *maleficium* from *Vinniani* and I have italicized alterations and additions which concern us. The author of *Columbani* retained the triad on lethal, love and abortifacient *maleficium*. In *Vinniani* 18–20 *decipere* had described lethal and love *maleficium* while *perdere* described abortifacient *maleficium*. In *Columbani* B6 these verbs were effectively switched around. *Perdere* is straightforward: to kill or destroy. But *decipere* is much trickier. It means to trap, ensnare, beguile, deceive – or perhaps, more literally, take away.[52] Grammatically, however, the object of this verb was the offspring, not the woman, so translating the segment on abortion (*mulieris partum quis deceperit*) is tricky. Valerie Flint found it 'puzzling' and other translators have injected clarity at the cost of grammatical sense.[53]

A clue to making sense of it lies in the connotations of love magic, which Jacqueline Borsje has examined in a range of Irish sources including penitentials together with vernacular Irish law compiled in c. 800. One Old Irish tract, *Cethairshlicht athgabálae*, listed glosses on fragments of ancient law. One

---

[50] T. M. Charles-Edwards, 'The Penitential of Columbanus', in *Columbanus: Studies on the Latin Writings*, ed. M. Lapidge (Woodbridge, 1997), especially pp. 217–25, 235–6; see too Meens, *Penance*, pp. 52–7, on *Columbani*. On the theme of penance as spiritual medicine, see J. T. McNeill, 'Medicine for Sin as Prescribed in the Penitentials', *Church History* 1.1 (1932), 14–26; T. O'Loughlin, 'Penitentials and Pastoral Care', in *A History of Pastoral Care*, ed. G. R. Evans (London, 2000), pp. 95–7.

[51] 'Si quis maleficio suo aliquem perdiderit [etc.]. Si autem pro amore quis maleficus sit et neminem perdiderit [etc.]; maxime, si per hoc mulieris partum quis[que] deceperit, ideo vi quadragesimas unus quisque insuper augeat, ne homicidii reus est', *P. Columbani* B6, ed. Bieler, *Irish Penitentials*, p. 100 (my italics).

[52] Cf. J. Borsje, 'Rules and Legislation on Love Charms in Medieval Ireland', *Peritia* 21 (2010), 178.

[53] Flint, *Rise of Magic*, p. 237. J. T. McNeill and H. M. Gamer, *Medieval Handbooks of Penance: A Translation of the Principal Libri Poenitentiales and Selections from Related Documents* (New York, 1938), p. 253, take *mulieris* as the object of *deceperit* for the sake of sense: 'Especially if by this means anyone deceives a woman with respect to the birth of a child'.

such list of glosses for the '[supernatural] attack of a bed', included attempts to estrange marriage partners or render a man impotent. The next list of glosses for another offence, 'destruction of a birth', included the 'taking of power or of [the ability to have] offspring (?)' and, again, causing male impotence. Together with the penitentials these glosses point to a common mental association between love magic and forms of magic which impeded birth or hindered fertility one way or another.[54]

After love magic, literally 'being a *maleficus* out of love', the ruling in *Columbani* B6 turned to the scenario of a woman's child affected 'through this [*per hoc*]'. If the kind of association which Borsje identifies in early Irish law was at play, in this context *decipere* probably meant something not entirely precise along the lines of 'cursing' or 'jinxing' a woman's child. Making clean distinctions between contraception and abortion may be misleading.[55] The intriguing final clause (*ne reus homicidii reus sit*), which has mystified some commentators, suggests that the ruling was self-consciously vague.[56] Given the possibilities of love magic, the final clause amounted to a precautionary penance: add six Lents in case you are guilty of murder. The real point is that between the vague way of describing the effect of *maleficium* on a woman's child and this precautionary clause which held out the possibility of taking life, the author was grappling with the ambiguous means and ends of taking potions to prevent birth or otherwise impede fertility.

If a deacon, if a priest: Clerical sexuality

The other noticeable change in *Columbani* B6 concerns gender. Despite using *Vinniani* as a source, the ruling on the lapsed nun, which is key to understanding the concern over abortion in *Vinniani*, was not used in *Columbani*. Moreover, the protagonists were male. The specification of different clerical ranks – cleric, deacon, priest, though, unusually for B(i) a layman is mentioned too – suggests the thought process was connected to clerical sexual sin. If not quite as pronounced as in *Vinniani*, concern over clerical sexual sin was still discernible in *Columbani*. A cleric who fathered a child fell into *maxima ruina* and had to do penance as an exile for seven years.[57] He received a shorter penance, three years, if he fornicated with women 'but he has not begotten a child and has not come to people's attention', with escalating penances for

---

[54] Borsje, 'Rules and Legislation', translations at 180, 183 (parentheses in original); see too J. Borsje, 'Love Magic in Medieval Irish Penitentials, Law and Literature: A Dynamic Perspective', *Studia Neophilologica* 84.1 (2012), 6–23.
[55] Flint, *Rise of Magic*, p. 237, refers to 'contraceptive magic'.
[56] Connery, *Abortion*, p. 71, writes, 'the meaning of this clause is not entirely clear, but it does connect the sin of abortion with homicide', without quite explaining what the connection might have been; cf. Honings, 'L'aborto nei libri penitenziali Irlandesi', pp. 165–6.
[57] *P. Columbani* B2, p. 98.

deacons, monks, priests and bishops.[58] Similarly, a cleric of any grade who slept with his spouse after *conversio* was likened to an adulterer.[59] *Columbani*, like *Vinniani*, was concerned with social repercussions of sexual transgression and took for granted that 'penance formed one of the means to restore social relations'.[60] One ruling even addressed a scenario in which a layman fathered a child with someone else's wife; he not only had to undergo penance (for three years as opposed to a cleric's seven years) and refrain from tastier food, but also had to pay some kind of compensation, literally a 'chastity price' (*praetium pudititiae*), to the humiliated husband.[61]

Columbani shows how different compilers could use the same basic penitential ruling to address and convey different concerns. Nonetheless, there are some commonalities between *Columbani* and *Vinniani*: first, an anxiety over sexual sin committed by those held to higher sexual standards within Christian communities; second, an envisaged context in which penitential practice interacted with forms of social discipline and even dispute settlement. A cleric who murdered someone would be exiled for ten years, doing penance for seven of them. Upon his return (at his abbot's or priest's discretion) he had to enact a form of restorative justice by offering himself to the parents of the slain as a surrogate son.[62] Finally, neither *Columbani* nor *Vinniani* clearly addressed voluntary abortion as a lay sin and, indeed, *Columbani* did not address abortion by women at all. This began to change with a family of early Frankish penitentials which drew upon *Columbani* as an important source.

Voluntary abortion and clerical reform: *The Simplices*

Simplices is the scholarly designation for a group of Frankish penitentials which originated perhaps as early as the later seventh century.[63] Each of these relatively short penitentials is known from one or two manuscript copies. They share the same basic core of forty or so penitential rulings not organized around any particular structure. This core combined material from *Columbani* B followed by other rulings including some conciliar material, the latest of which comes from a council of Auxerre held at some point after 585. Newer rulings were added after this core in some *simplices*. A group of eight *simplices* have been edited by Raymund Kottje, though one (*Sangallense simplex*) did not

---

[58] 'sed non filium generaverit et in notitiam hominum non venerit', P. *Columbani* B4, p. 100.
[59] P. *Columbani* B8, p. 100.
[60] Meens, *Penance*, p. 56.
[61] P. *Columbani* B14, p. 102.
[62] P. *Vinniani* 23, pp. 82–3; cf. P. *Columbani* B1. Other examples of restorative justice and dispute settlement mingling with penances include monetary compensation for serious violence (P. *Vinniani* 8) and the 'price of chastity' in P. *Columbani* B14.
[63] For an overview of the *simplices*, see Meens, *Penance*, pp. 76–81.

contain any rulings on abortion while another (*Hubertense*) was compiled in the ninth century and will be examined in the next chapter. This leaves four penitentials which contained both rulings (*Burgundense, Bobbiense, Oxoniense I* and *Floriacense*) and two (*Parisiense simplex* and *Sletstatense*) which contained one or other.

Dating is not straightforward. Judging by surviving manuscripts it is safe to assume that they were circulating by the eighth century, though, as we shall see, the hypothetical original was produced earlier and the youngest *simplices* survive in manuscripts from as late as the tenth century.[64] What the *simplices* allow us to see are minor variants and small flickers of deliberation on abortion in two relevant rulings, one derived from *Columbani* and the other an altogether new ruling.

Voluntarily: The new ruling on abortion
First, the new ruling. It will be useful to start with *Bobbiense*, which reproduced almost the entire core and was possibly produced before *c.* 700 (we turn to its intriguing manuscript context below). The newer ruling appeared after the concentration of Columbanan material in the first half or so:

> If any woman has voluntarily caused abortion, she should do penance for three years, one on bread and water.[65]

The same canon appeared in almost identical form across other *simplices*; the only significant variant was that one (*Floriacense*) gave a penance of one year instead of three.[66] The key word is the adverb *voluntarie*, which suggests the scenario of a pregnant woman who voluntarily undergoes abortion herself, though a later penitential identified an ambiguity when adding to this ruling, 'that is has done this by any sort of way to herself or someone else'.[67] Distinguishing between deliberate abortion and spontaneous miscarriage was far from straightforward in societies where reproductive failures were not infrequent. Such a distinction relied in part upon a woman's testimony, which might have provided cover for a woman who had deliberately undergone abortion, though it might also have fed suspicions over genuinely

---

[64] See Kottje, *Paenitentialia*, pp. xxii–xxv, xxxiii–xlii. Kottje's edition prints both individual editions and a synoptic edition of eight *simplices*. When referring to rulings from multiple penitentials in comparison, I quote from the latter; otherwise I quote from individual editions.

[65] 'Si quis mulier avorsum fecerit voluntarie, III annus peneteat, I in pane et aqua', P. *Bobbiense* 31, p. 70.

[66] P. *Floriacense* 32, P. *Burgundense* 35, P. *Parisiense simplex* 27, P. *Oxoniense I* 30, pp. 53–6. P. *Sletstatense* did not include this ruling.

[67] 'id est qualecunque causa sibi aut alii fecerit', P. *Merseburgense A* (V_{23}), ed. Kottje, *Paenitentialia*, p. 135; this was a late ninth-century recension of *Merseburgense A*, to which we turn below at p. 192; cf. Elsakkers, RBL, p. 405.

spontaneous miscarriage.⁶⁸ The allusion to volition might have raised a question over involuntary abortion in a reader's mind. A woman could be forced into abortion including through violence.⁶⁹ Did some believe that women had to undergo a purificatory penance after spontaneous miscarriage? Additions to this ruling in some later penitentials, which reduced penances for women who had an abortion without volition (*sine voluntate*) or unwillingly (*invite*), point in this direction.⁷⁰ Even more unambiguously, a shorter penance effectively for unintentional miscarriage was tacked onto this ruling in some later eighth-century compilations.⁷¹

Three years was not the longest penance – homicide required ten years and cutting off someone's limb five years⁷² – but it was the penance for a diverse array of sins: perjury under duress, love magic, usury, abduction of virgins or widows, observing the Kalends and so on.⁷³ *Parisiense simplex* added several rulings to the core and the final two provided condensed rationales for working out the duration of penances. Three years was the base penance for laypeople guilty of capital sins (*capitalia peccata*), while ecclesiastical ranks from clerics up to bishops received longer penances from five to twelve years; and minor sins (the author used theft and false witness as markers to indicate 'any similar sins') warranted one year of lay penance, again with penances escalating according to clerical grade.⁷⁴ This was one compiler's retrospective guideline for categorizing penances and it made abortion a *capitale peccatum*. But there was one final commonality across the *simplices*. Every single one included a canon on men or women who killed their infants by smothering or overlaying (*opprimere*) them. Causing infant death, albeit in this scenario where culpability was complicated, warranted three years just as voluntary abortion did.⁷⁵

---

⁶⁸ Early modern Venetian state archives reveal that both prosecutors and defence counsels had to contend with the physiological ambiguities of miscarriage and stillbirth; see the extraordinary and often appalling cases discussed by Ferraro, *Nefarious Crimes*, especially pp. 86–115, 118–36.

⁶⁹ See pp. 213–26 below on this scenario in Frankish law-codes and royal capitularies.

⁷⁰ *P. Silense* 65–6, ed. F. Bezler, *Paenitentialia Hispaniae*, CCSL 156A (Turnhout, 1998), p. 23; *P. Vallicellianum* C.6 37, ed. A.H. Gaastra, 'Between Liturgy and Canon Law: A Study of Books of Confession and Penance in Eleventh- and Twelfth-Century Italy' (unpublished Ph.D. dissertation, University of Utrecht, 2007), p. 277; see too Elsakkers, RBL, pp. 451–2, on voluntary/involuntary abortion in penitentials.

⁷¹ 'si nolens III XL', *P. Capitula Iudiciorum* 3.1c; cf. *P. Sangallense tripartitum* (I) 28, both ed. Meens, *Boeteboek*, pp. 438, 334.

⁷² *P. Bobbiense* 1, 19, p. 69.

⁷³ *P. Bobbiense* 7, 10, 17, 20, 33, 30, pp. 69–70.

⁷⁴ *P. Parisiense simplex* 61–2, p. 79. This penitential was probably written at the nunnery of Chelles or Jouarre in the mid eighth century; see Meens, *Penance*, pp. 79–80.

⁷⁵ *P. Burgundense* 19, *P. Bobbiense* 17, *P. Parisiense simplex* 11, *P. Sletstatense* 18, *P. Oxoniense I* 14, *P. Floriacense* 18, *P. Sangallense simplex* 10, pp. 29–32; *P. Floriacense* increased the penance to five years if the smothering was due to drunkenness

Rereading Columbani
Alongside this ruling on voluntary abortion most *simplices* also contained versions of *Columbani* B6 on *maleficium*. After eight penitential rulings on homicide, fornication, perjury and theft, all derived from *Columbani*, *Bobbiense* reproduced its own version:

> If anyone has destroyed someone by his *maleficium*, let him do penance for ten years, three on bread and water.
>
> If anyone has wrought *veneficium* for love and has destroyed no-one, let him do penance for three years, one on bread and water. If anyone has ensnared a woman's child, let him do six Lents on bread and water.[76]

Simplices tended to abbreviate their source material and the abbreviations were particularly compressed in *Bobbiense*. The alterations were not dramatic, though they give hints of a compiler thinking about his material. For instance, the penance for lethal *maleficium* became ten years, presumably to match the penance for homicide in the opening ruling on clerics who committed murder. The ruling on abortifacient magic excised the final clause (*ne reus homicidii sit*) and spoke of doing (*agere*) rather than adding (*augere*) six Lents in penance so that in effect the penance was lower than in *Columbani*.

Comparable changes are discernible in other *simplices*.[77] For instance, two of them (*Sletstatense* and *Floriacense*) effectively broke the triad by excising the first segment on lethal *maleficium* and only including the ruling on love and abortifacient magic. More broadly, *simplices* oscillated between *maleficium* and *veneficium*. *Burgundense*, like *Bobbiense*, referred to lethal *maleficium* but love and abortifacient *veneficium*.[78] The point was possibly to distinguish between various magical means and poisons standing for potions.

Two further changes are worth noting. First, a couple of penitentials increased the penance. Both *Oxoniense I* and *Floriacense* stipulated four years in total for abortifacient magic. The latter change is especially intriguing because *Floriacense* had reduced the penance in the *voluntarie* ruling down to one year; this compiler appears to have viewed clerical entanglement with abortion through *maleficium* as a graver sin than voluntary female abortion. Second, two *simplices* contained small alterations to the final clause. *Floriacense* reproduced it without the negative: 'if someone has ensnared a woman's offspring, he must add three years on bread and water, *he would be guilty of homicide*'.[79]

---

or (presumably culpable) negligence; cf. Honings, 'L'aborto nei libri penitenziali Irlandesi', p. 174.

[76] 'Si quis maleficium suum aliquid perdederit [etc]'; 'Si quis pro amore veneficium fecerit et neminem perdederit [etc]. Si quis mulieri partum deceperit [etc]', *P. Bobbiense* 9–10, p. 69.

[77] *P. Burgundense* 9–10, *P. Sletstatense* 9, *P. Oxoniense I* 7–8, *P. Floriacense* 10, pp. 17–23.

[78] *P. Burgundense* 9–10, pp. 63–4.

[79] '… in pane et aqua, *reus sit homicidii*', *P. Floriacense* 10, p. 98 (my italics).

Floriacense, to which we shall return, was admittedly not the tidiest penitential composition but as it stood the wording emphasized that this *was* murder. *Sletstatense*, by contrast, seems to have gone in the opposite direction. The final clause has *nec* rather than *ne*, possibly meaning: 'and he would not be guilty of homicide'.[80] Scribal errors cannot be definitively ruled out in either case, of course, but these alterations might well be hints of divergent views on whether or not abortion was murder.

The Bobbio Missal and the context of clerical reform
One final feature of the *simplices* brings us to *Bobbiense*'s manuscript context. Four other *simplices* graded penances for love or abortifacient magic by ecclesiastical rank (*Floriacense* alone also mentioned laymen). This typifies a concerted focus on clerics across many *simplices*. *Bobbiense* was unusual in that it did not grade *maleficium* penances by ecclesiastical rank. Its content and manuscript context, however, suggests that its compiler primarily had clerical perpetrators in mind too. *Bobbiense* forms part of the Bobbio Missal, a Merovingian liturgical manuscript, which also contained a lectionary, sacramentary, catechetical material and other liturgical texts, from blessings for newly married couples to *formulae* for exorcisms or ordinations of abbesses. The missal has been described as a 'vade mecum for a Merovingian priest'.[81] Furthermore, Rosamond McKitterick's palaeographical analysis of its scripts points to composition in south-east Provence, perhaps Vienne, as early as the close of the seventh century, which would make the Bobbio Missal the oldest surviving manuscript to contain a penitential.[82]

The Bobbio Missal provided for liturgical functions for a broader community or communities, but it primarily served a clerical community, as an aid in both disciplining and educating clerics. For instance, the Bobbio Missal contains the earliest missal rubric in which a priest asked for pardon of his own sins.[83] *Bobbiense* itself was tailored for a priest to hear confessions from other clerics with some scope for administering penance among laypeople too. Where perpetrators were identified, they were clerics; the one occasion when penances were graded by ecclesiastical rank makes no mention of

---

[80] '.. in pane et aqua *nec homicidium reus sit*', P. Sletstatense 9, p. 83 (my italics).
[81] R. Meens and Y. Hen, 'Conclusion', in *The Bobbio Missal: Liturgy and Religious Culture in Merovingian Gaul*, ed. R. Meens and Y. Hen (Cambridge, 2004), p. 219; cf. in the same volume Y. Hen, 'The Liturgy of the Bobbio Missal', pp. 152–3.
[82] R. McKitterick, 'The Scripts of the Bobbio Missal', in *Bobbio Missal*, pp. 19–52 on Paris, Bibliothèque nationale de France, MS lat. 13246; cf. in the same volume R. Meens, 'Reforming the Clergy: A Context for the Use of the Bobbio Missal', pp. 155–6. If so, the Bobbio Missal would predate the version of *Excarpsus Cummeani* in Copenhagen, Kongelige Bibliotek, MS Ny. Kgl. S. 58 8° 229, conventionally assigned to the first half of the eighth century: see R. Meens, 'The Oldest Manuscript Witness of the *Collectio canonum Hibernensis*', *Peritia* 14 (2000), 1–19.
[83] Meens, 'Reforming', pp. 165–6.

laymen.[84] Further, several rulings which did not specify perpetrators, from the now familiar reference to the *ruina maxima* of fathering a child to improper handling of the Eucharist, necessarily had clerics in mind.[85] And the sixteen rulings added onto the *simplices* core focussed on clerics' purity and ritual propriety.[86]

Of course, because many rulings simply started with *quis*, anyone, a reader could easily have consulted *Bobbiense* for guidelines in administering lay penance. But the point here is about context of compilation. Clerical perpetrators were something approaching the default setting in *Bobbiense* and some other *simplices*. Certainly *Burgundense*, which survives in an early eighth-century manuscript but is the most formally primitive of the *simplices*, regularly included gradations in penance according to ecclesiastical rank without consideration of the laity. Assuming the *simplices* originated from a now lost original, it is fairly certain that it too was compiled with clerical sin and penance foregrounded.[87] A thread from *Columbani* to the *simplices* connected men, principally clerics, to abortion.

Intriguingly, it was in this very context that the new ruling on voluntary abortion by women emerged. This and the ruling on smothering infants were the only rulings which deliberately specified female perpetrators. One possible explanation is a response to real-life practice. Alternatively, perhaps more plausibly, the reason was textual. Wanting to join up the dots, the compiler of the hypothetical original added it in after encountering Columbanan material on abortifacient magic perpetrated by men, clerical or otherwise.

Fetal positions: The Theodorean Penitentials

The third ruling to enter penitential tradition was markedly different. It entered via a different route from the *decipere partum* and *voluntarie* rulings, and graded penances for abortion according to the stage of pregnancy or fetal development. In one surviving form it explicitly demonstrated awareness of canonical precedent.

The ruling appeared in a number of penitentials associated with Theodore of Canterbury (d. 690). Born at Tarsus, deep in Asia Minor, and educated in the Greek east, Theodore had arrived in Rome as a monk at some point in the 660s. He was appointed archbishop of Canterbury by Pope Vitalian

---

[84] *P. Bobbiense* 11, p. 69 (on those who slept with their wives after ordination; mentions clerics, deacons, priests and bishops).
[85] *P. Bobbiense* 2, 16, p. 69.
[86] Meens, 'Reforming', pp. 157–9. These were adapted from the sixth-century *Ambrosianum*, on which see Meens, *Penance*, pp. 45–7.
[87] See Meens, *Penance*, pp. 76–7. *P. Burgundense* survives in a manuscript also containing the text of the later sixth-century council of Auxerre, the oldest surviving record of a synod held by a bishop for his own clerics.

in 668 before journeying to England with his companion Hadrian in 669. Theodore has long been recognized as an important spearhead of reform in the Anglo-Saxon church. Scholarship on his cultural background and impact was catalysed in the 1990s by the identification of two texts with Theodore and his circle. First, Bernhard Bischoff and Michael Lapidge demonstrated that previously unpublished biblical commentaries were notes taken by anonymous students from Theodore's and Hadrian's scriptural teaching. These commentaries provide the most extensive evidence for Theodore's teaching in England and for his background before reaching Britain.[88] The second text, the *Laterculus Malalianus*, is an exegetical text which Jane Stevenson has argued was composed in later seventh century Canterbury probably by Theodore himself.[89] Both texts give a more granular sense of the intellectual resources in exegesis, canon law and medicine with which Theodore and Hadrian transformed the Anglo-Saxon church.[90]

Although the penitentials associated with Theodore might not have been written by him, they certainly bear the distinctive imprint of his learning and background. The Theodorean penitentials have survived in multiple recensions, of which five have been edited: *Capitula Dacheriana* (D), *Canones Gregorii* (G), *Canones Cottoniani* (C), *Canones Basilienses* (B) and *Discipulus Umbrensium* (U).[91] The precise relation between these recensions is yet to be fully unravelled but it is clear that they represent different receptions of Theodore's penitential teaching. *Capitula Dacheriana* and *Canones Cottoniani* were probably from an early stage prior to 673. *Canones Gregorii*, a more influential recension, was probably compiled after 673.[92] *Discipulus Umbrensium*, the longest and

---

[88] B. Bischoff and M. Lapidge, *Biblical Commentaries from the Canterbury School of Theodore and Hadrian* (Cambridge, 1994), with pp. 5–189, for the fullest available biography of Theodore and Hadrian; see too M. Lapidge, 'The Career of Archbishop Theodore', in *Archbishop Theodore: Commemorative Studies on his Life and Influence*, ed. M. Lapidge (Cambridge, 1995), pp. 1–29.

[89] J. Stevenson, *The* Laterculus Malalianus *and the School of Archbishop Theodore* (Cambridge, 1995), pp. 8–20. See too J. Stevenson, 'Theodore and the *Laterculus Malalianus*', in *Archbishop Theodore*, pp. 204–21; Bischoff and Lapidge, *Biblical Commentaries*, pp. 180–2; J. Siemens, *The Christology of Theodore of Tarsus: The* Laterculus Malalianus *and the Person and Work of Christ* (Turnhout, 2010), pp. 46–8.

[90] On the learning of Greek contemporaries, see G. Cavallo, 'Theodore of Tarsus and the Greek Culture of his time', in *Archbishop Theodore*, pp. 54–67.

[91] On the composition and content of these recensions, see T. N. Charles-Edwards, 'The Penitential of Theodore and the *Iudicia Theodori*', in *Archbishop Theodore*, pp. 141–74; R. Flechner, 'The Making of the Canons of Theodore', *Peritia* 17–18 (2003–4), 121–43; Meens, *Penance*, pp. 88–96.

[92] Flechner 'Making', 123–6, argues this on the basis that *Capitula Dacheriana* and *Canones Cottoniani* permitted a man to remarry after divorcing an adulterous wife, a ruling derived from Basil of Caesarea, whereas *Canones Gregorii* did not; a right to remarry was condemned, however, by the council of Hertford (673) which Theodore attended. See Meens, *Penance*, p. 226, for a list of fifteen manuscripts containing *Canones Gregorii*.

most carefully organized Theodorean penitential, was the work of an eighth-century editor (the self-styled 'Discipulus Umbrensium') who combined a book of canonical judgments with a thematically organized penitential. This editor effectively reedited and reordered existing versions of Theodore's penitential teaching. His prologue emphasized Theodore's authority on penance and canonical judgments during his lifetime and after his death. Men and even women, the Discipulus noted, were fascinated by his teaching. The main body of his penitential, the Discipulus went on, was derived from answers which Theodore gave to questions posed to him by a certain Eoda from an Irish book (*ex scottorum libello*). Various versions of Theodore's penitential teaching were in circulation and the Discipulus wanted to disentangle what he called the 'diverse and confused summary' already in existence.[93] The versions of abortion rulings in *Discipulus Umbrensium* allow us to see how an early eighth century editor interpreted and arranged this material. But, before this, the different versions were variations on the same basic idea. To take first the two pre-673 texts, the version from *Capitula Dacheriana* is the only recension to use *partus*:

> A woman destroying offspring if before 40 days of conception a year, but if after 40 she should do penance for three years.[94]

The other early recension, *Canones Cottoniani*, included two versions. The first one appeared after rulings on infanticide and the death of unbaptized infants:

> A woman who has conceived a child in the womb before 40 days should do penance for one year. If she kills after forty days she should do penance as a murderer.[95]

A ruling on women who practised divination appeared next, before another version:

> Women who perpetrate abortion should be judged from the same ruling before they have soul and after, that is after 40 days from the reception of the seed she should do penance as a murderer, that is three years [etc.].[96]

---

[93] 'diversa confusaque digestio', *P. Theodori (U)*, ed. Finsterwalder, *Canones*, p. 288. Charles-Edwards, 'Penitential of Theodore', identifies this with *Cummeani* but in the course of a broader argument that Theodore's penitential teaching is not reducible to the effect of Irish influence.

[94] 'Mulier perdens partum si ante XL dies conceptionis annum si vero post XL peniteat III annos', *P. Theodori (D)* 114, ed. Finsterwalder, *Canones*, p. 248.

[95] 'Mulier que concepit filium in utero ante XL dies I annum peniteat'; 'Si post quadraginta dies occidit quasi homicida peniteat', *P. Theodori (C)* 143–4, ed. Finsterwalder, *Canones*, p. 280.

[96] 'Mulieres que abortivum faciunt ex eodem sententiam iudicentur antequam animam habent et postea, id est post XL dies acceptatione seminis ut homicida peniteat [etc]', *P. Theodori (C)* 147, p. 280.

A similar version of this second ruling appeared in *Canones Basilienses*.[97] Finally (we turn to *Discipulus Umbrensium* below) *Canones Gregorii*, like *Canones Cottoniani*, included the ruling amid other rulings on infanticide and the death of unbaptized infants. Here the arrangement of the canons is especially intriguing. Rulings covered both accidental and deliberate deaths of unbaptized infants, next came the abortion ruling followed immediately by another on baptism:

> A woman who conceives and kills her child in the womb before 40 days should do penance for one year. If she kills after 40 days she ought to do penance like a murderer.
>
> If it dies without someone's bloodshed and without baptism [he/she?] should do penance for three years.[98]

Responsibility for deaths of unbaptized infants cast its shadow over the versions in *Canones Cottoniani*. In the case of *Canones Gregorii*, the proximity of the ruling on baptism might have implied culpability for the death of an unbaptized infant even where abortion was not deliberate.

The terminology across the versions differed: destroying offspring (*partum perdere*), killing one's own child in the womb (*filium suum in utero occidere*), causing abortion (*abortivum facere*). What they shared in common was the significance of forty days in judging whether a woman who aborted should do penance as a murderer. As *Canones Basilienses* and *Canones Cottoniani* made explicit, forty days marked whether or not the fetus had *anima*, soul; they assumed what modern theologians would call a theory of delayed animation.[99] Here, a subtle caveat is necessary. In modern theological language delayed animation can refer to the theory that the soul enters an existing body after conception in the sense of the product of union between sperm and ovum. In the Theodorean penitentials conception appears to have meant reception of seed, the moment of intercourse. Nonetheless, coming into being within the womb was not instantaneous.

What would Jesus do? The Laterculus Malalianus and embryological knowledge
A moral distinction based on a key moment in fetal development had entered an early medieval ecclesiastical text. To understand how and why requires getting closer to Theodore's learning through the *Laterculus Malalianus*. A

---

[97] 'Mulieres quae abhortivum faciunt eodem modo II annis antequam animam habent et postea id est XL diebus post conceptionem seminis ut homicidae in tertia XLmis', *P. Theodori (B)* 62, ed. Asbach, *Poenitentiale*, supplement, p. 85.

[98] 'Mulier qui concepit et occidit filium suum in utero ante XL dies unum annum peniteat. Si post XL dies occidit quasi homicida debet penitere'; 'Si moriatur sine nece hominis et sine baptism III annos peniteat', *P. Theodori (G)* 105–6, ed. Finsterwalder, *Canones*, p. 263.

[99] Connery, *Abortion*, p. 73.

short exegetical treatise divided into two parts, the first part (*LM* 1–11) comprised a universal history of the world from Eden to the sixth century closely derived from John Malalas's *Chronographia*. The second part (*LM* 12–25) was a more original composition which worked through the life of Christ in painstaking exegetical detail. The date of Christ's conception at the annunciation (25 March) was mentioned early in the first part. This was a special date on which God had done all sorts of astounding things across and even before time: the Israelites' crossing of the Red Sea, Satan's expulsion from heaven and the very beginning of creation.[100]

The exegetical part returned to Christ's conception when considering how 'all things were done in full humanity with God'.[101] The passage from Christ's conception to birth took 276 days (the period from 25 March to 25 December) 'since all birth of males touches the beginning of the tenth month'.[102] Another allegorical hinge connected the building of the first temple at Jerusalem to the conception and birth of Christ. Following John 2. 20, it had taken forty-six years to build the temple. In the *Laterculus Malalianus* this signified the forty-six days in which Jesus was formed within Mary's womb. In fact, formation normally took forty-five days. But '[t]here is one day over the forty-five in the [case of] the Lord alone, on account of his unique incarnation from a virgin, without sin or the drawing-together of semen', adding up to forty-six days in total. Christ shared in our humanity from its humblest inception, but in a special way: the incarnation was both typical and distinct.[103] The *Laterculus Malalianus* is a good example of how pre-modern embryologies were often not about the embryo as a literal, physical entity. Embryological knowledge constituted a kind of 'narrative knowing' which expressed and explained other ideas.[104] Nonetheless, what interests us is how Theodore accounted for the normal process by which seed was converted and coagulated into incipient human form in the womb:

> For in this order, according to the authority of our seniors and predecessors, is said, and read, to be the conception of the human race; that for six days the semen remains in the womb, having the appearance of milk. Then it is

---

[100] *LM* 2, ed. and trans. Stevenson, *Laterculus Malalianus*, p. 123.

[101] 'Omnia gesta sunt in hominem plenum cum Deo', *LM* 12, pp. 136–7.

[102] 'quia omnis nativitas masculi decimi mensis tangit initia', *LM* 12, pp. 138–9. Galen's figure was 280 days and he also differentiated between male and female fetuses; see ibid., pp. 196–7.

[103] 'Et ideo quod in Domino solo una cadit dies super .xlv., propter singularem eius incarnationem de virgine sine corruptionem sive gluttinatio seminis', ibid.; on Theodore's incarnational theology, see J. Siemens, 'Christ's Restoration of Humankind in *Laterculus Malalianus*, 14', *Heythrop Journal* 48.1 (2007), especially 20–4.

[104] F. Garrett, 'Ordering Human Growth in Tibetan Medical and Religious Embryologies', in *Textual Healing: Essays on Medieval and Early Modern Medicine*, ed. E. L. Furdell (Leiden, 2005), p. 52. We return to this theme in chapter eight.

Abortion in the Early Middle Ages

turned into blood for nine days, then it grows for twelve days, and after that it adds eighteen days: it is soon coagulated, and grows towards the outline of limbs.[105]

This passage indicates the kind of intellectual resources upon which Theodore could draw, a 'strange mixture of embryology, number-theory, allegory ... and historical data'.[106] He was well schooled in both intricate exegesis and standard works in the seventh-century Byzantine medical curriculum.[107] Though the *Laterculus Malalianus* was original in how it imagined Christ's inception in the womb, its embryological assumptions drew ultimately on an allegorical essay by Augustine on the building of the temple, which itself refracted ideas associated with Galen. It is little surprise that a distinction in fetal development compatible with Galen and articulated in dense scriptural exegesis entered rulings on abortion in penitentials associated with Theodore. Of course, forty-five days was not the same thing as forty days; and the identification of *anima* with the end of this embryonic period was spelled out in penitentials, but not in the *Laterculus Malalianus*. Certainly, forty days was easier to remember. Moreover, a symbolic function cannot be entirely ruled out: the forty days of postpartum abstinence required in Theodorean penitentials might have recalled, for example, Christ's forty days in the desert.[108] Additionally, as Jane Stevenson has plausibly suggested, the difference might have been about 'erring on the side of severity, given the difficulty of actually calculating dates and the tendency, in the circumstances, of the mother to underestimate'.[109] The forty days specified in the penitentials reflected precaution rather than precision.

When read alongside the *Laterculus Malalianus* and with awareness of Theodore's medical learning, Theodorean penitentials provide a unique opportunity to connect measures against abortion with an embryological text. Such a connection is an exception, not the rule, just as Theodore's learning was exceptional by British (and, really, western) standards. But not all recipients of Theodore's penitential ideas in seventh-century England and

---

[105] 'Nam hoc ordine, secundum auctoritate maiorum nostrorum adque priorum, dicitur aut legiture: generis humani conceptio quod per .vi. diebus lactis similitudinem habens manet semen in vulva. Dehinc convertetur in sanguinem usque ad dies .viiii. Deinde augetur usque ad .xii., et dehinc adduntur .x. et .viii.: qui mox coagulatur et tendit ad liniamenta membrorum', *LM* 13, pp. 138–9.

[106] Stevenson, *Laterculus Malalianus*, p. 194, with pp. 196–7 on Augustine's *De annis quadraginta sex aedificandi templi*, in *De diversis quaestionibus* 56, PL 40, col. 39.

[107] Bischoff and Lapidge, *Biblical Commentaries*, pp. 243–55.

[108] *P. Theodori (U)* 1.14.19, p. 309. Numerological significance in the penitentials has not been examined in any detail, but for a sounding in this direction see A. Angenendt, T. Braucks, R. Busch and H. Lutterbach, 'Counting Piety in the Early and High Middle Ages', in *Ordering Medieval Society: Perspectives on Intellectual and Practical Modes of Shaping Social Relations*, ed. B. Jussen, trans. P. E. Selwyn (Philadelphia, 2001), pp. 23–31.

[109] Stevenson, *Laterculus Malalianus*, p. 13.

beyond shared the kind of intellectual resources embedded in the *Laterculus Malalianus*. In, *Canones Cottoniani* the early recension of Theodore's penitential teaching quoted above, which contained two versions of the abortion ruling, there is a fascinating suggestion that not all contemporaries grasped the forty days distinction straight away. The best explanation for why *Canones Cottoniani* contained two rulings is that the second one deliberately clarified the first. The first had simply mentioned forty days with two penances for before and after. The second referred back to it and, in effect, had to spell out the rationale and its practical applicability: this (a) was a question of before and after having soul and (b) had to be calculated from forty days after reception of seed. We might speculate whether this early recension of Theodorean penitential teaching captured a *viva voce* moment when the learned bishop had had to explain his penitential teaching to a questioning student much as the biblical commentaries captured students' notes from *viva voce* explanations of scripture.[110] At any rate, something had needed explaining.

The alignment of forty days with some classical embryologies – and the subsequent influence of Theodorean penitential teaching – should not obscure the likelihood that not all churchmen had the same instincts when it came to evaluating abortion according to the stage of fetal development. A different approach survives in a far less influential penitential, *Bigotianum*. Composed on the continent in *c.* 800, *Bigotianum* drew mainly on Irish material though also some Theodorean material. *Bigotianum* arranged its material according to eight principal sins. The relevant rulings appeared within the section on 'Anger', though a little incongruously under the heading, 'On those who kill themselves. I. Theodore', and after a Theodorean canon on suicide. 'The penance,' it began, 'for the destruction of the liquid matter of the infant in the womb of a woman is three years on bread and water'.[111] The penance for 'destruction of flesh and soul in the womb' was fourteen years.[112] And, finally, the 'price for the soul of a woman dying from destruction of flesh with soul: fourteen female slaves'.[113] Despite the proximity to Theodorean material on suicide, these terms appear to have been derived (with increased penances) from the Latin canons of an Irish synod contained within the so-called *Canones Hibernenses*, dating from no later than the middle of the seventh century.[114] A different take appeared in the vernacular *Old Irish Penitential*.

---

[110] Bischoff and Lapidge, *Biblical Commentaries*, pp. 173–80.
[111] 'Penitentia perditionis liquoris materiae infantis in utero mulieris .iii. anni in pane et aqua', *P. Bigotianum* 4.2.2, ed. Bieler, *Irish Penitentials*, p. 228. Bieler's translation ('destruction of the embryo of the child') rather loads the die.
[112] 'perditionis carnis et animae in utero', *P. Bigotianum* 4.2.3, p. 228.
[113] 'Praetium animae mulieris morientis de perditio carnis cum anima: xiiii. ancelle', *P. Bigotianum* 4.2.4, p. 228.
[114] *Canones Hibernenses* 1.6–8 (with slightly different penances: respectively, three and a half years, seven and a half years, and twelve female slaves), ed. Bieler, *Irish Penitentials*, p. 160, with pp. 8–9 on dating.

Three and a half years for a 'woman who causes miscarriage of that which she has conceived after it has been established in the womb'; seven years '[i]f the flesh has formed'; fourteen years '[i]f the soul has entered it'; fourteen cumals [a set value, literally meaning female slaves] or fourteen years '[i]f the woman dies of the miscarriage, that is, the death of body and soul'.[115] 'Flesh' and 'soul' did not coincide in the *Old Irish Penitential*, whereas they did explicitly in *Bigotianum* and implicitly in the Theodorean penitentials. In this sense, *Bigotianum* and the Theodorean penitentials were not miles apart. But the moral conclusions were different. Theodore's teaching explicitly likened destruction after forty days to murder. *Bigotianum* went even further. The penance of fourteen years for 'destruction of flesh and soul' was matched by the penance for parricide and exceeded penances for other forms of murder.[116]

Unlike *Bigotianum* or the *Old Irish Penitential*, the forty days approach circulated fairly widely, as we shall see, in mixed compilations being produced from the eighth century. But its fate in one family of penitential texts provides a further clue that not everyone received Theodore's teaching in the same way. During the course of the later eighth to mid ninth century, a penitential attributed to Bede (which contained the Theodorean *XL dies* ruling) and a penitential attributed to Egbert of York (which contained no abortion rulings) were joined together resulting in several Bede-Egbert penitentials compiled in the ninth century. Roughly by the mid ninth century, the version in an innovative and influential penitential, *Pseudo-Bedae*, had come to read:

> If any woman has *voluntarily* destroyed her offspring in the womb before 40 days, she should do penance for one year. But if she has killed it after 40 days, she should do penance for three years; *if indeed she has destroyed it after it was animated, she should do penance as a murderer[.]*[117]

Clearly some churchmen appreciated the questions raised by the Theodorean approach more than the precise answer given.

Reediting Theodore's teaching: The Discipulus
We finish with *Discipulus Umbrensium* to see how the Discipulus arranged two abortion rulings within his penitential. The Discipulus categorized and

---

[115] *Old Irish Penitential* 5.6, trans. D. A. Binchy, in Bieler, *Irish Penitentials*, p. 272.
[116] *P. Bigotianum* 4.1.–2, pp. 226–8.
[117] 'Si qua mulier partum suum ante XL dies in utero sponte perdiderit, I annum peniteat. Si vero post XL dies eum occiderit, III annos peniteat; si vero postquam animatus fuerit eum perdiderit, quasi homicida peniteat[.]', *P. Pseudo-Bedae* 14.1, ed. Wasserschleben, *Bußordnungen*, pp. 265–6 (my italics). For a more detailed overview of the evolution of abortion rulings – *P. Pseudo-Bedae* represents the end of a process with intermediary texts – see Elsakkers, RBL, pp. 407–14, and Elsakkers, 'Vocabulary', pp. 393–4. Note that following Wasserschleben I call *P. Pseudo-Bedae* what Elsakkers refers to as *P. Mixtum* following the painstaking study of the Bede and Egbert penitentials by R. Haggenmüller, *Die Überlieferung der Beda und Egbert zugeschrieben Bussbücher* (Frankfurt, 1991). We return to *P. Pseudo-Bedae* in the next chapter.

collected sins thematically. The abortion rulings appeared in a lengthy section, 'On penance specifically for the married (*De penitentia nubentium specialiter*)'. Offences encompassed marriage regulations (including on bigamy and divorce), forms of adultery and questions of purity and sexual practice. One ruling warned against any woman who used her husband's semen in food as a sort of aphrodisiac.[118] Others insisted that women should not enter church during menstruation or for forty days after childbirth.[119]

The first abortion ruling appeared after condemnations of sexual sin. Intercourse from behind (*retro nubere*) warranted forty days of penance; intercourse literally in the back (*in tergo nubere*), presumably anal intercourse, required penance as if someone had committed bestiality.[120] The other three related to sex on Sundays or other improper times. Next came the first abortion ruling (with two differences from other Theodorean versions italicized):

> Women who perpetrate abortion before it has soul should do one year or three Lents or forty days *according to the nature of their guilt*. And after, that is after 40 days of the seed being received they should do penance as murderers that is three years on Wednesdays and Fridays and in the three Lents. *This is judged ten years according to the canons*.[121]

Between this and the other version of the abortion ruling came two on child murder. If a mother killed her child (*filius*), she received fifteen years without any change except on Sundays. Next, in what was effectively a mitigating poverty clause, if the woman was a pauper (*paupercula*) she had to do penance for seven years; in the (unspecified) canon, the ruling added, if she was a murderer (*homicida*) she had to do penance for ten years.[122] Then came the other abortion ruling: 'A woman who has conceived and kills her infant in the womb before 40 days should do penance for one year. But if after 40 days she should do penance as a murderer.'[123] The final three rulings all concerned infant baptism. If a sickly pagan infant entrusted to a priest died, the priest would be deposed.[124] If an infant died through parental negligence, mother and father had to do a year's penance; three years if the infant was unbaptized

---

[118] *P. Theodori (U)* 1.14.15, p. 308.
[119] *P. Theodori (U)* 1.14.17–18, pp. 308–9.
[120] *P. Theodori (U)* 1.14.21–2, p. 309; cf. the euphemisms 'unnatural intercourse' and 'a graver offence of this kind', with Latin footnotes, in McNeill and Gamer, *Medieval Handbooks*, p. 197. The distinction between these terms, *retro* and *in terga*, was not always clear to later compilers; see P. J. Payer, 'Early Medieval Regulations concerning Marital Sexual Relations', *Journal of Medieval History* 6.4 (1980), 357–8.
[121] 'Mulieres quae abortivum faciunt antequam animam habeat [etc.] iuxta qualitatem culpae peniteant. et post id est post XL dies accepti seminis ut homicidae peniteant [etc.]. Hoc secundum canones decennium iudicatur', *P. Theodori (U)* 1.14.24, p. 309.
[122] *P. Theodori (U)* 1.14.25–6, p. 309.
[123] 'Mulier quae concepit et occidit infantem suum in utero ante XL dies [etc]', *P. Theodori (U)* 1.14.27, p. 310.
[124] *P. Theodori (U)* 1.14.28, p. 310.

and up to three years old. This appears to have been based on a real-life case, for the Discipulus added, 'he [i.e. Theodore] judged this at a certain moment because it happened to be referred to him'.[125] Finally, whoever killed an unbaptized child had to do ten years of penance following the canon, but seven years under discretion.[126]

The Discipulus's editing accentuated tendencies found across the Theodorean recensions. First, abortion, like infanticide, was a lay sin – indeed, a woman's sin. Fathers were mentioned only in the 'real-life' ruling on unbaptized infants. Second, the proximity to rulings on unbaptized infants implied a moral association between abortion/infanticide and the death of unbaptized infants.

A slightly more puzzling editorial decision was to retain two abortion rulings covering similar ground. Unlike in *Canones Cottoniani*, which also had two rulings, the second ruling did not clarify the first. Possibly, the answer lay in a desire to retain two different descriptions of intentional action: in the first, immediately after rulings on married intercourse, to have an abortion (*abortivum facere*); in the second, after infanticide and before infant baptism, to kill one's infant in the womb (*infantem suum in utero occidere*).

Thinking in terms of intentionality also complicates the references to murder. Both of the intervening rulings on child murder implied that being a murderer (*homicida*) or committing murder (*homicidium*) were in some way distinct from or additional to causing the death of a child. The second one of these (the poverty clause) stipulated a longer penance 'if she is a murderer (*homicida*)'. The distinction surely rested on intentionality. This raises a complication in the abortion rulings, which also referred to judging a woman as a murderer (*homicida*) after forty days. Ostensibly – and quite plausibly – whether or not a woman who aborted was a *homicida* depended on whether or not the fetus had *anima*; in dangerously modern terms, whether or not the fetus was a 'person'. But *homicida* also signalled the question of intentionality, the extent to which a woman could be held guilty of murder when the very possibility of being pregnant was not absolutely clear. Forty days was a short period of time very early in pregnancy and was certainly without the kind of obvious external manifestation which presumably underlay a canon in the second book requiring sexual abstinence between spouses from three months before birth.[127]

Finally, we should note the two additional features in the Discipulus's first abortion ruling. First, he added the phrase, 'according to the nature of guilt', to the penances for abortion before forty days. Penitentials were not meant to be read and used mechanistically. Instructions to the contrary which empha-

---

[125] 'Hoc quodam tempore quo contigit ad eum delatum sic iudicavit', *P. Theodori (U)* 1.14.29, p. 310.
[126] *P. Theodori (U)* 1.14.30, p. 310.
[127] *P. Theodori (U)* 2.12.3, p. 326.

sized the need for pastoral discretion and practical reason were outlined in prologues and were sometimes embedded within penitential rulings themselves.[128] Here was an explicit reminder within an abortion ruling. Its context, the surrounding rulings, provided implicit reminders. The preceding rulings on sexual sin suggested an aggravating factor, fornication; the subsequent rulings on infanticide suggested a mitigating factor, poverty. Later compilers drawing on Theodorean material transplanted the poverty clause onto the abortion ruling.[129]

Second, the Discipulus explicitly referred to canonical judgment: 'This is judged 10 years according to the canons'. Which canons did he have in mind? Ancyra is the obvious answer. But given Theodore's eastern background another possible source might have been Basil's letter to Amphilochius, which had also stipulated ten years. There are really two questions here, one regarding the Discipulus and the other regarding Theodore himself. In the case of the Discipulus the matter is not overly complicated. The only canonical source for *Discipulus Umbrensium* is the *Sanblasiana*, an early sixth century collection of Italian origin which also happens to be the only sixth- or seventh-century collection which has survived in an early English manuscript. The *Sanblasiana* used Dionysius Exiguus as a source.[130] The Discipulus had Ancyra in mind.

Theodore's case is a little more complicated. In journeying to England from the Greek East via Rome and Gaul, Theodore had traversed 'four distinct zones in the study of canonical texts'. Disentangling which canonical texts he knew, which he brought with him and which influenced subsequent texts (three distinct questions) remains problematic.[131] One complication is that various works associated with Theodore reflect his high regard for and knowledge of Basil. Theodorean penitentials contain five rulings which explicitly referred to Basil together with several possible derivations.[132] This residue of Basil's canonical judgments probably did not amount to textual resources, for Latin versions of his letters to Amphilochius only survive from the Later Middle Ages.[133] At the same time, it is difficult to assume that Theodore had not encountered them somewhere between Tarsus and Canterbury. Basil's canon on abortion had explicitly rejected hair-splitting over fetal development when assigning moral culpability for abortion. The intention, Basil had

---

[128] Cf. P. J. Payer, 'The Humanism of the Penitentials and the Continuity of Penitential Tradition', *Mediaeval Studies* 46 (1984), 342–6.

[129] See below p. 160 on *P. Bedae*.

[130] M. Brett, 'Theodore and the Latin Canon Law', in *Archbishop Theodore*, pp. 125, 136–7; M. Lapidge, 'The School of Theodore and Hadrian', *Anglo-Saxon England* 15 (1986), 66. On the *Sanblasiana*, see too Kéry, *Canonical Collections*, pp. 29–30.

[131] Brett, 'Theodore and the Latin Canon Law', pp. 120–38 (quotation at p. 121).

[132] Bischoff and Lapidge, *Biblical Commentaries*, p. 151; R. E. Reynolds, 'Basil and the Early Medieval Latin Canonical Collections', in *Basil of Caesarea: Christian, Humanist, Ascetic*, 2 vols., ed. P. J. Fedwick (Toronto, 1981), II, pp. 521–2.

[133] P. J. Fedwick, 'The Translation of the Works of Basil before 1400', in *Basil of Caesarea*, II, pp. 455–73.

reasoned, was always to be treated as murder. Theodore was more likely to have been aware of Basil's approach to abortion than any western churchmen in the Early Middle Ages. Ironically, it was in penitentials associated with Theodore's teaching – and which drew elsewhere on Basil as an authority – that the very sort of distinction which the Greek father had rejected gained a broad clerical readership.

Compilers and readers: Abortion rulings in later penitentials

Roughly by the turn of the eighth century three penitential rulings on abortion had emerged independently:

- *Decipere partum* ('If anyone has *decipere*-d a woman's child ...'), from the Columbanan tradition; included in the *simplices*;
- *Voluntarie* ('If a woman has voluntarily perpetrated abortion ...'), from the *simplices* tradition;
- *XL dies* ('If a woman kills her child before 40 days ...'), from the Theodorean tradition.

The genealogy of these rulings elaborated above demonstrates how different moral priorities and concerns generated ecclesiastical action against abortion. But these genealogies were obscured to subsequent readers for the simple reason that the majority read them in mixed compilations, which drew on multiple penitential traditions and outnumbered older penitentials. From an early stage, compilers drew on textual resources. But as the textual resources available to compilers grew in size and quantity, they needed to find ways to arrange their works in order to help readers pinpoint rulings on specific sins and, more broadly, to enhance the pedagogic function of their texts by grouping related rulings together. To observe how compilers went about this task is also to observe how the majority of clerical readers encountered penitential rulings on abortion.

The practical problem is demonstrated well by *Merseburgense A*, composed in Francia or northern Italy in the later eighth or early ninth century.[134] It reproduced the basic *simplices* core, onto which the compiler added material from *Cummeani*, some Theodorean penitential rulings (*Canones Gregorii* 91–103, i.e., not including the abortion ruling) and a mixed penitential, *Excarpsus Cummeani*, to which we turn in a moment. Following the order in the *simplices*, *Decipere partum* appeared early on and *Voluntarie* a little later after the Columbanan material. *Merseburgense A* also added a version of the Ancyran canon after the core. A reader of *Merseburgense A* interested in, for example, intentional abortion by a woman would have been able to consult

---

[134] Kottje, *Paenitentialia*, pp. xxv–xxvii, xlii; Meens, *Penance*, p. 112.

two rulings, *Voluntarie* and the Ancyran canon; but he would have had to read *Merseburgense A* through from start to finish in order to find them.[135]

The more material a compiler drew upon, the more acute the problem became. Consequently several found different ways of categorizing and reordering their material, sometimes under specific headings and with ascriptions to sources. One simple solution appeared in *Sangallense tripartitum* structured in three distinct parts, each following a distinct penitential tradition (*simplices*, Theodorean, Cummeanic). Canons were carefully grouped under clear headings within each part. In the first section, derived from the *simplices* tradition, a version of *Decipere partum* appeared (substituting *conceptum* for *partum*) alongside the ruling on smothering infants under the heading, 'On abortions' (*De avorsis*); *Voluntarie* appeared under the heading, *De maleficis*[136]; *XL dies* appeared among rulings on homicide ascribed to Theodore.[137]

Sangellense tripartitum was not, however, representative of most penitentials, for it only survives in a single manuscript produced at St Gall in the second quarter of the ninth century.[138] A more representative example is *Excarpsus Cummeani*, which contained all three rulings on abortion together with the Ancyra canon. This influential penitential was probably produced around the second quarter of the eighth century and had connections with the monastery of Corbie, where a compilation of the *Vetus Gallica* was produced in c. 740. *Excarpsus Cummeani* was an especially popular work surviving in twenty-eight manuscripts (six or so from the eighth century).[139] In this long compilation rulings were categorized in thematic sections under sometimes lengthy titles. Within these sections, rulings from ascribed sources tended to be bunched together. The Ancyran canon appeared ascribed under one such lengthy title ('On adultery and *raptus* and incest and dismissed wives, illicit times of intercourse, vices of lechery or with beasts, and who, after he has vowed himself to God, has returned to the world and scorned vows').[140] Next, under another lengthy title ('On murder and spilling of blood without death and smothered infants, those who die without baptism and abortion and

---

[135] *P. Merseburgense A* 10, 33, 46, pp. 128, 135, 140–1.
[136] *P. Sangallense tripartitum* (I) 18, 28, ed. Meens, *Boeteboek*, pp. 333–4. This version of *Voluntarie* included a reduced penance for unintentional miscarriage; see p. 142 n. 71 above.
[137] *P. Sangallense tripartitum* (II) 5, p. 336.
[138] *P. Sangellense tripartitum* must nonetheless be older since it used *P. Capitula iudiciorum*, discussed below, as a source; see Meens, *Boeteboek*, pp. 565–6. Both penitentials substituted *conceptum* for *partum* in the *Decipere partum* ruling.
[139] Meens, *Penance*, pp. 108–11, with pp. 229–30, for a list of over two dozen manuscripts and possible connections with Boniface.
[140] *P. Excarpsus Cummeani* 3.23, ed. Wasserschleben, *Bußordnungen*, pp. 473–4 (as *P. Cummeani*). The form of the canon included the addition about female accomplices; it mentioned the ten-year penance without reference to the earlier ruling of lifetime excommunication. This was the third of three rulings in a row derived from Ancyra, the first of which (3.21) was ascribed to Ancyra.

Abortion in the Early Middle Ages

those who cut off their limbs and those who offer leadership to barbarians') appeared three rulings: Ancyra (ascribed), *XL dies* (ascribed to Theodore and in a form akin to *Canones Gregorii* 105–6 and *Discipulus Umbrensium* 1.14.27); and *Voluntarie* ('from another penitential').[141] Finally, the triad on *maleficium* including *Decipere partum* appeared (unascribed) in a section under a heading listing various proscribed magical and superstitious practices beginning with magicians (*maleficos*) and poisoners (*veneficos*).[142] The double appearance of the Ancyran canon was no mistake, for the arrangement in *Excarpsus Cummeani* was deliberate. The compiler had made a good job of making the abortion rulings accessible. Three rulings (Ancyra, *XL dies* and *Voluntarie*) appeared under a heading on murder which included reference to abortion. Others could be found in sections on fornication and sexual sin (Ancyra, again) and magic (*Decipere partum*).

Other 'mixed' or 'tripartite' penitentials also demonstrate careful organization of material with varying degrees of ascription to authorities. The arrangement and ascriptions in the later eighth century *Remense* were similar to *Excarpsus Cummeani*.[143] *Vindobense B*, probably compiled in Salzburg around the turn of the ninth century under the influence of its bishop, Arn, drew on *Excarpsus Cummeani*, Theodorean material (from the *Discipulus Umbrensium* recension) and, unusually, *Vinniani*.[144] *Vindobense B* did not tend to ascribe its sources but otherwise the compiler made a comparable arrangement: abortion rulings amid rulings on murder, violence, etc., with Ancyra connected to sexual sin and *Decipere partum* to magical and superstitious practices.[145] A version of *Vinniani* 20–1 (abortifacient magic and the woman who bears a child in *ruina maxima*) also appeared earlier amid material derived from *Vinniani*, but separately from *Vinniani* 18–19 on lethal and love magic.[146]

One final example from a compiler who was even more diligent. *Capitula Iudiciorum* was a later eighth century penitential which survives in eight

---

[141] P. *Excarpsus Cummeani* 6.3, 11, 21, pp. 478–9; this version of Ancyra (6.3) did refer to the 'more humane' ten-year penance.

[142] P. *Excarpsus Cummeani* 7.1–2, pp. 480–1.

[143] P. *Remense* 8.20 (*Voluntarie*; ascribed to 'another penitential'), 8.26 (*XL Dies*, as in P. *Theodori (U)* 1.14.24; from a 'Roman penitential…Theodore said'), 8.46 (*XL Dies*, as in P. *Theodori (U)* 1.14.27; 'another penitential. Theodore said'), 8.49 (Ancyra), all under a heading on murder, spilling of blood, abortion etc.; 9.1–2 (*Maleficium* triad; unascribed), under a heading on magicians, poisoners, etc., ed. Asbach, *Poenitentiale*, supplement, pp. 51–4, 56.

[144] Meens, *Boeteboek*, pp. 566–7.

[145] P. *Vindobense B* 33.9 (*XL Dies*, as in P. *Theodori (U)* 1.14.27), 33.21 (*Voluntarie*), under *De homicidio* (etc.) heading derived from P. *Excarpsus Cummeani*; 30.3 (Ancyra) under heading, 'What we say should be observed about incestuous unions', in a section on marital and sexual offences; 34.1–2 (*Decipere partum*), under the *De maleficis* (etc.) heading derived from P. *Excarpsus Cummeani*: ed. Meens, *Boeteboek*, pp. 408–9, 400, 412.

[146] P. *Vindobense B* 12.6–7, separated from 18.1–2, pp. 378–80, 384.

manuscripts and was used in subsequent canonical and penitential works.[147] Following rulings under headings on murder and on bloodshed, the compiler collected all of the relevant abortion rulings in one place under the heading, 'On smothered infants and abortions' (*De oppressis infantis vel abortis*). The heading is suggestive, especially given that other infanticide rulings appeared with rulings on murder. The implication was that ambiguities surrounding parental culpability for overlain infants were comparable to those which affected culpability for abortion.[148] A version of *Decipere partum* (substituting *conceptum* for *partum*), *Voluntarie* and the Ancyran canon appeared ascribed to 'judgement of the canons', and a short version of *XL dies* ascribed to the 'judgment of Theodore'.[149]

One of Theodore's biblical commentaries warned that mandrake was a soporific if eaten in large quantities.[150] Sifting through longer penitential compilations risks much the same effect, but they are important because they are far more representative of clerical readers' encounters with abortion rulings than earlier penitentials. There are more surviving manuscript copies of *Excarpsus Cummeani*, which contained all three penitential rulings as well as the Ancyran canon, than manuscript copies of *Vinniani*, *Columbani* and the *simplices* combined. Further, penitentials which did not contain one or other ruling often survived in manuscripts alongside other penitentials which filled the gap.[151] With a few exceptions, a cleric reading a penitential from, say, the second half of the eighth century had access one way or another to multiple abortion rulings.

Certain tendencies shaped how readers encountered these rulings – and, indeed, who these readers were, for by the middle of the eighth century we can discern a growing number of manuscripts intended for use in pastoral care.[152] First, owing to the arrangement of rulings, there was a far stronger association between abortion and forms of murder and violence – these were the sections where most abortion rulings ended up – than in earlier penitentials. Second, rulings specifying female culprits (*Voluntarie, XL Dies*, Ancyran canon) were not infrequently grouped together. Consequently, there was a stronger association of abortion with female culprits than in the Columbanan/ *simplices* tradition, though it should be stressed that the gender of culprits in

---

[147] Meens, *Boeteboek*, p. 567.
[148] *P. Capitula Iudiciorum* 1.2h–I, ed. Meens, *Boeteboek*, p. 438.
[149] *P. Capitula Iudiciorum* 3.1b–d, 2a, with 1a (*opprimere* ruling from *simplices*) and 2b (unbaptized infants ruling from Theodorean penitentials), pp. 438–40. 3.1c was another version of *Voluntarie* which included a reduced penance for unintentional abortion.
[150] PentI 173, Bischoff and Lapidge, *Biblical Commentaries*, p. 334.
[151] For example, *P. Sangallense simplex*, the only one of the *simplices* to contain no abortion rulings, survives in the same manuscript as *P. Sangallense tripartitum* and *P. Vinniani*; see p. 133 n. 29 above.
[152] Meens, *Penance*, p. 114.

Decipere partum was either male or unspecified.¹⁵³ Third, penitential rulings were not devoid of a sense of authority. Not every compiler ascribed rulings or ascribed them accurately (if by our standards rather than theirs) but where they did there was a mingling – certainly no palpable dichotomy – between canonical and penitential judgment. Clearly conciliar tradition – Ancyra – was important, but Theodore was also remembered as an important authority through the Early Middle Ages and beyond.¹⁵⁴

A fourth tendency, related to the fact that readers encountered a variety of rulings on abortion, requires elaboration. Penitential rulings yield traces of active deliberation by compilers but they were also guidelines with which to think about abortion. They imply thought on the part of readers insofar as they invited thought by readers. The practical reasoning intrinsic to the application of rulings in juridical, catechetical or confessional contexts, reasoning which had to negotiate circumstantial and personal factors affecting culpability as well as ambiguities specific to abortion, was only occasionally explicit in rulings themselves. But this practical reasoning was nonetheless crucial.¹⁵⁵

Suppose a reader of *Excarpsus Cummeani* looked up abortion rulings. He would have found them fairly straightforward to locate. He would have also encountered variations in penances, behavioural contexts, aggravating and mitigating factors, and the question of whether or not abortion really was murder. How did a clerical reader make sense of these variations? A clue lies in a penitential spuriously attributed to Bede and probably composed earlier than its oldest manuscript witness from the early ninth century. *Bedae*, a fairly short penitential with a strong insular flavour, reproduced a version of *XL dies* with an addition: 'But it makes a great difference whether a poor woman (*paupercula*) does this because of the difficulty of rearing or a fornicating woman for the sake of hiding her crime'.¹⁵⁶ The *paupercula* clause, originally qualifying Theodorean rulings on infanticide, was now applied to highlight a mitigat-

---

[153] The version of Ancyra in some copies of *P. Remense* did not clearly specify that accomplices to abortion were female. Cf. 'De mulieribus *qui* fornicantur et partus suos necant sed et de his *qui* agunt ut uterus conceptus excutiant', *Remense* 8.49, p. 54 (my italics); given use of *qui* instead of *quae* in the opening words, this might have been a case of sloppy grammar as much as careful wording.

[154] See J. J. Contreni, 'Glossing the Bible in the Early Middle Ages: Theodore and Hadrian of Canterbury and John Scottus (Eriugena)', in *The Study of the Bible in the Carolingian Era*, ed. C. Chazelle and B. Van Name Edwards (Turnhout, 2003), p. 19, on a tenth-century genealogy of great teachers ending with Eriugena which, passing along the likes of Bede and Rabanus Maurus en route, began with Theodore and Hadrian, and on an image in a twelfth-century manuscript depicting Theodore and Eriugena seated together in debate.

[155] Cf. Payer, 'Humanism', 242–6.

[156] 'Sed distat multum, utrum paupercula pro difficultate nutriendi an fornicaria causa sui sceleris celandi faciat', *P. Bedae* 4.12, ed. Wasserschleben, *Bußordnungen*, p. 225. The same clause appears in the version of this ruling in *P. Pseudo-Bedae*, quoted above at p. 152; see Elsakkers, RBL, p. 407 (note that I call *P. Bedae* what Elsakkers refers to as *P. Ps.-Bedae*).

ing factor in abortion with an aggravating factor (fornication) added in too. The compiler of *Bedae* had read between the lines and joined up the dots.[157] Compilers constitute a special subset of reader in that they have left traces of how they read their sources in the form of usually inconspicuous, occasionally more conspicuous, variants. But when considering readers in general, the necessary absence of evidence does not entail evidence of absence. The proximity between penitential rulings on abortion and infant baptism implied a mental connection which was given explicit expression in a miscellany of sources which we will encounter in subsequent chapters. We should assume readers too read between the lines and joined up the dots. They were certainly nudged in that direction by the texts which they were reading. The variation which our reader of *Excarpsus Cummeani* would have encountered reflected moral complexities and ambiguities of abortion as defined by ecclesiastical compilers. But variation also had a practical function. The mixed rulings were prompts for negotiating key questions concerning abortion. Did she really have an abortion on purpose? Why did she resort to it? Did she have something to hide? Is she a *paupercula*? Did she realize that she was killing her own child? Did she know she was pregnant? Did any other man or woman help her? (Perhaps) he who fathered her child?

Absence of contraception?
The final consideration concerns an absence. Attentive readers might have noticed it. Where were penitential rulings which clearly addressed attempts to prevent conception? John Noonan assumed that such rulings existed from an early stage in the form of 'prohibitions of various forms of marital intercourse in which procreation was intentionally avoided'. For Noonan, a number of sexual practices which could not be procreative (my references above to intercourse *in terga* or semen as an aphrodisiac had a purpose beyond prurience) were effectively condemned as contraceptive practices.[158] Historians have rightly criticized Noonan for eliding intention and effect. Rulings on sexual offences often addressed practices which were non-procreative in effect – but there was no indication that this is why such practices were being condemned.[159] Whoever performed intercourse *in terga* 'ought to do penance like he who [did it] with animals'. The problem lay in transgression of what we might call the moral aesthetic of sex in the clerical imaginary.[160] Likewise,

---

[157] One can trace similar dynamics in distinct mini-traditions of penitential composition in, respectively, France, Italy and Spain in the tenth century and beyond; see Elsakkers, RBL, pp. 426–34.
[158] *Contraception*, p. 161. Noonan distinguished between these and unequivocal condemnations of preventing conception, though conventional dating of penitentials when he wrote led him to place the latter in the eighth century.
[159] P. Payer, *Sex and the Penitentials: The Development of a Sexual Code, 550–1150* (Toronto, 1984), pp. 33–4.
[160] 'penitere debet quasi ille qui cum animalibus', *P. Theodori* (U) 1.14.22, p. 309.

Abortion in the Early Middle Ages

disgust at use of semen in food, like disgust at uses of other bodily fluids such as blood, rested on semi-articulate notions of pollution; the aphrodisiac use of semen also connected this form of pollution to adultery and other sexual sin.[161] As Jean-Louis Flandrin put it, Noonan read back the later medieval or certainly modern Catholic 'unitary concept of the "crime against nature"' into early medieval penitentials.[162] Of course, preventing conception could exist in varying degrees of haziness alongside attempts to cause abortion. But, if we exclude the ambiguity of *Decipere partum*, there were no such rulings in penitentials until the ninth century, to which we shall turn in the next chapter.

If penitential compilers did not apply a coherent procreative norm to the sexual sins which they listed, some readers might well have brought such a norm to penitentials – not least when texts within the same manuscript outlined such a norm. Possible examples are numerous, so I restrict myself to two. First, as Rob Meens has shown, Theodorean penitentials often circulated with versions of Gregory the Great's famous *Libellus responsionum*, his set of answers to Augustine of Canterbury's questions about ritual and sexual taboos.[163] The *Libellus* conveyed something of Gregory's theology of marriage. Lawful intercourse was for procreation and not lust, for 'fleshly intercourse must be for the sake of producing children and not the satisfaction of vicious instincts'.[164] Readers of a fair number of manuscripts had access to penitential rulings on sexual offences and Gregory's theology of marriage.[165]

The second example is more specific. The St Gall manuscript containing *Sangallense tripartitum* also contained *Vinniani*. One curious feature of *Vinniani* not mentioned above was a potted theology of marriage in a ruling on lay chastity. Vinniaus urged continence in marriage 'because marriage without continence is not licit but a sin and [marriage] is granted by God's authority not for lust but for the sake of children, just as it is written, "And they will be two in one flesh" [Gen. 2. 24, Mt. 19. 5]'. He then listed periods of sexual abstinence required for liturgical or physiological reasons (including abstinence

---

[161] *P. Theodori (U)* 1.14.15, p. 308, mentions semen as aphrodisiac ('ut inde plus amoris accipiat') in a ruling on adultery; the next two rulings address tasting blood for medicinal purposes and menstruating women.

[162] Flandrin, 'Contraception', p. 29.

[163] R. Meens, 'Questioning Ritual Purity: The Influence of Gregory the Great's answers to Augustine's Queries about Childbirth, Menstruation and Sexuality', in *St Augustine and the Conversion of England*, ed. R. Gameson (Sutton, 1999), pp. 174–86.

[164] 'carnis commixtio creandorum liberorum sit gratia, non satisfactio vitiorum', Bede, *Historia Ecclesiastica Gentis Anglorum*, 1.27.8, ed. and trans. B. Colgrave and R. A. B. Mynors, *Bede's Ecclesiastical History of the English People* (Oxford, 1969), pp. 96–7; cf. d'Avray, *Medieval Marriage*, pp. 66–7, for a nuanced appreciation of Gregory's theology of marriage in another widely circulated work, *Regula pastoralis*.

[165] Some examples: Munich, Bayerische Staatsbibliothek, Clm 14780 contained *P. Burgundense*, *P. Theodori (G)*, and the *Libellus*; Oxford, Bodleian Library, MS Bodl. 311 (2122) contained *P. Oxoniense I*, *P. Theodori (G)* and the *Libellus*: Kottje, *Paenitentialia*, pp. xxxiv, xxxviii.

from conception up to birth).¹⁶⁶ For Gregory and Vinniaus alike – and we have already seen this in Caesarius's case – procreation was normative because of the relation between lust and carnality rather than because of any proto-natural law argument. Nonetheless, procreation defined the proper exercise of married sexuality and it is plausible that some readers of penitentials joined up the dots intertextually.

* * *

It is time to catch a breath. Between the sixth and ninth centuries a growing range of rulings on abortion circulated in penitentials. At their points of origin these rulings were generated by specific concerns: the sexual status of clerics and nuns; magical practices and recourse to poisons; voluntary abortion as a female sin. From the eighth century the specificity of these original concerns was obscured in larger and more widely circulated compilations which brought these rulings together. One common factor across early and later penitentials was a sense of the moral complexity of abortion. The idiom in which rulings were articulated varied significantly: to ensnare offspring, to perpetrate abortion, to kill a child in the womb. But in different ways, from the phrasing of rulings to the organization of material, compilers of penitentials navigated the difficulty of ascertaining whether abortion entailed a form of murder. The prospect that abortion was a response to sexual sin cast its shadow. Noticeably, too, abortion was one of a few sins in which female perpetrators were explicitly specified. At the same time, with the exception of penitentials drawing exclusively on Theodorean material, penitentials contained rulings which implied the possibility of male, especially clerical, entanglement with abortion.

Some older dismissals of the penitentials contain a kernel of truth. On one such view, penitentials were little more than 'abstract compendi[a] of suppositious crimes and unnatural sins, thought up in the cloister by the tortuous intellect of the clerical scribe'.¹⁶⁷ What penitentials reveal is clerical thought, the thought of compilers but also the textual prompts by which readers were prompted to think about the messy realities of sin in catechetical, juridical or confessional contexts. Rather than functioning as condensed versions of moral arguments, the practical function of rulings on abortion was to raise as much as resolve moral questions surrounding abortion. To the extent that penances listed in penitentials were administered in actual confessional encounters, there was a final kind of thought they invited: penitents' reflection on their sins. Abortion rulings, like other rulings, depended on the penitent's

---

166 'quia matrimonium sine continentia non ligitimum sed peccatum est et non ad libidinem sed causa filiorum Deo auctore concessum est, sicut scriptum est: Et erunt duo in carne una'; cf. 'postquam conceperit uxor non intrabit ad eam usquequo genuerit filium', *P. Vinniani* 46, pp. 90–2.
167 Nora Chadwick, quoted in Glasser, 'Early Anglo-Saxon Penitentials', 49.

complicity in confessing sins and receiving the spiritual medicine of remedial penance. If penitential compilers were right to be concerned that men and women, clerical and lay, might resort to abortion (or infanticide) to conceal sexual sin, we cannot take this complicity for granted.

Penitentials demonstrate how rejection of abortion was being both integrated into and shaped by programmes of church reform, clerical education and pastoral practice. But as bishops reflected intensively on the textual resources underlying these programmes in the early decades of the ninth century, concerns over the authority of ecclesiastical legislation gave rise to concerns over the extent to which penitentials helped or hindered pastoral practice. This moment in the history of the Carolingian church has profoundly shaped narratives of church tradition on abortion. But the story is complicated, for concerns over canonical authority affected the handling of abortion in more intricate ways than historians have recognized.

5
Tradition In Practice: Handling Abortion under the Carolingians

In *c.* 781 Alcuin sent what he called a small gift to Charlemagne. It took the form of two collections of letters supposedly exchanged between ancient figures: a correspondence between the Roman philosopher Seneca and the apostle Paul, and a correspondence between Alexander the Great and Dindimus, king of the Brahmans. Alcuin's dedicatory epigram is the earliest surviving reference to what came to be known as the *Collatio Alexandri et Dindimi*, an imaginary correspondence in which Alexander and Dindimus debated the moral superiority of their kingdoms. The Brahmans led a proudly ascetic life, whose excessive rigours Alexander rejected as a form of *dementia*.[1]

Although Alcuin's dedicatory epigram is the earliest reference to the *Collatio* and the oldest surviving copies date from the ninth century, it was not a Carolingian composition. Scholars roughly agree that it was written between the later fourth and sixth centuries. Interpretations of its original purpose – in effect, whether Alexander or Dindimus (or neither) was meant to be the winner in this epistolary contest – have varied remarkably. The *Collatio* has been read as an attack upon Alexander by late antique Cynic philosophers; as an attack on the austerity of the Cynics parodied in the figure of Dindimus; as an anti-ascetic tract associated with the likes of Jerome's *bête noire*, Jovinian; and as a late antique Christian attack on Alexander.[2] The history of the Brahmans' reputation and medieval reception of the *Collatio* is much clearer. Already in Late Antiquity the Brahmans enjoyed a laudable reputation among Christian writers and later medieval intellectuals would regard Dindimus as the 'virtuous heathen *par excellence*'.[3] Alcuin was very much aligned with this historical trajectory. Making no mention of Alexander he drew Charlemagne's attention to the Brahman people, the *gens Bragmana*,

---

[1] *Collatio Alexandri et Dindimi* 3, ed. T. Pritchard, 'The Collatio Alexandri et Dindimi: A Revised Text', *Classica et mediaevalia* 46 (1995), 270. The *Collatio* consists of five responses and counter-responses, with Alexander getting the first, middle and last word in the exchange.

[2] Pritchard, 'Collatio', 255–60; G. Cary, *The Medieval Alexander* (Cambridge, 1956), pp. 13–14.

[3] T. Hahn, 'The Indian Tradition in Western Medieval Intellectual History', *Viator* 9 (1978), 225 (italics in original); cf. Cary, *Medieval Alexander*, pp. 91–4.

which 'stands out for its admirable ways' and in which a 'reader can see faith with his mind'.[4]

What would Charlemagne have made of the *gens Bragmana*? The Brahmans lived out an equality of poverty. Their temples were not adorned with precious metals and gems.[5] They took bodily renunciation so seriously that they refused to rely on medicinal herbs to cure ailments.[6] Charlemagne might have found the Brahman approach to warfare and law-making especially alien. The Brahmans were staunch pacifists and shunned all legislation because laws educated people in the crimes they were meant to prohibit.[7] But Charlemagne might have found Brahman claims about sexual mores more recognizable. No one, the Brahman king declared, could accuse the *gens Bragmana* of incest, adultery or other sexual deviations. To prove his point Dindimus turned to abortion:

> It is not lust but love of offspring which reminds us of intercourse. We do not know love unless it is holy. We do not prevent the nascent young from growing by drinking up abortions or search after the death of another within a living body. Still less do we deprive God of his due by conceiving people in a sterile way[.][8]

Dindimus associated abortion with sexual transgression, the taking of life and even a kind of theological violence, ideas about abortion which would scarcely raise an eyebrow if they had been written by an early medieval bishop. It is significant that the closest we can place the most famous Carolingian king to the question of abortion is by looking at what one of his most famous scholars invited him to read. Thinking about readers of texts will be crucial in this chapter. To examine the handling of abortion under the Carolingians is to examine readers' encounters with texts.

The *Collatio* is also a reminder of a larger mass of material on abortion copied and read in Carolingian manuscripts. The overwhelming majority of Latin sources examined in preceding chapters had at least some Carolingian readers. We will come to canonical collections, conciliar decrees, penitentials and other prescriptive ecclesiastical texts. *Vitae* of saints and their strange 'abortion miracles' were being read too. By the ninth century Fortunatus's story of Germanus's miraculous birth had evidently entered Parisian lore.

---

[4] 'miribus extat ... lector mente fidem videat', PL 101, col. 1375C.
[5] *Collatio* 2.2, 16, pp. 263, 267.
[6] *Collatio* 2.2, 11, pp. 263, 266. On interest in medicinal herb-collecting at Charlemagne's court, see L. MacKinney, *Early Medieval Medicine, with special reference to France and Chartres* (Baltimore, 1937), pp. 86–7.
[7] *Collatio* 2.8, 3, pp. 265, 263.
[8] 'Ad concubitum non admonet nos libido sed subolis amor. Non novimus amorem nisi pium. Abortivis haustibus procedere feta nascentia non vetamus nec intra vivum corpus mortem investigamus alterius. In hominibus concipiendis sterilitatis obitu minime Deum suo iure privamus[.]', *Collatio* 2.7, pp. 264–5.

Abortion under the Carolingians

After the Viking siege of Paris in 885–6, Abbo, a monk of Saint-Germain-des-Prés, celebrated Germanus's supernatural thwarting of the Northmen in their ships. Recalling Germanus's very first miracle, Abbo likened his favourite saint to a biblical figure who had also given prophetic signs from the womb:

> In mother's womb he learned to spread his signs around
> And show his lofty power before he saw day's light.
> Say reader, please, if any saint has ever done
> Such deeds? Well maybe John the Baptist did them too,
> So let my Germain be revered with equal awe!⁹

Not just ecclesiastical texts but also a significant but still understudied corpus of medical writings – copies or adaptations of older works alongside some original texts – could be found in Carolingian libraries.¹⁰ There was also a number of relevant literary texts from antiquity. The oldest manuscript copies of Ovid's *Amores* date from the ninth century, probably derived from an original made *c.* 800.¹¹ Juvenal's *Saturae* nestled on the shelves of Charlemagne's court library and the late Carolingian biblical scholar Remigius of Auxerre even wrote a (now lost) commentary on Juvenal.¹²

Hints of precisely how the Carolingian literati interpreted Ovid's response to his mistress Corinna's attempted abortion or Juvenal's biting satire on wealthy adulteresses are elusive.¹³ But it is inconceivable that interpretative

---

⁹ 'Fundere signa prius didicit genetricis in alvo / Anteque virtutem celsam quam cernere lucem. / Talia quis, lector, sanctorum gesserit umquam, / Cedo! sacer forsan, sodes, babtista Iohannes; / Ergo meus similis Germanus huic habeatur', *Bella Parisiacae urbis* 2.373–7, MGH Poetae 4.1, p. 108; trans. A. Adams and A. G. Rigg, 'A Verse Translation of Abbo of St. Germain's *Bella Parisiacae urbis*', *Journal of Medieval Latin* 14 (2004), 14. See p. 177 n.62 below on Brigit of Kildare.

¹⁰ Manuscripts: Beccaria, *Codici*; Wickersheimer, *Manuscrits*. On the place of medical learning in the Carolingian renaissance, see J. J. Contreni, 'Masters and Medicine in Northern France during the Reign of Charles the Bald', in *Charles the Bald: Court and Kingdom*, 2nd edn, ed. M. T. Gibson and J. L. Nelson (Aldershot, 1990), pp. 267–82; see too F. S. Paxton, 'Curing Bodies – Curing Souls: Hrabanus Maurus, Medical Education, and the Clergy in Ninth-Century Francia', *JHMAS* 50.2 (1995), 230–52.

¹¹ E. J. Kenney, 'The Manuscript Tradition of Ovid's Amores, Ars Amatoria, and Remedia Amoris', *Classical Quarterly*, n.s., 12.1 (1962), 1–3, 6–9; R. J. Tarrant, 'Ovid', in *Texts and Transmission: A Survey of the Latin Classics*, ed. L. D. Reynolds (Oxford, 1983), pp. 259–61.

¹² H. N. Parker, 'Manuscripts of Juvenal and Persius', and H. N. Parker and S. Braund, 'Imperial Satire and the Scholars', both in *A Companion to Persius and Juvenal*, ed. S. Braund and J. Osgood (Oxford, 2012), respectively, pp. 155–7 (Charlemagne's library and more generally in the Carolingian renaissance), 441 (Remigius). On manuscripts: R. J. Tarrant, 'Juvenal', in *Texts and Transmission*, pp. 200–3; C. E. Finch, 'Juvenal in Codex Vat. Lat. 5204', *Classical Philology* 65.1 (1970), 47–8.

¹³ The copy of *Amores* 2.14 in Paris, Bibliothèque nationale de France, MS latin 8242, a Corbie manuscript from the last quarter of the ninth century, had the title: 'to a lover who perpetrated abortion [*ad amicam quae fecit abortum*]': see Kenney, *P. Ovidi Nasonis*, p. 60 (P in critical apparatus). On Alcuin's familiarity with Corinna's

habits were not shaped by Carolingian ecclesiastical action on abortion. A pseudo-Bonifatian sermon produced by a north Frankish bishop just after the turn of the ninth century counted 'causing abortion' among the sins to be renounced at baptism.[14] A rule drawn up for a council at Aachen convened under Louis the Pious in 816 reproduced Jerome's letter to Eustochium, including the passage on the triple guilt of religious women who resorted to abortion.[15] The Vulgate version of Exodus 21. 22–5 addressed abortion in the collection of capitularies put together by the mysterious Benedictus Levita.[16] Condemnation of abortion was deeply embedded within Carolingian programmes for pastoral care, clerical education and social reform. It was under the Carolingians that a sense of church tradition on abortion was really consolidated. But Carolingian texts also provide examples of a growing pastoral and juridical reflexivity on abortion, and perhaps even responsiveness to real-life behaviour. The handling of abortion in Carolingian ecclesiastical texts was shaped by a creative tension between authority and innovation, between respecting the past and responding to the present. As we shall see, this tension has shaped modern interpretations of these texts too.

Epicentres of condemnation: Abortion and Carolingian reform

The focus of much of this chapter is on the ninth century. But this should not imply an earlier vacuum and we will make an important detour into the eighth century below. Penitentials were not the only relevant sources produced before the intensification of Carolingian reform from the last decades or so of the eighth century. Manuals produced for missionaries in the Frankish frontierland, like the eighth-century Würzburg homiliary containing some of Caesarius's sermons communicated important material on abortion.[17] Further south and a little earlier Pirminius, founder of the monastery at Reichenau in 724, wove Caesarius's formulation on preventing conception as murder into his own manual for priests.[18] A pseudo-Augustinian homiliary surviving in an early eighth century manuscript was more unusual in smearing the practice of abortion with paganism. Any person 'who through *maleficia* makes it so

---

nightingale in *Amores* 2.6, if not her abortion attempts in *Amores* 2.13–14, see M. L. Kim, 'A Parrot and Piety: Alcuin's Nightingale and Ovid's "*Amores*" 2.6', *Latomus* 51.4 (1992), 881–91.

[14] 'abortum facere', Pseudo-Boniface, *Sermo* 15.1, PL 89, col. 870A–B; on the pseudo-Bonifatian sermons, see Hall, 'Early Medieval Sermon', p. 240.
[15] *Institutio sanctimonialium Aquisgranensis*, MGH Conc. 2.1, p. 426.
[16] *Capitularia* 6.12–13, MGH LL 2.2, p. 75.
[17] See pp. 62–3 above.
[18] *Scarapsus* 21, MGH QQ 25, pp. 73–4.

that women do not conceive or throw out conceived infants, are not Christians but pagans'.[19]

There are, nonetheless, reasons for concentrating mainly on the ninth century. First, some of the most intriguing texts lie roughly around the middle decades of the ninth century. Second, action by reform councils in the 810s–820s have been particularly significant in historiographical narratives of church tradition on abortion. Third, the historical context inaugurated by Charlemagne's reform efforts from c. 789 and extending throughout the ninth century, an ongoing 'program, educational in nature and religious in content, aimed at the thorough Christianization of all of society'.[20] The impulses underlying reform were not altogether novel but the scale and resources with which it was pursued were.[21] Carolingian reform also generated a particular focus on the priest in his locality as a 'sole contact between the people and the world of learning'.[22] Priestly responsibility for the education, guidance and salvation of communities was intensively emphasized. To this end priests needed to be equipped with the requisite education and textual tools. The remnants of attempts to translate the ideals of *correctio* into practice are the diverse manuscripts containing different combinations of liturgical, pedagogical, canonical and penitential texts. The sources examined in this chapter were all produced as part of the 'top-down' *correctio* of Carolingian society and typically emanated from episcopal epicentres of reform; they articulated the ends and provided the means by which the vision of a Christian society was to be put into practice.

Shepherding resources: Abortion within episcopal statutes

Not every ecclesiastical text circulating along reforming currents offers glimpses of intricate deliberation on abortion. But some are nonetheless important in demonstrating that condemnation of abortion was woven into initiatives designed to reach local priests. This is especially visible in episcopal statutes, the scholarly designation for a kind of ecclesiastical memorandum issued from episcopal centres by Carolingian bishops.[23]

Abortion made it into some, though certainly not all, episcopal statutes.

[19] 'qui per maleficia mulieribus facit, ut non concipiant aut conceptos infantes foras egiciant, non christiani, sed pagani sunt', *Homilia de sacrilegiis* 6.18, ed. C. P. Caspari, *Eine Augustin fälschlich beigelegte 'Homilia de Sacrilegiis'* (Christiania, 1886), p. 11. See too Elsakkers, RBL, pp. 389–90, on all three texts.

[20] S. A. Keefe, *Water and the Word: Baptism and the Education of the Clergy in the Carolingian Empire*, 2 vols. (Notre Dame, 2002) I, p. 1; for an overview of Carolingian reform, see R. McKitterick, *The Frankish Church and the Carolingian Reforms, 789–895* (London, 1977).

[21] Cf. G. Brown, 'Introduction: The Carolingian Renaissance', in *Carolingian Culture: Emulation and Innovation*, ed. R. McKitterick (Cambridge, 1994), pp. 1–17.

[22] Keefe, *Water*, I, p. 5.

[23] C. van Rhijn, *Shepherds of the Lord: Priests and Episcopal Statutes in the Carolingian Period* (Turnhout, 2007); see too J. Gaudemet, 'Les statuts épiscopaux de la première

A good example is a statute issued in the first decade of the ninth century by Gerbald of Liège, a bishop close to the Carolingian political centre. Gerbald instructed his priests to be on the lookout for any *malefici*. Who were these *malefici*? Diviners, soothsayers, the kinds of people who 'interpret dreams and wear those amulets around their neck with who knows what written on, [female] poisoners, that is women who give certain potions to strike out offspring, and make any divinations so that through this they receive greater affection from their husbands'.[24] Gerbald urged his priests to make these malefactors 'come before us, so that their cases can be discussed before us'.[25]

Most statutes continued the sharp gendering of Gerald's statute. Thus, Radulf of Bourges' statute (853/66) quoted Martin of Braga's canon, which had similarly focussed exclusively on women, though it addressed demand as well as supply.[26] In 858 Herard of Tours included 'female *venefici*' in a list of suspect characters who ought to be 'prohibited and punished with public penance', though he did not spell out precisely which kinds of poisons they dabbled in.[27] Other episcopal statutes followed Gerbald's terms more closely including the specific mention of potions for abortion. Wherever such malefactors were found, urged one, they had to be 'severely curbed until they come to correction'.[28] But, finally, another statute took pains not to limit the search for malefactors implicated in abortion to women. 'We want to know and ask if you know', began one measure, '[any] women who deal potions to strike out offspring and who make divinations or give poisons for killing people, *men or women noted*'.[29]

The significance of episcopal statutes lies in practice as much as thought. In

---

décade du IXe siècle', reprinted in J. Gaudemet, *La formation du droit canonique médiéval* (Aldershot, 1980), XIII, pp. 309–49.

[24] 'qui somnia observant et ista filacteria circa collum portant, nescimus quibus verbis scriptis, et veneficas id est mulieres, quae potiones aliquas donant, ut partus excutiant, et aliquas divinationes faciunt per hoc, ut a maritis suis maiorem amorem habeant', *Capitula II* 10, MGH Capit. episc. 1, p. 29. On Gerbald's capitularies, see too J. Maquet, '*Faire justice*' *dans le diocèse de Liège au Moyen Âge (VIIIe–XIIe siècles): Essai du droit judiciare reconstitué* (Liège, 2008), pp. 89–102.

[25] 'Omnes maleficos ... ante nos adducere faciatis, ut causae eorum ante nos discutiantur', *Capitula II* 10, p. 29.

[26] *Capitula* 41, MGH Capit. episc. 1, p. 264.

[27] 'mulieribus veneficis ... ut prohibeantur et publicę paenitentiae multentur', *Capitula* 3, MGH Capit. episc. 2, p. 128. Such lists can be found in other kinds of text. Ansegisus's influential collection of royal capitularies included lists of magical practitioners and other wrongdoers, including *malefici*: *Collectio capitularium* 1.21, 62, MGH Capit., N.S., 1, pp. 451, 463–4.

[28] 'severiter corrigiant, donec ad emendationem venient', *Capitula Silvanectensia prima* 11, MGH Capit. episc. 3, p. 83.

[29] 'Volumus scire et inquirare, si sciatic ... mulieres, quę potiones tribuunt, ut partus excutiant, et quę divinationes faciant aut veneficia donent hominem interficiendum, *eos vel eas notatę*', *Capitula Treverensia* 5, MGH Capit. episc. 1, p. 55 (my italics). Neither this nor the *Capitula Silvanectensia prima* can be dated securely.

her recent study Carine van Rhijn has emphasized that they were 'devised as specific tools of communication between city-based bishops and village-based priests'. Statutes were attempts to bridge the gap between the 'world of ideals of reform and that in which those ideals ought to be carried out'. In Gerbald's case suspicion of specifically female *veneficae* doling out abortifacients and aphrodisiacs emanated from the very 'imperial epicentre of reform'.[30] More broadly, episcopal statutes captured moments of communication between ecclesiastical centre and periphery. Abortion was very much on the agenda.

Canonical authority and the history of abortion: Tradition in practice

Another kind of text was more significant in Carolingian reform: canon law collections. Ostensibly, the story is simple. Ancyra continued its longstanding circulation in collections either copied or composed in the later eighth and ninth centuries. It appeared in major Carolingian collections, from the *Dionysiana-Hadriana*, sent to Charlemagne by Pope Hadrian I in 774 and derived in part from the *Dionysiana*, to the systematically arranged *Dacheriana*, and also in other older collections such as the *Vetus Gallica, Quesnelliana* and *Sanblasiana*.[31] Relevant conciliar canons from late antique and Visigothic Spain – Elvira, Lérida, Martin of Braga/Braga III and Toledo – were also available through copies of the *Hispana* circulating outside the Iberian peninsula or through Frankish collections which incorporated Hispanic material one way or another such as the *Hispana Gallica Augustodensis* and the famous pseudo-Isidorean *Decretales*.[32]

For a number of modern theologians, the story of church tradition on abortion in the Early Middle Ages starts and ends with these collections. One reason lies in misgivings about penitential ministry and outright hostility towards penitentials expressed by some Carolingian bishops at a series of reform councils in the early decades of the ninth century. The council of Chalon-sur-Saône (813) voiced concerns that priests were departing from church norms when administering penances, sometimes out of personal fondness or animosity towards penitents. Priests were ordered not to depart from sacred canons, the authority of sacred scripture and the established tradition of the church (*ecclesiastica consuetudo*), and to shun 'those small books, which they call penitentials, whose errors are certain, authors uncertain ... [which]

---

[30] Van Rhijn, *Shepherds of the Lord*, pp. 55–68 (quotations at pp. 50, 60).
[31] Cf. Huser, *Crime*, pp. 34, 39–47; Palazzini, *Ius fetus*, pp. 98–103. On the *Dacheriana*, see A. Firey, 'Ghostly Recensions in Early Medieval Canon Law: The Problem of the Collectio Dacheriana and its Shades', *Tijdschrift voor rechtgeschiedenis* 68 (2000), 63–82.
[32] *Decretales*, ed. P. Hinschius, *Decretales Pseudo-Isidorianae et Capitula Angilramni* (Leipzig, 1863), pp. 263 (Ancyra), 342 (Elvira), 346–7 (Lérida), 432 (Braga II); see p. 96 n.10 above on the *Hispana Gallica Augustodensis*.

impose light and odd measures of penance for grave sins'.³³ In the same year the council of Tours urged caution when assigning penances because some priests were handing them out varyingly (*varie*) and indiscriminately (*indiscrete*). The bishops at Tours were not entirely opposed to penitentials and advised using the best of the older ones.³⁴ Far more fiery judgment was passed some years later at the council of Paris (829). Through a mixture of apathy and neglect priests were meting out penances 'using those small codices, which are called penitentials, written against canonical authority, and because of this they are not curing but caressing and fomenting the wounds of sinners'.³⁵ The assembled bishops ordered 'each and every bishop to carefully search out those erroneous little codices in his district and consign them to flames when found, so that at last no ignorant priests can mislead people through them'.³⁶

The reform councils appeared to capture a crucial moment in the history of penance. Until fairly recently the conventional historiographical story told of a distinctively Carolingian approach to penance (public penance for public sins, private penance for private sins) and the ultimate displacement of older-style penitentials by newer reform-minded works by Halitgar of Cambrai and Rabanus Maurus. On this view penitentials were an 'ephemeral and ultimately despised intrusion into the frankish church' because of their 'variety and multiplicity, external signs of particularism and dispersed authority'.³⁷

For theologians interested in abortion it was as if Carolingian criticisms of penitential *codicelli* were criticisms of penitential rulings on abortion. The bishops' concerns over the authority of ecclesiastical texts provided not just a moment within a story but the framework for a grand narrative of church tradition on abortion. The likes of Halitgar and Rabanus Maurus manfully consolidated conciliar tradition to remedy what one theologian described as *marasma penitenziale*, penitential confusion.³⁸ The 'unauthorized improvising' of the penitentials deviated from the 'common teaching' of the church.³⁹

---

[33] 'libellis, quos paenitentiales vocant, quorum sunt certi errores, incerti auctores... pro peccatis gravibus leves quosdam et inusitatos imponunt paenitentiae modos', Council of Chalon (813), c.38, with c.34 on personal feelings intruding upon the confessional, MGH Conc. 2.1, pp. 280–1.

[34] Council of Tours (813), c.22, MGH Conc. 2.1, p. 289.

[35] 'utentes scilicet quibusdam codicellis contra canonicam auctoritatem scriptis, quos paenitentiales vocant, et ob id non vulnera peccatorum curant, sed potius foventes palpant', Council of Paris (829), c.32, MGH Conc. 2.2, p. 633.

[36] 'unusquisque episcoporum in sua parroechia eosdem erroneos codicellos diligenter perquirat et inventos igni tradat, ne per eos ulterius sacerdotes imperiti homines decipiant', Council of Paris (829), c.32, p. 633.

[37] Rosamond Pierce [McKitterick], 'The "Frankish" Penitentials', in *The Materials, Sources and Methods of Ecclesiastical History*, SCH 11, ed. D. Baker (Oxford, 1975), pp. 31–9 (quotations at pp. 34, 38); cf. C. Vogel, *Le pécheur et la penitence au Moyen Âge* (Paris, 1969), pp. 24–45.

[38] B. Honings, 'L'aborto in alcuni decreti episcopali', 201–17 (quotation at 206); cf. Palazzini, *Ius fetus*, pp. 98–107.

[39] Grisez, *Abortion*, pp. 150–5 (quotations at pp. 150–1); see too Huser, *Crime*, p. 40.

This common teaching was identified above all with Ancyra. Against the 'individualism' of the penitentials, the 'arbitrariness of their penances', and their 'initially local use' stood 'general acceptance ... given to the ten-year penance of Ancyra'.[40] Important revisionist scholarship has since problematized the history of penance which underlies these accounts.[41] At the time they were writing, however, the theologians' picture of corporate canonical authority versus penitential individualism was historically respectable insofar as its contours overlapped with conventional histories of penance. It also held implications for modern abortion debates insofar as what were taken to be the salient features of Ancyra – the long, ten-year penance and the absence of any distinctions based on fetal development – formed the core of firm church doctrine. Unwavering tradition survived transient bands of unofficial improvisers scribbling away at the ecclesiastical margins.

This picture of Carolingian ecclesiastical action and, by extension, church tradition on abortion across the Early Middle Ages is misleading. But it does at least reflect a real tension which lay at the heart of different kinds of ecclesiastical regulations. On the one hand, there was a need – and under the Carolingians an increasing desire – for legislation derived from reputable, preferably cited, authorities, whether conciliar, papal, patristic or, more vaguely, part of what the council of Chalon-sur-Saône had called *ecclesiastica consuetudo*. Especially troubling were uncertainties surrounding the provenance as much as the substance of ecclesiastical legislation. But, on the other hand, there was also a need for renewing legislation where necessary and to absorb lessons learned from episcopal and pastoral experience.[42] Innovation is a useful shorthand, though innovation was not about changing doctrine so much as making it workable by anticipating disciplinary and pastoral needs. The tension between authority and innovation was a creative tension rather than a zero-sum game. We have already seen the creative tension at play in different Latin versions of the Ancyran canon circulating from the fifth century, most obviously Martin of Braga's version, which condemned preventing conception as well as abortion and situated such behaviour within as well as outside marriage.[43] The broad brushes with which the theologians' picture of

---

[40] Connery, *Abortion*, p. 68.
[41] Against the public/private dichotomy, see M. de Jong, 'What was Public about Public Penance? *Paenitentia publica* and Justice in the Carolingian World', in *La giustizia nell'alto medioevo (secoli IX–XI)*, Settimane 42 (Spoleto, 1997), II, pp. 863–902; Meens, 'Frequency', pp. 47–50. See too Meens, *Penance*, pp. 115–23, who argues that the councils, concentrated in northern Francia, represented specific concerns in 'regions where the canonical tradition met the penitential tradition' (p. 116); penitentials had yet to make significant inroads further south, while further east penitentials were more seamlessly integrated into ecclesiastical culture.
[42] Cf. R. Flechner, 'The Problem of Originality in Early Medieval Canon Law: Legislating by Means of Contradictions in the *Collectio Hibernensis*', *Viator* 43.2 (2012), 30–1.
[43] See pp. 97–9, 104–5 above.

corporate canonical authority trumping penitential individualism is drawn render invisible the finer detail of how Carolingian churchmen actually negotiated the tension between authority and innovation when handling abortion. The devil is very much in this detail.

An immense forest of writers: The texture of authority
What counted as authoritative tradition on abortion? The problem with identifying this tradition solely with Ancyra is illustrated by two penitentials in the same manuscript which, ironically enough, might well have been the kinds of works which some bishops wanted to see consigned to the penitential bonfire.[44] *Martenianum*, a particularly chaotic penitential probably produced c. 800, contained five rulings on abortion. The opening pair were both ascribed to Ancyra. There was a problem. The second of these reproduced the Ancyran canon, but the first reproduced a slightly messy version of Theodore's *XL dies* as if it came from Ancyra.[45] Next came a spurious quotation attributed to Augustine: 'Any woman who destroys her offspring or kills her child, has perpetrated murder. Those complicit in this sin, woman or man, should do penance for seven years'.[46] The final two rulings adapted Jerome to Eustochium on abortion. The first reproduced one segment adding a penance of fourteen years.[47] The second reproduced another segment, possibly with a striking scribal error: abortion was the murder of a 'not damned' (instead of not yet born) person.[48] Another penitential within the same manuscript, *Floriacense*, was one of the *simplices* considered in the previous chapter. At the very end the compiler added extra rulings, all derived from *Martenianum*, and interestingly the compiler made a deliberate decision to add new abortion rulings. There was a catch. The final rulings were set out under the heading, 'Ancyran Synod'. It was a promisingly canonical start but *Floriacense* was even more muddled than *Martenianum*. The actual Ancyran canon was nowhere to be seen. Instead, the compiler had hastily jotted down *XL dies* and the pseudo-Augustinian ruling as if from Ancyra.[49]

Errors are certain, authors uncertain. It is little coincidence that

---

[44] The manuscript in question is Florence, Biblioteca Medicea-Laurenziana, MS Ashburnham 82 (32): see Kottje, *Paenitentialia*, pp. xxxix–xl.

[45] P. *Martenianum* 43–4, ed. v. Hörmann, 'Bußbücherstudien IV', 379; see Elsakkers, 'Vocabulary', p. 408, on the messy adaptation of *XL dies*.

[46] 'Quaecunque mulier aut partum suum disperdit aut filium necavit, homicidium perpetravit. Mulier sive vir consentientes in hoc peccato, VII annos poeniteant', P. *Martenianum* 45, p. 390.

[47] 'Quaecunque mulier hanc detestationem fecerit, rea ab his constituitur aut suae animae aut homicidii. Inde XIIII annos peniteat', P. *Martenianum* 46, p. 390.

[48] The edition in Wasserschleben, *Bußordnungen*, p. 291, reads, 'nec damnati hominis homicidium' (*nec damnati* for *nec dum nati*), though von Hörmann's edition contains the ungarbled rendering at 390, while noting Wasserschleben's reading.

[49] Cf. 'Quaecumquae mulier a<ut> partu<m suum> disperdit aut filius negavit, hom<icidium perpetrauit>', P. *Floriacense* 64–5, p. 103.

Martenianum is typically regarded as exactly the sort of penitential which Carolingian bishops at Chalon-sur-Saône and Paris had in mind.[50] But although these are good examples of scribes mucking things up, they are not examples of scribes altogether making things up. *Martenianum* had derived all but one of its rulings on abortion (*XL dies* is the exception) from an innovative canonical collection, the *Collectio canonum Hibernensis*.[51] Originally composed in Ireland in the early eighth century, the *Hibernensis* was the longest and most sophisticated systematic collection produced in the Early Middle Ages. As they explained in their prologue to the *Hibernensis*, its innovative compilers had wanted to create an 'exposition, brief and clear and harmonious, into a text of one volume, from an immense forest of writers'.[52] The abortion rulings in the *Hibernensis*, taken from Jerome and Caesarius (the latter cited as Augustine – perfectly normal by early medieval standards), typified the broader approach. The authors supplemented conciliar canons with sources new to canonical legislation and one book, entitled *De contrariis causis*, which listed statements for and against specific precepts, anticipated *sic et non* texts in later medieval universities and functioned as a methodological manual for the collection as a whole.[53] There are flickers that some ecclesiastical figures rejected the *Hibernensis*. It was not a niche text, though; it was certainly being read in Carolingian Francia and beyond. Churchmen drew upon it in their own compilations and even referred to it in the course of settling ecclesiastical disputes.[54] In sum, conciliar canons were undoubtedly important reference points in ecclesiastical texts. But this pair of slightly muddled penitentials and, through them the *Hibernensis*, suggest that the texture of canonical authority on abortion in the ninth century was more variegated than the theologians' insistence on Ancyra suggests.[55]

---

[50] Frantzen, *Mise à jour*, p. 32.
[51] *Hibernensis* 44.3–5, ed. Flechner, pp. 392–3. This is the collection quoted at the start of chapter two, though *P. Martenianum* did not reproduce the two quotations from Caesarius ascribed to Augustine at *Hibernensis* 44.4.
[52] Prologue translated in D. Howlett, 'The Prologue to the *Collectio Canonum Hibernensis*', *Peritia* 17–18 (2003–4), 146. On the innovation of the authors and the context in which they were writing, see T. M. Charles–Edwards, 'The Construction of the *Hibernensis*', *Peritia* 12 (1998), 209–37.
[53] Flechner, 'Problem of Originality'.
[54] On the influence of the *Hibernensis*, see R. E. Reynolds, 'Unity and Diversity in Carolingian Canon Law Collections: The Case of the *Collectio Hibernensis* and its Derivatives', in *Carolingian Essays: Andrew W. Mellon Lectures in Early Christian Studies*, ed. U.-R. Blumenthal (Washington D.C., 1983), pp. 99–135. See Flechner, 'Problem of Originality', 31 n.8, for further references to Pope Leo IV's (possible) rejection and also to Alcuin's use of the *Hibernensis* in a dispute with Theodulf of Orléans over rights of sanctuary.
[55] It is worth stressing that a very large number of early medieval canonical collections remain either unedited or lacking up-to-date critical editions which adequately record manuscript variants: cf. Kéry, *Canonical Collections*, pp. 1–201. It is a fair

Authority and innovation in reform works on penance

Three so-called reform works on penance appeared to inaugurate a return to conciliar tradition on abortion. Closer inspection of these works suggests a more complicated picture, however. Probably not too long before his death in 831 Halitgar of Cambrai wrote a work on penitential practice in response to a request by Ebbo of Rheims, one of the senior bishops at Paris in 829. What troubled Ebbo most, he explained in a letter to Halitgar, was that 'in the works for our priests judgments for penitents are so confused, and so diverse, divergent between themselves and supported by no-one's authority' that they were almost useless.[56] Rising to the task Halitgar put together a work on penance comprised of six books. The first two outlined vices and spiritual virtues while three more outlined canonical guidelines for administering penance, with separate books on the laity and the clergy and religious. The Ancyran canon appeared in the fourth book, on lay sins.[57] The final book, however, was a stand-alone penitential which Halitgar claimed to have found in the archive of the Roman church. In all likelihood Halitgar had not composed this penitential, but had come up with a useful fiction about it: here was a penitential of respectably Roman provenance. Halitgar included it, he explained, because it contained many things which were not in the canons and because some bog-standard priests (Halitgar calls them *simpliciores*) would benefit from a less complicated and voluminous work.[58] Like the earlier book, Halitgar's penitential included Ancyra on abortion but also two rulings which had long been circulating in the *simplices* penitentials: *Decipere partum* and *Voluntarie*.[59] Moreover, at the end Halitgar integrated a miscellany of penitential rulings, including several which addressed practical problems encountered in pastoral ministry: for instance, what to do if a man could not remember how many women he had fornicated with (extra fasting) or if the penitent was a pregnant woman (she could fast if she wished to).[60] The miscellany also contained a ruling on dealers in probably abortifacient drugs: any '*herbarius*, male or female, killers of infants', could only be received back into communion if on the verge of death after a lifetime of repentance.[61]

Halitgar's work proved influential. His 'Roman penitential' circulated both as part of the whole work and separately in manuscripts designed for multi-

---

bet that future research will uncover at least some interesting variants (or even additions).

[56] 'ita confusa sunt iudicia paenitentum in presbitorum nostrorum opusculis, atque ita diversa et inter se discrepantia et nullius auctoritate suffulta', *Ad epistolas variorum supplementum* 2.1 (Ebbo to Halitgar), MGH Epp. 5, p. 617; see too Meens, *Penance*, pp. 130–2, on the background.

[57] *P. Halitgarii* 4.3, ed. Schmitz, *Bußbücher*, II, pp. 279–80.

[58] All from Halitgar's prologue at p. 266; see Meens, 'Historiography', pp. 76–7, with pp. 74–82 on the history (and 'myth') of the 'Roman penitential'.

[59] *P. Halitgarii*, 6.21 (Ancyra), 6.31–2 (*Decipere partum*), 6.46 (*Voluntarie*), pp. 295–6.

[60] *P. Halitgarii* 6.87, 96, pp. 299–300.

[61] 'Herbarius, vir aut mulier interfectores infantum', *P. Halitgarii* 6.97, p. 300.

ple purposes; one manuscript, incidentally, contained Halitgar's penitential and the oldest copy of Cogitosus's *Vita Brigitae*.[62] In terms of abortion, if Halitgar's Roman penitential is what a canonically respectable Carolingian penitential looked like, it did not look all that different to other penitentials – except that Halitgar's canonically respectable work actually added a slightly obscure ruling on *herbarii*.[63]

Two other reform-minded penitentials, both composed by the Carolingian scholar Rabanus Maurus in the middle decades of the ninth century, stuck closely to conciliar precedent. In 842 Rabanus, then abbot of Fulda, sent his first penitential to Otgar, his predecessor as archbishop of Mainz. Otgar had asked him for a single volume on penance based on canonical and patristic teaching. Rabanus's reply to Otgar suggests one significant practical subtext following the military victory of Louis the German and Charles the Bald at Fontenoy in 841: a debate over whether soldiers returning victorious from battle needed to undergo confessional scrutiny and, if necessary, penitential purification (Rabanus sided with those who thought they did).[64] A decade or so later Rabanus, now archbishop of Mainz, responded to questions from another bishop, Heribald of Auxerre, with a similar penitential prefaced with comments on serious sins like homicide and adultery, and also with advice on seeking answers to pastoral questions in scripture.[65] Despite being familiar, as we shall shortly see, with some penitential rulings, Rabanus almost completely shunned them in his own compilations and broached abortion entirely through conciliar canons. Unlike most non-Hispanic canonical collections or, for that matter, penitentials, Rabanus reproduced three relevant conciliar rulings: Ancyra, Elvira and Lérida.[66] He did not end there. When Rabanus succeeded Otgar as archbishop of Mainz in 847 he presided over the council of Mainz in the same year on Louis the German's order.[67] Drawing upon his first

[62] Meens, 'Frequency', pp. 41–6; see Meens, *Penance*, pp. 234–7, for a list of manuscripts. The manuscript in question (Paris, Bibliothèque nationale de France, MS latin 2999) written in north-eastern France around the middle of the ninth century survives in a mutilated form and most of Cogitosus's *Vita Brigitae* is lost. However, the index survives, including the section heading, 'About the pregnant [woman] blessed without pain [*De pregnante benedicta sine dolore*]': M. Esposito, 'On the Earliest Latin Life of St. Brigid of Kildare', *Proceedings of the Royal Irish Academy, Section C: Archaeology, Celtic Studies, History, Linguistics, Literature* 30 (1912–13), 313–14, with R. Sharpe, *Medieval Irish Saints' Lives: An Introduction to Vitae Sanctorum Hiberniae* (Oxford, 1991), p. 18, on dating and provenance.

[63] A clear antecedent can be found in the eighth-century *P. Oxoniense II*, to which we turn on an eighth-century detour below.

[64] D. S. Bachrach, *Religion and the Conduct of War, c.300–1215* (Woodbridge, 2003), pp. 61–2. Rabanus's letter to Otgar: *Ep.* 32, MGH Epp. 5, pp. 462–4.

[65] *Ep.* 56, MGH Epp. 5, pp. 510–12.

[66] *P. ad Otgarum* 9 (all three canons following a canon on *parricidium* alluding to Cain and Abel), PL 112, cols. 1410c–11d; *P. ad Heribaldum* 8 (Ancyra and Elvira), 9 (Lérida), PL 110, cols. 474b–c.

[67] *Annals of Fulda* a.847, trans. T. Reuter, *The Annals of Fulda* (Manchester, 1992), p. 26.

penitential, the three abortion rulings formed one of the council's enactments, a copy of which was sent to the king himself.⁶⁸

Unlike Halitgar's 'Roman penitential', neither of Rabanus's works looked like a conventional penitential and they addressed abortion entirely through conciliar canons. So how do they complicate, rather than confirm, the theologians' picture? The answer lies in how these canons were actually used in practice. Unlike the predominantly anonymous compilers of penitentials or canonical collections, we have some sense of how Rabanus used canons in practice. In his personal correspondences and occasional treatises Rabanus responded to queries from colleagues about particular (and sometimes peculiar) scenarios. Could masses be celebrated for slaves who had absconded from their masters? What should happen to a man who frequently fornicated with cows? What about calves later born of cows which had once been sexually abused? Some of these scenarios were prompted by real-life cases, others by intellectual speculation. Rabanus was evidently something of a go-to man for colleagues faced with perplexing moral or pastoral questions. His responses provide glimpses of how longstanding precepts were actually used in encounters, real and imagined, with the messiness of sin.⁶⁹

In c. 842 Rabanus answered a series of questions posed by Reginbald, a *chorepiscopus*, a kind of auxiliary bishop who roamed the countryside.⁷⁰ Judging from Rabanus's reply, one question concerned infants found dead next to their parents. A more detailed treatise by Ratramnus of Corbie on this same scenario (incidentally, also a response to a question) points to an emerging Carolingian discourse on the overlaying of children, no abstract thought experiment in societies where parents and children often slept in the same bed.⁷¹ The conundrum lay in the fact that because the tragic accident of overlaying was neither implausible nor utterly rare, it also provided a cover for less accidental tragedies. Rabanus's response is revealing:

---

⁶⁸ Council of Mainz (847), c.21, MGH Concilia 3, pp. 171–2, with the prefatory letter to Louis at pp. 159–62.

⁶⁹ On Rabanus's thoughtful understanding and application of ecclesiastical law in his letters, see W. Hartmann, 'Raban et le droit', in *Raban Maur et son temps*, ed. P. Depreux et al. (Turnhout, 2010), pp. 91–104; P. Corbet, *Autours de Burchard de Worms: L'église allemande et les interdits de parenté (IXème–XIIème siècle)* (Frankfurt, 2001), pp. 8–16. Two of Rabanus's correspondences concern us; the second of these will be discussed in the next chapter.

⁷⁰ On Rabanus's support for the chorepiscopate in opposition to several western bishops and his close relations with various *chorepiscopi* including Reginbald, see G. Bührer-Thierry, 'Raban Maur et l'épiscopat de son temps', in *Raban Maur*, pp. 67–9.

⁷¹ Cf. Hartmann, 'Raban', p. 95. Ratramnus's treatise was first published in G. Schmitz, 'Schuld und Strafe: Eine unbekannte Stellungnahme des Rathramnus von Corbie zur Kindestötung', *Deutsches Archiv für Erforschung des Mittelalters* 38 (1982), 363–87 (edition at 384–7). On the *longue durée* of premodern sleeping arrangements and their ecclesiastical critics, see J.-L. Flandrin, *Families in Former Times: Kinship, Household and Sexuality*, trans. R. Southern (Cambridge, 1979), pp. 98–102.

Next, [in the case of] infants who are found dead with their father and mother and it is not clear whether the infant has been smothered [*oppressus*] or suffocated by them, or expired by its own death, the parents ought not to be untroubled nor without penance. Where the cause of death was an accident, not design, there should nonetheless be an inquiry into [their] love. But if it is revealed that they were the killers, they should realize that they have sinned gravely, which is recognized as follows by the council of Ancyra [etc.].[72]

Rabanus quoted the Ancyran canon on abortion and infanticide in its entirety before noting that others (*alii*) prescribed a penance of three years for anyone 'who recklessly smothered their infant'. The penance (three years) and verb (*opprimere*) are giveaways. The precept Rabanus had in mind clearly originated in penitentials.[73] Penitential rulings, it seems, had their uses and Rabanus integrated an *opprimere* ruling at another council of Mainz in 852.[74] There was a feedback loop connecting Reginbald's question with subsequent conciliar legislation at Mainz, and the feedback loop demonstrates pastoral reflexivity. It is not absolutely certain whether or not Reginbald's original question had been hypothetical.[75] Nonetheless, responsiveness to real-life concerns, if not to real-life cases, is easily missed just because Rabanus's sources were centuries old.

A canon on women who committed infanticide or had abortions because of fornication shed light on the problem of infants killed by their parents accidentally or otherwise. This is how an ancient precept was actually applied in practice. Rabanus's reply undermines overly literalist readings of Ancyra. Significance depended on application, meaning depended on use. It is not difficult to imagine how the three conciliar canons on abortion which Rabanus brought together in his penitentials were mined for different meanings and applications. For instance, each canon framed abortion and infanticide as a response to sexual sin, but each gave a different penance. The divergence underlined the importance of adapting penances to circumstances and individuals instead of treating the ten-year penance as a fixed sacred number. The letter of the law was the means to discerning the spirit of the law. Rabanus testifies to the broader consolidation of conciliar tradition on abortion under the Carolingians at the same time as he also testifies to an ecclesiastical culture

---

[72] 'De infantibus autem, qui mortem cum patre et matre inveniuntur et non apparet, utrum ab eis oppressus sit ipse infans sive suffocatus, an propria morte defunctus, nec debent inde securi esse, nec sine paenitentia ipsi parentes. Sed tamen in eis consideratio debet esse pietatis, ubi non voluntas, sed eventus mortis causa fuit. Si autem eos non latet ipsos eius esse interfectores, scire debent graviter se deliquisse, quod in Ancirano concilio hoc modo probatur.', *Ep.* 30.2, MGH Epp. 5, p. 449.

[73] 'qui infantem suum incaute oppresserit', ibid., p. 450, and see p. 142 above on *opprimere* rulings in the *simplices*. Cf. Hartmann, 'Raban', p. 95.

[74] Council of Mainz (852), c.9, MGH Concilia 3, p. 247.

[75] Some of Reginbald's other questions clearly were: for instance, what if a father and son, or two brothers, or an uncle and nephew had fornicated with the same woman: *Ep.* 30.4, pp. 450–2.

in which conciliar canons were a starting point, not the final word, in thinking about pastoral problems.

If otherwise depends on the priest's judgement: Canonical awareness in penitentials
Canonical awareness and concern with authority left their mark on some penitentials before the reform councils. As we saw in the previous chapter, the most widely circulated penitentials included Ancyra on abortion, and in some cases individual rulings or even entire texts were being read as if they were the words of significant figures like Theodore and Bede.

Thoughtful use of conciliar precedent and glimpses of canonical awareness appear in some ninth-century penitentials too. Here the historiographical picture has shifted since the theologians were writing. Evidently not all Carolingian bishops were opposed to penitentials. Some encouraged priests under their supervision to familiarize themselves with them.[76] Moreover, copying of older penitentials continued right through the ninth century and the production line of new penitential compilations did not completely grind to a halt either.[77]

Some of them were every bit as much infused with reform principles as Halitgar's penitential – but they were still penitentials.[78] One penitential composed around the middle of the ninth century, *Pseudo-Gregorii III*, began a section headed, 'On women who fornicate and cause abortion', with the Ancyran canon (more precisely, Martin of Braga's version). But the compiler then added the mitigating *paupercula* clause, originally found in Theodorean infanticide rulings, with a seven-year penance also attributed to the canon (*in canone*). Finally, he reproduced *XL dies*, with the penance for murder after forty days simply given as *quasi homicida*, and concluded, 'If otherwise depends on the priest's judgement'.[79] The compiler had effectively tried to harmonize Ancyra and two segments from the Theodorean penitentials, and had stressed that all of this was subject to prudential judgement.

A comparable approach is evident in a recently re-edited penitential, *Pseudo-Theodori*, an especially extensive work composed c. 830–847 in northern France. The meticulous compiler evidently wanted to assemble as comprehensive and comprehensible a text as possible. His wide-ranging source material included patristic texts, canonical collections and scripture together with an array of penitentials including Theodorean penitentials (the Discipulus's recension), *Excarpsus Cummeani*, Halitgar's penitential and *Pseudo-Bedae*. The

---

[76] See Hammer, 'Country Churches', pp. 7, 11, on Gerbald of Liège and Haito of Basel.
[77] Meens, 'Frequency'; A. J. Frantzen, 'The Significance of the Frankish Penitentials', *Journal of Ecclesiastical History* 30.4 (1979), 409–21.
[78] Meens, *Penance*, pp. 135–6.
[79] 'Sin aliter, in iudicio pendeat sacerdotis', P. Ps.-Gregorii III 17, ed. Kerff, 'Paenitentiale Pseudo-Gregorii III', pp. 177–8, which also included *XL dies* (with pp. 161–2 on dating).

source material was nothing new, but the scale and expertise with which the compiler brought together his material was more exceptional.[80]

The section on homicide opened with a distinction effectively between murder and manslaughter followed by abortion rulings: Ancyra, *XL Dies* and *Voluntarie*. The version of *XL Dies* was one of the three-tier versions which had emerged in Bede–Egbert penitentials: before forty days (one year of penance), after forty days (three years) and after animation (*quasi homicida*). *Pseudo-Theodori* harmonized these sources by glossing the final permutation, 'that is, ten years', followed by the *paupercula* clause, and also by changing the customary *Voluntarie* penance from three to ten years.[81] Both here and in *Pseudo-Gregorii III* compilers had streamlined abortion rulings according to Ancyra and its ten-year penance. But the flipside of canonical awareness was interpreting Ancyra in light of other penitential rulings. In effect, because 'it ma[de] a big difference whether a *paupercula* does this because of the difficulty of rearing or a *fornicaria* in order to hide her crime', Ancyra became a canon on abortion in the specific context of fornication and perhaps also on abortion as homicide after forty days or after animation.

Pseudo-Theodori also made a measured repetition. The Ancyran canon appeared in a lengthy section on clerical and religious sexual sin too. Again, so much of the material is familiar from other penitentials. But the attention to detail with which specific circumstances and culprits were compressed into rulings is noticeable. Many rulings followed a recurring structure: a basic scenario of sexual sin with penances according to clerical or monastic grade; an equivalent penance for nuns where relevant (*similiter et illae peniteant*); an intensified penance if children were born from the illicit union; and yet another penance if these illicitly conceived children were killed.[82] As in the earliest penitentials, especially *Vinniani*, there was a palpable concern over members of the Christian community whose role was defined by their sexual status. By the time of *Pseudo-Theodori*, however, this concern had been refracted through accumulated church tradition. The compiler was careful to emphasize that if generating children in illicit unions compounded sexual sin, then killing those children went one step even further.[83] Equivalent penances for nuns as well as clerics were consistently reiterated because, as one ruling on fornication with laypeople explained, the 'Christian religion condemns fornication by the same measure in either sex'. Immediately after this the compiler reproduced

---

[80] See C. Van Rhijn and M. Saan, 'Correcting Sinners, Correcting Texts: A Context for the *Paenitentiale pseudo-Theodori*', EME 14.1 (2006), 23–40.

[81] P. Pseudo-Theodori 15.3–5, ed. van Rhijn, *Paenitentiale*, p. 37. See p. 152 above on the evolution of a 'three-tier' *XL dies*; I borrow the term 'three-tier' from Elsakkers, 'Vocabulary'.

[82] The components of this pattern are established at P. Pseudo-Theodori 12.1–3; see too 12.4 (adultery with someone else's spouse), 12.10 (fornication with *propinquae*) and 12.12 (fornication with many women), among other examples, pp. 21–4.

[83] P. Pseudo-Theodori 12.3, pp. 19–20.

Ancyra. Admittedly, he had not altered the canon's specific mention of female perpetrators but this was a tiny slip (or a slightly too precise citation) in an otherwise thorough section. In context the implication was very much that the Ancyran canon spoke more broadly to the question of clerical and monastic, male and female, sexual sin.[84]

Concerns over clerical and religious fornication were not new but the scale and urgency with which Carolingian ecclesiastical and royal texts addressed the problem of fornication by clerics, monks and nuns is noticeable. The contagion of clerical or religious sexual impurity grotesquely distorted the sacred topography of Carolingian society. At the local level it profoundly damaged the reputation of the church. 'Top-down' demands made of clerics by kings and bishops are occasionally mirrored in sources by hints of what van Rhijn has called the '"bottom-up" *correctio*' of local communities scandalized by priests' sexual misadventures.[85] The extent of such concerns is reflected by occasional intrusions in unexpected places. A seventh-century letter from Chrodobert of Tours advising an abbess, Boba, on what to do with nuns who perpetrated 'adultery' after religious profession was the opening item in a slightly unusual ninth-century formulary.[86]

The most striking Carolingian representation of how sexual sin impacted upon religious and local communities alike appears in a ninth-century life about an eighth-century saint Leoba (d. 782), abbess of Bischofsheim in northern Bavaria. Its author, Rudolf of Fulda, had written it in 837/8 at the request of Rabanus Maurus.[87] The story went that the nuns at Bischofsheim regularly clothed and fed a crippled *paupercula* who begged for alms at the gates of the monastery. Led astray by the devil's suggestions, however, the woman had fornicated. She pretended to be ill 'when she could not hide the fetus conceived in her swelling womb'.[88] After giving birth in secret, she flung the infant into a nearby pool. The story was not about a nun who had committed sexual sin – but that was precisely the point. After a local woman made a grisly discovery when she went to draw water from the pool, her fellow locals turned against the nuns:

---

[84] 'quia christiana religio fornicationem in utroque sexu pari ratione condemnat', *P. Pseudo-Theodori* 12.7, with 12.8 (Ancyra), p. 21.

[85] van Rhijn, *Shepherds*, pp. 200–10 (quotation at p. 201); see too M. de Jong, '*Imitatio morum*: The Cloister and Clerical Purity in the Carolingian World', in *Medieval Purity and Piety: Essays on Medieval Clerical Celibacy and Religious Reform*, ed. M. Frassetto (New York, 1998), pp. 49–80.

[86] *Formulae collectionis S. Dionysii* 1, MGH Formulae, pp. 494–6, with Rio, *Legal Practice*, pp. 48–9, 141–4.

[87] On the background to the *Vita Leobae* and the translation of Leoba's relics to Fulda, see S. Hollis, *Anglo-Saxon Women and the Church: Sharing a Common Fate* (Woodbridge, 1992), pp. 271–300.

[88] 'Cumque intumescente utero conceptum foetum celare non posset', *Vita Leobae* 12, MGH SS 15.1, p. 127.

[I]ncensed with female rage, she filled the entire village with jumbled shouting and spoke with indignation as she reproached the nuns: 'Oh what a chaste community, how glorious is the habit of virgins, who give birth to children beneath their veils and, at once discharging the duties of mothers and priests, baptize those to whom they have given birth!'[89]

The infant's body polluted the villagers' pool just as sexual hypocrisy polluted Leoba's community at Bischofsheim.[90] The finger of suspicion pointed to a nun, who, the locals quickly learned, had left to visit her parents a few days earlier. Leoba prayed fervently and organized the recitation of the entire psalter by the nuns. Finally, the *paupercula* confessed to her crime. But this was not a warm-hearted story of reconciliation. There was no redemption for the anonymous *paupercula*, the 'wretch who did not deserve to be cleansed'. She remained in thrall to the devil for the rest of her life.[91] The real menace to society in Rudolf's story was not child-murder but the damage of scandal (*infamia*) and disgusting rumour (*foedus rumor*) to a monastery's standing. The culmination of the narrative, the crux of Leoba's miracle, lay in making Bischofsheim's 'virginal reputation, which the devil tried to obscure with his sinister rumour, even clearer'.[92]

Ecclesiastical legislation, royal capitularies, saints' lives and even formularies expressed Carolingian anxieties over the repercussions of sexual sin by clerics, monks and nuns. *Pseudo-Theodori* epitomized such anxieties too. But, in a good example of tradition in practice, *Pseudo-Theodori* had addressed these anxieties through an ancient canon which predated the rise of monasticism and which had never framed abortion in terms of sexual sin by the clergy or religious.

Ultimately, there was no dichotomy between the mainstream of penitential rulings on abortion and conciliar tradition in canonical collections. The reality conforms to what Rob Meens calls the 'conflation of penitentials and canon law': the inclusion of penitentials and canonical collections within the same manuscripts, incorporation of some penitential rulings in other forms of ecclesiastical legislation, and absorption of some canons into penitentials.[93] One final thought concerns a counter-intuitive possibility. Canonical collections

---

[89] 'femineoque accensa furore, villam omnem clamore inordinato complevit et sanctis virginibus cum indignatione improperans ait: "O quam casta congregatio, quam gloriosa conversatio virginum, quae sub velo positae filios pariunt, et matrum pariter ac presbiterorum fungentes officio, eosdem quos genuerint ipsae baptizant!"', *Vita Leobae* 12, p. 127.

[90] See A. Firey, *A Contrite Heart: Prosecution and Redemption in the Carolingian Empire* (Leiden, 2009), pp. 20–30, for ideas about physical and spiritual pollution in the *Vita Leobae*; see pp. 201–2 n.173 below on the sometimes sinister connotations of pools.

[91] 'Misera tamen illa purgari non meruit', *Vita Leobae* 12, p. 127.

[92] 'ut nomen virginale, quod diabolus sinistra fama obruere conatus est, magis claresceret', *Vita Leobae* 12, p. 127.

[93] Meens, 'Frequency', p. 47.

undoubtedly enjoyed greater prestige value than penitentials in the hierarchy of ecclesiastical texts. Even taking into account the higher rate of attrition among smaller, portable manuscripts containing penitentials designed for local priests, the most influential canonical collections outnumbered penitentials.[94] By the ninth century relevant conciliar canons on abortion were available to clerical readers through canonical collections: always Ancyra and sometimes, in the case of collections with direct or indirect affinities to the *Hispana*, Elvira and Lérida. Conciliar canons were available, that is, if anyone needed or wanted to look them up and – crucially – also knew where to look for one or, at most, three relevant canons within voluminous collections, most of which were arranged chronologically (the systematic *Dacheriana* was perhaps the most widely disseminated exception). The mere existence of large numbers of these compendious works did not guarantee that specific entries would be easily consulted or readily remembered. Knowing where to look is awareness of canonical precedent by another name, for it presupposes that a conciliar canon had become synonymous with a specific topic. Widely disseminated canonical collections can be misleading because in themselves they do not provide historians with traces of this knowing where to look. Certainly without aids like the *Excerpta Hispana*, the extent to which single rulings within large collections like the *Dionysiana-Hadriana* actually generated awareness of canonical precedent on abortion should not be overstated. Ironically, at least in the case of Ancyra, it might well have been popular penitentials which offer historians better traces of knowing where to look. This counter-intuitive possibility should not be overstated either. Nonetheless, it is plausible that at least some penitentials generated wider awareness of canonical precedent on abortion, together with relevant penitential rulings, than some of the great Carolingian canonical collections.

These perilous times: Reflecting on abortion in the ninth century

The story of how Carolingian clerics and bishops handled abortion has concentrated so far on questions of authority, on how ecclesiastical authors thought with and about largely older rulings on abortion, and on a common stock of conciliar canons, penitential rulings and patristic quotations. There might have been some variations across texts, variations which offer us glimpses of thought, but this common stock is largely representative of the resources which clerics and bishops learned from and consulted in pastoral ministry and otherwise regulating their communities.

Other ninth-century texts preserve more unusual moments of deliberation on abortion. These moments provide insights into a growing pastoral and juridical reflexivity. Some, as we shall see, are more representative than others

---

[94] Ibid., p. 46.

of resources circulating among the Carolingian clergy and episcopate. How representative are the thought processes captured in these moments? And is it possible that they also capture responses to real life? In the survey that follows the possibility becomes progressively stronger.

Without a doubt: Papal asides on abortion as murder
Ninth-century letters preserve two moments when abortion intruded upon conversations between senior ecclesiastical figures. Both occurred in letters from popes to archbishops of Mainz. First, Pope Nicholas I writing to Charles of Mainz, Rabanus's successor and the grandson of Louis the Pious, at some point between 858 and 863 on how to address various offences. Nicholas went into a fair amount of detail on the taking of life. Murderers could not take up arms after completing penance (except against pagans) whereas those who killed involuntarily should be excluded from communion for five years with a detailed programme of fasting and prayers for a further five years. 'But,' Nicholas continued:

> women who voluntarily strike out infants conceived from the womb before the fullness of time should without doubt be considered murderers. But those [women] who seem to suffocate their children in their sleep, it is right to judge about these lightly, because they have not tumbled into this fault deliberately.[95]

Was Nicholas replying to a specific question on the overlaying of infants or perhaps even on abortion? Very likely not. His reply gives scant indication that Charles had asked such a question. Here was a pope using intentional abortion and accidental overlaying to illustrate the difference between murder and manslaughter.

The second example – a later pope to a later archbishop of Mainz – was certainly a response to a specific question, perhaps prompted by a specific case, but it was not a question about abortion. 'You have asked', Stephen V wrote in 887/8 to Liutbert, Charles's long-serving successor, in 887/8, 'regarding infants, who are discovered dead in bed with their parents'. Liutbert wanted Stephen's advice on whether to resort to the ordeal of hot iron or ordeal of hot water to get at the truth.[96] But Stephen utterly rejected any form of ordeal as so much superstition. Instead, he insisted that Liutbert rely on voluntary confessions and testimony from witnesses, leaving judgment of hidden matters to

---

[95] 'Mulieres autem, quae ante temporis plenitudinem conceptos utero infantes voluntate excutiunt, ut homicidae procul dubio iudicandae sunt. Illae vero, quae dormiendo filios suos suffocare videntur, leviter de his iudicare oportet, quia nolentes et non sentiendo ad hunc devolutae sunt casum', *Ep.* 155, MGH Epp. 6, pp. 670–1.

[96] 'Consuluisti etiam de infantibus, qui in uno lecto cum parentibus dormientes mortui reperiuntur, utrum ferro candente an aqua fervente seu alio quolibet examine parentes se purificare debeant eos non oppressisse.', *Fragmenta registri Stephani V papae* 25, MGH Epp. 7, p. 347.

God. But those who confessed, Stephen concluded, or were otherwise proven guilty of such terrible things had to be censured 'because if someone who has destroyed what has been conceived in the womb through abortion is a murderer, then by how much less will someone who has killed a little child of even just a day be able to absolve themselves of murder?'.[97]

It is an accident of survival that Mainz looks like the epicentre of Carolingian discussion on the overlaying of infants. The mental reflex of treating overlaying and abortion together had, of course, been conditioned much earlier. Both papal statements became important authoritative pronouncements in their own right. In 868 the council of Worms drew upon Nicholas's letter to Charles for some of its canons; the excerpt quoted above became a canon which emphasized leniency for (presumably accidental) overlaying at the same time as it emphasized that abortion, driving out infants conceived in the womb before the fullness of time, was indubitably homicide.[98] Further down the line, Stephen's rhetorical question ultimately entered Gratian's *Decretum*.[99] In both cases what became authoritative statements had originally been rhetorical asides. To illustrate a point about the overlaying of infants two popes referred to the moral certainty that abortion crossed over into murder territory.

Traces of hard cases (i): Obstetric emergencies
There was moral certainty on abortion – in theory. Mitigating voices wrestling with the complexities of abortion in the Early Middle Ages are harder to hear – but not impossible. As we have already seen, explicit references to the pressures of poverty and subtler intimations of the ambiguities of early pregnancy demonstrate that ecclesiastical authors wrestled with some complications. Two further complications are the paradigmatic hard cases on abortion: obstetric or gynaecological emergencies pitting a mother's life against her child's and the aftermath of rape or sexual abuse.

Hitherto, these hard cases have been absent. The first hard case, the question of therapeutic abortion, generated significant moral and medical discussion among later medieval intellectuals, and obstetric emergencies provided a scenario for later medieval miracle stories.[100] What about in earlier centuries?

---

[97] 'quia si conceptum in utero qui per aborsum deleverit, homicida est, quanto magis qui unius saltem diei puerulum peremerit, homicidam se esse excusare nequibit?', *Fragmenta* 25, p. 348.
[98] Council of Worms (868), c.18, MGH Conc. 4, p. 271; it is possible that there was a collection of papal letters at Mainz which was drawn upon at Worms in 868: D. Jasper and H. Fuhrmann, *Papal Letters in the Early Middle Ages* (Washington DC, 2001), p. 116.
[99] Müller, *Criminalization*, pp. 23–4.
[100] Moral and medical discourse: Biller, *Measure of Multitude*, pp. 148–53; Müller, *Criminalization*, pp. 110–16. Miracle stories: R. Finucane, *The Rescue of the Innocents: Endangered Children in Medieval Miracles* (Basingstoke, 1997) pp. 23–33; H. Powell, 'The 'Miracle of Childbirth': The Portrayal of Parturient Women in Medieval Miracle Narratives', *SHM* 25.4 (2012), 795–811.

Abortion under the Carolingians

There were discussions or references to therapeutic abortion or extraction of dead fetuses from the womb in copies of various late antique texts ranging from Theodorus Priscianus's *Euporiston* to Augustine's *De civitate Dei*.[101] Obstetric emergencies also featured in some early medieval hagiography.[102] Awareness of the complications of childbirth and pregnancy is even embedded within an emergency baptism provision in *Martenianum*.[103] Terrible obstetric emergencies occurred in the eighth and ninth centuries just as they had done in antiquity and just as they would do later in the Middle Ages.[104] But the contrast with later centuries is clear; original scrutiny of the moral quandaries is not easy to find in the Early Middle Ages.

The reticence of the sources was broken by one penitential. *Arundel* included an abortion ruling with a ten-year penance (Ancyra in spirit, but not in letter[105]) before adding two novel rulings which effectively distinguished between serious and frivolous reasons for abortion:

> If a woman arranges by any *maleficium* that she can never conceive in order to hide her lust, she should do penance for 10 years in the same way. But women who do this to escape death or narrowness in childbirth should do penance for three years.[106]

> If any woman has caused abortion for her convenience, she do penance for one year; if for a necessary reason, 40 days as a Lent.[107]

The irresistible conclusion is that these rulings consciously anticipated the difficult real-life decisions prompted by obstetric emergencies or gynaecological

---

[101] See Beccaria, *Codici*, pp. 197–8, 281–4, for ninth- or tenth-century manuscripts of the third book of the *Euporiston* and see p. 30 above on Priscianus. On *De civitate Dei*, see below pp. 267–8.

[102] Schulenburg, *Forgetful of their Sex*, pp. 229–31.

[103] Cf. 'Baptizare autem praegnantem vel enixam mulierem vel hoc quod genuerit si mortis periculo urguetur vel ipsam hora eadem qua gignit vel hoc quod gignitur eadem qua natum est nullo modo prohibetur', *P. Martenianum* 67, 439.

[104] See V. Garver, 'Childbearing and Infancy in the Carolingian World', *Journal of the History of Sexuality* 21.2 (2012), 228–9, together with K. L. Pearson, 'Nutrition and the Early-Medieval Diet', *Speculum* 72.1 (1997), 29–30, and V. L. Bullough and C. Campbell, 'Female Longevity and Diet in the Middle Ages', *Speculum* 55.2 (1980), 323, for speculative disease profiles of pregnant women in the period.

[105] 'Mulieres, qui partus suos sponte necaverint, aut aliquo maleficio vel herbarum potione excutiant, juxta hilerdense concilium X annis poeniteant, et omnibus diebus vitae suae fletibus insistant', *P. Arundel* 17, ed. Schmitz, *Bußbücher*, I, p. 443. This is a noticeably reworked version of Ancyra – the mention of *maleficium* and herbs is novel – but mistakenly attributed to Lérida.

[106] 'Mulier si aliquo maleficio ad occultandum libidinem suam obtinet, se numquam concipere posse, eodem modo X annos poeniteat. Quae vero ad vitandam mortem vel partus augustiam hoc faciunt, triennio poeniteat', *P. Arundel* 18, p. 443; I have read 'angustiam' for 'augustiam'.

[107] 'Si qua mulier pro sua levitate avorsum fecerit, uno anno peniteat; si pro utilitate necessaria, XL diebus more quadragesimali', *P. Arundel* 20, p. 444. The intervening ruling concerned the overlaying of infants.

morbidity.[108] The catch, however, is that *Arundel* is a late text, probably from the tenth or eleventh century, and its material on abortion is idiosyncratic.[109] In terms of content and chronology *Arundel* is not representative of Carolingian (or post-Carolingian) ecclesiastical texts. More interesting is to speculate whether *Arundel* represents thought-processes in users of these earlier texts. In terms of the questions it addressed, quite probably; in terms of the exact calibrations of circumstances and penances in the answers given, it is harder to say.

Traces of hard cases (ii): Rape
The other hard case, the aftermath of rape or sexual abuse, yields stronger traces. For the first trace we must shift back in time to at least the middle of the eighth century, perhaps even earlier. It appears in *Oxoniense II*, which Rob Meens has argued might well have been authored by the Anglo-Saxon missionary Willibrord (d. 739).[110] Willibrord had been sent to evangelize Frisia by Egbert of York and *Oxoniense II* fits with a missionary context. It is, in Ian Wood's words, a 'remarkable text [which] would certainly have been appropriate for work on either side of the Frisian frontier, dealing as it does with practices which are unquestionably non-Christian in origin, such as infanticide'.[111] We might quibble whether infanticide (or abortion) was inherently a non-Christian practice in origin. The important point is that *Oxoniense II* noticeably grappled with social customs and cultural norms which sanctioned child-murder in a society where public morality was thinly Christianized at most. The possibility of a Frisian connection is intriguing because later Carolingian texts also made a connection between infanticide or abortion and Frisian custom. To Carolingian eyes Frisia looked like a backwater where they murdered their children.[112]

At any rate, *Oxoniense II* is an unusual penitential. Its social detail is as tantalizing as its Latin is occasionally perplexing, and penances, often expressed in weeks rather than years, were noticeably more lenient than in most penitentials. A sequence of rulings on deliberate and accidental infant deaths carefully thought in terms of both Christian (*fidelis*) and pagan (*gentilis*) infants, and even referred to placing infants 'in a cradle[?] or some other place according to custom'.[113] Here was an author, probably a missionary, taking pains to place sin in social context.

---

[108] Elsakkers, RBL, pp. 450–1.
[109] Frantzen, *Mise à jour*, p. 39, on dating.
[110] Meens, *Penance*, pp. 102–6.
[111] I. Wood, *The Missionary Life: Saints and the Evangelisation of Europe, 400–1050* (Harlow, 2001), p. 79.
[112] See below pp. 230–5 on the *Lex Frisionum* and *Vita Liudgeri*.
[113] 'secundum consuetudinem sive in cuna sive in alio loco', P. Oxoniense II 28, with cc.25–30 on infant deaths, ed. Kottje, *Paenitentialia*, pp. 195–6.

Our first trace appears immediately after the rulings on infant deaths. *Oxoniense II* turned to scenarios involving childbirth in captivity (*in hostem*). The compiler tailored rulings according to customs and norms surrounding the social recognition of young infants. The ceremonial raising of an infant from the ground was a significant social rite. A woman who 'gave birth to an infant in captivity and raised him up from the ground and did not care[?] into infancy, should fast as much as she wanted'.[114] But if she had (literally) raised and nursed the infant, 'and later threw him out [*proiecit*] unwillingly', she had to fast for 28 weeks.[115] Next comes our first trace:

> On a woman who throws out [*proicit*] an unwanted infant in captivity. If a woman throws out [*proicit*] an unwanted infant because she could not carry or feed him, she should not be blamed, but should nonetheless fast for three weeks.[116]

Was this about abortion? We have already seen that *proicere* could describe infant exposure as well as abortion.[117] It is plausible, perhaps more likely, that the author of *Oxoniense II* had infant exposure in mind because the preceding ruling used *proicere* in this sense and the subsequent ruling addressed the social recognition of young infants.[118] On the other hand, the preceding ruling is absent from the oldest (but fragmentary) manuscript witness and, perhaps, carrying (*portare*) was a figurative reference to pregnancy.[119] To find the next trace we move to northern Italy in around 800. A penitential which we have already encountered, *Merseburgense A*, adapted this ruling:

> If a woman abducted (*rapta*) by an enemy throws out her unwanted child [because] she cannot sustain or nourish [the child], she should not be blamed but should nonetheless do penance for three weeks.[120]

---

[114] 'Si autem mulier in hostem peperit infantem et eum sustulerit a terra nec captavit ad infantem, illa ieiunet quantum voluerit', P. *Oxoniense II* 31, p. 196.

[115] '… et lactavit sibi in filium et iterum proiecit eum nolendo', P. *Oxoniense II* 32, p. 196.

[116] 'De eam, qui in hostem invitum proicit infantem. Si autem mulier invitus proicit infantem sive quia non potuit eum portare vel nutrire, illa non est culpanda, sed tamen ieiunet ebdomada III', P. *Oxoniense II* 33, p. 196; following manuscript variants, I read *invitus* as *invitum*.

[117] See above pp. 87–8 on the expression, *proice puerperium*, in Gregory of Tours' *De miraculis Andreae*.

[118] The meaning of P. *Oxoniense II* 34, p. 196, is not crystal clear, though again the compiler tailored rulings to fit the local social environment: 'If a Christian woman bears an infant and does not raise him from the ground, so that she does not suffer[?], and does not suckle the infant, so that she does not seem shameful or unfaithful in her own husband's eyes, should fast for 35 weeks [*Si autem mulier christiana peperit infantem et non sustulit eum a terra, ut non laboret, neque nutriat infantem, ut non videtur <tur>pes vel infidelis coram proprio maritu suo, illa ieiunet ebdomada XXXV*]'.

[119] P. *Oxoniense II* 28–32 is missing from Stuttgart, Würtemmbergische Landesbibliothek, Cod. fragm. 100 A: Kottje, *Paenitentialia*, pp. xvli, 196 (as St_6).

[120] 'Si mulier ab hoste rapta infantem suum invitum proicit vel que non potest stare aut nutrire, non est culpanda, se<d> tamen III ebdomadas peneteat', P. *Merseburgense*

Again, there is a question mark over whether the compiler had abortion rather than infant exposure in mind.[121] But in both cases note the mental association: a woman faced with an unwanted child in an implied context of coerced intercourse ought not to be held culpable for her actions, though she should still undergo a brief penance. Even if the authors of *Oxoniense II* and *Merseburgense A* were consciously addressing infant exposure, the meaning could easily have been extended to abortion given the mental associations and the double meaning of *proicere*.

These rulings appeared in texts which were not quite as singular as *Arundel*. Halitgar's ruling on *herbarii* had a clear antecedent in *Oxoniense II* and affinities with another ninth-century penitential, *Hubertense*, can be discerned too.[122] But *Oxoniense II*'s ultimate influence largely came later in the tenth and eleventh centuries and specifically in Italy.[123] Despite appearing in texts produced at the top and tail of the Carolingian empire, neither ruling entered the mainstream of ninth-century ecclesiastical texts. Later ninth- or early tenth-century recensions of *Merseburgense A*, to which we turn below, did not include it.

The scenario addressed, however, reflected a broader Carolingian social concern. The clue lies in the addition made in *Merseburgense A* referring to an abducted (*rapta*) woman. We must tread carefully. *Raptus*, the relevant noun, was an inconsistent term which did not typically mean rape in the modern sense of coerced or non-consensual intercourse. It is best translated as abduction and its meaning ranged from consensual elopement to violent, sexual abduction, with various shades of grey in between. *Raptus* evidently troubled Carolingian rulers, jurists and intellectuals. As Rachel Stone has shown in her study of a treatise on *raptus* by Hincmar of Rheims, Carolingian discourse tended to focus on the social repercussions of *raptus* as a marital strategy among young noblemen and the subsequent validity or otherwise of 'abduction marriage'.[124] On a sidenote, the negative impact of *raptus* on relations between kin-groups and between parents and daughters suggest further social pressures through which children could become unwanted.

Certain texts do convey the social, if not quite the psychological, cost of rape in the modern sense. Marianne Elsakkers has argued that at least some

---

A 115, pp. 158–9; see pp. 156–7 above on abortion rulings in *Merseburgense A. Invitus* is usually best translated as unwilling, but it is difficult to translate otherwise here.

[121] Schulenburg, *Forgetful of their Sex*, p. 250, follows Boswell, *Kindness*, p. 220, in reading a version of this ruling in a later penitential, *Vallicellianum I* 40, ed. Schmitz, *Bußbücher*, I, p. 285, as a reference to exposure.

[122] P. *Oxoniense II* 43, p. 198. Examples of affinities: P. *Hubertense* 53, 55, 58–61, ed. Kottje, *Paenitentialia*, pp. 113–15.

[123] See A. Gaastra, 'Penance and the Law: The Penitential Canons of the *Collection in Nine Books*', *EME* 14.1 (2006), 85–102.

[124] R. Stone, 'The Invention of a Theology of Abduction: Hincmar of Rheims on Raptus', *JEH* 60.3 (2009), 433–48; more broadly, see too Stone, *Morality and Masculinity*, pp. 249–55; J. Chélini, *L'aube du Moyen Age: Naissance de la chrétienté occidentale: La vie religieuse des laïcs dans l'Europe carolingienne (750–900)* (Paris, 1991), pp. 177–83.

measures within later eighth- and ninth-century law-codes and capitularies produced for peripheral or recently conquered territories like Saxony, Frisia and Thuringia addressed *raptus* in a way which implied sexual violation.[125] The *Lex Frisionum*, for example, stipulated that anyone who 'abducted (*rapuerit*) a virgin girl and sent her back violated' had to pay a set compensation to her and to the king, with another third to her father or guardian.[126] Some penitentials addressed coercive or manipulative sexual violation of women too. Unusually, but not unsurprisingly, *Oxoniense II* went into detail and even slipped into the second-person in its advice on how to deal with victims of rape:

> If anyone has violated someone else's woman and fornicated with her either in captivity or in the road, where she was alone, or in some other place, where she could not defend herself from the person who violated her, you should not force her, who unwillingly fornicated and is now as if someone had killed her, to fast. But if she wanted to fast herself, you should not prohibit it.[127]

Perhaps *Oxoniense II* likened rape to physical death because it could be a socially fatal injury. Concern over victims' welfare mingled with the perspectives of male relations; this is what happened when 'someone else's woman' was violated. From the perspective of a husband, rape gravely compromised his wife's honour and, therefore, his own; from the perspective of a father or guardian, rape compromised marriageability and thereby increased the burden of unmarried women.[128]

The dismissive idea of 'unauthorized improvising' with which the entire corpus of penitential rulings on abortion has been marginalized has its uses. Provisions on hard cases in *Arundel*, *Oxoniense II* and *Merseburgense A* point to casuistic gaps in Carolingian ecclesiastical texts at the same time as they point to social realities to which Carolingian clerics had to respond. The authors of these works improvised just as Hincmar of Rheims had to when addressing

---

[125] M. Elsakkers, 'Raptus ultra Rhenum: Early Ninth-Century Saxon Laws on Abduction and Rape', *Amsterdamer Beiträge zur Älteren Germanistik* 52 (1999), 27–53; see too Oliver, *Body Legal*, pp. 180–202.

[126] 'Si quis puellam virginem rapuerit et violatam dimiserit', *LF* 9.8–9, MGH Fontes iuris 12, p. 48.

[127] 'Si quis mulierem alterius violaverit et fornicaverit cum ea sive in hoste sive in via, ubi sola erat, sive in alio loco, ubi se non potuit defendere ab homine, qui eam violavit, nec cogatis illam ieiunare, qui invitus fornicavit et sic est, quasi aliquis interfecisset eam. Si autem voluerit ipsam ieiunare, non prohibeatis', P. *Oxoniense II* 59, p. 201; the rapist had to fast for twenty-eight weeks and any accomplices ('Qui et consensit ei') had to fast for fourteen weeks. On rape (but also *raptus*) in penitentials, see too J. A. Smith, *Ordering Women's Lives: Penitentials and Nunnery Rules in the Early Medieval West* (Aldershot, 2001), pp. 56–8; Brundage, *Law, Sex, and Christian Society*, p. 165.

[128] Cf. Elsakkers, 'Raptus', p. 44.

raptus in the absence of a developed patristic tradition.[129] They do not represent the mainstream of ecclesiastical legislation on abortion. Precisely for this reason, they do represent the need to improvise. The likelihood is that in their encounters with women who had suffered obstetric emergencies or rape many Carolingian priests and bishops likewise improvised too, albeit in ways which have not left written traces.

The dog not barking in the night: The intrusion of 'contraception'
Before the turn of the ninth century clear condemnation of preventing conception was absent from penitentials and the majority of canonical collections. The entry of 'contraception' into pastoral and episcopal texts occurred over the course of the ninth century.[130] How and why did this happen, and what does this say about the handling of abortion?

These questions are not premised upon an earlier absence of thought on preventing conception. Consider two recensions of *Merseburgense A* dating from the later ninth or early tenth century. *Merseburgense A* had contained both *Voluntarie* and the Ancyran canon. In one recension, Ancyra was read in terms of the murder of children born in sin; in another, Ancyra was read in a way specifically tied to abortion after fornication. In both, compilers had harmonized older rulings while simultaneously straddling the line between abortion and preventing conception:

> If any woman has voluntarily caused abortion, that is, has done something to herself or another so that [she] does not conceive or kills what has been conceived, she should do penance for three years on bread and water. And if she fornicated and killed what is born, she should do penance for 10 years.[131]

> If any woman voluntarily causes abortion so that she does not conceive or kills what have been conceived, she should do penance for three years on bread and water. And if she has fornicated and killed, she should do penance for 10 years.[132]

---

[129] Stone, 'Invention', 448.
[130] Cf. Callewaert, 'Les pénitentiels', 357; Payer, *Sex and the Penitentials*, p. 34. Noonan, *Contraception*, pp. 152–5, places some of the relevant texts, since re-dated to the ninth century, in the eighth century.
[131] 'Si quis mulier voluntarie aborsum, id est qualecunque causa sibi aut alii fecerit, ut non concipiat aut conceptos occidat, III annos in pane et aqua peniteat. Et si fornicaverit et occiderit, quod nascitur, X annos peniteat', *Merseburgense A (V_{23})*, p. 135; on the manuscript (Vatican City, Biblioteca Apostolica Vaticana, MS Vat. Lat. 5751) see Kottje, *Paenitentialia*, p. xliii.
[132] 'Si quis mulier voluntarie aborsum fecerit, ut non concipiat aut conceptos occidat, III annos in pane et aqua peniteat. Et si fornicaverit et occiderit, X annos peniteat', *Merseburgense A (W_{10})*, p. 135; on the manuscript (Vienna, Österreichische Nationalbibliothek, Cod. lat. 2225) see ibid., p. xlv.

Abortion under the Carolingians

The early medieval vocabulary of preventing conception was not as developed or flexible as its later medieval equivalent. It lacked expressions such as *vitatio prolis* (avoidance of offspring). The search for thought on preventing conception is really an exercise in grammatical sleuthing, a hunt for relevant *ut*-clauses.[133] But we have already encountered such *ut*-clauses and the thinking they embody in Martin of Braga's reworked version of Ancyra and Caesarius's condemnation of preventing conception (often circulating under Augustine's authority). Outside ecclesiastical texts comparable clauses can also be found in Salic law.[134] Like the oldest relevant penitential ruling, *Decipere partum*, these were responses, albeit not plainly expressed, to the ambiguity of distinguishing between abortion and preventing conception. In sum, the later recensions of *Merseburgense A* made explicit what was already latent in many ecclesiastical texts.

To clarify, then, the core questions surrounding what Peter Biller has called the 'intrusion of "contraception" in the ninth century concern why provisions which addressed preventing conception more (if not completely) distinctly from abortion entered ninth-century texts within penitential sub-traditions from which such provisions had previously been absent.[135] Why then and there? Before turning to Biller's answer, here are the three main pieces of evidence.

The earliest intrusion appears in *Pseudo-Bedae*, produced by the second quarter of the ninth century. This was one of the penitentials containing a three-tier version of *XL dies* (before forty days, after forty days, after animation) as well as Ancyra.[136] *Pseudo-Bedae* also included an *ordo ad dandam penitentiam* preceding the main body of penitential tariffs. Such *ordines* or liturgies of penance began to proliferate in the ninth century. Whether or not *Pseudo-Bedae* pre-dates the reform councils, penitential *ordines* were a textual innovation designed to regularize and support penitential ministry. Halitgar's 'Roman penitential', for example, contained an *ordo*. The *ordo* in *Pseudo-Bedae* also included an interrogatory, a list of questions for priests to ask penitents. 'Make him confess all his sins by saying this,' instructed *Pseudo-Bedae's* interrogatory.[137] Abortion appeared in a list of superstitious practices. 'Have you committed sacrilege,' one question began, going on to mention soothsaying, making offerings at springs and so on until, 'or have you drawn lots, or caused abortion? You will do penance for five years or three.'[138] Later, immediately after a question on overlaying, came more:

---

[133] E.g. *ut non concipiat* (so that she does not conceive).
[134] See pp. 224–5 below on Salic measures against harming the fertility of others.
[135] Biller, *Measure of Multitude*, p. 181.
[136] See above p. 152.
[137] 'Tunc fac eum confiteri omnia peccata sua, ita dicendo', *P. Pseudo-Bedae*, p. 253.
[138] 'Fecisti sacrilegium ... aut sortitus fuisti, aut avorsum fecisti? V annos vel III poeniteas', *P. Pseudo-Bedae* (interrogatory), p. 254.

> Have you drunk any *maleficium*, that is herbs or other things, so that you were not able to have infants, or have given [this] to someone else, or wanted to kill someone by a potion, or [drunk] from the blood or semen of your husband so that he has a greater love for you, or have you tasted or drunk holy oil? Seven years or five or three.[139]

> Have you killed your offspring (*partus*)? Ten years, and if you have killed a son or daughter (*filium aut filiam*), you should do penance for 12 years, and if in the womb before being conceived, you should do penance for one year, if after being conceived, three years.[140]

The underlying thought process is not easy to grasp when one tries to match penances to sins. In the interrogatory *maleficium* to prevent conception was dealt with more stringently than abortion, while the distinction between killing a *partus* (a fetus, a newborn, an infant?) and killing a son or daughter is not entirely clear. The different approach of the three-tier version of XL *dies* in the main body of tariffs complicates matters further. What is clearer is that the author of *Pseudo-Bedae* was fumbling for ways to address the avoidance of offspring beyond abortion.

The next intrusion appears in a penitential elaborating on the *simplices* tradition and composed by the middle of the ninth century, *Hubertense*. Like other *simplices* it included *Decipere partum* and *Voluntarie*.[141] *Hubertense* also added novel canons to the basic *simplices* core. One of them, on potions for abortion or preventing conception *and* other physical means of avoiding offspring under the (slightly misleading) title, 'On the potions of women', simply contradicts Philippe Ariès's thesis on *l'impensabilité* of avoiding conception before modernity:

> If anyone has taken potions so that a woman does not conceive or has killed what has been conceived, or a man has poured out his semen from intercourse with a woman so that [she] does not conceive, as the sons of Judah did in Thamar, let each one fast for ten years.[142]

It is worth pausing to notice *Hubertense*'s highly resourceful use of scripture. The reference was to Genesis 38, the story of Thamar's single-minded pur-

---

[139] 'Bibisti ullum maleficium, id est herbas vel alias causas, ut non potuisses infantes habere, aut alio donasti, aut hominem per pocionem occidere voluisti, aut de sanguine vel semine mariti tui, ut majorem de te haberet amorem, aut gustati aut chrisma bibisti? VII annos vel V aut III poeniteas', P. *Pseudo-Bedae* (interrogatory) 30, p. 255.

[140] 'Necasti partus tuos? X annos, et si filium aut filiam occidisti, XII annos poeniteas, et si in utero ante conceptum, annum I poeniteas, si post conceptum, III annos', P. *Pseudo-Bedae* (interrogatory) 31, p. 255.

[141] P. *Hubertense* 10, 37, pp. 109, 112.

[142] 'Si quis potiones acceperit, ut mulier non concipiat, aut conceptos occiderit aut vir semen effuderit a coitu mulieris, ut non concipiat, sicut filii Iudae fecerunt in Thamar, ieiunet unusquisque annos X', P. *Hubertense* 56, p. 114. On *l'impensabilité*, see P. Ariès, 'Sur les origines de la contraception en France', *Population* 3 (1953), 465–72.

suit of offspring from her husband's line. After the death of her husband, Er, Thamar's father-in-law Judah instructed his other son, Onan, to provide her with offspring as the Levirate law demanded. But Onan spilled his seed on the ground and was struck dead by God. After losing two of his sons, Judah refused to give his youngest, Shelah, to Thamar. She took the law into her own hands. While disguised as a temple prostitute, Thamar was impregnated by her unknowing father-in-law. When news of Thamar's prostitution and pregnancy reached Judah, he ordered her to be burned alive. But the narrative culminated in the revelation of her secret conception and Judah's recognition of Thamar's righteousness in contrast to his refusal to give his youngest son in marriage. Thamar gave birth to the twins, Pharez and Zerah. One of Thamar's twins, Pharez, appeared in both Gospel genealogies of Christ (Thamar is also mentioned in Matt. 1. 3).[143]

The understanding of Onan's sin in Carolingian and earlier exegesis was mutable. The most significant precursor (nothing suggests direct influence) came in an anti-Manichaean treatise by Augustine, in which he construed Onan's action as deliberately contraceptive.[144] But others read Onan's sin differently. John Cassian, for example, anticipated onanism as a synonym for masturbation when he distinguished between fornication which 'takes place in the union of the sexes' and fornication which 'occurs without touching a woman'.[145] In the ninth century Theodulph of Orléans spoke of the 'pollution and detestable sin of lying unnaturally with a woman, from where it is read that Onan son of Judah, who would pour his seed onto the ground having entered the woman, was struck by God'. In context, Theodulph was mentally categorizing forms of sexual impurity, including incest, rather than avoidance of offspring.[146] Theodulph was not the only Carolingian author to use Onan as an example.[147] Onan is the name from Genesis 38 most familiar to a modern audience, but this was probably not true in the ninth century. Late antique and early medieval exegesis of Genesis 38 focussed upon the allegorical significance of Judah and Thamar. All three of Alcuin's *Interrogationes* on Genesis 38 focussed on Thamar and Judah. Where Alcuin addressed sexual sin, he

---

[143] See E. M. Menn, *Judah and Tamar (Genesis 38) in Ancient Jewish Exegesis: Studies in Literary Form and Hermeneutics* (Leiden, 1997), including pp. 82–6 on genealogies.
[144] Cf. 'in terram fundebat, ne semen daret ad fecundandam Thamar', *Contra Faustum* 22.84, PL 42, col. 456.
[145] *Conferences* 5.11.4, trans. B. Ramsey, *John Cassian: The Conferences* (New York, 1997), p. 191.
[146] 'immunditia vel detestabile peccatum cum femina non naturaliter concumbere, unde Honas filius Iudae a deo percussus legitur, qui semen fundebat in terram ingressus ad mulierem', *Capitula II* 7.11, MGH Capit. episc. 1, p. 168; this ruling also speaks of bestiality, homosexuality, incest and inter-femoral sex. Cf. Biller, *Measure of Multitude*, p. 182 n.21.
[147] See p. 257 below on Hincmar of Rheims.

Abortion in the Early Middle Ages

contrasted Judah's lustfulness with Thamar's desire to produce children. He did not even mention Er or Onan by name.[148]

Nor, tellingly, did *Hubertense*. Scriptural references in a penitential were justificatory references to authority. But the reference to the 'sons of Judah' also had an illustrative purpose for the primary audience: clerics. The author had cleverly referred to a story whose principal figures, Thamar and Judah, were likely to have been familiar to Carolingian clerical readers, certainly if the popularity of Alcuin's work on Genesis is anything to go by.[149] The author was even a little exegetically daring in ascribing coital withdrawal to both of Judah's sons. Like any Carolingian compiler worth his salt, *Hubertense*'s author was interested in producing an authoritative text but possibly did not have access to a large stock of canonical or penitential source material. Scripture partly filled the gap.[150] Yet, the author also seems to have known conciliar tradition: the ten-year penance here and also in the version of *Voluntarie* suggests awareness of the Ancyran penance. The result was a subtly novel ruling which clearly distinguished between killing what has been conceived, preventing conception from taking place and avoiding the possibility of conception through coital withdrawal, but also subjected all three offences to what looks like a deliberately canonical penance. Here was authority and innovation in symbiosis.

The final piece of evidence dates from just after the turn of the tenth century. It takes the form of an influential manual for bishops written by Regino of Prüm *c.* 906. We will return to Regino's work in more detail below. More immediately, Regino included two novel provisions which addressed preventing conception. First, in an interrogatory for bishops during episcopal visitations to local communities, which opened with questions on homicide, including abortion and infanticide. After a model question asking whether any woman had killed anyone through poisonous herbs (*herbae venenatae*) or death-dealing potions (*mortiferae potiones*) or shown anyone else how to prepare them, came another which very carefully specified the possibility of male as well as female perpetrators: 'Is there any man or woman who has done this or taught another how to do it, that a man cannot generate or a woman conceive?'.[151] The second addition was the counterpart to this question in the

---

[148] *Interrogationes et responsiones in Genesim* 257–9, PL 100, cols. 554D–5B; see H. U. von Balthasar, *Explorations in Theology II: Spouse of the Word*, trans. A. V. Littledale (San Francisco, 1991), pp. 264–70, on the exegetical tradition more generally.

[149] On the popularity of Alcuin's work, which survives in fifty-two manuscripts, seventeen from the ninth century, see M. Fox, 'Alcuin the Exegete: The Evidence of the *Quaestiones in Genesim*', in *Study of the Bible*, pp. 41–3.

[150] Just under a third of the newer rulings added onto the *simplices* core quote or allude to scripture: P. *Hubertense* 44, 46, 48, 55–6, 62, pp. 113–15.

[151] 'Est aliquis vel aliqua, qui hoc fecerit vel alium facere docuerit, ut vir non possit generare aut femina concipere?', *De synodalibus causis et disciplinis ecclesiasticis* 2.1.9, ed. W. Hartmann, *Das Sendhandbuch des Regino von Prüm* (Darmstadt, 2004), p. 238.

main body of canons: 'If someone for the sake of satisfying lust or deliberate hatred has done something to a man or woman so that children are not born from him [or her], or has given [something] to drink, so that he [or she] cannot generate or conceive, he [or she] should be regarded as a murderer'.[152] Peter Biller has sketched out the chronology to the 'intrusion of 'contraception':

> Such material is *entirely* absent from the earlier penitentials. The dog not barking in the night really is significant, given that the penitentials were preoccupied with virtually every form of sex under the sun ... The chronology is clear: silence earlier on and then very strong presence, attested in three texts whose firm dates go from c.825–850 to 906. What lies behind this?[153]

Biller's answer hinges around a coincidence in the written record. A polyptych or estate survey listing the monastery of Prüm's land holdings and dues owed by tenants survives from 893. Georges Duby among others noted that the Prüm polyptych points to population pressures. The basic unit in polyptychs was the manse, an area of land for cultivation and habitation seen as appropriate for a family unit, including unmarried children and, perhaps, servants or slaves. In the Prüm polyptych this typically ranged between twelve and thirty-seven acres.[154] But, as particularly detailed entries for Prüm's westernmost estates in the Ardennes show, peasant holdings did not always translate into a single family on a single manse. Villance, a village in the Ardennes belonging to Prüm, had 116 families packed into thirty-five manses, with eighty-eight occupying twenty-two manses.[155] Yoshiki Morimoto's more recent study of the Prüm polyptych complements this picture. In addition to overcrowded manses there were a number of fractional manses (peasant holdings of half- or quarter-manses). While the Ardennes entries listed tenants one by one, entries for estates elsewhere used model manses without giving details of other tenants. In other words, the form of most entries in the Prüm polyptych very likely masked the scale of overcrowded manses. Overpopulated or fractional manses might have constituted over twenty per cent of holdings on Prüm's estates.[156]

Although Regino wrote his manual at Trier c. 906, he had earlier served as abbot of Prüm from 892 until his deposition in 899. If the Prüm polyptych coincided with the start of his abbacy, then Regino must have been aware of it. There is another coincidence. The Prüm polyptych provides a picture

---

[152] 'Si aliquis causa explendae libidinis vel odii meditatione, ut non ex eo soboles nascatur, homini aut mulieri aliquid fecerit vel ad potandum dederit, ut non possit generare aut concipere, ut homicida teneatur', *De synodalibus causis* 2.88, p. 292.

[153] *Measure of Multitude*, pp. 181–2 (italics in original); c. 825–850 refers to the dating of the earliest manuscript copy of *P. Pseudo-Bedae*.

[154] Y. Morimoto, 'Aspects of the Early Medieval Peasant Economy as Revealed in the Polyptych of Prüm', in *The Medieval World*, ed. P. Linehan and J.L. Nelson (London, 2001), p. 609.

[155] G. Duby, *Rural Economy and Country Life in the Medieval West*, trans. C. Postan (Columbia, SC, 1968), pp. 12–13; cf. Biller, *Measure of Multitude*, p. 184.

[156] Morimoto, 'Aspects', pp. 609–13.

of overcrowded manses in the Ardennes, the very region from which the St Hubert manuscript containing *Hubertense* comes. As Biller puts it, 'Noonan did not read polyptychs, and Duby did not read these penitentials'. The remarkable coincidence leads to the 'hypothesis that the pastoral concern with avoiding conception, which emerged and then intensified between the early ninth century and around 900, was an alert response to patterns of sin among the flock: one sin was being committed more than it had been, in an area suffering what we call over-population'.[157]

The hypothesis is ingenious. But it is worth briefly considering some doubts or, at least, complications over certain elements of the coincidence between *Hubertense*, Regino's manual and the Prüm polyptych. Some historians have asked whether the Prüm polyptych was not in fact put together after Regino's abbacy.[158] Nonetheless, as abbot Regino would have been better informed of Prüm's estates than most. Next, more significantly, was the ruling in *Hubertense* originally written in the Ardennes? Going by manuscript dating, *Hubertense*'s is the oldest version. But there are some faint grounds for wondering whether *Hubertense*'s ruling was in fact the original version.[159] Finally, the extent to which the Prüm polyptych points to overpopulation requires some nuance. It certainly points to overpopulation in the technical sense of divided or multi-occupied manses. But does this mean over-population with all of its connotations in a demographic sense? Based on details of reduced dues and services for multiple families within single manses or single families in subdivided manses, Morimoto argues that the manse system was sufficiently flexible to adapt to 'variation between family fortunes' and thereby provide a 'stable base for every peasant household at any given moment of its

---

[157] *Measure of Multitude*, pp. 184–5 (quotation at p. 185).

[158] Cf. S. Airlie, ' "Sad stories of the death of kings": Narrative Patterns and Structures of Authority in Regino of Prüm's *Chronicle*', in *Narrative and History in the Early Medieval West*, ed. E. M. Tyler and R. Balzaretti (Turnhout, 2006), pp. 109–10 n.14.

[159] For the coincidence to work it is relevant that the ruling was originally written and not just copied in the Ardennes. A version of the ruling also appears in the later ninth-century P. Merseburgense B. The precise relation between *P. Hubertense* and *P. Merseburgense B* is not clear though they have parallels; Kottje, *Paenitentialia*, pp. xxvii–xxix. Here is the version in *P. Merseburgense B*: 'Si quis potiones acceperit mulier, ut non concipiant, aut conceptus occiderit aut vir semen effude<rit> a cuitum mulieris, ut non concipiat, sicut filii Iude fecerunt in Thamar, ieiunet unusquisque annos II in pane et aqua', *P. Merseburgense B* 12, ed. Kottje, *Paenitentialia*, p. 174. This feels, for want of a better word, messier than *P. Hubertense*'s version; or, to put it differently, *P. Hubertense* feels tidier: 'Si quis' is deliberately gender inclusive rather than *P. Merseburgense B*'s 'Si quis … mulier' (shifting from gender-inclusive to gender-specific wording is the opposite of evolutionary tendencies in ecclesiastical texts on abortion); and the penance in *P. Merseburgense B* (two years) is more unusual, especially if a deliberate reduction from ten. Following the manuscript dating is perfectly plausible; but when penitential attrition is borne in mind it is also plausible, though necessarily speculative, that *P. Hubertense* represents a tidied version of a pre-existing ruling.

Abortion under the Carolingians

life-cycle'.[160] Moreover, Morimoto's study of the Prüm polyptych emphasizes a dynamic rather than static picture of how peasant landholding and estate management responded to demographic change. Indeed, it implies a dynamic picture of demographic change. Overpopulated manses in the Ardennes near the end of the ninth century do not necessarily mean overpopulated manses in the Ardennes a half century or so earlier when *Hubertense* was written.

I mention these complications because coincidences can be seductive. To focus solely on them, however, is to miss the wood for the trees. Biller's hypothesis remains compelling, especially in Regino's case. For Biller, the coincidence sheds light on a moment of proto-demographic medieval thought in the ninth century before its clearer articulation from the twelfth century and beyond, for 'inside the minds of Regino and other pastoral experts of this period, [we can discern] the *awareness* and *thought* of "many people", "they are poor", and "they are avoiding conceiving"'.[161] For our purposes, the real importance lies not in what the hypothesis says about Regino, but in what it says about the tradition of texts upon which he drew.

First, the boundary between the history of contraception and history of abortion is porous. *Pseudo-Bedae*, *Hubertense* and Regino's manual were novel because they addressed preventing conception increasingly, if not perfectly, distinctly from causing abortion. Their novelty underlines an important aspect already noted of older ecclesiastical texts which addressed abortion and preventing conception together: those older *ut*-clauses were attempts to address the ambiguity of abortion.

Second, the hypothesis is a reminder that ecclesiastical authors did put down their reed pens and lift up their heads to look at what was going on around them. They puzzled over difficult pastoral cases and asked one another for advice. But, at the same time, ecclesiastical regulations masked their authors' reflexivity. Biller has shown how some (but certainly not all) pastoral and university texts from the later twelfth to fourteenth centuries were inscribed with 'alert response[s] to patterns of sin' or explicit reflection on more singular pastoral cases. The formal qualities of Carolingian ecclesiastical texts – their terse style and conservative recycling – resisted, even precluded, such inscription. Regino of Prüm was no Peter the Chanter.[162] But the mistake would be to treat Biller's hypothesis as the model for a verification test as if determining pastoral responsiveness in Carolingian ecclesiastical texts depends only on identifying wholly novel provisions which can be substantiated with serendipitous documentary sources. Regino is unusually generous to historians (and we will see another connection with another source shortly). But, in general, such serendipity is in short supply. As we saw

---

[160] Morimoto, 'Aspects', pp. 612–13, 619 n.4 (quotation at p. 612); the picture of estate management and demographic picture in Duby, *Rural Economy*, p. 49, is less benign.
[161] *Measure of Multitude*, p. 185 (italics in original).
[162] See ibid., pp. 172–7, on pastoral details in Peter the Chanter and later quodlibets.

earlier, Rabanus's recycling of the oldest conciliar material on abortion coexisted with lively conversations between ecclesiastical colleagues on abortion and infanticide. In the case of both Rabanus and Regino, we are reliant on coincidences with other sources to see pastoral reflexivity in action. The real conclusion to be drawn from them – the real importance of Biller's hypothesis – is the possibility, or even probability, that authors of Carolingian ecclesiastical texts were far more pastorally alert than the formal qualities of their texts and the scarcity of germane coincidences might suggest.

Every priest should publicly announce: Regino's manual

Regino's *De synodalibus causis* has been read as a conduit of church tradition on abortion to the real intellectual business of later medieval thought: from Regino, through Burchard of Worms and Ivo of Chartres, to Gratian.[163] Looking backwards, rather than forwards, Regino's innovative work is a useful *summa* of church tradition on abortion over the preceding centuries. Regino wrote *De synodalibus causis* at the request of Rathbod, archbishop of Trier, and presented it to Hatto of Mainz. Regino's dedicatory preface makes clear how and why he had designed this work. Like an increasing number of bishops from the later ninth century, Hatto maintained a programme of visitations to local communities within his diocese. It was impractical for a bishop to haul his library around with him. Regino's little handbook (*manualis codicillus*) was a practical alternative.[164] He had thought carefully about its form and content. His manual brought together an interrogatory for bishops inquiring after the conduct of their priests, another episcopal interrogatory for synodal visitations to local communities, an *ordo* for priests to hear confession (including a penitential interrogatory) and a body of canons derived from multiple sources. Regino's approach to older legislation eschewed selectivity for comprehensiveness. He included all relevant provisions on any given topic. Moreover, Regino explicitly justified his inclusion of more recent provisions from Gaul and Germany because, he all but admitted, there were gaps in church tradition.[165] *De synodalibus causis* was cutting-edge canon law for bishops at the coalface.

What did Regino include on abortion? By the look of it, everything he could lay his hands on – and a few other things besides. We have some idea of his penitential sources from the final question in his interrogatory for clerics, which asked whether the priest had the Roman penitential (that is, Halitgar's), or penitentials by Theodore or Bede.[166] Adapted from *Pseudo-Bedae*, the

---

[163] Cf. Connery, *Abortion*, pp. 80–5.
[164] *De synodalibus causis* (preface), p. 20.
[165] On Regino's approach, see Meens, *Penance*, pp. 141–8; G. Austin, *Shaping Church Law around the year 1000: The Decretum of Burchard of Worms* (Farnham, 2009), pp. 39–41.
[166] *De synodalibus causis* 1.96, p. 38. On the ambiguity of the Latin (*Si habeat poenitentialem Romanum vel a Theodoro episcopo aut a venerabili Beda editum*) – did Regino mean one of three penitentials, or two different editions of the Roman penitential attributed to Theodore and Bede? – see Payer, *Sex and the Penitentials*, p. 78. Either

Abortion under the Carolingians

confessor's interrogatory in Regino's penitential *ordo* included the questions on drinking up *maleficium* and killing a *partus*, killing a *filius* or *filia*, and killing before or after conception in the womb.[167] In the main body of canons Regino included eleven on infanticide, infant abandonment and abortion. He quoted the council of Mainz (852) and Rabanus's letter to Reginbald on the overlaying of infants. Picking up the conciliar thread from Rabanus's allusion to Ancyra, next came the relevant conciliar canons on abortion and infanticide from Ancyra, Lérida and Elvira, followed by two longstanding penitential rulings: *XL dies* (a three-tier version derived from *Pseudo-Bedae*) and *Voluntarie* (with a ten-year penance). We turn to the next two canons shortly. The final pair, unusually derived from Roman law, addressed exposed infants.[168] Regino was not an early tenth-century Gratian. Rather than a *concordia canonum*, he had assembled a repository of potentially conflicting canonical and penitential provisions. Criticizing penitential (or, for that matter, canonical) *marasma* is anachronistic. For Regino, *marasma* was almost a methodology. As he elaborated in his dedication to Hatto, he had assembled 'diverse rulings of diverse fathers in order ... leaving to the reader's judgement what he prefers to extract and approve as the most pertinent'.[169]

Questions on preventing conception from Regino's innovative interrogatory for bishops conducting visitations have been quoted above.[170] The opening questions addressed murder and quickly turned to infants. Had any man or woman 'smothered their own infant or suffocated it by the weight of their clothes'? Was the child baptised?[171] Next:

> Is there any man or woman who has struck out someone else's offspring or, if a woman has through her own will struck out her offspring and caused abortion?[172]

> Is there any woman who, conceiving in fornication and fearing it should be discovered, has thrown out her own infant into water or hidden it in the ground, which they call *morth*?[173]

---

way, Regino's high regard for certain penitentials was inherited by Burchard of Worms: Austin, *Shaping Church Law*, pp. 120–1.

[167] *De synodalibus causis* 1.304, p. 164.
[168] *De synodalibus causis* 2.60–6, 69–70, pp. 280–6.
[169] 'diversorum patrum diversa statuta ... lectoris iudicio derelinquens, quid potissimum eligere ac approbare malit', *De synodalibus causis* (preface), p. 22.
[170] For a detailed analysis of the interrogatory for episcopal visitations which casts Regino as something of a pioneer in the history of questionnaires, see J.-P. Grémy, 'Une enquête au début du Xe siècle: le questionnaire synodal de Réginon de Prüm', *European Journal of Sociology* 49.2 (2008), 325–59.
[171] *De synodalibus causis* 2.1.4, p. 238.
[172] 'Est aliquis vel aliqua, qui alterius partum excusserit vel, si ipsa femina propria voluntate suum partum excusserit et abortivum fecerit?', *De synodalibus causis* 2.1.5, p. 238.
[173] 'Est aliqua femina, quae in fornicatione concipiens, timens, ne manifestaretur,

Questions in interrogatories for confession were asked in one-to-one encounters between priests and penitents. Preserving anonymity was a possibility. Questions for episcopal visitations, by contrast, were public spectacles. The local archdeacon was supposed to publicize the visitation a few days in advance so that everyone could attend the synod on the designated day. Questions would be posed to seven men under oath about offences within the community.[174] If confession was about the state of an individual's soul, episcopal visitations scrutinized a community's collective conscience. It is notable that the visitation interrogatory did not specify penances and it is probable that responses to offences (were these penances or punishments?) were co-ordinated variously by ecclesiastical or secular authorities in different locales.[175] Regino's valuable detail on episcopal visitations begins to smudge the boundaries between personal fault and public offence, perhaps even between ecclesiastical regulation and secular regulation, to which we turn in the next chapter. It also brings to the surface an ambiguity affecting all of the ecclesiastical sources examined in the last two chapters, an ambiguity which boils down to a deceptively simple question: was the handling of abortion envisaged in ecclesiastical texts a public or private affair? The emergence of a regularized system of episcopal visitations dealing in part with offences against public morality, to which Regino's details attest, only took off from the later ninth century. But the manuscript contexts of penitentials point to bishops operating in a judicial capacity as well as priests operating in a pastoral capacity, and idealized visions of Carolingian justice envisaged a 'shared judicial responsibility' between secular officials and bishops.[176] In other words, while some ecclesiastical sources on abortion were geared towards shaping individuals' consciences in ways which offered some degree of protective anonymity, others were used to shape community values and shame sinners in a decidedly more public way.

Presumably next to no one wanted personal sins to be broadcast to a wider

---

infantem proprium aut in aquam proiecerit aut in terra occulataverit, quod morth dicunt?', *De synodalibus causis* 2.1.6, p. 238. Biller, *Measure of Multitude*, pp. 183–4, notes Regino's use of the vernacular and suggests that the 'text draws close to real people here' (p. 184). Biller also makes a connection to the story in the *Vita Leobae*, discussed above at pp. 182–3, in which an illegitimately conceived infant was drowned in a pool. Evidently pools of water held sinister connotations. Alamannic law contains a provision on anyone who used a water-lock (*clausura in aquam*) to drown someone's cattle, a servant or an infant: LA (A) 79, MGH LNG 5.1, p. 144.

[174] *De synodalibus causis* 2.1–2, pp. 234–6.
[175] G. Austin, 'Bishops and Religious Law, 900–1050', in *The Bishop Reformed: Studies of Episcopal Power and Culture in the Central Middle Ages*, ed. J. S. Ott and A. T. Jones (Aldershot, 2007), p. 47.
[176] J. R. Davis, 'A Pattern for Power: Charlemagne's Delegation of Judicial Responsibilities', in *The Long Morning of Medieval Europe: New Directions in Early Medieval Studies*, ed. J. R. Davis and M. McCormick (Aldershot, 2008), pp. 235–46 (quotation at p. 243).

community save for the small minority who could find the spiritual benefits of humility in public humiliation. The stakes were even higher with abortion and infanticide. The presumption in so many ecclesiastical texts was that these sins were designed to conceal yet other sins. We have recurrently flirted with the core tension. Did 'top-down' measures against sexual sin (to mention nothing of 'bottom-up' attitudes) risk making abortion a temptation? One of Regino's other rulings within the main body of canons sets out precisely the kind of measure which might have generated this tension:

> As has reached the attention of the sacred council, there are certain women who conceiving in fornication and fearing that their crime, which they had perpetrated secretly, should be discovered, have killed the infants which they have given birth to, and buried them in mounds of earth or thrown them out into waters; the canons of the council[s] of Ancyra, Elvira and Lérida are witnesses to how great an outrage this is.[177]

The next measure echoed the vocabulary of older measures and pronouncements which had generated this tension from late antiquity onward. But it also demonstrates that Regino had recognized and reflected upon the tension:

> Because such things are being perpetrated so often when the devil persuades and the flesh's weakness entices and works together, we, wanting that any woman whatsoever to be healed from a single death-dealing potion lest the crime, that is of adultery and homicide, should be twinned give the resolution that every single priest should announce publicly in his community that, if any woman corrupted in secret has conceived and given birth, she should absolutely not kill her son or daughter at the devil's encouragement, but, by whichever method works, she should carry and expose her offspring before the doors of the church, so that brought to the priest the next morning it can be adopted and nourished, and she will avoid the guilt of homicide and, which is worse, parricide in such an occasion. For, who kills a son or daughter is always considered a parricide.[178]

---

[177] 'Sunt quaedam mulieres, ut ad notitiam sancti concilii pervenit, quae ex fornicatione concipientes, metuentes, ne scelus, quod occulte perpetrarunt, manifestum fieret, infantes, quos pepererunt, occiderunt, et terrae congerie cooperuerunt aut in aquas proiecerunt; quod quantum nefas sit, canones Ancyrani, Eliberitani atque Ilerdensis concilii testes sunt', *De synodalibus causis* 2.67, pp. 282–4. This measure and the following one are attributed to a council of Rouen, though the source is unknown and Regino might well have written both.

[178] 'Igitur quia diabolo suadente et carnis fragilitate delectante et ideo consentiente, multoties talia perpetrantur, ideo ex una mortifera potione aliam utcunque mederi cupientes, ne geminetur scelus, scilicet adulterii et homicidii, damus consilium, ut unusquisque sacerdos in sua plebe publice adnunciet, ut, si aliqua femina clanculo corrupta conceperit et pepererit, nequaquam diabolo cohortante filium aut filiam suam interficiat, sed, quocumque praevalet ingenio, ante ianuas ecclesiae partum deportari faciat ibique proici, ut coram sacerdote in crastinum delatus ab aliquo fideli suscipiatur et nutriatur, et tali ex causa homicidii reatum et, quod maius est,

Abortion in the Early Middle Ages

Regino was not alone. The Carolingian *vita* of a Merovingian saint, Goar, contains a relevant social detail. The story goes that Goar was challenged by Rusticus, the bishop of Trier, to reveal who the parents of a three-day-old abandoned infant really were. Readers can probably guess what happened next. Goar prayed to the Trinity and the infant miraculously revealed that the father was none other than Rusticus. Though the episode is rich in detail, the motif of the tiny infant revealing its father was not original.[179] What interests us is the more unusual social detail captured in the introduction to the story:

> It was then the custom at Trier that when by some sort of lapse a woman bore an infant, whose parents she did not want to be known or whom she did not have nearly enough to rear because of a want of basic means, she would expose the tiny newborn in a particular marble bowl which had been constructed for this very thing ... and when the exposed infant was found, there would be someone moved by pity who would adopt and rear it.[180]

The marble bowl at Trier anticipated the rotating cradles and revolving boxes for receiving foundlings in early modern Italian cities.[181] The *vita Goaris* gave further details of social rituals surrounding the rescue of abandoned infants. If wardens or the poor attached to a church (*matricularii*) recovered the exposed infant, they made inquiries in the community. If any prospective foster parents came forward, the infant was taken to the bishop, who conferred the right to rear the child.[182]

For John Boswell, purged of its miraculous elements, the story and its social detail points to the 'quotidian reality of abandonment'.[183] But imagine

    parricidii evadat. Nam, qui filium aut filiam interficit, parricida omnimodis tenetur', *De synodalibus causis* 2.68, p. 284.

[179] Gregory of Tours, *LH* 2.1, pp. 37–8, relates how Martin of Tours' successor, Brictius, was wrongly accused of being the father of a foundling; a closer parallel occurs in the *Vita prima Brigitae* 39, trans. Connolly, 'Vita Prima', 23, in which Brigit resolves a paternity dispute during a council of bishops at the behest of Patrick by making an infant miraculously reveal that his father was sitting at the council table.

[180] 'Moris quippe tunc Trevirorum erat, ut, cum casu quaelibet femina infantem peperisset, cuius nollet sciri parentes aut certe quem pro inopia rei familiaris nequaquam nutrire sufficeret, ortum parvulum in quadam marmorea conca, quae ad hoc ipsum statuta erat, exponerat ... ut, cum expositus infans repperiretur, existeret aliquis, qui eum provocatus miseratione susciperet et enutriret', *Vita Goaris*, ed. H. E. Stiene, *Wandalbert von Prüm, Vita et miracula Sancti Goaris* (Frankfurt, 1981), pp. 23–4. The ellipsis in my translation is the same as in Boswell, *Kindness*, p. 218, though I return to the astonishing detail left out below.

[181] Ferraro, *Nefarious Crimes*, pp. 10, 161, 202, and see the photograph of the rotating cradle of Santa Maria della Pietà, Venice at p. 9.

[182] The same term, *matricularii*, is found in the formula on exposed infants in the *Formulae Andecavenses*, on which see p. 74 above. For a sense of the social profile and position of *matricularii* within the church community, see M.A. Claussen, *The Reform of the Frankish Church: Chrodegang of Metz and the Regula canonicorum in the eighth century* (Cambridge, 2004), pp. 107–13.

[183] *Kindness*, p. 218.

for a moment this detail from a Carolingian perspective as part of a story about a custom at Trier from the Merovingian past. Regino was almost certainly familiar with the story – and not just because he wrote *De synodalibus causis* at Trier. In fact, the *vita Goaris* was written at Prüm in 839 and its author, Wandalbert, was one of the monastery's foremost intellectual figures. The connection between Goar and Prüm does not end there. Wandalbert noted in a parenthesis (it comes at the point marked by the ellipsis in the quotation above) that the marble bowl could be found in the refectory at Prüm thanks to a donation by Pippin.[184] Regino's provision in *De synodalibus causis* came from the pen of an expert aware of pastoral challenges in the present and also shaped by the collective memory of a custom from the past. As Regino wrote his manual in Trier he might well have remembered the stories and sins of tenants on Prüm's lands together with the sensation when he felt the marble of the foundling bowl with his fingertips and washed his palms in its water.

* * *

Historians should not take Carolingian ecclesiastical texts on abortion at face value. Subtle novelties lie beneath surface continuities. But claims of novelty also mask deeper continuities. Regino politely warned that he had included newer provisions in *De synodalibus causis*, 'things which I have deemed more pertinent to these our perilous times'.[185] His justification? Many new offences were being perpetrated 'which were unheard of in olden times because they were not committed and thus were not written and condemned in established rulings'.[186]

Perhaps Regino genuinely believed that moral decline and its novelties in sinning explained gaps in church tradition and perhaps similar thoughts occurred to others as they scanned ecclesiastical texts for details relevant to specific cases. There is a half-truth in Regino's justification. We may be sceptical that genuinely new lay behaviour was the primary cause of new measures. But in at least some cases committing perceptions or anticipations of behaviour to writing was new. The real novelty of Carolingian ecclesiastical texts on abortion lay in clerical behaviour. Even if we make allowances for the higher survival rate of texts from the Carolingian period, the corpus of material testifies to the unprecedented integration of condemnation of abortion

---

[184] Cf. 'quae etiam conca nunc in monasterio Prumia dono Pippini clarissimi regis aquaeductui mancipata fratribus aquam coram refectorio praebet', *Vita Goaris*, pp. 23–4; some manuscripts add that the bowl had since been placed in the vestiary, and presbyters and deacons washed their hands in it before and after mass. On the strong connections between Prüm and the Carolingian dynasty, see Airlie, 'Sad Stories', pp. 114–18.

[185] 'quae his periculosis temporibus nostris necessariora esse cognovi', *De synodalibus causis* (preface), p. 20.

[186] 'quae priscis temporibus inaudita, quia non facta, et ideo non scripta et fixis sententiis damnata', *De synodalibus causis* (preface), pp. 20–2.

within textual tools designed for clerical education, pastoral ministry and episcopal practice. Of course, we cannot take for granted how deeply ideas on abortion within these texts penetrated the murky world of the local priest and, through him, his flock. Modern Catholic history offers a cautionary tale. Amid the emergence of new forms of mass communication and the politicization of birth control, the early decades of the twentieth century witnessed an intensification of official reiterations of church doctrine on marital morality. Pius XI's papal encyclical *Casti Connubii*, a response to the Anglican approval of birth control at the Lambeth Conference in 1930, was published in the same year. Some committed Catholics became public witnesses to papal doctrine. In the 1930s American Catholics could tune into the radio preacher Fulton Sheen's fulminations against artificial contraception on the wireless or hear mission preachers at spiritual retreats speak with increasing directness on the ills of perverting marital morality. Yet, at precisely the same time, many priests across parishes in the USA were neither as vocal nor as articulate on such questions in the pulpit and confessional.[187]

Paradoxically, Carolingian ecclesiastical texts appear at the surface to be the most repetitive and, thus, least promising material for discerning active deliberation on abortion in the Early Middle Ages; but, when read closely, they suggest a quantitative and qualitative shift in the scale and extent of ecclesiastical action on abortion. Compared with their Visigothic and Merovingian counterparts, more Carolingian priests (or, for that matter, bishops) were invited to think and act about abortion through a mainstream of canons and rulings together with some more unusual outliers. Carolingian textual tools communicated traditional condemnation of abortion as a set of moral prompts, starting points for thought. These prompts were not meticulously coherent. They did not provide an entirely settled moral theory of abortion; in Regino's euphemism, they were 'diverse rulings' (*diversa statuta*). Rather, they provided guidance for the moral parameters within which to negotiate abortion in practice. Users of these texts confronted with the practice of abortion did what their authors had done. They navigated creative tensions between authority and innovation, between doctrines from the past and needs in the present, and between the spirit and letter of the law.

---

[187] Tentler, *Catholics and Contraception*, especially pp. 73–129.

6

Legislative Energies: Disputing Abortion in Law-codes

Imagine that a man hits a pregnant woman and unintentionally causes her to have an abortion. How should he make amends for killing a fetus? Would he have to pay compensation for the woman's injuries too? Did compensation depend on her status? What if she died? And suppose the man had meant to harm or kill her? Would he then also have to pay for killing what was in her womb? The thoughts of jurists who raised and wrestled with these questions have survived in a legal commentary, the *Liber Papiensis*, designed to guide legal practitioners in eleventh-century Pavia.[1] Evidence from multiple jurisdictions in subsequent centuries shows unequivocally that such cases really occurred. A fifteenth-century compilation of verdicts by a lay judicial panel operating in Leipzig, for example, included a verdict on two armed men who had broken into another man's house. The intruders came across his pregnant wife. Shaken by the ordeal, she fell ill and miscarried the child within a few days. If the homeowner could prove that his wife really had fallen ill out of fright and if the unintended abortion could be confirmed by two reputable women, the men would have to pay monetary compensation.[2]

The norms underlying the Leipzig verdict, if not quite the specific procedures, are reminiscent of norms embedded in post-Roman law-codes. The specific law on which the Pavian jurists were commenting had originally been issued by a seventh-century Lombard king. The legal approach addressed in theory at Pavia and in practice at Leipzig ultimately originated in early medieval law. What we lack for the Early Middle Ages, however, are equivalents of the *Liber Papiensis* and the Leipzig verdict: jurisprudential discussions of legal regulations on abortion and cases which allow us to see how such regulations were applied in practice. All that we have to work with are the regulations themselves in several *leges barbarorum* issued in post-Roman kingdoms.[3]

Theoretically, abortion could constitute an offence in a number of different

---

[1] *Liber Papiensis* Roth. 75, MGH LL 4, pp. 307–8. On the *Liber Papiensis*, see C. Radding, 'Legal Theory and Practice in Eleventh-Century Italy', *Law and History Review* 21.2 (2003), 377–81.
[2] Case quoted and discussed in Müller, *Criminalization*, pp. 128–9.
[3] For overviews of early medieval law-codes on abortion, see Elsakkers, RBL, pp. 329–71; Schwarz, *Schutz des Kindes*, pp. 35–79; Oliver, *Body Legal*, pp. 180–202. Unfortunately P. Tyszka, *The Human Body in Barbarian Laws, c.500–800*, trans. G. R. Torr (Frankfurt, 2013), came to my attention too late to incorporate in my findings.

ways. Third-party abortion, a useful shorthand for miscarriage induced through violence or other means, intentionally or accidentally, by someone other than the pregnant woman, appeared in all promulgated law-codes which clearly addressed abortion. People who supplied medicinal herbs or magical potions to cause abortion or otherwise affect fertility also featured in some codes – sometimes specified as women, sometimes not. But women who voluntarily underwent abortion were conspicuous by their absence in almost all the *leges barbarorum*. The most conspicuous exception was Visigothic law, which had come to address abortion from multiple angles by the seventh century for several reasons including a style of public morality peculiar to Visigothic Spain and the slowly dissolving residue of Roman legal ideas.[4]

This chapter will examine the handling of abortion in other early medieval law-codes with two questions, or clusters of questions, in the background. The first cluster relates to Wolfgang Müller's thesis on the criminalization of abortion. For Müller, we recall, abortion was handled as a sin and as a tort by early medieval authorities – but not as a crime. Laws on abortion in early medieval law-codes were designed to operate in the legal landscape of 'communal justice', a landscape where legal measures largely took the form of monetary compensation for specific offences. Compensation was designed to facilitate the settlement of disputes as an alternative to extra-legal violence and thereby maintain social order within relatively small communities.[5] If we accept that criminalization does not require a formal theory of crime, Visigothic law, I argued in chapter three, is an exception to Müller's scheme. The articles examined in this chapter, however, do not so obviously provide further exceptions. They were shaped by the underlying rationality of 'communal justice'; to put it more bluntly, this chapter will be dealing mainly in torts. Sin, tort and crime are useful ideal types in historical study of medieval legal systems. But were understandings of torts in early medieval law unaffected by ideas about sin? Was the boundary between tort and sin impermeable? Was abortion as crime unthinkable?

The second question concerns the relation between ecclesiastical and secular legal norms more directly. At the surface, law-codes provide a sustained non-ecclesiastical voice on abortion. But any contrast is complicated when we think of readers and interpretative communities. The cumulative impact of Christian norms on communities in which the law was contested and interpreted is like a glacier: shifts over time are as certain as they are imperceptible. In the Carolingian period, certainly, numerous ecclesiastical figures had knowledge, interests and expertise in law, including some figures we have

---

[4] See pp. 109–20 above. The other possible exception is Burgundian law, which adopted Constantinian laws on divorce. A man had a right to divorce if it was proven that his wife had dabbled in *maleficium*, Liber Constitutionum 34.3, MGH LNG 2.1, p. 68, or was a *venefica*, Lex Romana Burgundionum 21.2, MGH LNG 2.1, p. 143; see Elsakkers, RBL, pp. 333–4, on the possibility that this encompassed abortion.

[5] Müller, *Criminalization*, p. 42.

Abortion in Law-codes

already encountered. Alongside his episcopal statutes Gerbald of Liège circulated comments on tariffs in Salic and Ripuarian law.[6] In the later eighth and early ninth century, Arn of Salzburg, who might have overseen the composition of a penitential, *Vindobense B*, was also something of an 'authority figure' in the theory and practice of Bavarian law.[7]

Patrick Wormald once described the dissonance between legal and ecclesiastical approaches to murder as the 'central paradox of Carolingian law-giving'. Alongside 'all possible deference to the *leges*' came a 'massive output' of edicts which were 'by and large ecclesiastical in tone': '[I]t seems to have struck no legislator as unacceptably anomalous,' he noted, 'that capitularies were declaring homicide to be an unacceptable blot on a God-fearing and Bible-reading society, while the repeatedly endorsed *leges* continued to provide blithely for the rhythms of personal vengeance'.[8] Wormald's paradox can be switched to abortion (though this chapter's response is not intended to be switched back to address the original paradox). As we shall see, unlike ecclesiastical texts, most law-codes were seemingly uninterested in women's voluntary abortions. Were treatments of abortion circulating in law-codes further manifestations of Wormald's paradox? Ecclesiastical opposition to voluntary abortion alongside secular legal tolerance? If so, it was a paradox in which the likes of Gerbald and Arn acquiesced; and it was unthinkingly perpetuated in ecclesiastical scriptoria like the scriptorium at Cologne, where copies of canonical collections were produced alongside copies of the *Lex Salica* and *Lex Ribuaria* under the direction of the bishop and sometime courtier, Hildebald.[9]

The limits of law-codes

While the law-codes under examination in this chapter originated over a broad chronological and geographical span, it will be instructive to keep the Carolingian context in mind because copies of all of these codes (with one exception) survive in a large number of Carolingian manuscripts.[10] Carolingian

---

[6] R. McKitterick, 'Charlemagne's *Missi* and their Books', in *Early Medieval Studies in Memory of Patrick Wormald*, ed. S. Baxter *et al.* (Farnham, 2009), p. 264.

[7] W. Brown, *Unjust Seizure: Conflict, Interest, and Authority in an Early Medieval Society* (Ithaca, NY, 2001), pp. 102–23 (quotation at p. 105); M. Innes, 'Charlemagne, Justice and Written Law', in *Law, Custom and Justice in Late Antiquity and the Early Middle Ages*, ed. A. Rio (London, 2011), pp. 180–5. On the *P. Vindobense B* connection, see Meens, *Boeteboek*, p. 566.

[8] Wormald, '*Leges barbarorum*', p. 45.

[9] McKitterick, *Frankish Church*, p. 33. On Hildebald's career, see D. Bullough, 'Charlemagne's "Men of God": Alcuin, Hildebald and Arn', in *Charlemagne: Empire and Society*, ed. J. Storey (Manchester, 2005), pp. 142–6.

[10] R. McKitterick, *The Carolingians and the Written Word* (Cambridge, 1989), pp. 23–75. The exception (on a technicality) is the final law-code examined in this chapter, the *Lex Frisionum*. Owing to my linguistic limitations, I omit discussion of Anglo-Saxon

rulers, like other early medieval rulers, cultivated a 'lively tradition of admiration for the Christian emperors as lawgivers'.[11] But the ideological capital of law-giving for kings is clearer than the practical ramifications of law-codes for regions and communities within their kingdoms. The problem is not a dearth of sources. A large mass of Carolingian manuscripts contained copies of law-codes and Rosamond McKitterick has identified three principal manuscript contexts: law-books, which typically contained several *leges* together with Carolingian capitularies; school books; and ecclesiastical collections, which tended to bring together canon and secular law. In the law-books the *Lex Salica* was typically found alongside the *Lex Ribuaria* and *Lex Alamannorum*, though sometimes also with Lombard, Burgundian and Bavarian codes.[12] The manuscript evidence points to practical interest in written law within an empire defined by legal pluralism. Law-codes were transmitted in manuscripts containing other law-codes as well as other kinds of legal and ecclesiastical texts, and these manuscripts were being read by ecclesiastical as well as royal officials.

The relative abundance of law-codes in Carolingian manuscripts, however, contrasts with the relative paucity of direct evidence for how – and, in fact, whether – their laws were actually applied in practice. Typically cast as the arch-sceptic on the practicality of law-codes, Wormald contended that a large amount of early medieval legislation 'gives the impression that its purpose was simply to get something into writing that *looked* like a written law-code, more or less regardless of its actual value to judges sitting in court'.[13] As Alice Rio has cautioned, it is easy to overlook the nuance of Wormald's scepticism, which is 'often caricatured as an outright rejection of laws' relationship to reality'. Meagre references to law-codes in other sources like charters, which more directly reflect processes of dispute settlement and legal practice, and the textual conservatism of law-codes themselves (which we will see below in the case of the *Lex Salica*) problematize assumptions about the relationship between law-codes and evolving social practice across time and space.[14] For law-codes, in which almost all legal discussion of abortion is to be found, were the most static kind of legal text. No allusions to abortion appear in texts which are closer to legal practice and dispute settlement on the ground, such

---

law, on which see Elsakkers, RBL, pp. 348–50, though much of the discussion in this chapter is applicable to the treatment of abortion in Anglo-Saxon law.

[11] J.L. Nelson, 'Translating Images of Authority: The Christian Roman Emperors in the Carolingian World', reprinted in J.L. Nelson, *The Frankish World, 750–900* (London, 1996), p. 91.

[12] McKitterick, *Written Word*, pp. 46–55.

[13] P. Wormald, '*Lex scripta* and *Verbum regis*: Legislation and Germanic Kingship from Euric to Cnut', reprinted in P. Wormald, *Legal Culture in the Early Medieval West: Text, Image, and Experience* (London, 1999), pp. 1–44 (quotation at p. 13, italics in original).

[14] A. Rio, 'Introduction', in *Law, Custom, and Justice*, p. 7.

as formularies, or (with one Merovingian exception) in texts which represent more up-to-date written regulations, capitularies.

In light of these problems the first point to stress is that social offences anticipated by legislators were not phantasms. Nestled around specific laws on abortion were other laws addressing such offences as homicide, physical violence and *raptus*. The imprint of these offences in the documentary record, as opposed to narrative or prescriptive sources, is slight. There was an incentive to produce and preserve documents on property disputes and, for this reason, charters have rightly eclipsed law-codes as the starting point for the study of dispute settlement. But charters are of little use for present purposes: abortion and property rights are not natural bedfellows.[15] Compared with documentary practices relating to land-ownership, there was certainly less incentive to produce and preserve documents on homicide, assault and so on.[16] But less does not mean none at all. Formularies, relatively sidelined by historians until Alice Rio's important recent monograph, contain some model documents on homicide, violent assault, *raptus* and, as we saw in connection with Caesarius of Arles's sermons, infant abandonment – in other words, traces of actual cases and/or anticipations of future cases.[17] Admittedly, no

---

[15] Charters may yield more to historians interested in infertility and childlessness: see N. L. Taylor, 'Women and Wills: Sterility and Intestacy in Catalonia in the Eleventh and Twelfth Centuries', *Medieval Encounters* 12.1 (2006), 87–96. The one possible exception of which I know is problematic. A Lombard charter, ostensibly from 787, for a foundling hospital in Milan supposedly established by a certain Datheus justified the foundation because of the fate of unbaptized souls killed through abortion and infanticide by those who wanted to hide sexual sin. Boswell, *Kindness*, p. 225 n.158, suspected that it was a later medieval forgery, a view echoed more recently by R. Balzaretti, 'Women, Property and Urban Space in Tenth-Century Italy', *Gender & History* 23.3 (2011), 572 n.13; the question of authenticity is, to use the most relevant Obamaism, above my paygrade. The charter certainly contains intriguing details (including, for example, a request for wet-nurses) and, for what it is worth, here is the relevant passage: 'Because the race of mankind is frequently deceived through lust, and from here the evil of murder is born, since those who conceive in adultery kill tender fetuses so that they are not betrayed in public, and send the little ones to hell without the cleansing of baptism, because they found no place in which they could deliver [infants] alive and hide the disgrace of adultery; but in fact, they throw them in drains and feculent streams, and thus each time a child is conceived out of fornication, murders are perpetrated in the world [*Et quia frequenter per luxuriam hominum genus decipitur, et exinde malum homicidii generatur, dum concipientes et adultero, ne prodantur in publico, foetos teneros necant, et absque baptismatis lavacro parvulos ad tartara mittunt, quia nullum reperiunt locum, in quo servare vivos valeant et celare possint adulterii stuprum; set per cloacas et sterquilinia fluminaque proiciunt, atque per hoc toties exercentur homicidia in orbe, quoties ex fornicatione conceptus fuerit infans*]', no. 61, ed. G. Porro-Lambertenghi, *Codex diplomaticus Langobardiae* (Turin, 1873), p. 115.

[16] Oliver, *Body Legal*, pp. 28–9.

[17] For examples of formulae dealing with homicide, assault and *raptus*, see *Formulary of Angers* 6, 12, 26, 44, 50, *Formulary of Marculf* 1.2, 37, 2.16, 18, 29, trans. Rio, *Formularies*, pp. 53, 59–60, 69–70, 85–6, 91–2, 161–2, 171–2, 199–202, 211–13. For a summary of

surviving formulary contains model documents about abortion. But comparative material shows that the kinds of scenarios discussed hypothetically in early medieval law-codes became the substance of numerous later medieval cases.[18] The earlier absence of documentary evidence for abortion cases makes for a weak argument from silence on social practice, for it is doubtful that violence against women, pregnant or otherwise, suddenly proliferated only at some point after the millennium. While it is impossible to write case histories of abortion for the Early Middle Ages, this is almost certainly not because there were no cases.

But the extent to which law-codes reflect the norms and procedures by which these lost cases were mediated, adjudicated and settled – to mention nothing of social attitudes – is a different matter. Recent scholarship on legal practice emphasizes that law-codes were one resource among many with which to frame legal arguments. Law-codes functioned as a 'point of reference, not a straightjacket'. They provided guidelines to be consulted and adapted flexibly to local circumstances and particular situations.[19] Furthermore, the norms embedded in legal articles are reducible neither to top-down royal impositions nor to bottom-up codifications of timeless tribal custom. It is more accurate (though also necessarily vaguer) to regard law-codes as part of a 'dialogue between legal norms and social norms'.[20]

If law-codes represent one voice in a dialogue between written norms and unwritten custom, other voices are less audible. Unlike formularies, law-codes do not provide a worm's-eye perspective, a window onto 'legal processes from the point of view of practitioners and litigants'. Alice Rio has demonstrated that the relatively rigid approach to freedom and unfreedom in law-codes co-existed with a more complex and negotiable picture in formularies. Salic law and Carolingian capitularies, for instance, stipulated that free women who married *servi* would lose their free status along with their children; the formulae evidence shows legal provisions for masters to forego claims on *servi* and their wives.[21] Legal articles, as we shall see, set out guiding principles for adjudication, culpability and redress in highly condensed form. In the absence of the kind of beneficial complications provided by formularies, law-codes provide a simplified picture of both social problems and attempts to resolve them. We do well to remember this.

Frankish and Lombard cases involving assault, see Oliver, *Body Legal*, pp. 53–61. On infant abandonment, see pp. 74 above; on poisoning, p. 225 n. 77 below.

[18] Müller, *Criminalization*; Butler, 'Abortion by Assault'; S. Butler, 'Abortion Medieval Style? Assaults on Pregnant Women in Later Medieval England', *Women's Studies* 40.6 (2011), 778–99.

[19] Innes, 'Charlemagne', pp. 171–2 (quotation at p. 171); see too T. Faulkner, 'Carolingian Kings and the *Leges barbarorum*', *Historical Research* 86.233 (2013), 456.

[20] Rio, 'Introduction', p. 3.

[21] Rio, *Legal Practice*, pp. 212–37, with pp. 216–23 on mixed marriages.

The feud should end there: The rationality of legal articles on abortion

There is a surface paradox. Churchmen were interested in voluntary abortion. Legislators, by contrast, seemed disinterested in it. To understand why, we begin with four older law-codes circulating in Carolingian manuscripts: the *Lex Salica*, *Lex Ribuaria*, *Lex Alamannorum* and *Edictum Rothari*. The initial focus will be on the texts and contexts, the genesis and logic, of their articles on abortion. The approach is slightly artificial – we may well dissect articles from law-codes in a way that most early medieval users did not – but is nonetheless important in elucidating the thought processes of legislators and the dispute contexts which they were anticipating from clues in their texts. The handling of abortion across law-codes was not identical and we must avoid false assimilations. But they shared an underlying rationality: dispute settlement.

Unnamed infants: Abortion in Salic and Ripuarian law
Salic law originated in the early sixth century.[22] Two Merovingian redactions (A and C) have survived alongside other Carolingian redactions. The *Lex Salica Karolina*, an emended Carolingian edition of Salic law, was produced under Charlemagne around the turn of the ninth century. This redaction of Salic law survives in over sixty manuscript copies (fifty-four from the ninth or tenth centuries) and greatly outnumbers other Carolingian redactions: three copies survive of a redaction made under Pippin between 751 and 768 (D), and six of another redaction compiled earlier under Charlemagne at the end of eighth century (E). The *Lex Salica Karolina*, the 'redaction sanctioned by the Carolingian king and his advisors', was, in effect, an official text.[23]

A great deal of Salic law established compensation tariffs for bodily injuries and other offences escalating up to homicide, for which perpetrators had to compensate the victim's kin with his or her wergild or monetary value in the eyes of the law. Articles on many offences did not specify the status, gender, ethnicity and so on of perpetrator or victim. But the social profile of victims, including gender, was particularly important in the case of murder because it constituted a 'definitive loss for the family, so that the worth of the

---

[22] I. Wood, *The Merovingian Kingdoms 450–751* (London, 1994), pp. 108–14.
[23] McKitterick, *Written Word*, p. 41. Despite differences of interpretation, I am indebted to M. Elsakkers, 'Abortion, Poisoning, Magic, and Contraception in Eckhardt's *Pactus legis Salicae*', *Amsterdamer Beitrage zur älteren Gemanistik* 57 (2002), 233–68, as a guide to the principal modern edition. Eckhardt's *Pactus* is a reconstructed text which absorbed all textual variants. The resulting text, which contains four relevant articles, does not accurately represent any of the surviving Merovingian or Carolingian redactions. The *Pactus* forms the main body of the edition in MGH LNG 4.1, but four A-recension texts (A1–4), two C-recension texts (C5–6) and an edition of the *Lex Salica Karolina* are printed synoptically beneath the main text; the other Carolingian recensions (D and E) are edited by Eckhardt in MGH LNG 4.2.

victim needed to be assessed more precisely'.[24] One sequence of articles in the *Lex Salica Karolina* addressed the killing of women or children (literally boys, *pueri*) separately from murder in general. Amounts of compensation were listed for killing a boy under twelve years of age (600 *solidi*), for cutting the hair of a long-haired boy (*puer crinitus*) without parental consent (45 *solidi*) and for doing the same to a girl (62½ *solidi*).[25] The next article turned to the killing of pregnant women, whose wergild was set at 700 *solidi*. (By way of comparison, the standard wergild stipulated elsewhere for Frankish freemen was 200 *solidi*.)[26] The envisaged scenario might well have been a violent one, for the relevant verb in older redactions and variant manuscripts oscillated between killing (*occidere* or *interficere*) and beating (*battuere*).[27] This was followed by an article covering abortion and infanticide: 'If anyone has killed an infant in its mother's belly or born before it has a name within nine nights, he should be judged culpable for 4,000 *denarii* which makes 100 *solidi*'.[28] Subsequent articles in the sequence calibrated the compensation for killing women according to their reproductive capacity: 200 *solidi* for killing a 'free girl within the years before she can have infants' or a 'woman after she has not been able to have infants',[29] but 600 *solidi* for killing a 'free woman after she has begun to have infants'.[30]

Textual conservatism, an instinct to 'maintain the integrity of the traditions that the *Lex* symbolized', insulated the *Lex Salica* from major changes over the centuries.[31] Nonetheless, it is possible to trace fragments of how legal thinking evolved across Merovingian and Carolingian redactions. Compensation for pregnant women (but not infants) varied and so too did details in the wording. One manuscript of the earliest Merovingian redaction contained an article on killing a pregnant women followed by an article on killing an infant in the belly of its mother without any mention of nine nights, naming or birth; in other words, an article on third-party abortion but not infanticide.[32]

---

[24] J. L. Nelson and A. Rio, 'Women and Laws in Early Medieval Europe', in *The Oxford Handbook of Women and Gender in Medieval Europe*, ed. J. M. Bennett and R. M. Karras (Oxford, 2013), pp. 104–6 (quotation at p. 106).
[25] *Lex Salica Karolina* 26.1–3, pp. 89, 91.
[26] *Lex Salica Karolina* 43.1, p. 155.
[27] *Lex Salica Karolina* 26.4, p. 91.
[28] 'Si quis infantem in ventre matris suae aut natum antequam nomen habeat infra IX noctes occiderit, IVM denariis qui faciunt solidos C culpabilis iudicetur', *Lex Salica Karolina* 26.5, p. 91.
[29] 'puellam ingenuam infra annos antequam infantes possit habere possit habere'; 'feminam postquam infantes habere non potuerit', *Lex Salica Karolina* 26.6, 8, p. 93.
[30] 'feminam ingenuam postquam infantes coeperit habere', *Lex Salica Karolina* 26.7, p. 93. In some manuscripts of the Merovingian A-redaction equivalents of these articles on women's wergilds are also inserted into the compensation tariffs for homicide in general: *Lex Salica* (A3) 41.13–15, (A4) 41.10–12, p. 160.
[31] Wormald, '*Leges barbarorum*', p. 41.
[32] *Lex Salica* (A4) 24.5–6, p. 90.

The two older Carolingian recensions followed this in spirit: an article on anyone who fatally struck (*debattuere* or, in the E-recension, *percutere*, the same verb used in Latin versions of Exodus on abortion) a pregnant woman, and the next on anyone who killed an infant in its mother's womb (*uterus* now, rather than *venter*): again, abortion but not infanticide.[33] The first additions appeared in three other manuscripts of the earliest Merovingian redaction, which extended the article by adding, 'or before it has a name'. All of them, incidentally, phrased the preceding article in terms of physical violence against pregnant women.[34] Versions in another Merovingian redaction made the further addition, 'within nine nights'.[35] Finally, in the *Lex Salica Karolina* this was further glossed with 'having been born'. The chronological sequence indicates that originally legislators were thinking in terms of violence against pregnant women. There might even have been an associated vernacular term.[36] Initially, subsequent additions (nine nights, naming) look like further permutations of the original scenario: an infant which survived the assault on its mother and a violently induced birth but later died. This was the explicit function of a reference to nine nights in Alamannic law, to which we shortly turn. By the time of the *Lex Salica Karolina*, however, the article had come to cover both abortion and infanticide.

The most common companion to the *Lex Salica* in Carolingian manuscripts was the *Lex Ribuaria*, which probably originated in seventh-century Austrasia, perhaps under Dagobert I (d. 639).[37] The relevant Ripuarian article was evidently derived from Salic law. The spirit of the law was the same, though the organization and wording were slightly different. The article on third-party abortion appeared alongside others in which wergild was affected by some dimension of the victim's ethnicity or ecclesiastical rank. Four articles set out compensation that varied according to the victim's ethnic group (so, for

---

[33] *Lex Salica (D)* 30.2–3, *(E)* 30.2–3 (*percutere* in the latter, which also sets the wergild for pregnant women at 300 *solidi*), pp. 70–3.

[34] E.g. 'Si quis femina ingenua et gravida trabaterit si moritur', *Lex Salica (A1)* 24.3–4, with comparable variants in *(A2)* 24.3–4, *(A3)* 24.5–6, p. 90; A1 and A2 set the wergild for a pregnant woman at 800 *solidi*.

[35] *Lex Salica (C5)* 24.5, *(C6)* 24.7, p. 91; C6 sets the wergild for a pregnant woman at 300 *solidi*.

[36] Vernacular glosses in some manuscripts of the A-, C- and D-redactions, the so-called Malberg glosses, contain variants of Old Germanic terms. In most cases slightly different terms appear in, respectively, the article on pregnant women and the article on abortion/infanticide (e.g. *adnouaddo* and *anne ando* in A2, *annouuano* and *annouuado* in C6), though D9 contains the same term (*anno ano*) in both articles. The meaning(s) is not certain, though 'unborn' and 'unnamed' are two plausible possibilities: see Elsakkers, 'Abortion, Poisoning', 249–51, with further references. Settling the question is well beyond my linguistic expertise. However, if this etymology is on the right track, the inclusion of these vernacular terms in multiple manuscripts of the D-redaction, in which articles addressed abortion but not infanticide, suggests to me that 'unborn' is more likely.

[37] Wood, *Merovingian Kingdoms*, pp. 115–17; Wormald, '*Leges barbarorum*', pp. 40–1.

example, a Frank was worth 200 *solidi* while a Frisian or Alaman was worth 160 *solidi*). Five more elaborated escalating amounts of compensation for different members of the clergy, rising up to 900 *solidi* for a bishop.[38] Tucked on at the end before commutation tariffs for converting *solidi* into silver or livestock came the article on abortion and infanticide: 'If anyone has killed the offspring in a woman or born, before it has a name, he should be judged culpable for 100 *solidi*. And if he killed the mother with offspring, he should be fined 700 *solidi*'.[39] The connection with violence against pregnant women was not as explicit as in some Salic redactions insofar as the wergild for a childbearing woman was defined elsewhere in the text, though with noticeable precision: 600 *solidi* for a woman 'after she has begun to bear all the way to her fortieth year'.[40]

The arithmetic is straightforward; 700 *solidi* for killing a pregnant woman equals 600 *solidi* for a woman of childbearing age plus 100 *solidi* for the *infans*. Drawing a comparison with compensation for wounds and injuries, Elsakkers has argued that the 100 *solidi* fine 'indicates that abortion and infanticide were regarded [respectively] as serious injuries or attempted murder [sic], but not as homicide'.[41] But by the same logic, the compensation for killing a *Romanus* or a cleric, whose wergilds were set at 100 *solidi* in Ripuarian law, also signals that their murders were somehow seen as not really homicide. The most straightforward reading of the text and context of the Salic and Ripuarian articles – in both cases articles appeared in sections stipulating the wergilds for specific members of society – is that 100 *solidi* simply was the wergild for a fetus or very young infant, whatever views defendants or plaintiffs might have held about the humanity of the fetus or very young infant – or, for that matter, about the humanity of a *Romanus* or a cleric.[42]

---

[38] *LR* 40.1–9, MGH LNG 3.2, pp. 92–4; articles dealing with clerics or affairs connected to the church (e.g. church freedman) are one example of subtle differences between Salic and Ripuarian law, on which see I. Wood, 'Jural Relations among the Franks and Alamanni', in *Franks and Alamanni in the Merovingian Period*, ed. I. Wood (Woodbridge, 1998), pp. 219–21.

[39] 'Si quis partum in feminam interfecerit seu natum, priusquam nomen habeat, bis quinquagenos solid. culpabilis iudicetur. Quod si matrem cum partu interfecerit, septingentos solid. multetur', *LR* 40.10, p. 94.

[40] 'postquam parere coeperit usque ad quadragesimum annum', *LR* 12.1, p. 78. The same principle that reproductive capacity affects a woman's wergild appears in the *Lex Thuringorum* 48–9, MGH LL 5, p. 136, where it also interacted with the social status of women.

[41] Elsakkers, 'Abortion, Poisoning', 243. Oliver, *Body Legal*, pp. 195–6, follows Elsakkers but also adds that the 100 *solidi* fine was for 'killing a late-period fetus' (p. 196), which is plausible but certainly not explicit.

[42] As the *reductio ad absurdum* suggests, I have reservations over this argument even if there were a strong numerical correspondence between wergilds; but, at any rate, the correspondence is weak. Out of all the Salic articles on injuries (*Lex Salica Karolina* 31.1–19 or Eckhardt's *Pactus* 29.1–18) only three set compensation at 100 *solidi*: amputating hands, feet, eyes or noses (*Lex Salica Karolina* 31.1), chopping

Boy or girl? Abortion in Alamannic law

The *Lex Alamannorum* represents a later stage in the production of early medieval law-codes. Alamannic law possibly originated at roughly the same time as Ripuarian law in the early seventh century; the fragmentary *Pactus legis Alamannorum* might approximate to these origins. A later code, the *Lex Alamannorum*, associated with the Alamannic duke Lantfrid (d. 730) was issued in the early eighth century. The *Lex Alamannorum* bears a stronger ecclesiastical impression than the *Lex Salica* or *Lex Ribuaria*. An opening sequence of articles dealt with matters of church property, rights of asylum and the murder of clerics, while later articles addressed subjects also covered in ecclesiastical regulations, such as observing the sabbath and incest.[43]

The two relevant articles on abortion, however, do not show palpable ecclesiastical influence. The first dealt with a scenario of abortion caused by a third party: 'If any woman was pregnant and through another's action the infant is born dead, or if it was born alive and does not live nine nights, he who has been accused should pay 40 *solidi* or swear with 12, half chosen.'[44] Again the wergild was relatively low (by way of comparison a freeman's wergild was 160 *solidi* and a freewoman's wergild was doubled, 320 *solidi* without consideration of reproductive capacity).[45] Noticeably this was not an article on infanticide. The period of nine nights was explicitly tied to the aftermath of abortion caused by another party.

The second article appeared later in the *Lex Alamannorum* and approached the question in a different way:

> If anyone makes a pregnant woman abort in such a way that you are able to recognize whether it had been a male or female: if it should be male, he should compensate with 12 *solidi*; but if female, with 24.[46]

---

out someone's tongue (31.16) and castrating a freeborn man (31.18). None of the articles on wounds (*Lex Salica Karolina* 19.1–10 or *Pactus* 17.1–12) did. Many compensations, including that for attempted murder (*Lex Salica Karolina* 19.1), were set at 62½ *solidi*.

[43] Wood, 'Jural Relations', pp. 221–4.

[44] 'Si qua mulier gravida fuerit, et per factum alterum infans natus mortuus fuerit, aut si vivus natus et novem noctes non vivit, cui reputatum fuerit, 40 solidos solvat aut cum 12 medios electos iuret', LA (A) 70, MGH LNG 5.1, p. 137. This edition prints the A- and B-redaction texts together; the prologue to the A-redaction mentions the renovation of the *lex* at the time of Lantfrid; the B-redaction is younger but claims an older heritage going back to the time of Clothar II (d. 629). Here and below I quote from the A-redaction text. There are no significant variants in the B-redaction text, though in this case LA (B) 77 specifies eight rather than nine nights (and other manuscripts oscillate between eight/nine and nights/days).

[45] LA (A) 60.1–2, pp. 129–30.

[46] 'Si quis aliquis mulierem prignantem aborsum fecerit, ita ut iam cognoscere possis, utrum vir aut femina fuisset: si vir debuit esse, cum 12 solidis conponat; si autem femina, cum 24', LA (A) 88.1, p. 150.

And if he cannot recognize whether [it had been male or female] and it was not yet formed in the outlines of a body, he should compensate 12 *solidi*. If he [i.e. the plaintiff] seeks more, he [the plaintiff or the defendant?] should clear himself with oath-swearers.[47]

The rationale underlying the wergilds is difficult to ascertain. They were lower than in the earlier article (24 or 12 *solidi* versus 40 *solidi*). Was the difference because legislators were consciously addressing different scenarios (perhaps the earlier article envisaged a scenario later in pregnancy)? Or had they simply not joined up the dots? The relevance of the sex of the fetus is even more tantalizing. The distinction hinged on visible, even tangible, physical features, the 'outlines of a body', rather than on metaphysical ideas about the soul.[48] Visigothic legal measures, as we saw in chapter four, made an unformed/formed distinction too. But in Alamannic law the distinction was a means to an end. Both an unformed fetus of indeterminate sex *and* a recognizably male fetus warranted the same amount. The key point was that the female fetus warranted more. Fetal development differentiated compensation according to sex, not the other way around.[49]

There are other early medieval legal texts for comparison but comparison does not necessarily bring clarity. Two Merovingian additions to Salic law also drew attention to the sex of fetuses after abortion by assault. To complicate matters, however, one raised the wergild for female fetuses and the other for male fetuses. First, a capitulary issued by Chilperic I (d. 584). Within a series of articles on offences against women (under the heading, 'On a woman sliced or cropped [*caesa et excapillata*]') came a sequence beginning with an article which described forms of violence against pregnant women in conspicuous anatomical detail:

[47] 'Si nec utrum cognoscere potest, et iam non fuit formatus in liniamenta corporis, 12 solidos conponat. Si amplius requiret, cum sacramentalis se edoniet', LA (A) 88.2, pp. 150–1. It is not entirely clear whether oathswearing was required of the plaintiff asking for greater compensation or the defendant; perhaps the more intuitive (but also more grammatically awkward) assumption is the latter, though the admittedly much later Leipzig verdict shows how oathswearing could be used to assess plaintiffs' claims in such cases.
[48] Elsakkers, 'Vocabulary', pp. 383–4, 389, 410, notes that the term *liniamenta corporis* echoes the term used by Macrobius and Augustine to describe fetal formation at, respectively, the thirty-fifth to forty-ninth or forty-fifth days, but also acknowledges that it is unclear whether the *Lex Alamannorum* envisaged abortion quite so early in pregnancy. If there is an affinity, it seems very faint; and, even if by chance our author had actually read and remembered Macrobius or Augustine on fetal formation, it is highly unlikely that readers read *liniamenta corporis* as a reference to a specific embryological theory. In other words, despite the verbal echo, the embryological texts shed less light on the thought processes underlying the distinction in Alamannic law than first meets the eye.
[49] Cf. 'Alamannic law also uses the criterion of formation, and defines the difference between early term and late abortion in terms of gender differentiation', Elsakkers, 'Vocabulary', p. 389.

If anyone has struck a pregnant free woman in the belly or kidneys with a fist or a heel and does not strike the fetus out and on account of this she is stricken almost to the point of death, he should be judged culpable for 200 *solidi*.[50]

But if anyone strikes the fetus out dead and she herself escapes, he should be judged culpable for 600 *solidi*.[51]

The sequence continued: if the woman died, 900 *solidi*; if she had been under the protection of the king, 1,200 *solidi*; and finally 'if the infant who is struck out is a girl', a huge 2,400 *solidi*.[52] This staggering sum might have been connected to the preceding article: in other words, the infant conceived by a woman under the protection of the king, in which case perhaps (though this is still not entirely satisfying) the huge wergild reflected the importance of marriageable daughters to families in the upper echelons of Merovingian society. The second Merovingian addition to Salic law is textually problematic. It is nonetheless worth quoting. Yet another redaction stipulated a 600 *solidi* wergild for killing a pregnant woman but then added: 'And if it was proved that the offspring was a boy, he should be judged culpable for 600 *solidi* on similar terms for the boy himself'.[53]

Why did a female fetus warrant greater compensation in Alamannic law? One suggestion is that the doubling of the wergild reflected the 'precariousness of a girl's life as well as her sexual value as an adult'.[54] Another way of

[50] 'Si quis mulierem ingenuam pregnantem in ventre aut in renis percusserit pugno aut calce et ei pecus non excutiat et illa propter hoc gravata fuerit quasi usque ad mortem, CC solidos culpabilis iudicetur', *Capitula legi Salicae addita* 3.104.4, MGH LNG 4.1, p. 260. The word *pecus* literally means cattle, but it was also used to describe the fetus in some medical texts. For example, when Muscio addressed suitable care for pregnant women in the seventh month of pregnancy, he warned against too much exertion 'in case the already perfected fetus is thrown outside [*pecus iam perfectum foris excutiatur*]', *Genecia* 44, p. 16; cf. Elsakkers, RBL, p. 363.
[51] 'Si quis vero pecus mortuum excusserit et ipsa evaserit, DC solidos culpabilis iudicetur', *Capitula legi Salicae addita* 3.104.5, p. 260.
[52] 'Si vero infans puella est, qui excutetur, MMCCCC solidos conponat', *Capitula legi Salicae addita* 3.104.6–8, p. 260.
[53] 'Et si probatum fuerit, quod partus ille puer fuerit, simili conditione pro ipso puero DC solidos culpabilis iudicetur', *Pactus legis Salicae* 65e.1, p. 235. This is quoted from Eckhardt's *Pactus*, which in turn incorporated it from a sixteenth-century edition by Johannes Herold. According to Eckhardt, Herold based his edition on now-lost manuscripts including a putative B-redaction manuscript from which this article supposedly derives: Elsakkers, 'Abortion, Poisoning', 233–7, provides a helpful textual overview. Even if authentic, the article is unrepresentative of Salic legal tradition. Its inclusion in the main body of Eckhardt's *Pactus* is misleading.
[54] E. Coleman, 'Infanticide in the Early Middle Ages', in *Women in Medieval Society*, ed. S. M. Stuard (Philadelphia, 1976), p. 60. Coleman, it should be stressed, uses Alamannic law as a counter-example ('[t]he Alamannic Code shows a consistent care for females') to the evidence she draws upon for her thesis on female infanticide in the Early Middle Ages. If there were a connection between articles on

thinking about this requires a mental shift from the general to the particular, from a putative tribal custom to the significance of what losing a girl might have meant to an individual family. Did the article arise out of the experience of a specific case or cases?

There are flickers of such a possibility. The first thing to note is chronology. The earlier Alamannic article might have been fairly old, for it survives in a fragment of the *Pactus legis Alamannorum*.[55] The second article, however, does not. It was quite probably a subsequent addition to Alamannic law. The next point is that noticeably specific details in any regulation can reflect specific circumstances in which it arose.[56] Consider the article which immediately follows. It clarified husbands' rights to inherit property when their wives died in childbirth. A husband could take hold of his wife's property if the infant, surviving its mother for an hour or so, had been able to open its eyes and see the roof and four walls of the house before dying.[57] A woman's natal and marital families had conflicting interests in the destination of her property, and the fine detail drew a much needed line. The specificity of detail both here and in the preceding abortion article does not, of course, automatically mean that the articles originated in individual cases. But, at the same time, it is likely that such specific details entered legislators' minds after the kinds of disputes they were meant to resolve had occurred; or, to put it the other way around, that such specific details were less likely to arise purely out of thought experiments on dispute scenarios.[58]

There is, finally, one grammatical detail in the abortion article which could conceivably be a stray trace of a particular judgment. It is easy to miss. The third-person was the staple of legal articles just as it was the staple of penitential rulings. But the opening to the article briefly lapsed into the second-person: 'If anyone makes a pregnant woman abort in such a way that *you* are able [*possis*] to recognize', etc. For a moment, compare formularies. Compilers

abortion and socially sanctioned undervaluing of girls we would expect the opposite: a *higher* valuing of male fetuses.

[55] *Pactus legis Alamannorum* 12, MGH LNG 5.1, p. 24.
[56] A good example takes the form of a unique provision in Bavarian law regulating both the killing and deposition of bishops, LB 1.10, MGH LNG 5.2, pp. 281–3. The law looks like a trace of the historical circumstances surrounding the death of Emmeram of Regensburg in the seventh century according to C. I. Hammer, 'Arbeo of Freising's "Life and Passion" of St. Emmeram: The Martyr and his Critics', *Revue d'histoire écclesiastique* 101.1 (2006), 30–4. We turn to Arbeo of Freising's *vita* of Emmeram below.
[57] *LA (A)* 89.1–2, pp. 151–2.
[58] In one sense this is true of many articles: *pace* Dindimus and the Brahmans, murders predate written laws on murder. But the basic structure of many such laws – a wergild, further calibrated according to status, gender and so on – could plausibly be the product of hypothetical thinking about murder. It seems to me less likely, though it is certainly not impossible, that the articles in question emerged quite so hypothetically.

of formulae often, though certainly not always, transformed documents on specific cases into model documents by erasing particular details: a name replaced with a pronoun like *ille*, and so on.[59] It is possible that the lapse into the second-person was similar to an imperfectly *ille*-fied formula, a tiny trace of a particular judgment or correspondence on a case. Scribal error, of course, is always a convenient get-out and the relevant manuscript by a certain Wandalgarius, the oldest dateable witness to the *Lex Alamannorum*, is infamous for its errors.[60] But, in this case, what we have is a scribal error one way or another. The question is which way. An unusual mistake introduced into the text by a scribe who certainly made other mistakes? Or an original feature of the text which this slightly haphazard scribe, unlike at least some other scribes, did not correct? The fact that the only other manuscript in which this reading occurs belongs to a separate family of *Lex Alamannorum* manuscripts makes the latter more likely.[61] It is conceivable that the legislative response to the scenario of third-party abortion incorporated guidance from a real case or from the accumulated experience of real cases by extending a broader principle in Alamannic law: a woman's wergild was twice that of a man's.

Legislative energies: The rationality of law-codes
Our final examples appeared in the edict issued by the Lombard king, Rothari, in 643. It contains two – or four, depending on how one sees it – relevant articles. One article addressed pregnant slave-girls and abortion by assault: 'If someone has struck a pregnant slave-girl and caused abortion, he should compensate three *solidi*. But if she dies from the blow, he shall compensate for her as well as for what died in her womb'.[62] The principle was clear: two separate amounts of compensation, one for the mother and the other for 'what died in her womb'. Jarringly, this article appeared amid a sequence on animals and livestock: the two preceding articles addressed the same scenario with the same clear principle but in the cases of cows and mares. In all three

---

[59] Rio, *Legal Practice*, pp. 47–8.
[60] *Possis* is the reading in both Eckhardt's edition of the *Lex Alamannorum*, quoted above, and in an older edition in MGH LL 5, p. 115. This reading only occurs in two of the 12 A-recension manuscripts which Eckhardt used in his edition (A1 = St Gall, Stiftsbibliothek, Ms. 731, A12 = Paris, Bibliothèque nationale de France, Lat. 10753); the others all have the third-person (*possit*, and in one case, *posset*). However, Eckhardt regarded A1 as the oldest and most authoritative witness to the *Lex Alamannorum* (A): see MGH LNG 5.1, pp. 12–14. Copied in 793, A1 is well known for what McKitterick, *Written Word*, p. 46, calls its 'notorious mistakes' ('Sermo valde corruptus est', Eckhardt warned in his introduction before listing examples).
[61] See MGH LNG 5.1, p. 14.
[62] 'Si quis percusserit ancilla gravida et avortum fecirit, conponat solidos tres. Si autem ex ipsa percussura mortua fuerit, conponat eam, simul et quod in utero eius mortuum est', *Edictum Rothari* 334, MGH LL 4, p. 76.

cases compensation went to owners.⁶³ The other relevant Lombard article appeared elsewhere in the *Edictum Rothari*. This law, later discussed by Pavian jurists in the *Liber Papiensis*, addressed abortion by assault in the case of free-women in more detail:

> If an infant in its mother's womb has been accidentally killed by someone: if the woman is a freewoman and has escaped, she should be assessed as a freewoman according to her nobility, and the infant should be compensated for at half of what she has been valued. But if she has died, he should compensate for her according to her rank in addition to what was dead in her womb, as above, the feud ceasing because he did it accidentally.⁶⁴

This encapsulated the rationality of most legal articles on abortion. Law-codes provided guidelines to help resolve disputes between kin-groups in the aftermath of offences precisely in order to prevent disputes from degenerating into feuds. One significant corollary is that law-codes encoded social values more than moral values. Wergilds and other compensations were attempts to convert the social value of individuals (or their body parts) into monetary form. The relatively high wergild for childbearing women in Salic and Ripuarian law ultimately reflected women's value to families in the formation of marriage alliances, which is also mirrored in Merovingian grave good patterns whereby women of childbearing age received more materially lavish burials.⁶⁵ Similarly, the relatively lower wergild for an infant or fetus – a commonality across law-codes with the exception of the Merovingian additions – also attempted to quantify the social loss of a future family member.

Personhood is a treacherously loaded term but, following the lead of anthropologists, conceiving of personhood relationally, thinking in terms of social personhood, is instructive. Concepts of animation and formation ought not to be understood solely or primarily in terms of the application of metaphysical theories but as 'attempts to establish the identity of the foetus [sic] in terms of a continuous social community'.⁶⁶ Across different societies ritual

---

⁶³ *Edictum Rothari* 332–3, p. 76. Both articles, incidentally, use *pecus* to describe fetal calves and foals.

⁶⁴ 'Si infans in utero matris suae nolendo ab aliquem occisus fuerit: si ipsa mulier libera est et evaserit, adpretietur ut libera secundum nobilitatem suam, et medietatem quod ipsa valuerit, infans ipse conponatur. Nam si mortua fuerit, conponat eam secundum generositatem suam, excepto quod in utero eius mortuum fuerit, ut supra, cessanta faida, eo quod nolendo fecit', *Edictum Rothari* 75, p. 24; translation adapted from K. Fischer Drew, *The Lombard Laws* (Philadelphia, 1973), p. 65. In ninth-century Anglo-Saxon law, the wergild in such a scenario was calculated as half of the father's value: see Elsakkers, 'Genre Hopping', p. 83.

⁶⁵ G. Halsall, 'Female Status and Power in Early Merovingian Central Austrasia: The Burial Evidence', *EME* 5.1 (1996), 1–24.

⁶⁶ G. Aijmer, 'Introduction: Coming into Existence', in *Coming into Existence: Birth and Metaphors of Birth*, ed. G. Aijmer (Gothenburg, 1992), p. 11. See W. R. James, 'Placing the Unborn: On the Social Recognition of New Life', *Anthropology & Medicine* 7.2

and symbolic markers provide means by which parents, families and wider communities initiate, develop and deepen their relationships with incipient social persons. The social personhood of new members of society develops over time, certainly after but sometimes even before birth. In the case of the Old Testament story of Hannah's conception of Samuel, which provided the template for the conception of saints in hagiography and the scriptural justification for child oblation, this development began at conception.[67] The details embedded in law-codes – nine nights, naming – were symbolic markers relevant to assessing the loss of nascent social beings. Fetuses and infants have scarcely begun to enter the 'mutually defining network of anticipatory relations with others over time'.[68] Their lower wergilds reflected the ambiguity of nascent social persons who had scarcely crossed the thresholds of families and communities.

Wergild is subject to two further interpretative complications. First, the scenarios addressed by most law-codes implied injuries sustained by pregnant women who survived abortion by assault or other means: injuries from whatever caused abortion including violence (sometimes explicit) and injuries or risk of injuries from undergoing labour under duress (always implicit). But law-codes did not always or even often individuate offences and forms of recompense with care. Nor, for that matter, did other sources.[69] Chilperic I's capitulary, quoted above, was clear. It explicitly stipulated compensation when violence resulted in neither maternal death nor fetal expulsion. But this clarity was exceptional. Lombard law did not explicitly make provisions for injuries sustained by a pregnant woman.[70] Other legal articles did not clearly factor such injuries in either and, as argued above in the case of Salic and Ripuarian law, the tendency was to stipulate wergilds for infants or fetuses

---

(2000), 169–89, for an anthropological critique of concepts of personhood which ignore relational and social dimensions; see too B. A. Conklin and L. M. Morgan, 'Babies, Bodies, and the Production of Personhood in North America and a Native Amazonian Society', *Ethos* 24.4 (1996), 657–94.

[67] See de Jong, *In Samuel's Image*, pp. 156–64, on the story of Hannah in the context of child oblation.

[68] James, 'Placing the Unborn', p. 177.

[69] *Cartae Senonicae* 51, MGH Formulae, p. 207, stipulated that a woman who had wounded a man in the knees before killing his daughter had to pay the *leod* or wergild, without making it clear whether the injury to the man's knees had been factored in; see Oliver, *Body Legal*, pp. 58–9, on this case. Incidentally, the manuscript containing the *Cartae Senonicae* also contained a D-redaction of Salic law: on the collection and ninth-century manuscript (Paris, Bibliothèque nationale, MS latin 4627), see Rio, *Legal Practice*, pp. 121–6, 256–7.

[70] The Pavian jurists appear to have deliberately injected clarity into the law when they distinguished between compensation for injury (*iniuria*), which applied when wrongdoing was deliberate, and compensation for harm (*damnum*), which applied (as in this scenario) when wrongdoing was unintentional: *Liber Papiensis* Roth. 75, pp. 307–8.

rather than compensation for bodily injuries.[71] Of course, plaintiffs in disputes involving abortion induced by violence might well have sought compensation for injuries sustained by their kinswomen and wives too. But judges and disputing parties would not have found guidelines in most legal articles on abortion particularly helpful on how to address such injuries.

The other complication concerns the contestability of third-party abortion. In later medieval cases the ambiguity of the causal connection between injuring a pregnant woman and a subsequent miscarriage is palpable.[72] There are hints of contestation in some early medieval articles. The first Alamannic article contains a faint hint in its reference to whoever was alleged (*reputatus*) to have caused abortion while the second article anticipated that plaintiffs might ask for greater compensation for male or sexually ill-defined fetuses. Lombard law was even clearer in its aside on intentionality and plea that the feud should end there: the implication, of course, was that the feud might not end there. These are important reminders that disputes, including those on abortion, were contested by both parties. Far from enshrining consensual custom or applying a tribal embryology to which all assented, law-codes offered approximations of the physical harm and social damage wrought by offences and they supplied terms on which disputing parties could agree to disagree.

Provisions concerning fertility in Salic law with no precise equivalents in other codes ought to be interpreted in light of the dispute settlement framework. The relevant provisions appeared amid articles on *maleficium*. All redactions of Salic law contained articles stipulating the compensation for giving someone herbs to drink: if the person died, 200 *solidi*, if the person survived, 62 *solidi*.[73] A provision on *maleficium* affecting a woman's fertility entered through one manuscript of the later C-redaction: 'If any woman causes *maleficium* to another woman from where she could not have infants, she should be judged culpable for 62½ *solidi*'.[74] This provision was, as Elsakkers has noted, unique in Salic law for designating women as offenders and victims of an offence, and it may offer a 'glimpse of Frankish women amongst themselves, of the world of *secreta mulierum*, where women, who were knowledgeable about *maleficia*, prepare abortifacients and contraceptives for other women'.[75] Tidied versions in all Carolingian redactions, however, substituted herbs

---

[71] As we saw in chapter four, Visigothic law addressed bodily injuries but in a slightly haphazard way; see p. 117 above.
[72] Butler, 'Abortion by Assault'.
[73] *Lex Salica (A1)* 19.1–2, pp. 80, 82, with other A-redaction variants; *A1* lists the second compensation as 63 *solidi*, but the other texts all give 62 *solidi*. For a detailed textual analysis of this provision across the Salic redactions see Elsakkers, 'Abortion, Poisoning', 251–64.
[74] 'Si quis mulier altera mulieri maleficium fecerit unde infantes non potuerit habere, sol. LXII [semis] cul. iud.', *Lex Salica (C5)* 19.4, p. 83; I have read *altera* as *alterae*.
[75] Elsakkers, 'Abortion, Poisoning', 258.

(*herbae*) for *maleficium* and the gender inclusive *quis* for the gender specific *quis mulier*.[76] What was the point of this provision? It is possible that plaintiffs might have pursued cases in which someone had harmed a kinswoman's fertility with no ill will intended: in other words, cases of birth control, menstrual regulation or other kinds of gynaecological therapy gone wrong. But social pressures would have disinclined the male kin of an unmarried woman from pursuing such a case because it could have publicly compromised her sexual reputation, while an ecclesiastical pressure, which would have increased over the centuries (and which would have been stronger where bishops or abbots were integrated into judicial procedures), might have disinclined husbands of married women from pursuing such cases. It is far more likely that the provision was intended for accusations that someone had intentionally, that is, maliciously harmed a woman's reproductive capacity. We ought to take such an anxiety as seriously as other sources took use of herbs and *maleficium* to murder and harm others or adversely affect male sexual virility.[77]

The ostensible paradox – ecclesiastical interest alongside legal disinterest in women who voluntarily underwent abortion or otherwise impeded fertility – dissolves once we recognize the distinct practices underlying ecclesiastical and legal texts: dispensing penances or canonical sentences for individual sinners versus settling disputes between kin-groups. The surface paradox of early medieval ecclesiastical and legal texts on abortion is comparable to the surface paradox of eastern imperial and western conciliar legislation on suicide in the sixth century, explored masterfully by Alexander Murray. Both kinds of sixth-century legislation emanated from zealously Christian authorities, yet both authorities treated suicide in almost opposite ways. Justinian's team of jurists assembled a corpus of texts which 'treated suicide as intrinsically innocent', while groups of assembled clergy treated suicide as 'equally intrinsically, heinously culpable'. As Murray has shown, the paradox only lies at the surface. Jurists and lawyers were interested in property, clerics and bishops in posthumous rites. Imperial and conciliar legislation on suicide captured 'respective legislative energies [which] went in different directions and answered to forces … coming at them from different quarters'.[78]

---

[76] *Lex Salica* (D) 25.3, (E) 24.3, pp. 66–7, *Lex Salica Karolina* 21.4, p. 83.

[77] See *Formulae Andecavenses* 12 for a *solsadia*, a document on a defendant's failure to turn up at court, from a case in which a woman was accused of killing someone through *maleficium*, and *Cartae Senonicae* 22 for an oath for a woman to swear that she had never prepared or dispensed *herbae maleficiae* to kill or make someone unwell or insane: MGH Formulae, pp. 9, 194–5. See C. Rider, *Magic and Impotence in the Middle Ages* (Oxford, 2006), pp. 29–52, on early medieval discussion of impotence magic. In light of the pervasive gendering of *maleficium* as a female offence, the gender inclusivity of this article in Carolingian redactions of Salic law is all the more noticeable.

[78] Murray, *Curse on Self-Murder*, pp. 152–88 (quotations at pp. 153, 187).

Like sixth-century legislation on suicide, ecclesiastical texts and law-codes were speaking about different things in different legal languages. Insofar as law-codes addressed social offences through wergild and compensation, they were relatively inarticulate on offences committed within families or kin-groups. Alamannic law, for example, reasoned that anyone who killed a close relative should be cut off from inheritance and 'undergo penance following the canons'. It even moralized that such a wrongdoer should realize that he had acted against God. But no mention was made of compensation or oathswearers.[79] Likewise, many law-codes effectively devolved repercussions for adulterous wives to their husbands. Some, like the *Edictum Rothari*, explicitly allowed husbands to kill adulterous wives and their lovers with impunity. Others, however, including Salic law, did not explicitly address the fate of adulterous wives.[80] Legal absence was not a sign of social tolerance. As bishops were all too aware, some Frankish men killed their wives on the whiff, let alone the proof, of adultery.[81] The absence of voluntary abortion in most law-codes is best understood as a legislative blind-spot. A dispute over a woman who voluntarily had an abortion did not compute with the rationality of most law-codes.

Shifting contexts: Abortion in younger law-codes

One piece of evidence fills the vacuum between the distinct energies of secular and ecclesiastical legislation. In 847 Rabanus replied to a certain Regimbod on a question concerning a violently induced abortion. A noticeable detail leaves little doubt that we are dealing with a real-life case: by implication, the woman in question was pregnant with triplets. Regimbod wanted to know the best course of action after a man 'by lashing his wife had killed his two children in birth in such a way that they were unable to attain the grace of baptism'.[82] A third child survived its birth but was grievously wounded and expired soon after being baptized. 'Here it is clear,' Rabanus responded, 'that he has fallen into the crime of parricide because of his immoderate assault'. Perhaps gently chiding Regimbod, Rabanus urged that 'what the sacred canons decree on homicide is not unknown to you'. He quoted Ancyra – not on abortion, but on

---

[79] 'penitentiam autem secundum canones agat', *LA (A)* 40, pp. 99–100.
[80] Nelson and Rio, 'Women and Laws', p. 110.
[81] See for example Hincmar, *De divortio Lothari et Theutbergae* (resp. 5), MGH Conc. 4.1, p. 145, with Stone, 'Invention', 439, and council of Tribur (895), c.46, which outlined how a bishop should try to prevent an angry husband from killing an adulterous wife, MGH Capit. 2, pp. 239–40; see too Nelson and Rio, 'Women and Laws', p. 110; Chélini, *L'aube du moyen âge*, pp. 225–8.
[82] 'flagellando uxorem suam, duos filios suos in partu occidit, ita ut ad baptismi gratiam pervenire non potuerint', *Ep.* 41, MGH Epp. 5, p. 479.

the difference between intentional murder and unintentional manslaughter, and it was left to Regimbod to apply the distinction.[83]

Legal regulations were ill-equipped to deal with such a case of domestic violence. Ecclesiastical regulations did not directly address the scenario either, though Rabanus's improvisation was another example of how canonical tradition worked in practice. One of Rabanus's observations is of particular interest: the twins had died unbaptized.[84] This was a religious interpretation of abortion by assault. Such moral colouring was absent in the law-codes examined so far. But two younger law-codes absorbed ideas about the theological significance of miscarried infants and the public morality of abortion. They raise questions about how Christianization affected the contexts in which law was interpreted at the same time as they render perceptible the boundaries which constrained legislative energy.

Compensation for damnation: Bavarian law on abortion
In its extant form the *Lex Baiwariorum* was probably codified in the 730s or 740s under the Agilolfing duke Odilo (d. 748), a generation or so before the toppling of his son, Tassilo, in the Carolingian takeover of Bavaria in 788.[85] It drew on multiple sources including Visigothic law, albeit in the form of the older *Lex Eurici* rather than the code issued by Recceswinth in 654.[86] Moreover, the code itself and other Bavarian legislative activity point to the miscegenation of secular and ecclesiastical in Bavarian legal thought and practice.[87]

All of the relevant articles were drawn together in a section, 'On wives and cases which often pertain to them'.[88] Most of these laws addressed offences like adultery and *raptus*, sometimes in noticeable detail. A would-be adulterer

---

[83] 'Ubi liquido patet, quod propter inmoderatam correptionem in crimen cecidit parricidii. Quid autem de homicidio sancti canones sanciant, tibi non ignotum est, cum in Ancyrano concilio ita scriptum est', *Ep*. 41, p. 479. Judging by the citation from Ancyra, Rabanus entertained the possibility that there was an ulterior motive behind the man's assault; on the same possibility in some later medieval cases, see Butler, 'Abortion by Assault'.

[84] See Cramer, *Baptism*, p. 140, on a fragmentary letter in which Rabanus urged the necessity of baptizing infants without delay.

[85] For an overview of theories on the *Lex Baiwariorum*'s origins and an argument that it was produced in 736–8, earlier than the conventional view of 744–8, see J. Couser, '"Let them make him Duke to rule that people": The *Law of the Bavarians* and Regime Change in Early Medieval Europe', *Law and History Review* 30.3 (2012), 865–99. On the Carolingian takeover, see S. Airlie, 'Narratives of Triumph and Rituals of Submission: Charlemagne's Mastery of Bavaria', *Transactions of the Royal Historical Society*, 6th s., 9 (1999), 93–119.

[86] Cf. Couser, 'Law of the Bavarians', 870–2.

[87] Thus, for example, the council of Ascheim (755/60), c.15, stipulated that a priest had to be present in court so that judges would not be swayed by bribes and so that settlements would be religiously sound; see Firey, *Contrite Heart*, pp. 182–6, on Ascheim and other councils held under Tassilo in the 750s–770s.

[88] 'De uxoribus et causis, quae sepe contingunt', *LB* 8, p. 353.

had to compensate a husband if he had managed to plant one foot onto the marriage bed before the wife stopped things from going any further.[89] The section concluded with six articles on abortion. The first has some affinities with Visigothic law: 'If any woman has given a potion to cause abortion, if she is a slave-girl, she should receive 200 lashes, and if a freewoman, she should lose her freedom [and] be classed in servitude to whom the duke has ordered'.[90] As with Salic law on female fertility, this Bavarian law might have envisaged those who maliciously harmed another woman's fertility.[91] But there was a crucial difference. What had been handled as a tort in Salic law was effectively handled as a public offence in Bavarian law. The remaining articles addressed abortion by assault:

> If anyone has caused abortion in a woman by any sort of blow, if the woman has died, he should be held as a murderer. But if only the offspring is destroyed, if the offspring was not hitherto alive, he should compensate 20 *solidi*. But if [the offspring] was already living, he should pay wergild, 53½ *solidi*.[92]

Another law-code, another kind of fetal distinction. The same distinction was applied if a 'slave-girl has been wounded by any person whatsoever, so that it causes abortion': 4 *solidi* if not yet alive, 10 *solidi* if already alive.[93] Whether this *non vivus/vivens* distinction was synonymous with the formed/unformed distinction in both Old Testament and Visigothic law is not altogether clear; acknowledging uncertainty here is more informative than rendering these distinctions dangerously intelligible by simply assimilating them. Moreover, manuscript variants suggest divergences over the social values embedded in monetary compositions.[94] The function of the distinction, however, was clear: the law explicitly framed compensation as a wergild only if the *partus* was already *vivus*. The most interesting details appeared in a highly unusual

---

[89] *LB* 8.1, p. 354.

[90] 'Si qua mulier potionem, ut avorsum faceret, dederit, si ancilla est, CC flagella suscipiat, et si ingenua, careat libertate servitio deputanda cui dux iusserit', *LB* 8.18, pp. 361–2. The affinities are with Eurician legislation; the later *Lex Visigothorum* expanded this law to include women who asked for such potions too, on which see pp. 111–13 above.

[91] This is certainly how Zeumer read the original Eurician provision; see p. 112 above.

[92] 'Si quis mulieri ictu quolibet avorsum fecerit, si mulier mortua fuerit, tamquam homicida teneatur. Si autem tantum partus extinguitur, si adhuc partus vivus non fuit, XX sold. conponat. Si autem iam vivens fuit, weregeldum persolvat L et III sold. et tremisse.', *LB* 8.19, pp. 362–3; cf. Elsakkers, RBL, pp. 344–5.

[93] 'Si vero ancilla a quaecumque persona debilitata fuerit, ut avorsum faceret', *LB* 8. 22–3, p. 365.

[94] This is not actually clear from von Schwind's edition, from which I have quoted. The older edition by Merkel prints two texts for *LB* 8.19, MGH LL 3, p. 301. The B-text stipulates 20 *solidi* in the first permutation, but the A-text stipulates 40 *solidi*; moreover, both texts simply refer to paying the wergild in the second permutation without specifying the amount.

description of how monetary recompense for abortion ought to be paid. The perpetrator had to pay 12 *solidi* initially. Then he and his descendants had to make an annual payment of a single *solidus* each autumn for up to seven generations from father to son. If they defaulted on a single payment, they had to pay 12 *solidi* again before returning to the sequence until it was complete.[95] The rationale was spelled out. The longstanding compensation deliberately mirrored the longstanding grief of parents and the longstanding suffering of unbaptized souls:

> On this account, after the religion of Christianity grew in the world, our ancestors and judges pronounced a longstanding composition because the soul, after it has received flesh but has scarcely reached the light of birth, suffers a longstanding punishment because it was handed over to hell in an abortive way without the sacrament of regeneration.[96]

This intergenerational payment plan attempted to establish a form of restorative justice which took seriously the theological implications of social conduct. Remarkably, one of the clearest articulations of the connection between abortion and the fate of unbaptized souls appeared in the rationale for a compensation in a law-code, one manifestation of the 'intensification of Bavarian Christian culture' from the eighth century.[97] A further suggestion that this connection was being made by contemporaries appears in a letter written by one of the figures synonymous with Bavarian religious intensification, Boniface, to the Mercian king Ethelbert in 745/6. This letter, it is worth stressing, was not just a formulaic rehashing of moral tropes. Boniface's praise for Ethelbert's almsgiving soon gave way to a stinging rebuke of wayward morals in his kingdom, including the king's failure to take a lawful wife. Boniface pointedly used pagan *exempla* to shame the supposedly Christian king. Even the pagans respected marriage. Bands of Saxon women chased after adulterous women with knives and rods while the Wends, the lowest of races, revered marriage so deeply that wives joined their husbands on the funeral pyre in a barbarian precursor of *sati*. The personal was political. If the English kept acting like the Sodomites they would produce a degenerate people. Recent Saracen routs in Spain and southern France, Boniface warned,

---

[95] Cf. 'Si avorsum fecerit, inprimis XII sold cogatur exsolvere. Deinde ipse et posteri sui per singulos annos, id est autumnus, singulum solidum solvent usque in septimam propinquitatem de patre in filios. Et si neglectum unius anni fecerint, tunc iterum XII sold solvere cogantur et deinceps ordine praefato, donec series rationabilis impleatur', *LB* 8.20, pp. 363–4.

[96] 'Propterea diuturnam iudicaverunt antecessores nostri conpositionem et iudices, postquam religio christianitatis inolevit in mundo, quia diuturnam, postquam incarnationem suscepit anima, quamvis ad nativitatis lucem minime pervenisset, patitur poenam, quia sine sacramento regenerationis avortivo modo tradita est ad inferos', *LB* 8.21, p. 364. The title, 'On the long-standing grief of parents [*De diuturna dolore parentum*]', appears in a few manuscripts.

[97] Airlie, 'Narratives of Triumph', 94.

were divine punishments for such sins. Boniface, the *au courant* moralist, also warned about the fate of unbaptized souls when dealing with rumours of sexual crimes involving nuns in Ethelbert's kingdom:

> And it should be noted that beneath that crime lurks another immense outrage, namely murder. Because, when those whores, nuns or otherwise, give birth to their offspring wrongly conceived in sins, they more often than not kill them; rather than filling the churches of Christ with adoptive children, they instead fill up tombs with bodies and hell with wretched souls.[98]

The connection between Boniface's letter and the *Lex Baiwariorum* is not direct. But Boniface was writing to Ethelbert a few years after an invitation to Bavaria from Odilo in 739.[99] His letter certainly suggests that something was in the air in Bavaria and it is revealing that the legal rationale for the intergenerational wergild in the *Lex Baiwariorum* was explicitly framed as a tradition borne of religious conversion.

Bavarian law demonstrates how religion could inform the handling of abortion within a traditional dispute settlement framework. But it also shows the limits of the framework. Admittedly the first provision on supply of abortifacient potions edged closer to crime than to tort. Nonetheless, the theological significance of abortion, which in theory carried implications for the loss of any unbaptized soul, was limited to a scenario of third-party abortion. In this sense, the *Lex Baiwariorum* highlights the boundary of much early medieval legislation on abortion. The final law-code under consideration, however, traversed that boundary.

Women's rights and wrongs: Child-murder in the Lex Frisionum
Disentangling the interplay between top-down and bottom-up impulses within early medieval law-codes is difficult. The *Lex Frisionum* is unusual because it clearly captured both Frisian social custom and Carolingian legal initiatives. The text, which survives through an early modern edition of a now lost manuscript, is unusual in another sense too. It dates roughly from the later eighth century, somewhere between 785, when the Carolingians fully conquered Frisia, and the turn of the ninth century. Crucially, the surviving text was not a promulgated code. As the very last words, *Hęc hactenus* (effectively, 'here's where we've got up to') make clear, it was self-consciously incomplete. A work in transition for a society in transition, the *Lex Frisionum*

---

[98] 'Et notandum, quod in illo scelere aliud inmane flagitium subterlatet, id est homicidium, quia, dum ille meretrices, sive monasteriales sive sęculares, male conceptas soboles in peccatis genuerint, et sepe maxima ex parte occidunt non inplentes Christi ęcclesias filiis adoptivis, sed tumulos corporibus et inferos miseris animabus satiantes', *Ep.* 73, MGH Epp. sel. 1, p. 151.

[99] Boniface's time in Bavaria is described by his hagiographer Willibald, *Life of Saint Boniface* 7, trans. C. H. Talbot, in *Soldiers of Christ: Saints and Saints' Lives from Late Antiquity and the Early Middle Ages*, ed. T. F. X. Noble and T. Head (London, 1995), pp. 130–1.

represented documentation compiled in preparation for a code which was either never promulgated or has not survived. Its laws, as we shall see, were notes and surveys of Frisian legal custom in the process of being revised in accordance with more recognizably Carolingian legal impulses.[100]

The *Lex Frisionum* was, in part, a kind of condensed ethnography. Interest in local customs, including regional differences within Frisia, was woven into the *Lex Frisionum*.[101] One consequence was the incorporation of some decidedly non-Christian norms. The most glaring example was the final entry, a description of a custom more than a legal provision per se. Anyone who despoiled a temple would be led to the seashore to suffer a grisly fate. After his ears and genitals had been cut off, the offender would become a human sacrifice to the gods.[102] Such norms might not have passed the censor in subsequent drafts, for elsewhere the *Lex Frisionum* captured attempts to inject Christian values into a still Christianizing society in the form of fines for working on Sundays.[103] Even more significant was the imposition of royal prerogatives, partly through the payment of wergild to the king in the case of certain offences (to which we turn below). In sum, the *Lex Frisionum*, which probably originated in a manuscript containing other Germanic codes, represents a Carolingian perspective on nascent Frisian law. Through its mixture of specifically Frisian, generically Germanic and decidedly royal components, it offers a snapshot of legislation as a process.[104] Deciphering the relevant measures, as we shall see, depends on navigating through the distinctive layers of the text as well as grasping its provisional nature.

Unlike other law-codes the *Lex Frisionum* did not address abortion by assault,[105] but it did address voluntary child-murder. The relevant provision (*LF* 5.1) was deeply embedded within a list of those who could be killed

---

[100] The *Lex Frisionum* survives in a 1557 edition by Johannes Herold. The fundamental study remains H. Siems, *Studien zur Lex Frisionum* (Ebelsbach, 1980); see too N. E. Algra, 'The *Lex Frisionum*: The Genesis of a Legalized Life', in *The Law's Beginnings*, ed. F. J. M. Feldbrugge (Leiden, 2003), pp. 77–92; D. J. Henstra, *The Evolution of the Money Standard in Medieval Frisia: A Treatise on the Systems of Money of Account in the former Frisia (c.600–c.1500)* (Amsterdam, 1999), pp. 277–9.

[101] For example, a serf who denied an accusation of killing a nobleman needed the support of thirty-five oathswearers in central Frisia (literally between the rivers Lauwer and Weser) but forty-seven further west (literally beyond the Fli), while the procedure outlined to deal with anyone accused of killing someone else's slaves or animals included the observation that this was the custom in central and western Frisia (between the Lauwer and Zwin): *LF* 1.8, 4.1–3, pp. 36, 44–6.

[102] *LF*, additio, 11.1, p. 102; cf. Siems, *Lex Frisionum*, pp. 338–50; Algra, 'Lex Frisionum', pp. 78–9.

[103] *LF* 18.1–2, p. 62.

[104] Siems, *Lex Frisionum*, especially pp. 115–28, 366–71; see too the summary of Siems's conclusions in Henstra, *Evolution*, pp. 277–8.

[105] Vernacular Old Frisian law codified from the eleventh century onward did, on which see M. Elsakkers, 'Her anda neylar: An Intriguing Criterion for Abortion in Old Frisian Law', *Scientarium Historia* 30 (2004), 107–54.

without having to pay compensation. From soldiers to arsonists, most members of the list are not surprising. They were individuals whose professional conduct or social misconduct put their lives at risk. But the final entry was altogether more striking:

> A champion; and he who was killed in battle; and an adulterer; and a thief if he was found in a ditch by which he is trying to get into another's house; and he who wanting to burn down another's house holds a torch in his hand so that the flame touches the roof or wall of the house; whoever breaks open a shrine; and the infant taken out of the womb and killed by the mother.[106]

The line between abortion and infanticide was not always sharply defined. This might have been describing infanticide or abortion (or both).[107] Certainly many ecclesiastical and legal texts, as we have repeatedly seen, treated abortion and infanticide together. There was a degree of polyvalence to the effect that what was said about one offence could easily have been applied to the other. Particularly relevant in this regard is the penitential possibly written for Frisia earlier in the eighth century, *Oxoniense II*, and its enigmatic ruling on the *proiectus* (abandoned or aborted?) infant. Even if the exemption clause in the *Lex Frisionum* dealt with newborns, it carried implications for abortion insofar as it appeared to enshrine a right for mothers to kill their own infants.

To complicate matters further, the exemption list (*LF* 5.1) was immediately followed by another provision (*LF* 5.2): 'And if any woman has done this, she should pay her wergild to the king; and if she denied, she should swear with five'.[108] How do we make sense of the apparent legal sanction of child-murder and this provision which followed it?

The first clue is that the last two entries in the exemption list do not quite fit with the grammatical construction of the preceding entries, a hint that they were subsequent additions to an original list.[109] What these two entries share in common is that they were observations of specifically (and, one presumes to Carolingian eyes, peculiarly) Frisian customs. The penultimate entry is almost identical to the opening words describing the gruesome fate awaiting anyone who violated a Frisian temple.[110] In the case of the last entry on the

---

[106] 'Campionem; et eum qui in praelio fuerit occisus; et adulterum; et furem si in fossa, qua domum alterius effodere conatur, fuerit repertus; et eum qui domum alterius incendere volens facem manu tenet, ita ut ignis tectum vel parietem domus tangat; qui franum effregit; et infans ab utero sublatus et enecatus a matre', *LF* 5.1, p. 46.
[107] Cf. Elsakkers, RBL, pp. 346–7.
[108] 'Et si hoc quaelibet femina fecerit, leudem suam regi componat; et si negaverit, cum V iuret', *LF* 5.2, p. 46.
[109] As noted by Siems, *Lex Frisionum*, p. 334. Grammatically speaking the list was full of accusative nouns (e.g. 'campionem', 'furem') or accusative pronouns followed by a relative clause (e.g. 'eum qui in praelio [etc]', 'eum qui domum [etc]'). The penultimate item is simply a relative clause ('qui franum effregit'), while the final item begins with a nominative noun ('infans').
[110] Cf. 'Qui fanum effregerit', *LF*, additio, 11.1, p. 102.

Abortion in Law-codes

infans ab utero sublatus, there is a connection to a story in the *vita* of Liudger (d. 809), missionary to the Frisians, written by his nephew Altfrid in the middle of the ninth century. The story concerned the circumstances surrounding the birth of Liudger's mother, Liafburg. Her paternal grandmother was a staunch pagan who completely rejected the Catholic faith. Angered that her daughter-in-law only gave birth to girls, this pagan matriarch sent men to 'snatch that daughter [i.e., Liafburg] now born from the mother's lap and kill her before she drank her mother's milk; because such was the custom of pagans, that if they wanted to kill a son or a daughter, they would be killed before [eating] earthly food'. But a female neighbour managed to steal away the infant Liafburg from an attempted drowning and feed her some honey.[111] Scholars have long connected this social detail in a saint's life about the conversion of Frisia to the exemption clause in the *Lex Frisionum*.[112] To this connection can be added the eighth-century penitential, *Oxoniense II*, examined in the previous chapter, which might also have identified comparable Frisian social customs concerning the social acceptance of infants.[113] What the authors of *Oxoniense II* and the *Lex Frisionum* observed as a social norm in the eighth century had become part of the historical reputation of Frisia when Altfrid recalled the 'custom of the pagans' in the 840s.

Clearly some forms of infanticide and, perhaps by extension, abortion received public sanction in Frisian society. The real question, however, concerns what the author(s) of the *Lex Frisionum* did with this social fact. What was the significance of the clause which followed the exemption: any woman (*quaelibet femina*) who did this had to pay her wergild to the king? Several historians have interpreted the exemption list (*LF* 5.1) as enshrining a maternal right to child-murder. Explicitly or implicitly, a necessary corollary is that the additional clause (*LF* 5.2) concerned any *other* woman, that is, any woman other than the mother. On this interpretation the provision following the exemption punished women, perhaps from outside a family, who did what a mother was entitled to do.[114]

If we recognize the different layers operating within what was a work in

---

[111] 'qui raperent eandem filiam tunc natam de sinu matris, et necarent priusquam lac sugeret matris; quia sic mos erat paganorum, ut si filium aut filiam necare voluissent, absque cibo terreno necarentur', *Vita Liudgeri* 6–7, MGH SS 2, p. 406. See Wood, *Missionary Life*, pp. 113–15, on the background to the *Vita Liudgeri*.

[112] Boswell, *Kindness*, p. 211. See too Siems, *Lex Frisionum*, pp. 334–6, with references to older German scholarship. Siems rightly critiques the tenacious assumption among older legal scholars that Germanic law gave fathers the right to decide on the social acceptance of their children, and their sometimes tortuous attempts to make the *Lex Frisionum* and *Vita Liudgeri* fit with such an assumption to the extent of suggesting that *patre* should replace *matre* in the text of *LF* 5.1.

[113] See pp. 188–9 above.

[114] This is explicit in Elsakkers, RBL, p. 347 and Oliver, *Body Legal*, pp. 198–9 (though Oliver reads *quaelibet femina* as another woman but *leudem suam* as the mother's wergild – another woman pays the mother's wergild to the king); it is implicit in

progress, an alternative interpretation becomes necessary.[115] Payment to the king is one significant clue. Countless provisions in the *Lex Frisionum* supplemented payments of compensation or wergild to victims or kin with *fredus* or 'peace money', an additional payment to the king. *Fredus* was not a novel legal concept. It appeared in a few articles in Salic law, though, as Warren Brown has recently argued, Salic *fredus* denoted a fine when specific royal prerogatives were disrupted more than a 'fine for breach of a general peace'.[116] In the *Lex Frisionum* the ideological function of peace-money was different and not just because it referred to *freda* in the feminine. It was qualitatively and quantitatively different. Provisions on violence, theft and manslaughter established *fredus* in abstract.[117] Numerous other provisions added *fredus* too.[118] In a recently conquered territory *fredus* had a sharp ideological edge which cut deeper than simply safeguarding specific royal prerogatives. Through *fredus* the shadow of royal justice extended over the customary settlement of all kinds of disputes. Within the legal vision sketched out in the *Lex Frisionum*, social order was circumscribed by the Carolingian king

Not just the social order, but the moral order too. Payment to the king did not always take the form of *fredus* in the sense of payment additional to compensation or wergild due to victims or their kin. Certain provisions stipulating payment to the king alone betray an aspiration to redefine Frisian public morality through legislation. Thus, anyone who swore falsely on the relics of the saints or sold a slave to pagan *gentes* had to pay his own wergild to the king.[119] Similarly, a woman, by implication unmarried, who 'mixed herself in fornication with any man', also had to pay her wergild to the king. How was such a woman described? *Femina quaelibet*, any woman.[120] This brings us back to the *quaelibet femina* of *LF* 5.2. As Harald Siems noted and as this final example suggests (to mention nothing of other uses of the masculine *quilibet* across the *Lex Frisionum*), reading *quaelibet* as referring to any *other* woman is problematic. The additional clause, 'Any woman who does this should pay her own wergild to the king', was doing the same ideological work as provisions on female fornication and enslavement to pagans: legislating public morality, in part, because of what Siems has called 'Christian fervour'.[121] The provisional nature of the *Lex Frisionum* is the ultimate interpretative key. The

---

Boswell, *Kindness*, p. 211. Algra, 'Lex Frisionum', p. 86, including n.41, is slightly laconic on this question.

[115] My line of argument here expands on insights in Siems, *Lex Frisionum*, pp. 334–8.
[116] W. Brown, *Violence in Medieval Society* (Harlow, 2010), pp. 52–3 (quotation at p. 53).
[117] *LF* 16.1 (manslaughter), additio, 9.1 (violence and theft), pp. 60, 100.
[118] E.g. *LF* 3.2 (theft by a noble), 3.3 (theft by a freeman), 17.2 (killing someone in church or at the court of a duke), 22.65 (pulling someone's hair), 22.83 (pushing someone into water), 22.89–90 (touching the breasts or genitals of a woman who is 'non suam', not one's own), pp. 44, 62, 78. This list is not exhaustive.
[119] *LF* 10.1, 17.5, pp. 52, 62.
[120] 'Si femina quaelibet homini cuilibet fornicando se miscuerit', *LF* 9.1, p. 48.
[121] 'christlichen Eifer', Siems, *Lex Frisionum*, p. 337.

law in *LF* 5.2 was a Carolingian legal initiative which effectively counteracted the Frisian social custom recorded in *LF* 5.1. Those tasked with preparing a law-code for Frisia had been sufficiently unsettled by a Frisian custom to record it and then leave a comment on it.

* * *

The *Lex Baiwariorum* and the *Lex Frisionum* captured legislative moments when the conventional framework of Germanic law-codes was infused with ideas about religious principles, public morality and the body politic. The *Lex Baiwariorum* shows how the dispute settlement framework could absorb religious perspectives on the eschatological significance of abortion while the *Lex Frisionum* demonstrates that just as Carolingian discourse on the theory and practice of justice was beginning to intensify, extending the framework of the law to address such offences as child-murder by mothers was an intelligible legislative possibility. We do not know whether and, if so, in what form a Frisian law-code was actually promulgated, but the idea itself is nonetheless suggestive. If the idea does not entirely satisfy modern definitions of crime, it certainly goes beyond modern definitions of tort. Both codes, especially the *Lex Frisionum*, are not representative of the content of most early medieval law-codes. Their value lies in glimpses of what the textual conservatism of older law-codes obscures: the evolving impact of religious and political ideas on the drafting of written law, on the clerical and secular officials entrusted with overseeing legal procedures and on the broader cultural climate in which disputes arose and law was interpreted and contested in attempts to resolve such disputes.

Two final thoughts draw attention to the importance of recognizing what law-codes do not show us. The first concerns the pressures and processes underlying unwanted pregnancies. Such pressures certainly existed and they exploded onto the pages of a saint's life written by Arbeo of Freising at some point between 765 and 772, in which the repercussions of an unwanted pregnancy within the ranks of the Bavarian nobility catalysed a chain of events culminating in the horrific martyrdom of Emmeram. Ota, the unmarried daughter of an eminent Bavarian duke, Theodo, had conceived a child from a certain Sigibald, the son of a judge. The pair began to panic 'when they could now barely hide the disgrace'.[122] They approached the bishop and soon-to-be martyr Emmeram for help, 'fearing, as is the wont of sinners, present punishments more than the perpetual agonies of souls'.[123] Emmeram reproved them for their sin but also counselled them. Deliberating on their predicament, he

---

[122] 'dum iam minime stuprum abscondere potuerunt', *Vita Haimrhammi* 9, MGH SRG 13, p. 39. Here and below I quote from the older (and more clumsily expressed) A-recension, though I have used the B-recension to clarify the meaning where relevant. On the background to the *Vita Haimrhammi*, see Hammer, 'Arbeo'.

[123] 'Plus enim, ut peccantium mos est, praesentes poenas pertimescebant quam perpetuae cruciatus animarum', *Vita Haimhrammi* 9, p. 39.

advised naming himself as the father of the child because 'he realized that if this crime was uncovered in public, he would not in any way be able to obtain mercy for them from the girl's father'.[124] Once the pregnancy was revealed, Ota was ultimately condemned to live out the rest of her days in exile while Emmeram met his sickening end at the sword of her brother, Lantpert, dismembered, emasculated and left to die by the road.[125]

Emmeram's instincts about Ota's father were correct. When he realized what had happened, Theodo angrily quizzed Ota to find out who had dared to violate the 'offspring of such a great man'.[126] When she confessed along the lines Emmeram had advised, he erupted in anger. Theodo's own men had to stop him from attacking Ota and, perhaps, from cutting out the infant within her, a graphic imagining of how an unwanted child could threaten familial honour.[127] This grisly story dramatized the fraught repercussions of unwanted pregnancies. Law-codes, especially their provisions on adultery and other sexual offences, provide more sober traces of pressures which might have made abortion or infanticide intelligible recourses.[128] The key point is that the substance of legal articles on abortion did not capture these social pressures; and the absence of articles on voluntary abortion did not signal tacit tolerance.

The second thought concerns the ideals and practice of justice, specifically under the Carolingians. Ecclesiastical and legal texts were abundantly copied in Carolingian manuscripts. Distinguishing between genres of ecclesiastical texts (whether canonical collections or penitentials) and law-codes is not anachronistic. These really were distinct kinds of texts, originating in distinct kinds of practices (or anticipations of practices). Yet, at the same time, Carolingian justice had a genre-blind, *ad hoc* quality. From Charlemagne's reign onward, the provision of justice was idealized as a cooperation between secular and ecclesiastical officials. Moreover, responsibility for responding to particularly serious offences which harmed the public body was often entrusted to bishops. The idea that bishops exercised an important judicial function for the 'elimination of moral impurity from the Frankish kingdoms' can be clearly traced in royal capitularies and conciliar documents right through the ninth century and beyond.[129] For example, in 846 Lothar I (d. 855)

---

[124] 'Praesciebat ... ut, si hoc in publicum everteret [evolveretur, B] crimen, nullo modo his veniam a patre puelle impetrare potuisset', *Vita Haimhrammi* 9, p. 39.
[125] *Vita Haimhrammi* 13, 17–18, p. 44, 50–3.
[126] 'tanti viri sobolem', *Vita Haimhrammi* 12, p. 44.
[127] It is not perfectly clear from the Latin whether Theodo wanted to strike Ota or the fetus within her; cf. 'in vehementissimam exarsit iram, ita a suis vix contentus, ut proprias in eam non inmitteretur manus et suam ense prostraretur sopolam', *Vita Haimhrammi* 12, p. 44. In his summary of this episode, Brown, *Unjust Seizure*, p. 38, takes *sopolam* to mean the latter: 'Enraged, [Theodo] would have drawn his sword to kill the baby in the womb had not his men restrained him'.
[128] See pp. 121–3 on excavating such social pressures from the *Lex Visigothorum*.
[129] S. Hamilton, 'Inquiring into Adultery and other Wicked Deeds: Episcopal Justice in tenth- and early eleventh-century Italy', *Viator* 41.2 (2010), 21–44, esp. 26–36 (quo-

enjoined the bishops of his kingdom to investigate anyone guilty of *publica flagitia*, public disgraces, including adultery, incest, homicide and sacrilege, and subject them to public penance or even excommunication until they changed their ways.[130] As Abigail Firey has recently put it, in the Carolingian empire 'religious perspectives on spiritual disorders migrated into legal definitions of public hazards and ... religious remedies became incorporated into jurisprudence'.[131] Peter Brown has called this the 'peccatization' of the early medieval world.[132] Within this world, a neat distinction between sin and crime – or between ecclesiastical and secular legislation – quickly breaks down. Offences against the Carolingian public body were conceptualized and counteracted as sins.

Was abortion too regarded as a *publicum flagitium* by the ninth century? This is distinctly possible, though the gaps between genres and the absence of case histories makes demonstrating it difficult. The *Lex Frisionum* suggests that the idea of child-murder as a public offence was intelligible, while Regino's material for episcopal visitations, examined in the previous chapter, hints at the convergence of religious and social regulation of communities. Only one instance of a real abortion accusation – though not quite documentation from a real case – survives from the early medieval west, and it too points in this direction. When a woman was accused of sexual sin and abortion in the 850s, the decision to assess the accusations by an ordeal was made 'by the judgment of lay nobles, by the advice of bishops and with the consent of the king'.[133] The episode in question, which has been passed over in silence within histories of abortion, merits close microhistorical examination. This was no ordinary case. The accused woman was a Carolingian queen; her accusers were working on behalf of her husband, the king; and the accusation was the opening act in a decade-long political drama which had profound consequences for Carolingian history.

---

tation at p. 24); cf. W. Ullmann, *The Carolingian Renaissance and the Idea of Kingship: The Birkbeck Lectures 1968–9* (London, 1969), pp. 21–42; Davis, 'Pattern for Power'.

[130] *Capitulare de expeditione contra Sarracenos facienda* (Nr. 203), c.6, MGH Capit. 2, p. 66.
[131] *Contrite Heart*, p. 61.
[132] 'The Decline of the Empire of God: Amnesty, Penance, and the Afterlife from Late Antiquity to the Middle Ages', in *Last Things: Death and the Apocalypse in the Middle Ages*, ed. C. W. Bynum and P. Freedman (Philadelphia, 2000), p. 58.
[133] 'iudicio laicorum nobilium et consultu episcoporum atque ipsius regis conensu', Hincmar, *De divortio* (interrogatio 1), p. 114.

7

Interior Wound: The Rumour of Abortion in the Divorce of Lothar II and Theutberga

Writing in the early tenth century, Regino of Prüm looked back on 855 as a watershed year. Lothar II, the new ruler of the Carolingian middle kingdom, married a noblewoman, Theutberga. 'The greatest ruin resulted from this union,' rued Regino, 'not only for him, but also for his whole kingdom'.[1] The marriage quickly unravelled. Within a few years, Lothar and his supporters had made their first moves to dissolve the union in a way which left the young king free to remarry. Theutberga was accused of the most sordid crimes, including incest and abortion. The attempt to engineer a divorce quickly escalated into a *cause célèbre*. It sucked in an expanding ensemble cast, a who's-who of church and state in the mid ninth century. Debate over the divorce dragged on for over a decade. It finally ended in 869, when Lothar died en route back from Rome, believing that he had finally obtained approval for his marriage to another woman from a pope whose predecessor had been his most implacable opponent. To examine the only abortion accusation surviving from the early medieval west requires delving deep into this Charles-and-Diana moment in Carolingian history.

Such lurid accusations against the wife of a Christian ruler were not utterly without a precedent, though we must shift back in time to early Byzantium to find it. In the sixth century, Procopius recounted squalid stories about the empress Theodora. An eager participant in drunken orgies, 'though [Theodora] was pregnant many times, yet practically always she was able to contrive to bring about an abortion immediately'.[2] Theodora's name, like Theutberga's, was dragged through the mud. But there are important differences too. Procopius's picaresque narrative was not just a character assassination of the empress. Theodora's abortions unveiled the true character of her husband Justinian, 'who did not disdain ... to lie with a woman who had not only encompassed herself round about with every other rank defilement but had also practised infanticide time and again by voluntary abortions. And I think that I need to make mention of nothing else whatever in regard to the

---

[1] *Chronicon* a.856, trans. S. MacLean, *History and Politics in Late Carolingian and Ottonian Europe: The Chronicle of Regino of Prüm and Adalbert of Magdeburg* (Manchester, 2009), p. 135.
[2] *Anecdota* 9.18–19, ed. and trans. H. B. Dewing, *The Anecdota or Secret History* (Cambridge MA, 1935), p. 109; cf. *Anecdota* 17.16–23, pp. 203–4, on another scandalous story involving a failed abortion attempt.

character of this man.'³ Moreover, Procopius's *Secret History* was a secretive history, almost certainly not circulated in the sixth century and perhaps scarcely read until several centuries later.⁴ The string of accusations against Theutberga, by contrast, was unfurled with her husband's acquiescence. Far from being private, the defamation of Theutberga was painfully public. As one protagonist complained in 860, rumours about her had trickled down to the *plebs*. Women gossiped about the affair as they sat weaving.⁵

The spirit of this chapter is microhistorical. Its task is to unravel what it meant to accuse a woman, a Carolingian queen no less, of abortion in the ninth century. The task is complicated, however, by an easily missed blip in the conventional narrative of the divorce. The case is grist to the mill of historians interested in Carolingian political culture, Christian marriage doctrine and the early medieval papacy. They have quite rightly not focussed on the abortion angle. In the early 860s, when Lothar's chances of remarrying looked promising, Theutberga's alleged incest, not her alleged abortion, was the crucial argument. But, if anything, abortion was even more peripheral than has been recognized. If the divorce of Lothar and Theutberga was ever adapted for a film by a screenwriter who did a fair amount of historiographical reading, the abortion accusation would be the MacGuffin. A plot device at the beginning of the story, it initially appears important to the villains for reasons which are never fully explained – and then quietly disappears.

This chapter requires some careful detective work to establish that the accusation of abortion entered and exited the confusing swirl of sources earlier than historians have recognized. This might seem counter-intuitive. Isn't it mad to minimize meticulously the role of an abortion accusation in our only surviving case? There is method in the madness. The detective work is necessary to understand the significance and repercussions of the abortion accusation, and the friction between the interests of those who made it (or made it up) and of those who questioned it. For some contemporaries at least did question it, including our most important witness to the early stages of the divorce, Hincmar of Rheims. The final portion of this chapter will turn to how this 'marriage guru of ninth-century Francia' attempted to make sense of rumours which baffled and appalled contemporaries in equal measure.⁶

---

³ *Anecdota* 10.3, p. 121.
⁴ L. Brubaker, 'Sex, Lies and Textuality: The *Secret History* of Prokopios and the Rhetoric of Gender in Sixth-Century Byzantium', in *Gender in the Early Medieval World: East and West, 300–900*, ed. L. Brubaker and J. M. H. Smith (Cambridge, 2004), pp. 83–101.
⁵ Hincmar, *De divortio* (*responsio* 3), p. 130. Translations are my own, though I have consulted R. Stone and C. West, *Hincmar of Rheims, The Divorce of King Lothar II and Queen Theutberga* (Manchester, forthcoming). I am grateful to Rachel Stone and Charles West for giving me an electronic copy of their translation prior to publication.
⁶ d'Avray, *Medieval Marriage*, p. 85. On Hincmar's involvement in other ninth-century

Background: The events of 855–63

Lothar I died in 855.[7] His kingdom, flanked by those of his brothers, Charles the Bald to the west and Louis the German to the east, was split between his sons. Louis II (d. 875), the eldest, inherited Italy; Charles (d. 863), the youngest, inherited Provence; and Lothar II inherited the northernmost part, so-called Lotharingia. Like several other young Carolingian aristocrats in the mid ninth century, Lothar had already been in a sexual relationship by the time he entered marriage.[8] In Lothar's case, the status of his relationship with an Alsatian noblewoman, Waldrada, would be hotly contested in the years to come. By the time of his death in 869, the couple had had a son and three daughters together. One of these sons, Hugh, probably born in 855, points to the status of their union when Lothar inherited his father's kingdom. Hugh was not a royal Carolingian name. In other words, the relationship with Waldrada, whatever term we use to describe it, was not initially intended to evolve into a royal marriage.[9] Instead, in 855 Lothar married another noblewoman, Theutberga, in what was very likely a politically calculated marriage. Theutberga's father, Boso, had been one of Lothar I's counsellors and her brother, the married cleric Hubert, held strategically important land in the south of Lothar's kingdom. Fearful of his brother Louis II's intentions, the marriage cemented an alliance with a noble who controlled a strategically important transalpine passage between Lotharingia and Italy.[10]

marriage cases, see R. Stone, '"Bound from either side": The Limits of Power in Carolingian Marriage Disputes, 840–870', *Gender & History* 19.3 (2007), 467–82.

[7] There is a sizeable and still growing body of historiography on the case. This summary (and chapter) is particularly indebted to several works. K. Heidecker, *The Divorce of Lothar II: Christian Marriage and Political Power in the Carolingian World*, trans. T. M. Guest (Ithaca NY, 2010) is now the most detailed study in English and is indispensable, among other reasons, as a guide to the large body of sources, including several which have been relatively neglected by scholars. S. Airlie, 'Private Bodies and the Body Politic in the Divorce Case of Lothar II', *Past & Present* 161 (1998), 3–38, remains one of the most illuminating readings of the divorce. More recently, Firey, *Contrite Heart*, pp. 9–60, provides an intricate examination of penitential and legal processes in the early phases of the divorce. For the papal perspective, see now D. L. d'Avray, *Papacy, Monarchy, and Marriage, 860–1600* (Cambridge, forthcoming), pp. 48–63, together with translation of some of Nicholas I's letters in D. L. d'Avray, *Dissolving Royal Marriages: A Documentary History, 860–1600* (Cambridge, 2014), pp. 11–43. I am grateful to David d'Avray for sharing both works with me prior to publication. I am also grateful to him and to Rachel Stone for illuminating discussion and correspondence on the divorce.

[8] R. Le Jan, *Famille et pouvoir dans le monde Franc (VIIe–Xe siècle): Essai d'anthropologie sociale* (Paris, 1995), pp. 274–7.

[9] Airlie, 'Private Bodies', p. 17. For a critique of the concept of *Friedelehe*, a form of Germanic marriage which historians have hypostatized to contrast with unions conforming to church regulations, see R. M. Karras, 'The History of Marriage and the Myth of Friedelehe', *EME* 14.2 (2006), 119–51.

[10] On Theutberga's family and, more broadly, the role of the nobility in royal marriage

Matters had changed dramatically within a couple of years.[11] Theutberga was publicly accused of terrible offences, which she denied. (We will turn to various rumours, accusations and confessions in detail below.) Probably in 858 the matter was referred to an ordeal. Theutberga's name was cleared and she was restored as Lothar's wife. The ordeal was only the beginning, however; Lothar's side quickly pursued a different route. Councils at Aachen in January and February 860 brought king and queen together before gatherings of bishops and nobles. In carefully choreographed presentations of oral and written confessions, Theutberga appeared to confirm that at least some rumours were true, though she would soon write (or had already written) to Pope Nicholas I warning of forced confessions.[12] After interrogating both king and queen, Lothar's bishops concluded that she was not fit to be a wife, still less the wife of a king, and should enter a convent as a penitent.

It appeared that Lothar was going to get a divorce on the terms he wanted. Significantly, though, the first mutterings of opposition came from within his own kingdom. Not everyone in Lothar's kingdom was satisfied with the *fait accompli*.[13] Our main source for the events summarized so far owes its existence to the concerns of anonymous dissenters in Lotharingia who referred documentation and questions on the case to bishops in neighbouring kingdoms; fatefully, Hincmar of Rheims was one of these bishops.[14] He had already turned down an invitation to the February council from Adventius of Metz, one of Lothar's episcopal supporters, on grounds of ill health. By March 860, Hincmar had received the dissenters' summary of events, including one report of the Aachen (January 860) council, together with a list of their

alliances, see Heidecker, *Divorce*, pp. 51–62; M. Gaillard, 'Du pouvoir des femmes en Francia Media: épouses et filles des souverains (ca. 850–ca. 950)', in *De la mer du Nord à la Méditerranée. Francia media: Une région au coeur de l'Europe (c.840–c.1050)*, ed. M. Gaillard *et al.* (Luxembourg, 2011), pp. 301–14.

[11] J. L. Nelson, *Charles the Bald* (London, 1992), p. 199, notes sagely that 'though political factors count very nicely for the making of the marriage, they do so much less convincingly for its failure'.

[12] Though they have not survived, Nicholas I later referred to and appeared to quote from Theutberga's letters, on which see p. 250 below.

[13] Evidence of later opposition is detectable in a short précis of the case in Ado of Vienne's *Chronicon*. Ado served as a bishop under Lothar from 863 until 869. His short narrative focussed on the nefarious role of two other bishops, Gunther of Cologne and Theutgaud of Trier, in misleading the young king, who, 'deceived by depraved counsellors, incited almost the entire church against him by vacillating between marriage to two women for a long time [*a pravis conciliaris deceptus, diu de duarum feminarum connubio vacillando, pene totam ecclesiam contra se concitavit*]', *Chronicon*, MGH SS 2, p. 323. Ado's framing of the case, which effectively presented Lothar as a bigamist, was very likely influenced by Nicholas I's take on the case: see Nicholas's letter to Ado written in 863, *Ep.* 18, MGH Epp. 6, pp. 284–6. For further evidence of Lotharingian opposition to the divorce, see p. 248 below.

[14] Hincmar protected their anonymity but noted at *De divortio*, p. 112, that this group was comprised of both ecclesiastical and lay figures.

questions about the case. He entered the debate with at least apparent reluctance. Hincmar's lengthy responses to the dissenters' questions including one about sexual scandal and abortion form the first part of his treatise on the case (its title, *De divortio Lotharii regis et Theutbergae reginae*, is modern). Later that year the dissenters sent a second list of questions, and Hincmar's responses to these formed the second part of the *De divortio*. A third part, on another marriage case, was added late in 860.[15]

There is a risk that our picture of the earliest phases in the divorce will become overly Hincmarocentric. We should not overestimate the circulation of *De divortio* – nor altogether neglect it. Hincmar addressed his work to the kings and bishops of Francia and at least some parts did circulate among contemporaries.[16] At the same time, other dossiers on the case were evidently being produced too and Hincmar quoted from more than one. In this sense, *De divortio* is a layered text. *De divortio* also had another, often neglected, kind of textual layering. The treatise survives in a single manuscript copy from Rheims. Interspersed around the main body of the text are dozens of often lengthy marginal additions added by several contemporary hands known from other Rheims manuscripts. In effect, Hincmar and a team of scribes added information, augmented authorities and elaborated arguments on the case; and they subsequently continued to expand the text as a living compendium of citations for use beyond the divorce.[17]

If Hincmar's *De divortio* remains the key source for the early stages of the divorce, it was overtaken by events. Already by 860 Theutberga had fled west into Charles the Bald's kingdom. Back in Lotharingia, Lothar evidently still needed permission to take Waldrada as his queen. Further councils at Aachen in April 862 and Metz in June 863 rehearsed the legitimacy of the divorce and effectively cleared the way for a marriage with Waldrada.[18] For our purposes

---

[15] Heidecker, *Divorce*, pp. 46–8. Hincmar mentioned his meeting with Adventius in late January 860 in *De divortio* (*responsio* 3), p. 130. On Adventius's career and involvement in the divorce, see M. Gaillard, 'Un évêque et son temps, Advence de Metz (858–875)', in *Lotharingia: eine europäische Kernlandschaft um das Jahr 1000*, ed. H.-W. Herrmann and R. Schneider (Saarbrücken, 1995), pp. 89–119.

[16] *De divortio*, p. 107. See Heidecker, *Divorce*, pp. 47–8, on evidence for circulation in 860.

[17] The manuscript in question is Paris, Bibliothèque nationale, MS latin 2866. Not all of the marginalia were added as part of discussion on the case, though the substance of the marginalia to which I shall draw attention below suggests that they almost certainly were. K. Heidecker, 'Gathering and Recycling Authoritative Texts: The Importance of Marginalia in Hincmar of Reims' Treatise about King Lothar's Divorce', in *Organizing the Written Word: Scripts, Manuscripts and Texts*, ed. Marco Mostert (Turnhout, forthcoming), provides helpful orientation accompanying Letha Böhringer's detailed comments in MGH Conc. 4.1, pp. 39–65. The additions are marked in the margins and notes of Böhringer's edition (it is worth keeping a bookmark at pp. 40–2, which provides a table of marginal additions). I am very grateful to Karl Heidecker for sharing his book chapter with me prior to publication.

[18] On events from 860 to 862, see Heidecker, *Divorce*, pp. 100–48.

the Metz council, which was attended by papal legates, marks a watershed; Nicholas I had entered the ring. Papal involvement prompted an important argumentative shift in the debate: away from the argument that Theutberga was not fit to be a royal wife because of the offences to which she confessed, and towards the argument that Lothar's prior union with Waldrada had in fact been a legitimate marriage, though the memory of Lothar's treatment of Theutberga haunted all subsequent discussion of the case.

So the disgrace would be hidden: The defamation of Theutberga

The accusations against Theutberga appalled her contemporaries. Or, if we follow some sources and many historians in regarding them as calculated fabrications (*insidiae*), they were designed to appal contemporaries.[19] David d'Avray puts it bluntly; in terms of shock value, they were the 'equivalent of child abuse allegations today'.[20] As Stuart Airlie has emphasized, to grasp why they struck contemporaries so sharply, the accusations should be set against Carolingian political theology and ideas about queenship. Certainly from the reign of Louis the Pious, understandings of what it meant to be a queen were illuminated in the shimmering light of biblical exemplars. Queens were not only expected to emulate virtuous wives and fruitful mothers like Esther and Judith, but even the Virgin Mary. The accusations turned Theutberga into a 'ghastly parody of Carolingian queenship ... almost as an antithesis of the Virgin Mary herself'.[21] If the allegation of abortion was unique, the treatment of Theutberga was not. She stands in a line of Carolingian queens after Judith (d. 843), wife of Louis the Pious, subjected to lurid accusations of adultery and other sexual offences.[22] Given the place of queens in Carolingian political culture, such accusations were experienced as nothing less than pollutions which threatened to 'corrupt the entire social and cosmic order'.[23]

We may well feel that the 'malignly inventive humiliation Lothar and his advisors devised for Theutberga was so extreme that it is hard not to be pleased at its failure'.[24] But what exactly was Theutberga accused of? What did she confess to? And are the answers to both of these questions

---

[19] *Annales Bertiniani* a.860, ed. F. Grat *et al.*, *Annales de Saint-Bertin* (Paris, 1964), p. 84.
[20] *Papacy, Monarchy, and Marriage*, p. 55.
[21] Airlie, 'Private Bodies', 20–2 (quotation at 22).
[22] See G. Bührer-Thierry, 'La reine adultère', *Cahiers de civilisation médiévale* 35.4 (1992), 299–312, on sexual accusations against Carolingian queens, including Judith, Richardis (d. 894/6) and Uta (d. 899/903); see too T. Reuter, 'Sex, Lies and Oath-Helpers: The Trial of Queen Uota', in T. Reuter, *Medieval Polities and Modern Mentalities* (Cambridge, 2006), pp. 217–30.
[23] See M. de Jong, *The Penitential State: Authority and Atonement in the Age of Louis the Pious* (Cambridge, 2009), pp. 185–204 (quotation at p. 202) on the political and social meaning of sexual slander against Judith.
[24] Wickham, *Inheritance of Rome*, p. 421.

Abortion in the Early Middle Ages

identical? Modern historians typically refer to three distinct but connected offences when summarizing or narrating the divorce: incest with Hubert; unnatural intercourse, specified as anal intercourse or sodomy in a fair amount of recent historiography; and abortion. The assumption is that these were the accusations which 'uncoiled at Aachen' in 860, where Theutberga's confession supplied Lothar's team with the requisite grounds for dissolving the marriage.[25] (As if generalizing from a royal divorce was not treacherous enough, our only surviving abortion accusation sounds disappointingly absurd: abortion after incestuous sodomy?). Reference to all three offences can be found in the sources. Detective work, however, raises questions about the role played by abortion in the defamation of Theutberga. The accusation of abortion evaporated from the sources well before the argumentative shift in 863.

Disappearing act: Theutberga's offence(s) in the written record
If the allusion to abortion is our missing person, we must start where our missing person was last seen. Early on in *De divortio* Hincmar quoted the brief sent to him in the early months of 860 by dissenters in Lothar's kingdom. The brief included a potted narrative to bring him up to speed with events:

> They [the Lotharingian dissenters] say in the first chapter: The wife [Theutberga] of the lord and king Lothar was initially accused of *stuprum*, that her brother [Hubert] had committed with her the crime of masculine intercourse between the thighs, just as men are accustomed to commit shamefulness with men [Rom. 1. 27], and from this she conceived; and that because of this, she took a drink and aborted the offspring so that the disgrace would be hidden.[26]

Quoted by Hincmar, the dissenters were writing in 860, but at this point their narrative was still in 857/8. Theutberga denied the charges and, in the absence of witnesses, proof was sought in an ordeal:

---

[25] Incest, anal intercourse and abortion: Airlie, 'Private Bodies', p. 22 (quotation at p. 20); Nelson, *Charles the Bald*, p. 199; V. L. Garver, *Women and Aristocratic Culture in the Carolingian World* (Ithaca NY, 2009), p. 165; E. J. Goldberg, *Struggle for Empire: Kingship and Conflict under Louis the German, 817–876* (Ithaca NY, 2006), p. 292; MacLean, *History and Politics*, p. 140 n.77; Wickham, *Inheritance of Rome*, pp. 420–1. J. Devisse, *Hincmar, archévêque de Reims, 845–882*, 3 vols. (Geneva, 1975–6), I, p. 369, refers to incest, unnatural intercourse and abortion. Firey, *Contrite Heart*, p. 14, refers to incestuous 'sodomy' and abortion, but notes the semantic ambiguity of key sources.

[26] 'Aiunt enim primo capitulo: Uxor domni regis Hlotharii primo quidem reputata est de stupro, quasi frater suus cum ea masculino concubitu inter femora, sicut solent masculi in masculos turpitudinem operari, scelus fuerit operatus et inde ipsa conceperit; quapropter, ut celaretur flagitium, potum hausit et partum abortivit', *De divortio* (*interrogatio* 1), p. 114.

by the judgment of lay nobles, by the advice of bishops and with the consent of the king, a proxy for that woman went to the judgment of boiling water [the ordeal], and after he was found uncooked, the same woman was restored to the marriage bed and decreed royal union from which she had been suspended.[27]

Only then did the brief turn to more recent events: 'after a space of time, the booklet [the first report of the Aachen (January 860) council], just as we sent to you, was written by some bishops, [but] *we do not know whether about the same matter or about something committed after the beginning of the union*'.[28] The Lotharingian dissenters were not entirely certain whether what Theutberga had recently confessed to in 860 was identical to what she had been accused of in the run-up to the ordeal in 858. As it happens, those advancing the case against Theutberga did connect her confession to the ordeal, though the connection appeared in an account of the February council which Hincmar subsequently obtained from elsewhere.[29] But when we turn to the reports of the councils at Aachen in 860 – two versions of the January council and one of the February council – at which Theutberga's confession was extracted and publicized, a subtle shift becomes clear. Incest and unnatural fornication were still there; abortion was absent.

Admittedly, the two reports of the January council reproduced by Hincmar in *De divortio* were vague on Theutberga's actual offence. In the first report, which the dissenters had sent to Hincmar, Theutberga swore (in direct speech) that she was not fit to remain in the royal union and referred the bishops to their colleague, Gunther of Cologne, to whom she had confessed.[30] The other two reports had not been sent by the dissenters but were inserted into *De divortio* after Hincmar had started writing.[31] The second report for Aachen (January

---

[27] 'Quae ipsa denegans probationis auctore testibusque deficientibus, iudicio laicorum nobilium et consultu episcoporum atque ipsius regis consensu vicarius eiusdem feminae ad iudicium aquae ferventis exiit et, postquam incoctus fuerat ipse repertus, eadem femina maritali thoro ac coniugio regio decreto, quo suspensa fuerat, est etiam restituta', *De divortio*, (*interrogatio* 1), p. 114.

[28] 'Sicque post spatium temporis, *nescimus utrum de eadem re an de commisso post initum coniugium, a quibusdam episcopis talis*, sicut vobis transmittimus, conscriptus habetur libellus', *De divortio* (*interrogatio* 1), p. 114 (my italics).

[29] Referring to this passage in the dissenters' brief, Airlie, 'Private Bodies', 19 n.51, writes that the 'accusations uttered in 860 are explicitly linked then with the ordeal of 858'. It is true, as we shall shortly see, that the link was made at the 860 councils; but, in fact, the brief itself explicitly questioned the link.

[30] *De divortio* (*interrogatio* 1, *Libellus octo capitulorum* 6), p. 115. For a detailed reading of this report, including an intriguing argument that Theutberga 'manipulate[d] the ambiguities in the juridical and penitential processes in order to gain both legal and moral advantage' (p. 22), see Firey, *Contrite Heart*, pp. 17–26.

[31] The folios on which they were written – fols. 15r–19v, corresponding to *De divortio* (*responsio* 1), pp. 119–25 – were subsequently added to the manuscript; see Böhringer's table of marginal additions at p. 40 (*Erg*. 2–2a). Hincmar wrote at least

860) gave slightly more detail on the substance of the confession, publicized through Gunther's testimony as confessor: '[Theutberga] confessed to God and to us that she had an interior wound within her, not by her own will, but violently inflicted upon her'.[32] The report of the February council was more direct.[33] A document containing Theutberga's confession (*cartula confessionis*) was read aloud, including the revelation that 'my brother, the cleric Hubert, corrupted me as an adolescent, and practised and perpetrated upon my body fornication against natural use'.[34] The bishops cross-examined Lothar in case – here the report risked protesting too much – 'this much discussed woman was lying out of any deception or fear of anyone'.[35] So, unlike the dissenting bishops who wrote to Hincmar, the Aachen (February 860) report did connect Theutberga's confession to the 858 ordeal, but it did not allude to abortion. Lothar revealed that he had 'accepted the false judgment [the 858 ordeal] as a truthful examination, while knowing [the truth], and tolerated it so that, if it could be possible, such an unbelievable disgrace could appear and then disappear from the world'. But he could no longer sustain the lie after journeys to Italy and Burgundy revealed just how far rumours had spread.[36]

Although they were quoted and critically dissected by Hincmar, the reports of the Aachen councils probably originated with Lothar's side. They were attempts at information control. An entry for 860 in the *Annales Bertiniani* may provide a glimpse of the limits of information control among contemporaries, though we cannot be absolutely certain that this was one of the last entries written by Prudentius of Troyes (d. 861) rather than a later revision by Hincmar, who took over the annals at some point between 861 and 866.[37] The

---

some, perhaps a significant portion, of *De divortio* before obtaining the more detailed information in these reports.

[32] 'Confessa est deo et nobis, quod vulnus in se haberet interius, non tamen sua sponte, sed violenter sibi inlatum', *De divortio* (*interrogatio* 1, Libellus septem capitulorum 4), p. 120.

[33] Hincmar, *De divortio* (*responsio* 1), p. 121, referred to another volume (*thomus*) which he did not reproduce in its entirety because of its length (*prolixitas*); he quoted cc.15–19 of this account of the February council. I set aside the possibility, proposed by Firey, *Contrite Heart*, p. 15 n.12, that a scribal error has generated the idea of two separate councils in January and February 860.

[34] 'germanus meus Hubertus clericus me adulescentiam corrupit et in meo corpore contra naturalem usum fornicationem exercuit et perpetravit', *De divortio* (*responsio* 1, c.15), p. 121.

[35] 'ne forte pro aliqua deceptione aut pro timore alicuius sepedicta mulier mentiretur', *De divortio* (*responsio* 1, c.15), p. 121.

[36] 'falsum iudicium se sciente pro verifica examinatione suscepit et toleravit, ut, si fieri posset, tanta turpitudo incredibilis appareret et sic in mundo evanesceret', *De divortio* (*responsio* 1, c.16), pp. 121–2.

[37] Prudentius authored the *Annales Bertiniani* from a.843 until his death in 861. Hincmar's entries start from a.861 with a prickly epitaph of Prudentius, though he certainly tinkered with some earlier entries: see J. L. Nelson, *The Annals of St. Bertin* (Manchester, 1991), pp. 14–15. Judging from *Annales Bertinani* a.853, in which

entry reported that 'Lothar hated his queen, Theutberga, with irreconcilable loathing, and after wearing her down with many acts of hostility, he finally forced her to confess before bishops that she had had sodomitical intercourse with her brother Hubert'. Lotharingian control of the narrative was far from total. Nonetheless, in the *Annales Bertiniani*, as in the accounts of the Aachen council, Theutberga confessed (albeit under duress) to incest and unnatural intercourse – but not to abortion.[38]

The pattern continues when we move beyond the events of 860 – in terms of the sources, beyond Hincmar's *De divortio* and the texts it quoted. The council at Aachen in April 862 amplified an idea already articulated in 860: the pollution of incest precluded Theutberga from any marriage, let alone a royal marriage.[39] Lothar's bishops now gave their case a canonical sheen. They referred to a canon from the council of Epaon (517), cited as the council of Agde (506), which banned incestuous marriage in the sense of marriage between partners related within the forbidden degrees of kinship, to back up the idea that those guilty of incest were precluded from entering into marriage.[40] Here, the temptation is to side with Regino, who dismissed the Lotharingian canon law case as a heady mixture of bad motives and bad learning. In Regino's account, there was 'not ... one learned bishop in Lothar's realm who had a clear grounding in the study of the canons'.[41] Regino might have been something of an expert on ecclesiastical regulations in his own day, but the reality of canonical culture was more complex than his picture suggests. As David d'Avray recently argued, when Nicholas I became involved, he did not address the canon law case presented to him on its own terms because, in part, he could not call upon the kind of canonical expertise that a Carolingian king could muster. The critical mass of legal learning was

---

he noted sourly that sons followed father in their devotion to adulterous liaisons, Prudentius did not hold Lothar I or his sons in high regard.

[38] 'Lotharius reginam suam Teutbergam inrecovabili odio habitam et multis contrarietatibus fatigatam ad hoc compulit ut ipsa coram episcopis confiteretur fratrem suum Hucbertum sibi sodomitico scelere commixtum', *Annales Bertiniani* a.860, p.82; trans. Nelson, *Annals of St. Bertin*, p. 92. The reference to *sodomoticum scelus* did not necessarily mean anal intercourse; see pp. 254–5 below.

[39] Different accounts of this council are edited in MGH Conc. 4, pp. 71–89; see Heidecker, *Divorce*, p. 43 n.27. One report (text A) is from a manuscript containing the letters of Adventius and Lothar, and while the other texts all appear in a sequence within a late ninth-century manuscript from Reims. One of these (text C) is an account of the bishops' decision. The other texts are a statement presented to the bishops by Lothar (text B), an anonymous treatise on the case which critically dismembered the canonical arguments made by Lothar's bishops (text D), and another anonymous and incomplete text which set out a list of pros and cons through quotations (text E).

[40] Council of Aachen (862), text A, c.9, p. 74.

[41] *Chronicon* a.865, trans. MacLean, *History and Politics*, pp. 141–2; *Chronicon* a.864, pp. 139–40, presents Gunther and Theutgaud of Trier as venal villain and dim-witted sidekick.

Abortion in the Early Middle Ages

concentrated in Francia, not Rome.[42] Given the ambiguities of church law on marriage, the Carolingian Renaissance's production line of savvy bishops, and the more general tendency by which ecclesiastical regulations, when applied in practice, were mental tools for thinking through cases flexibly (here we should recall Rabanus's use of conciliar canons in his letters on infanticide and abortion by assault), the line separating sophistry from sophistication was very fine indeed.[43] Admittedly, in the aftermath of Aachen (862) some Lotharingian bishops authored a formidable forensic analysis of patristic and conciliar authorities, which eviscerated the canonical case for the divorce, though the extent to which their anonymous text circulated is less clear.[44] But, anticipating the canonical case made by Lothar's bishops, in 860 Hincmar had already quoted the same canon from Epaon to make much the same point in the *De divortio*. Hincmar's doubts, to which we turn below, focussed on the alleged fact of Theutberga's offence and the procedures by which it had been publicized. But, like Lothar's bishops, Hincmar found their theory perfectly intelligible: incest, if proven, precluded Theutberga from entering into a marriage.[45] At any rate, the canonical case advanced at Aachen in 862 still rested on Theutberga's confession. If Theutberga 'had been fit for the conjugal bed, and had not been defiled by the pestilential pollution of incest nor publicly condemned by a *viva voce* confession, [Lothar] would have voluntarily kept her'.[46] But 'how could she, whom by her own admission her own brother had not shrunk from violating, be joined in matrimony'?[47] Over a couple of years, the argument about incest had sharpened. There was little need to mention abortion.

Moving ahead to second-hand accounts (no direct reports survive) of the council at Metz in 863, abortion had long since dropped off the radar.[48] One account appeared in a fragmentary letter written by Adventius in 863, which captured the moment when the two very different arguments advanced by Lothar's side sidled awkwardly past one another on parallel tracks. Adventius

---

[42] d'Avray, *Papacy, Monarchy, and Marriage*, pp. 50–4, which also provides a convincing account of Nicholas's approach to the case, neatly summarized as 'narrative as argument' (p. 58).

[43] See pp. 178–80, 226–7, above, on Rabanus's letters.

[44] Council of Aachen (862), text D, pp. 78–86, with Heidecker, *Divorce*, pp. 107–9, on this remarkable text, which complements d'Avray's picture of contrasting canonical expertise north and south of the Alps.

[45] Hincmar quoted the Epaon canon to make this point at *De divortio* (*responsio* 12), p. 195, (*responsio* 19), p. 219.

[46] 'Quam, si idonea fuisset coniugali thoro, et pestifera incestus pollutione foedata non esset, et vivae vocis confessione publice condemnata, sponte retineret', Council of Aachen (862), text A, c. 3, p. 72; cf. Council of Aachen (862), text B, p. 75.

[47] 'Quomodo enim posset matrimonio copulari, quam iuxta suam assertionem frater non pertimuit construpare?', Council of Aachen (862), text C, p. 76.

[48] On the sources for this council, effectively letters and annals, see Heidecker, *Divorce*, p. 149 n.2.

proposed that Lothar had in fact already been married to Waldrada in a public ceremony and with an exchange of gifts, and that it was only later that Hubert cowed Lothar into marrying his sister.[49] But, risking an argumentative overload, Adventius also emphasized that 'rumour of the worst disgrace followed Theutberga and she was declared guilty of incestuous intercourse with her brother Hubert', as had recently been reconfirmed at Metz.[50]

The pattern is clear. Abortion is absent from the mélange of other sources on the case, mainly annals or chronicles and letters, some contemporary, some written in retrospect – and most hostile to Lothar and his supporters.[51] Reference appears in only one early text (more precisely, in a text-within-the-text), Hincmar's *De divortio*, and specifically in relation to the ordeal of 858. Abortion had the ghostliest presence in the written record. Although he was writing roughly half a century after events, Regino, who had access to various kinds of documentation on the case, provides a rough litmus test. Theutberga was accused of 'very serious crimes'; specifically, she had been 'polluted by lying together incestuously with her own natural brother'.[52]

We can also conclude cautiously that the surviving record only captures some of the word-of-mouth information (and misinformation) which spread. The point is not just that some sources on the case have not survived.[53] Other sources deliberately avoided divulging precise details of the accusations against Theutberga, which makes it difficult to know precisely what their authors knew. Those who were suspicious about the veracity of the accusations against Theutberga resorted to a sensible rhetorical strategy: measured

---

[49] See Heidecker, *Divorce*, pp. 110–19, on the deployment of this argument by Adventius and other Lotharingian bishops.

[50] 'Fama pessimae turpitudinis Theutbergam sequitur et de incestuoso concubitu fratris sui Hucberti rea acclamatur', *Epistolae ad divortium Lotharii II regis pertinentes* 5, MGH Epp. 6, pp. 215–16.

[51] See Heidecker, *Divorce*, pp. 37–41, for an overview of the narrative sources. Terse entries in *Annales Laubacenses* a.855, 858, MGH SS 1, p. 15, and *Annales Lobienses* a.855, 858, 864, 870, MGH SS 13, p. 232, offer little detail. The more detailed narrative in *Liber Pontificalis* 107.44–50, trans. R. Davis, *The Lives of the Ninth-Century Popes*, TTH 20 (Liverpool, 1995), pp. 224–31, effectively begins with the council at Metz in 863 and focusses in particular on Lothar's bishops.

[52] 'gravia crimina ... semetipsam fratris germani incestuoso concubitu esse pollutam', *Chronicon* a.864, p. 81; trans. MacLean, *History and Politics*, p. 139. In addition, during his time as abbot, Regino had effectively acted as prison warden to Lothar's son, Hugh, who had been blinded and confined at Prüm from 885 on the orders of Charles the Fat following his involvement in an aborted rebellion; see S. Airlie, 'Unreal Kingdom: Francia Media under the Shadow of Lothar II', in *Francia Media*, pp. 353–5.

[53] The dossiers from which Hincmar quoted the second version of Aachen (January 860) and the report of Aachen (February 860), and Theutberga's correspondence with Nicholas I are obvious examples. In some cases, the loss of texts might have been deliberate: see Heidecker, *Divorce*, pp. 132–3, on an (ironically) extant letter from Adventius to Theutgaud of Trier with instructions to burn after reading.

reticence. Perhaps deliberately taciturn, the *Annales Xantenses* concisely described Theutberga as a 'legitimate wife repudiated on an unspeakable pretext'.⁵⁴ Nicholas I's letters offer clearer examples. In 'tearful letters' (*lacrimosis litteris*), he recounted, Theutberga had protested that she was 'pure and innocent of the crime of which she is accused'. Elsewhere, Nicholas lamented that 'compelled by force, [Theutberga] had composed a false confession of crime',⁵⁵ and he carefully avoided substantively repeating the slanderous detail which had been spewed out from the 'throat of iniquity'.⁵⁶

Cui bono? Making sense of rumour

One of the dangers with the divorce of Lothar and Theutberga is projecting later dynamics back onto earlier phases. Theutberga's supposed infertility is a case in point. It is misleading to read the initial momentum behind the case in terms of a succession crisis facing a king lumbered with a barren wife;⁵⁷ or, for that matter, that Theutberga was understood to be sterile as an after-effect of her abortion.⁵⁸ The problem of succession became increasingly fraught for Lothar as the 860s wore on. But allegations of Theutberga's barrenness, asserted, curiously enough, by Theutberga herself and addressed by Nicholas I in 867, only surfaced late on in the case.⁵⁹

The abortion accusation is the inverse of the sterility canard, a detail which needs to be firmly situated very early in the divorce. Why did it appear and disappear so quickly? The divorce defies those who prefer to tell history as it was. The machinations of Lothar's side may be the most immediately transparent, but no one side had a monopoly on character assassination, information manipulation and attempts to control narratives and interpretations of events.⁶⁰ After all, the flipside of the defence of Theutberga was the vilification of Waldrada, to whom Nicholas referred in one letter simply as the 'whore'

---

⁵⁴ 'legitimam uxorem ... ab eo nefanda occasione', *Annales Xantenses* a.866, MGH SRG 12, p. 23; on these annals, which were probably re-edited in Louis the German's kingdom in the 870s, see Heidecker, *Divorce*, p. 39.

⁵⁵ 'puram se quo accusatur crimine inquit atque insontem'; 'vi coactum falsum contra se composuisse piaculum', *Ep.* 3, 11, MGH Epp. 6, pp. 269, 277; trans. d'Avray, *Dissolving*, pp. 14, 18. In addition to these letters, Nicholas also referred to his correspondence with Theutberga in *Ep.* 10, p. 276.

⁵⁶ 'iniqua ... fauce', *Ep.* 53, p. 343; trans. d'Avray, *Dissolving*, p. 29.

⁵⁷ Cf. L. Dupraz, 'Deux préceptes de Lothaire II (867 et 868), ou les vestiges diplomatiques d'un divorce manqué', *Zeitschrift für schweizerische Kirchengeschichte* 59 (1965), 204: 'Mais Theutberge était stérile. Aussi Lothaire, qui voulait une posterité, entrepit-il tout ce qui était en son pouvoir pour obtenir l'annulation de son mariage.'

⁵⁸ Cf. V. I. J. Flint, 'Magic and Marriage in Ninth-Century Francia: Lothar, Hincmar – and Susanna', in *The Culture of Christendom: Essays in Medieval History in Commemoration of Denis L. T. Bethell*, ed. M. A. Meyer (London, 1993), p. 66.

⁵⁹ Airlie, 'Private Bodies', 12. See Nicholas I, *Ep.* 45 (to Theutberga), *Ep.* 46 (to Lothar), pp. 320, 324.

⁶⁰ P. Buc, *The Dangers of Ritual: Between Early Medieval Texts and Social Scientific Theory* (Princeton, 2001), pp. 55–80.

Divorce of Lothar II and Theutberga

(*scortum*).⁶¹ If we assume that the accusation of incest, unnatural fornication and abortion which led to the ordeal was a concoction or at least a manipulation, whose concoction or manipulation was it?

One intriguing possibility, recently proposed by Karl Heidecker, takes seriously the idea that Lothar's anonymous opponents twisted details to undermine the king every bit as much as his supporters did to undermine Theutberga. Heidecker has suggested that the reference to abortion in the dissenters' brief was intended to work against Lothar. Incest and even unnatural fornication were not dissenting fabrications (after all, they formed part of the case established by Lothar's side at Aachen in February 860). But abortion after conceiving through unnatural intercourse looks more suspect. 'It was in the interests of those who compiled the list of questions [i.e. the Lotharingian dissenters],' Heidecker argues, 'to make the accusation seem ridiculous and suggest that Lothar had simply made the whole thing up in order to obtain a divorce from Theutberga'.⁶² Certainly, if Hincmar's *De divortio* is anything to go by, the concatenation of accusations (incest, unnatural fornication, abortion) did Lothar's cause no favours. It raised not only perplexing physiological questions, but also perplexing juridical questions given that Theutberga had been cleared at the ordeal. Heidecker's reading implies that when the dissenters asked for Hincmar's evaluation of the validity of ordeals and the possibility of conceiving through unnatural intercourse, they were playing a clever game.⁶³

At the very least, the dissenters had an interest in representing Lothar's case in its weakest form. There is another possibility – and we can only deal in possibilities – which takes account of this. The dissenters were not altogether dissembling. The triple charge really had initially been brought against Theutberga, even if the dissenters reported it in a deliberately negative light.⁶⁴

---

⁶¹ *Ep.* 39 (to Adventius), p. 313. See Rider, *Magic and Impotence*, pp. 32–6, for Hincmar's discussion of aphrodisiac and impotence magic in relation to Waldrada.

⁶² Heidecker, *Divorce*, p. 68; at pp. 68–9 n.34, Heidecker cautiously suggests that we cannot entirely rule out the possibility that there was a grain of truth to the story of incestuous sexual abuse by Hubert. As Heidecker notes, some sources convey Hubert's reputation for violence and sexual depravity, most significantly a letter by Nicholas I's predecessor, Benedict III (d. 858), which did not look at Hubert through the prism of the allegations in the divorce; on Hubert's reputation, see too Chélini, *L'aube de moyen âge*, p. 158.

⁶³ Ordeal: *De divortio* (*interrogatio* 6, 7), pp. 146, 161. On gynaecological perplexities, see pp. 253–8, below, on *De divortio* (*interrogatio* 12), pp. 181–2. On the other hand, the dissenters had written with certainty about the ordeal and with uncertainty about what happened next. If they had wanted to undermine Lothar by ascribing a ridiculous assertion to him, they might well have extended it to the councils of 860. After all, the reticence of the *libellus* which they sent to Hincmar (who obtained, we recall, the other reports of the Aachen councils from elsewhere) provided an ideal opportunity.

⁶⁴ For example, there need not have been rumours about just one single act between Theutberga and Hubert, as d'Avray, *Papacy, Monarchy and Marriage*, p. 55 n.31, notes, or even a single version of the rumours.

It is faintly possible that abortion might have served a specific legal purpose beyond defamation.[65] But as Lothar and his supporters mapped out another route to divorce following the failure of the ordeal in 858, they dropped the abortion angle. It was counter-productive. Perhaps they had picked up on the kind of incredulous reaction captured by the dissenters' questions for Hincmar. More significantly, dropping the abortion angle complemented a calculated strategy adopted in 860, which Abigail Firey has recently brought to light in her examination of the Aachen (860) reports. These reports situated the 'explanation of cause or motive ... within the general domain of original sin, rather than within a more specific framework of sin or crime'. Theutberga's offence 'lay in having been polluted, not in having been led by a perverse will into sin. Her responsibility for the sin she confessed, despite the horror it evoked, was thus considerably mitigated.'[66] Far from being a confession of guilt or culpability, Theutberga's confession at 860 was a revelation of pollution or defilement. She had suffered an 'interior wound within her, not by her own will, but violently inflicted upon her'; in modern terms, she had been sexually abused or raped.[67] Theutberga was the unfortunately polluted victim whose involuntary defilement rendered her unfit for marriage. The bishops were the grieving agents of a sad but necessary course of action. With 'tearful sighs' (*lacrimosis suspiriis*) and other gestures carefully recorded in the reports, Lothar watched on as his wife was declared unfit for the royal bed.[68] The abortion accusation would have given this smooth narrative of involuntary pollution an abrasively rough edge.

In sum – and, by necessity, speculatively – abortion was included and dropped by Lothar's side once it became counter-productive, while the dissenters were careful not to forget the initial charge because its 'overkill' discredited Lothar.[69] Abortion was useful to more than one side in the debate. The

---

[65] The possibility occurred to me when reading Flint, 'Magic and Marriage', p. 73, who wrote (erroneously) that 'magically induced sterility and abortion merited the death penalty according to Salic law' (Flint then referred to *PLS* 19.4). Pace Flint, Salic law, on which see pp. 213–6, 224–5 above, contained no such provision. But one relevant body of law did provide a rationale for an abortion accusation. Drawing on late Roman law, Burgundian law granted husbands the right to divorce wives on specific grounds, including use of *maleficium*, on which see p. 208 n.4 above. The connection is possible insofar as it was intelligible that Theutberga could fall under the scope of Burgundian law; cf. Firey, *Contrite Heart*, pp. 18–19 n.18: '[the case raised] the question of how secular law and canon law might apply. Theutberga could possibly claim to be governed by Burgundian law, while Lothar's legal personality would have been that of a Salic Frank. As wife and queen, Theutberga would have come under the provisions of Lothar's law, but the relative force of laws with pagan (Salic) or Arian (Burgundian) associations had of Christian or scriptural legislation also had to be weighed.'

[66] *Contrite Heart*, pp. 27–37 (quotation at p. 35).

[67] *De divortio* (*interrogatio* 1), p. 120, with n.32 above; cf. Firey, *Contrite Heart*, p. 29.

[68] *De divortio* (*responsio* 1, c. 16), p. 122.

[69] d'Avray, *Papacy, Monarchy and Marriage*, p. 55.

ephemerality of the accusation hints at assumptions about abortion among contemporaries. First, and most obviously, abortion was a convenient charge to make in character assassinations of women.[70] Second, if abortion was deliberately dropped by the time of the Aachen (860) councils, to accuse a woman of abortion smacked of antagonism, the very impression which Lothar's side wanted to minimize in 860. Third, because abortion so naturally evoked concealment of sexual sin, it also become a cipher of sexual sin. The more explosive the sexual transgression, the more credible that transgressors might do everything they could to conceal it. Few sexual sins were more explosive than incest in ninth-century political culture. This tenacious mental reflex remains relevant even if the dissenting bishops had deliberately made up or massaged information to discredit Lothar. It had to be plausible that Lothar had come up with such an implausible charge if the likes of Hincmar were to be convinced. The mental reflex provided the requisite patina of plausibility.

Whose concoction was it anyway? It is impossible to know for certain. In one important sense, the question becomes moot when we turn to Hincmar's response. Whether a gamble which ultimately backfired on Lothar or a wily ruse concocted by dissenters in his kingdom, from Hincmar's perspective the triple charge of incest, unnatural fornication and abortion had been lodged against Theutberga by Lothar's side. When we examine his response, it becomes clear that the abortion accusation was one reason why some contemporaries viewed the case against Theutberga with suspicion.

On *stuprum* and abortion: Hincmar's response

Among their numerous questions, the Lotharingian dissenters asked Hincmar to write back to them on what scripture and patristic tradition had to say about *stuprum* and abortion. They wanted Hincmar's knowledge of sacred texts to illuminate 'whether a woman can conceive in such a way, as is said, and remain a virgin after abortion, as is said to have happened to this one; and if she has been discovered to have perpetrated these crimes before marriage, whether she should or can remain in marriage'. The dissenters also asked for full details of authors and book titles.[71] Hincmar did not disappoint,

---

[70] M. A. Kelleher, '"Like Man and Wife": Clerics' Concubines in the Diocese of Barcelona', *Journal of Medieval History* 28 (2002), 356, gives an example from late medieval Catalonia. When a cleric, Bernat Staproa, was accused of deflowering a girl and getting her pregnant, he responded that she already had a reputation for sexual promiscuity and abortion long before he had got to her, and that the child was not his. At the same time, this was a wholly different legal landscape, in which secular courts could (in theory) put to death men and women implicated in abortion and infanticide, on which see ibid., 356 n.28.

[71] 'utrum tali modo, sicut dicitur, femina possit concipere et post aborsum virgo valeat permanere, sicut de ista dicitur accedisse; et si deprehensa fuerit haec ante

responding with a lengthy, meandering answer crammed with citations, and later supplemented with extensive marginal additions.[72]

To begin, Hincmar quoted various scriptural passages on an array of sexual sins, including Leviticus on incest, Genesis on Onan's pouring out of his seed and Paul on '*men working shamefulness with men* and *women turning natural use into that use which is against nature*' (an extension of the passage quoted by the dissenters when describing the accusation), all backed up with patristic citations.[73] Hincmar had assembled this array of sexual offences to emphasize 'how great an evil incest of brother and sister with male sodomitical intercourse also is, if by chance this is the case'. Both offences – incest and unnatural fornication – Hincmar gravely noted, were punishable by death in Leviticus.[74]

But what exactly did sodomitical intercourse entail? The proliferation of references to anal intercourse in recent historiography belies the semantic flux which Hincmar and his contemporaries had to negotiate when speaking about sex.[75] The dissenters had referred to intercourse 'between the thighs' (*inter femora*). *Femur* carried sexual connotations and in Christian Latin, though less typically in classical Latin, *femora* could be a euphemism for (male or female) genitalia or intercourse.[76] Take, for example, a Carolingian episcopal statute which elaborated a wide range of sexual perversions to illustrate the 'worst crime in scriptures', including 'that impurity which a man exercises between his own thighs by himself or with someone else' (respectively, masturbation and inter-femoral intercourse).[77] This is significant. The dissenters were no innocent reporters, but it is highly questionable that they imputed that

---

coniugium crimina perpetrasse, utrum in coniugio debeat aut valeat permanere', *De divortio* (*interrogatio* 12), p. 177.

[72] *De divortio* (*responsio* 12), pp. 177–96. It is worth noting that Hincmar might well have drafted much of this *responsio* before obtaining or, at least, digesting the two reports of the Aachen council later inserted into the manuscript, on which see pp. 245–6 n.31 above. On this *responsio*, see Heidecker, 'Gathering and Recycling', and Garver, 'Childbearing and Infancy', 224–5. I do not discuss less relevant portions of *responsio* 12, which stressed the need to question Hubert and rulers' obligations to judge justly.

[73] '*masculos in masculos turpitudinem operantes* et *feminas naturalem usum in eum usum, qui est contra naturam, mutantes*', *De divortio* (*responsio* 12), pp. 177–8 (1 Rom. 27. 26, italicized).

[74] 'quantum mali sit fratris cum sorore incestus etiam concubitu masculi sodomitano, si forte causa ita se habet', *De divortio* (*responsio* 12), pp. 177–9 (quotation at p. 179).

[75] G. W. Olsen, *Of Sodomites, Effeminates, Hermaphrodites, and Androgynes: Sodomy in the Age of Peter Damian* (Toronto, 2011), pp. 31–41.

[76] J. N. Adams, *The Latin Sexual Vocabulary* (London, 1982), pp. 51, 93, 180; Olsen, *Sodomites*, pp. 35–8.

[77] 'in scripturis crimen pessimum', 'quid inter femora sua impuritatem solus cum se ipso vel cum alio exercet', Theodulph of Orléans, *Capitula II* 7.11, MGH Capit. episc. 1, p. 168.

Theutberga had been accused – absurdly – of conceiving a child through anal intercourse.

Judging by his response, nor did Hincmar. A long passage argued vehemently against those 'who assert that it is not the sodomitical sin except when one fornicates within the body, that is in the obscene part of the body, within the belly as it were'. Packed thick with patristic citations, the passage concluded, 'no one should say that he, who has worked shamefulness against nature in male or in female [another reference to 1 Rom. 27] and has made himself impure deliberately and eagerly through rubbing or touch or shameful movements, does not perpetrate the sodomitical sin'. Hincmar's point here, it seems, was that the 'sodomitical sin' was not limited to anal intercourse.[78] There is a complication. This long passage was a marginal addition written by two different hands.[79] Perhaps some contemporaries (erroneously, in Hincmar's eyes) thought that the allegation against Theutberga entailed fornication 'in the obscene part of the body'. Alternatively, perhaps the point was more theoretical than factual, an attempt to dispel confusion over the moral taxonomy of sexual acts.

At any rate, the response then turned to abortion. The marginalia notwithstanding, Hincmar reached the topic with one question foregrounded. To have aborted, Theutberga had to have conceived. But could she have conceived through unnatural intercourse? Hincmar began by quoting Exodus 21. 22–3 in the Vetus Latina version, that is, with the formed/unformed distinction. Next, he turned to what scripture had to say about conception:

> And about conception it is written in the gospel: *For what is born in her*,[80] which without doubt, as Gregory explains, is meant 'has been conceived' [*Moralia* 29.19.36]. For then Joseph first began to hesitate, because he saw the swelling womb of his bride. Here let us reflect from the law how conception happens according to nature. *Woman*, it says, who *bears male* or *female after receiving semen* [Leviticus 12. 2,5], and about parturition of the formed or, as we mentioned above, unformed, which a woman gives birth to or aborts of the male or female kind, it is written: *Everything, which* opens up *the vulva* [Exodus, *passim*].[81]

---

[78] 'qui asstruunt non esse scelus sodomitanum, nisi quando intra corpus, id est in membro obscenę partis corporae, videlicet aqualiculum, fornicatur'; 'Nemo igitur dicat non perpetrare eum peccatum sodomitanum, qui contra naturam in masculum vel in feminam turpitudinem operatur et attritu vel attactu seu motu inpudico ex deliberatione et studio inmundus efficitur', *De divortio* (*responsio* 12), pp. 179–81 (quotations at pp. 179, 181).

[79] See Böhringer's table of additions at p. 42 (*Erg.* 38–38a); the hand which wrote the first part of this addition is also the hand in which the inserted reports of the Aachen councils were written.

[80] This is quoted from Matt 1. 20. In context, an angel appeared to Joseph, counselling him not to dismiss Mary because what was born in her was from the Holy Spirit.

[81] 'Et de conceptu in evangelio scriptum est: *Quod enim in ea natum est*, quod sine dubio, ut exponit Gregorius, "conceptum est" dicitur. Nam tunc primum Ioseph

Hincmar's purpose in quoting Exodus was clear. The formed/unformed distinction allowed him to establish a relevant point about parturition. Even the abortion of an unformed fetus was a form of parturition, which opened up the womb; and any form of parturition required the reception of semen. Next (I temporarily skip over a marginal addition), Hincmar turned to the Virgin Mary to illustrate the relevance:

> [F]or ... it has not been heard of or ... read in the scripture of truth, that the *vulva* of a woman has received seed without coitus and given birth to something living or abortive with a closed womb and unopened *vulva* or untainted flesh, except singularly the happy and blessed Virgin Mary alone, whose conception was not of nature, but of grace[.][82]

Mary was the exception that proved the rule. She alone was mother and virgin, she alone had given birth with 'flesh intact and unopened *vulva*, that is, closed womb'.[83] The flesh of all other virgins was 'broken in them in their first intercourse, [for] nature does not allow them to remain whole in the emission of any sort of birth'.[84]

Two marginal additions clarified Hincmar's point. Both were evidently added for their bearing on the case and both conveyed a hardening of suspicion towards the Lotharingian argument. First, in between the two excerpts just quoted, came a supplement to the argument drawing on natural or, perhaps, medical reading (*fisica lectio*) to complement scripture.[85] A woman received semen 'through male coitus discharged through the genital vein into the secret of the vulva with the carrying womb ... and [she] does not, as this fabrication says, draw up emitted semen to herself or take it up in some other

---

hęsitare coepit, quia tumentem sponsę suae uterum vidit. Hinc revolvemus ex lege, quomodo fiat secundum naturam conceptio. *Mulier*, inquit, quae *suscepto semine pepererit masculum* sive *feminam*, et de parturitione sive formati sive, ut praemisimus, informati, quod mulier sive masculini sive feminini generis parit vel abortit, scriptum est: *Omne, quod* adaperit *vulvam'*, De divortio (*responsio* 12), p. 181 (scriptural citations italicised; see Böhringer's notes for further references). On the variable meanings of *vulva* in Latin, see p. 278 n.64 below.

[82] 'enim non est auditum nec ... in scriptura veritatis est lectum, ut vulva feminę sine coitu semen suceperit atque conceperit et clauso utero et inaperta vulva seu integra carne vivum vel abortivum pepererit, excepta sola singulariter beata et benedicta virgine Maria, cuius conceptio non naturę fuit, sed gratiae', *De divortio* (*responsio* 12), p. 182.

[83] 'carne integra et vulva non adaperta, id est clauso utero', *De divortio* (*responsio* 12), p. 182.

[84] 'in eis in concubitu primo corrumpitur, in emissione cuiuslibet partus integram permanere natura non patitur', *De divortio* (*responsio* 12), p. 182.

[85] This addition is written in the same hand mentioned in p. 255 n.79 above; see Böhringer's table of additions at p. 42 (*Erg.* 39). Böhringer suggests that this addition built on Isidore, *Etymologiae* 9.1.136ff, though the idea of the vulva's secrets echoes Rabanus Maurus's adaptation of the *Etymologiae* in *De universo* 6.1; see p. 288 below on both texts.

Divorce of Lothar II and Theutberga

place or fashion'. And scripture, the addition continued, showed that what was conceived from emitted semen threw open the womb. We should follow what we read, it concluded, and reject what we do not read.[86]

Appearing after the argument about the exceptional parturition of the Virgin Mary, the second marginal addition used the story of Onan to criticize 'that diabolical fabrication, which is reported about that woman and her brother'.[87] Onan had been struck dead by God because he 'would lie with his wife seeking to fulfil lust and not wanting children to be born ... From which we do not believe that this woman could have conceived from such intercourse.'[88] The addition, we should note, clearly construed Onan's act as a deliberate avoidance of offspring.

The argument was clear. So too were its implications for Lothar. If he had found Theutberga a virgin upon marriage, then why did Lothar let people speak about her as if she had been dishonoured (*stuprata*)? And if she was not a virgin, why had he kept her for all this time and gone along with the ordeal?[89] In the pre-marginalia text, Hincmar concluded with some caution. As a bishop, he only knew about the 'virginal secrets of girls and women [*puellarum virginialia vel feminarum secreta*]' through books, not experience. Married laymen and judges, 'who ought to judge on this, will be able to know from themselves and learn from their wives in marital license better and more quickly than us, whether any woman can conceive in such a way, as we have heard about this one'.[90] The marginalia on *fisica lectio* and Onan sharpened the argument. Perhaps they also lent Hincmar's caution a *faux-naif* tone.

In sum, the abortion accusation, a small detail in the early phase of the divorce, was one cog in a machine which slowly turned against Lothar. The

---

[86] 'coitu virili per genitalem venam inmissum in vulvae secretum baiulante matrice ... et non, ut haecadinventio dicit, semen sibi attrahere vel adsumere alibi vel aliunde emissum', *De divortio* (*responsio* 12, *Erg.* 39), p. 182.

[87] 'hac diabolica adinventione, quae de ista femina et suo frater refertur', *De divortio* (*responsio* 12, *Erg.* 40), p. 182. This addition was written in a different hand, which also wrote the second part of the addition referred to in n. 79 above; see Böhringer's table at p. 42 (*Erg.* 40).

[88] 'cum uxore sua quaerens explere libidinem et nolens nasci filios concumbebat ... Unde non credimus tali concubitu hanc feminam potuisse concipere', *De divortio* (*responsio* 12, Erg. 40), p. 182.

[89] *De divortio* (*responsio* 12), p. 182. Hincmar was probably remembering that the ordeal had been the last resort in the absence of proof – and his stinging questions suggest that he was writing before receiving the report from Aachen (February 860). Hincmar presumed that loss of virginity and subsequent parturition entailed some physical change in female bodies, though it is misleading to think of this as a reference to the hymen: Garver, 'Childbearing and Infancy', 225. On varying construals (and some rejections) of physical proofs of virginity in classical and medieval societies, see Kelly, *Performing Virginity*, pp. 17–39.

[90] 'qui de hoc iudicare debebunt, melius nobis et citius per se scire et licentia maritali ab uxoribus suis discere praevalebunt, utrum tali modo, sicut de ista audivimus, femina quaelibet possit concipere', *De divortio* (*responsio* 12), pp. 182–3.

record of the accusation to which Hincmar responded was a political gambit: an unsuccessful one by Lothar's side in 858 or a more successful one by Lothar's opponents in 860. Either way – and the possibilities are not mutually exclusive – it was a gambit which helped to undermine Lothar's case. The arguments over the divorce were not just arguments about canonical regulations, but also, perhaps even more fundamentally, arguments about narratives. Already in 860, Hincmar might not have questioned canonical theory – he accepted that incest, if proven, precluded Theutberga from marriage – but he did question the confusing narrative which he had to piece together from multiple accounts. The abortion accusation was one detail among others which fed Hincmar's suspicions. The only surviving instance of an early medieval woman accused of abortion did not quite turn out as we might have expected. In accusations, mud always sticks – but not always to the accused.

* * *

Generalizing from the divorce of Lothar and Theutberga is precarious. It was the ninth-century equivalent of a media frenzy. But we can nonetheless tease out certain insights from the divorce. The first concerns incest. The tempting conclusion relates to real-life practice. Incest could lead to attempted abortion.[91] But this slightly awkwardly glosses over the problematic nature of the allegations against Theutberga. In fact, it is comparative material rather than the isolated evidence of the divorce that provides surer grounds. Incest is the dirty secret in the broader history of abortion. Attempts at abortion, not always successful, stalk legal records of early modern cases involving incest.[92] Future research may well uncover similar tendencies in later medieval ecclesiastical and secular records. But there are traces in different versions of miracle motifs circulating from the thirteenth century onward, motifs which narrated stories of incestuous sexual abuse and abortion or infanticide culminating in miraculously thwarted suicide attempts by vulnerable women. These stories originated in works produced by preaching friars who 'fed on a collective pastoral experience and recorded some of it, thinly disguised, in *exempla* and *miracula*'.[93]

The real question concerns perceptions rather than practice, and hones in on an absence in early medieval regulations. Ecclesiastical regulations on abortion made connections with extra-marital fornication, adultery and even marital sexuality. Their authors, at least in stereotype, were obsessed with

[91] Elsakkers, RBL, p. 474.
[92] Ferraro, *Nefarious Crimes*; Egmond, 'Incestuous Relations'. See Christopoulos, 'Nonelite Male Perspectives', on a case involving incest in the sense of affinity (a man accused of deflowering his sister-in-law and then compelling her to have an abortion).
[93] A. Murray, *Suicide in the Middle Ages Volume I: The Violent against Themselves* (Oxford, 1998), pp. 264–7 (quotation at p. 265); cf. M. Rubin, *Mother of God: A History of the Virgin Mary* (London, 2009), p. 240.

sex. Regulations against abortion and regulations against incestuous sexual acts can be found across different ecclesiastical texts (and some law-codes). Yet none of these texts made an explicit connection between incest and abortion. If we assume that the pertinent difference between early modern and early medieval societies lay more in the capacity for judicial authorities to pursue *and* record cases than in the social occurrence of incest and consequent recourse to abortion, the question is why did no early medieval regulations address abortion in the context of incest? Explaining such absences is difficult – and dangerous. After all, few texts made an explicit connection between abortion and the fate of unbaptized souls, but some users of these texts did. At the same time, the exceptional connection between incest and abortion in the divorce quietly indicates the limited reach of ecclesiastical regulations on abortion. Early modern cases give a strong sense of *omertà*, the wall of silence which fiercely guarded family secrets from outside scrutiny and which even the judicial machinery of early modern states struggled to penetrate when prosecuting cases involving incest and abortion.[94] The capacity of early medieval authorities to breach this particular wall of silence is likely to have been weaker. Ecclesiastical regulations on abortion were devised and developed in societies where powerful but largely uncodified social and familial norms shaped how individuals and communities responded to abortion and its sexual contexts.

Another, more fundamental insight concerns the elusiveness of how ecclesiastical and secular authorities actually handled abortion in practice. Thinking within neatly distinguished genres has allowed us to reconstruct thought processes embedded within regulations in penitentials, law-codes and other kinds of texts. But these neat distinctions break down when we try to imagine how such regulations informed practice, and not just because abortion could be engulfed by sexual transgression within socially divisive inquests. The divorce suggests that the calibration of ecclesiastical and lay authorities in the provision of justice regarding marital disputes and sexual offences was far from fixed. It points to jurisdictional and procedural improvisation, certainly when cases were entangled with complex networks of power and influence at the top of society.[95]

Thus, when reflecting on procedures for adjudicating marital disputes, Hincmar recalled an episode from the court of Louis the Pious. In 822 a noblewoman called Northild complained to the emperor 'about certain disgraceful acts' (*de quibusdam inhonestis*) between her and her husband Agembert.[96]

---

[94] J. F. Harrington, *The Unwanted Child: The Fate of Foundlings, Orphans and Juvenile Criminals in Early Modern Germany* (Chicago, 2009), p. 29. Several of the cases discussed in Ferraro, *Nefarious Crimes*, point to the silence of local communities too.
[95] Cf. Stone, 'Bound from Either Side'.
[96] Chélini, *L'aube du moyen âge*, pp. 204–5, cautiously speculates whether these entailed deliberately non-procreative sexual acts, though this is not my reason for referring to Northild's case.

Both the ensuing jurisdictional shuffle and Hincmar's approval are revealing. Louis referred Northild to episcopal judgment. But bishops passed the case on to lay judges, agreeing that they would impose any requisite penance if the case was referred back to them after a crime was adjudged to have taken place. Their 'sacerdotal discretion', Hincmar noted, 'pleased the noble laymen, because judgment about their spouses was not taken from them nor was any prejudgement imposed on civil laws by the priestly order'.[97] Moreover – and this is sobering – just after addressing the question of abortion in *De divortio*, Hincmar took seriously the possibility that lay judges could decide to condemn Theutberga to death whether 'by Roman law or though their laws or those to which the woman is subject or those through which they should want to judge her'.[98] The fact that this possibility was intelligible to Hincmar underlines the gap between law-codes and judicial practice suggested in the previous chapter.

Finally, like Rabanus's letters, Hincmar's treatise gives us a precious glimpse of tradition in practice. When summing up his response to the dissenters' question on *stuprum* and abortion in *De divortio*, Hincmar slotted two citations on abortion from texts written centuries earlier into his argument. The first example appeared when Hincmar set out his belief that the tools of ecclesiastical discipline, namely separation from the church, could replace the function of execution in law, both old law and contemporary law. This depended, of course, on Theutberga being referred to episcopal hands if judges concluded she was guilty. To illustrate the point, Hincmar quoted Ancyra 'on those who fornicate irrationally, that is with men or animals, and those women, who fornicate and kill their offspring or those who act with them to strike them out of the womb'.[99] 'Castigated through a strict ten-year penance', Theutberga's life would be devoted to penance and she would be 'separated not just from the royal bed, but also from any conjugal union'.[100]

The second example formed the final words of his response on *stuprum* and abortion, to illustrate a point 'about he or she ... who, after perpetrating incest before the beginning of a legitimate marriage, takes away from himself [or herself] the legitimate marriage, which he [or she] had been able to have'.[101] Hincmar's final authority? Augustine on *libido crudelis*, perhaps the only clear

---

[97] 'Nobilibus ... laicis sacerdotalis discretio placuit, quia de suis coniugibus eis non tollebatur iudicium nec a sacerdotali ordine inferebatur legibus civilibus praeiudicium', *De divortio* (*responsio* 5), p. 142.

[98] 'sive per legam Romanam aut per illorum leges vel quibus illa femina est subiecta vel per quas illi eam voluerint iudicare', *De divortio* (*responsio* 12), p. 183.

[99] 'de his qui fornicantur inrationalibiliter, id est cum masculis vel pecoribus, et de illis mulieribus, quae fornicantur et partus suos necant, vel quae agunt secum, ut utero conceptos excutiant', *De divortio* (*responsio* 12), p. 194.

[100] 'per districtam decennalem poenitentiam castigate ... segregata non solum a toro regio, verum etiam ab omni coniugali', *De divortio* (*responsio* 12), p. 194.

[101] 'de ea vel eo ... qui ante initum legitimum coniugium perpetrato incestu legitimum, quod habere poterat, sibi tollit coniugium', *De divortio* (*responsio* 12), p. 195.

instance of an early medieval churchman leaning on this passage on abortion from *De nuptiis et concupiscentia* (quoted as *De bono coniugali*), which was less of a canonical text on abortion for early medieval churchmen than it has been for historians of church doctrine. Husbands and wives who used poisons of sterility did not deserve to be called spouses. The implications for the case were clear.[102]

If the divorce subtly underlines the elusiveness of the handling of abortion in the Early Middle Ages, it less subtly emphasizes the elusiveness of women who resorted to abortion, and of the men and women who collaborated with, coerced or confronted them. Theutberga might well have *not* been one of these women and her brother Hubert might well have *not* been one of these men. The experiences and emotional lives of early medieval women who decided to resort to abortion are even less recoverable than their later medieval or early modern counterparts. In the final chapter, we turn to a yet more elusive historical subject: the aborted fetus.

---

[102] *De divortio (responsio* 12), pp. 195–6.

8

Unnatural Symbol: Imagining *Abortivi* in the Early Middle Ages

According to Isidore of Seville, to genuflect was to recall our prenatal existence. The knees (*genua*) got their name from the cheeks (*genae*) 'because in the womb they are opposite the cheeks'.[1] Kneeling was the posture in which people wept because 'nature wants to remind them of the maternal womb, where they sat as if in darkness before they came into the light'.[2] Early medieval religious culture reverberated with remembrances and representations of fetal existence. Like so many hagiographers, Alcuin began his *vita* of Willibrord with 'signs of divine election in his mother's womb'.[3] Through these signs Willibrord emulated the 'most holy precursor of our lord Jesus Christ, blessed John the Baptist, sanctified by God in his mother's womb', while liturgies cultivated the memory of the Baptist, 'who not yet born sensed the voice of the lord's mother and still enclosed in the womb leapt with prophetic elation at the advent of human salvation'.[4] Even more fundamentally, it was the feast of the annunciation, not the feast of the nativity, which marked the central moment in Christian theology. Christ's incarnation began in Mary's womb. When Carolingian theologians debated the nature of the eucharist in the ninth century, they were debating how Christ's body, the same as 'that flesh created in the womb without seed from the Virgin Mary by the power of the Holy Spirit', could be made present each day at mass.[5] These

---

[1] 'eo quod in utero sint genis opposita', *Etymologiae* 9.1.108.
[2] 'Voluit enim eos natura uterum maternum rememorare, ubi quasi in tenebris consedebant antequam venirent ad lucem', *Etymologiae* 9.1.109.
[3] 'in utero matris divinae electionis ... praesagia', Alcuin, *Vita Willibrordi* 2, MGH SRM 7, p. 117.
[4] 'sanctissimus praecursor domini nostri Iesu Christi beatus Iohannes Baptista, ex utero matris Deo sanctificatus', ibid.; 'qui vocem matris domini nondum aeditus sensit, et adhuc clausus utero ad adventum salutis humanae profetica exultatione gestivit', *Sacramentarium Veronense* 254, ed. L. C. Mohlberg, with L. Eizenhöfer and P. Siffrin, *Sacramentarium Veronense (Cod. Bibl. Capit. Veron. LXXXV [80])* (Rome, 1978), p. 33.
[5] 'carnem illam ... de Maria virgine in utero sine semine potestate Spiritus Sancti creatam', Paschasius Radbertus, *De corpore et sanguino Domini* 4.86–90, ed. B. Paulus, CCCM 16 (Turnhout, 1969), p. 30. For a rich reading of ninth-century thought on the eucharist and its broader context, see R. Fulton, *From Judgment to Passion: Devotion to Christ and Mary, 800–1200* (Ithaca NY, 2002), pp. 9–59.

Imagining Abortivi

examples only scratch the surface. Medieval Christianity fostered multiple modes of imagining the fetus.

One modern meaning cultivated from medieval discussions of the embryonic Christ is the 'absolute inviolability of human life from conception ... revealed by the Redeemer in the womb'. But did the embryonic Christ and fetal saints hold similar medieval meanings? Perhaps it feels intuitive that they did.[6] A growing body of interdisciplinary and cross-cultural scholarship on conceptualizations of the fetus, however, suggests that what feels like an intuition about the historical relationship between representations of the fetus and perspectives on abortion is more like an unexamined assumption. Scholars have not only increasingly problematized assumed continuities in understandings of what the fetus is, but also understandings of what it has meant to speak about the fetus across different societies and times.[7] In particular, a number of scholars have carefully recovered symbolic meanings and narrative epistemologies of the pre-modern fetus, from intricate metaphors of spiritual growth and religious practice in medieval Buddhist embryologies to elaborate readings of the fetus as a symbol of Israel within rabbinic narratives and politicized early Islamic readings of Muhammed's gestation in Amina's womb.[8] As the editors of a recent volume on fetal symbolism in religious thought have argued, our eyes and ears are not naturally attuned to the diversity of fetal meanings in pre-modern and non-western cultures:

> In contemporary Western culture, the word 'fetus' introduces either a political subject or a literal, medicalized entity. Neither of these frameworks gives sufficient credit to the vast array of literature and oral traditions emerging from religious cultures around the world that see within the fetus a symbol, a metaphor, an imagination ... [T]hroughout much of human history and across most of the world's cultures, when the fetus was imagined, it enjoyed

---

[6] J. Saward, *Redeemer in the Womb: Christ Living in Mary* (San Francisco, 1993), quotation at p. 164; see too D. A. Jones, *The Soul of the Embryo: An Inquiry into the Status of the Human Embryo in the Christian Tradition* (London, 2004).

[7] The work of the early modern historian, Barbara Duden, has been particularly influential: B. Duden, *Disembodying Women: Perspectives on Pregnancy and the Unborn*, trans. L. Hoinacki (Cambridge MA, 1993); B. Duden, 'The Fetus on the "Farther Shore": Towards a History of the Unborn', in *Fetal Subjects, Feminist Positions*, ed. L. M. Morgan and M. W. Michaels (Philadelphia, 1999), pp. 13–25. See too, E. Keller, 'Embryonic Individuals: The Rhetoric of Seventeenth-Century Embryology and the Construction of Early-Modern Identity', *Eighteenth-Century Studies* 33.3 (2000), 321–48, and L. M. Morgan, *Icons of Life: A Cultural History of Human Embryos* (Berkeley, 2009), a provocative study of the deeper cultural impact of embryo collecting at the Carnegie Institute in the early twentieth century.

[8] F. Garrett, *Religion, Medicine and the Human Embryo in Tibet* (London, 2008); G. Kessler, *Conceiving Israel: The Fetus in Rabbinic Narratives* (Philadelphia, 2009); D. C. Peterson, 'A Prophet Emerging: Fetal Narratives in Islamic Literature', in *Imagining the Fetus: The Unborn in Myth, Religion, and Culture*, ed. V. R. Sasson and J. M. Law (Oxford, 2009), pp. 203–22.

a much wider range of symbolic and cultural subjectivities, often contributing possibilities of inclusivity, emergence, liminality, and transformation.[9]

A powerful contemporary cultural reflex, conditioned especially by the proliferation of visual representations of the fetus and decades of political debate over abortion rights, makes it almost natural to assume that speaking about the fetus carries implications about abortion. But the loose confederacy of recent scholarship emphasizes the necessity of 'denaturaliz[ing] the human embryo'; or, in plainer terms, to avoid automatically associating discourse on the fetus with discourse on abortion.[10]

From late antiquity right through to the end of the Middle Ages, countless authors and artists cultivated and communicated complex meanings of fetal existence within theological tracts, sacred narratives, devotional practices and, even, iconography. It is likely that certain theological ideas about the fetus informed moral ideas about abortion (and infanticide).[11] But automatically reading the varieties of early medieval discourse on the fetus as encrypted moral arguments about abortion is more revealing of modern, rather than medieval, mental associations. We cannot simply assume that when theologians like Maximus the Confessor traced the union of body and soul to the moment of conception when reflecting on the nature of Christ, their ideas were either intended or understood to have implications for abortion.[12]

Determining whether and how different modes of imagining the fetus in the Early Middle Ages related to moral ideas about abortion first requires a deeper history of what it meant to speak about the fetus physiologically, symbolically and theologically.[13] Such a task is well beyond the scope of this book. This chapter will focus more modestly on specific modes of imagining

---

[9] V. R. Sasson and J. M. Law, 'Introduction: Restoring Nuance to Imagining the Fetus', in *Imagining the Fetus*, p. 3.

[10] L. M. Morgan, 'Embryo Tales', in *Remaking Life and Death: Towards an Anthropology of the Biosciences*, ed. S. Franklin and M. Lock (Santa Fe, 2003), p. 262; cf. Kessler, *Conceiving Israel*, pp. 18–19.

[11] Cf. Koskenniemi, *Exposure*, pp. 23–4.

[12] On Maximus, see M.-H. Congourdeau, 'L'animation de l'embryon humain chez Maxime le Confesseur', *Nouvelle revue théologique* 111 (1984), 693–709; Saward, *Redeemer in the Womb*, pp. 8–13. On the theological concerns which underlay early and late antique Christian thought on the embryo, see M.-H. Congourdeau, 'Genèse d'un regard Chrétien sur l'embryon', in *Naissance et petite enfance*, pp. 349–62.

[13] M. van der Lugt, *Le ver, le démon et la vierge: Les théories médiévales de la génération extraordinaire* (Paris, 2004), especially pp. 365–504 on the intellectual resources, contexts and conclusions of later medieval thought on the conception of Christ, is a model for emulation. Other useful starting points include, on later medieval theology, literature and art, J. Tasioulas, '"Heaven and Earth in Little Space": The Foetal Existence of Christ in Medieval Literature and Thought', *Medium Aevum* 76.1 (2007), 24–48, and, on early Christian thought, C. Playoust and E. Bradshaw Aitken, 'The Leaping Child: Imagining the Unborn in Early Christian Literature', in *Imagining the Fetus*, pp. 157–83.

Imagining Abortivi

the fetus which we have intermittently encountered in previous chapters: the *abortivus* or *aborsus* in speculative thought and symbolic language. The *abortivus* was the stillborn infant, the fetus dead in the womb, the premature newborn, the product of abortion (deliberate or otherwise). Discussion of *abortivi* was not the same thing as discussion of abortion. 'Only death is certain,' Augustine once said in a sermon. 'A boy is conceived, perhaps he is born, perhaps he becomes an *aborsus*.' In societies where pregnancy loss was commonplace, unintended abortion encapsulated the contingency of mortality. Deliberately aborted fetuses were only a minority among *abortivi*.[14]

The flesh-and-blood contingencies of pregnancy loss were a social reality, imaginations of the *abortivus* haunted the margins of thought. Abortion has a long but neglected history as a symbol. In the Early Middle Ages this symbolism sometimes appeared in unexpected places. Take, for example, a bureaucratic letter from one government official to another in Ostrogothic Italy. In 507/11, Cassiodorus, a key figure in Theoderic's government, wrote to a local prefect, Faustus, to inquire after an overdue grain shipment. Faustus was either corrupt or incompetent, but aristocratic decorum forced Cassiodorus to envelop his criticism in sophisticated circumlocution. One digressive image described the poor harvest, which had made the grain shipment such an urgent matter, as an earthly miscarriage:

> Since the dryness of the present year, which is locally accustomed to rage at certain times, has not given birth so much as thrown out the aborted *fetus* of the harvests in imperfect fullness after the earthly organs have been hardened by too much heat[.][15]

Far more commonly, however, abortion symbolism expressed religious ideas and elaborated on scriptural texts. In early medieval thought, the *abortivus* came to symbolize wayward sinners, defiant Jews and obdurate heretics. But if the *abortivus* was an expressive symbol, it was also an elusive reality, a fleeting presence, which created conceptual problems for theologians. How did *abortivi* fit into God's salvific plan? Would they have a share in the world to come?

---

[14] 'Sola mors certa est ... Conceptus est puer, forte nascitur, forte aborsum facit', *Sermo* 97.3, PL 38, col. 590. For an attempt to generate a quantitative picture of fetal mortality from the seventeenth century onward, see R. Woods, *Death before Birth: Fetal Health and Mortality in Historical Perspective* (Oxford, 2009).

[15] 'Cum siccitas praesenti anni, quae localiter certis solet desaevire temporibus, terrenis visceribus nimio calore duratis abortivos messium fetus non tam edidit quam imperfecta ubertate proiecit', *Variae* 1.35, MGH AA 12, p. 33. *Fetus* (here in the plural) could of course mean fruits, as it does in *Variae* 4.50, p. 137. But it is clear from his language (*edere*, in the sense of giving birth, in addition to *viscera*, *abortivus* and *proicere*, terms which we have encountered many times already) that Cassiodorus was playing on the other meaning of *fetus*. See R. MacPherson, *Rome in Involution: Cassiodorus' Variae in their Literary and Historical Setting* (Poznan, 1989), pp. 165–9, on the context and content of *Variae* 1.35.

265

The prescriptive ecclesiastical and secular texts excavated in previous chapters were often laconic or, at best, allusive in terms of what they understood abortion to entail. As we shall see, there are problems with simply filling the gaps by using references to *abortivi* across the broad range of texts surveyed below, from eschatological speculations to exegetical digressions, from polemical letters to proto-encyclopaedias. Authors used *abortivi* to articulate and explore other ideas, which cannot simply be elided with moral perspectives on abortion. But surveying this corpus can nonetheless deepen our sense of early medieval, certainly learned ecclesiastical, *mentalités*. For when authors likened clerical opponents to *abortivi* or struggled to visualize the bodies of *abortivi*, they took for granted ideas and sensibilities about life and death in the womb.

Dead or alive: Augustine and his readers on the resurrection of *abortivi*

We begin at the end, or beyond the end, at the resurrection. From early Christianity the resurrection of the body was 'always connected to divine power ... [to] the extraordinary power necessary to create and recreate, to reward and punish, to bring life from death'.[16] In the vision of heaven sketched out by the fourth-century Syrian theologian Ephrem, whoever 'dies in the womb of his mother and never comes to life, will be quickened at the moment [of resurrection] by [Christ] who quickens the dead; he will then be brought forth as an adult'. For Ephrem, the resurrection would transfigure the calamity of death before birth into a celestial reunion between mother and child. 'If a woman dies while pregnant, and the child in her womb dies with her,' Ephrem continued, 'that child will at the resurrection grow up and know its mother; and she will know her child'.[17]

But the resurrection also threw up difficult conceptual tensions about identity and change, about the nature of bodies and souls, because at the resurrection we will be both the same as and different from our former bodily selves. Eschatology forced theologians to confront awkward metaphysical questions.[18] The residue of such intellectual challenges can be detected in an eighth-century catechetical creed. It emphasized that everyone, 'whether a small child, an old man, or after coming alive and dying in a mother's womb',

---

[16] C. W. Bynum, *The Resurrection of the Body in Western Christianity, 200–1336* (New York, 1995), p. 2.

[17] Quoted ibid., p. 77.

[18] In addition to Bynum, *Resurrection of the Body*, on later scholastic responses to such questions, see P. L. Reynolds, *Food and the Body: Some Peculiar Questions in High Medieval Theology* (Leiden, 1999); A. Fitzpatrick, 'Bodily Identity in Scholastic Theology' (unpublished Ph.D. thesis, University College London, 2013).

would be resurrected.[19] Like Ephrem, the creed used the resurrected fetus to illustrate the all-embracing power of the resurrection. Unlike Ephrem, its author had inherited a more complicated tradition of thought. The resurrected fetus had come alive in the womb. This precise detail was a trace of vexed questions which Augustine had once confronted. What made the resurrection of *abortivi* a hard case in eschatology makes the thought of Augustine and his early medieval readers of particular interest to us. Reflection on the resurrection of *abortivi* necessitated reflection on the beginning of bodies and souls in the womb.

Neither affirming nor denying: Augustine on abortivi
As he sat down at mealtime, Charlemagne enjoyed nothing more than listening to readings from great works, especially from his favourite work, Augustine's *De civitate Dei*. He might well have heard some odd questions at the dinner table. What would happen to nail clippings at the resurrection? Or hair cut off by barbers? These were the kinds of questions, Augustine complained in *De civitate Dei*, posed by those who wanted to ridicule belief in bodily resurrection. Questions about *abortivi* were another strategy of derision. Would aborted fetuses (*abortivi fetus*) rise again? If so, in what kind of bodies would *abortivi* be resurrected? Or, if *abortivi* would not rise up because they were poured out (*effusi*) rather than born, what would the resurrected bodies of small children (*parvuli*), who died in infancy, look like?[20]

Augustine was confident that young infants would attain perfected bodies at the resurrection. Dead infants lacked the bodily size with which they would one day be resurrected. But 'just as all body parts are already latently in seed, even though some of them are lacking in the born', the possibility of bodily perfection was inherent in everyone at least in principle (*in ratione*). At the resurrection *parvuli* would be resurrected in the bodies, tall or short, big or small, they would otherwise have attained.[21] Augustine's confidence quickly evaporated, however, when he turned to *abortivi*:

> I dare neither to affirm nor to deny that aborted fetuses, which, when they had already lived in the womb, died there, will be resurrected; although I do not see how, if they are not discounted from the number of the dead, the resurrection of the dead should not extend to them. For either not all the dead will rise up and there will be some human souls, which had human bodies albeit within the maternal organs, without bodies in eternity; or if all

[19] 'aut parvulus, aut senex, aut in utero matris vivificatus et mortuus fuerat', Pirminius, *Scarapsus* 28a, p. 113.
[20] *De civitate Dei*, 22.12, ed. B. Dombart and A. Kalb, *Augustinus, De civitate dei*, CCSL 48 (Turnhout, 1955), p. 831. On Charlemagne's literary tastes, see Einhard, *Life of Charlemagne* 24, trans. P. E. Dutton, *Charlemagne's Courtier: The Complete Einhard* (Peterborough, Ontario, 1998), p. 31.
[21] 'sicut ipsa membra omnia iam sunt latenter in semine, cum etiam natis nonnulla adhuc desint', *De civitate Dei*, 22.13, pp. 833–4.

human souls will receive their risen bodies, which they had wherever they left them in life and death, I do not understand how I can say that those who died in the wombs of mothers do not partake of the resurrection of the dead. But whichever of these someone thinks, what we will say about born infants ought to be understood about them too, if they will rise up.[22]

Augustine's hesitation gravitated around whether or not bodily resurrection embraced all of the dead. If bodily resurrection did not apply to all of the dead, the disembodied souls of *abortivi* would float around for eternity. Alternatively, if it did apply to all of the dead, *abortivi* who died in their mothers' wombs would be resurrected in perfected bodies just as infants would be.

In *De civitate Dei* Augustine referred to *abortivi* who numbered among the dead – or, to put it differently, to *abortivi* who had once been alive, if only fleetingly. The *Enchiridion*, which also had a wide readership in the Early Middle Ages, makes clear that the beginnings of life troubled Augustine more deeply.[23] Here Augustine's speculation was more intricate, more intensely personal and more openly riven with doubts. He introduced his section on the resurrection with one confident proposition: no Christian should doubt that all those who had been born and who would be born, who had died and would die in the future, would be resurrected. But 'I have not worked out,' he confessed, 'how I can briefly discuss [resurrection] and satisfy all the questions which are typically raised about this subject'.[24]

The first question concerned aborted fetuses, 'who have been born as it were in the wombs of the mothers, but not yet in such a way that they can be reborn'.[25] Effectively this was about very young, undeveloped fetuses. If *they* would be resurrected, then formed fetuses (*formati*) certainly would be. Augustine initially leaned towards excluding unformed abortions (*informes*

---

[22] 'Abortivos fetus, qui, cum iam vixissent in utero, ibi sunt mortui, resurrecturos ut adfirmare, ita negare non audeo; quamvis non videam quo modo ad eos non pertineat resurrectio mortuorum, si non eximuntur de numero mortuorum. Aut enim non omnes mortui resurgent et erunt aliquae humanae animae sine corporibus in aeternum, quae corpora humana, quamvis intra viscera materna, gestarunt; aut si omnes animae humanae recipient resurgentia sua corpora, quae habuerunt, ubicumque viventia et morientia reliquerunt, non invenio quem ad modum dicam ad resurrectionem non pertinere mortuorum quoscumque mortuos etiam in uteris matrum. Sed utrumlibet de his quisque sentiat, quod de iam natis infantibus dixerimus, hoc etiam de illis intellegendum est, si resurgent', *De civitate Dei*, 22.13, p. 833.

[23] See the list of manuscripts in *Augustinus, De fide rerum invisibilium; Enchiridion ad Laurentium de fide et spe et caritate* [etc], CCSL 46 (Turnhout, 1969), pp. viii–xiv, including around twenty from the ninth/tenth century or earlier.

[24] 'quemadmodum possim breviter disputare, et omnibus quaestionibus quae de hac re moveri assolent satisfacere, non invenio', *Enchiridion* 23.84, ed. M. Evans, CCSL 46, p. 95.

[25] 'qui iam quidem nati sunt in uteris matrum, sed nondum ita ut iam possint renasci', *Enchiridion* 23.85, p. 95. This appears to be Augustine's paraphrase of a question, not his answer.

Imagining Abortivi

abortus) from the resurrection: 'But who is not more inclined to think that unformed abortions perish, just like seeds which were not conceived?'[26] Yet he immediately began to vacillate. 'But does anyone dare to deny, though would he dare to affirm either,' Augustine equivocated, 'that the resurrection will bring it about that whatever lacked form will be filled, and in such a way that the perfection which would have come about in time is not lacking?'[27] Augustine felt the intuitive pull of the assumption that *informes abortus* would not be resurrected, but he also wondered whether this misconstrued the dramatic power of the resurrection, through which 'what is not yet whole will be made whole, just as what was deficient will be repaired'.[28] Since anyone who had died would be resurrected, the real question concerned when life – and the possibility of numbering among the dead – began in the womb:

> And through this [the question] can be asked and discussed very carefully among the most learned – I do not know whether it can be ascertained by man – namely when does a person begin to live in the womb, whether there is some kind of hidden life which does not yet appear with the movements of something living? For it seems overly rash to deny that infants, who are cut out limb by limb and thrown out of the wombs of pregnant women so that they do not kill their mothers too if they remained dead there, had ever lived. But once a person begins to live, he is then certainly able to die: and dead, wherever death managed to befall him, I cannot understand how he cannot pertain to the resurrection of the dead.[29]

Augustine knew the answer to the question of the resurrection of *abortivi* in theory. If they had been alive, and thus had been able to die, *abortivi* would also be resurrected in perfected bodies. His allusion to embryotomy – in this case, referring to the excision of dead fetuses dangerously retained in their mothers' wombs, fetuses which were presumably *formati* if they could be cut out limb by limb – illustrated the theory. But Augustine was by his own admission unsure whether the status of *informes abortus* could be ascertained.[30]

---

[26] 'Informes vero abortus quis non proclivius perire arbitretur, sicut semina quae concepta non fuerint?', *Enchiridion* 23.85, p. 95.

[27] 'Sed quis negare audeat, etsi affirmare non audeat, id acturam resurrectionem ut quidquid formae defuit impleatur, atque ita non desit perfectio quae accessura erat tempore', *Enchiridion* 23.85, pp. 95–6.

[28] 'sed integretur quod nondum erat integrum, sicut instaurabitur quod fuerat vitiatum', *Enchiridion* 23.85, p. 96.

[29] 'Ac per hoc scrupulosissime quidem inter doctissimos quaeri ac disputari potest, quod utrum ab homine inueniri possit ignore, quando incipiat in utero homo vivere, utrum sit quaedam vita et occulta quae nondum motibus viventis appareat. Nam negare vixisse puerperia quae propterea membratim exsecantur et eiciuntur ex uteris praegnantium ne matres quoque, si mortua ibi relinquantur, occident, impudentia nimia videtur. Ex quo autem incipit homo vivere, ex illo utique iam mori potest: mortuus vero, ubicumque illi mors potuit evenire, quomodo ad resurrectionem non pertineat mortuorum reperire non possum', *Enchiridion* 23.86, p. 96.

[30] Shanzer, 'Voices', 348–9, referring to Augustine's 'bolder treatment' in the

In both works Augustine puzzled over the fate of *abortivi* at the resurrection. He did not directly address what would happen to them if they were resurrected. The logic of his ideas on grace and original sin dictated that *abortivi*, like unbaptized infants, were beyond redemption; moreover, fetuses still in the womb, unlike infants, were necessarily unbaptizable. Despite controversy among contemporaries, Augustine stood by his ideas on grace, baptism and original sin, which he spelled out in debate with the Pelagian theologian Julian of Eclanum.[31] But Augustine was also chafed by the mental abrasion between eschatology and theodicy. As he confessed in a letter to Jerome in 415, he was not entirely satisfied with his handling of the consequences of original sin for infants and acknowledged that objections to his ideas were borne in part out of compassion.[32] Although he rejected the idea of some kind of middle place for the unbaptized who had committed no sin, Augustine felt compelled to declare that the sinless unbaptized would receive the 'lightest punishment of all'.[33]

Augustine's intricacy and self-conscious uncertainty have been the most significant casualties in later interpretations and appropriations of his thinking. To reconstruct Augustine's position on abortion modern interpreters have filled the silences of his moral treatises on marriage, in which he addressed the morality of abortion or otherwise avoiding offspring without explicitly addressing when life begins, with his eschatology. The various Augustines resurrected as interlocutors in modern debate have been shorn of imperfections; after all, the resurrection perfects whatever lacked form. The assurance of these resurrected Augustines contrasts with the vacillating Augustine of the *Enchiridion* (and we will encounter another uncertain Augustine commenting on Exodus below). Thus, one modern Augustine does not regard the undeveloped fetus as a 'human person'.[34] Another modern Augustine, by contrast, embraces the 'value of all life, actual or potential' in the face of uncertainty over when life begins.[35]

Enchiridion, interprets Augustine's position as the 'unformed *foetus* cannot be said to have lived, because it had never been born' (at 348, italics in original). Nardi, *Aborto*, p. 556, provides a more acute summary of the *Enchiridion*: 'il feto formato ha l'anima, è vivo, è uomo; il feto ancora informe è un *rebus*: può essere e non essere vivo' (italics in original).

[31] On Augustine's ideas on grace, original sin and baptism, see S. Lancel, *St Augustine*, trans. A. Nevill (London, 2002), pp. 413–38, 443–53; J. A. Trumbower, *Rescue for the Dead: The Posthumous Salvation of Non-Christians in Early Christianity* (Oxford, 2001), pp. 133–40. For a detailed examination of Augustine's preaching on infant baptism, see A. Dupont, *Gratia in Augustine's Sermones ad Populum during the Pelagian Controversy*, trans. B. Doyle (Leiden, 2013), pp. 203–96.

[32] *Ep.* 166.16–18, trans. W. Parsons, *Saint Augustine: Letters Volume IV (165–203)* (Washington DC, 1955), pp. 20–3.

[33] *Enchiridion* 93, p. 99; cf. *Ep.* 184A, trans. Parsons, *Augustine*, p. 137.

[34] Dombrowski and Deltete, *Defense of Abortion*, p. 23.

[35] Gorman, *Abortion*, pp. 71–2. Jones, *Soul of the Embryo*, p. 228, appears to assume

Imagining Abortivi

The Augustine whom early medieval readers encountered did not speak in the tongues of personhood or sanctity of life. But, like modern readers, early medieval readers extracted different ideas from the same texts. Of course, they did not just inherit Augustine's writings, but also less intricate, more definite articulations of Augustinian ideas. Canon law collections broadcast the rulings of a council which Augustine attended at Carthage in 418, for example, which reiterated the necessity of infant baptism and the rejection of a medial place short of damnation.[36] In a letter to a monk inquiring after the souls of *parvuli* who had died unbaptized, Gregory the Great conceded uncertainty over the metaphysical origin of the soul, but wrote that the bind of original sin on the souls of those who had not been reborn in baptism was certain.[37] Fulgentius of Ruspe (d. 527/35) declared with even less subtlety that small children who died unbaptized, including those 'who begin to live in the wombs of mothers and die there ... will be punished with everlasting punishment of eternal fire'.[38]

Most of Augustine's readers presumably recognized the complexity of the questions which he had addressed. Some of them also recognized the complexity of the answers he gave. The potted biography of Augustine written at the end of the fifth century by Gennadius of Marseille referred, remarkably enough, to the resurrection of *abortivi*. After stressing the quantity and quality of his oeuvre (Augustine wrote so much that not everything he wrote could be found and, anyway, who read his works with the same care with which he wrote them?) Gennadius noted that Augustine 'went over the resurrection of the dead with similar sincerity, though he created doubt over *abortivi* for the less capable'.[39] When a pair of Visigothic bishops reflected on resurrected

---

that Augustine was attempting to imagine the bodies of resurrected fetuses in heaven.

[36] Council of Carthage (418), cc.2–3, ed. Munier, *Conciliae Africae*, p. 69.

[37] Gregory the Great, *Ep.* 9.147, MGH Epp. 2, pp. 147–8. See pp. 279–82 below on Gregory's *Moralia in Iob*.

[38] 'qui sive in uteris matrum vivere incipient et ibi moriuntur ... ignis aeterni sempiterno supplicio puniendos', *De fide* 70, ed. J. Fraipont, *Opera (Fulgentius Ruspensis)*, CCSL 91A (Turnhout, 1968), p. 753. On the subtly different tradition of thought on the problem of unbaptized infants in theology from the Greek east, see G. Gould, 'Childhood in Eastern Patristic Thought: Some Problems of Theology and Theological Anthropology', and J. Baun, 'The Fate of Babies Dying before Baptism in Byzantium', both in *The Church and Childhood*, SCH 31, ed. D. Wood (Oxford, 1994), pp. 39–52, 115–25.

[39] 'De Resurrectione etiam mortuorum simili cucurrit sinceritate; licet minus capacibus dubitationem de abortivis fecerit', *De scriptoribus ecclesiasticis* 38, PL 58, col. 1080A. Gennadius's work suggests that the resurrection of *abortivi* was something of an eye-catching topic in late antique theology, for *abortivi* are also mentioned in his biography of a Donatist bishop, Tyconius. According to Gennadius, Tyconius believed that there would be a single resurrection, in which even *abortivi deformati*, unformed abortions, would be resurrected, though he distinguished between a resurrection of the baptized and a general resurrection, *De scriptoribus ecclesiasticis*

bodies in the seventh century, they both read Augustine's hesitancy, his *dubitatio*, differently.

Resurrection of the damned: Julian of Toledo's Prognosticum

One example comes in a work by an important late Visigothic bishop, Julian of Toledo (d. 690). A patristic expert, in 688/9 Julian wrote the *Prognosticum*, a carefully assembled anthology of what church fathers had said on important theological questions about the nature of death and divine judgment.[40]

A portion of the third book turned to the resurrection. It ranged from general principles, such as whether the resurrection applied to all of the dead, to more specific questions, such as how the physically deformed would be resurrected. Significantly, *abortivi* merited their own little section. Julian began with his précis of the central issue: 'If it can be ascertained *when man begins to live in the mother's womb*, then it can be truly determined that what had been able to die, that is he who had life and was able to die, is restored at the time of the resurrection'.[41] He then quoted Augustine's theoretical assertion in the *Enchiridion* that anyone who had begun to live and was thus capable of dying should not be resurrected.[42] But the manner in which Julian introduced the quotation delicately underlined Augustine's hesitancy: 'For blessed Augustine, not so much arguing this matter as proposing, said this among other things'.[43] Finally, Julian ended with a quotation from another fifth-century thinker originally from North Africa, Julianus Pomerius, which illuminated what had been shaded in Augustine's speculation:

> Of course those who are thrown forth from the womb will be resurrected if they lived, not for judgment but for punishment; because, since they were condemned by Adam's condemnation, they have not been loosened from the bonds of their damnation. Nonetheless, whether infants are deprived of life in the womb or already born, it is believed that they will be resurrected at that age to which they would certainly have been if they lived, reaching

---

18, cols. 1071B–2A. On Tyconius's influence upon Augustine's eschatology, see A. Fredriksen, 'Tyconius and Augustine on the Apocalypse', in *The Apocalypse in the Middle Ages*, ed. R. K. Emmerson and B. McGinn (Ithaca NY, 1992), pp. 20–37. For Gennadius's own views on the resurrection, see *De ecclesiasticis dogmatis* 6–9, PL 58, cols. 982C–3C.

[40] On Julian's life and writings see J. N. Hillgarth, *Sancti Iuliani Toletanae sedis episcopi opera, pars I*, CCSL 115 (Turnhout, 1976), pp. viii–xxi.

[41] 'Si potest certum haberi *quando incipit homo in matris utero vivere*, ex tunc veraciter definiri potest quod et mori utique potuisset, sicque eum qui vitam habuit et mori potuit, resurrectionis tempore reparari', *Prognosticum* 3.27, ed. Hillgarth, CCSL 115, pp. 100–1; I have italicized the quotation from *Enchiridion* 23.86.

[42] From, 'But once a person begins to live', to the end of the indented quotation from the *Enchiridion* above at p. 269.

[43] 'Nam beatus Augustinus hanc quaestionem non tam disserens quam proponens, inter caetera sic ait', *Prognosticum* 3.27, p. 101.

advanced years; because if resurrection will repair nature, nothing will be able to lack the fullness of nature.⁴⁴

Through his choice of quotations and brief comments, Julian had effectively woven together the logical threads of original sin and resurrection. If resurrected, *abortivi* would rise up in the perfected bodies of the damned. The *Prognosticum* was a hugely influential work which proliferated in monastic and church libraries from the ninth century.⁴⁵ Julian's concision distilled for his readers two significant assumptions about *abortivi*. If resurrected, *abortivi* were necessarily excluded from salvation; and the status of *abortivi* was so ambiguous that even Augustine had been tentative.

Lack of humour: Braulio of Saragossa on bodily fluids at the resurrection
A few decades earlier, aborted fetuses entered a discussion on relics written by another important Visigothic bishop, Braulio of Saragossa (d. 651). In 649/50 Braulio wrote to an abbot, Taio. Judging from Braulio's reply, Taio had expressed concerns over the authenticity of a very special kind of relic, the blood of Christ. Jerome had once written about a column at Jerusalem spattered with Christ's blood. This troubled Taio. Why was his blood there? Was Christ's blood not restored to him at his resurrection? Would our blood not be restored to us? As Caroline Walker Bynum has emphasized, from the turn of the fifth century relic cults were an important catalyst for thought on the resurrection. Taio's concerns were neither eccentric nor altogether theoretical in a world of relics. It seemed repugnant that a 'mere fragment' or 'tiny bit' of a saint which held such power on earth would not be restored at the resurrection.⁴⁶

Although blood would once again course through our resurrected veins, Braulio explained, not all the superfluous blood which flowed through us over the course of our lives would resurge. Similarly, body parts, from limbs to hair, would be appropriately refashioned at the resurrection, but 'not the

---

⁴⁴ 'Sane illi qui proiciuntur ex utero, resurrecturi sunt si vixerunt, non iudicandi sed puniendi; quia, cum essent Adae damnatione damnati, non sunt suae damnationis nexibus absoluti. Et tamen sive in utero sive iam nati vita priventur infantes, in ea resurrecturi creduntur aetate, ad quam profecto essent, si viverent, annis procedentibus perventuri; quia si naturam resurrectio reparabit, aliquid deese plenitudini naturae non poterit', *Prognosticum* 3.27, p. 101.

⁴⁵ A little over a dozen of the 162 surviving manuscripts listed by Hillgarth in CCSL 115, pp. xxv–xxxiv, date from the ninth century; additionally, the *Prognosticum* is listed in most church library catalogues from the ninth to twelfth centuries, pp. xx–xxi. On the *Prognosticum*'s influence on later medieval theology, see J. N. Hillgarth, 'St. Julian of Toledo in the Middle Ages', *Journal of the Warburg and Courtauld Institutes* 21.1/2 (1958), 15–20; Bynum, *Resurrection of the Body*, pp. 121–2.

⁴⁶ Bynum, *Resurrection of the Body*, pp. 104–8 (quotations at p. 106); see too C. W. Bynum, *Wonderful Blood: Theology and Practice in Late Medieval Northern Germany and Beyond* (Philadelphia, 2007), pp. 96–111, on debate over blood relics from the thirteenth century onward.

superfluous humours by which corruptions are born or vices generated'.[47] It was reasonably clear that 'at the resurrection every person will have a body created reasonably and wholly ... with corruptions and vices removed'.[48] Superfluity was Braulio's key concept for thinking about resurrected bodies – and superfluity was the conceptual channel through which abortions entered the discussion:

> But we should be cautious in this inquiry ... in case we go so far that we are guilty of being superstitious, like those who ask about aborted fetuses, which exist from the body of either sex, [and] what could be thought about menstrual blood and the impure humour,[49] which in almost every life it is necessary to discharge naturally, [questions] in which they are superfluously superstitious.[50]

Braulio had advised Taio to read Augustine, for he claimed not to believe anything beyond 'what has been argued with prudent thought and elegant language by holy Augustine in several of his works, which have reached my hands'.[51] But none of Augustine's hesitation, which Julian of Toledo would politely signal a few decades later, trickled through into Braulio's account. For Braulio, the *abortivus* was a disgusting flux scarcely distinct from menstrual blood or semen:

> Why should it not be believed that human blood perishes once it is drawn off, since the generative humour itself, and blood,[52] as well as the *aborsus* are restored to neither parent in the resurrection: if indeed one should speak of a parent, whose disgusting fluid or inanimate fetus is poured forth. But there are some who assure us that this is the true blood of Christ which is held as relics by several people, as you say, and that this blood was not assumed in the resurrection of the body of the Lord[.][53]

[47] 'Non tamen superfluos humores, a quibus aut corruptela nascuntur aut vitia generantur', *Ep.* 42, ed. J. Madoz, *Epistólario de S. Braulio de Zaragoza* (Madrid, 1941), p. 180.

[48] 'unumquemque in resurrectione, exceptis corruptionibus et vitiis ... eius habere corpus rationabiliter integerrime constitutum', *Ep.* 42, p. 181.

[49] Presumably, semen.

[50] 'Cauti tamen in hac inquisitione esse debemus ... ne forte eo usque progrediamur ut superstitiosi reputemur. Sicut hi, qui de abortivis quaerunt fetibus, quae utique consistunt ex corpore utriusque sexus, quid de menstruo posset sanguine atque impuro sentiri humore, quem in omni paene vita necesse est etiam naturaliter egeri, in quibus superflue erunt superstitiosi', *Ep.* 42, p. 181.

[51] 'quae a sancto Augustino per diversa opuscula sua, quae ad manus venerunt meas, prudenti ingenio et eleganti sunt dissertata sermone', *Ep.* 42, pp. 179–80. Braulio explained that he had not gone to the trouble of seeking out these works – he almost certainly had *De civitate Dei* and *Enchiridion* in mind – because it was clear from Taio's letter that he had them at hand.

[52] Here I think Braulio meant menstrual blood.

[53] 'Sed cur non credatur et sanguis humanus perire detractus, cum et ipse humor generabilis atque sanguis, sicut et aborsus neutri reddatur in resurrectione parenti, si tamen parens iam dicendus est cuius aut liquor foedus, aut inanimatus profunditur

Imagining Abortivi

A comparable mental association between aborted fetuses and objects of disgust – in this case, carrion and the flesh of unclean animals – appeared in a slightly later text, the *Revelationes* of Pseudo-Methodius, written around the early eighth century.[54] This hugely influential apocalyptic text imagined Alexander the Great's encounter with the sons of Japheth, the tribe of Gog and Magog, who would one day run rampage at the end times:

> These are the sons of Japheth, whose uncleanness he saw and shuddered at. For all of them eat in the semblance of the beetle every polluted and filthy thing, dogs, mice, snakes, carrion, abortions, miscarriage, and those which in the womb because of softening had not yet formed a solid from a liquid or a structure made of any part of the limbs which might in form and figure produce an appearance or imitate a shape, and the miscarriages of animals[.][55]

For the author of the *Revelationes*, as for Braulio, shapeless fetuses were disgusting pollutants. Braulio not only thought that inanimate fetuses (*inanimati fetus*) were little more than a vile effusion, but, most strikingly of all, he made precisely the opposite conceptual move from so much church legislation. Could men and women really be called parents when the fetus was just a revolting *liquor* in the womb?

Both Julian and Braulio were familiar with Visigothic ecclesiastical and

---

fetus? Verumtamen non sunt hi qui nobis adfirmant verum esse cruorem Domini, qui pro reliquiis, ut ipse dicis, ab aliquibus habetur, ita istum cruorem non fuisse adsumptum in resurrectione corporis Domini, sicut nequaquam assumptus est', *Ep.* 42, p. 181.

[54] The *Revelationes* was a vulgar Merovingian Latin translation of a Greek text, itself a translation of a Syriac text composed in the later seventh century during the Arab invasions. On the earliest manuscript, Berne, Burgerbibliothek, MS 611, see M. Verhelst, 'Pseudo-Methodius, Revelationes: Textgeschichte und kritische Edition', in *The Use and Abuse of Eschatology in the Middle Ages*, ed. D. Verbeke *et al.* (Leuven, 1988), p. 114.

[55] 'Sunt autem ex filiis Iapeth nepotes, quorum inmunditiam videns exorruit. Commendebant enim hi omnes cantharo speciem omnem coinquinabilem vel spurcebilem, id est canes, mures, serpentes, morticinorum carnes, aborticia, informabilia corpore et ea, que in alvo necdum † per leniamenta † coaculata sunt vel ex aliqua parte † membrorum producta conpago † formam figmenti possit perficere vultum vel figuram expremere et haec iumentorum', Pseudo-Methodius, *Revelationes* 8.4, and cf. *Revelationes* 13.20, ed. and trans. B. Garstad, *Apocalypse Pseudo-Methodius: An Alexandrian World Chronicle* (Cambridge MA, 2012), pp. 96–7, 130–3. The Latin *Revelationes* is palpably more detailed on *aborticia* and other shapeless forms in the womb than the Greek *Apocalypse*, which refers to 'abortions, miscarriages, fetuses not completely formed or some preserving the marks of formation [amblōmata, ektrōmata, embrua mēpō teleiōs apartisthenta ē tina tēs diaplaseōs aposōzonta charatēra]', trans. Garstad, *Apocalypse*, pp. 22–3, or the Syriac *Apocalypse*, which refers to 'embryos which the women aborted they ate as if they were some delicacy', trans. P.J. Alexander, *The Byzantine Apocalyptic Tradition* (Berkeley, 1985), p. 40. I am grateful to James Palmer for references to Pseudo-Methodius.

Abortion in the Early Middle Ages

secular legislation against abortion.⁵⁶ But connecting the thought of Augustine and his interpreters on *abortivi* to ecclesiastical discourse on the morality of abortion requires caution. Eschatological thought certainly illuminates ideas and instincts which were relatively shaded in church regulations. Lurking in the small gaps between rulings on abortion and infant baptism grouped closely together in some penitentials was an idea explicit in eschatology: the fate of *abortivi*, necessarily condemned to eternal perdition. Eschatological speculation dramatized the conceptual problem of imagining the beginning and end of life in the womb, though there was firmer consensus on the fate of the unbaptized.

But what is the significance of the assumption which a conflicted Augustine had admitted felt plausible and which an altogether more confident Braulio had amplified: unformed abortions were more like semen or menstrual blood than infant? There are two answers, both of which are significant but neither of which is sufficient by itself. The intuitive answer is that some strands of eschatology articulated assumptions which also underlay the idea that deliberate abortion of the unformed fetus simply was not murder and was perhaps even justifiable or at least mitigable. This idea found surprising expression in the Latin *vita* of an Irish saint, Ciarán of Saigir, a text which is difficult to date with any precision but which bears some affinities to other Irish *vitae* in which the pregnancies of nuns miraculously disappeared. After a woman named Bruinech, who had joined a female religious community formed by Ciarán's mother, had been abducted by a local despot, Dimma, the saint managed to rescue her. In this story *raptus* had a coercive sexual dimension. When they returned to the monastery the 'girl confessed that she had conceived in her womb', and so Ciarán, the 'man of God, stirred by a zeal for justice, not wanting the serpent's seed to come alive, by imprinting the sign of the cross on her belly made it be empty'.⁵⁷

A second, less intuitive answer draws attention to a contrast: the ambiguous beginnings of life were addressed in eschatology in a detail and spirit which is lacking in other sources. On this reading, it is misleading simply to plug the gaps in church legislation, sermons and so on with Braulio's confident dismissal of the *abortivus fetus* as inanimate flux. Questions addressed in eschatology threw up answers which were not meant to be applied to the questions addressed in pastoral texts. For Braulio, it was almost unintelligible to speak of parents of the abortive flux. For Caesarius and at least some other

---

⁵⁶ Julian produced a recension of the *Hispana*, the so-called Iuliana, *c.* 681. On Braulio's involvement in preparing the *Lex Visigothorum* for Recceswinth, see Lynch, *Saint Braulio*, pp. 136–40.

⁵⁷ 'confessa est puella se conceptum habere in utero. Tunc vir Dei, zelo iustitie ductus, viperium semen animari nolens, impresso ventri eius signo crucis, fecit illud exinaniri', *Vita Ciarani* 5, ed. Heist, *Vitae*, p. 348. For a more detailed reading of this episode and editorial censoring of it in a later medieval manuscript, see Mistry, 'Sexual Shame', 612–14.

churchmen, it was almost unintelligible *not* to speak of parents of what might have been conceived. Eschatology and pastoral practice generated different perspectives on the *aborsus*. Some ecclesiastical authors like Regino, who collected together rulings which took different approaches to abortion in his episcopal manual, were reluctant to settle definitively the moral problem of abortion along the lines represented by Braulio's eschatological thought or Ciarán's miracle.

Alienated from the womb: Abortion symbolism in the Early Middle Ages

Some thinkers might have preferred to avoid thinking about the *abortivus* altogether. But the *abortivus* was unavoidable in scripture. In the Old Testament, abortion imagery expressed spiritual dislocation and ruin. The book of Ecclesiastes, for example, declared that the greedy man who accumulated worldly possessions was worse off than the *abortivus*.[58] The apostle Paul extended this imagistic tradition when he likened himself to an abortion (*ektrōma* in the Greek, *abortivus* in the Latin) upon encountering the risen Christ (1 Cor. 15. 8). Modern biblical scholars continue to debate exactly what Paul meant literally and figuratively.[59] Early medieval exegetes developed their own interpretations from different literal meanings of *abortivus*. One sixth-century commentary offered two definitions of the *abortivus* as 'who is born outside the period, or who is drawn out alive from a dead mother'; Paul called himself an *abortivus* in the first sense because he came to faith outside the period of Jesus's preaching.[60] Similarly, in a commentary on the Pauline epistles which circulated widely in the Middle Ages, Haimo of Auxerre (d. *c*. 878) defined *abortivus* as 'someone born without the right time for birth; out-

---

[58] The author 'added this hyperbolically [*illud hyperbolice addidit*]', Alcuin explained in his commentary on Ecclesiastes 6. 3, because anyone consumed with desire and greed ultimately experienced a deep sadness which the *abortivus* was destined never to experience: *Commentaria super Ecclesiasten*, PL 100, col. 692A. Below we will encounter other examples from Job and Numbers.

[59] G. W. E. Nickelsburg, 'An [*ektrōma*], though Appointed from the Womb: Paul's Apostolic Self-Description in 1 Corinthians 15 and Galatians 1', *Harvard Theological Review* 79.1/3 (1986), 198–205; H. W. Hollander and G. E. Van Der Hout, 'The Apostle Paul Calling Himself an Abortion: 1 Cor. 15.8 within the context of 1 Cor. 15.8–10', *Novum Testamentum* 38.3 (1996), 224–36.

[60] 'Abortivus dicitur, qui extra tempus nascitur, seu qui mortua matre vivus educitur', Pseudo-Primasius, *Commentaria in Epistolas B. Pauli*, PL 68, col. 543D. This commentary, once attributed to Primasius of Hadrumetum, was in fact Cassiodorus's revision of a commentary on Paul's epistles originally by Pelagius: see A. Souter, *Pelagius's Expositions of Thirteen Epistles of St Paul. Volume 1, Introduction* (Cambridge, 1922), pp. 318–26; K. L. Hughes, *Constructing Antichrist: Paul, Biblical Commentary, and the Development of Doctrine in the Early Middle Ages* (Washington DC, 2005), pp. 117–18.

side the appropriate time, either before he ought to be born, or after'.[61] Julius Caesar's birth was a literal example of the latter, 'just as the apostle was *abortivus* in a certain sense, because he was born in Christ after the time'.[62] More typically, however, the *abortivus* tended to mean literally the product of miscarriage, premature birth, stillbirth, or the infant dead in the womb. Figuratively, the *abortivus* signified prematurity, imperfection and mortality.

Abortion imagery from the Bible was further refracted through a tradition of thought without direct scriptural basis: the idea of *mater ecclesia*, the conceptualization of the church as mother. *Mater ecclesia* first appeared in the works of second-century authors, but it was intensely developed in both pastoral practice and polemical debate from the third century among North African theologians including Tertullian, Cyprian and Augustine.[63] Conception, gestation in the womb and birth became a rich way of imagining baptism. As Robin Jensen has emphasized, *mater ecclesia* was not a dull, intangible metaphor but a vivid, even graphic, anthropomorphization of the church. *Mater ecclesia* had lactating breasts and a fertile womb. Like human mothers, she conceived, gave birth and nurtured her infants. She suffered too. She miscarried her infants and grieved at their loss.[64]

When Caesarius of Arles likened catechumens to gestating fetuses awaiting their rebirth and warned them not to bring about their own abortions, he was channelling a rich symbolic tradition, which has scarcely been explored in its medieval manifestations.[65] Informed by the scriptural resonance of the *abortivus* and one specific strand of *mater ecclesia* imagery, pregnancy loss, much of the symbolic language of abortion in the Early Middle Ages was

---

[61] 'Abortivus est, qui sine legitimo tempore nascendi nascitur: extra tempus videlicet congruum aut antequam debeat nasci, aut post', Haimo, *Enarratio in divi Pauli epistolis*, PL 117, col. 594C. On the historical significance and historiographical neglect of Haimo's work, see J. Heil, 'Haimo's Commentary on Paul: Sources, Methods and Theology', in *Études d'exégèse Carolingienne: Autour d'Haymon d'Auxerre*, ed. S. Shimahara (Turnhout, 2007), pp. 103–21.

[62] 'sic et Apostolus abortivus quodammodo exstitit, quia post tempus natus est in Christo', *Enarratio in divi Pauli epistolas*, cols. 594C–D.

[63] For an analysis of *mater ecclesia* as an often polemical ecclesiological concept in North African Christian thought, which also contains a helpful overview of older theological scholarship, see B. M. Peper, 'The Development of *Mater ecclesia* in North African Ecclesiology' (unpublished Ph.D. thesis, Vanderbilt University, 2011). For a flavour of this older scholarship, see J. C. Plumpe, *Mater Ecclesia: An Inquiry into the Concept of the Church as Mother in Early Christianity* (Washington DC, 1943).

[64] R. Jensen, '*Mater ecclesia* and *Fons aeterna*: The Church and her Womb in Ancient Christian Tradition', in *A Feminist Companion to Patristic Literature*, ed. A.-J. Levine (London, 2008), pp. 137–55, who persuasively connects this concept to a remarkable baptismal font from fifth-century Sufetula (modern-day Sbeitla, Tunisia). The font is shaped like a vulva, here in the modern sense of the external female genitalia. As we shall see below, the Latin *vulva*, which I will keep italicized in translations, could also mean vagina or even womb.

[65] See p. 61 above on *Sermo* 200.

inherently negative. Several images we will encounter were exclusionist ecclesiological statements of who was in and who was out of the church's womb.[66]

Reprehensible words: Gregory the Great on Job's curses
Gregory the Great's *Moralia* contained an extensive exegetical interaction with one of the most significant sources of *abortivus* imagery in the Old Testament: the book of Job. In the midst of his troubles, Job had repeatedly cursed his conception, survival in the womb and subsequent birth. Gregory not only offered intricate interpretations of these curses, but also used their literal meaning as a paradigmatic example of moving beyond the letter to the spirit of the word.

In the fourth book of the *Moralia*, Gregory offered layered allegorical and tropological or moral interpretations of Job's curses. The fourfold structure of one curse – 'Why did I not die in the *vulva*? Why did I not perish upon leaving the womb? Why was I taken up on knees? Why suckled with breasts?' (Job 3. 11–12)[67] – held multiple moral meanings. These four moments at the beginning of life, from conception in the womb to suckling in infancy, denoted four stages by which sin was perpetrated in the heart (suggestion, pleasure, consent and audacity to justify one's actions); and four stages by which sin was consummated in action (secretly, openly, increasingly and habitually).[68] Within each scheme, different developmental stages and anatomical details carried different meanings. Thus, in the first scheme, the '*vulva* of conception was the tongue of evil suggestion'.[69] In the latter scheme, the *vulva* was the 'hidden sin of man which secretly conceives the sinner and hides his guilt still in darkness'.[70]

Another one of Job's curses – 'Or why did I not cease to be like a concealed *abortivus*, or like those conceived who never see the light?' (Job 3. 16)[71] – became an allegory of salvation history. 'An *abortivus*,' Gregory explained,

[66] It is worth stressing certain limitations in the survey that follows. First, I have not included each and every example which I have found; and it is highly unlikely that I have exhausted the early medieval supply of this imagery. Second, there is a wealth of other reproductive and physiological metaphors in exegesis and theology which I do not discuss. Third, I largely avoid going into detail about affiliations with and borrowings from older works, especially by Augustine, Jerome and the Latin Origen. In part, this is because the task of disentangling originality from derivations is rendered particularly difficult by the lack of up-to-date critical editions. One beneficial side-effect, however, is avoiding the anachronistic trap of over-privileging originality.
[67] 'Quare non in vulva mortuus sum; egressus ex utero non statim perii? cur exceptus genibus? cur lactatus uberibus?', *Moralia* 4.27.48, ed. M. Adriaen, *Moralia in Iob*, CCSL 143 (Turnhout, 1979), p. 193.
[68] *Moralia* 4.27.49–51, pp. 193–6.
[69] 'vulva conceptionis fuit lingua malae suggestionis', *Moralia* 4.27.50, p. 194.
[70] 'Vulva quippe peccantis, est hominis culpa latens quae occulte peccatorem concipit et reum suum adhuc in tenebris abscondit', *Moralia* 4.27.51, p. 194.
[71] 'Aut sicut abortivum absconditum non subsisterem: vel qui concepti non viderunt lucem' *Moralia* 4.32.63, p. 207.

'because it arises before the full period [and] is immediately hidden away at death'.[72] Noah, Abraham and Jacob, who lived before the advent of the law, 'dead, as it were, from the womb' in the sense that they mortified their pleasures as best as they could.[73] Moreover, this murky period in salvation history was 'aptly called a hidden *abortivus* because from the beginnings of the world, while we know about a certain few through Moses' writings, the large part of humankind is concealed from us'.[74] The 'conceived who never the saw the light' represented those who were 'born in this world after receiving the [Mosaic] law' and thus had never seen the light of Christ's incarnation.[75] The 'interior conceiving brought forth the form of faith', but an 'intervening death seized them from this world before the truth made manifest lightened the world'.[76] Gregory's moral and allegorical reading hinged on connotations of uterine concealment and premature mortality.

The fourth book had opened with a crucial methodological moment in the *Moralia*.[77] Anyone who neglected the spiritual meaning of the sacred word, Gregory warned, would be confounded by uncertainty. Why? Because scriptural words sometimes contradict themselves in their literal meaning. The dissonance of words in their outer sense was a sign that the reader had to delve deeper for their inner sense.[78] What interests us is the example which Gregory offered as a paradigm of scriptural words which were palpably contradictory in their surface sense, another one of Job's curses: 'Let the day perish when I was born, and the night in which it was said: a man has been conceived' (Job 3. 3).[79] 'If the meaning is studied at the surface,' Gregory asserted, 'what is more reprehensible than these words?'[80] But what was so reprehensible? Gregory's first explanation was admittedly a little pedantic. In effect, the curse made no sense because one cannot undo the past; the curse was irrational.[81] The

---

[72] 'Abortivum quia ante plenum tempus oritur, exstinctum protinus occultatur', *Moralia* 4.32.63, p. 207.

[73] 'quasi ab utero mortui sunt', *Moralia* 4.32.63, p. 207.

[74] 'Bene autem abortivum hoc absconditum dicitur quia a mundi primordiis, dum quosdam paucos Moyse scribente cognoscimus, pars nobis maxima humani generis occultatur', *Moralia* 4.32.63, p. 207.

[75] 'concepti non viderunt lucem ... qui post acceptam legem in hoc mundo nati sunt', *Moralia* 4.32.64, p. 208.

[76] 'conceptus interior formam fidei edidit ... prius hos a mundo mors interveniens rapuit, quam manifesta mundum Veritas illustravit', *Moralia* 4.32.64, p. 208.

[77] S. E. Schreiner, 'Perception in Gregory's *Moralia in Job*', *Studia Patristica* 28 (1993), 90–1; M. Parmentier, 'Job the Rebel: From the Rabbis to the Church Fathers', in *Saints and Role Models in Judaism and Christianity*, ed. J. Schwartz and M. Poorthius (Leiden, 2004), pp. 240–2.

[78] *Moralia* 4.1, p. 158.

[79] 'Pereat dies in qua natus sum, et nox in qua dictum est: Conceptus est homo', *Moralia* 4.2, p. 159.

[80] 'si superficie tenus attenditur, quid his verbis reprehensibilius invenitur?', *Moralia* 4.2, p. 159.

[81] *Moralia* 4.1.2, p. 159.

second explanation, which quoted Job 3. 11–12 for support, was altogether more elaborate – and more intriguing for what Gregory assumed was obvious about *abortivi*:

> But if [Job] had died immediately upon leaving the womb, would he have conceived that he deserved a reward for this same perdition? Do the *abortivi* enjoy eternal rest? For whoever is not set free by the water of rebirth is held bound by guilt of the original bond. Indeed what the water of baptism effects among us, faith alone did for small children or the virtue of sacrifice for adults did among the ancients, or the witness of circumcision for those who proceeded from Abraham's line.[82]

Gregory used Psalm 51. 5 and John 3. 11–12 as scriptural support for the punishment of the unbaptized before continuing:

> How, then, does [Job] desire his own death in the womb, and hope to have been able to find rest in the benefits of his own death, when it is certain that the rest of life [i.e. eternal life] would not have received him from life if the sacraments of divine knowledge had in no way freed him from original sin?[83]

In other words, how could Job wish for his own damnation by cursing his conception? Job's curse illustrated the confusion of reading 'words [which] are opposed to reason at the surface' without sensitivity to deeper meanings.[84] The manner in which Gregory construed the literal dissonance of Job's curse was emphatic. As he later reiterated, 'far be it from us to believe that holy Job, so gifted with spiritual knowledge ... should have wished that he died as an *abortivus*'.[85] The surface contradiction was so obvious that he could pose a rhetorical question: 'Do *abortivi* enjoy eternal rest?'. For Gregory in particular and the early medieval church more generally, there was a significant practical subtext: the growing insistence on the necessity of infant baptism. In several letters Gregory insisted that bishops and clerics made proper provisions for the baptism of infants so that none of them 'died in the darkness with the filth of sin unwashed'.[86] Gregory's exegesis, like certain strands of eschatological

---

[82] 'Numquid si egressus ex utero statim periisset, retributionis meritum ex hac ipsa perditione conciperet? Numquid aeterna requie abortivi perfruuntur? Quisquis enim regenerationis unda non solvitur, reatu primi vinculi ligatus tenetur. Quod vero apud nos valet aqua baptismatis, hoc egit apud veteres vel pro parvulis sola fides, vel pro maioribus virtus sacrificii, vel pro his qui ex Abrahae stirpe prodierant, mysterium circumcisionis', *Moralia* 4.3, p. 160.

[83] 'Quid est ergo quod in vulva mortuum se fuisse desiderat et potuisse se quiescere eiusdem mortis beneficiis sperat, dum constet quod nequaquam eum requies vitae susciperet, si a reatu illum originalis culpae nequaquam divinae cognitionis sacramenta liberassent?', *Moralia* 4.3, p. 160.

[84] 'verba ... in superficie a ratione discordant', *Moralia* 4.3, p. 161.

[85] 'Absit nos credere quod beatus Iob, tanta spiritus scientia praeditus ... abortivum se optet interiisse', *Moralia* 4.27.48, p. 193.

[86] 'inabluta sorde peccati defunctis in tenebris', *Ep.* 3.7, MGH Epp. 1, p. 166; in this

speculation, brought to the surface a stark but simple truth. Death in the womb, to be conceived but never to see the light, was to die bound to original sin.

The womb of the church: The abortivus as outsider
Following the lead of their late antique sources, early medieval churchmen used the *abortivus* to describe groups or individuals who were in some way outside the church. The full range of interpretative possibilities appeared in a later commentary on the psalms which was falsely attributed to the Carolingian scholar Remigius of Auxerre (d. 908) in the twelfth century.[87] Nonetheless, it is worth quoting, partly as an invitation to later medievalists, but also because of the clarity with which it brought together different ways of interpreting Psalm 58. 3: 'Sinners are alienated from the *vulva*, they have wandered from the womb, they have spoken lies'.[88] First, *alienati* could signify sinners. Through his foreknowledge God rejected some sinners, like Esau, in their very conception.[89] Second, Jews were 'alienated from the *vulva* of the Catholic mother, that is, in the rites of the church, in which they ought to have been conceived for life in her as it were'.[90] Jews had wandered away 'from the womb of the church in which they should have been informed and instructed', a play on the physical and figurative connotations of formation.[91] But, finally, *alienati* also stood for 'heretics, [who] by leaving from [the mother church] and daring to preach what they have not learned, cause an abortion before they have been formed and instructed in the womb of the mother'.[92]

letter Gregory was adjudicating a dispute between bishops which included accusations that one of them had deliberately prohibited infant baptism. For examples of Gregory overseeing practical provisions for infant baptism in the course of papal administration, see *Ep.* 1.15, 1.17, 1.51, 4.9, 6.38, 13.22, MGH Epp. 1, pp. 16, 23, 77, 242, 415, MGH Epp. 2, pp. 388–9.

[87] C. Jeudy, 'L'oeuvre de Remi d'Auxerre: État de la question', in *L'école carolingienne d'Auxerre: De Murethach à Remi 830–908*, ed. D. Iogna-Prat et al. (Paris, 1991), pp. 374–7. A few extracts from unpublished psalm commentaries genuinely by Remigius have been edited in P.A. Vaccari, 'Il genuino commento ai Salmi di Remigio di Auxerre', *Biblica* 26.1–2 (1945) 52–99; an edition of both extant versions is being prepared for CCCM. See too C. Jeudy, 'Remigii autissiodorensis opera (*Clavis*)', in *L'école carolingienne d'Auxerre*, pp. 466–7.

[88] 'Alienati sunt peccatores a vulva, erraverunt ab utero, locuti sunt falsa', Pseudo-Remigius, *Enarrationes in Psalmos*, PL 131, cols. 431C–D.

[89] This is a reference to Genesis 25. 19–26, in which Jacob and Esau, the sons of Isaac, struggled in the womb of Rebekah; God told Rebekah, 'Two nations are in your womb', and the elder (Esau was born first) would serve the younger. On rabbinic readings of Jacob as Israel and Esau as Christian Rome, see Kessler, *Conceiving Israel*, pp. 47–64.

[90] 'alienati sunt a vulva catholicae matris, id est in ipsis initiamentis Ecclesiae, in quibus quasi in ea ad vitam concipi debuerunt', *Enarrationes in Psalmos*, col. 431D.

[91] 'ab Ecclesiae utero in quo debuerunt informari et instrui', *Enarrationes in Psalmos*, col. 432A.

[92] 'vel haeretici, antequam in utero illius matris formati et eruditi essent, exeuntes ab ea,

Imagining Abortivi

Each of these interpretations in the pseudo-Remigian commentary had older precedents. One central physiological aspect of development in the womb made the *abortivus* a suitable metaphor for Jews or fledgling Christians: premature and imperfect formation. The metaphor can be found in some of the oldest surviving commentaries on Paul's epistles. Paul had written, 'My little children, again I am in labour until Christ is formed in you' (Gal. 4. 19), one late antique commentary explained, because 'first he had given birth to them by faith in baptism, but because they were born through *abortus*, [and] turned out to be unformed and infirm', he was now trying to reform them.[93] Similarly, the Benedictine abbot Smaragdus (d. *c*. 840) explained that Paul was 'dead in the synagogue and born in the church like an *abortivus*, about the life of which it had been despaired of [sic], if he had not been violently pulled through God's grace'.[94] In another sense, there was even a hint of the moral association between sexual sin and defective offspring; Paul was also like an *abortivus* because the 'mother synagogue bore him imperfect and badly conceived'.[95]

While the *abortivus* as Jews played on connotations of prematurity and imperfection, the *abortivus* as sinner and, especially, heretic emphasized expulsion from the womb. After warning his flock against sins like abortion in one sermon, Caesarius had later warned that catechumens should avoid sin 'in case by chance they convulse the maternal organs through their wrongdoing and the holy mother throws them forth like an abortion before a proper birth'.[96] The image was ultimately derived from Augustine's preaching. On more than one occasion Augustine drew on uterine imagery to describe *mater ecclesia* and her children. 'See the womb of the church,' he addressed catechumens, 'see how she bears you, and brings you forth into the light of faith and toils with her groaning. Do not let your impatience convulse the maternal

---

et praedicere praesumentes quod non didicerunt, abortivum fecerunt', *Enarrationes in Psalmos* PL 131, col. 432A. See too the comparable approach in a pseudo-Bedan commentary, *Commentaria in Psalmos*, PL 93, col. 784B. Although some sections of the commentary were derived from Theodore of Mopsuetia and Cassiodorus, the relevant exegesis came from a section composed in the late eleventh century or later: cf. T. Gross-Diaz, *The Psalms Commentary of Gilbert of Poitiers: From Lectio Divina to the Lecture Room* (Leiden, 1996), p. 113.

[93] 'Filii mei, quos iterum parturio, donec Christus formetur in vobis. Primum per fidem illos genuerat in baptism, sed quia velut per abortum nati, deformati et infirmes inventi sunt', Ambrosiaster, *Ad Galatas* 4.19, ed. H. J. Vogels, *Ambrosiastri qui dicitur Commentarius in epistulas Paulinas*, CSEL 81.3 (Vienna, 1969), p. 49.

[94] 'quia est Synagogae mortuus et natus Ecclesiae tanquam abortivo, de cujus vita fuerat desperatum, nisi per gratia Domini violenter fuisset attractus', Smaragdus, *Collectiones in epistolas et evangelii*, PL 102, col. 434D; see H. Barré, *Les homéliares carolingiens de l'école d'Auxerre: Authenticité, inventaire tableaux comparatifs, initia* (Vatican City, 1962), pp. 12–13, on Smaragdus's text.

[95] 'quia mater synagoga eum male conceptum imperfectumque peperit', *Collectiones*, col. 435A.

[96] See p. 61 above.

Abortion in the Early Middle Ages

organs and narrow the doors of your birth.'[97] Elsewhere, the image of the heretic aborted from the church's womb illuminated other scriptural passages which did not explicitly refer to the *abortivus*. A pseudo-Bedan commentary explained Leviticus 24. 10–11, in which the son of an Israelite mother and Egyptian father cursed God following a fight in the Israelite camp, in terms of heresy. He signified 'heretics, born from the devilish father, and thrown out of the womb of the mother church like *abortivi*'.[98]

Metaphors of expulsion from the womb of the church blended the scriptural connotations of the *aborsus* with the ecclesiological imagery of *mater ecclesia*. They also played on the physiological connotations of miscarriage and, one suspects, moral connotations of abortion. Authors had to take care because the mother in question was the church. Sinners or heretics became, in effect, both cause and product of their grieving mother's abortion. These uterine ecclesiologies are good examples of what Mary Douglas hypothesized as the 'concordance between symbolic and social experience', the body and its functions representing the social body and its processes.[99] Adapting Douglas's famous expression, insofar as it was a bodily malfunction, abortion was a powerful unnatural symbol which expressed social expulsion. As its use in pastoral rhetoric suggests, this was not simply an arcane metaphor circulating within a restricted circle of biblical scholars. In his letter to the Visigothic king, the monk Tarra, as we have already seen, framed his unjust expulsion from the monastery at Cauliana as an abortion.[100] Moreover, in the course of often polemical and personal disputes over theology and doctrine, churchmen resorted to the *abortivus* as an insult. A complex disagreement over Christ's nature as God and man erupted in the later eighth century when the Spanish bishops, Felix of Urgel and Elipandus of Toledo, were accused of espousing the idea that Christ was born as a man and only subsequently adopted the divine nature. In a treatise attacking Felix (and not necessarily representing his position accurately), Paulinus of Aquileia accused his adversary of Christological inconsistency. Sometimes Felix spoke of Christ's

---

[97] 'Ecce uterus matris Ecclesiae, ecce ut te pariat, atque in lucem fidei producat, laborat in gemitu suo. Nolite vestra impatentia viscera materna concutere, et partus vestri januas angustare', *Sermo* 216.7, PL 38, col. 1080; for other examples, see Augustine, *Ep.* 243.8, PL 33, col. 1057; *Enarrationes in Psalmos* 57.6, ed. H. Müller, *Augustinus, Enarrationes in Psalmos 51–60*, CSEL 94.1 (Vienna, 2004), p. 274; *Contra Faustum* 12.47, PL 42, col. 280. More broadly, on uterine imagery in Augustine's outreach to catechumens, see W. Harmless, *Augustine and the Catechumenate* (Collegeville, 1995), pp. 244–96.

[98] 'significat haereticos, qui de patre diabolo geniti, et ex utero matris Ecclesiae tanquam abortivi ejecti', Pseudo-Bede, *Commentarii in Pentateuchum*, PL 91, col. 356C. According to M. Gorman, 'The Commentary on the Pentateuch Attributed to Bede in PL 91.189–394', *Revue Bénédictine* 106 (1996), 61–108, 255–307, this commentary was written in Spain in around 700.

[99] M. Douglas, *Natural Symbols*, 2nd edn (London, 2006), p. xxxvi.

[100] See pp. 93–4 above on Tarra's letter to Reccared.

Imagining Abortivi

divinity as something nominal or adoptive, at other times he spoke of Christ as true God and true man. Paulinus concluded that Felix's constant backtracking was not driven by a desire for theological truth, but by fear, 'in case by chance he would be thrown forth from the womb of the holy mother church like an *abortivus* before the glimmer of light'.[101]

Another example, less closely related to scriptural or exegetical imagery, appeared in Julian of Toledo's *Historia Wambae*, which recalled an abortive rebellion against the Visigothic king Wamba in 672–3 led by the duke Flavius Paulus, who had gained the support of several towns in southern Gaul. One part of his account, the *Insultatio in tyrannidem Galliae*, was a sarcastic invective against the region personified as an adulterous woman, Gallia, who had conceived and given birth to pain and sorrow.[102] 'You still cannot deny,' Julian sneered, 'that the fetus is yours by conception'.[103] In an insulting image which elided the possibility of infanticide and abortion, Julian sarcastically asked Gallia why she had not gotten rid of her offspring:

> But if you gave birth, why did you not cut off the monstrous birth before they grew up? Or is it not more a mark of virtue for respectable women to have killed monsters born of them; indeed, of crime, if they destroyed ordained fetuses, of order, if they killed unformed ones?[104]

A few centuries earlier, another Spanish author was even blunter in the midst of the heresiological tumult over Priscillianism, to which we turned in chapter three. While Turibius of Astorga's letter to Leo I has not survived, his letter to fellow bishops Hydatius and Ceponius has. Northern Spain, he complained, was swarming with heretics. A bishop's choice was plain: 'either one compels them, scolded in the lap of a faithful parent, to change or, [if] utterly incorrigible, one expels them from the association of sacred heredity like abortive

---

[101] 'ne forte ex utero sacrosanctae matris Ecclesia[e] tanquam abortivus ante lucis projiciatur crepusculum', Paulinus of Aquileia, *Contra Felicem* 1.9, PL 99, col. 362a. The fundamental study of the Adoptionist controversy is J. C. Cavadiani, *The Last Christology of the West: Adoptionism in Spain and Gaul, 785–820* (Philadelphia, 1993); see too C. Chazelle, *The Crucified God in the Carolingian Era: Theology and Art of Christ's Passion* (Cambridge, 2001), pp. 52–70.

[102] *Historiae Wambae* 3, *Insultatio* 3, MGH SRM 5, p. 527. On the political background, see M. de Jong, 'Adding Insult to Injury: Julian of Toledo and his *Historia Wambae*', in *The Visigoths*, pp. 373–89; J. Martínez Pizarro, *The Story of Wamba: Julian of Toledo's Historia Wambae regis* (Washington DC, 2005).

[103] 'conceptione tamen fetus tui, negare non poteris', *Insultatio* 4, p. 527.

[104] 'Si autem tu genuisti, quare genita monstruosa, priusquam adolescerent, non secasti? An non potius mulieres idoneas monstra ex se genita abnecasse, virtutis erit indicium; criminis quidem, si ordinatos fetus perimerent, ordinis, si informes necarent?', *Insultatio* 4, p. 527. Pizarro, *Story of Wamba*, p. 225, not unreasonably takes *ordinati fetus* and *informes* to mean a distinction between 'healthy' and 'misshapen' offspring, in which case the image might well have been one of infanticide rather than abortion. But, if so, it is another example of how language describing abortion and infanticide was frequently interchangeable.

births and illegitimate offspring'.[105] To put it crudely, but not altogether inaccurately: either make them mend their ways or else abort the bastards.

It is understandable to conclude that Julian (or Turibius) had 'somehow managed to forget the fulminations of the Spanish church councils against abortion and infanticide'.[106] But it is also conceivable that Julian and Turibius had penned the closest things to early medieval jokes on abortion. In antiquity, Ovid had joked about abortion in the sense of satirizing Roman public morality. Here, the joke was different. Rather like an opponent of torture suggesting that advocates of so-called enhanced interrogations ought to be waterboarded, Julian and Turibus were trading in a jarring, even grotesque, brand of humour. Their images gained their force because of, not in spite of, moral discourse on abortion. Indeed, it is tempting to conclude that Spain was a particularly fertile ground for *abortivus* imagery because, as we have seen, Spain was also where moral rhetoric on abortion found its most febrile expression.

Rabanus Maurus and scripturally informed abortion
The final figure under examination was not only well acquainted with *abortivus* imagery, but he was also an expert on ecclesiastical measures against abortion. We have already examined Rabanus Maurus's penitentials and letters addressing abortion. The majority of his literary output, however, took the form of biblical commentaries and other exegetical works.[107] Plenty of them contained *abortivus* imagery. Rabanus's reading of an episode involving Moses and his siblings, Aaron and Miriam, in the book of Numbers was especially graphic. After Miriam had spoken against Moses because he had married a Cushite woman, God punished her with leprosy. Aaron begged his brother to intervene on Miriam's behalf:

> 'Do not let her be like something dead, like the *aborsus* thrown out of the mother's womb with half of its flesh consumed' [Numbers 12. 12]. He wants to show in this, because the people was formed in the *vulva* of its mother synagogue, it was still unable to reach a completed and whole birth; for it

---

[105] 'aut correctos piae parentis gremio reformari compellit, aut pertinaciter contumaces, veluti abortivos partus ac non legitimam sobolem ex consortio sanctae haereditatis expellit', PL 54, col. 693B.

[106] Pizarro, *Story of Wamba*, pp. 170–1 (quotation at p. 170), notes that Julian might well have adapted his idea about getting rid of monstrous births from classical sources.

[107] Scholars have only relatively recently begun to mine Rabanus's commentaries as rich sources for cultural history: see M. A. Mayeski, '"Let women not despair": Rabanus Maurus on Women as Prophets', *Journal of Theological Studies* 58.2 (1997), 237–50; M. de Jong, 'Exegesis for an Empress', in *Medieval Transformations*, pp. 69–100; A. Firey, 'The Letter of the Law: Carolingian Exegetes and the Old Testament', in *With Reverence for the Word: Medieval Scriptural Exegesis in Judaism, Christianity, and Islam*, ed. J. D. McAuliffe et al. (Oxford, 2003), pp. 204–24; L. Coon, '"What is the Word if not Semen?" Priestly Bodies in Carolingian Exegesis', in *Gender in the Early Medieval World, East and West, 300–900*, ed. L. Brubaker and J. M. H. Smith (Cambridge, 2004), pp. 278–300.

Imagining Abortivi

is a birth like an imperfect and disarranged *aborsus*, in such a way that the people is for some time placed within the mother's *vulva*, that is, within the institution of the synagogue; but with sins interrupting it could not be formed to wholeness and come alive. And indeed they were thrown forth like an imperfect and immature *aborsus* with sin, as it were, consuming half, as it says, of its flesh.[108]

Like all Carolingian biblical scholars, Rabanus drew heavily on patristic and earlier Carolingian sources. Rabanus and his peers have often been cursorily treated as derivative and unoriginal. Certainly, much of the *abortivus* imagery in his oeuvre is familiar because it was a significant conduit for the broader percolation of late antique ideas to Carolingian audiences. The avaricious man was no better off than an *abortivus* because 'both will be seized away in the same end': death in this world and divine judgment in the world to come.[109] Paul was like an *abortivus* because he was 'dead to the synagogue', which had 'born him badly conceived and imperfect'.[110] But Rabanus's works clearly filled a pedagogical need among the Carolingian clergy, laity and even royalty. Commentaries by Rabanus and others skilfully combined ideas from multiple sources and broadcast their images to an audience broader than a cadre of biblical experts.[111]

A case in point is Rabanus's popular encyclopaedia, *De rerum naturis*, which laced together natural history and folk etymology with theological and scriptural reflections. Where Rabanus addressed human physiology, the result was a theology of the body. Of particular interest is Rabanus's explanation for *vulva*, which followed his explanation of *matrix*, the womb, 'that

[108] 'ne fiat simile morte, et ut aborsus ejectus de vulva matris. Et comedit dimidium carnis ejus. Vult in hoc ostendere, quia populus ille formatus in vulva quidem fuerit suae matris synagogae, non tamen pervenire potuerit ad effectum et integrum partum; sicut enim aborsus imperfectus et incompositus est partus, ita et ille populus aliquanto quidem tempore intra vulvam matris, hoc est, intra synagogae institutionem positus est; sed peccatis intercedentibus formari ad integrum, vivificarique non potuit. Et ideo abjecti sunt velut aborsus imperfectus et immaturus, peccato scilicet consumente dimidium, ut ait, carnis ejus', *Enarrationes in librum Numerorum* 2.9, PL 108, col. 665D; cf. Coon, 'Priestly Bodies', on the flesh-and-blood physicality of metaphors of priestly *semen* in Rabanus's exegesis.

[109] 'tamen ambo aequali fine rapientur', *Commentaria in Ecclesiasticum* 3.9, PL 109, col. 856B; cf. Alcuin, *Commentaria super Ecclesiasten*, PL 100, cols. 692A–B.

[110] 'est synagogae mortuus ... eum male conceptum imperfectumque peperit', *Homilia in evangelia et epistolas* 140, PL 110, col. 416A, with a comparable idea in his *Enarrationes in epistolas B. Pauli*, PL 111, col. 1529D; cf. Smaragdus, *Collectiones*, quoted above in n.95.

[111] The previous quotation, for example, is taken from a homiliary which Rabanus produced c. 854/5 at the request of Lothar I. Rabanus's accompanying letters, *Ep.* 50–1, MGH Epp. 5, pp. 504–6, expressed his hope that the readings would benefit both Lothar and his people; cf. Barré, *Les homéliares*, pp. 13–17; M. Pollheimer, 'Hrabanus Maurus – The Compiler, the Preacher, and his Audience', in *Sermo Doctorum*, pp. 203–28.

in which the fetus is generated: for the received seed warms up; warmed up it forms a body; embodied it divides into limbs'.[112] The *vulva* was the gateway to the *matrix*. It was 'so-called, like a *valva*, that is the door of the belly, which receives semen or from which the fetus comes out'. This was lifted verbatim from one of Rabanus's important sources, Isidore's *Etymologiae*.[113] But Rabanus went well beyond Isidore. *Vulva* meant much more. It signified inner secrets, the doorway to God's hidden knowledge. Moreover, there were souls within the *vulva*, where good and bad were conceived. Finally, the *vulva* was also the 'inner faith of the church, from which depraved heretics bring on the mother's abortion, as is said about them in the psalms: Sinners are alienated from the *vulva*, they have wandered from the womb, they have spoken falsehoods.'[114]

Rabanus's most extensive engagement with scriptural abortion took the form of interpretations of Mosaic law on abortion by assault. Combining portions from Augustine and the Latin Origen with his own reflections, Rabanus's commentary on Exodus 21. 22–5 expanded at considerable length on what such spiritual interpretation looked like.[115] Rabanus began with the Vulgate text, that is, the Latin text without the formed/unformed distinction. This was pure Rabanus, for Augustine and Origen had commented on Vetus Latina or Septuagint versions of the passage which contained the unformed/ formed distinction. Though Rabanus was primarily interested in the spiritual meanings, he first had to establish the literal meaning. 'Here, so it seems to me, the meaning is as follows', he began.[116] If someone struck a woman 'after conceiving the seed, and through this he has caused an abortion while she still lives', he would have to pay monetary compensation according to what was demanded and the judges decreed. If the woman also died, then he would

---

[112] 'Matrix dicitur quod foetus in eo generetur: semen enim receptum confovet, confotum corporat, corporatum in membra distinguit', *De rerum naturis* 6.1, PL 111, col. 173C. On the background to this work, see W. Schipper, 'The Earliest Manuscripts of Rabanus Maurus' *De Rerum Naturis*', in *Pre-modern Encylopaedic Texts: Proceedings of the Second Comers Congress, Groningen, 1–4 July 1996*, ed. P. Binkley (Leiden, 1997), pp. 363–5.

[113] 'Vulva vocata, quasi valva, id est, janua ventris: vel quod semen recipit: vel quod ex ea foetus procedat', *De rerum naturis* 6.1, col. 173C; cf. Isidore, *Etymologiae* 11.1.136–7.

[114] 'Est et vulva Ecclesiae fides interior a qua haeretici depravati aborsum matris intulerunt, sicut in psalmo de eisdem dicitur: Alienati sunt peccatores a vulva, erraverunt ab utero, locuti sunt falsa', *De rerum naturis* 6.1, col. 173D; the quotation is from Psalm 58. 3.

[115] Rabanus's two key sources were Augustine, *Quaestiones in Heptateuchum* 2.80, ed. I. Fraipont, *Quaestiones in Heptateuchum libri VII* (etc.), CCSL 33 (Turnhout, 1958), pp. 110–12, and Rufinus's Latin version of Origen, *Homilia in Exodum* 10, PG 12, cols. 369B–74C. No Greek fragments of *Homilia* 10 have survived.

[116] 'Hic, ut mihi videtur, talis est sensus', *Commentaria in Exodum* 3.1, PL 108, col. 112D.

be punished, 'in this case now guilty of homicide'.[117] Rabanus now shifted to his primary interest: reading spiritually (*mystice*). In its deeper meaning, the Exodus text distinguished between different kinds of spiritual harm. On the one hand, a person who 'through neglect or deceit has harmed someone's soul after the seed of the word has been conceived', for which the spiritual assailant, *percussor*, would have to undergo penance.[118] On the other hand, the *seductor* of a 'soul killed through error, after an abortion has been produced, that is, a fatal act', would be 'condemned to eternal death, like a true murderer'.[119]

'But it should be noted,' Rabanus continued, 'that another edition has it thus', before quoting the Vetus Latina version.[120] The spiritual interpretation of this version, including its formed/unformed distinction, drew heavily on the Latin Origen.[121] Again, the law imparted lessons for those in positions of teaching authority within the church. The two men fighting stood for those who 'quarrel about dogmas or teachings of the law' and thereby scandalized (literally, caused to stumble) souls at different stages of spiritual formation.[122] The unformed infant stood for those who had recently conceived the word of God. They were liable for a penalty (*damnum*) 'when [such a] soul is made to stumble through [their] strife, in such a way that it throws out and loses the word of faith, which it had scarcely conceived, not yet formed'.[123] In the case of the formed infant, the repercussions were even graver:

> The formed infant can be seen as the word of God in the heart of that soul which has followed the grace of baptism, or [which] has conceived the word of faith more manifestly and clearly. Therefore if this soul has been struck by the strife of teachers, has thrown out the word and has been found to be among those about whom the Apostle said, 'For already some have turned away after Satan' [1 Tim. 15], he [i.e. the offender] will give a soul for a soul, either he ought to be received on judgment day in front of the judge who can destroy soul and body in hell; or it certainly could be applied to he who aware that he has been such a great scandal, places his own soul in the place

---

[117] 'post conceptum semen, pro hoc abortivum quidem fecerit ... tunc jam homicidii reus', ibid.
[118] 'quis alicujus animam post conceptum semen verbi, per incuriam vel fraudem laeserit', ibid.
[119] 'anima per errorem necata, post prolatum abortivum, hoc est opus mortiferum ... seductor illius, quasi verus homicida, aeterna morte reus erit', *Commentaria in Exodum* 3.1, col. 113A.
[120] 'Notandum autem quod alia editio sic habet', ibid.
[121] Origen (Rufinus), *Homilia in Exodum* 10.4, cols. 373A–74C; cf. Koskenniemi, 'Right to Life', pp. 64–5.
[122] 'duo disputantes sunt de dogmatibus vel quaestionibus legis', *Commentaria in Exodum* 3.1, col. 113C.
[123] 'Haec ... anima cum per contentionem aliquorum scandalizabitur, ita ut verbum fidei quod tenuiter conceperat, abjiciat et perdat nondum formatum', *Commentaria in Exodum* 3.1, col. 113D.

of the soul of the person whom he has scandalized; and continually to death makes efforts over how he may give back, repair and restore [that soul] to faith.[124]

The remainder of Rabanus's explanation showed how the different bodily parts mentioned in the *Lex talionis* in Exodus 21. 24–5, an eye for an eye, a tooth for a tooth, and so on, corresponded to different forms of spiritual harm wrought by bad teachers.

Although it borrowed heavily from Origen, woven into Rabanus's exegesis was an important thread of thought about the literal meaning of the law. In the case of the Vetus Latina text and its formed/unformed distinction, he did this by selectively quoting from Augustine. 'Here,' he explained, 'a question about the soul is typically thrown up, whether what is not formed can be understood as not [having] a soul; and indeed [whether] it is not murder because it cannot be said to be animated if it did not have a soul up to this point'.[125] Following Augustine, if we have to forgive our debtors just as we wish to be forgiven by others (Matt 6. 12), we need to know what it is we are forgiving: 'Thus the law did not want an unformed child to pertain to murder, because a soul cannot yet be said to be alive in a body which lacks sensation, if such [a body] has not yet been formed and thus has not yet been endowed with sensations'.[126]

Rabanus, like Augustine, can easily be misunderstood here. The point was above all epistemological. The law made the distinction because it was uncertain ('it cannot be said') whether the unformed infant has a living soul. Admittedly, Rabanus's selectivity has slightly diluted the epistemological uncertainty found in Augustine's reading of Exodus, for Rabanus trimmed away something Augustine had said about the unformed child (*informe puerperium*) which raised the possibility that formation was not identical with animation: 'but up to now animated in an unformed way since the great question about the soul ought not to be rushed along in the temerity of fragmented

---

[124] 'Formatus infans potest videri sermo Dei in corde ejus animae quae gratiam baptismi consecuta est, vel evidentius et clarius, verbum fidei concepit. Haec ergo si anima, contentione doctorum percussa, abjecerit verbum et inventa fuerit esse de illis de quibus dicebat Apostolus: Jam enim quaedam conversae sunt retro post Satanam, animam pro anima dabit, vel in die judicii accipiendum est, apud eum judicem, qui potest animam et corpus perdere in gehenna; vel certe potest fortassis etiam illud aptari, ut qui sibi conscius tanti scandali fuerit, ponat animam suam pro anima illius, quem scandalizaverit; et usque ad mortem det operam, quomodo redeat, quomodo reparetur, quomodo restituatur ad fidem', *Commentaria in Exodum*, cols. 114A–B. The passage continued by explaining Exodus 21. 24–5, an eye for an eye, a tooth for a tooth, etc.

[125] 'Hic de anima quaestio solet agitari, utrum quod formatum non est, ne anima quidem possit intelligi; et ideo non sit homicidium, quia non exanimatum dici potest, si adhuc animam non habebat', *Commentaria in Exodum* 3.1, cols. 113A–B.

[126] 'Ideo ergo informe puerperium lex noluit ad homicidium pertinere, quia nondum dici potest anima viva in eo corpore quod sensu caret, si talis est in carne nondum formata, et ideo nondum sensibus praedita', ibid., col. 113C.

thought'.[127] Not all of Augustine's readers have followed his advice that this was a question which demanded slow, rather than hasty, thought.[128] But, despite not quoting Augustine on this point, Rabanus's adaptation of Origen on the spiritual meaning of the Vetus Latina text did indirectly recognize the epistemological point when it distinguished between figuratively giving a soul for a soul (*anima pro anima*) and a penalty for a soul (*damnum pro anima*): in other words, there was a soul at stake in both permutations.[129]

No one writing the history of abortion appears to have found Rabanus's biblical commentaries to be of any interest. But Rabanus's interpretations of Exodus carry more than one implication for those who have been inclined either to maximize or minimize the significance of concepts of formation and animation within church tradition on abortion. Simply filling the silences in ecclesiastical legislation with Rabanus's (or Augustine's) interpretations of the literal meaning of Exodus 21. 22–3 may be as misleading as filling them with ideas from eschatological speculation. Centuries earlier, thinkers had used Mosaic law as a springboard for commenting on the ethics of abortion and infant exposure, though the clearest example was a Jewish writer.[130] The authority of scripture notwithstanding, there is only limited evidence to suggest that early medieval churchmen actually drew upon Mosaic law on accidental abortion for ecclesiastical regulations. Moreover, in its literal meaning, the Mosaic law spoke more directly to scenarios addressed in secular law-codes than to voluntary abortions addressed in ecclesiastical texts.[131]

[127] 'Si ergo illud informe puerperium iam quidem fuerat, *sed adhuc quodam modo informiter animatum* – *quoniam magna de anima quaestio non est praecipitanda indiscussae temeritate sententiae*', Augustine, *Quaestiones in Heptateuchum* 2.80, p. 111 (my italics). The common reading is that Augustine effectively treated formation and animation as synonymous; cf. Elsakkers, 'Vocabulary', p. 385. But the (as it were) articulately inarticulate expression – *quodammodo informiter animatum* – points in the opposite direction; or, at least, that Augustine took seriously the possibility that animation and formation were not the same thing.

[128] For example, Dombrowski and Deltete, *Defense of Abortion*, p. 24, trim off the previous quotation when they quote *Quaestiones in Heptateuchum* and summarize it rather hastily ('the question of homicide is not even pertinent with respect to the unformed fetus'); additionally, they mistakenly imply that the passage is about voluntary abortion ('the pregnant woman who has an abortion is *not* to be accused of murder', italics in original). As with his eschatological speculation, Augustine's thought here is distorted if readers ignore his uncertainty (and his actual words). Incidentally, the quotation is also trimmed off from citations of *Quaestiones in Heptateuchum* in Tasioulas, 'Heaven and Earth', 39, and Elsakkers, 'Vocabulary of Abortion', p. 385.

[129] Respectively, *Commentaria in Exodum* 3.1, cols. 114A, 113D.

[130] See Koskinniemi, *Exposure*, pp. 30–4, on Philo.

[131] Affinities between the Vetus Latina version of Exodus and Visigothic *antiquae* on abortion remain the strongest evidence for scripture informing legislation; see pp. 113–17 above. Incidentally, one of the few prescriptive texts to cite Exodus on abortion quoted the Vulgate version: Benedictus Levita, *Capitularia* 6.12–13, MGH LL 2.2, p. 75. Hincmar quoted the Vetus Latina text in *De divortio*, but in order to clarify

A further caveat is that while the Vulgate did not simply supersede Vetus Latina texts of the Bible, progressively fewer churchmen encountered the Vetus Latina version of Exodus over the course of the Early Middle Ages, especially after the turn of the ninth century.[132]

On the other hand, however, to regard the complicating question of fetal formation as somehow outside church tradition is to fail to understand that tradition as it appeared to Rabanus and his contemporaries. Measures which graduated penance according to fetal development were conspicuously absent in Rabanus's penitentials, though we have already seen reasons for not reading their absence as a deliberate avoidance to purge ecclesiastical law of penitential improvisations.[133] Rabanus's commentary on Exodus makes clear that such distinctions were perfectly intelligible to him. Moreover, they had a scriptural basis and a history of patristic attention.[134]

In sum, readers could certainly discern in Exodus concepts for negotiating abortion. The extent to which they actually did must necessarily be guessed at. If attempted reconstructions of Augustine's ideas about abortion are a good guide, one suspects that the temptation of overstatement outweighs the temptation of understatement. When read closely, Rabanus's interpretation did not see in Exodus a definitive or binding theory for knowing precisely when human life begins and, thus, when abortion was and was not the taking of a life. What he did see, as he explained in *De rerum naturis*, was a moral lesson for those in positions of teaching authority within the church.

> Pregnant souls of the faithful recently conceive the word of God and do not yet give birth in works: as it is said in Exodus for teachers of controversy: if two men are fighting, and [one] has struck a pregnant woman, and she has an abortion; that is, has lost the word of faith.[135]

For Rabanus, the real lesson of Exodus on abortion was the care of souls.

* * *

whether or not Theutberga had really had an abortion, not to assess the morality of abortion.

[132] The most significant exception for our purposes is Hincmar's citation of the Vetus Latina version, *De divortio, interrogatio* 12, p. 182. On the history of the Vulgate and Vetus Latina texts in the Early Middle Ages, see R. Loewe, 'The Medieval History of the Latin Vulgate', in *The Cambridge History of the Bible: The West from the Fathers to the Reformation*, ed. G. W. H. Lampe (Cambridge, 1969), pp. 102–42; F. van Liere, *An Introduction to the Medieval Bible* (Cambridge, 2014), pp. 80–95.

[133] See pp. 177–80 above.

[134] It is telling that none of the theologians mentioned in chapter five, who have claimed Rabanus's penitentials as a return to authentic church tradition, refer to his *Commentaria in Exodum*.

[135] 'Praegnantes animae fidelium verbum Dei nuper concipientes et necdum in opera parturientes: sicut in Exodo pro contentionis doctoribus dicitur: Si duo viri rixantes, et percusserit quis mulierem praegnantem, et abortivum fecerit; id est, fidei verbum perdiderit', *De rerum naturis* 7.1, col. 181D.

Like pastoral and legal thought on abortion, eschatological speculation on the fate of the *abortivi* had to contend with the ambiguities of life and death in the womb. What made these areas of thought and practice conceptually challenging also made the *abortivus* a powerful if protean symbol. Depending on interpretative contexts, different authors amplified different connotations of the *abortivus*: imperfect formation, obscure concealment, uterine expulsion, untimely birth and premature death.

The texts examined in this chapter represent accumulated fragments of thought rather than a fully-fledged discourse on *abortivi*. Nonetheless, three broad conclusions emerge. First, the cumulative effect of reading these texts strengthens the impression that there was not total uniformity to the contexts and intellectual resources with which early medieval churchmen visualized, represented and imagined life and death in the womb – or, indeed, to the conclusions which they drew.[136] Embryological fragments floating around in early medieval texts provide deceptively reassuring numerical figures. Isidore's *Etymologiae* – and, following him, Rabanus's *De rerum naturis* – circulated the idea that the fetus was formed by the fortieth day, an idea also found in Theodorean penitentials. It is easy to miss that the figure was surrounded by different theories and expressed in what we might call a 'so-they-say' tone. The heart, the seat of life and wisdom, was formed first, some people said, and 'then the whole work is filled out by the fortieth day, which has been gathered, they say, from abortions'. But others, Isidore quickly added, said that the fetus started from the head down.[137] When Hincmar, who knew Isidore's work, tried to make sense of the terrible accusations lodged against Theutberga, he imagined how 'Joseph began to hesitate, because he saw the swelling womb of his spouse'.[138] The gendering of reproductive knowledge was complicated by religious status. As a bishop, Hincmar professed ignorance over women's secrets and was tempted to outsource the investigative task to married laymen.[139] Paschasius Radbertus went even further by questioning female reproductive knowledge when he wrote, 'each of us hitherto closed in a mother's womb receives a soul secretly as it were, so that there may for some time be a *man in a living soul* [Gen. 2. 7] in such a way that a mother does not know when life enters in him through her before it departs'. Certainly, Carolingian theologians were not afraid of uncertainty on such questions.[140] Symbolic

---

[136] On what van der Lugt has called 'la faiblesse d'une unicité des théories de la génération' later in the Middle Ages, see *Le ver*, pp. 31–93.

[137] 'deinde quadragesimo die totum opus expleri; quod ex abortionibus, ut ferunt, collecta sunt', *Etymologiae* 9.1.143; cf. Rabanus, *De rerum naturis* 6.1, col. 174C.

[138] 'Ioseph hesitare coepit, quia tumentem sponse suae uterum vidit', *De divortio* (responsio 12), p. 181.

[139] *De divortio* (responsio 12), p. 182.

[140] 'unusquisque nostrum utero matris adhuc clausus accipiat licet occulte animam, ut sit *homo in animam viventem* ita interdum, ut mater nesciat quando per eam in illo priusquam exeat vita ingrediatur', Paschasius Radbertus, *De corpore et sanguine*

representations of the *abortivus* flourished because of the same uncertainty on which eschatological speculation sometimes floundered.

But if thinking about the *abortivi* was to think in the darkness of the womb, there was, second, a kind of doctrinal clarity about what would ultimately happen to *abortivi* who never saw the light of day. In both eschatology and exegesis the eternal perdition awaiting *abortivi* and unbaptized infants was taken for granted. Here, fragments of thought on *abortivi*, together with other texts like the *Lex Baiwariorum*, brought out mental associations which were latent in penitential rulings. Death and divine judgment awaited the avaricious man and the *abortivus* alike.[141] We ought to tread carefully. It is not uncommonly assumed that original sin cast a dark shadow over moral perspectives on abortion to the extent that 'abortion came to be considered *worse* than murder'.[142] But this is underdetermined by the evidence, certainly for the Early Middle Ages. This is not to deny the social afterlife of religious doctrine in the *longue durée*, the haunting of individuals and communities by the memories of the unbaptized, which is hard to discern for the Early Middle Ages but becomes increasingly visible in burial practices and folkloric traditions right through to modernity.[143] Strikingly, however, while connections between baptism and the murder or death of infants were made, no surviving early medieval text explicitly drew the conclusion that abortion was '*worse* than murder'.

In contemporary pro-life thought and practice, aborted fetuses have become the 'holy innocents' of modernity.[144] The idea of infant martyrs was not alien to early medieval Christianity. Liturgical and theological traditions commemorated the holy innocents slaughtered by Herod as martyrs who attained

---

Domini 3.50–4, ed. B. Paul, CCCM 16 (Turnhout, 1969), p. 25 (my italics). On Carolingian uncertainty over the origin of the soul, see P. Boucaud, '*Factus est homo in animam viventem*: Anthropologie chrétienne dans l'exégèse de Claude de Turin († ca. 827/828)', in *The Multiple Meaning of Scripture: The Role of Exegesis in Early Christian and Medieval Culture*, ed. I. Van 't Spijker (Leiden, 2009), pp. 125–51.

[141] Alcuin, *Commentaria super Ecclesiasten*, cols. 691D–2B.

[142] Feldman, *Birth Control in Jewish Law*, pp. 269–70 (italics in original), after citing Fulgentius, *De Fide* 70 on unbaptized infants (quoted above at p. 271) and before moving on to baptismal syringes used by some early modern doctors over a millennium later. Readers of Fulgentius through Feldman have gone one step further, if the Wikipedia entry for 'History of abortion law debate' is anything to go by: 'St. Fulgentius opposed abortion even for the purpose of saving the woman's life'. The misleading idea that Christian opposition to abortion ultimately originated in the theology of original sin has a long history: see, for example, Lecky, *History of European Morals*, II, pp. 22–3.

[143] See A. O'Connor, *The Blessed and the Damned: Sinful Women and Unbaptised Children in Irish Folklore* (Bern, 2005), which, despite its title, contains relevant material on burial and folkloric practices outside Ireland; cf. J.-C. Schmitt, *Ghosts in the Middle Ages: The Living and the Dead*, trans. T. L. Fagan (Chicago, 1998), p. 145.

[144] P. Jobert, 'Holy Innocents in our Times', in *Abortion and Martyrdom: The Papers of the Solesme Consultation and an Appeal to the Catholic Church*, ed. A. Nichols (Leominster, 2002), pp. 120–5.

salvation despite not being baptized.[145] But, there is little to suggest that this tradition embraced the minority of *abortivi* deliberately expelled from the womb. The most revealing thing, finally, about the early medieval *abortivus* was that it was not naturally regarded as an innocent victim of misfortune or misdeed. What made Tarra's self-image as an abortion flung from the monastic womb so exceptional was his emphasis on innocence.[146] The image was an anomaly within a mental universe in which the *abortivus* could symbolize heretics and sinners. This symbolic possibility defies modern expectations of what a religious culture antipathetic to abortion looks like. Far from being a paragon of innocence, the early medieval *abortivus* was a symbol of alienation.

---

[145] P. A. Hayward, 'Suffering and Innocence in Latin Sermons for the Feast of the Holy Innocents', in *Church and Childhood*, ed. Wood, pp. 67–80; see too P. H. Wasyliw, *Martyrdom, Murder, and Magic: Child Saints and Their Cults in Medieval Europe* (New York, 2008).

[146] The only other comparable example which I have come across appears in a twelfth-century *vita* of Thomas Becket, which reimagined the physical location of his murder as the womb of the church: the 'sons killed the father in the womb of their mother [*Occiderunt filii patrem in utero matris suae*]', William FitzStephen, *Vita Thomae* 143, ed. J. C. Robertson, *Materials for the History of Thomas Becket, Archbishop of Canterbury, Volume III* (London, 1877), p. 143; cf. D. Baraz, *Medieval Cruelty: Changing Perceptions, Late Antiquity to the Early Modern Period* (Ithaca NY, 2003), p. 83.

Afterword

Most of the stories people told about abortion in the Early Middle Ages are hidden. We have whispers of only a few like the unpleasant story with which Theutberga was slandered. In the eighth century, an author took it upon himself to retell the life of Germanus in an abridged form; the *Vita Germani brevior* runs to just a few pages. The author had abbreviated the life so that he could 'now relate what the story teaches so truly'.[1] The first lesson in this distilled life of Germanus nevertheless remained the saint's miraculous survival in the womb:

> The land of Autun earned the increase of his birth; a native within its boundaries, his father Eleutherius and also his mother Eusebia were descended from a noble and distinguished line. So when the mother had felt him in the womb not much time after the birth of a previous son, she wanted to extinguish inside her he whom Christ was calling to himself as a soldier to heaven; and after she received a drink, she sipped poisons mixed with swallowed wine. In the mouth of death the mother drank what she knew to be abortive, aiming to inflict danger. Behold! The bundle did not know the suffering of being thrown out. The extraordinary boy felt the pain in his mother's flesh more than he had feared the risk to his life. The mother, whom the punishment for parricide had encircled, was snatched away from her crime. Let the wondrous and clear sign be obvious to all, that blessed Germanus was known as a miracle worker before he reached the light from his mother's womb![2]

---

[1] 'quod verius historia edocet ad presens loquamur', *Vita Germani brevior* 1, MGH SRM 7, p. 419; on the eighth-century dating, see Bruno Krusch's comments at p. 367.

[2] 'Huius nativitatis augmentum arva Augustedunensis promeruit, cuius in terminis genitor eius Eleotherius indigena simulque et mater ipsius Eusebia nobili honestoque genere degebantur. Hunc igitur cum post partum filii prioris non multum post tempore in utero mater sensisset, cupiebat introrsus extinguere, quem sibi Christus ut militem ad superna evocabat, acceptoque poculo, venena mixta cum mero austo libavit. Ore bibens mortis conscia mater abortiva, quaerens nocendi causam periculi. En! foris eiectum nesciret sarcina damnum: magis namque sensit materna caro dolorem, quam puer aegregius timuisset pericula vitae ... Eripitur mater a crimine, quem noxa vincxerat parricidae. Mirum videlicet atque perspicuum cunctis pateat sacramentum, beatum Germanum ante virtutum fateri artificem, quam ex matris utero ad hoc lumine perveniret!', *Vita Germani brevior* 1, p. 419.

Afterword

We have heard it all before. By this third telling, I can no longer surprise my reader. But one lesson which the story 'teaches so truly' is to resist the numbness of repetition. Reams of repetitive texts addressing abortion recirculated across the Early Middle Ages. As this book has traced, they were reread with new eyes, reinvigorated with new meanings and revised in what Regino of Prüm had called 'these, our perilous times'.[3]

But Germanus's story and its reincarnations are exceptions. The very practice of marshalling tradition on abortion had inclined Regino to ask difficult questions about it. As he wondered whether the heavy weight of church tradition created the very sins it was meant to curb, it is hard to avoid thinking that he recalled the marble bowl at Prüm and the story of its old resting place in Trier where it had once cradled tiny infants whose parents did not want to be known. Maybe he also remembered the struggles of men and women on the estates of the monastery he had once led. When authors like Regino looked around them, they saw societies in which abortion was conceivable, but we have only the merest whispers of the stories which made abortion conceivable to them.

* * *

The sins and crimes of women and men – what people really did – are also hidden. Scholars can create long lists of possible motives and possible means painstakingly assembled from the voices of those who condemned them.[4] But the truth is that we still have to imagine actively their sins and crimes, the blows landed upon pregnant women desperate to keep their children and the poisons mixed with wine sipped by other women desperate to lose theirs.

We must take care with our imaginations.[5] One imagined space where abortion took place is the world of *secreta mulierum*. In a later eighth-century edict, a Beneventan duke, Arechis II, claimed to have an insight into this world. 'Released from marital control,' he complained in an edict, women whose husbands had died were 'enjoying the freedom of their own authority licentiously'.[6] They secretly took up nuns' habits to avoid falling back under marital authority but their habits concealed the most sordid sins. The 'kindlings of the flesh burn them, so much that they are secretly spread beneath the prostitutions of not just one ... but of many; and unless the womb has swollen up, it is not easily proven'.[7]

We must avoid joining the ranks of Arechis who imagined that women were, as it were, out of control. Early medieval women exercised agency

---

[3] See p. 205 above.
[4] See the helpful summary in Elsakkers, RBL, pp. 469–93.
[5] Green, 'Gendering', especially 503–7, is a model for emulation.
[6] 'maritalis dominaturae solutae, licentius proprii arbitrii libertatem fruuntur', *Capitula* 1.12, MGH Fontes iuris 2, p. 174.
[7] 'exurunt eas carnis incentiba, adeo ut non solum unius ... plurimorum prostitutionibus clanculo substernantur; et nisi uterus intumuerit, non facile comprobatur', ibid.

within a space tightly circumscribed by powerful social and cultural forces. The church, including its teachings on abortion and the causes of abortion, was one force. It is conspicuous to us because it has countless spokesmen in the historical record. But there were other, less clearly documented forces of family honour and social reputation. These forces collided spectacularly in the story of Ota's unwanted pregnancy in the *Vita Haimhrammi*.[8] Ota's father tried to cut open his daughter's belly after she told him, on Emmeram's advice, that the bishop had fathered her child. When imagining the experiences of women, like Ota, faced with unwanted pregnancies, we must also imagine the powerful but conflicting social forces through which pregnancies could become unwanted by individuals, families and communities. Women bore the brunt of these forces but men were subject to them too. Emmeram had been approached not only by Ota, but also by the young father of her child. The bishop had effectively saved the boy's life (tellingly, saving Ota's was out of his control). Alongside a pervasive tendency across early medieval texts to associate abortion with female sexual sin lies a counter-strain embodied in inconspicuous gender switches in some texts: *quae* becomes *quis*, and so on. If this corpus of material really does bear the imprint, albeit distorted, of abortion as it was practised in early medieval societies, then do we need to imagine some sort of place for men within the world of *secreta mulierum*?

* * *

'If out of the seed of a tree something can be produced which cannot [yet] be seen, why is it different with the dust of human flesh that is not seen, out of which form can be retrieved?'[9] This question is taken from a sermon which appears in an early ninth century sermonary designed for pastoral practice in Bavaria.[10] The sermon continued a few lines later:

> Certainly you, the human who says these things, you were once the froth of blood in your mother's womb; then out of father's seed and mother's blood you were a small liquid ball. Say, I ask, if you know how the humour of seed hardened into bones, how liquid remained in marrow, how it solidified in muscles, how it grew into flesh, how it stretched into skin, how it separated in hairs and nails ... Grant to the power of your creator what you cannot

---

[8] See pp. 235–6 above.
[9] 'Si ergo ex semine arboris produci potest quod videri non potest, cur de pulvere carnis humanae diffiditur, quod ex eo reparari forma valeat, que non videtur?', *Sermo Augustini de resurrectione* (= *Sermo* 81, Salzburg Sermonary), ed. A. Wilmart, 'Un sermon sur la résurrection corporelle emprunté à S. Grégoire passé sous le nom de S. Augustin', *Revue Bénédictine* 47 (1935), 5.
[10] The sermon was not, in fact, Augustinian, though large parts of were adapted from a homily by Gregory the Great, *Homilia in Ezechielem* 2.8.7–8, PL 76, cols. 1032A–3B. On the sermonary in which it appeared, see J. C. McCune, 'An Edition and Study of Select Sermons from the Carolingian Sermonary of Salzburg' (unpublished Ph.D. dissertation, University of London, 2006), with pp. 209–11 on the sermon.

Afterword

understand by reason, so that he who can make you out of nothing can revive you out of dust.[11]

Unlike Braulio of Saragossa, who had struggled to see the inanimate fetus as anything more than disgusting blood or semen, this sermon traced each human back to the froth of blood in the womb. Like Braulio, however, the sermon was not addressing abortion.[12] The argument that life began at (or before?) conception was designed to deflect doubtful questions about resurrected bodies. If God was able to transform us within the womb from a fleck of nothingness into a unified body, then he had the power to resurrect us in the world to come. This book has traced an intricate pattern of different perspectives on abortion. Explicit debates are largely hidden from view. Were the contrasting ideas expressed by the sermon and by Braulio the kinds of arguments advanced in such debates or are we turning fragments of thought into a discourse? This is a sobering question which emphasizes how much of the thought-worlds of our authors remains hidden.

There is an even more sobering question. What about the audience of the sermon? In ninth-century Bavaria they did not speak the language in which the sermon was written. How would a preacher have translated ideas about the froth of blood and power to create *ex nihilo*? Did his audience speak the same conceptual language? What ordinary men and women *thought* about abortion and about churchmen's ideas on abortion is a deeply hidden history. How did they react to preachers who warned them against aborting their children and threatened that, if they did, then they too would be alienated from the womb of the church? Gregory the Great was right. Much of the past is like a concealed *abortivus* which has perished in the darkness of the womb, for 'while we know about a certain few through ... writings, the large part of humankind is hidden from us'.

---

[11] 'Certe tu, homo qui haec loqueris, aliquando in matris utero sanguinis spuma fuisti; ibi quippe ex semine patris et matris sanguine parvus ac liquidus globus eras. Dic rogo, si nosti, qualiter ille humor seminis in ossibus duruit, qualiter in medullis liquidus remansit, qualiter in nervis solidatus est, qualiter in carne concrevit, qualiter in cute extensus est, qualiter in capillis atque unguibus distinctus ... Da potentiae creatoris tui quod ratione comprehendere non vales, ut ipse te possit resuscitare ex pulvere, qui te potuit ex nihilo facere', *Sermo Augustini de resurrectione*, 6.

[12] See pp. 273–7 above on Braulio.

BIBLIOGRAPHY

Primary sources

Abbo of St-Germain, *Bella Parisiacae urbis*, ed. P. de Winterfeld, MGH Poetae 4.1 (Berlin, 1899), pp. 72–122
  English translation: A. Adams and A. G. Rigg, 'A Verse Translation of Abbo of St. Germain's *Bella Parisiacae urbis*', *Journal of Medieval Latin* 14 (2004), 1–68
Acta Andreae, ed. and trans. J.-M. Prieur, *Acta Andreae*, CCSA 5–6 (Turnhout, 1989)
The Acts of Andrew and the Acts of Andrew and Matthias in the City of the Cannibals, ed. and trans. D. R. MacDonald, (Atlanta, 1990)
Ad epistolas variorum supplementum, ed. E. Dümmler, MGH Epp. 5 (Berlin, 1899), pp. 615–40
Ado of Vienne, *Chronicon*, ed. G. H. Pertz, MGH SS 2 (Hannover, 1829), pp. 315–23
Alcuin, *Commentaria super Ecclesiasten*, PL 100, cols. 665–722
—— *Interrogationes et responsiones in Genesim*, PL 100, cols. 515–70
—— *Vita Willibrordi*, ed. W. Levison, MGH SRM 7 (Hannover/Leipzig, 1920), pp. 81–141
Altfrid, *Vita Liudgeri*, ed. G. H. Pertz, MGH SS 2 (Hannover, 1829), pp. 403–19
Ambrose, *Hexameron*, ed. C. Schenkl, *Sancti Ambrosii opera, pars prima*, CSEL 32.1 (Vienna, 1896), pp. 1–261
Ambrosiaster, *Ad Galatas*, ed. H. J. Vogels, *Ambrosiastri qui dicitur Commentarius in epistulas Paulinas*, CSEL 81.3 (Vienna, 1969), pp. 1–68
Annales Bertiniani, ed. F. Grat et al., *Annales de Saint-Bertin* (Paris, 1964) English translation: J. L. Nelson, *The Annals of St. Bertin* (Manchester, 1991)
Annales Fuldenses, trans. T. Reuter, *The Annals of Fulda* (Manchester, 1992)
Annales Laubacenses (pars secunda a. 796–885), ed. G. H. Pertz, MGH SS 1 (Hannover, 1826), p. 15
Annales Lobienses, ed. G. Waitz, MGH SS 13 (Hannover, 1881), pp. 224–35
Annales Xantenses, ed. B. de Simson, MGH SRG 12 (Hannover/Leipzig, 1909), pp. 1–39
Ansegisus, *Collectio capitularium*, ed. G. Schmitz, MGH Capit., n.s., 1 (Hannover, 1996)
Apocalypse of Peter, ed. and trans. D. D. Buchholz, *Your Eyes Will Be Opened: A Study of the Greek (Ethiopic) Apocalypse of Peter* (Atlanta, 1988)
The Apocryphal New Testament: A Collection of Apocryphal Christian Literature in an English Translation, trans. J. K. Elliott (Oxford, 1993)
Apophthegmata Patrum, trans. B. Ward, *The Sayings of the Desert Fathers: The Alphabetical Collection* (London, 1975)

Bibliography

Arbeo, *Vita Haimhrammi*, ed. B. Krusch, MGH SRG 13 (Hannover, 1920), pp. 1–99
Athenagoras, *Legatio*, ed. and trans. W. R. Schoedel, *Athenagoras: Legatio and De Resurrectione* (Oxford, 1972)
Augustine, *Contra Faustum*, PL 42, cols. 207–518
—— *De bono coniugali*, ed. and trans. M. Walsh, *Augustine: De bono coniugali, De sancta virginitate* (Oxford, 2001)
—— *De civitate dei*, ed. B. Dombart and A. Kalb, *Augustinus, De civitate dei*, CCSL 47–8 (Turnhout, 1955)
—— *De diversis quaestionibus octoginta tribus*, PL 40, cols. 11–147
—— *De nuptiis et concupiscentia*, ed. C. F. Vrba and J. Zycha, *Sancti Aureli Augustini (sect. VIII, pars II)*, CSEL 42 (Vienna, 1902), pp. 207–319
—— *Enchiridion*, ed. M. Evans, *Augustinus, De fide rerum invisibilium; Enchiridion ad Laurentium de fide et spe et caritate* (etc.), CCSL 46 (Turnhout, 1969), pp. 20–114
—— *Enarrationes in Psalmos*, ed. H. Müller, *Augustinus, Enarrationes in Psalmos 51–60*, CSEL 94.1 (Vienna, 2003)
—— *Epistolae*, PL 33
   Partial English translation: W. Parsons, *Saint Augustine: Letters, Volume IV (165–203)* (Washington DC, 1955)
—— *Quaestiones in Heptateuchum*, ed. I. Fraipont, *Quaestionum in Heptateuchum libri VII* (etc.), CCSL 33 (Turnhout, 1958), pp. 1–377
—— *Sermones*, PL 38–9, 46–7
Aulus Gellius, *Noctes Atticae*, ed. C. Hosius, *A. Gellii Noctium Atticarum libri XX*, 2 vols. (Leipzig, 1967)
Ausonius, *Professores*, ed. C. Schenkl, MGH AA 5.2 (Berlin, 1883), pp. 55–71
—— *De ratione puerperii maturi*, ed. C. Schenkl, MGH AA 5.2 (Berlin, 1883), pp. 155–6
Basil, *Epistolae*, ed. and trans. R. Deferrari, *Saint Basil: The Letters*, 4 vols. (London, 1926–34)
Bede, *Historia Ecclesiastica Gentis Anglorum*, ed. and trans. B. Colgrave and R. Mynors, *Bede's Ecclesiatical History of the English People* (Oxford, 1969)
Pseudo-Bede, *Commentarii in Pentateuchum*, PL 91, cols. 189–394
Benedictus Levita, *Capitularia*, ed. G. H. Pertz, MGH LL 2.2 (Hannover, 1837), pp. 17–158
Boniface, *Epistolae*, ed. M. Tangl, MGH Epp. sel. 1 (Berlin, 1916)
Pseudo-Boniface, *Sermones*, PL 89, cols. 843–79
Braulio, *Epistolae*, ed. J. Madoz, *Epistólario de S. Braulio de Zaragoza* (Madrid, 1941)
Breviarium Alarici, ed. G. Haenel, *Lex Romana Visigothorum* (Leipzig, 1849)
Breviarium Gothicum, PL 86, cols. 47–1314
Butler's Lives of the Saints, new edn, ed. P. Burns (London, 2003)
Caesarius, *Sermones*, ed. G. Morin, *Sancti Caesarii Arelatensis Sermones*, CCSL 103–4 (Turnhout, 1953)
—— ed. and trans., M.-J. Delage, *Césaire d'Arles: Sermons au people I*, SC 175 (Paris, 1971)
Canones Hibernenses, ed. Bieler, *Irish Penitentials*, pp. 160–75
Capitula Silvanectensia prima, ed. R. Pokorny, MGH Capit. episc. 3 (Hannover, 1995), pp. 74–83
Capitula Treverensia, ed. P. Brommer, MGH Capit. episc. 1 (Hannover, 1984), pp. 53–6

Capitulare de expeditione contra Sarracenos facienda, ed. A. Boretius and V. Krause, MGH Capit. 2 (Hannover, 1897), pp. 65–8

Cartae Senonicae, ed. K. Zeumer, MGH Formulae (Hannover, 1886), pp. 185–207

Cassiodorus, *Variae*, ed. T. Mommsen (Berlin, 1894)

Chariton, *Callirhoe*, ed. and trans. G. P. Goold, *Callirhoe: Chariton* (Cambridge MA, 1995)

Codex diplomaticus Langobardiae, ed. G. Porro-Lambertenghi (Turin, 1873)

Codex Iustinianus, ed. P. Krueger, *Corpus Iuris Civilis*, vol. 2 (Berlin, 1915)

Codex Theodosianus, ed. T. Mommsen and P. M. Meyer, *Theodosiani Libri xvi cum Constitutionibus Simmondianis*, vol. I.2, 2nd edn (Berlin, 1954)

Cogitosus, *Vita Brigitae*, AS Feb. I, cols. 135B–41E

—— PL 72, cols. 775–90

    English translation: S. Connolly and J.-M. Picard, 'Cogitosus's *Life of St. Brigit*: Content and Value', *Journal of the Royal Society of Antiquaries of Ireland* 117 (1987), 5–27

Collatio Alexandri et Dindimi, ed. T. Pritchard, 'The Collatio Alexandri et Dindimi: A Revised Text', *Classica et mediaevalia* 46 (1995), 255–83

Collectio canonum Hibernensis, ed. F. W. H. Wasserschleben, *Die irische Kanonensammlung* (Leipzig, 1885)

—— ed. and trans. R. Flechner, *A Study, Edition and Translation of the Hibernensis with Commentary* (Dublin, forthcoming)

Collectio Quesnelliana, PL 56, cols. 359–746

Council of Aachen (862), ed. W. Hartmann, MGH Conc. 4 (Hannover, 1998), pp. 68–89

Council of Agde (506), ed. Munier, *Conciliae Galliae*, pp. 189–228

Council of Ancyra (314), ed. R. B. Rackham, 'The Text of the Canons of Ancyra', *Studia biblica et ecclesiastica* 3 (1891), 139–216

Council of Arles (c.442/506), ed. Munier, *Conciliae Galliae*, pp. 111–30

Council of Braga – see Martin of Braga

Council of Carthage (418), ed. Munier, *Conciliae Africae*, pp. 69–78

Council of Chalon-sur-Saône (813), ed. A. Werminghoff, MGH Conc. 2.1 (Hannover/Leipzig, 1906), pp. 273–85

Council of Elvira (c. 300), *CCH 4*, pp. 233–68

Council of Lérida (546), *CCH 4*, pp. 297–311

Council of Mainz (847), ed. W. Hartmann, MGH Conc. 3 (Hannover, 1984), pp. 159–77

Council of Mainz (852), ed. W. Hartmann, MGH Conc. 3 (Hannover, 1984), pp. 235–52

Council of Paris (829), ed. A. Werminghoff, MGH Conc. 2.2 (Hannover/Leipzig, 1908), pp. 605–80

Council of Toledo I (400), *CCH 4*, pp. 323–44

Council of Toledo III (589), *CCH 5*, pp. 49–159

Council of Toledo IV (633), *CCH 5*, pp. 160–70

Council of Toledo IX (655), *CCH 5*, pp. 487–514

Council of Tours (813), ed. A. Werminghoff, MGH Conc. 2.1 (Hannover/Leipzig), pp. 286–93

Bibliography

Council of Tribur (895), ed. A. Boretius and V. Krause, MGH Capit. 2 (Hannover, 1897), pp. 196–249
Council of Vaison (442), ed. Munier, *Conciliae Galliae*, pp. 94–104
Council of Worms (868), ed. W. Hartmann, MGH Conc. 4 (Hannover, 1998), pp. 259–307
Cresconius, *Concordia canonum*, PL 88, cols. 829–942
Cyprian of Carthage, *Epistolae*, ed. G. F. Diercks, *Cyprianus, Epistularium: Epistulae 1–57*, CCSL 3B (Turnhout, 1994)
De vita et miraculis beatissimi Germani antistitis, ed. P. de Winterfeld, MGH Poetae 4.1 (Berlin, 1899), pp. 124–30
Decretales Pseudo-Isidorianae, ed. P. Hinschius, *Decretales Pseudo-Isidorianae et Capitula Angilramni* (Leipzig, 1863)
Didache, ed. and trans. A. Milavec, *The Didache: Faith, Hope, and Life of the Earliest Christian Communities, 50–70 C.E.* (New York, 2003)
Digest, ed. T. Mommsen with P. Krueger, trans. A. Watson, *The Digest of Justinian*, 4 vols. (Philadelphia, 1985)
Dionysius Exiguus, *Codex canonum ecclesiasticum*, PL 67, cols. 137–316
Dracontius, *De laudibus Dei*, ed. and trans. C. Moussy, *Dracontius Œuvres tome I: Louanges de Dieu, Livres I et II* (Paris, 1985)
Edictum Rothari, ed. F. Bluhme, MGH LL 4 (Hannover, 1868), pp. 3–90
English translation: K. Fischer Drew, *The Lombard Laws* (Philadelphia, 1973)
Einhard, *Life of Charlemagne*, trans. P. E. Dutton, *Charlemagne's Courtier: The Complete Einhard* (Peterborough, Ontario, 1998), pp. 15–39
Epistolae ad divortium Lotharii II regis pertinentes, ed. E. Dümmler, MGH Epp. 6 (Berlin, 1925), pp. 207–240
Excerpta Hispana, CCH 2, pp. 43–214
Formulae Andecavenses, ed. K. Zeumer, MGH Formulae (Hannover, 1886), pp. 1–25
Formulae collectionis s. Dionysii, ed. K. Zeumer, MGH Formulae (Hannover, 1886), pp. 494–500
Formulae Turonenses, ed. K. Zeumer, MGH Formulae (Hannover, 1886), pp. 128–65
The Formularies of Angers and Marculf: Two Merovingian Legal Handbooks, TTH 46, trans. A. Rio (Liverpool, 2008)
Fulgentius Ferrandus, *Breviatio canonum*, ed. Munier, *Conciliae Africae*, pp. 287–306
Fulgentius of Ruspe, *De fide*, ed. J. Fraipont, *Opera (Fulgentius Ruspensis)*, CCSL 91A (Turnhout, 1968), pp. 709–60
Gennadius, *De ecclesiasticis dogmatis*, PL 58, cols. 979–1055
—— *De scriptoribus ecclesiasticis*, PL 58, cols. 1053–1120
Gerbald of Liège, *Capitula II*, ed. P. Brommer, MGH Capit. episc. 1 (Hannover, 1984), pp. 22–32
Gregory I, *Epistolae*, ed. P. Ewald and L. M. Hartmann, MGH Epp. 1–2 (Berlin, 1891–9)
—— *Homiliae in Ezechielem*, PL 76, cols. 785–1072
—— *Moralia*, ed. M. Adriaen, *Moralia in Iob*, CCSL 143–143B (Turnhout, 1979)
Gregory of Tours, *De miraculis beati Andreae apostoli*, ed. M. Bonnet, MGH SRM 1.2 (Hannover, 1885), pp. 371–96
—— PL 71, cols. 1261–4

—— *Liber in gloria martyrum*, ed. B. Krusch, MGH SRM 1.2 (Hannover, 1885), pp. 34–111

    English translation: R. Van Dam, *Gregory of Tours: Glory of the Martys*, TTH 3 (Liverpool, 1988)

—— *Liber vitae patrum*, ed. B. Krusch, MGH SRM 1.2 (Hannover, 1885), pp. 211–94

—— *Libri Historiarum decem*, ed. B. Krusch and W. Levison, MGH SRM 1.1 (Hannover, 1951)

    English translation: L. Thorpe, *History of the Franks* (Harmondsworth, 1974)

—— *De virtutibus Martini*, ed. B. Krusch, MGH SRM 1.2 (Hannover, 1885), pp. 134–211

Haimo of Auxerre, *Enarratio in D. Pauli epistolis*, PL 117, cols. 361–938

Halitgar of Cambrai, *P. Halitgarii*, (books 3–6) ed. Schmitz, *Bußbücher*, II, pp. 252–300

Herard of Tours, *Capitula*, ed. R. Pokorny and M. Stratmann, MGH Capit. episc. 2 (Hannover, 1995), pp. 115–57

Hincmar of Rheims, *De divortio Lotharii regis et Theutbergae reginae*, ed. L. Böhringer, MGH Conc. 4.1 (Hannover, 1992)

    English translation: R. Stone and C. West, *Hincmar of Rheims, The Divorce of King Lothar II and Queen Theutberga* (Manchester, forthcoming)

Homilia de sacrilegiis, ed. C. P. Caspari, *Eine Augustin fälschlich beigelegte 'Homilia de Sacrilegiis'* (Christiania, 1886)

Institutio sanctimonialium Aquisgranensis, ed. A. Werminghoff, (Hannover/Leipzig, 1906), pp. 421–56

Isidore of Seville, *Etymologiae*, ed. W. M. Lindsay, *Isidori Hispalensis episcopi Etymologiarum sive Originum Libri XX* (Oxford, 1911)

Jerome, *Epistolae*, ed. I. Hilberg, *Sancti Eusebii Hieronymi epistulae*, CSEL 54–6 (Vienna, 1910–18)

John Cassian, *Conferences*, trans. B. Ramsey, *John Cassian: The Conferences* (New York, 1997)

John Chrysostom, *Homiliae XXXII in Epistolam ad Romanos*, PG 60, cols. 583–682

    English translation: J. B. Morris and W. H. Simcox, *The Homilies of S. John Chrysostom, Archbishop of Constantinople on the Epistle of S. Paul the Apostle to the Romans*, 3rd edn (Oxford, 1877)

Jonas of Orléans, *De institutione laicali*, PL 106, cols. 121–278

Jordanes, *Getica*, ed. T. Mommsen, MGH AA 5.1 (Berlin, 1882)

Julian of Toledo, *Historia Wambae*, ed. W. Levison, MGH SRM 5 (Hannover/Leipzig, 1910), pp. 486–535

    English translation: J. Martínez Pizarro, *The Story of Wamba: Julian of Toledo's Historia Wambae regis* (Washington DC, 2005)

—— *Prognosticum*, ed. J. N. Hillgarth, *Sancti Iuliani Toletanae sedis episcopi opera, pars I*, CCSL 115 (Turnhout, 1976)

Juvenal, *Saturae*, ed. and trans. S. M. Braund, *Juvenal and Persius* (Cambridge MA, 2004)

Leo I, *Epistolae*, PL 54, cols. 593–1218

Lex Alamannorum, ed. K. Lehmann and K. A. Eckhardt, MGH LNG 5.1, 2nd edn (Hannover, 1966)

—— ed. J. Merkel, MGH LL 3 (Hannover, 1863), pp. 84–119

Lex Baiwariorum, ed. E. von Schwind, MGH LNG 5.2 (Hannover, 1926)
—— ed. J. Merkel, MGH LL 3 (Hannover, 1863), pp. 183–496
Lex Frisionum, ed. K. A. Eckhardt and A. Eckhardt, MGH Fontes iuris 12 (Hannover, 1982)
Lex Ribuaria, ed. F. Beyerle and R. Buchner, MGH LNG 3.2 (Hannover, 1954)
Lex Romana Burgundionum, ed. L. R. von Salis, MGH LNG 2.1 (Hannover, 1892), pp. 123–70
Lex Salica (includes *Pactus Legis Salicae*, Merovingian redactions, *Lex Salica Karolina* and additions to Salic law), ed. K. A. Eckhardt, MGH LNG 4.1 (Hannover, 1962)
—— *Lex Salica* (D and E redactions), ed. K. A. Eckhardt, MGH LNG 4.2 (Hannover, 1969)
Lex Thuringorum, ed. K. F. von Richthofen, MGH LL 5 (Hannover, 1875–89), pp. 103–44
Lex Visigothorum, ed. K. Zeumer, MGH LNG 1 (Hannover/Leipzig, 1902)
Liber Constitutionum, ed. L. R. von Salis, MGH LNG 2.1 (Hannover, 1892), pp. 1–122
Liber Papiensis, ed. A. Boretius, MGH LL 4 (Hannover, 1868), pp. 289–585
Liber Pontificalis, trans. R. Davis, *The Lives of the Ninth-Century Popes*, TTH 20 (Liverpool, 1995)
Martial, *Epigrammata*, ed. D. R. Shackleton-Bailey, *M. Valerii Martialis Epigrammata* (Stuttgart, 1990)
Martin of Braga, *Opera omnia*, ed. C. W. Barlow, *Martini episcopi Bracarensi opera omnia* (New Haven CT, 1950)
Medieval Handbooks of Penance: A Translation from the Principal Libri paenitentiales *and selections from related documents*, trans. J. T. McNeill and H. M. Gamer (New York, 1938)
Methodius, *Symposium*, trans. H. Musurillo, *The Symposium: A Treatise on Charity* (New York, 1958)
Pseudo-Methodius, *Revelationes*, ed. and trans. B. Garstad, *Apocalypse Pseudo-Methodius: An Alexandrian World Chronicle* (Cambridge MA, 2012)
Minucius Felix, *Octavius*, ed. C. Halm, *M. Minucii Felicis Octavius*, CSEL 2 (Vienna, 1867)
Muscio, *Genecia*, ed. V. Rose, *Sorani Gynaeciorum vetus translatio latina* (Leipzig, 1882)
Musonius Rufus, *Fragments*, ed. and trans. C. Lutz, 'Musonius Rufus: The Roman Socrates', *Yale Classical Studies* 10 (1947), 3–147
Nicholas I, *Epistolae*, ed. E. Perels, MGH Epp. 6 (Berlin, 1925), pp. 257–690
Novellae, ed. R. Schoell and G. Kroll, *Corpus Iuris Civilis*, vol. 3 (Berlin, 1912)
Old Irish Penitential, trans. D. A. Binchy, in Bieler, *Irish Penitentials*, 258–74
Origen, *Homiliae in Exodum*, PG 12, cols. 297–395
Ovid, *Amores*, ed. E. J. Kenney, *P. Ovidii Nasonis Amores: Medicamina faciei femineae; Ars amatoria; Remedia amoris* (Oxford, 1961)
—— *Heroides*, ed. and trans. G. Showerman, *Ovid: Heroides and Amores* (London, 1914)
P. Ambrosianum, ed. L. Körntgen, *Studien zu den Quellen der frühmittelalterlichen Bußbücher* (Sigmaringen, 1993), pp. 257–70
P. Arundel, ed. Schmitz, *Bußbücher*, I, pp. 432–65
P. Bedae, ed. Wasserschleben, *Bußordnungen*, pp. 220–30
P. Bigotianum, ed. Bieler, *Irish Penitentials*, pp. 198–239

P. Bobbiense, ed. Kottje, Paenitentialia, pp. 66–71
P. Burgundense, ed. Kottje, Paenitentialia, pp. 61–5
P. Capitula iudiciorum, ed. Meens, Boeteboek, pp. 434–85
P. Columbani, ed. Bieler, Irish Penitentials, pp. 96–107
P. Cummeani, ed. Bieler, Irish Penitentials, pp. 108–35
P. Excarpsus Cummeani, ed. Wasserschleben, Bußordnungen, pp. 460–93
P. Floriacense, ed. Kottje, Paenitentialia, pp. 95–103
P. Hubertense, ed. Kottje, Paenitentialia, pp. 105–15
P. Martenianum, ed. v. Hörmann, Bußbücher studien IV, pp. 358–483
P. Merseburgense A, ed. Kottje, Paenitentialia, pp. 123–69
P. Merseburgense B, ed. Kottje, Paenitentialia, pp. 169–79
P. Oxoniense I, ed. Kottje, Paenitentialia, pp. 87–93
P. Oxoniense II, ed. Kottje, Paenitentialia, pp. 179–205
P. Parisiense simplex, ed. Kottje, Paenitentialia, pp. 73–9
P. Pseudo-Bedae, ed. Wasserschleben, Bußordnungen, pp. 248–83
P. Ps.-Gregory III, ed. Kerff, 'Paenitentiale Pseudo-Gregorii', pp. 161–88
P. Pseudo-Theodori, ed. van Rhijn, Paenitentiale
P. Remense, ed. Asbach, Poenitentiale, appendix, pp. 1–77
P. Sangallense simplex, ed. Kottje, Paenitentialia, pp. 117–21
P. Sangallense tripartitum, ed. Meens, Boeteboek, pp. 326–53
P. Silense, ed. Bezler, Paenitentialia, pp. 15–42
P. Sletstatense, ed. Kottje, Paenitentiale, pp. 81–5
P. Theodori
—— Canones Basilienses (B), ed. Asbach, Poenitentiale, appendix, pp. 79–89
—— Canones Cottoniani (C), ed. Finsterwalder, Canones, pp. 271–84
—— Canones Gregorii (G), ed. Finsterwalder, Canones, pp. 253–70
—— Capitula Dacheriana (D), ed. Finsterwalder, Canones, pp. 239–52
—— Discipulus Umbrensium (U), ed. Finsterwalder, Canones, pp. 285–334
P. Vallicellianum I, ed. Schmitz, Bußbücher, I, pp. 227–342
P. Vallicellianum C.6, ed. A. H. Gaastra, 'Between Liturgy and Canon Law: A Study of Books of Confession and Penance in Eleventh- and Twelfth-Century Italy' (unpublished Ph.D. dissertation, University of Utrecht, 2007), pp. 274–81, available at http://dspace.library.uu.nl/handle/1874/23216 [accessed 2 June 2015]
P. Vindobense B, ed. Meens, Boeteboek, pp. 354–433
P. Vinniani, ed. Bieler, Irish Penitentials, pp. 74–95
Paschasius Radbertus, De corpore et sanguino domini, ed. B. Paulus, De corpore et sanguine domini, Epistola ad Fredugardum, CCCM 16 (Turnhout, 1969)
Paulinus of Aquileia, Contra Felicem, PL 99, cols. 313–467
Pirminius, Scarapsus, ed. E. Hauswald, MGH QQ 25 (Hannover, 2010)
Pliny the Elder, Naturalis Historia, ed. C. Mayhoff, C. Plinii Secundi Naturalis historiae libri XXXVII, 6 vols. (Stuttgart, 1967–70)
Pliny the Younger, Epistolae, ed. R. A. B. Mynors, C. Plinii Caecili Secundi epistolarum libri decem (Oxford, 1963)
Plutarch, Moralia, ed. and trans. F. C. Babbitt, Plutarch's Moralia, vol. 3, 172a–263c (s.l., 1931)
Prefaces to Canon Law Books in Latin Christianity: Selected Translations, 500–1245, trans. R. Somerville and B. C. Brasington (New Haven CT, 1998)

Pseudo-Primasius, *Commentaria in epistolas B. Pauli*, PL 68, cols. 417–793
Procopius, *Anecdota*, ed. and trans. H. B. Dewing, *The Anecdota or Secret History* (Cambridge MA, 1935)
Rabanus Maurus, *Commentaria in Ecclesiasticum*, PL 109, cols. 763–1127
—— *Commentaria in Exodum*, PL 108, cols. 9–245
—— *De rerum naturis*, PL 111, cols. 9–614
—— *Enarrationes in epistolas B. Pauli*, PL 111, cols. 1273–1616
—— *Enarrationes in librum Numerorum*, PL 108, cols. 587–837
—— *Epistolae*, ed. E. Dümmler, MGH Epp. 5 (Berlin, 1899), pp. 379–533
—— *Homiliae in evangelia et epistolas*, PL 110, cols. 135–467
—— *P. ad Heribaldum*, PL 110, cols. 467–94
—— *P. ad Otgarum*, PL 112, cols. 1397–424
Radulf of Bourges, *Capitula*, ed. P. Brommer, MGH Capit. episc. 1 (Hannover, 1984), pp. 227–68
Regino of Prüm, *Chronicon*, ed. F. Kurze, MGH SRG 50 (Hannover, 1890)
  English translation: S. MacLean, *History and Politics in Late Carolingian and Ottonian Europe: The Chronicle of Regino of Prüm and Adalbert of Magdeburg* (Manchester, 2009)
—— *De synodalibus causis et disciplinis ecclesiasticis*, ed. W. Hartmann, *Das Sendhandbuch des Regino von Prüm* (Darmstadt, 2004)
Pseudo-Remigius, *Enarrationes in Psalmos*, PL 131, cols. 134–845
Rudolf of Fulda, *Vita Leobae*, ed. G. Waitz, MGH SS 15.1 (Hannover, 1887), pp. 121–31
Sacramentarium Veronense, ed. L. C. Mohlberg, with L. Eizenhöfer and P. Siffrin, *Sacramentarium Veronense (Cod. Bibl. Capit. Veron. LXXXV [80])* (Rome, 1978)
Salzburg Sermonary, *Sermo* 81, ed. A. Wilmart, 'Un sermon sur la résurrection corporelle emprunté à S. Gregoire passé sous le nom de S. Augustin', *Revue Bénédictine* 47 (1935), 3–7
Scribonius Largus, *Compositiones*, ed. S. Sconocchia, *Scribonii Largi Compositiones* (Leipzig, 1983)
Seneca the Younger, *De consolatione ad Helviam*, ed. L. D. Reynolds, *L. Annaei Senecae Dialogorum libri duodecim* (Oxford, 1977), pp. 291–317
Sibylline Oracles, ed. and trans. J. L. Lightfoot, *The Sibylline Oracles: With Introduction, Translation, and Commentary on the First and Second Books* (Oxford, 2007)
Smaragdus, *Collectiones in epistolas et evangelii*, PL 102, cols. 15–583
Soranus, *Gynecology*, trans. O. Temkin, *Soranus' Gynecology* (Baltimore, 1956)
Stephen V, *Fragmenta registri Stephani V papae*, ed. E. Caspar, MGH Epp. 7 (Berlin, 1928), pp. 334–53
St Galler Receptarium (A), ed. J. Jörimann, *Frühmittelalterliche Rezeptarien* (Zurich, 1925), pp. 5–37
Suetonius, *De vita Caesarum*, ed. and trans. J. C. Rolfe, *Suetonius* (s.l., 1914)
Sulpicius Severus, *Chronica*, ed. and trans. G. de Senneville-Grave, *Chroniques, Sulpice Sévère*, SC 441 (Paris, 1999)
Tacitus, *Germania*, ed. M. Winterbottom and R. M. Ogilvie, *Cornelii Taciti Opera Minora* (Oxford, 1975)
Tarra, *Epistola*, ed. J. Gil, *Miscellanea Wisigothicae* (Sevilla, 1972), pp. 28–9

Tertullian, *Ad Nationes*, ed. J. G. Ph. Borleefs, *Tertullianus: Opera I*, CCSL 1 (Turnhout, 1954), pp. 9–75

—— *Ad Uxorem*, ed. A. Kroymann, *Tertullianus: Opera I*, CCSL 1 (Turnhout, 1954), pp. 373–94

—— *Apologeticum*, ed. E. Dekkers, *Tertullianus: Opera I*, CCSL 1 (Turnhout, 1954), pp. 77–171

—— *De anima*, ed. J. H. Waszink, *Tertullianus: Opera II*, CCSL 2 (Turnhout, 1954), pp. 779–869

—— *De exhortatione castitatis*, ed. A. Kroymann, *Tertullianus: Opera II*, CCSL 2 (Turnhout, 1954), pp. 1013–35

—— *De virginibus velandis*, ed. E. Dekkers, *Tertullianus: Opera II*, CCSL 2 (Turnhout, 1954), pp. 1207–26

Theodore of Canterbury, *Laterculus Malalianus*, ed. and trans. J. Stevenson, *The Laterculus Malalianus and the School of Archbishop Theodore* (Cambridge, 1995)

Theodorus Priscianus, *Euporiston*, ed. V. Rose, *Theodori Prisciani Euporiston libri III* (Leipzig, 1894)

Theodulph of Orléans, *Capitula I*, ed. P. Brommer, MGH Capit. episc. 1 (Hannover, 1984), pp. 73–142

—— *Capitula II*, ed. P. Brommer, MGH Capit. episc. 1 (Hannover, 1984), pp. 142–84

Turibius, *Epistola*, PL 54, cols. 693–5

Venantius Fortunatus, *De virtutibus sancti Hilarii*, ed. B. Krusch, MGH AA 4.2 (Berlin, 1885), pp. 7–11

—— *Opera poetica*, ed. F. Leo, MGH Auct. ant. 4.1 (Berlin, 1881)

—— *Vita Germani*, ed. B. Krusch, MGH SRM 7 (Hannover, 1920), pp. 372–418, revised edn of *Vita Germani*, ed. B. Krusch, MGH AA 4.2 (Berlin, 1885), pp. 11–27

—— *Vita Marcelli*, ed. B. Krusch, MGH AA 4.2 (Berlin, 1885), pp. 49–54

Visio Pauli, ed. T. Silverstein and A. Hilhorst, *Apocalypse of Paul: A New Critical Edition of Three Long Latin Versions* (Geneva, 1997)

Vita Aidi, ed. Heist, *Vitae*, pp. 167–81

—— ed. Plummer, *Vitae*, I, pp. 34–45

Vita Balthildis, ed. B. Krusch, MGH SRM 2 (Hannover, 1888), 475–508

Vita prima Brigitae, AS Feb. I, cols. 119E–35B

    English translation: S. Connolly, 'Vita Prima Sanctae Brigitae: Background and Historical Value', *Journal of the Royal Society of Antiquaries of Ireland* 119 (1989), 5–49

Vita Caesarii, ed. B. Krusch, MGH SRM 3 (Hannover, 1896), pp. 433–501

    English translation: W. E. Klingshirn, *Caesarius of Arles: Life, Testament, Letters*, TTH 19 (Liverpool, 1994)

Vita Ciarani, ed. Heist, *Vitae*, pp. 346–53

Vita Eparchii, ed. B. Krusch, MGH SRM 3 (Hannover, 1896), pp. 550–64

Vita Germani episcopi Parisiaci II. Brevior, ed. B. Krusch (Hannover/Leipzig, 1920), pp. 419–22

Wandalbert of Prüm, *Vita Goaris*, ed. H. E. Stiene, *Wandalbert von Prüm, Vita et miracula Sancti Goaris* (Frankfurt, 1981)

William FitzStephen, *Vita Thomae*, ed. J. C. Robertson, *Materials for the History of Thomas Becket, Archbishop of Canterbury, Volume III* (London, 1877)

Willibald, *Life of Saint Boniface*, trans. C. H. Talbot, in *Soldiers of Christ: Saints and Saints' Lives from Late Antiquity and the Early Middle Ages*, ed. T. F. X. Noble and T. Head (London, 1995), pp. 107–64

Secondary sources

Abbot, E., *A History of Celibacy* (Cambridge MA, 2001)
Adamik, T., 'Eroticism in the *Liber de miraculis beati Andreae apostoli* of Gregory of Tours', in *The Apocryphal Acts of Andrew*, ed. J. N. Bremmer (Leuven, 2000), pp. 35–46
Adams, J. N., *The Latin Sexual Vocabulary* (London, 1982)
Adkin, N., *Jerome on Virginity: A Commentary on the* Libellus de virginitate servanda *(Letter 22)* (Cambridge, 2003)
Aijmer, G., 'Introduction: Coming into Existence', in *Coming into Existence: Birth and Metaphors of Birth*, ed. G. Aijmer (Gothenburg, 1992), pp. 1–19
Airlie, S., 'Private Bodies and the Body Politic in the Divorce Case of Lothar II', *P&P* 161 (1998), 3–38
—— 'Narratives of Triumph and Rituals of Submission: Charlemagne's Mastering of Bavaria', *Transactions of the Royal Historical Society*, 6th s., 9 (1999), 93–121
—— '"Sad stories of the death of kings": Narrative Patterns and Structures of Authority in Regino of Prüm's *Chronicle*', in *Narrative and History in the Early Medieval West*, ed. E. M. Tyler and R. Balzaretti (Turnhout, 2006), pp. 105–31
—— 'Unreal Kingdom: Francia Media under the Shadow of Lothar II', in *De la mer du Nord à la Méditerranée. Francia Media. Une région au coeur de l'Europe (c.840–c.1050)*, ed. M. Gaillard *et al.* (Luxembourg, 2011), pp. 339–56
Alexander, P. J., *The Byzantine Apocalyptic Tradition* (Berkeley CA, 1985)
Algra, N. E., 'The *Lex Frisionum*: The Genesis of a Legalized Life', in *The Law's Beginnings*, ed. F. J. M. Feldbrugge (Leiden, 2003), pp. 77–92
Amerini, F., *Aquinas on the Beginning and End of Human Life*, trans. M. Henninger (Cambridge MA, 2013)
Amos, T. L., 'Preaching and the Sermon in the Carolingian World', in *De Ore Domini: Preacher and Word in the Middle Ages*, ed. T. L. Amos *et al.* (Kalamazoo, 1989), pp. 41–60
Amundsen, D. W., 'Visigothic Medical Legislation', *Bulletin of the History of Medicine* 45.6 (1971), 553–69
Angenendt, A., Braucks, T., Busch, R. and Lutterbach, H., 'Counting Piety in the Early and High Middle Ages', in *Ordering Medieval Society: Perspectives on Intellectual and Practical Modes of Shaping Social Relations*, ed. B. Jussen, trans. P. E. Selwyn (Philadelphia, 2001), pp. 15–54
Ariès, P., 'Sur les origines de la contraception en France', *Population* (French edn) 3 (1953), 465–72
Atkinson, C. W., *The Oldest Vocation: Christian Motherhood in the Middle Ages* (Ithaca NY, 1991)
Auerbach, E., *Literary Language and its Public in Late Latin Antiquity and in the Middle Ages*, trans. R. Manheim (Princeton, 1965)

Ausenda, G., 'Kinship and Marriage among the Visigoths', in *The Visigoths from the Migration Period to the Seventh Century: An Ethnographic Perspective*, ed. P. Heather (Woodbridge, 1999), pp. 129–69

Austin, G., 'Bishops and Religious Law, 900–1050', in *The Bishop Reformed: Studies of Episcopal Power and Culture in the Central Middle Ages*, ed. J. S. Ott and A. T. Jones (Aldershot, 2007), pp. 40–57

—— *Shaping Church Law around 1000: The Decretum of Burchard of Worms* (Farnham, 2009)

Bachrach, D. S., 'Confession in the *Regnum Francorum* (742–900): The Sources Revisited', *JEH* 54.1 (2003), 3–22

—— *Religion and the Conduct of War, c.300–1215* (Woodbridge, 2003)

Baernstein, B. R. and Christopoulos, J., 'Interpreting the Body in Early Modern Italy: Pregnancy, Abortion and Adulthood', *P&P* 223 (2014), 41–75

Bailey, L. K., '"These are not men": Sex and Drink in the Sermons of Caesarius of Arles', *JECS* 15.1 (2007), 23–43

—— *Christianity's Quiet Success: The Eusebius Gallicanus Sermon Collection and the Power of the Church in Late Antique Gaul* (Notre Dame IN, 2010)

von Balthasar, H. U., *Explorations in Theology II: Spouse of the Word*, trans. A. V. Littledale (San Francisco, 1991)

Balzaretti, R., 'Women, Property and Urban Space in Tenth-Century Milan', *Gender & History* 23.3 (2011), 547–75

Baraz, D., *Medieval Cruelty: Changing Perceptions, Late Antiquity to the Early Modern Period* (Ithaca NY, 2003)

Barbero, A. and Loring, M. I., 'The Catholic Visigothic Kingdom', in *The New Cambridge Medieval History Volume 1: c.500–c.700*, ed. P. Fouracre (Cambridge, 2005), pp. 346–70

Barilan, Y. M., 'Abortion in Jewish Religious Law: Neighbourly Love, Imago Dei, and a Hypothesis on the Medieval Blood Libel', *Review of Rabbinic Judaism* 8.1 (2005), 1–34

Barr, J. A., 'Tertullian's Attitude to Uterine Offspring' (unpublished Ph.D. dissertation, University of Queensland, 2013)

Barré, H., *Les homéliaires carolingiens de l'école d'Auxerre: authenticité, inventaire tableaux comparatifs, initia* (Vatican City, 1962)

Baun, J., 'The Fate of Babies Dying before Baptism in Byzantium', in *The Church and Childhood*, SCH 31, ed. D. Wood (Oxford, 1994), pp. 115–25

Beccaria, A., *I codici di medicina del periodo presalernitano (secoli IX, X e XI)* (Rome, 1956)

Beck, H. G. J., *The Pastoral Care of Souls in South-East France during the Sixth Century* (Rome, 1950)

Bernard, C., Deleury, E., Dion, F. and Gaudette, P., 'Le statut de l'embryon humain dans l'Antiquité gréco-romaine', *Laval Théoloqique et Philosophique* 45.2 (1989), 179–95

Biller, P., 'Birth-Control in the West in the Thirteenth and Early Fourteenth Centuries', *P&P* 94 (1982), 3–26

—— 'Confessors' Manuals and the Avoidance of Offspring', in *Handling Sin: Confession in the Middle Ages*, ed. P. Biller and A. J. Minnis (York, 1998), pp. 165–87

—— *The Measure of Multitude: Population in Medieval Thought* (Oxford, 2000)

Bibliography

Bischoff, B. and Lapidge, M., *Biblical Commentaries from the Canterbury School of Theodore* (Cambridge, 1994)

Bitel, L. M., 'Sex, Sin, and Celibacy in Early Ireland', *Proceedings of the Harvard Celtic Colloquium* 7 (1987), 65–95

—— *Land of Women: Tales of Sex and Gender from Early Ireland* (Ithaca NY, 1996)

Blair, J., *The Church in Anglo-Saxon Society* (Oxford, 2005)

Bledsoe, C. H., *Contingent Lives: Fertility, Time, and Aging in West Africa* (Chicago, 2002)

Bologne, J.-C., *La naissance interdite: Sterilité, avortement, et contraception au moyen âge* (Paris, 1988)

Bonner, G., 'Abortion and Early Christian Thought', in *Abortion and the Sanctity of Human Life*, ed. J. H. Channer (Exeter, 1985), pp. 93–122

Bonnet-Cadilhac, C., 'Si l'enfant se trouve dans une présentation contre nature, que doit faire la sage-femme?', in *Naissance et petite enfance dans l'antiquité*, ed. V. Dasen (Fribourg, 2004), pp. 199–208

Borsje, J., 'Rules and Legislation on Love Charms in Early Medieval Ireland', *Peritia* 21 (2010), 172–90

—— 'Love Magic in Medieval Irish Penitentials, Law and Literature: A Dynamic Perspective', *Studia Neophilologica* 84.1 (2012), 6–23

Boswell, J. E., *The Kindness of Strangers: The Abandonment of Children from Late Antiquity to the Renaissance* (London, 1988)

Boucaud, P., '*Factus est homo in animam viventem*: anthropologie chrétienne et psychologie dans l'exégèse de Claude de Turin', in *The Multiple Meaning of Scripture: The Role of Exegesis in Early-Christian and Medieval Culture*, ed. I. van 't Spijker (Leiden, 2009), pp. 125–51

Boudon-Millot, V., 'La naissance de la vie dans la théorie médicale et philosophique de Galien', in *L'embryon formation et animation: Antiquité grecque et latine traditions hébraïque, chrétienne et islamique*, ed. L. Brisson *et al.* (Paris, 2008), pp. 79–94

Brennan, B., 'The Career of Venantius Fortunatus', *Traditio* 41 (1985), 49–78

—— 'The Image of the Merovingian Bishop in the Poetry of Venantius Fortunatus', *Journal of Medieval History* 18 (1992), 115–39

—— 'Deathless Marriage and Spiritual Fecundity in Venantius Fortunatus's "De Virginitate"', *Traditio* 51 (1996), 73–97

Brent, A., *Hippolytus and the Roman Church in the Third Century: Communities in Tension before the Emergence of a Monarch-Bishop* (Leiden, 1995)

Brett, M., 'Theodore and the Latin Canon Law', in *Archbishop Theodore: Commemorative Studies on his Life and Influence*, ed. M. Lapidge (Cambridge, 1995), pp. 120–40

Brown, G., 'Introduction: The Carolingian Renaissance', in *Carolingian Culture: Emulation and Innovation*, ed. R. McKitterick (Cambridge, 1994), pp. 1–51

Brown, P., *The Body and Society: Men, Women and Sexual Renunciation in Early Christianity* (London, 1988)

—— *Augustine of Hippo: A Biography*, new edn (London, 2000)

—— 'The Decline of the Empire of God: Amnesty, Penance, and the Afterlife from Late Antiquity to the Middle Ages', in *Last Things: Death and the Apocalypse in the Middle Ages*, ed. C. W. Bynum and P. Freedman (Philadelphia, 2000), pp. 41–59

—— *The Rise of Western Christendom*, 2nd edn (Oxford, 2003)

Brown, W. C., *Unjust Seizure: Conflict, Interest, and Authority in an Early Medieval Society* (Ithaca NY, 2001)
— *Violence in Medieval Europe* (Harlow, 2010)
Brundage, J. A., *Law, Sex, and Christian Society in Medieval Europe* (Chicago, 1987)
Buc, P., *The Dangers of Ritual: Between Early Medieval Texts and Social Scientific Theory* (Princeton, 2001)
Bührer-Thierry, G., 'La reine adultère', *Cahiers de civilisation médiévale* 35.4 (1992), 299–312
— 'Raban Maur et l'épiscopat de son temps', in *Raban Maur et son temps*, ed. P. Depreux *et al.* (Turnhout, 2010), pp. 63–76
Bullough, D., 'Charlemagne's Men of God: Alcuin, Hildebald and Arn', in *Charlemagne: Empire and Society*, ed. J. Storey (Manchester, 2005), pp. 136–50
Bullough, V. and Campbell, C., 'Female Longevity and Diet in the Middle Ages', *Speculum* 55.2 (1980), 317–25
Burrus, V., *The Making of a Heretic: Gender, Authority, and the Priscillianist Controversy* (Berkeley CA, 1995)
Butler, S. M., 'Abortion by Assault: Violence against Pregnant Women in Thirteenth and Fourteenth-Century England', *Journal of Women's History* 17.4 (2005), 9–31
— 'Abortion Medieval Style? Assaults on Pregnant Women in Later Medieval England', *Women's Studies* 40.6 (2011), 778–99
Bynum, C. W., *The Resurrection of the Body in Western Christianity, 200–1336* (New York, 1995)
— *Wonderful Blood: Theology and Practice in Late Medieval Northern Germany and Beyond* (Philadelphia, 2007)
Cadden, J., *Meanings of Sex Difference in the Middle Ages: Medicine, Science, and Culture* (Cambridge, 1995)
Cain, A., *The Letters of Jerome: Asceticism, Biblical Exegesis, and the Construction of Christian Authority in Late Antiquity* (Oxford, 2009)
Callan, M.B., 'Of Vanishing Fetuses and Maidens Made-Again: Abortion, Restored Virginity, and Similar Scenarios in Medieval Irish Hagiography and Penitentials', *JHS* 21.2 (2012) 282–96
Callewaert, P. S., 'Les pénitentiels au moyen âge et les pratiques anticonceptionelles', *La vie spirituelle*, suppl. 74 (1965), 339–66
Carrick, P., *Medical Ethics in Antiquity: Philosophical Perspectives on Abortion and Euthanasia* (Dordrecht, 1985)
Cary, G., *The Medieval Alexander* (Cambridge, 1956)
Cassidy, K., 'A Convenient Untruth: The Pro-Choice Invention of an Era of Abortion Freedom', in *Catholicism and Historical Narrative: A Catholic Engagement with Historical Scholarship* (Lanham MD, 2014), pp. 73–102
Castellanos, S., 'The Significance of Social Unanimity in a Visigothic Hagiography: Keys to an Ideological Screen', *JECS* 11.3 (2003), 387–419
— 'Creating New Constantines at the End of the Sixth Century', *Historical Research* 85 (2012), 556–75
Castelli, E. A., 'Gender, Theory, and the Rise of Christianity: A Response to Rodney Stark', *JECS* 6.2 (1998), 227–57
Cavadini, J.C., *The Last Christology of the West: Adoptionism in Spain and Gaul, 785–820* (Philadelphia, 1993)

Cavallo, G., 'Theodore of Tarsus and the Greek Culture of his time', in *Archbishop Theodore: Commemorative Studies on his Life and Influence*, ed. M. Lapidge (Cambridge, 1995), pp. 54–67

Chadwick, H., *Priscillian of Avila: The Occult and the Charismatic in the Early Church* (Oxford, 1976)

Charles-Edwards, T. M., 'The Penitential of Theodore and the *Iudicia Theodori*', in *Archbishop Theodore: Commemorative Studies on his Life and Influence*, ed. M. Lapidge (Cambridge, 1995), pp. 141–74

—— 'The Penitential of Columbanus', in *Columbanus: Studies on the Latin Writings*, ed. M. Lapidge (Woodbridge, 1997), pp. 217–39

—— 'The Construction of the *Hibernensis*', *Peritia* 12 (1998), 209–37

—— *Early Christian Ireland* (Cambridge, 2000)

Chattopadhayay-Dutt, P., *Loops and Roots: The Conflict between Official and Traditional Family Planning in India* (New Delhi, 1995)

Chazelle, C., *The Crucified God in the Carolingian Era: Theology and Art of Christ's Passion* (Cambridge, 2001)

Chélini, J., *L'aube du Moyen Age: Naissance de la chrétienté occidentale: La vie religieuse des laïcs dans l'Europe carolingienne (750–900)* (Paris, 1991)

Christopoulos, J., 'Abortion and the Confessional in Counter-Reformation Italy', *Renaissance Quarterly* 65.2 (2012), 443–84

—— 'Nonelite Male Perspectives on Procured Abortion, Rome circa 1600', *I Tatti Studies in the Italian Renaissance* 17.1 (2014), 155–74

Cilliers, L., 'Vindicianus' *Gynaecia* and Theories on Generation and Embryology from the Babylonians up to Graeco-Roman Times', in *Magic and Rationality in Ancient Near Eastern and Graeco-Roman Medicine*, ed. H. J. Horstmanshoff (Leiden, 2004), pp. 343–67

Clark, G., *Women in Late Antiquity: Pagan and Christian Lifestyles* (Oxford, 1994)

Claussen, M. A., *The Reform of the Frankish Church: Chrodegang of Metz and the* Regula canonicorum *in the Eighth Century* (Cambridge, 2004)

Coates, S., 'Regendering Radegund? Fortunatus, Baudonivia and the Problem of Female Sanctity in Merovingian Gaul', in *Gender and Christian Religion*, SCH 34, ed. R. N. Swanson (Woodbridge, 1998), pp. 37–50

—— 'Venantius Fortunatus and the Image of Episcopal Authority in Late Antique and Early Merovingian Gaul', *English Historical Review* 115.464 (2000), 1109–37

Coleman, E., 'Infanticide in the Early Middle Ages', in *Women in Medieval Society*, ed. S. M. Stuard (Philadelphia, 1976), pp. 47–70

Collins, J. J., 'Sibylline Oracles', in *The Old Testament Pseudepigrapha*, 2 vols., ed. J. H. Charlesworth (London, 1983), I, pp. 317–472

Collins, R[ichard], 'Observations on the Form, Language and Public of the Prose Biographies of Venantius Fortunatus in the Hagiography of Merovingian Gaul', in *Columbanus and Merovingian Monasticism*, ed. H. B. Clarke and M. Brennan (Oxford, 1981), pp. 105–31

Collins, R[oger], '"Sicut lex Gothorum continet": Laws and Charters in Ninth- and Tenth-Century León and Catalonia', *English Historical Review* 100, no.396 (1985), 485–512

—— *Early Medieval Spain: Unity in Diversity, 400–1000*, 2nd edn (New York, 1995)

Condit, C. M., *Decoding Abortion Rhetoric: Communicating Social Change* (Urbana IL, 1990)

Condren, M., *The Serpent and the Goddess: Women, Religion, and Power in Celtic Ireland* (San Francisco, 1989)

Congourdeau, M. H., 'L'animation de l'embryon humain chez Maxime le Confesseur', *Nouvelle revue théologique* 111 (1984), 693–709

—— 'Genèse d'un regard Chrétien sur l'embryon', in *Naissance et petite enfance dans l'antiquité*, ed. V. Dasen (Fribourg, 2004), pp. 349–62

—— 'Les variations du désir d'enfant à Byzance', in *Becoming Byzantine: Children and Childhood in Byzantium*, ed. A. Papaconstantinou and A.-M. Talbot (Washington DC, 2009), pp. 35–63

Conklin, B. A. and Morgan, L. M., 'Babies, Bodies, and the Production of Personhood in North America and a Native Amazonian Society', *Ethos* 24.4 (1996), 657–94

Connery, J. R., *Abortion: The Development of the Roman Catholic Perspective* (Chicago, 1977)

—— 'The Ancients and the Medievals on Abortion: The Consensus the Court Ignored', in *Abortion and the Constitution: Reversing Roe v. Wade through the Courts*, ed. D. J. Horan et al. (Washington DC, 1987), pp. 123–35

Connolly, H., *The Irish Penitentials: Their Significance for the Sacrament of Penance Today* (Dublin, 1995)

Contreni, J. J., 'Masters and Medicine in Northern France during the Reign of Charles the Bald', in *Charles the Bald: Court and Kingdom*, 2nd edn, ed. M. T. Gibson and J. L. Nelson (Aldershot, 1990), pp. 267–82

—— 'Reading Gregory of Tours in the Middle Ages', in *The World of Gregory of Tours*, ed. K. Mitchell and I. Wood (Leiden, 2002), pp. 418–30

—— 'Glossing the Bible in the Early Middle Ages: Theodore and Hadrian of Canterbury and John Scottus (Eriugena)', in *The Study of the Bible in the Carolingian Era*, ed. C. Chazelle and B. Van Name Edwards (Turnhout, 2003), pp. 39–60

Coon, L., '"What is the word if not semen?" Priestly Bodies in Carolingian Exegesis', in *Gender in the Early Medieval World: East and West, 300–900*, ed. L. Brubaker and J. M. H. Smith (Cambridge, 2004), pp. 274–300

Corbet, P., *Autour de Burchard de Worms: L'église allemande et les interdits de parenté (IXème–XIIème siècle)* (Frankurt, 2001)

Couser, J., 'Inventing Paganism in Eighth-Century Bavaria', *EME* 18.1 (2010), 26–42

—— '"Let them make him duke to rule the people": The *Law of the Bavarians* and Regime Change in Early Medieval Europe', *Law and History Review* 30.3 (2012), 865–99

Crahay, R., 'Les moralistes anciens et l'avortement', *L'antiquité classique* 10 (1941), 9–23

Cramer, P., *Baptism and Change in the Early Middle Ages, c.200–c.1150* (Cambridge, 1993)

Crawford, S., 'Infanticide, Abandonment and Abortion in the Graeco-Roman and Early Medieval World: Archaeological Perspectives', in *Childhood and Violence in the Western Tradition*, ed. L. Brockliss and H. Montgomery (Oxford, 2010), pp. 59–67

Czachesz, I., 'Torture in Hell and Reality: The Visio Pauli', in *The Visio Pauli and the Gnostic Apocalypse of Paul*, ed. J. M. Bremmer and I. Czachesz (Leuven, 2007), pp. 130–43

Daly, W., 'Caesarius of Arles: A Precursor of Medieval Christendom', *Traditio* 26 (1970), 1–28

Davis, J. R., 'A Pattern for Power: Charlemagne's Delegation of Judicial Responsibilities', in *The Long Morning of Europe: New Directions in Early Medieval Studies*, ed. J. R. Davis and M. McCormick (Aldershot, 2008), pp. 235–46

Davis, P. J., *Ovid and Augustus: A Political Reading of Ovid's Erotic Poems* (London, 2006)

d'Avray, D. L., *Medieval Marriage: Symbolism and Society* (Oxford, 2005)

—— 'Slavery, Marriage and the Holy See: From the Ancient World to the New World', *Rechtgeschichte/Legal History* 20 (2012), 347–51

—— *Dissolving Royal Marriages: A Documentary History, 860–1600* (Cambridge, 2014)

—— *Papacy, Monarchy and Marriage, 860–1600* (Cambridge, forthcoming)

Dean-Jones, L.A., *Women's Bodies in Classical Greek Science* (Oxford, 1994)

Delage, M.-J., 'Un évêque au temps du invasion', in *Césaire d'Arles et la Christianisation de la Provence*, ed. D. Bertrand *et al.* (Paris, 1994), pp. 21–43

Dellapenna, J. W., *Dispelling the Myths of Abortion History* (Durham NC, 2006)

Devisse, J., *Hincmar, archevêque de Reims, 845–882*, 3 vols. (Geneva, 1975–6)

Díaz, P. C. and Valverde, M. R., 'The Theoretical Strength and Practical Weakness of the Visigothic Monarchy of Toledo', in *Rituals of Power from Late Antiquity to the Early Middle Ages*, ed. F. Theuws and J. L. Nelson (Leiden, 2000), pp. 59–93

Dickison, S. K., 'Abortion in Antiquity', *Arethusa* 6.1 (1973), 159–66

Dixon, S., *Reading Roman Women: Sources, Genres and Real Life* (London, 2001)

Dölger, F. J., 'Das Lebensrecht des ungeborenen Kindes und die Fruchtabtreibung in der Bewertung der heidnischen und christlichen Antike', *Antike und Christentum: Kultur und religionsgeschichte Studien* 4 (1934), 1–61

Dombrowski, D. A., 'St. Augustine, Abortion and Libido Crudelis', *Journal of the History of Ideas* 49.1 (1988), 151–6

Dombrowski, D. A. and Deltete, R., *A Brief, Liberal, Catholic Defense of Abortion* (Urbana IL, 2000)

Douglas, M., 'Population Control in Primitive Groups', *British Journal of Sociology* 17.3 (1966), 263–73

—— *Purity and Danger: An Analysis of Concepts of Pollution and Taboo*, new edn (London, 2002)

—— *Natural Symbols*, 2nd edn (London, 2006)

Dubarle, A.-M., 'La Bible et les pères ont-ils parlé de la contraception?', *La vie spirituelle*, suppl. 63 (1962), 573–610

—— 'La contraception chez Césaire d'Arles', *La vie spirituelle*, suppl. 67 (1963), 515–19

Duby, G., *Rural Economy and Country Life in the Medieval West*, trans. C. Paston (Columbia SC, 1968)

Duden, B., *Disembodying Women: Perspectives on Pregnancy and the Unborn*, trans. L. Hoinacki (Cambridge MA, 1993)

—— 'The Fetus on the "Farther Shore": Towards a History of the Unborn', in *Fetal Subjects, Feminist Positions*, ed. L. M. Morgan and M. W. Michaels (Philadelphia, 1999), pp. 13–25

Dunstan, G. R., 'The Moral Status of the Human Embryo: A Tradition Recalled', *Journal of Medical Ethics* 10.1 (1984), 38–44
—— 'The Human Embryo in the Western Moral Tradition', in *The Status of the Embryo: Perspectives from Moral Tradition*, ed. G. R. Dunstan and M. J. Sellers (London, 1988), pp. 39–57
Dupont, A., *Gratia in Augustine's* Sermones ad Populum *during the Pelagian Controversy*, trans. B. Doyle (Leiden, 2013)
Dupraz, L., 'Deux préceptes de Lothaire II (867 et 868), ou les vestiges diplomatiques d'un divorce manqué', *Zeitschrift für schweizerische Kirchengeschichte* 59 (1965), 193–236
Edelstein, L., 'The Hippocratic Oath: Text, Translation and Interpretation', reprinted in *Ancient Medicine: Selected Papers of Ludwig Edelstein*, ed. O. Temkin and C. L. Temkin (Baltimore, 1967), pp. 3–63
Edwards, C., *The Politics of Immorality in Ancient Rome* (Cambridge, 1993)
Egmond, F., 'Incestuous Relations and their Punishment in the Dutch Republic', *Eighteenth-Century Life* 25.3 (2001), 20–42
Elliott, D., *The Bride of Christ Goes to Hell: Metaphor and Embodiment in the Lives of Pious Women, 200–1500* (Philadelphia, 2012)
Elsakkers, M., 'Raptus Ultra Rhenum: Early Ninth-Century Saxon Laws on Abduction and Rape', *Amsterdamer Beiträge zur Älteren Germanistik* 52 (1999), 27–53
—— 'Genre-Hopping: Aristotelian Criteria for Abortion in Germania', in *Germanic Texts and Latin Models: Medieval Reconstructions*, ed. K. E. Olsen et al. (Leuven, 2001), pp. 73–92
—— 'Inflicting Serious Bodily Harm: The Visigothic *Antiquae* on Violence and Abortion', *Tijdschrift voor Rechtgeschiedenis* 71 (2003), 55–63
—— 'Abortion, Poisoning, Magic and Contraception in Eckhardt's *Pactus Legis Salicae*', *Amsterdamer Beiträge zur Älteren Germanistik* 57 (2003), 233–267
—— '*Her anda Neylar*: an Intriguing Criterion for Abortion in Old Frisian Law', *Scientiarum Historia* 30 (2004), 107–154
—— 'Gothic Bible, Vetus Latina and Visigothic Law: Evidence for a Septuagint-based Gothic version of Exodus', *Sacris Eruditi* 44 (2005), 37–76
—— 'The Early Medieval Latin and Vernacular Vocabulary of Abortion and Embryology', in *Science Translated: Latin and Vernacular Translations of Scientific Treatises in Medieval Europe*, ed. P. de Leemans et al. (Leuven, 2008), pp. 377–413
—— 'Reading Between the Lines: Old Germanic and Early Christian Views on Abortion' (unpublished Ph.D. dissertation, University of Amsterdam, 2010)
Esposito, M., 'On the Earliest Latin Life of St. Brigid of Kildare', *Proceedings of the Royal Irish Academy. Section C: Archaeology, Celtic Studies, History, Linguistics, Literature* 30 (1912/13), 307–26
Etienne, R., 'La conscience médicale antique et la vie des enfants', *Annales de démographie historique* (1973), 16–46
Evans Grubb, J., 'Infanticide and Infant Exposure', in *The Oxford Handbook of Childhood and Education in the Classical World*, ed. J. Evans Grubb et al. (Oxford, 2013), pp. 83–107
Eyben, E., 'Family Planning in Graeco-Roman Antiquity', *Ancient Society* 11/12 (1980/1), 5–82

Faulkner, T., 'Carolingian Kings and the *Leges Barbarorum*', *Historical Research* 86.233 (2013), 443–64

Fear, A., 'God and Caesar: The Dynamics of Visigothic Monarchy', in *Every Inch a King: Comparative Studies on Kings and Kingship in the Ancient and Medieval Worlds*, ed. L. Mitchell and C. Melville (Leiden, 2013), pp. 285–302

Fedwick, P. J., 'The Translation of the Works of Basil before 1400', in *Basil of Caesarea: Christian, Humanist, Ascetic*, 2 vols., ed. P.J. Fedwick (Toronto, 1981) II, pp. 439–512

Feldman, D. M., *Birth Control in Jewish Law: Marital Relations, Contraception, and Abortion as set forth in the Classic Texts of Jewish Law* (New York, 1968)

Ferraro, J. M., *Nefarious Crimes, Contested Justice: Illicit Sex and Infanticide in the Republic of Venice, 1557–1789* (Baltimore, 2008)

Ferreiro, A., 'The Missionary Labors of St. Martin of Braga in 6th Century Galicia', *Studia Monastica* 23 (1981), 11–26

—— 'Early Medieval Missionary Tactics: The Example of Martin and Caesarius', *Studia Historica Antigua* 6 (1988), 225–38

—— '"Frequenter legere": The Propagation of Literacy, Education, and Divine Wisdom in Caesarius of Arles', *JEH* 43.1 (1992), 5–15

—— 'Jerome's Polemic against Priscillian in his *Letter* to Ctesiphon (133,4)', reprinted in A. Ferreiro, *Simon Magus in Patristic, Medieval and Early Modern Traditions* (Leiden, 2005), pp. 83–110

—— 'Priscillianism and Nicolaitism', reprinted in A. Ferreiro, *Simon Magus in Patristic, Medieval and Early Modern Traditions* (Leiden, 2005), pp. 111–22

Filotas, B., *Pagan Survivals, Superstitions and Popular Cultures in Early Medieval Pastoral Literature* (Toronto, 2005)

Finch, C. E., 'Juvenal in Codex Vat. Lat. 5204', *Classical Philology* 65.1 (1970), 47–8

Finucane, R. C., *The Rescue of the Innocents: Endangered Children in Medieval Miracles* (Basingstoke, 1997)

Firey, A., 'Ghostly Recensions in Early Medieval Canon Law: The Problem of the *Collectio Dacheriana* and its Shades', *Tijdschrift voor rechtsgeschiedenis* 68 (2000), 63–82

—— 'The Letter of the Law: Carolingian Exegetes and the Old Testament', in *With Reverence for the Word: Medieval Scriptural Exegesis in Judaism, Christianity, and Islam*, ed. J. D. McAuliffe et al. (Oxford, 2003), pp. 204–24

—— *A Contrite Heart: Prosecution and Redemption in the Carolingian Empire* (Leiden, 2009)

Fischer, B., 'Impedimenta mundi fecerunt eos miseros', *Vigiliae Christianae* 5 (1951), 84–7

Fitzpatrick, A., 'Bodily Identity in Scholastic Theology' (unpublished Ph.D. dissertation, University College London, 2013), available at http://discovery.ucl.ac.uk/1411124/1/FITZPATRICK_730544%20PhD%20Thesis.pdf [accessed 17 December 2014]

Flamion, J., *Les Actes Apocryphes de l'Apôtre André: Les Actes d'André et de Mathias, de Pierre et d'André et les textes apparentés* (Paris, 1911)

Flandrin, J.-L., *Families in Former Times: Kingship, Household and Sexuality*, trans. R. Southern (Cambridge, 1979)

—— *Un temps pour embrasser: Aux origines de la morale sexuelle occidentale (VIe–IXe siècle)* (Paris, 1983)
—— 'Contraception, Marriage, and Sexual Relations in the Christian West', reprinted in *Biology of Man in History: Selections from the Annales – Économies, Sociétés, Civilisations*, ed. R. Forster and O. Ranum, trans. E. Forster and P. Ranum (Baltimore, 1975), pp. 23–47

Flechner, R., 'The Making of the Canons of Theodore', *Peritia* 17–18 (2003–4), 121–43
—— 'The Problem of Originality in Early Medieval Canon Law: Legislating by Means of Contradictions in the *Collectio Hibernensis*', *Viator* 43.2 (2012), 29–48

Flemming, R., *Medicine and the Making of Roman Women: Gender, Nature, and Authority from Celsus to Galen* (Oxford, 2000)

Flint, V. I. J., *The Rise of Magic in Early Medieval Europe* (Oxford, 1991)
—— 'Magic and Marriage in Ninth-Century Francia: Lothar, Hincmar – and Susanna', in *The Culture of Christendom: Essays in Medieval History in Commemoration of Denis L.T. Bethell*, ed. M.A. Meyer (London, 1993), pp. 61–74

Fontanille, M.-T., *Avortement et contraception dans la médécine gréco-romaine* (Montrouge, 1977)

Fox, M., 'Alcuin the Exegete: The Evidence of the *Quaestiones in Genesim*', in *The Study of the Bible in the Carolingian Era*, ed. C. Chazelle and B. Van Name Edwards (Turnhout, 2003), pp. 39–60

Frantzen, A. J., 'The Significance of the Frankish Penitentials', *JEH* 30.4 (1979) 409–21
—— *The Literature of Penance in Anglo-Saxon England* (New Brunswick NJ, 1983)
—— *Mise à jour du fascicule no. 27* (Turnhout, 1985) [revision of Vogel, *Les 'Libri Paenitentiales*]
—— *Before the Closet: Same-Sex Love from* Beowulf *to* Angels in America (Chicago, 1998)

Frederiksen, A., 'Tyconius and Augustine on the Apocalypse', in *The Apocalypse in the Middle Ages*, ed. R.K. Emmerson and B. McGinn (Ithaca NY, 1992), pp. 20–37

Fulton, R., *From Judgment to Passion: Devotion to Christ and Mary, 800–1200* (Ithaca NY, 2002)

Gaastra, A. H., 'Penance and the Law: The Penitential Canons of the *Collection in Nine Books*', *EME* 14.1 (2006), 85–102

Gaca, K. L., 'The Reproductive Technology of the Pythagoreans', *Classical Philology* 95.2 (2000), 113–32

Gaillard, M., 'Un évêque et son temps: Advence de Metz (858–875)', in *Lotharingia – une région au centre de l'Europe autour de l'an Mil*, ed. H.-W. Herrmann and R. Schneider (Saarbrücken, 1995), pp. 89–119
—— 'Du pouvoir des femmes en Francia Media: épouses et filles des souverains (ca. 850–ca. 950)', in *De la mer du Nord à la Méditerranée. Francia Media. Une région au coeur de l'Europe (c.840–c.1050)*, ed. M. Gaillard *et al.* (Luxembourg, 2011), pp. 301–14

Galvão-Sobrinho, C., 'Hippocratic Ideals, Medical Ethics, and the Practice of Medicine in the Early Middle Ages: The Legacy of the Hippocratic Oath', *JHMAS* 51.4 (1996), 438–55

Gamel, M.-K., '*Non sine caede*: Abortion Politics and Poetics in Ovid's *Amores*', *Helios* 16 (1989), 183–206.

Garrett, F., 'Ordering Human Growth in Tibetan Medical and Religious

Embryologies', in *Textual Healing: Essays on Medieval and Early Modern Medicine*, ed. E. Furdel (Leiden, 2005), pp. 31–52
—— *Religion, Medicine and the Human Embryo in Tibet* (London, 2008)
Garver, V. L., *Women and Aristocratic Culture in the Carolingian World* (Ithaca NY, 2009)
—— 'Childbearing and Infancy in the Carolingian World', *JHS* 21.2 (2012), 208–44
Gaudemet, J., 'Les statuts épiscopaux de la première décade du IXe siècle', reprinted in *La formation du droit canonique médiéval* (Aldershot, 1980) XIII, pp. 303–49
George, J., *Venantius Fortunatus: A Latin Poet in Merovingian Gaul* (Oxford, 1992)
Glasser, M., 'Marriage in Medieval Hagiography', *Studies in Medieval and Renaissance History*, n.s., 4 (1981), 1–34
Goffart, W., *The Narrators of Barbarian History (A.D. 550–800): Jordanes, Gregory of Tours, Bede, and Paul the Deacon* (Princeton, 1988)
Goldberg, E. J., *Struggle for Empire: Kingship and Courtship under Louis the German, 817–876* (Ithaca NY, 2006)
Gorman, M. J., *Abortion and the Early Church: Christian, Jewish and Pagan Attitudes in the Greco-Roman World* (Downers Grove IL, 1982)
Gorman, M. [M.], 'The Commentary on the Pentateuch Attributed to Bede in PL 91.189–394', *Revue Bénédictine* 106 (1996), 61–108, 255–307.
Gould, G., 'Childhood in Eastern Patristic Thought: Some Problems of Theology and Theological Anthropology', in *The Church and Childhood*, SCH 31, ed. D. Wood (Oxford, 1994), pp. 39–52
Gourevitch, D., 'Chirurgie obstétricale dans le monde romain', in *Naissance et petite enfance dans l'antiquité*, ed. V. Dasen (Fribourg, 2004), pp. 291–333
Gourinat, J.-B., 'L'embryon végétatif et la formation de l'âme selon les stoïcens', in *L'embryon formation et animation: Antiquité grecque et latine, traditions hébraïque, chrétienne et islamique*, ed. L. Brisson et al. (Paris, 2008), pp. 59–77
Gray, P., 'Abortion, Infanticide, and the Social Rhetoric of the *Apocalypse of Peter*', *JECS* 9.3 (2001), 313–37
Green, M. H., 'The Transmission of Ancient Theories of Female Physiology and Disease through the Early Middle Ages' (unpublished Ph.D. dissertation, Princeton University, 1985)
—— 'Gendering the History of Women's Healthcare', *Gender & History* 20 (2008), 487–518
Grémy, J.-P., 'Une enquête au début de Xe siècle: le questionnaire synodal de Réginon de Prüm', *European Journal of Sociology* 49.2 (2008), 325–59
Grisez, G., *Abortion: The Myths, the Realities, and the Arguments* (New York, 1970)
Gross-Diaz, T., *The Psalms Commentary of Gilbert of Poitiers: From Lectio Divina to the Lecture Room* (Leiden, 1996)
Gudorf, C. E., 'Contraception and Abortion in Roman Catholicism', in *Sacred Rights: The Case for Contraception and Abortion in World Religions*, ed. D. C. Maguire (Oxford, 2003), pp. 55–78
Hahn, T., 'The Indian Tradition in Western Medieval Intellectual History', *Viator* 9 (1978), 213–34
Hall, T. N., 'The Early Medieval Sermon', in *The Sermon*, Typologie des sources du Moyen Age Occidental 81–3, ed. B. M. Kienzle (Turnhout, 2000), pp. 203–47

Halsall, G., 'Female Status and Power in Early Merovingian Central Austrasia: The Burial Evidence', *EME* 5.1 (1996), 1–24
—— 'Material Culture, Sex, Gender, Sexuality and Transgression in Sixth-Century Gaul', in G. Halsall, *Cemeteries and Society in Merovingian Gaul: Selected Studies in History and Archaeology, 1992–2009* (Leiden, 2010), pp. 327–55
Hamilton, S., *The Practice of Penance, 900–1050* (London, 2001)
—— 'Inquiring into Adultery and Other Wicked Deeds: Episcopal Justice in Tenth- and Eleventh-Century Italy', *Viator* 41.2 (2010), 21–44
Hammer, C. I., 'Country Churches, Clerical Inventories and the Carolingian Renaissance in Bavaria', *Church History* 49.1 (1980), 5–17
—— 'Arbeo of Freising's "Life and Passion" of St Emmeram', *Revue d'histoire ecclésiastique* 100.1 (2006), 5–36
Hanson, A. E., 'Continuity and Change: Three Case Studies in Hippocratic Gynecological Therapy and Theory', in *Women's History and Ancient History*, ed. S. B. Pomeroy (Chapel Hill NC, 1991), pp. 73–110
Hanson, A. E. and Green, M. H., 'Soranus of Ephesus: *Methodicorum princeps*', in *Aufstieg und Niedergang der römischen Welt* II, 37, ed. W. Hasse and H. Temporini (Berlin, 1994), pp. 968–1075
Hardt, M., 'The Bavarians', in *Regna and Gentes: The Relationship between Late Antique and Early Medieval Peoples and Kingdoms in the Transformation of the Roman World*, ed. H.-W. Goetz et al. (Leiden, 2003), pp. 429–61
Harmless, W., *Augustine and the Catechumenate* (Collegeville MN, 1995)
Harper, K., *Slavery in the Late Roman World, AD 275–425* (Cambridge, 2011)
—— *From Shame to Sin: The Christian Transformation of Sexual Morality in Late Antiquity* (Cambridge MA, 2013)
Harrington, C., *Women in a Celtic Church: Ireland, 450–1150* (Oxford, 2002)
Harrington, J. F., *The Unwanted Child: The Fate of Foundlings, Orphans and Juvenile Criminals in Early Modern Germany* (Chicago, 2009)
Harris-Stoertz, F., 'Pregnancy and Childbirth in Twelfth- and Thirteenth-Century French and English Law', *JHS* 21.2 (2012), 263–81
Hartmann, W., 'Raban et le droit', in *Raban Maur et son temps*, ed. P. Depreux et al. (Turnhout, 2010), pp. 91–104
Hayward, P. A., 'Suffering and Innocence in Latin Sermons for the Feast of the Holy Innocents, c.400–800', in *The Church and Childhood*, SCH 31, ed. D. Wood (Woodbridge, 1994), pp. 67–80
Heene, K., *The Legacy of Paradise: Marriage, Motherhood and Woman in Carolingian Edifying Literature* (Frankfurt, 1997)
Heidecker, K., *The Divorce of Lothar II: Christian Marriage and Political Power in the Carolingian World*, trans. T. M. Guest (Ithaca NY, 2010)
—— 'Gathering and Recycling Authoritative Texts: The Importance of Marginalia in Hincmar of Reims' Treatise about King Lothar's Divorce', in *Organizing the Written Word: Scripts, Manuscripts and Texts*, ed. Marco Mostert (Turnhout, forthcoming).
Heil, J., 'Haimo's Commentary on Paul: Sources, Methods and Theology', in *Études d'exégèse carolingienne: Autour d'Haymon d'Auxerre*, ed. S. Shimahara (Turnhout, 2007), pp. 103–21.
Hen, Y., *Culture and Religion in Merovingian Gaul, A.D. 481–751* (Leiden, 1995)

Bibliography

—— 'Knowledge of Canon Law among Rural Priests: The Evidence of Two Carolingian Manuscripts from around 800', *Journal of Theological Studies*, n.s., 50.1 (1999), 117–34
—— 'Martin of Braga's *De correctione rusticorum* and Its Uses in Frankish Gaul', in *Medieval Transformations: Texts, Power, and Gifts in Context*, ed. E. Cohen and M. B. de Jong (Leiden, 2001), pp. 35–49
—— 'Paganism and Superstitions in the Time of Gregory of Tours: *Une question mal posée!*', in *The World of Gregory of Tours*, ed. K. Mitchell and I. Wood (Leiden, 2002), pp. 229–40
—— 'The Liturgy of the Bobbio Missal', in *The Bobbio Missal: Liturgy and Religious Culture in Merovingian Gaul*, ed. Y. Hen and R. Meens (Cambridge, 2004), pp. 140–53
—— 'The Contents and Aims of the so-called Homiliary of Burchard of Würzburg', in *Sermo Doctorum: Compilers, Preachers, and Their Audiences in the Early Medieval West*, ed. M. Diesenberger *et al.* (Turnhout, 2013), pp. 127–52
Hen, Y. and Meens, R., 'Conclusion', in *The Bobbio Missal: Liturgy and Religious Culture in Merovingian Gaul*, ed. Y. Hen and R. Meens (Cambridge, 2004), pp. 219–22
Henstra, D. J., *The Evolution of the Money Standard in Medieval Frisia: A Treatise on the History of Systems of Money of Account in the former Frisia (c.600–c.1500)* (Amsterdam, 1999)
Herlihy, D., 'Households in the Early Middle Ages: Symmetry and Sainthood', in *Households: Comparative and Historical Studies of the Domestic Group*, ed. R. McC. Netting *et al.* (Berkeley CA, 1984), pp. 383–406
Hilhorst, A., 'The Apocalypse of Paul: Previous History and Afterlife', in *The Visio Pauli and the Gnostic Apocalypse of Paul*, ed. J. M. Bremmer and I. Czachesz (Leuven, 2007) pp. 1–23
Hillgarth, J. N., 'St. Julian of Toledo in the Middle Ages', *Journal of the Warburg and Courtauld Institutes* 21.1/2 (1958), 7–26
Himes, N. E., *Medical History of Contraception* (Baltimore, 1936)
Hirt, M., 'La législation romaine et les droits de l'enfant', in *Naissance et petite enfance dans l'antiquité*, ed. V. Dasen (Fribourg, 2004), pp. 281–91
Hollander, H. W. and van der Hout, G. E., 'The Apostle Paul calling himself an Abortion: 1 Cor. 15:8 within the context of 1 Cor. 15:8–10', *Novum Testamentum* 38.3 (1996), 224–36
Hollis, S., *Anglo-Saxon Women: Sharing a Common Fate* (Woodbridge, 1992)
Honings, B., 'L'aborto in alcuni decretali episopali: una reazione decretale all'arbitrarietà penitenziale', *Apollinaris* 49 (1976), 201–17
—— 'L'aborto nei libri penitenziali Irlandesi: convergenza morale e divergenze pastorali', reprinted in *Una componente della mentalità occidentale: penitenziali nell'alto medio evo*, ed. M. G. Muzzarelli (Bologna, 1980), pp. 155–84
Hopkins, K., 'Contraception in the Roman Empire', *Comparative Studies in Society and History* 8 (1965), 124–51
Horden, P., 'What's Wrong with Early Medieval Medicine?', *SHM* 24.1 (2011), 5–25
Horn, C. B. and Martens, J. W., *'Let the Little Children Come to Me': Childhood and Children in Early Christianity* (Washington DC, 2009)

Howlett, D., 'The Prologue to the *Collectio Canonum Hibernensis*', *Peritia* 17–18 (2003–4), 144–49

Hughes, K. L., *Constructing Antichrist: Paul, Biblical Commentary, and the Development of Doctrine in the Early Middle Ages* (Washington DC, 2005)

Huser, R. J., *The Crime of Abortion in Canon Law: An Historical Synopsis and Commentary* (Washington DC, 1942)

Innes, M., 'Charlemagne, Justice and Written Law', in *Law, Custom, and Justice in Late Antiquity and the Early Middle Ages*, ed. A. Rio (London, 2011), pp. 155–203

Jackson, B. S., 'The Problem of Exod. XXI 22–5 (*Ius talionis*)', *Vetus Testamentum* 23.3 (1973), 273–304

Jacobsen Buckley, J., 'Libertines or Not: Fruit, Bread, Semen and Other Body Fluids in Gnosticism', *JECS* 2.1 (1994), 15–31

Jakab, A., 'The Reception of the Apocalypse of Peter in Ancient Christianity', in *The Apocalypse of Peter*, ed. J. N. Bremmer and I. Czachesz (Leuven, 2003), pp. 174–86

James, W. R., 'Placing the Unborn: On the Social Recognition of New Life', *Anthropology and Medicine* 7.2 (2000), 169–89

Janes, D., 'Sex and Text: The Afterlife of Medieval Penance in Britain and Ireland', in *Medieval Sexuality: A Casebook*, ed. A. Harper and C. Proctor (London, 2008), pp. 32–44

Jasper, D. and Fuhrmann, H., *Papal Letters in the Early Middle Ages* (Washington DC, 2001)

Jensen, R. M., '*Mater Ecclesia* and *Fons Aeterna*: The Church and Her Womb in Ancient Christian Tradition', in *A Feminist Companion to Patristic Literature*, ed. A.-J. Levine (London, 2008), pp. 137–55

Jeudy, C., 'L'oeuvre de Remi', in *L'école carolingienne d'Auxerre: De Murethach à Remi 830–908*, ed. D. Iogna-Prat *et al.* (Paris, 1991), pp. 373–97

—— 'Remigii autissiodorensis opera (Clavis)', in *L'école carolingienne d'Auxerre: De Murethach à Remi 830–908*, ed. D. Iogna-Prat *et al.* (Paris, 1991), pp. 457–500

Jobert, P., 'Holy Innocents in Our Times', in *Abortion and Martyrdom: The Papers of the Solesme Consultation and an Appeal to the Catholic Church*, ed. A. Nichols (Leominster, 2002), pp. 120–5

Jones, A. E., *Social Mobility in Late Antique Gaul: Strategies and Opportunities for the Non-Elite* (Cambridge, 2009)

Jones, D. A., *The Soul of the Embryo: An Inquiry into the Status of the Human Embryo in the Christian Tradition* (London, 2004)

de Jong, M., *In Samuel's Image: Child Oblation in the Early Medieval West* (Leiden, 1996)

—— 'What was Public about Public Penance? *Paenitentia publica* and Justice in the Carolingian World', in *La giustizia nell'alto medioevo*, Settimane di studio del Centro Italiano di studi sull'alto Medioevo 42 (Spoleto, 1997), pp. 863–904

—— '*Imitatio morum*: The Cloister and Clerical Purity in the Carolingian World', in *Medieval Purity and Piety: Essays on Medieval Clerical Celibacy and Religious Reform*, ed. M. Frassetto (New York, 1998), pp. 49–80

—— 'Adding Insult to Injury: Julian of Toledo and his *Historia Wambae*', in *The Visigoths from the Migration Period to the Seventh Century: An Ethnographic Perspective*, ed. P. Heather (Woodbridge, 1999), pp. 373–89

Bibliography

—— 'Transformations of Penance', in *Rituals of Power from Late Antiquity to the Early Middle Ages*, ed. F. Theuws and J. L. Nelson (Leiden, 2000), pp. 185–224
—— 'Exegesis for an Empress', in *Medieval Transformations: Texts, Power, and Gifts in Context*, ed. E. Cohen and M. de Jong (Leiden, 2001), pp. 69–100
—— *The Penitential State: Authority and Atonement in the Age of Louis the Pious* (Cambridge, 2009)
Jütte, R., *Contraception: A History*, trans. V. Russell (Cambridge, 2008)
van Kampen, L., 'Acta Andreae and Gregory's "De Miraculis Andreae"', *Vigiliae Christianae* 45.1 (1991), 18–26
Kapparis, K., *Abortion in the Ancient World* (London, 2002)
Karras, R. M., 'The History of Marriage and the Myth of Friedelehe', *EME* 14.2 (2006), 119–51
Kasten, B., 'Stepmothers in Frankish Legal Life', in *Law, Laity and Solidarities: Essays in honour of Susan Reynolds*, ed. P. Stafford *et al.* (Manchester, 2001), pp. 47–67
Keefe, S. A., *Water and the Word: Baptism and the Education of the Clergy in the Carolingian Empire*, 2 vols. (Notre Dame IN, 2002)
Kelleher, M. A., '"Like man and wife": Clerics' Concubines in the Diocese of Barcelona', *Journal of Medieval History* 28 (2002), 349–60
Keller, A., *Die Abortiva in der römischen Kaiserzeit* (Stuttgart, 1988)
Keller, E., 'Embryonic Individuals: The Rhetoric of Seventeenth-Century Embryology and the Construction of Early-Modern Identity', *Eighteenth-Century Studies* 33.3 (2000), 321–48
Kelly, K. C., *Performing Virginity and Testing Chastity in the Middle Ages* (London, 2000)
Kenney, E. J., 'The Manuscript Tradition of Ovid's Amores, Ars Amatoria and Remedia Amoris', *Classical Quarterly*, n.s., 12.1 (1962), 1–31
Kéry, L., *Canonical Collections of the Early Middle Ages (ca. 400–1140): A Bibliographical Guide to the Manuscripts and Literature* (Washington DC, 1999)
Kessler, G., *Conceiving Israel: The Fetus in Rabbinic Narratives* (Philadelphia, 2009)
Keulen, W., *Gellius the Satirist: Roman Cultural Authority in the Attic Nights* (Leiden, 2009)
Kim, M. I., 'A Parrot and Piety: Alcuin's Nightingale and Ovid's "Amores" 2.6', *Latomus* 51.4 (1992), 881–91
King, H., *Hippocrates' Woman: Reading the Female Body in Ancient Greece* (London, 1998)
King, P. D., *Law and Society in the Visigothic Kingdom* (Cambridge, 1972)
—— 'King Chindasvind and the First Territorial Law-Code of the Visigothic Kingdom', in *Visigothic Spain: New Approaches*, ed. E. James (Oxford, 1980), pp. 131–57
Kitchen, J., *Saints' Lives and the Rhetoric of Gender* (Oxford, 1998)
Klingshirn, W. E., 'Charity and Power: Caesarius of Arles and the Ransoming of Captives in Sub-Roman Gaul', *Journal of Roman Studies* 75 (1985), 183–203
—— 'Church Politics and Chronology: Dating the Episcopacy of Caesarius of Arles', *Revue des études augustiniennes* 38 (1992), 80–88
—— *Caesarius of Arles: The Making of a Christian Community* (Cambridge, 1994)
Koon, S. and Wood, J., 'Unity from Disunity: Law, Rhetoric and Power in the Visigothic Kingdom', *European Review of History* 16.6 (2009), 793–808

Körntgen, L., 'Canon Law and the Practice of Penance: Burchard of Worms's Penitential', *EME* 14.1 (2006), 103–17

Koskenniemi, E., *The Exposure of Infants among Jews and Christians in Antiquity* (Sheffield, 2009)

—— 'Right to Life and Jewish-Christian Ethics in the Roman World: A Case Study of the Fighting Men and the Unhappy Birth', in *Encounters of the Children of Abraham from Ancient to Modern Times*, ed. A. Laato and P. Lindqvist (Leiden, 2010), pp. 47–73

Kudlien, F., 'Medical Ethics and Popular Ethics in Greece and Rome', *Clio Medica* 5 (1970), 91–121

Laeuchli, S., *Power and Sexuality: The Emergence of Canon Law at the Synod of Elvira* (Philadelphia, 1972)

Lancel, S., *Saint Augustine*, trans. A. Nevill (London, 2002)

Langlands, R., *Sexual Morality in Ancient Rome* (Cambridge, 2006)

Lapidge, M., 'The School of Theodore and Hadrian', *Anglo-Saxon England* 15 (1986), 45–72

—— 'The Career of Archbishop Theodore', in *Archbishop Theodore: Commemorative Studies on his Life and Influence*, ed. M. Lapidge (Cambridge, 1995), pp. 1–29

Lassen, E. M., 'The Ultimate Crime: Parricidium and the Concept of Family in the Late Roman Republic and Early Empire', *Classica et mediaevalia* 43 (1993), 147–62

Le Jan, R., *Famille et pouvoir dans le monde franc (VIIe–Xe siècle): Essai d'anthropologie sociale* (Paris, 1995)

Lecky, W. E. H., *History of European Morals from Augustus to Charlemagne*, 2 vols., 3rd edn (London, 1877)

Lemmens, M., *Lexical Perspectives on Transitivity and Ergativity: Causative Constructions in English* (Amsterdam, 1998)

Lepicard, E., 'The Embryo in Ancient Rabbinic Literature: Between Religious Law and Didactic Narratives: An Interpretative Essay', *History and Philosophy of the Life Sciences* 32 (2010), 21–42

Levi, G., 'On Microhistory', in *New Perspectives on Historical Writing*, ed. P. Burke (Cambridge, 1991), pp. 93–113

Leyser, C., '"This Sainted Isle": Panegyrics, Nostalgia, and the Invention of Lerinian Monasticism', in *The Limits of Ancient Christianity: Essays on Late Antique Thought and Culture in honour of R. A. Markus*, ed. W. E. Klingshirn and M. Vessey (Ann Arbor MI, 1999) pp. 188–206

—— *Authority and Asceticism from Augustine to Gregory the Great* (Oxford, 2000)

van Liere, F., *An Introduction to the Medieval Bible* (Cambridge, 2014)

Loewe, R., 'The Medieval History of the Latin Vulgate', in *The Cambridge History of the Bible: The West from the Fathers to the Reformation*, ed. G. W. H. Lampe (Cambridge, 1969), pp. 102–54

Lövkrona, I., 'Gender, Power and Honour: Child Murder in Premodern Sweden', *Ethnologia Europaea* 32.1 (2004), 5–14

van der Lugt, M., *Le ver, le démon et la vierge: Les théories médiévales de la generation extraordinaire* (Paris, 2004)

Lynch, C. H., *Saint Braulio, Bishop of Saragossa (631–51): His Life and Writings* (Washington DC, 1938)

MacIntyre, A., *After Virtue: A Study in Moral Theory*, 2nd edn (London, 1985)
MacKinney, L. C., *Early Medieval Medicine: With special reference to France and Chartres* (Baltimore, 1937)
—— 'Medical Ethics and Etiquette in the Early Middle Ages: The Persistence of Hippocratic Ideals', *Bulletin of the History of Medicine* 26.1 (1952), 1–31
MacLean, S., *Kingship and Politics in the Late Ninth Century: Charles the Fat and the End of the Carolingian Empire* (Cambridge, 2003)
MacPherson, R. M., *Rome in Involution: Cassiodorus' Variae in their Literary and Historical Setting* (Poznan, 1989)
Maguire, D. C. and Burtchaell, J., 'The Catholic Legacy on Abortion: A Debate', in *On Moral Medicine: Theological Perspectives in Medical Ethics*, ed. S. E. Lammers and A. Verhey (Grand Rapids MN, 1998), pp. 586–99
Manselli, R., 'Vie familiale et éthique sexuelle dans les pénitentiels', in *Famille et parenté dans l'Occident médiéval*, ed. G. Duby and J. le Goff (Rome, 1977), pp. 363–78
Maquet, J., *'Faire justice' dans le diocèse de Liège au Moyen Âge (VIIIe–XIIe siècles): Essai du droit judiciare reconstitué* (Liège, 2008)
Markus, R. A., *The End of Ancient Christianity* (Cambridge, 1990)
—— 'From Caesarius to Boniface: Christianity and Paganism in Gaul', in *The Seventh Century: Continuity and Change*, ed. J. Fontaine and J. N. Hillgarth (London, 1992), pp. 154–68
Martin, C., *La géographie du pouvoir dans l'Espagne visigothique* (Villeneuve-d'Asq, 2003)
Mathisen, R., 'The "Second Council of Arles" and the Spirit of Compilation and Codification in Late Roman Gaul', *JECS* 5.4 (1997), 511–54
Mayeski, M. A., '"Let women not despair": Rabanus Maurus on Women as Prophets', *Journal of Theological Studies* 58.2 (1997), 237–50
McClanan, A. L., '"Weapons to probe the womb": The Material Culture of Abortion and Contraception in the Early Byzantine Period', in *The Material Culture of Sex, Procreation, and Marriage in Premodern Europe*, ed. A. L. McClanan and E. R. Encarnación (New York, 2002), pp. 33–58
McCune, J. C., 'An Edition and Study of Select Sermons from the Carolingian Sermonary of Salzburg' (unpublished Ph.D. dissertation, University of London, 2006), available at https://kclpure.kcl.ac.uk/portal/files/2930713/441286.pdf [accessed 17 December 2014]
McKeon, P. R., *Hincmar of Laon and Carolingian Politics* (Urbana IL, 1978)
McKitterick, R., [as Pierce, R.], 'The "Frankish" Penitentials', in *The Materials, Sources and Methods of Ecclesiastical History*, SCH 11, ed. D. Baker (Oxford, 1975), pp. 31–9
—— *The Frankish Church and the Carolingian Reforms, 789–895* (London, 1977)
—— 'Some Carolingian Law-books and their Function', in *Authority and Power: Studies on Medieval Law and Government presented to Walter Ullmann on his Seventieth Birthday* (Cambridge, 1980), pp. 13–28
—— 'Knowledge of Canon Law in the Frankish Kingdoms before 789: The Manuscript Evidence', *Journal of Theological Studies* 36.1 (1985), 91–117
—— *The Carolingians and the Written Word* (Cambridge, 1989)
—— 'The Scripts of the Bobbio Missal', in *The Bobbio Missal: Liturgy and Religious*

Culture in Merovingian Gaul, ed. Y. Hen and R. Meens (Cambridge, 2004), pp. 19–52

—— 'Charlemagne's *Missi* and their Books', in *Early Medieval Studies in memory of Patrick Wormald*, ed. S. Baxter (Farnham, 2009), pp. 253–67

McLaren, A., *A History of Contraception: From Antiquity to the Present Day* (Oxford, 1990)

McNamara, J. A., 'Chastity as a Third Gender in the History and Hagiography of Gregory of Tours', in *The World of Gregory of Tours*, ed. K. Mitchell and I. Wood (Leiden, 2002), pp. 199–209

McNeill, J. T., 'Medicine for Sin as Prescribed in the Penitentials', *Church History* 1.1 (1932), 14–26

Meens, R., 'The Frequency and Nature of Early Medieval Penance', in *Handling Sin: Confession in the Middle Ages*, ed. P. Biller and A. J. Minnis (York, 1998), pp. 35–61

—— 'Questioning Ritual Purity: The Influence of Gregory the Great's Answers to Augustine's Queries about Childbirth, Menstruation and Sexuality', in *St Augustine and the Conversion of England*, ed. R. Gameson (Stroud, 1999), pp. 174–86

—— 'Religious Instruction in the Frankish Kingdoms', in *Medieval Transformations: Texts, Power, and Gifts in Context*, ed. E. Cohen and M. de Jong (Leiden, 2001), pp. 51–68

—— 'The Oldest Manuscript Witness of the *Collectio Canonum Hibernensis*', *Peritia* 14 (2001), 1–19

—— 'Reforming the Clergy: A Context for the Use of the Bobbio Missal', in *The Bobbio Missal: Liturgy and Religious Culture in Merovingian Gaul*, ed. Y. Hen and R. Meens (Cambridge, 2004), pp. 168–86

—— '"Aliud benitenciale": The Ninth-Century *Paenitentiale Vindobense C*', *Medieval Studies* 66 (2004), 1–26

—— 'Introduction: Penitential Questions: Sin, Satisfaction and Reconciliation in the Tenth and Eleventh Centuries', *EME* 14.1 (2006), 1–6

—— 'Penitentials and the Practice of Penance in the Tenth and Eleventh Centuries', *EME* 14.1 (2006), 7–21

—— 'The Historiography of Early Medieval Penance', in *A New History of Penance*, ed. A. Firey (Leiden, 2009), pp. 73–95

—— *Penance in Medieval Europe 600–1200* (Cambridge, 2014)

Menn, E. M., *Judah and Tamar (Genesis 38) in Ancient Jewish Exegesis: Studies in Literary Form and Hermeneutics* (Leiden, 1997)

Meyer, M. A., 'Early Anglo-Saxon Penitentials and the Position of Women', *Haskins Society Journal* 2 (1990), 47–61

Miles, S. H., *The Hippocratic Oath and the Ethics of Medicine* (Oxford, 2004)

Miller, B. D. H., 'She who hath drunk any potion...', *Medium Aevum* 31 (1962), 188–93

Miller, T. S., *The Orphans of Byzantium: Child Welfare in the Christian Empire* (Washington DC, 2003)

Mistry, Z., 'The Sexual Shame of the Chaste: "Abortion Miracles" in Early Medieval Saints' Lives', *Gender & History* 25.3 (2013), 607–20

Moreira, I., *Dreams, Visions, and Spiritual Authority in Merovingian Gaul* (Ithaca NY, 2000)

—— 'Dreams and Divination in Early Medieval Canonical and Narrative Sources: The Question of Clerical Control', *Catholic Historical Review* 89 (2003), 607–23

Morgan, L. M., 'Imagining the Unborn in the Ecuadorean Andes', *Feminist Studies* 23.2 (1997), 322–50

—— 'Embryo Tales', in *Remaking Life and Death: Toward an Anthropology of the Biosciences*, ed. S. Franklin and M. Lock (Santa Fe, 2003), pp. 261–91

—— *Icons of Life: A Cultural History of Human Embryos* (Berkeley CA, 2009)

Morimoto, Y., 'Aspects of the Early Medieval Peasant Economy as Revealed in the Polyptych of Prüm', in *The Medieval World*, ed. P. Linehan and J. Nelson (London, 2001), pp. 605–21

Morin, G., 'L'homéliaire de Burchard de Würzburg: Contribution à la critique des sermons de St. Césaire d'Arles', *Revue bénédictine* 13 (1896), 97–111

Moskowitz, M. L., *The Haunting Fetus: Abortion, Sexuality, and the Spirit World in Taiwan* (Honolulu, 2001)

Müller, W. P., *Die Abtreibung: Anfänge der Kriminalisierung* (Cologne, 2000)

—— *The Criminalization of Abortion in the West: Its Origins in Medieval Law* (Ithaca NY, 2012)

Murgatroyd, P., 'Tacitus on the Death of Octavia', *Greece & Rome* 55.2 (2008), 263–73

Murray, A., 'Confession before 1215', *Transactions of the Royal Historical Society* 6th s. 3(1993), 51–81

—— *Suicide in the Middle Ages, volume I: The Violent against Themselves* (Oxford, 1998)

—— *Suicide in the Middle Ages, volume II: The Curse on Self-Murder* (Oxford, 2000)

Nardi, E., *Procurato aborto nel mondo greco romano* (Milan, 1971)

Nelson, J. L., *Charles the Bald* (London, 1992)

—— 'Translating Images of Authority: The Christian Roman Emperors in the Carolingian World', reprinted in J. L. Nelson, *The Frankish World 750–900* (London, 1996), pp. 89–98

Nelson, J. L. and Rio, A., 'Women and Laws in Early Medieval Europe', in *The Oxford Handbook of Women and Gender in Medieval Europe*, ed. J. M. Bennett and R. M. Karras (Oxford, 2013), pp. 103–17

de Nie, G., '"Consciousness fecund through God": From Male Fighters to Spiritual Bride-Mother in Late Antique Female Spirituality', in *Sanctity and Motherhood: Essays on Holy Mothers in the Middle Ages*, ed. A. Mulder-Bakker (New York, 1995), pp. 101–61

—— 'Caesarius of Arles and Gregory of Tours: Two Sixth-Century Gallic Bishops and "Christian Magic"', reprinted in G. de Nie, *Word, Image and Experience: Dynamics of Miracle and Self-perception in Sixth-Century Gaul* (Aldershot, 2003), V, pp. 170–96

—— 'Fatherly and Motherly Curing in Sixth-Century Gaul: Saint Radegund's *Mysterium*', reprinted in G. de Nie, *Word, Image and Experience: Dynamics of Miracle and Self-perception in Sixth-Century Gaul* (Aldershot, 2003), XIII, pp. 53–86

Noonan, J. T., *Contraception: A History of its Treatment by the Catholic Theologians and Canonists* (Cambridge MA, 1965)

—— 'An Almost Absolute Value in History', in *The Morality of Abortion: Legal and Historical Perspectives*, ed. J. T. Noonan (Cambridge MA, 1970), pp. 1–59

Nussbaum, M. C., 'The Incomplete Feminism of Musonius Rufus, Platonist, Stoic, and Roman', in *The Sleep of Reason: Erotic Experience and Sexual Ethics in Ancient Greece and Rome*, ed. M. Nussbaum and J. Sihvola (Chicago, 2002), pp. 283–326

Nutton, V., 'Beyond the Hippocratic Oath', *Clio Medica* 24 (1993), 10–37

—— *Ancient Medicine* (London, 2004)

O'Connor, A., *The Blessed and the Damned: Sinful Women and Unbaptised Children in Irish Folklore* (Bern, 2005)

Oliver, L., *The Body Legal in Barbarian Law* (Toronto, 2011)

O'Loughlin, T., *Celtic Theology: Humanity, World, and God in Early Irish Writings* (London, 2000)

—— 'Penitentials and Pastoral Care', in *A History of Pastoral Care*, ed. G. R. Evans (London, 2000), pp. 93–111

Olsen, G. W., *Of Sodomites, Effeminates, Hermaphrodites, and Androgynes: Sodomy in the Age of Peter Damian* (Toronto, 2011)

Osiek, C. and Balch, D. L., *Families in the New Testament World: Households and House Churches* (Louisville KY, 1997)

Palazzini, G., *Ius fetus ad vitam eiusque tutela in fontibus ac doctrina canonica usque ad saeculum xvi* (Urbania, 1943)

Palmer, J., 'Defining Paganism in the Carolingian World', *EME* 15.4 (2007), 402–25

Parker, H. N., 'Manuscripts of Juvenal and Persius', in *A Companion to Persius and Juvenal*, ed. S. Braund and J. Osgood (Oxford, 2012), pp. 137–62

Parker, H. N. and Braund, S., 'Imperial Satire and the Scholars', in *A Companion to Persius and Juvenal*, ed. S. Braund and J. Osgood (Oxford, 2012), pp. 436–64

Parmentier, M., 'Job the Rebel: From the Rabbis to the Church Fathers', in *Saints and Role Models in Judaism and Christianity*, ed. M. Poorthuis and J. Schwartz (Leiden, 2004), pp. 227–42

Patlagean, É., 'Birth Control in the Early Byzantine Empire', in *Biology of Man in History: Selections from the Annales – Économies, Sociétés, Civilisations*, ed. R. Forster and O. Ranum, trans. E. Forster and P. M. Ranum (Baltimore, 1975), pp. 1–22

Paxton, F. S., 'Curing Bodies–Curing Souls: Hrabanus Maurus, Medical Education, and the Clergy in Ninth-Century Francia', *JHMAS* 50.2 (1995), 230–52

—— 'Birth and Death', in *The Cambridge History of Christianity Volume 3: Early Medieval Christianities, c. 600–c. 1100*, ed. T. F. X. Noble and J. M. H. Smith (Cambridge, 2008), pp. 383–98

Payer, P. J., 'The Humanism of the Penitentials and the Continuity of the Penitential Tradition', *Mediaeval Studies* 46 (1984), 340–54

—— *Sex and the Penitentials: The Development of a Sexual Code 550–1150* (Toronto, 1984)

—— 'Confession and the Study of Sex in the Middle Ages', in *Handbook of Medieval Sexuality*, ed. V. Bullough and J. A. Brundage (New York, 1996), pp. 3–31

Pearson, K. L., 'Nutrition and the Early-Medieval Diet', *Speculum* 71.2 (1997), 1–32

Peper, B. M., 'The Development of *Mater Ecclesia* in North African Ecclesiology' (unpublished Ph.D. dissertation, Vanderbilt University, 2011), available at http://etd.library.vanderbilt.edu/available/etd-03242011-105708/unrestricted/Title-Table.pdf [accessed 17 December 2014]

Peterson, D. C., 'A Prophet Emerging: Fetal Narratives in Islamic Literature', in *Imagining the Fetus: The Unborn in Myth, Religion, and Culture*, ed. V. R. Sasson and J. M. Law (Oxford, 2009), pp. 203–22

Playoust, C. and Bradshaw Aitken, E., 'The Leaping Child: Imagining the Unborn in Early Christian Literature', in *Imagining the Fetus: The Unborn in Myth, Religion, and Culture*, ed. V. R. Sasson and J. M. Law (Oxford, 2009), pp. 157–84

Plumpe, J. C., *Mater Ecclesia: An Inquiry into the Concept of Church as Mother in Early Christianity* (Washington DC, 1943)

Pollheimer, M., 'Hrabanus Maurus – The Compiler, the Preacher, and his Audience', in *Sermo Doctorum: Compilers, Preachers, and their Audiences in the Early Medieval West*, ed. M. Diesenberger *et al.* (Turnhout, 2013), pp. 203–28

Poulakou-Rebelakou, E., Lascaratos, J. and Marketos, S. G., 'Abortions in Byzantine Times (325–1453 AD)', *Vesalius* 2.1 (1996), 19–25

Powell, H., 'The "Miracle of Childbirth": The Portrayal of Parturient Women in Medieval Miracle Narratives', *SHM* 25.4 (2012), 795–811

Price, R., 'Informal Penance in Early Medieval Christendom', in *Retribution, Repentance, and Reconciliation*, SCH 40, ed. K. Cooper and J. Gregory (Woodbridge, 2004), pp. 29–38

Prioreschi, P., 'Contraception and Abortion in the Graeco-Roman World', *Vesalius* 1.2 (1995), 77–87

Quispel, G., 'An Unknown Fragment of the Acts of Andrew (Pap. Copt. Utrecht N. 1)', *Vigiliae Christianae* 10.1 (1956), 129–48

Radding, C., 'Legal Theory and Practice in Eleventh-Century Italy', *Law and History Review* 21.2 (2003), 377–81

Réal, I., *Vies des saints, vie de famille: Représentation et système de la parenté dans le royaume mérovingien (481–751) après les sources hagiographiques* (Turnhout, 2001)

Reuter, T., 'Sex, Lies and Oath-helpers: The Trial of Queen Uota', reprinted in T. Reuter, *Medieval Polities and Modern Mentalities* (Cambridge, 2006), pp. 217–30

Reynolds, P.L., *Marriage in the Western Church: The Christianization of Marriage in the Patristic and Early Medieval Periods* (Leiden, 1994)

—— *Food and the Body: Some Peculiar Questions in High Medieval Theology* (Leiden, 1999)

Reynolds, R. E., 'Basil and the Early Medieval Latin Canonical Collections', in *Basil of Caesarea: Christian, Humanist, Ascetic*, 2 vols., ed. P. J. Fedwick (Toronto, 1981) II, pp. 513–32

—— 'Unity and Diversity in Carolingian Canon Law Collections: The Case of the *Collectio Hibernensis* and its Derivatives', in *Carolingian Lectures: Andrew W. Mellon Lectures in Early Christian Studies*, ed. U.-R. Blumenthal (Washington DC, 1983), pp. 71–98

van Rhijn, C., *Shepherds of the Lord: Priests and Episcopal Statutes in the Carolingian Period* (Turnhout, 2007)

van Rhijn, C. and Saan, M., 'Correcting Sinners, Correcting Texts: A Context for the *Paenitentiale Pseudo-Theodori*', *EME* 14.1 (2006), 23–40

Richlin, A., *The Garden of Priapus: Sexuality and Aggression in Roman Humour*, rev. edn (New Haven CT, 1992)

Riddle, J. M., *Contraception and Abortion from the Ancient World to the Renaissance* (Cambridge MA, 1992)

—— *Eve's Herbs: A History of Contraception and Abortion in the West* (Cambridge MA, 1997)

Rider, C., *Magic and Impotence in the Middle Ages* (Oxford, 2006)

Rimell, V., *Martial's Rome: Empire and the Ideology of Epigram* (Cambridge, 2008)

Rio, A., 'Introduction', in *Law, Custom, and Justice in Late Antiquity and the Early Middle Ages*, ed. A. Rio (London, 2011), pp. 1–22

—— *Legal Practice and the Written Word in the Early Middle Ages* (Cambridge, 2009)

Riquet, M., 'Christianisme et population', *Population* 4 (1949), 615–30

Ritari, K., *Saints and Sinners in Early Christian Ireland: Moral Theology in the Lives of Saints Brigit and Columba* (Turnhout, 2009)

—— 'The Image of Brigit as a Saint: Reading the Latin Lives', *Peritia* 21 (2010), 191–207

Rives, J. B., 'Magic, Religion, and Law: The Case of the *Lex Cornelia de sicariis et veneficiis*', in *Religion and Law in Classical Rome*, ed. C. Ando and J. Rüpke (Stuttgart, 2006), pp. 47–67

Roberts, M., *The Humblest Sparrow: The Poetry of Venantius Fortunatus* (Ann Arbor MI, 2009)

Rosenwein, B. H., *Emotional Communities in the Early Middle Ages* (Ithaca NY, 2006)

Rousselle, A., *Porneia: On Desire and the Body in Antiquity*, trans. F. Pheasant (Oxford, 1988)

—— 'Body Politics in Ancient Rome', in *A History of Women, vol. 1: From Ancient Goddesses to Christian Saints*, ed. P. S. Pantel (Cambridge MA, 1992), pp. 296–337

Rubin, M., *Mother of God: A History of the Virgin Mary* (London, 2009)

Salmon, P., *La limitation des naissances dans la société romaine* (Brussels, 1999)

Salvatore, A., *Sermo humilis, sensus mysticus: esegesi e linguaggio da Paulino di Nola a Cesario di Arles* (Naples, 1995)

Saward, J., *Redeemer in the Womb: Christ Living in Mary* (San Francisco, 1993)

Schiff, D., *Abortion in Judaism* (Cambridge, 2002)

Schipper, W., 'The Earliest Manuscripts of Rabanus Maurus' *De rerum naturis* (Karlsruhe, Badische Landesbibliothek, Ms Aug. 68 and Vienna, Osterreichische Nationalbibliothek 121)', in *Pre-Modern Encyclopaedic Texts: Proceedings of the Second Comers Congress, Groningen, 1–4 July 1996* (Leiden, 1997), pp. 363–78

Schmitt, J.-C., *Ghosts in the Middle Ages: The Living and the Dead*, trans. T. L. Fagan (Chicago, 1998)

Schmitz, G., 'Schuld und Strafe: Eine unbekannte Stellungnahme des Rathramnus von Corbie zur Kindestötung', *Deutsches Archiv für die Erforschung des Mittelalters* 38 (1982), 363–87

Schreiner, S. A., 'The Role of Perception in Gregory's *Moralia in Job*', *Studia Patristica* 28 (1993), 96–105

Schroeder, C. T., 'Francia as "Christendom": The Merovingian *Vita Domnae Balthildis*', *Medieval Encounters* 4.3 (1998), 265–84

—— 'Child Sacrifice in Egyptian Monastic Culture: From Familial Renunciation to Jephthah's Lost Daughter', *JECS* 20.2 (2012), 269–302

Schulenburg, J. T., *Forgetful of Their Sex: Female Sanctity and Society, ca. 500–1100* (Chicago, 1998)

Schwarz, H., *Der Schutz des Kindes im Recht des frühen Mittelalters* (Bonn, 1993)

Shanzer, D., 'History, Romance, Love, and Sex in Gregory of Tours' *Decem libri his-*

toriarum', in *The World of Gregory of Tours*, ed. K. Mitchell and I. Wood (Leiden, 2002), pp. 395–413
—— 'Voices and Bodies: The Afterlife of the Unborn', *Numen* 56 (2009), 326–65
Sharpe, R., *Medieval Irish Saints' Lives: An Introduction to* Vitae Sanctorum Hiberniae (Oxford, 1991)
—— 'Churches and Communities in Early Medieval Ireland: Towards a Pastoral Model', in *Pastoral Care before the Parish*, ed. J. Blair and R. Sharpe (Leicester, 1992), 81–109
Shaw, B. D., 'The Family in Late Antiquity: The Experience of Augustine', *P&P* 115 (1987), 3–51
Shepard, M.B., 'The St. Germain Windows from the Thirteenth-Century Lady Chapel at Saint-Germain-des-Prés', in *The Cloisters: Studies in Honor of the Fiftieth Anniversary*, ed. E.C. Parker (New York, 1992), pp. 283–302.
Siemens, J. R., 'Christ's Restoration of Humankind in the Laterculus Malalianus, 14', *Heythrop Journal* 48.1 (2007), 18–28
—— *The Christology of Theodore of Tarsus: The* Laterculus Malalianus *and the Person and Work of Christ* (Turnhout, 2010)
Siems, H., *Studien zur Lex Frisionum* (Ebelsbach, 1980)
Skemer, D., *Binding Words: Textual Amulets in the Middle Ages* (University Park PA, 2006)
Smith, J. A., *Ordering Women's Lives: Penitentials and Nunnery Rules in the Early Medieval West* (Aldershot, 2001)
Smith, J. E., *Humanae Vitae: A Generation Later* (Washington DC, 1991)
Smith, J. M. H., *Europe after Rome: A New Cultural History 500–1100* (Oxford, 2005)
Souter, A., *Pelagius's Expositions of Thirteen Epistles of St. Paul, Volume 1, Introduction* (Cambridge, 1922)
Southon, E., 'Fatherhood in Late Antique Gaul', in *Families in the Roman and Late Antique World*, ed. M. Harlow and L. Larsson Lovén (London, 2012), pp. 238–53
van Staalduine-Sullivan, E., 'Between Legislative and Linguistic Parallels: Exodus 21:22–25 in Its Context', in *The Interpretation of Exodus: Studies in honour of Cornelis Houtman*, ed. R. Roukema (Leuven, 2006), pp. 207–24
von Staden, H., '"In a pure and holy way": Personal and Professional Conduct in the Hippocratic Oath', *JHMAS* 51.4 (1996), 404–37
Stark, R., *The Rise of Christianity: A Sociologist Reconsiders History* (Princeton, 1996)
Starr, K., 'Judge John T. Noonan, Jr.: A Brief Biography', *Journal of Law and Religion* 11.1 (1994–5), 151–76
Stevenson, J., 'Theodore and the *Laterculus Malalianus*', in *Archbishop Theodore: Commemorative Studies on his Life and Influence*, ed. M. Lapidge (Cambridge, 1995), pp. 204–21
Stocking, R. L., *Bishops, Councils, and Consensus in the Visigothic Kingdom, 589–633* (Ann Arbor MI, 2000)
Stone, R., '"Bound from either side": The Limits of Power in Carolingian Marriage Disputes, 840–870', *Gender & History* 19.3 (2007), 467–82
—— 'The Invention of a Theology of Abduction: Hincmar of Rheims on Raptus', *JEH* 60.3 (2009), 433–48
—— *Morality and Masculinity in the Carolingian Empire* (Cambridge, 2012)

—— 'Gender and Hierarchy: Archbishop Hincmar of Rheims (845–882) as a Religious Man', in *Religious Men and Masculine Identity in the Middle Ages*, ed. P. H. Cullum and K. J. Lewis (Woodbridge, 2013), pp. 28–45

Streeter, J., 'Appendix to chapter 2: The Date of the Council of Elvira', in G. E. M. de Ste Croix, *Christian Persecution, Martyrdom, and Orthodoxy*, ed. M. Whitby and J. Streeter (Oxford, 2006), pp. 99–104

Szreter, S. and Fisher, K., *Sex before the Sexual Revolution: Intimate Life in England 1918–1963* (Cambridge, 2010)

Tarrant, R. J., 'Juvenal', 'Ovid', in *Texts and Transmission: A Survey of the Latin Classics*, ed. L. D. Reynolds (Oxford, 1983), pp. 200–3, 257–65

Tasioulas, J., '"Heaven and Earth in Little Space": The Foetal Existence of Christ in Medieval Literature and Thought', *Medium Aevum* 76.1 (2007), 24–48

Taylor, N. L., 'Women and Wills: Sterility and Intestacy in Catalonia in the Eleventh and Twelfth Centuries', *Medieval Encounters* 12.1 (2006), 87–96

Temkin, O., 'The Idea of Respect for Life in the History of Medicine', in *Respect for Life in Medicine, Philosophy, and the Law*, ed. O. Temkin (Baltimore, 1977), pp. 1–23

Tentler, L. W., *Catholics and Contraception: An American History* (Ithaca NY, 2004)

Tentler, T. N., *Sin and Confession on the Eve of the Reformation* (Princeton, 1977)

Thompson, E. A., 'The Conversion of the Spanish Suevi to Catholicism', in *Visigothic Spain: New Approaches*, ed. E. James (Oxford, 1980), pp. 77–92

Thomson, J. J., 'A Defense of Abortion', *Philosophy and Public Affairs* 1.1 (1971), 47–66

Totelin, L., 'Old Recipes, New Practice? The Latin Adaptations of the Hippocratic Gynaecological Treatises', *SHM* 24.1 (2011), 74–91

Toubert, P., 'La théorie du mariage chez les moralistes carolingiennes', in *Il matrimonio nella società altomedievale: 22–28 aprile 1976*, 2 vols., Settimane di studio del Centro italiano di studi sull'alto medioevo 24 (Spoleto, 1977), I, pp. 233–82

—— 'The Carolingian Moment (Eighth–Tenth Century)', in *A History of the Family, volume I: Distant Worlds, Ancient Worlds*, ed. A. Burguière *et al.*, trans. S. Hanbury *et al.* (Cambridge, 1996) pp. 379–406

Trout, D. E., *Paulinus of Nola: Life, Letters, and Poems* (Berkeley CA, 1999).

Trumbower, J. A., *Rescue for the Dead: The Posthumous Salvation of Non-Christians in Early Christianity* (Oxford, 2001)

Ullmann, W., *The Carolingian Renaissance and the Idea of Kingship* (London, 1969)

Vaccari, P. A., 'Il genuino commento ai Salmi di Remigio di Auxerre', *Biblica* 26.1–2 (1945), 52–99

Van Dam, R., *Leadership and Community in Late Antique Gaul* (Berkeley CA, 1985)

—— *Saints and their Miracles in Late Antique Gaul* (Princeton, 1993)

Velázquez, I., 'El *Suggerendum* de Tarra a Reccaredo', *Antiquité Tardive* 4 (1996), 291–98

Verhelst, M., 'Pseudo-Methodius, Revelationes: Textgeschichte und kritische Edition', in *The Use and Abuse of Eschatology in the Middle Ages*, ed. D. Verbeke *et al.* (Leuven, 1988), pp. 112–36

Violante Branco, M. J., 'St. Martin of Braga, the Sueves and Gallaecia', in *The Visigoths: Studies in Culture and Society*, ed. A. Ferreiro (Leiden, 1999), pp. 63–98

Vogel, C., *Le pécheur et la pénitence au Moyen Âge* (Paris, 1969)

Bibliography

—— Les 'libri paenitentiales', Typologies des sources du Moyen Age occidental, vol. 27 (Turnhout, 1978)

Wallace-Hadrill, J.M., *The Frankish Church* (Oxford, 1983)

Wasyliw, P. H., *Martyrdom, Murder, and Magic: Child Saints and their Cults in Medieval Europe* (New York, 2008)

Watson, P., 'Juvenal's *scripta matrona*: Elegaic Resonances in Satire 6', *Mnemosyne* 4th s., 60.4 (2007), 628–40

Watts, W. J., 'Ovid, the Law and Roman Society on Abortion', *Acta Classica* 16 (1973), 89–101

Wemple, S. F., *Women in Frankish Society: Marriage and the Cloister 500 to 900* (Philadelphia, 1981)

Wickersheimer, E., *Les manuscrits latins de médecine du haut Moyen Âge dans les bibliothèques de France* (Paris, 1966)

Wickham, C., *The Inheritance of Rome: A History of Europe from 400 to 1000* (London, 2009)

Wilkinson, L. P., 'Classical Approaches to Population and Family Planning', *Population and Development Review* 4.3 (1978), 439–55

Williams, M. A., *Rethinking 'Gnosticism': An Argument for Dismantling a Dubious Category* (Princeton, 1996)

Wilson, W. T., *The Sentences of Pseudo-Phocylides* (Berlin, 2005)

Wood, I., *The Merovingian Kingdoms 450–751* (London, 1994)

—— 'Jural Relations among the Franks and Alamanni', in *Franks and Alamanni in the Merovingian Period: An Ethnographic Perspective*, ed. I. Wood (Woodbridge, 1998), pp. 213–25

—— 'The Individuality of Gregory of Tours', in *The World of Gregory of Tours*, ed. K. Mitchell and I. Wood (Leiden, 2002), pp. 29–46

—— *The Missionary Life: Saints and the Evangelisation of Europe 400–1050* (Harlow, 2001)

Woods, D., 'On the Death of the Empress Fausta', *Greece & Rome* 45.1 (1998), 70–86

Woods, R., *Death before Birth: Fetal Health and Mortality in Historical Perspective* (Oxford, 2009)

Wormald, P., '*Lex scripta* and *Verbum regis*: Legislation and Germanic Kingship from Euric to Cnut', reprinted in *Legal Culture in the Early Medieval West: Law as Text, Image and Experience* (London, 1999), pp. 1–44

—— 'The *Leges barbarorum*: Law and Ethnicity in the post-Roman West', in *Regna and Gentes: The Relationship between Late Antique and Early Medieval Peoples and Kingdoms in the Transformation of the Roman World*, ed. H.-W. Goetz et al. (Leiden, 2003), pp. 21–46

Zurek, A., 'L'etica coniugale in Cesario di Arles: Rapporti con Agostino e nuovi orientamenti', *Augustinianum* 25 (1985), 565–78

INDEX

Abbo of St. Germain 167
abortion *see also* childbearing and childbirth; embryology; embryotomy; fetus; medicine; miscarriage; *parricidium*; sterility
  adultery 35–6, 40, 43, 44–5, 95–6, 98
  ambiguity 139, 143–4, 162
  by assault or violence *see under* miscarriage
  baptism 148, 153–4, 161, 226–7, 229–30, 294
  clerics 95–7, 122, 124–5 n.112, 138, 139–40, 143, 144–5, 181–2, 253 n.70
  concealing sexual transgression 40–1, 42, 44–5, 49, 96, 121–2, 160–1, 192, 203, 253, 297
  damnation of culprits 23, 40, 59, 67
  dangers for women 10, 29–30, 34, 47, 115, 117
  early term/late term distinction 10, 115
  female autonomy 34 n.54, 297–8
  female culpability 32, 35, 42, 44–5, 51–2, 69–73, 98, 99, 114, 141–2, 145, 154, 159–60, 163, 170, 297–8
  female obsession with appearance 33, 34, 52–3
  formed/unformed distinction 51–2, 113–16, 255, 267–8, 276, 289–92, 293–4
  forty days, before and after 147–8, 150–2, 181
  incest and sexual abuse 36, 238, 244–5, 258–9

  and infanticide 1, 33, 38, 39, 40, 45, 59, 61, 77, 95, 97, 98, 107, 108, 111, 117–18, 121, 123, 134, 142, 179, 185, 214, 232, 285
  intentionality 52, 154, 155–6
  male culpability 36, 43, 53, 96–7, 113–14, 117, 121, 137, 139–40, 143, 145, 160, 163, 170, 174, 196, 297–8
  male interests 26, 35–6, 110, 117
  married couples 42, 48–9, 53, 98, 106–7, 123, 261
  motherhood 70–1, 81–2
  as murder 52, 59, 60, 143–4, 147–8, 152–3, 154, 159, 180, 185–6, 197
  nuns and virgins 2, 42, 47, 64, 133, 135–7, 181–2
  paganism 168–9
  parental pressure 75, 236
  polytheism 38, 76
  poverty 160, 180–1
  premarital sex 34 n.54, 62
  preventing conception 7, 29, 49, 59, 98, 139, 193–4, 196, 201
  proicere 87–8, 189–90, 232
  rape 188–92 *see also raptus*
  self-harm 59, 65, 71
  sex of fetus 217–20
  social status 35–6, 43, 46, 62, 64, 69, 71, 114, 117
  stepmothers 70–1
  supernatural or superstitious means 63, 76, 132
  suppliers of abortifacients 95, 97–8, 111–12, 170, 176, 228
  vivens/non vivus distinction 228
  voluntary/involuntary distinction 141–2
abortion symbolism 93–4, 265–6, 277–92, 293

Index

catechumens 61, 283
heretics 282, 284, 288
innocent victims 93–4, 294–5
Jews 282–3, 286–7
salvation history 279–80
sin 279
sinners 61, 282, 284
abortivi/aborted infants 265, 277–8
  see also abortion symbolism;
  Augustine; baptism
  damnation 268, 270, 272–3,
    281–2, 294
  as insult or joke 285–6
  resurrection 266–77
  salvation 40–1, 266
Acts of Andrew 86
Adamik, Tamás 87
Ado of Vienne 241 n.13
adultery 89–90, 120, 122, 140,
  226, 227–8, 229, 232, 243,
  285 *see also* adultery *under*
  abortion
Adventius of Metz 241, 242 n.15,
  247 n.39, 248–9
Áed 2, 3
Aetherius of Lisieux 88
Airlie, Stuart 243
Alcuin 165–6, 167–8 n.13, 195–6,
  262
Alexander the Great 37, 165
Altfrid of Hildesheim 233
Ambrose of Milan 46, 47
Annales Bertiniani 246–7
Annales Xantenses 250
Annunciation 149, 262
aphrodisiacs *see* love magic *under*
  magic
Apocalypse of Peter 40–1
apocrypha 39, 41, 66 *see also Acts
  of Andrew; Apocalypse of Peter;
  Visio Pauli*
apologetics 37–9
Apophthegmata Patrum 43–4
Arbeo of Freising 235
Ardennes 197–8
Arechis II 297–8
Arianism 100, 102, 106, 113
Arn of Salzburg 158, 209
Athenagoras 38
Augustine 5, 48–50, 54, 55, 60, 72,
  73, 100, 114, 150, 187, 195,
  218 n.48, 260–1, 265, 267–70,
  272–3, 274, 276, 278, 283–4,
  288, 290–1
  texts wrongly attributed to 50,
    174, 175
Aulus Gellius 33
Ausonius of Bordeaux 14 n.49,
  103–4

Bailey, Lisa 68, 69–70
Balthild 91–2
baptism 41, 61, 278 *see also* baptism
  under abortion
  catechumens 60–1
  unbaptized infants 81–2, 148,
    153–4, 157, 187, 201, 229–30,
    270, 271, 281–2
Basil of Caesarea 51–2, 155–6
Bede 152, 160, 180, 200
Benedictus Levita 168, 291–2 n.131
Bertchramnus of Bordeaux 90
bestiality 153, 178
bible 196 *see also* apocrypha;
  biblical commentaries
  Ecclesiastes 277, 287
  Exodus 51, 113–14, 116, 118, 168,
    215, 228, 255–6, 288–92
  Genesis 136, 194–6 *see also* Onan
  Jeremiah 39, 79
  Job 279–82
  Leviticus 254, 255, 284
  Numbers 286–7
  Pauline epistles 1, 165, 254, 277,
    283, 287
  Psalms 282–3
biblical commentaries 1, 146, 151,
  196
Biller, Peter 10–11, 21, 130, 193,
  197–200, 201–2 n.173
Bischoff, Bernhard 146
bishops 59, 84, 97, 104–5, 108–9,
  129, 196, 236–7, 257 *see also*
  episcopal statutes
  episcopal visitations 200–2
  sexual behaviour 90, 90–1 n.147,
    139–40
blood *see* menstruation
Boba, abbess 182
Bobbio Missal 144–5
Boniface 63, 229–30
Borsje, Jacqueline 138–9
Boswell, John 4 n.10, 204–5, 211
  n.15

Braulio of Saragossa   124, 273–7, 299
breastfeeding   33, 47 n.113
Brictius of Tours   90
Brigit of Kildare   3, 135–6, 177 n.62
Brown, Peter   42, 45, 48, 237
Brown, Warren   234
Buddhism   263
Burchard of Worms   200
Burchard of Würzburg   63
Burrus, Virginia   102 n.30, 103 n.34
Bynum, Caroline Walker   273

Caesarius of Arles   57–78, 80, 83, 84, 87, 91, 123, 163, 168, 175, 193, 211, 276–7, 278, 283
Callan, Maeve   136
Callirhoe   25
Callistus I, pope   43
Canones Hibernenses   151
canonical collections   52, 95–6, 98–9, 99–100 n.21, 105, 155–6, 171, 174–5, 183–4, 247–8 *see also* Martin of Braga; penitentials
  Dacheriana   171
  Dionysiana-Hadriana   171, 184
  Dionysius Exiguus   99, 171
  Hibernensis   56, 174–5
  Hispana   96, 106, 171, 184
  Quesnelliana   99, 171
  Sanblasiana   155, 171
  Vetus Gallica   157, 171
Carolingian reform   168–9, 171–2, 182
Cassiodorus   265, 277 n.60
Catholicism
  artificial contraception   5–7, 58, 162, 206
  debate over abortion   5 n.15, 6, 49
  tradition   172–3
Chadwick, Henry   104
Charlemagne   165–6, 167, 213, 267
Charles-Edwards, Thomas   137
Charles the Bald   177, 240, 242
Charles of Mainz   185
charters   211
childbearing and childbirth
  birth-spacing   64, 80, 83
  caesarean   278
  dangers   30, 81, 82, 86–7, 186–8, 220, 266

postpartum abstinence   83, 150
  salvific   1, 2, 81–2, 84
  social rituals after childbirth   189
Chilperic I   218–19, 223
Chindaswinth   94, 110, 116, 117–19, 120, 123
Christ   150, 195, 273
  conception in Mary's womb   39, 149–50, 256, 262
Chrodobert of Tours   90–1 n.147, 182
church   *see also* bishops; canonical collections; clergy; penitentials
  and classical society   4–5, 25, 38, 54
  councils   94, 225, 236–7
    councils of Aachen (860)   241, 244, 245–7, 251, 252, 257 n.89
    council of Aachen (862)   242, 247–8
    council of Ancyra (314)   45–6, 52 n.135, 91, 95–6, 98, 99, 128, 134, 155, 157, 158, 159, 160, 173, 174, 176, 177, 179, 180, 181–2, 184, 187, 192, 196, 201, 203, 226–7, 260 *see also* Martin of Braga
    council of Arles (late fifth century)   74
    council of Braga I (561)   100–4
    council of Braga II (572)   98, 125
    council of Chalon-sur-Saône (813)   171–2, 173, 175
    council of Elvira (early fourth century)   44–5, 46, 95–6, 171, 177, 184, 201, 203
    council of Lérida (546)   94–7, 98, 122, 124, 125, 171, 177, 184, 187 n.105, 201, 203
    council of Mainz (847)   177–8
    council of Mainz (852)   179, 201
    council of Metz (863)   242–3, 248–9
    council of Paris (829)   172, 175, 176
    council of Toledo I (400)   101
    council of Toledo III (589)   93, 106–9, 118, 119, 123, 171
    council of Toledo IV (633)   121 n.98

council of Toledo IX
(655) 121–2
council of Tours (813) 172
council of Vaison (442) 74
council of Worms (868) 186
as mother 278–9
pastoral care 56, 129, 159, 176, 177–9, 193, 199
tradition 13, 56–7, 66, 171, 179–80, 192–3
Ciarán of Saigir 276
Cicero 26
Clement of Alexandria 41
clergy 17, 132 see also clerics under abortion
instruction 100, 104–5, 129, 144, 169–71, 176, 180, 196, 205–6
sexual behaviour 88, 90–1, 121–2, 132, 133, 134–5, 139–40, 145, 181–3
Cogitosus of Kildare 135, 177
Collatio Alexandri et Dindimi 165–6
Columbanus 131, 137
conception 256, 264, 299
of saints 79–80
Connery, John 6 n.17, 139 n.56
Connolly, Hugh 134
Constantine 27, 28 n.23
contraception 4 n.10, 29, 30, 99, 161–3, 192–3, 195, 199, 257 see also preventing conception under abortion
as murder 56, 75–7, 197
Corinna 34, 167
councils see under church
crime see under law
Cyprian of Carthage 43, 45–6, 278

Dagaulf, husband of Vilithuta 81
Dagulf, abbot 88
Datheus of Milan 211 n.15
d'Avray, David 243, 247–8
devil 61, 64–5, 66, 76, 183
Didache 37
Digest see Roman under law
Dindimus 165–6
Dixon, Suzanne 34
Domitian 36
Douglas, Mary 284
Dracontius 70

drunkenness 52, 69–70
Duby, Georges 197–8, 199 n.160

Ebbo of Rheims 176
Elipandus of Toledo 284–5
Elsakkers, Marianne 9–10, 18, 111 n.61, 112 n.62, 113–14, 115–16, 118, 190–1, 218 n.48, 224
embryology 14–15, 24 n.8, 36, 148, 150, 218 n.48, 293 see also *Laterculus Malalianus*
embryotomy 30–1, 269
Emmeram of Regensburg 235–6, 298
Ephrem the Syrian 266
Epiphanius of Salamis 42
episcopal statutes 169–71
Epistle of Barnabas 37
eschatology 41, 266–7, 270 276, 291 see also *abortivi*/aborted infants; Augustine
eucharist 262
Eusebia 78–9, 80, 82–3, 87, 296
Eustochium 47
Eve 1, 71, 136
Exodus see under bible

family honour 88–9, 122, 235–6, 298
Favorinus 33, 47 n.113
Felix of Urgel 284–5
fetus 134, 137 see also abortion; *abortivi*/aborted infants; embryology; soul
beginnings of life 49, 50, 298–9
consumption of 42, 67, 275
dead in womb 18, 30, 187, 269
divine care 41, 65
formed/unformed distinction see under abortion
forty days, before and after see under abortion
as *homo* 35–6, 38
social recognition 216, 222–3
stages of development 10, 52, 97 n.11, 148–9, 151–2, 217–8, 228, 275
as symbol 15, 61, 263–5 see also abortion symbolism
Firey, Abigail 237, 252
Flandrin, Jean-Louis 8, 162
Flint, Valerie 138, 252 n.65

formularies 211–12, 220–1
 Cartae Senonicae 223 n. 69, 225 n.77
 Formulae Andecavenses 74, 204 n.182, 225 n.77
 Formulae collectio S. Dionysii 182
 Formulae Senonenses 90–1 n.147
 Formulae Turonenses 74 n.80
Frisia 188, 190, 230–1, 232–3 see also Frisian under law; P. Oxoniense II under penitentials; Vita Liudgeri
Fulgentius Ferrandus 105 n.42
Fulgentius of Ruspe 271, 294 n.142

Galen 29, 150
Gennadius of Marseille 271
Gerbald of Liège 170, 209
Germanus of Paris 1–2, 3, 78–80, 84, 87, 166–7, 296–7
 Saint Germain-des-Prés 3
Goar 204
Goffart, Walter 89
Gratian 50, 55, 186, 200
Green, Monica 18 n.65
Gregory I, pope 162–3, 271, 279–82, 298 n.10, 299
Gregory of Nyssa 41 n.87
Gregory of Tours 70, 71 n.63, 73 n.70, 73 nn.72–3, 79–80, 83 n.114, 85–91
Gunther of Cologne 241 n.13, 245–6, 247 n.41

Hadrian of Canterbury 146
hagiography 1–3, 7, 57, 58, 71, 78, 79–80, 81, 136, 187, 223, 276 see also Venantius Fortunatus
Haimo of Auxerre 277–8
Halitgar of Cambrai 172, 176–7, 180, 190, 193, 200
Hatto of Mainz 200
Heidecker, Karl 251
Hen, Yitzhak 63
Herard of Tours 170
heresy 7, 42, 48, 100, 104–5 see also Manichaeism; Noonan, John; Priscillianism
Heribald of Auxerre 177
Hincmar of Rheims 190, 226 n.81, 241–2, 244–8, 249, 251, 253–60, 291–2 n.111, 293

Hippocratic Oath 28 n.25, 29, 30, 31 n.40
Hippolytus of Rome 43
holy innocents see under infanticide
homosexuality 118, 244, 254
Honings, Bonifacio 172
Hubert, brother of Theutberga 240, 244, 246, 247, 249
Hugh, son of Lothar II 240, 249 n.52
Huser, Roger John 5, 13

Importunus of Paris 90–1 n.147
impotence 139, 225
incest 86, 195, 244–5, 247–9, 253, 254 see also incest and sexual abuse under abortion
Indicia 47
infant abandonment 4 n.10, 27, 32, 40, 46, 189, 201 see also proicere under abortion
 reception of foundlings 74–5, 87–8, 203–5, 211 n.15
infanticide 44, 85, 91–2, 153, 182–3, 188, 201, 233 see also and infanticide under abortion; overlaying of infants
 female infanticide 219 n.54–5, 233
 holy innocents 294–5
infertility see sterility
Isidore of Seville 262, 288, 293
Islam 263
Ivo of Chartres 50, 200

Jacob and Esau 39, 282 n.89
Jerome 47, 48, 50, 51, 165, 270, 273
 letter to Eustochium 47, 64, 168, 174, 175
John the Baptist 2, 39, 167, 262
John Cassian 195
John Chrysostom 52–3
Josephus 51
Jovinian 48, 165
Judah 194–6
Judaism 5 n.15, 23, 31 n.39, 37, 51, 53, 55, 263
Judith, empress 243
Julia Flavia 36
Julian of Eclanum 48, 270
Julian of Toledo 272–3, 274, 275, 285–6
Julianus Pomerius 57, 272–3

Index

Justinian 27, 225, 238–9
Juvenal 35, 36, 55, 167

King, Helen 18 n.65
Kitchen, John 80, 80–1 n.102
Koskenniemi, Erkki 37, 51
Kottje, Raymund 140

Lapidge, Michael 146
Laterculus Malalianus 146, 148–51
law 14, 16, 109, 190–1, 202, 209–12, 222, 224, 225–6, 230, 235–7 *see also* canonical collections; charters; councils; formularies; Müller, Wolfgang
   Alamannic 201–2 n.173, 210, 217–21, 224, 226
   Anglo-Saxon 209–10 n.10, 222 n.64
   Bavarian 209, 210, 220 n.56, 227–30, 235, 294
   Burgundian 208 n.4, 210, 252 n.65
   capitularies 211, 212, 218–19, 236–7
   crime 11–12, 113, 114, 119–20, 124, 208, 235, 237
   fredus 234
   Frisian 191, 230–5, 237
   Lombard 207, 210, 221–2, 223, 226
   Ripuarian 210, 215–16, 217, 223
   Roman 26–8, 39, 54–5, 109, 110, 112, 201, 208, 225
   Salic 109, 193, 210, 212, 213–6, 217, 223, 224–5, 226, 228, 234, 252 n.65
   tort 11–12, 113, 114, 119–20, 228
   Visigothic 107, 109–20, 122, 124, 208, 218, 227–8, 275–6
   wergild 213–4, 216, 217–18, 222, 223–4, 228–9, 230, 233–4
Leo I, pope 101–4
Leoba of Bischofsheim 182–3
Leovigild 97, 108, 110, 112
Leyser, Conrad 69
Liafburg 233
Liber Papiensis 207, 222, 223 n.70
liturgy 262
Liutbert of Mainz 185
Lothar I 236–7, 240, 247–8 n.37, 287 n.111

Lothar II 238–44, 246–53, 257–8
Louis the German 177, 240
Louis the Pious 168, 185, 243, 259
Lucretius of Braga 100–1

Macrobius 14 n.49, 218 n.48
magic 63, 139
   love magic 132, 138–9, 142, 144, 162 n.161, 170
maleficium 132, 132 n.24, 133, 138, 143, 170, 187, 194, 201, 224–5
Manichaeism 88, 100, 101–2, 195 *see also* Priscillianism
marriage 8, 26, 32–3, 43, 101–2, 118, 123, 190, 212, 248, 257 *see also* adultery
   heretical misogamy 101–2
   incest rules 247–8
   sexual morality 48–9, 72–3, 153, 162
Martin of Braga 97–100, 104–5, 123, 170, 171, 173, 180, 193 *see also* councils
Martin of Tours 73 n.70
Mary 39, 72, 149, 243, 256–7
masturbation 35, 195, 254
Maximus the Confessor 264
McKitterick, Rosamond 144, 210
medicine 17–19, 150, 167, 256 *see also* embryotomy
   medical ethics 28–31, 33
   methods for abortion 18, 19, 24 n.6, 29, 30, 63–4
Meens, Rob 126 n.3, 129, 130, 162, 183, 188
menstruation 18, 72, 153, 162 n.161 *see also* sexual abstinence
   menstrual blood 274, 276
Methodius of Olympus 39–40
Minucius Felix 38–9, 54
miracles 1, 2, 3, 84, 85, 87–8, 136, 186 *see also* hagiography
miscarriage 82, 141–2
   abortion by assault or violence 10, 43–4, 51, 73, 113–17, 207–8, 214, 217, 218–19, 221–2 *see also* Exodus *under* bible
   animals 115, 221–2
   health hazard 115

339

Modestinus 39, 54
monasticism 74, 131–2
  child oblation 4 n.10, 223
  renunciation of sexuality 2, 47, 82, 133
  sexual scandal 47, 93, 135, 181–3
Moreira, Isabel 80
Morimoto, Yoshiki 197–9
Muhammed 263
Müller, Wolfgang 11–12, 119, 124, 208
Murray, Alexander 20, 128, 129–30, 131, 225–6
Muscio 29 n.29, 219 n.50
Musonius Rufus 32, 47 n.113, 48, 54

Nardi, Enzo 4, 5 n.13
Nero 36
Nicetius of Lyon 79–80
Nicholas I, pope 185–6, 241, 243, 247, 250–1
Nitigisius of Lugo 98
Noonan, John 6–7, 42, 48, 49, 56, 99, 100–1, 104–5, 161–2
Northild 259–60
Novatus 43
nuns *see under* abortion

Octavia, empress 36
Onan 195–6, 254, 257
ordeal 89–90, 185, 241, 244–5, 249, 251, 257 n.89
Origen 114, 288, 289, 290, 291
Ota, daughter of Theodo 235–6, 298
Otgar of Mainz 177
overlaying of infants 142, 157, 159, 178–9, 185–6, 193, 201
overpopulation 197–9
Ovid 34–5, 36, 55, 167, 286

paganism 63, 75–6, 136, 153, 168–9, 188–9, 229, 230, 233, 234
Palazzini, Giuseppe 5, 13
parenthood 41, 46, 63–4, 123
parricidium 39, 42, 43, 46, 65, 79, 84, 123, 203, 226
Paschasius Radbertus 293
Paul, apostle *see* Pauline epistles *under* bible
Paulinus of Aquileia 284–5
Payer, Pierre 127
Pelagius 42 n.93, 277 n.60
penance 126, 127, 137–8, 140, 142, 147, 171–3, 176, 185, 226
penitentials 126–31, 137, 154–5, 156–7, 159–61, 163–4, 176–7, 180, 193 *see also* Halitgar of Cambrai; Rabanus Maurus
  and canonical authority 147, 160, 171–5, 176–80, 183–4
  Old Irish Penitential 151–2
  P. Arundel 187–8, 190, 191
  P. Bedae 160–1,
  P. Bigotianum 151–2
  P. Bobbiense 141, 143, 144–5
  P. Burgundense 141, 143, 145
  P. Capitula Iudiciorum 142 n.71, 158–9
  P. Columbani 131, 137–40, 141, 143, 145, 159
  P. Cummeani 127 n.5, 131
  P. Egberti 127 n.5
  P. Excarpsus Cummeani 157–8, 159, 160–1, 180
  P. Floriacense 141, 143–4, 174–5
  P. Hubertense 142, 190, 194–6, 198
  P. Martenianum 174–5, 187
  P. Merseburgense A 156–7, 189–90, 191
  later recensions 192–3
  P. Merseburgense B 198 n.159
  P. Oxoniense I 141, 143–4
  P. Oxoniense II 177 n.63, 188–90, 191, 232, 233
  P. Parisiense simplex 141, 142
  P. Pseudo-Bedae 152, 180, 193–4, 200–1
  P. Pseudo-Gregorii III 180
  P. Pseudo-Theodori 180–2, 183
  P. Remense 158
  P. Sangallense simplex 140
  P. Sangallense tripartitum 142 n.71, 157, 162
  P. Silense 142 n.70
  P. Sletstatense 141, 143
  P. Vallicellianum C.6 142 n.70
  P. Vindobense B 158, 209
  P. Vinniani 131–7, 138, 139, 140, 158, 159, 162–3, 181
  simplices 140–5, 159, 194
  Theodorean 145–7, 293
    Canones Basilienses 146–8
    Canones Cottoniani 146–8, 151
    Canones Gregorii 146–8

Capitula Dacheriana 146–7
Discipulus Umbrensium 146–7, 152–5, 180
penitential rulings on abortion 156
   Decipere partum 156, 157, 158, 159, 160, 162, 176, 193, 194
   Voluntarie 156, 157, 158, 159, 176, 181, 192, 194, 196, 201
   XL dies 157, 158, 159, 174, 180, 181, 201
Philo of Alexandria 51
Pirminius 168, 266–7
Pius XI, pope 206
Pliny the Elder 30, 32
Plutarch 34 n.54
poisons 27, 79, 83, 111–12 *see also maleficium; veneficium*
polyptychs 197–9
pregnancy *see* childbearing and childbirth; conception
Priscillian 100, 102, 103–4
Priscillianism 88, 100–4, 285
Procopius 238–9
procreation 72, 162–3
Procula 103–4
promiscuity 176, 238
prostitution 33, 52–3, 85, 93, 195
   prostitute as insult 88, 230, 250–1
Prudentius of Troyes 246–7
Prüm 197, 205
Pseudo-Bede 284
Pseudo-Boniface 168
Pseudo-Methodius 275
Pseudo-Phocylides 23, 37
Pseudo-Primasius 1 n.1, 277 n.60
Pseudo-Remigius 282–3

queenship 243

Rabanus Maurus 172, 177–80, 185, 200, 201, 226–7, 248, 256 n.85, 260, 286–92
Radegund 81, 82
Radulf of Bourges 170
raptus 190–2, 211, 227, 276 *see also* rape *under* abortion
Rathbod of Trier 200
Ratramnus of Corbie 178
Rebecca 39
Reccared 93, 94, 106, 107–8
Recceswinth 109, 116, 118, 119, 120, 124

Regimbod 226–7
Reginbald 178
Regino of Prüm 196, 197–200, 200–5, 237, 238, 247, 249, 277, 297
Remigius of Auxerre 167, 282
resurrection 101–2, 272, 273–4 *see also abortivi*/aborted infants
van Rhijn, Carine 170–1
Riddle, John 18 n.65
Rio, Alice 90–1 n.147, 210, 211, 212
Rudolf of Fulda 182–3

satire 35–6, 89
Scribonius Largus 29
semen 153, 161–2, 194–5, 255, 256, 257, 274, 276
Seneca the Younger 33, 47 n.113, 53
Septuagint *see* Exodus *under* bible
sermons 62–3, 68–9, 77–8, 168–9, 298–9 *see also* Caesarius of Arles; John Chrysostom
sexual abstinence 59, 61, 65, 154, 162–3
   during menstruation 72
   during pregnancy 72, 83
sexual abuse *see* incest and sexual abuse *under* abortion
sexual intercourse *see also* sodomy/sodomitical intercourse
   anal 153, 161, 244, 254–5
   inter-femoral 254
   unnatural 195, 244–6, 251, 254–5
Shanzer, Danuta 41, 84–5 n.118, 269–70 n.30
Sibylline Oracles 23, 37, 53
Siems, Harald 234
Smaragdus of Saint-Mihiel 283
sodomites 118 n.89
sodomy/sodomitical intercourse 244, 247, 254–5
Soranus of Ephesus 29, 30, 33
soul 36, 148, 151–2
Stephen V, pope 185–6
sterility
   infertility 63–4, 211 n.15, 250
   sterilitas and abortion 35, 47, 59, 65, 69
Stevenson, Jane 146, 150
St Gall *receptarium* 18–19
Stocking, Rachel 108
Stone, Rachel 190

suicide   151, 225
Sulpicius Severus   103–4

Tacitus   32, 36, 48
Taio   273
Tarra   93–4, 284, 295
Tertullian   30–1, 38, 39, 42, 54, 278
Thamar   194–6
Theodora, empress   238–9
Theodore of Canterbury   145–7, 149–51, 154, 155–6, 159, 160, 180, 200 see also Laterculus Malalianus; Theodorean under penitentials
Theodorus Priscianus   30, 187
Theodulph of Orléans   195, 254 n.77
Theutberga   238–53, 255–8, 260–1
Theutgaud of Trier   241 n.13, 247 n.41, 249 n.53
Thomas Becket   295 n.146
tort   see under law
Trier   204–5
Tryphoninus   26
Turibius of Astorga   101, 285–6

Van Dam, Raymond   102
Venantius Fortunatus   70, 78–84, 85, 91, 166–7
veneficium   27–8, 97, 112, 170–1, 196
Vetus Latina   see Exodus under bible
Vilithuta   81
Vindicianus   14 n.49

violence   116, 211, 211–12 n.17 see also abortion by assault or violence *under* miscarriage
against women   73, 207, 214, 218–19, 223–4, 226–7
bodily injuries   116, 211, 213
Visio Pauli   66–7
Vita Balthildis   91–2
Vita Germani brevior   296
Vita Goaris   204–6
Vita Haimhrammi   220 n.56, 235–6, 298
Vita Leobae   182–3, 201–2 n.173
Vita Liudgeri   233
vulva   256, 278 n.64, 287–8

Waldrada   240, 242–3, 249, 250–1
Wandalbert of Prüm   205
Wandalgarius   221
Wemple, Suzanne   73
wergild   see under law
Whether what is carried in the womb is a living being   36–7
widows   122, 229
Willibrord   188, 262
womb   256–7, 262, 287–8
  blessing   2
  symbol of church   61, 71–2, 282, 283–4, 287–8
Wood, Ian   188
Wormald, Patrick   110, 209, 210

Zurek, Antoni   72

www.ingramcontent.com/pod-product-compliance
Lightning Source LLC
Chambersburg PA
CBHW052056300426
44117CB00013B/2151